Medieval Iberia

Published by
University of Pennsylvania Press
Philadelphia, Pennsylvania 19104-4112
www.upenn.edu/pennpress

Printed in the United States of America on acid-free paper
10 9 8 7 6 5 4 3 2

Library of Congress Cataloging-in-Publication Data

Medieval Iberia : readings from Christian, Muslim, and Jewish sources / edited
by Olivia Remie Constable, with the assistance of Damian Zurro. — 2nd ed.
    p.   cm. — (The Middle Ages series)
Includes bibliographical references and index.
ISBN 978-0-8122-2168-8 (pbk. : alk. paper)
    1. Spain—Civilization—711-1516—Sources. 2. Portugal—Civilization—To
1500—Sources. 3. Spain—Ethnic relations—Sources. 4. Portugal—Ethnic
relations—Sources. 5. Civilization, Medieval—Sources. I. Constable, Olivia
Remie. II. Zurro, Damian. III. Series: Middle Ages series.
DP97.4.M43   2011
306.0946'0902—dc23   2011022411

Dedicated to the Memory of
JOHN BOSWELL and ELKA KLEIN

Contents

Contents According to Subject

Many items are listed under more than one subject, and often only part of the text relates to the subject listed.

Conquest and Reconquest
(see also Warfare and Military Administration)

Education

Festivals, Ceremonies, and Entertainment

Food, Drink, Daily Life, and Household Affairs

Interfaith Relations

Catholics and Arians

Christians and Jews

Christians and Muslims

Jews and Muslims

Philosophy, Theology, and Morality

Politics, Nobility, and the Royal Court

Slavery and Unfreedom

Travel, Geography, and Natural History

Urban Life and Town Administration

Warfare and Military Administration

Women, Marriage, and Family

Illustrations

Preface to the Second Edition

Since the first edition of *Medieval Iberia* appeared in 1997, many more medieval Iberian sources have been published in English translations, and in a few cases new translations have appeared of texts that were included in the first edition. This second edition takes advantage of these new resources, as well as including a number of original new translations. The intention throughout has been to broaden and deepen coverage, with special attention to adding materials relating to Portugal and to women. Twenty-five new chapters have been added (and roughly thirty-five new texts), but none of the sources included in the original edition have been removed, although one appears in a new translation (the *Book of Deeds* of Jaume I). This second edition also includes illustrations, bringing a visual dimension to complement the written texts. As in the first edition, special care has been taken to collect texts together that provide different perspectives on the same event.

Introduction

The medieval Iberian Peninsula was remarkable for its political, religious, cultural, linguistic, and ethnic diversity. Some historians have emphasized the positive side of the mélange of Iberian peoples in the Middle Ages, describing their society as one of coexistence, or *convivencia*. It is true that Jews, Christians, and Muslims lived together on the peninsula for nearly eight centuries. Not only did Christian and Muslim kingdoms exist side by side, but people of different faiths lived within each region. As in other Islamic lands, Jews and Christians enjoyed a special protected status in Muslim Spain as "People of the Book" (*dhimmī*). Protection for the *dhimmī* did not imply equality, but it allowed Jews and Christians to practice their faith under Muslim rule. Later, Muslims and Jews would also be afforded a certain degree of protection under Christian rule.

In contrast to the arguments for *convivencia*, other scholars have discerned a more hostile scenario for Iberian history, in which Muslims and Christians were engaged in an ongoing contest for political, religious, and economic advantage. From the medieval Christian point of view, the military struggle against the Muslims was often presented as a *reconquista*, which by the twelfth century had taken on the character of a crusade to regain territory lost when the Muslims conquered much of the peninsula from the Visigoths in the early eighth century. Whether the Christian military advance, culminating in the fall of Muslim Granada in the late fifteenth century, represented a conquest or a reconquest has been the subject of much scholarly debate.

The diversities of Iberian history cannot be fully explained by either harmonious *convivencia* or hostile *reconquista*. Both of these concepts reflect facts of life in the medieval peninsula, yet both are myths that have been overused in historical explanations. Iberian reality was more complex. Christian and Muslim rulers were often at odds, as were the Christian rulers of Castile and Portugal and the Muslim rulers of Córdoba and Zaragoza, but at times they cooperated. This collection of medieval Iberian texts attempts to show the differences and hostilities that distinguished peoples living on the peninsula while also demonstrating points of contact between them. Some selections describe interactions between different groups in the peninsula; others were produced by and for individual communities.

The texts written in medieval Iberia are as diverse as the peoples who wrote them. No collection can ever fully reflect the richness, variety, and beauty of the writings produced in a region over a period of many centuries. All the materials in this volume have been chosen for their historical content, but they also represent a wide variety of genres.

Likewise, these medieval texts were written in many different languages. Christians wrote in Latin and later in Romance vernaculars, including Castilian, Catalan, Portuguese, and Galician. Muslims generally wrote in Arabic, though the Mudejars (Muslims living under Christian rule in the later Middle Ages) gradually created Aljamiado, a version of the Romance vernacular written in Arabic characters. Some Christians also used Arabic, particularly if they were Mozarabs (Arabized Christians, usually living under Muslim rule). Similarly, Jews living in Muslim Spain often wrote in Arabic (or Judeo-Arabic, a version of Arabic written in Hebrew characters), especially for secular documents, but their primary literary and religious language was Hebrew.

Language was a primary tool of identity and segregation, marking off one community from another, yet it was also a means for communication, a way of crossing boundaries between communities. Many people were comfortable in more than one language, and it was normal for literate people to write in one language while using another for everyday conversation. For example, a Jewish merchant in Muslim Spain might generally have spoken Arabic with his clients and family, and probably also a Romance dialect when needed; he would have corresponded with business partners in Judeo-Arabic, but would have used Hebrew for religious matters at home and in the Jewish community.

Different groups of people produced different types of texts, but not all kinds of materials have survived equally over the centuries. Some documents were carefully preserved so that they could be read by future generations, whereas others have survived only by chance. Countless other documents have not survived, because they were purposely destroyed; lost in the course of war, emigration, and political change; or merely forgotten and left to decay. The centuries have been particularly hard on Arabic and Hebrew materials from the Iberian Peninsula, of which many disappeared in the course of medieval conquests, conversions, and expulsions. Christian texts have survived much better: there is a greater variety of genres reflected in the Christian sources, and consequently more modern scholars work with Christian materials. These inequalities, inevitably, are reflected in this collection.

Territorial and linguistic differences in the medieval Iberian Peninsula created an almost endless diversity in the names of persons and places. A personal name in Latin or Castilian was not necessarily written or pronounced in the same way as its Catalan or Portuguese counterpart, while Arabic and Hebrew names were often adapted to suit the spelling of non-Semitic languages. It is at times impossible to choose the "correct" version of a name, between modern and medieval versions, or among Latin, Arabic, Hebrew, Portuguese, Castilian, and Catalan variants. As a general rule, most place-names in this collection are given in their modern Castilian versions, as are personal names except in the case of some regional or medieval spellings, or Anglicized versions (as in Saint James). In most cases, Arabic and Hebrew personal names have been transliterated according to established systems, though here again there are some inconsistencies (as when a Hebrew name was written in Arabic or an Arabic name in Latin).

Dates also present a problem. Jewish and Muslim calendars follow a lunar cycle, whereas Christians use solar calculations. Thus Jewish and Muslim years are slightly shorter than Christian years, and their reckoning begins at a different point in time. The Jewish calendar is reckoned from the Creation; the Muslim calendar begins in 622 C.E., the date of Muḥammad's flight from Mecca to Medina. Thus, when Granada surrendered in late 1491 according to Christian reckoning, it was 897 for the Muslims and 5252 by the Jewish calendar. To complicate matters further, earlier Iberian Christians calculated their dates differently than did Christians elsewhere in Europe, taking 38 B.C.E. as a starting point and thereby putting Spanish dates thirty-eight years ahead of those elsewhere in Christian Europe. This system was used in Spain during the Visigothic period and persisted in some regions of the peninsula until the early fifteenth century. For the sake of simplicity, most dates in this volume have been converted to modern western usage (C.E.).

This collection represents the efforts of many people, including those who originally wrote the texts and those who translated them into English. Not surprisingly, therefore, the materials reflect a variety of styles of composition and translation. No attempt has been made to impose a misleading homogeneity on the collection, although there has been an effort to ensure that the translations are clear, coherent, and readable renditions of the original texts.

Each chapter is preceded by a brief introduction giving historical, biographical, and other contextual details to assist the reader. The collection does not attempt to provide a comprehensive survey of medieval Iberian history, although there is a brief chronology listing major periods and political events. Readers seeking a general historical outline or looking for further information on a particular topic should consult the bibliography, which lists a number of recent studies in English along with older classics.

The Visigothic Kingdom
(Sixth and Seventh Centuries)

1. IN PRAISE OF SPAIN

Isidore of Seville, *History of the Goths,*
Vandals, and Suevi (624)

Translated from Latin by Kenneth B. Wolf

Isidore of Seville, one of the most influential figures in the early medieval church, was born about 560, probably in Byzantine-held Cartagena. As a boy he moved with his family to Seville, which was then under Visigothic control. In 600 he became bishop of Seville, a post he occupied until his death in 636. Isidore was the author of many books, including three historical works. One of them, the Historiae Gothorum Vandalorum et Sueborum *[History of the Goths, Vandals, and Suevi], completed in 624, chronicled the history of the Visigoths from 256 until the time in which Isidore was writing, with brief additional sections describing the Vandals and the Suevi. Although this book had an important influence on later Spanish historiography, it was less known outside the peninsula. The prologue to Isidore's history (translated here) was composed with classical literary models in mind and was designed to praise Spain and glorify the Goths. Isidore's panegyric was echoed in later literature, including the thirteenth-century Castilian* Primera crónica general. *(ORC)*

Of all the lands from the west to the Indies, you, Spain, O sacred and always fortunate mother of princes and peoples, are the most beautiful. Rightly are you now the queen of all provinces, from which not only the west but also the east borrows its shining lights. You are the pride and the ornament of the world, the more illustrious part of the earth, in which the Getic people are gloriously prolific, rejoicing much and flourishing greatly.

Indulgent nature has deservedly enriched you with an abundance of everything fruitful. You are rich with olives, overflowing with grapes, fertile with harvests. You are dressed in corn, shaded with olive trees, covered with the vine. Your fields are full of flowers, your mountains full of trees, and your shores full of fish. You are located in the most favorable region in the world; neither are you parched by the summer heat of the sun, nor do you languish under icy cold, but girded by a temperate band of sky, you are nourished by fertile west winds. You bring forth the fruits of the fields, the wealth of the mines, and beautiful and useful plants and animals. Nor are you to be held inferior in rivers, which the brilliant fame of your fair flocks ennobles.

Alpheus yields to you in horses and Clitumnus in cattle, although

English text from *Conquerors and Chroniclers of Early Medieval Spain*, edited and translated by Kenneth B. Wolf (Liverpool: Liverpool University Press, 1990), pp. 81–83. Reprinted with permission of the publisher.

Alpheus, regarded as sacred for his Olympic victories, exercised fleet chariots on the track of Pisa, and Clitumnus once sacrificed great oxen as victims on the Capitol.[1] You do not need the fields of Etruria,[2] for you have more abundant pasturage, nor do you marvel at the groves of Molorchus,[3] for you have palm trees in plenty, nor do your horses run less swiftly than the Elian chariots.[4] You are fertile with overflowing rivers, you are tawny with gold-flowing torrents, you have a spring that fathered a horse. You have fleeces, dyed with native purples, that glow with Tyrian crimson.[5] You have rock, shining in the shadowy depths of the mountains, that is aflame with radiance like the sun.

Yet you are as rich in purple-clad rulers[6] as you are in native gems, and, rich in imperial gifts, you are as wealthy in adorning your princes as you are blessed in producing them. Rightly did golden Rome, the head of the nations, desire you long ago. And although this same Romulean[7] power, initially victorious, betrothed you to itself, now it is the most flourishing people of the Goths, who in their turn, after many victories all over the world, have eagerly seized you and loved you: they enjoy you up to the present time amidst royal emblems and great wealth, secure in the good fortune of empire.

1. The Alpheus is a river in the Peloponnese. According to tradition, it flowed through an underwater channel to Sicily. There, as Isidore observed in his *Etymologies* (14.6.33), it watered a pasture renowned for the quality of its horses. These horses were famous for their success at the Olympic games held near Pisa and Elis in the Peloponnese. The Clitumnus is a small river in the Umbria region of Italy. Isidore referred to it in his *Etymologies* (13.13.6) as a lake known for the size of the cattle that grazed nearby. These cattle were the preferred victims of sacrifices to the gods. Isidore's intention throughout his famous prologue (known as the *Laus Spaniae*) was to compare Spain favorably to the Italy and Greece of the Roman poets, using their own points of classical reference.

2. In west-central Italy.

3. Molorchus was a poor farmer who, according to tradition, entertained Heracles.

4. "Elian chariots" is a poetic way of referring to the chariots of the Olympic games, held near Elis.

5. A reference to the famous Tyrian dyes that were extracted from a particular kind of mollusc.

6. A reference to the Roman emperors who were born in Spain.

7. Referring to Romulus, the traditional founder of Rome.

2. A CATHOLIC BISHOP AND AN ARIAN KING

Lives of the Holy Fathers of Mérida (ca. 630)
Translated from Latin by Joseph N. Garvin

The author of this work is unknown, although he is sometimes identified as a certain Paul, a deacon of Mérida. The Lives was probably composed in the 630s. It chronicles the lives and works of the Catholic bishops of Mérida in the period before the conversion of the Visigoths from Arianism to Catholicism in 589. Although Catholics formed a majority in the Iberian population during the sixth century, the ruling Visigoths tried to impose Arian beliefs. Primary among these was the tenet that Christ was subordinate to God the Father and created by God in time. In contrast, Catholic doctrine taught that Father and Son were coequal, coeternal, and of the same substance.

This selection describes events in the life of Masona, the bishop of Mérida under Leovigild (r. 569–586), the last Arian king before the Visigothic conversion to Catholicism. The author clearly portrays the king as a demonic obstructer of the true faith, but the monarch may also be seen as attempting to preserve his own religious beliefs in the face of popular pressure. (ORC)

Whence it happened that his [Masona's] virtue, through report, reached the ears of Leovigild, the savage and cruel king of the Visigoths, and the monstrous demon of his jealousy, always envious of good works, stung into action by sharper goadings, wounded the soul of the king with its viperous venom and poured into his being its poisoned potion. At once, the king, armed with diabolical cunning by the drinking of this lethal cup, urged on by hate, again and again commanded the holy man by messengers who went back and forth between them to abandon the Catholic Faith and to turn to the Arian heresy together with all the people who were entrusted to him. And when the man who had dedicated himself to God replied courageously and told the king as the messengers kept coming back that he would never abandon the true faith he had learned once, he also rebuked the Arian king as he was in duty bound and with proper reproofs refused to embrace the heresy.

When the messengers returned to him, the king began to tempt his soul by various persuasions in the hope that in some way he might incline him to his wicked pleasure. But the bishop scorned his many crafty persuasions, rejected his gift as so much dross, and heroically defended his Catholic Faith. He was unwilling to remain silent about the heresy lest by keeping silent he

English text from *Vitas sanctorum patrum emeritensium*, translated by Joseph N. Garvin (Washington, D.C.: Catholic University of America Press, 1946), pp. 199–219. Reprinted with permission of the publisher.

seemed to give assent, and with all his powers he fought against its madness, sounding forth with the trumpet of truth.

When the king saw himself failing and his efforts fruitless, he became furious and began to terrorize him, thinking that he could by threats shatter the constancy of one whom he had been unable to overcome by blandishments. But the holy man was not broken by the terrorizing nor persuaded by the blandishments; but fighting the fierce tyrant in brave encounter, he remained unconquered in defense of justice.

Realizing that neither by threats nor by bribes could he make the man of God turn from the true faith to his heresy, the cruel tyrant, wholly a vessel of wrath, fomenter of vice, and root of damnation, whose breast the fierce enemy and crafty serpent occupied and held in his control, gave to his people bitter instead of sweet things, harsh instead of mild measures, death-dealing potions instead of health. With the object of arousing seditious uprisings and of disturbing the bishop and all his people he appointed as bishop of the Arian party in the city a certain wicked man, an out-and-out supporter of the Arian heresy, whose name was Sunna. He was a supporter of wicked doctrine, a baleful and harsh-featured man; his brow was wild, his eyes savage, his aspect hateful, his movements horrifying; he was sinister in mind, depraved in character, of lying tongue and obscene speech, turgid exteriorly, empty interiorly, puffed up without, vapid within, inflated externally, devoid of all virtue internally, deformed both within and without, lacking in goodness, abounding in evil, guilty of crime, exceedingly reckless of eternal death.

This fosterer of heresy came to Mérida and at the command of the king boldly took some churches and all their privileges from their rightful bishop, appropriating them for himself.

Now after the heretical bishop had sought with all his might to perturb the servant of God and all the faithful by well-devised measures but could not, he relying on the king's favor attempted to attack the basilica of the holy virgin Eulalia in order to wrest it from the authority of its bishop and to have it for the Arians. When the holy bishop Masona and all his people resisted keenly and fought back sturdily the false bishop Sunna made many written accusations to the king against the holy man and suggested to him that the basilica which he longed to lay hold of be taken from the authority of the Catholics by royal order and handed over to his control. In answer to this request the king is said to have promulgated the following decree: that both bishops be cited and appear before judges who were to sit in the Bishop's House, and in their presence engage in oral conflict in defense of either side and, arguing against each other alternately, fortify and back up by arguments drawn from the books of Holy Scripture whatever claims each one made; and that he whose side won the triumph of victory should likewise possess the church of St. Eulalia.

When this decree, as rumor spread, sounded in the ears of the devout Masona he went at once in haste to the basilica of the holy virgin Eulalia and lay prostrate upon the floor before the altar under which lay the venerable body of the holy martyr, persevering for three days and as many nights in fasting and weeping. On the third day he returned to his home, which is built within the walls of the city, and with such readiness and steadfastness of mind did he return that to none of the faithful did it seem doubtful that He was coming to aid him Who said: "Be not thoughtful beforehand what you shall speak; but whatever shall be said to you in that hour that speak you. For it is not you that speak, but the Holy Spirit."

When he came into the city and, entering his house, took his seat, he took away the grief of all the faithful by the joyfulness of his countenance and exhorted them not to be uncertain of his victory, and awaiting the shameless Arian bishop and the judges he waited a long time. Finally the Arian bishop and the judges came in, accompanied by throngs of people and puffed up with arrogant pride. When the bishops were seated the judges who in the majority were supporters of the Arian party and of the impious king also seated themselves. When they were seated, the holy bishop Masona, with his usual dignity and good judgment, pointedly remained silent with his eyes fixed upon heaven. Since he was silent Sunna, the bishop of the heretics, spoke first and poured forth shameless, strident, harsh, scabrous, and undisciplined words. After the man of God patiently, gently, and sweetly answered him and brilliantly set forth the whole truth and he in reply hissed in insolent words as though with the mouth of a dragon, the two carried on a mighty verbal struggle with each other. But fleshly power could in no way resist the wisdom of God and the Holy Spirit who spoke through the mouth of His servant, Bishop Masona.

But why go on? Beaten and overthrown on every point Sunna fell silent and flushed, covered with great shame, and likewise his perverse partisans who tried earnestly to help him, not only blushed in their confusion but hearing the amazingly learned exposition that proceeded in mellifluous speech from his mouth, in consternation of mind and deep admiration praised him whom a little before they had tried to overcome. For the Lord vouchsafed that day to give so great favor to his lips that never before had anyone seen him so brilliant in eloquent discourse, and although he always taught eloquently he was more eloquent that day than on all other days.

Then did the righteous see and rejoice and all iniquity stilled its mouth because God stopped the mouth of them that spoke wicked things. All the faithful marvelled exceedingly because although they had known before that the man was eloquent they could not remember that he had ever uttered such scholarly and brilliant words with such clear and fluent speech.

Although the above-mentioned heretical bishop Sunna had been refuted by every argument and the truth, he remained obdurate in his former religion and could not advance with free steps to the haven of salvation, for the ancient enemy had with God's permission hardened his stony heart as he had Pharaoh's.[1]

After the debate, seeing himself utterly defeated, he began ever more wildly with clever scheming to devise complaints and false charges against the servant of God and, supported by every sort of weapon, to hurl them against the soldier of Christ, attacking therein rather himself, and privily to lodge many charges against the blessed bishop Masona in the ears of the Arian king Leovigild. But the craft of the adversary did not avail, his calamitous wickedness in no way harmed the man of God, for the grace of the Redeemer armed him with weapons of the spirit.

Finally the evil spirit impelled the oft-named king of the Arians to remove the holy man from his see and to have him brought before him. His ministers, sharing in his crime, quickly obeyed the command of their king and coming to Mérida forced the blessed man to go in all haste to Toledo[2] where the king lived.

When the holy bishop Masona, suddenly torn from the bosom of his holy Church, was being taken away from Mérida and, though innocent, was being led into exile like a condemned person, the voice of all the citizens of Mérida resounded loudly with great cries and unbearable tears. With immense groaning and immense wailing they proclaimed that they were being robbed of the help of their great bishop, shouting in these words: "Why are you abandoning your fold, loving shepherd? Why are you leaving your flock to perish? Do not, we beg, cast us into the jaws of wolves, lest your sheep fed until now on honeyed flowers be torn by devouring wolves, with no shepherd to care for them." He, moved by so much weeping, full of compassion in the Lord as always, is said to have burst into tears. Then addressing them in many words, he with marvelous subtlety consoled them. Then he bade farewell to all and accompanied by the blessing of God left them with tranquil mind, constant soul, and joyful countenance as was his wont.

When he arrived at Toledo and stood in the presence of the fierce tyrant,

1. Referring to the Pharaoh in the biblical book of Exodus, whose heart was hardened against the pleas of Moses.
2. Toledo was the capital city of the Visigothic rulers.

the king reviling him with many insults and assailing him with many threats sought with all the power of his depraved will to draw him to Arianism. Although the man of God willingly bore all the abuse that was heaped upon him and calmly put up with everything he meekly but boldly answered what the rabid dog barked at him and, disregarding personal insults but pained at the outrage to the Catholic Faith, replied to the tyrant bravely.

More and more enraged by his imperturbability, the maddened king even more savagely raged against the servant of God with more rabid barkings. Then he demanded with terrible threats that he give him the tunic of the holy virgin Eulalia that he might have it in the basilica of the Arian heresy there in Toledo. To this demand the man of God answered: "Be it known to you that I shall never soil my heart with the sordidness of Arian unbelief, never shall I sully my mind with the foulness of its perverted doctrine. Never shall I permit the tunic of my Lady Eulalia to be polluted by the sacrilegious hands of heretics or even to be touched by the tips of their fingers. Never can you find it and get it into your possession." On hearing this the profane king flew into a frenzy of madness and quickly and speedily sent emissaries to Mérida to look carefully everywhere for the sacred tunic, searching diligently in the treasure of the church of St. Eulalia and in the treasure of the older church that is called Sancta Jerusalem, until they should find it and bring it to him.

They came and looked for it everywhere diligently but did not find it and so returned empty-handed to their king. When they reported their failure to him the devil raged more furiously against the man of God, gnashing his teeth. When the bishop was brought before him the king said: "Either tell me where that is which I demand or know that if you do not tell you will be subjected to severe tortures and then sent into exile in a distant land where you will be subjected to many trials and intolerably tortured by want of all necessities and die a cruel death." To this threat the man of God is said to have answered thus: "You threaten me with exile? Be it known to you that I do not fear your threats nor am I afraid of exile and therefore I beg of you that if you know of any place where God is not present, you have me exiled there." The king said to him: "Where is not God present, you death-seeker?" The man of God replied: "If you know that God is everywhere, why do you threaten me with exile? Wherever you send me I know that the love of God will not abandon me. And I am sure of this, that the more cruelly you rage against me the more will His mercy accompany me and His clemency console me."

Because of the bishop's constancy the maddened tyrant was stricken within by a greater torment of his wicked mind and, moved by exceeding gall and bitterness, said to him: "Either give me the tunic that you have surreptitiously taken away or if you do not give it to me I shall have your members torn apart by various tortures." The soldier of God fearlessly made this reply: "I have already told you once and again that I shall not fear your threats. Let your perverted mind devise against me whatever more it can. I still do not fear you nor shall I, terrified by fear, give you what you ask for. But know this, that I have burned the tunic in fire and reduced it to ashes and mixed them in water and drunk them," and touching his stomach with his hand he said, "Look! here it is within upon my stomach. Never shall I give it to you." This he said because without anyone knowing it he had folded it and wrapped it in linen cloths and wound it about his stomach under his clothes and wore it thus, God alone aware of it. But God so blinded the eyes of the king and all his attendants that not one understood how the man of God did it.

While these and similar remarks were being made the sky was very clear. Suddenly the majesty of God thundered from heaven with a great rumble so that king Leovigild fell trembling in great terror from his throne upon the ground. Then the man of God with great exultation said boldly: "If we must fear a king, behold the king we should fear, not such as you."

Then the evil spirit who is always armed with revilings opened the sacrilegious mouth of the tyrant to noxious words and he growled this impious sentence: "We command that Masona, always hostile to our way of life, the enemy of our faith and opposed to our religion, be speedily taken from our presence and sent into exile."

As soon as the hostile and impious king gave this unjust sentence his ministers, who shared in his crime, withdrew the bishop from his presence and, at the bidding of the king, prepared an untamed horse for him to ride in the hope that it would throw him headlong so that in falling he would break his neck and perish cruelly. So wild was the horse that no rider dared to mount it because it had already thrown many headlong. While it was being made ready for the man of God to mount it, the cruel king emerged from a window of the palace and looking on waited for the holy man to fall from the horse and give him a great spectacle. At once the holy bishop made the sign of the cross and mounted the untamed horse which the Lord made like a gentle lamb. It began with all gentleness and care to pursue the course of its journey although a little while before it had as though with scorn refused with great snorting and blowing and incessant motion of its entire body to carry another. When they saw this miracle all were astounded and marvelled exceedingly and the attitude of the king himself was changed into great wonder. But of what advantage could the blazing splendor of the sun be to a blind man whose heart the savage enemy had darkened entirely!

God's holy bishop Masona went to the appointed place accompanied by only three of his servants, with whom the men who had been sent by the king to punish him put him away in exile in a monastery.

Bishop Masona lived in exile for three years until St. Eulalia appeared to king Leovigild in a dream. In this dream, the saint beat the king, and demanded that Masona be reinstated in Mérida. Fearing further punishment, the king complied with her wishes.

3. THE VISIGOTHIC CONVERSION
TO CATHOLICISM

The Third Council of Toledo, Sixty-Two Bishops Attending, in Which the Arian Heresy Was Condemned in Spain (589)

Translated from Latin by David Nirenberg

The records of the ecclesiastical councils celebrated by the bishops of the Iberian Peninsula from the fourth century to the Arab conquest are among the most important sources for the history of Visigothic Spain.

The councils offer much information, but it is rarely easy to interpret. Because church councils were interested in condemning non-normative practices, we do not know how common these practices were nor in what contexts they occurred. Further, the fact that councils often repeat much older legislation makes it difficult to use them as indicators of contemporary social reality.

Toledo III is the most famous of the councils, representing the moment when the riding Visigoths converted from their traditional Arian form of Christianity to the Catholic Christianity of the Hispano-Roman peoples they had conquered. In Toledo III the Visigothic king Reccared (r. 586–601) endorsed an assimilationist policy; in it one can already see a symbiosis between Visigothic and Catholic peoples. This cooperation would have had a profound effect on the later stability and prosperity of the Visigothic kingdom. (DN)

In the name of our Lord Jesus Christ, in the fourth year of the reign of the most glorious, most pious and most faithful to God Lord Reccared, king, on the eighth day of the Ides of May, era 627 [589], this sacred council was celebrated in the royal city of Toledo, by the bishops of all Spain and of the Gauls who are inscribed below.

This most glorious prince having commanded, because of the sincerity of his faith, that all the prelates of his kingdom should convene in one [council] in order that they might exult in the Lord, both for his conversion and for the renewal of the Gothic people, and that they should at the same time give thanks to the divine dignity for such an extraordinary gift, this same most blessed prince addressed the venerable council saying: "I do not believe that you are unaware of the fact, most reverend bishops, that I have summoned you into our serene presence for the restoration of ecclesiastical discipline.

Translated from José Vives, Tomás Marín Martínez, and Gonzalo Martínez Díez, *Concilios visigóticos e hispano-romanos* (Barcelona: C.S.I.C., 1963), with emendations provided by Gonzalo Martínez Díez and Felix Rodríguez's critical edition in *La colección canónica hispana*, vol. 5, *Concilios hispanos: Segunda parte* (Madrid: C.S.I.C., 1992), pp. 49–148.

Because of space limitations here, the text of some chapters is omitted. Their subjects are generally clear from the headings.

And because throughout past times the threatening heresy [of Arianism] did not allow a synod of all the Catholic Church to be convened, God, whom it pleased to eliminate the said heresy through us, admonished us to repair the institutions of the customs of the church. . . ."

Upon [hearing] this, the entire council, giving thanks to God and acclaiming the most religious prince, decreed in that instant a fast of three days. And all the bishops of God having come together again on the eighth day of the Ides of May, after the preliminary oration, each of the bishops was again seated in his proper place, when behold, among them appeared the most serene prince, having joined himself to the oration of the bishops of God, and filled thereafter with divine inspiration, he began to address [the bishops] saying: "We do not believe that your holinesses are unaware of how long a time Spain labored under the error of the Arians, and how, not long after our father's death, when it was known that we had associated ourselves with your holy Catholic faith, there [arose] everywhere a great and eternal rejoicing. And therefore, venerable fathers, we decided to unite you [in order] to celebrate this council, so that you yourselves may give eternal thanks to the Lord for the peoples newly come to Christ. The rest of the agenda which we present before your priestliness concerning our faith and hope which we profess, we have written down in this book. Read it, therefore, among yourselves. And [then] approved by the judgment of council and decorated with this testimony of faith, our glory shall shine throughout all times to come."

The . . . book the king offered was received, therefore, by all the bishops of God, and [it] being read in a clear voice by the clerk, the following was heard: Although the omnipotent God has, for the benefit of the populace, given us charge of the kingdom, and has delivered the governance of not a few peoples into our royal stewardship, nevertheless we remember that we too are of mortal condition, and that we cannot merit the happiness of future blessedness unless we esteem the cult of the true faith, and, at least, please our creator with the creed of which he is worthy. For which reason, the higher we are extolled above our subjects by royal dignity, the more we should provide for those things that pertain to God, both to increase our faith, and to take thought for the people God has entrusted to us. . . .

Therefore, most holy fathers, these most noble peoples, who have been brought near to the Lord by our diligence, I offer to the eternal God through your hands, as a holy and propitiating sacrifice. Truly it shall be for me an unfading crown and a delight in the reward of the just if these peoples, who because of our dexterity have rushed to the unity of the church, remain rooted and firm within it. And truly, just as it was [entrusted] to our care by the divine will to bring these peoples to the unity of the Church of Christ, it is your duty to instruct them in the dogmas of the Catholics so that, instructed in the full knowledge of the truth, they [shall] know [how] stolidly to reject the errors of the pernicious heresy, and to keep to the path of the true faith through love, embracing the communion of the Catholic Church with an ever more ardent desire. . . .

To these my true confessions I added the sacred decrees of the above-mentioned councils, and I signed them, with God [as my] witness, in all innocence of heart. . . .

I, Reccared, king, faithful to this holy and true creed, which is believed by the Catholic Church throughout the world, holding it in my heart, affirming it with my mouth, signed it with my right hand, [under] God's protection.

I, Bado, glorious queen, signed with my hand and with all my heart this creed, which I believed and professed.

Then the entire council broke into acclamations, praising God and applauding the prince: I. Glory be to God, Father, Son, and Holy Spirit, whose care it is to bestow peace and unity upon His Holy Catholic Church. II. Glory to our Lord Jesus Christ, who with the price of His blood assembled the Catholic Church from [among] all peoples. III. Glory to our Lord Jesus Christ, who joined such an illustrious people to the unity of the true faith, and established [but] one flock and one shepherd. IV. Who has [been given] eternal merit [by] God, if not the true and Catholic king Reccared? V. To whom [has] God [given] an eternal crown, if not the true [and] orthodox king Reccared? VI. [To] whom present and eternal glory, if not [to] the true lover of God, king Reccared? VII. He is the recruiter of new peoples for the church. VIII. May he be beloved of God and of men, who so admirably glorified God on earth, with the help of the Lord Jesus Christ, who with God the Father lives and reigns, one with the Holy Spirit, for ever and ever, amen. . . .

Here begin the decrees which, in the name of God, were established by the third holy synod in the city of Toledo.

I. That the Statutes of the Councils and the Decrees of the Roman Pontiffs Be Maintained

After the condemnation of the Arian heresy and the exposition of the holy Catholic faith, the holy council decreed the following: that since in some Spanish churches, whether because of heresy or paganism, canonical discipline was passed over, license for transgression abounded, and the option of discipline was denied, so that any excess of heresy found favor and an abundance of evil made lukewarm the strictness of discipline, [because of these things,] the mercy of Christ having restored peace to the church, [we order that] all that which the authority of the ancient canons prohibited, let it also be restricted by the revived discipline, and let that be performed which [the canons said] ought to be performed. Let the determinations of all the councils retain their vigor, and also the synodal letters of the holy Roman pontiffs. Henceforth let no unworthy [person], contravening the ancient councils, aspire to be worthy of the honors of episcopal office. And let nothing be done of that which the holy fathers, filled with the spirit of God, decreed should not be done, and let any who presume to do [such a thing] be restrained by the severity of the ancient canons.

II. That in All the Churches the Creed Should Be Recited on Sunday

III. That No One May Alienate Church Goods Unless out of Necessity

This holy council gives no bishop license to alienate the goods of the church, for this is forbidden in the ancient canons. But if they should give something that does not prejudice the well-being of the church for the benefit of the monks or churches of their parish, [the donation] shall remain valid. They are also permitted to provide for the necessities of pilgrims, clerics, and the poor to the extent that they are able, excepting the rights of the church.

IV. That It Is Permitted the Bishop to Convert a Church in His Parish into a Monastery

V. That Bishops and Deacons Should Live Chastely with Their Wives

It has come to the attention of the holy council that the bishops, presbyters, and deacons who are coming out of heresy [i.e., Arians] copulate with their wives out of carnal desire. So that this shall not be done in the future, we decree what prior canons had already determined: that they are not allowed to live in libidinous union, but rather with the conjugal bond remaining between them they should mutually help each other, without living in the same room. Or if [his] virtue is strong enough, let him make his wife live in some other house, as good witness to [his] chastity, not only before God, but also before men. But if any should choose to live obscenely with his wife after this accord, let him be a lector. [And concerning any of] those who have always been subjected to ecclesiastical canons [i.e., Catholics], if against ancient command they have had consort in their cells with women who could provoke a suspicion of infamy, let them be punished canonically, the women being sold [into slavery] by the bishop, their price being distributed to the poor.

VI. That a Slave of the Church Who Is Manumitted by the Bishop Must Remain a Dependent of the Church, and That Those Manumitted by Others Should Be Defended by the Bishop

VII. That Divine Scriptures Be Read at the Bishop's Table

Out of reverence for the bishops of God the entire council decreed the following: that because idle tales are often told at table, the divine scriptures should be read at all episcopal gatherings, for in this fashion the soul will be edified and unnecessary tales will be prohibited.

VIII. That the Prince May Not Give Away Clerics Dependent on the Fisc

By command and consent of our lord the most pious king Reccared the council of bishops decrees as follows: that no one dare ask the prince for [unfree] clerics belonging to the fisc as a present, but rather, with their personal tribute paid, let them serve the church to which they are bound so long as they live according to their rule.

IX. That the Churches of the Arians Shall Belong to the Catholic Bishops in Whose Dioceses They Are Located

X. That No One Commit Violence Against the Chastity of a Widow, and That No One Marry a Woman Against Her Will

In the interests of chastity (the increase of which the council should most avidly incite) and with the agreement of our most glorious lord king Reccared, this holy council affirms that widows who wish to maintain their chastity may not be forced with any violence into a second marriage. And if before taking a vow of chastity they wish to be married, let them marry him who of their own free will they wish to have as husband. The same should be maintained concerning virgins, [for] they should not be forced to take a husband against their parents' will or their own. If anyone impedes the desire of a widow or virgin to remain chaste, let him be held a stranger from holy communion and the thresholds of the church.

XI. That Penitents Do Penance

[We are] aware of the fact that in some churches of Spain men do penitence for their sins, not in accordance with the canons, but in a disgusting way: as often as they wish to sin, they ask the presbyter to be reconciled. Therefore, in order to eliminate such an execrable presumption, the council decrees that penitence be given in accordance with the form of the ancient canons, that is: that he who repents should first be separated from communion, and he should avail himself often of the laying on of hands, along with the other penitents. Once his time of satisfaction is finished, he should be restored to communion as the bishop sees fit. But those who return to their old vice, whether during the time of penitence or afterwards, shall be condemned in accordance with the severity of the ancient canons.

XII. Concerning Those Who Ask for Penance: If They Are Male, First Tonsure Them; If Female, [Let Them] First Change Their Dress

. . . [Because] often, out of eagerness to administer penance to lay people, [lay people] relapse into lamentable crimes after receiving it.

XIII. That Clerics Who Appeal to Secular Judges Be Excommunicated

Prolonged lack of discipline and ingrown license have given rise to such illicit presumption, that clerics, abandoning their own bishop, summon other clerics to civil courts. Therefore we decree that henceforth they not presume to do so, and if any one does, let him lose the case and be excommunicated.

XIV. Concerning the Jews

At the suggestion of the council, our most glorious lord has commanded [that the following] be inserted in the canons: It is not permitted for Jews to have Christian women as wives or concubines, nor to purchase slaves for their personal use. And if children are born of such a union, they should be taken to the baptismal font. They may not be assigned any public business by virtue of which they [might] have power to punish Christians. And if any Christians have been stained by them, [or] by Jewish ritual, or been circumcised, let them return to liberty and the Christian religion without paying the price [of their freedom].

XV. That Servants of the [Royal] Fisc Who Build a Church Should Endow It, and [Ask] Confirmation from the King

XVI. That Bishops Along with Judges Destroy the Idols, and That Lords Forbid Their Servants Idolatry

Because the sacrilege of idolatry is taking root in nearly all of Spain and Gaul, the holy synod, with the consent of the glorious prince, commands the following: that each bishop in his respective area, along with the judge of that region, should diligently search out the aforesaid sacrilege, and should not refrain from exterminating that which they find, and should correct those

who participate in such error with any punishment available, save that which
endangers life. . . .

XVII. That the Bishops and the Judges Correct with Bitter Discipline Those Who Murder Their Own Children

Among the many complaints which have come to the ears of the holy council,
there has been denounced to it a crime so great, that the ears of the present
bishops cannot bear it, and this is that in some parts of Spain, parents kill
their own children, [because they are] eager to fornicate, and know nothing
of piety. Those to whom it is troublesome to have many children should first
refrain from fornication. [For once] they have contracted marriage under the
pretext of procreation, they make themselves guilty of parricide and fornication, who, by murdering their own children, reveal that they were married
not for procreation but for libidinous union. Our most glorious lord king
Reccared, having taken account of such evil, his glory has deigned to instruct
the judges of those regions to inquire diligently concerning such a horrible
crime, in conjunction with the bishops, and to forbid it with all severity.
Therefore this sacred council sorrowfully urges the bishops of [those] regions
that together with the judges they diligently inquire [about this crime], and
forbid it with the most severe penalties, excepting death.

XVIII. That the Synod Meet Once a Year, and That the Judges and Agents of the [Royal] Fisc Attend

XIX. That the Church and All Its Goods Are Under the Administration of the Bishop

Many people, against that which is established in the canons, request the
consecration of churches which have been built [by them] in such a way that
the endowment they gave it not fall under the administration of the bishop,
which thing was displeasing in the past and is forbidden in the future. Rather,
everything is [now] under the administration and power of the bishop, in
accordance with the ancient edicts.

XX. That the Bishop May Not Impose Exactions or Tribute upon His Diocese

The complaints of many require this decree, because we have known that
bishops in their dioceses act, not in a sacerdotal manner, but cruelly, and . . .
impose tributes and afflictions upon their dioceses. Therefore, excepting that
which the ancient canons command the bishop should receive from his parishes, they shall be denied all that to which they now presume, that is: they

may not fatigue presbyters and deacons with exactions or taxes. Let it not appear in the Church of God that we deserve the name of tax collectors more than that of God's pontiffs. And those clerics who feel themselves oppressed by the bishop, whether local or from the diocese, should not hesitate to bring their complaints before the metropolitan. . . .

XXI. That It Is Forbidden for Judges to Make Exactions of Clerics and Servants of the Church

Because we are aware that in many towns servants of the church, of the bishops, and of all the clerics are bothered by diverse exactions from judges and [other] public authorities, the entire council has asked of the piety of our most glorious lord that henceforth he prohibit such abuses, and that the servants [or: slaves] of the above-mentioned officials [be free to] labor on their own or the church's business. And if any judge or civic official wishes to employ some cleric or some servant of a cleric or of the church in public or private business, let him be a stranger to the communion of the church, which he is obstructing.

XXII. That the Bodies of [Deceased] Religious Be Processed [to Burial] amid the Chanting of Psalms

The bodies of all religious who, called by God, depart from this life, should be carried to the grave amid psalms and the voices of the chanters only, but we absolutely forbid burial songs, which are commonly sung for the dead, and the accompaniment [of the corpse] by the family and dependents of the deceased, beating their breast. It suffices that, in the hope of the resurrection of the Christians, there be accorded to bodily remains the tribute of divine canticles. For the Apostle forbids us to mourn the dead, saying: "I do not wish you to sadden yourselves about those who are asleep, as do those who have no hope" [1 Thess. 4:12]. And the Lord did not mourn the dead Lazarus, but rather shed tears for his resurrection to the hardships of this world. Therefore if the bishop is able, he should not hesitate to forbid all Christians to do this. Clerics, too, should not act in any other way, for it is fitting that throughout the world deceased Christians should be buried thus.

XXIII. That Dances Be Prohibited on the Birthdays of the Saints

That unreligious custom which the vulgar people practice on the feast days of the saints must be completely destroyed. That is, that the people who ought to attend to the divine offices instead dedicate themselves to unseemly songs and dances, injuring not only themselves, but also interfering with the offices of the religious. The holy council commends [this] to the care of the bishops and judges: that this custom may be banished from all of Spain.

Here Begins the Edict of the King in Confirmation of the Council

Our most glorious lord, king Reccared: [That] divine truth which makes us lovers of all those living under the power of our rule, [also] primarily inspired our understanding to command all the bishops of Spain to present themselves to our highness, in order to restore ecclesiastical faith and discipline. And after careful and considerate deliberation, we know that [these things] have been decided, with all [due] maturity of feeling and weightiness of intelligence, concerning both what is convenient for the faith and the correction of customs. Therefore, we command with our authority all men who are [citizens] of our kingdom, that no one be allowed to disdain or presume to neglect anything that has been established in this holy council held in the city of Toledo in the fourth year of our felicitous reign. For these decrees which have so pleased our intelligence and which, [because they are] so much in accord with ecclesiastical discipline, have been promulgated by this synod, should be maintained and observed in all their authority by [everyone], as much clerics as laypeople, and by every manner of person. . . .

We decree that all these ecclesiastical rules which we have summarized briefly above [should be] maintained with eternal stability as is amply explained in the canons. If any cleric or layperson does not wish to obey these decrees, [let them be punished as follows]: If they are a bishop, presbyter, deacon, or cleric, let them be subject to excommunication by the entire council. If they are laypeople of substance in their region, let them give [as a fine] half of their possessions to the fisc, and if they are people of inferior status in their region, let them lose [all] their possessions and be sent into exile.

I, Flavius Reccared, have signed as confirmation these decrees which we established with the holy synod.

[There follow the signatures of the bishops, etc.]

4. VISIGOTHIC LEGISLATION CONCERNING THE JEWS

The laws issued under Visigothic rule were remarkable in that they continued the Roman tradition that the head of state had the right and responsibility to legislate. In contrast, other Germanic successor-states to the Roman Empire issued law codes that were little more than lists of penalties for specific offenses. They limited their lawmaking in that fashion because they held to the primitive Germanic conviction that law was the immemorial custom of the people. The following selections demonstrate Visigothic legislation concerning the Jews. Reccared (586–601) was the first Visigothic king to become a Catholic, and also the first king to pursue an active anti-Jewish policy. The influence of Visigothic policies toward the Jews was preserved in later Christian legislation in Iberia throughout the Middle Ages. (ORC & Jd'QA)

A. Canon III of the Sixth Council of Toledo (638)
Translated from Latin by Jeremy duQ. Adams

The third canon from the Sixth Council of Toledo (held in 638) added serious political consequences to a general principle regulating the relationship between Christians and Jews. The council was summoned by king Khintila (r. 636–639) and attended by forty-eight bishops from all of Spain and part of southeastern Gaul, as well as by clergymen representing five other dioceses (in other words, the entire church under Visigothic rule). This anti-Jewish legislation makes important statements about the vices these churchmen perceived as inherent in the Jewish community and seeks to bind present and future kings to that attitude. In order to combat these perceived vices, Khintila sought the conversion of all Iberian Jews to Christianity. (ORC & Jd'QA)

Keeping Watch on the Jewish Faith

It seems that the inflexible infidelity of the Jews has finally been forced to bend to the powerful piety of heaven. The whole world is aware how, thanks to the inspiration of God on high, the Most Excellent and Most Christian Sovereign [Khintila], inflamed with the ardor of the Faith and in union with the bishops of his kingdom,[1] has chosen to obliterate the very foundations of the superstitious prevarication [of the Jews], and does not permit anyone who is not Catholic to reside in his kingdom. We give thanks to God, the omnipotent King of Heaven, for the fervor of [the king's] faith, for having

Translated from *Concilios visigóticos e hispano-romanos*, edited by José Vives, Tomás Marín Martínez, and Gonzalo Martínez Díez (Madrid: C.S.I.C., 1963), pp. 236–37.

1. A union expressed by this council, which met at Toledo in the large church of St. Leocadia outside the city walls. As early as the Third Council of Toledo (589; see Chapter 3), these ecclesiastical councils had become symbols of the solidarity of church and state in Visigothic Spain.

Figure 1. Saint Ildefonso and a Jew (tenth century). Biblioteca Laurenziana, Florence, Italy. MS Laurenziana Ashburnham 17, fol. 18. Photo credit: Scala/Art Resource, NY.

created so brilliant a soul and filled it with His own wisdom; may He grant him long life in this world and eternal glory in the future. It is however our farsighted concern and a worthy object of our vigilant attention to issue a decree whereby neither his ardor nor our labor may grow lukewarm and be undone in time to come.

Therefore with one heart and voice fully in accord with [the king] we promulgate a judgment pleasing to God, and with the consensus of the magnates and illustrious men [of the kingdom] arising from their deliberation, we decree sanctions therefore: to wit, that whoever in time to come shall attain the highest authority in the kingdom shall not ascend the royal throne until he shall have sworn, among the other provisions of his oath, not to permit [the Jews] to violate the Catholic Faith; he shall not favor their infidelity in any way whatever, nor from neglect or covetousness shall he grant access to the prevarication of such as hover on the brink of faithlessness. Rather shall he see to it that what has been achieved in our time by great effort be maintained hereafter; for it is pointless to accomplish positive results if their preservation be not evident.

Indeed, if after having assumed the government of the kingdom in the aforesaid ritual, [any king] shall have the temerity to violate this promise, let him be anathema Maranatha[2] in the sight of the eternal God and let him become fuel for the eternal fire, along with any bishop, priest, or other Christian who shall have incurred the same condemnation. We for our part so decree and thereby confirm what has been written in previous general councils[3] concerning the Jews: we know that those provisions were necessary for their salvation, and hence judge it important that they be maintained in full vigor.

B. Selections from the *Lex Visigothorum*

The Lex Visigothorum, *also known as* Liber iudiciorum *[Book of Laws] or* Forum iudicum *(and hence as the* Fuero juzgo *in its influential thirteenth-century Castilian translation), is a comprehensive law code in twelve books, each dedicated to a specific topic. It was first promulgated in 654 under king Recceswinth, and later revised in 681 under king Ervig. This book's orderly structure and length make it unique among early medieval Germanic law codes. Book XII deals with religious deviancy, and the second of its subdivisions is entitled "On Amputating All the Errors of All Heretics and All Jews." Many of its articles address the problem of Jewish converts to Christianity who had*

---

2. That is, let him be excommunicated in the most serious manner possible.

3. This refers either to previous councils legislating for the church of Spain as a whole (rather than for one or another province thereof), or to councils of the whole church. Canons 57–66 of the Fourth Council of Toledo (633) deal with several issues of Jewish-Christian relations.

secretly returned to Judaism (sometimes called "judaizers" or "judaizing Christians").
(ORC & Jd'QA)

That Jews May Not Testify Against Christians [and When It Shall Be Lawful for Any of Their Descendants to Give Testimony] (654)

Translated from the Latin by Jeremy duQ. Adams

If a lie discovered before men both renders its perpetrator infamous and incurs a sentence of condemnation, how much the more should not one found defective in regard to the divine Faith be utterly excluded from giving testimony? Deservedly therefore Jews, whether baptized or not baptized, are forbidden to give testimony in court.

But if any born from their stock be found acceptable for upright behavior and integrity of faith, permission to testify truthfully along with Christians is granted them; but not unless they shall fully satisfy a priest, the king, or a judge in all particulars as to their behavior and faith.

Testimony of Faith by Converted Jews (654)

Translated from Latin by Jacob R. Marcus

To our most pious and noble lord and master, king Recceswinth:

We, Jews of the city of Toledo, who have hereto attached our signatures or seals, call your attention to the fact that formerly we were compelled to present a memorial to king Khintila, of holy memory, by which we bound ourselves to uphold the Catholic faith, as, in like manner, we do now. But, whereas the perfidy born of our obstinacy and the antipathy resulting from our ancestral errors influenced us to such an extent that we did not then truly believe in our Lord Jesus Christ and did not sincerely embrace the Catholic faith, therefore now, freely and voluntarily, we promise Your Majesty for ourselves, our wives, and our children, by this, our memorial, that henceforth we will observe no Jewish customs or rites whatever, and will not associate, or have any intercourse with any unbaptized Jews. Nor will we marry any person related to us by blood, within the sixth degree, which union has been declared to be incestuous and wicked.[1] Nor will we, or our children, or any

---

Translated from *Monumenta Germaniae Historica: Legum sectio I, Leges Visigothorum*, edited by Karl Zeumer (Hanover and Leipzig: Hahn, 1902; reprint, 1973), XII, 2, 10; pp. 416–17.

Text from *MGH: Leges Visigothorum*, XII, 2, 17; English text from *The Jew in the Medieval World: A Source Book, 315–1791*, edited by Jacob R. Marcus, revised edition with an introduction and updated biography by Marc Saperstein (Cincinnati: Hebrew Union College Press, 1999), pp. 22 24. Reprinted with permission of the publisher.

1. Canon law prohibited marriage even between distant cousins.

of our posterity, at any time hereafter, contract marriage outside our sect [Christianity]; and both sexes shall hereafter be united in marriage according to Christian rites. We will not practice the operation of circumcision. We will not celebrate the Passover, Sabbath, and other festival days, as enjoined by the Jewish ritual. We will not make any distinction in food, according to our ancient usages. We will not observe, in any way, ceremonies prescribed by the abominable practices and habits of the Hebrews.

But, with sincere faith, grateful hearts, and perfect devotion, we believe that Christ is the son of the living God, as declared by ecclesiastical and evangelical tradition; and we hereby acknowledge Him to be such, and venerate Him accordingly. Moreover, all the ceremonies enjoined by the Christian religion—whether said ceremonies relate to festivals, or to marriage and food—we will truly and exactly observe; and we will maintain the same with sincerity, without any objection or opposition thereto; and without any subterfuge on our part, by means of which we might hereafter deny our acts, return to what has been prohibited, or not completely fulfill all that we have promised.

With regard to the flesh of animals which we consider unclean, if we should be unable to eat the same on account of our ancient prejudices, nevertheless, when it is cooked along with other food, we hereby promise to partake of the latter with no manifestation of disgust or horror.

And if, at any time, we should be found to have transgressed, and to have violated any of the promises hereinbefore specified; or should presume to act contrary to the doctrines of the Christian faith; or if we should, in word or deed, neglect to fulfill the obligations to which we have bound ourselves, as being acceptable to the Catholic religion; we hereby swear by the Father, Son and Holy Spirit, who form one God in the Trinity, that, in case a single transgressor should be found among our people, he shall be burned, or stoned to death, either by ourselves, or by our sons. And should Your Majesty graciously grant such culprit his life, he shall at once be deprived of his freedom, so that Your Majesty may deliver him to be forever a slave to anyone whom Your Majesty may select; and Your Majesty shall have full authority to make whatever disposition of him and his property as may seem expedient; not only on account of the power attached to your royal office, but also by the authority granted by this our memorial.

Made in the name of God, at Toledo, on the Kalends of March, in the sixth year of Your Majesty's happy reign [1 March 654].

Jews Shall Not Remove Themselves or Their Children or Slaves from the Blessing of Baptism (681)

Translated from Latin by Jacob R. Marcus

Since truth itself teaches us to seek, to investigate, to knock [at the door of heaven and it will be opened], admonishing us that "ardent men inherit the kingdom of heaven," there is no doubt that he falls short of the reward of divine favor who does not exert himself to gain that favor (Matt. 7:7, 11:12).

Therefore, if any Jew—of those, naturally, who are as yet not baptized or who have postponed their own or their children's baptism—should prevent his slaves from being baptized in the presence of the priest, or should withhold himself and his family from baptism, or if any one of them should exceed the duration of one year after the promulgation of this law without being baptized, the transgressor of these [conditions], whoever he may be, shall have his head shaved, receive a hundred lashes, and pay the required penalty of exile. His property shall pass over into the power of the king; it shall remain perpetually in the possession of him to whom the king wishes to bestow it, inasmuch as the stubborn life [of the Jew] shows him to be incorrigible.

Text from *MGH: Leges Visigothorum* XII, 3, 3; English text from *The Jew in the Medieval World. A Source Book: 315–1791*, edited by Jacob R. Marcus, revised edition by Marc Saperstein (Cincinnati: Hebrew Union College Press, 1999), p. 24. Reprinted with permission of the publisher.

5. KING KHINDASWINTH AND QUEEN RECIBERGA

Eugenius II of Toledo, Poetic Epitaphs (ca. 650)
Translated from Latin by Jeremy duQ. Adams

This pair of royal epitaphs by Bishop Eugenius II of Toledo (646–657) suggests several things about the relationship of church and state in Visigothic Spain. Khindaswinth (r. 642–653) seized power after a civil war, but reestablished the shaky Gothic monarchy on firm bases of legislative redirection and cultural patronage. The dynasty he established produced the king (Roderic) who fell in the Muslim invasion of 711; later kings of León would claim descent from Khindaswinth's line.

  Eugenius, metropolitan bishop of Toledo, was a gentleman-versifier in the Roman tradition. The acute contrast between the deference shown in other epitaphs by Eugenius and the scathing language of his epitaph for the king (one wonders whether the monarch could still have been alive when it was written) is all the more striking since it was Khindaswinth who had appointed Eugenius bishop of Toledo, and hence the ranking prelate of the Spanish church. The ferocious criticism in this epitaph suggests the tensions inherent in any political office dependent on the approval of religious authorities. In contrast, the epitaph for Khindaswinth's young queen bespeaks a sympathy between the king and his bishop, each the embodiment of Hispano-Roman and Hispano-Gothic patriarchy. Of Reciberga we know practically nothing besides this poem: her signature appears on a charter (unfortunately dubious) to a monastery in the Asturian mountains.

  Roman culture was still desirable as an assertion of legitimacy in the middle of the seventh century, and Eugenius composed the king's epitaph in elegiac couplets, a metrical form made standard for funereal verse by Catullus and others. Reciberga's epitaph is composed in the heroic meter of poems by Virgil and Lucan, basic models for Latin verse in Spanish schools from those poets' lifetimes on. Lucan, whose family came from Córdoba, was a particular favorite. These free translations try to echo the rhythmic form as well as the highly rhetorical tone of the original poems. (ORC & Jd'QA)

For Khindaswinth

Mourn for me, all you within the orb of the world!
  So may your shame be cleansed by appropriate floods.
So may Christ in his clemency cancel your debts,
  So may the shining gate of high heaven swing open.
Let funereal wailing burst now from contrite hearts;
  Let them bring forth the tears of pious general grief.

Translated from *Monumenta Toletana Sacra* (Toledo: Comitatus pro XIII Jubilaeo Sancti Ildefonsi, 1972), pp. 33, 76–77; reprint of *Sanctorum patrum Toletanorum quotquot extant opera*, vol. I, edited by Francisco de Lorenzana (Madrid: Ibarra, 1782).

Send up your sighs to God, give vent to groans of sorrow,
    And on my wretched behalf cry mercy, I pray.
I am Khindaswinth, ever the friend of mischief;
    Perpetrator of crimes Khindaswinth am I.
Impious, obscene, scandalous, shameful, wicked,
    Never willing the best, always up to the worst.
Whatever depraved desire can do, injury seeking,
    That have I done, and have been even worse.
There was no crime I did not wish to commit,
    In vice I was always the best and the first.
Behold: these ashes that wore royal robes have yielded the scepter;
    The earth now weighs upon one who took off the purple.
The chartered trappings of kingship now profit me naught,
    Naught the green jewels, the diadem's luster.
Silver aids me not, there is no help in bright gold,
    The imperial seat does me harm, and treasure pleases me not.
All the glory of mud-sprung[1] life is deception:
    It flies away like a breath, melts in swift dissolution.
Happy indeed is he, in the grace of Christ happy,
    Who has always abhorred the weak, windy[2] wealth of the world.

For Reciberga

Were it allowed to exchange gold and jewels for death,
No ills could have broken apart the life of these monarchs.
But since one common lot shatters everything mortal,
Wealth cannot exempt kings, nor grieving the poor.
Hence I, O wife, unable to overcome fate,
Commit you with these rites to the care of the saints
So that, when devouring flames come to consume the earth,
You may arise a worthy member of their company.
So now Reciberga, my beloved, farewell:

---

1. English cannot convey the original play of words. The adjective *luteus*, with a short initial *u*, as here, means "made of mud" (from *lutum*, very like the material God shaped into Adam in Gen. 2:7); with a long initial *u*, *luteus* means "golden," or at least "yellowish in color."

2. Here there is either a problem with the manuscript or another entirely Eugenian pun: the *flagilis* of the oldest manuscript may be an error for *fragilis* ("weak") or *flabilis* ("windy"), or a highly exceptional construct playing on both meanings as well as suggesting the rare form *flaglo*, a variant for *flagro*, from which derives the English *flagrant*—all of which would be quite typical of the literary conceits favored by late survivors of the classical tradition like Eugenius. North of the Alps, the classical twilight had ended a century earlier.

Thus I, king Khindaswinth, prepare my beloved's bier.
All that remains is to state the brief span of time
That contained her life and our union.
The pact of our marriage endured almost seven years;
She was then twice eleven years old, plus eight months.

The Muslim Arrival and
Christian Reaction
(Eighth Century)

Map 1. The Iberian Peninsula, 711–1031.

6. ACCOUNTS OF THE
MUSLIM CONQUEST (711)

A. *Chronicle of 754*
Translated from Latin by Kenneth B. Wolf

The anonymous Latin Chronicle of 754 was written by a Christian living in al-Andalus during the second generation after the conquest of 711. It was designed as an installment in the ongoing "universal chronicle" begun by Eusebius and Jerome in the fourth century and continued by John of Biclaro and Isidore of Seville. Because the extant Arab histories postdate the Muslim conquest of Spain by hundreds of years, the Chronicle of 754 is the single most important source of information on the "settling in" period of Muslim rule—from the invasion to the eve of the establishment of the Umayyad emirate (756). The following selection describes the conquest itself. It is important to realize that, despite its rhetorical expressions of horror and grief, the chronicle as a whole treats the Muslim governors as legitimate rulers, evaluating them in terms of their ability to promote peace and order on the peninsula rather than dismissing them altogether as non-Christians. The dates in the translation reflect the usage in the original and are not always accurate. (KBW)

In Justinian's time,[1] in the aforesaid year, the first year of his rule and the eighty-ninth of the Arabs, Walīd held the kingship among the Arabs.[2] In Spain, Witiza continued to rule for his fifteenth year.

In Justinian's time, in the era 747 (709), in his fourth year [*sic*] as emperor and the ninety-first of the Arabs, Walīd received the scepter of the kingdom of the Saracens, as his father had arranged, and fought various peoples for four years. He was victorious and, endowed with great honors, exercised his rule for nine years. He was a man of great prudence in deploying his armies to the extent that, though lacking in divine favor, he crushed the forces of almost all neighboring peoples, made Romania[3] especially weak with constant raiding, nearly brought the islands to their destruction, raided and subdued the territory of India, brought cities to utter destitution, besieged fortresses, and, from the twisted paths of Libya, subjugated all of Mauretania.[4] In the western regions, Walīd, through a general of his army by the name of Mūsā,[5]

English text from *Conquerors and Chroniclers of Early Medieval Spain*, edited and translated by Kenneth B. Wolf (Liverpool: Liverpool University Press, 1990), pp. 130–35. Reprinted with permission of the publisher.

1. Justinian II, Byzantine emperor (r. 705–711).
2. Walīd I, Umayyad caliph in Damascus (r. 705–715).
3. Asia Minor.
4. Muslim armies had crossed North Africa to Morocco by 705.
5. Mūsā ibn Nuṣair was appointed governor of Ifrīqiya (roughly modern Tunisia) in 707.

attacked and conquered the kingdom of the Goths—which had been established with ancient solidity almost 350 years ago from its foundation in the era 400 (362) and which had been extended peacefully throughout Spain from the time of Leovigild for almost 140 years up to the era 750 (712)—and having seized the kingdom, he made it pay tribute.

In Justinian's time, in the era 749 (711), in his fourth year as emperor and the ninety-second of the Arabs, with Walīd retaining the scepter of the kingdom for the fifth year, Roderic rebelliously seized the kingdom at the instigation of the senate.[6] He ruled for only one year. Mustering his forces, he directed armies against the Arabs and the Moors sent by Mūsā, that is against Ṭāriq ibn Ziyād[7] and the others, who had long been raiding the province consigned to them and simultaneously devastating many cities. In the fifth year of Justinian's rule, the ninety-third of the Arabs, and the sixth of Walīd, in the era 750 (712), Roderic headed for the Transductine mountains[8] to fight them and in that battle the entire army of the Goths, which had come with him fraudulently and in rivalry out of ambition for the kingship, fled and he was killed. Thus Roderic wretchedly lost not only his rule but his homeland, his rivals also being killed, as Walīd was completing his sixth year of rule. . . .

In Justinian's time, in the era 749 (711),[9] in his fourth year as emperor, the ninety-second of the Arabs, and the fifth of Walīd, while Spain was being devastated by the aforesaid forces and was greatly afflicted not only by the enemy but also by domestic fury, Mūsā himself, approaching this wretched land across the straits of Cádiz and pressing on to the pillars of Hercules—which reveal the entrance to the port like an index to a book or like keys in his hand revealing and unlocking the passage to Spain—entered the long plundered and godlessly invaded Spain to destroy it.[10] After forcing his way to Toledo, the royal city, he imposed on the adjacent regions an evil and fraudulent peace. He decapitated on a scaffold those noble lords who had remained, arresting them in their flight from Toledo with the help of Oppa, King Egica's son. With Oppa's support, he killed them all with the sword. Thus he devastated not only Hispania Ulterior, but Hispania Citerior[11] up to and beyond

6. Roderic (r. 710–711). The term "senate" probably refers to the palace officials.

7. Ṭāriq ibn Ziyād, governor of Tangiers, had been appointed by Mūsā ibn Nuṣair to lead a force to Spain in 711.

8. Location unknown, but perhaps in the region of Medina Sidonia.

9. The author picks up again in 711 after a paragraph on the bishop Sindered, who fled from his post in Toledo in the face of the Arab conquest.

10. Mūsā entered Spain in 712 and, after taking Seville and Mérida, joined up with Ṭāriq in Toledo in 713.

11. Hispania Ulterior and Hispania Citerior refer to the Roman division of western and

the ancient and once flourishing city of Zaragoza, now, by the judgment of God, openly exposed to the sword, famine, and captivity. He ruined beautiful cities, burning them with fire; condemned lords and powerful men to the cross; and butchered youths and infants with the sword. While he terrorized everyone in this way, some of the cities that remained sued for peace under duress and, after persuading and mocking them with a certain craftiness, the Saracens granted their requests without delay. When the citizens subsequently rejected what they had accepted out of fear and terror, they tried to flee to the mountains where they risked hunger and various forms of death. The Saracens set up their savage kingdom in Spain, specifically in Córdoba, formerly a patrician see and always the most opulent in comparison to the rest of the cities, giving its first fruits to the kingdom of the Visigoths. . . .

In the era 750 (712), in Justinian's sixth year as emperor and the ninety-fourth of the Arabs, Mūsā, after fifteen months had elapsed, was summoned by order of the princes and, leaving his son 'Abd al-'Azīz in his place, he returned to his homeland and presented himself to the king Walīd in the last year of his reign. Mūsā brought with him from Spain some noblemen who had escaped the sword; gold and silver, assayed with zeal by the bankers; a large quantity of valuable ornaments, precious stones, and pearls; ointments to kindle women's desire; and many other things from the length and breadth of Spain that would be tedious to record. When he arrived, by God's will he found Walīd angry.[12] Mūsā was ignominiously removed from the prince's presence and paraded with a rope around his neck. . . .[13]

At the same time, in the era 753 (715), in Justinian's ninth year as emperor and the ninety-seventh of the Arabs, 'Abd al-'Azīz pacified all of Spain for three years under the yoke of tribute.[14] After he had taken all the riches and positions of honor in Seville, as well as the queen of Spain, whom he joined in marriage, and the daughters of kings and princes, whom he treated as concubines and then rashly repudiated, he was eventually killed on the advice of 'Ayyūb by a revolt of his own men while he was in prayer. After 'Ayyūb had held Spain for a full month, Al-Ḥurr succeeded to the throne of Hesperia by order of the prince,[15] who was informed about the death of 'Abd al-'Azīz in

---

eastern Spain. The division did not run exactly north-south and thus much of the southern peninsula was in Hispania Ulterior.

12. Actually, Walīd was ill and died shortly after the return of Mūsā and Ṭāriq (who left Spain in 714), leaving his successor, Sulaymān, to deal with the conquerors of Spain.

13. To humiliate him publicly.

14. 'Abd al-'Azīz, the son of Mūsā, ruled 714–716. His capital was in Seville; the Andalusi capital moved to Córdoba a few years later.

15. 'Ayyūb ibn Ḥabīb al-Lakhmī ruled briefly in 716, then was succeeded by al-Ḥurr ibn 'Abd al-Raḥmān al-Thaqafī (r. 716–718) by order of the Muslim governor of Ifrīqiya.

this way: that on the advice of queen Egilona, wife of the late king Roderic, whom he had joined to himself, he tried to throw off the Arab yoke from his neck and retain the conquered kingdom of Iberia for himself.

B. Ibn 'Abd al-Ḥakam, *Narrative of the Conquest of al-Andalus*
Translated from Arabic by David A. Cohen

The earliest surviving accounts of the Islamic conquest of Spain in Arabic date from the mid- to late ninth century. The best known of these is a collection of stories and legends contained in the Futūh Miṣr *[Conquest of Egypt] of Ibn 'Abd al-Ḥakam (d. 871), a member of a prominent Arab family of religious and legal scholars from Egypt.*

Ibn 'Abd al-Ḥakam's life and writing are typical of the Islamic culture of his time. The most characteristic feature of this culture was the transmission of ideas, religious rules, prophecies, and other knowledge in the form of anecdotes or narratives called ḥadīth. *The most important* ḥadīth *were tales about the prophet Muḥammad, which were used as the basis of Islamic religious law, but stories about profane historical events were told in the form of* ḥadīth *as well. Ibn 'Abd al-Ḥakam's history is essentially a collection of* ḥadīth. *In the first centuries of Islam, oral recitation was the principal means of transmission of the* ḥadīth. *Since devout Muslims wanted trustworthy reports of actual events, it became customary to preface the* ḥadīth *with authenticating sequences or chains of oral sources called* isnād. *This selection from the* Futūh Miṣr *includes several* isnād. *A modern reader should keep in mind the pious atmosphere of oral storytelling in which Ibn 'Abd al-Ḥakam gathered his material. The* ḥadīth *were often told by holy men inside the mosque, and hearing and learning them were considered forms of religious devotion, as well as instruction and entertainment. A history written from such stories may jar modern tastes, which are accustomed to a very different notion of the relevance of events. Historians in recent decades have tended to discount the usefulness of Ibn 'Abd al-Ḥakam and accounts like his for the study of the Islamic conquest of Spain. Some have doubted whether many of the persons mentioned, such as Julian and Ṭāriq, even existed. Nevertheless Ibn 'Abd al-Ḥakam's moralizing tales offer a telling glimpse into the world of mainstream, pious Muslims as they reflected on Islam's experience of conquest. (DAC)*

He said:[1] Mūsā ibn Nuṣair sent his son Marwān ibn Mūsā to Tangiers, stationing him on the coast. When he and his friends became tired, he left, and he bestowed the command of his army on Ṭāriq ibn 'Amrū. There were 1,700

Translated from *The History of the Conquest of Egypt, North Africa, and Spain Known as the Futūḥ Miṣr of Ibn 'Abd al-ḥakam*, edited by Charles C. Torrey, Yale Oriental Series—Researches III (New Haven, Conn.: Yale University Press, 1922), pp. 204–13.
1. The "he" of this and similar phrases throughout the text refers to the author. Such constructions recall the circumstances of oral recitation. The Arabic word translated as "narrative" in the title, *dhikr*, can also mean oral relating, remembrance, or recitation.

men, but it is also said there were 12,000 Berbers and 16 Arabs, though this is not true. . . .

There was a strait between [Tangiers] and the people of al-Andalus, and [ruling] over it was a non-Arab man called Julian [Arabic Yulyān], lord of Ceuta and of a city on the passage to al-Andalus called Algeciras.[2] Algeciras was one of the cities adjacent to Tangiers [i.e., on the Spanish coast opposite Tangiers], and it was Julian's, He was accustomed to obey Roderic [Ludhrīq], lord of al-Andalus, who lived in Toledo. Ṭāriq wrote to Julian and flattered him, until they exchanged presents. Now Julian had sent his daughter to Roderic, lord of al-Andalus, for her education and instruction, and Roderic made her pregnant. When this news reached Julian he said, "I do not see how I can punish him or pay him back except by sending the Arabs against him." So he sent word to Ṭāriq, saying, "It is I who will take you to al-Andalus." At that time Ṭāriq was in Tlemcen and Mūsā ibn Nuṣair was in Qairawan. Ṭāriq answered, "I will not trust you until you send me a hostage," so Julian sent him his two daughters. He had no children other than these two. Ṭāriq put them under secure guard in Tlemcen, and then he went out to Julian, who was in Ceuta on the straits. Julian rejoiced at his arrival and said to him, "I will take you over to al-Andalus." Now there was in the straits, between the two coasts, a mountain lying between Ceuta and al-Andalus called today Gibraltar [Jabal Ṭāriq].

When it was evening, Julian came to him with ships, and he carried him across the strait, and he lay in wait there during the day. The next evening he sent the ships back to the rest of his companions, and they were all brought to him. The people of al-Andalus did not know about them, nor did they think anything except that the ships going back and forth were similar to the [merchant] ships that [usually] went back and forth in the straits for their profit.

Ṭāriq was in the last group of riders, and when he went over to his companions, Julian and the merchants who were with him stayed behind in Algeciras, which was better for their spirit.[3] The report of Ṭāriq and those who were with him reached the people of al-Andalus and the places where they lived. Meanwhile Ṭāriq, followed by his companions, went his way over a bridge[4] from the mountains to a village called Qarṭājanna,[5] and they marched heading for Córdoba.

---

2. The identity of this place-name and a number of others in the text are disputed by scholars.

3. This phrase probably means that it was better for the morale of the Muslim soldiers if Julian and the ships remained on the Iberian side to provide a way of escape.

4. The Arabic word translated here as "bridge," qanṭara, can mean an arched bridge or a viaduct supported by arches. Ruins of a Moorish viaduct exist today at Algeciras, and in the eighteenth century remains of a viaduct could be found at Gibraltar.

5. Carteya, a Roman town now in ruins.

He said: As my father, 'Abd Allah ibn 'Abd al-Ḥakam, and Hishām ibn Isḥāq told me, there was a house of [many] locks in al-Andalus, and no king could hold power over them unless he added a lock of his own, until there came the king who was attacked by the Muslims. They [the people of al-Andalus] urged him to place a lock on the house just as the kings before him had done, but he refused. "I will not put anything on the house until I know what is inside," he declared, and he commanded that it be opened. In it were drawn pictures of the Arabs, and also there was writing, which said, "When this door is opened, these people will conquer this country."

Then he returned to the *ḥadīth* of 'Uthmān and of others. He said: As Ṭāriq marched, the warriors of Córdoba came out against him, and they were emboldened when they saw how few were his companions. They fought, and their fight increased in intensity until they were defeated. Then [the Muslims] did not stop killing them until they reached the city of Córdoba. When Roderic heard this, he marched out against them from Toledo. They met at a place called Sidonia [Shadūna] at a river called today Wādī Umm Ḥakīm.[6] They fought a fierce battle, and God, glory and greatness upon him, killed Roderic and those who were with him. . . . Ṭāriq then advanced to Toledo, and he entered it and asked after the table. He had no thought other than for this table, for it was the table of Sulaimān ibn Dā'ūd, as is alleged by the People of the Book.[7] Yaḥyā ibn Bukair told us that al-Laith ibn Sa'd told him that when al-Andalus was conquered by Mūsā ibn Nuṣair, the table and crown of Sulaimān ibn Dā'ūd, prayers and blessings of God be upon him, were seized. Ṭāriq was informed that the table was in a fortress called Firās, two days' journey from Toledo, and the lord of the fortress was the son of Roderic's sister. So Ṭāriq sent to him a guarantee of his safety and the safety of the people of his house, whereupon he surrendered to Ṭāriq, who kept him safe and carried out all he had promised him. Then Ṭāriq said to him, "Hand over the table," and he did so. On it were gold and gems such as had never been seen. Ṭāriq tore off one of the legs together with its gems and gold, and put in its place a similar one. The value of the table was estimated at 200,000 dinars, because of the gems that were on it. Ṭāriq then took what was his from the gems, weapons, gold, silver, and table service, and it amounted to the same value in money, the like of which had never been seen.

6. According to Ibn 'Abd al-Ḥakam, Umm Ḥakīm was the name of a slave girl of Ṭāriq. An island off the coast of southern Spain captured by Ṭāriq is also said to be named after her.

7. The term "People of the Book" in Islam refers to Christians and Jews, i.e., those who follow religions founded on the Bible. Sulaimān ibn Dā'ūd is the Arabic name for the biblical Solomon, son of David. The story of the finding of Solomon's table caught the imagination of medieval Islamic writers and was subsequently embellished. It appears in the *Thousand and One Nights*.

So he gathered it all up and returned to Córdoba and stayed there. He wrote to Mūsā ibn Nuṣair and told him of the conquest of al-Andalus and the booty he had won. Mūsā then wrote to al-Walīd ibn ʿAbd al-Malik informing him of this, and he threw himself on his mercy.[8] Mūsā also wrote to Ṭāriq saying that he should not move beyond Córdoba until he should come to him, and he reviled him bitterly. . . .

Ibn ʿAbd al-Ḥakam continues his account with various stories in which Mūsā, Ṭāriq, and members of the caliphal family in Syria quarrel and intrigue over sharing the vast spoils from al-Andalus. Both Ṭāriq and Mūsā are obliged to travel to the caliphal court to protect their claims and their lives.

. . . it is also said that Mūsā ibn Nuṣair came to al-Walīd ibn ʿAbd al-Malik when al-Walīd was sick, and Mūsā gave the table [of Solomon] to him as a present. But Ṭāriq declared, "It is I who won the table!" Mūsā called him a liar. So Ṭāriq said to al-Walīd, "Call for the table, and see whether any of the gold from it is missing." Al-Walīd called for it, and he saw how one of the legs was not the same as the others. And Ṭāriq said to him, "Ask him, O Commander of the Faithful, and if he can tell you truthfully about what you seek to know, then he is right." So al-Walīd asked him about the table leg, and he said, "I found it like this." Then Ṭāriq brought out the leg he had taken when he found [the table], and he said, "The Commander of the Faithful asked you about it in order to find the truth about what I have said, and indeed it is I who found it." So al-Walīd trusted him, graciously accepted his account, and valued his prize highly. . . .

Neither Mūsā nor Ṭāriq ever returned to Spain. Before his departure, Mūsā, as governor of Islamic North Africa, appointed his son ʿAbd al-ʿAzīz to rule as governor over Spain.

Then he returned to the *ḥadīth* of ʿUthmān and others, and he said: After his father departed, ʿAbd al-ʿAzīz married a Christian princess, daughter of a king of al-Andalus. It is said she was the daughter of Roderic, king of al-Andalus, whom Ṭāriq killed. She brought him a great fortune in worldly things, such as cannot be described. When she came to him, she said, "Why do I not see the people of your kingdom glorifying you? They do not prostrate themselves before you as the people of my father's kingdom glorified him and prostrated themselves before him." He did not know what to say

---

8. Literally, "he gave him his life," i.e., he gave the caliph the right to decide whether he should live or die.

to her, so he commanded that the side of his palace be pierced with a small door. He used to give audience to the people, and for this purpose he would come to the inside of the door, so that someone entering to see him would have to lower his head on account of the smallness of the door. She was in a [hidden] spot watching the people, and when she saw this, she said to ʿAbd al-ʿAzīz, "Now you are a great king!" The people heard, however, that he had constructed the door for this purpose, and some believed that she had made him a Christian. So Ḥabīb ibn Abī ʿUbaida al-Fihrī and Ziyād ibn al-Nābigha al-Tamīmī and their friends from the Arab tribes, when they heard about it, stirred up rebellion against him. They decided to kill ʿAbd al-ʿAzīz. They went to his muezzin and said, "Give the call to prayer at night so that we may come out for prayers." So the muezzin called out and intoned the call to prayer, and ʿAbd al-ʿAzīz came out and said to his muezzin, "You have rushed indeed, giving the call to prayer at night!" Then he went to the mosque. Those of the [rebel] party had already gathered there, as well as others who were present for the prayers. ʿAbd al-ʿAzīz went to the front and began to recite, "When the event happens—and there is no lie to the event—casting [some] low and raising [others] high" (Qurʾān 56:1–3), whereupon Ḥabīb struck his sword at ʿAbd al-ʿAzīz's head. ʿAbd al-ʿAzīz turned away in flight until he came to his house, and he went into his garden and hid there under a bush. Ḥabīb ibn Abī ʿUbaida and his companions fled, but Ziyād ibn al-Nābigha followed him. He came upon his tracks and found him under the bush. ʿAbd al-ʿAzīz said to him, "Be merciful, Ibn al-Nabigha, and I will give you whatever you ask." But he answered, "You may not taste life after this!" and finished him off, and he cut off his head.

Ḥabīb and Ziyād took the head to Syria and presented it to the caliph in the presence of Mūsā, the murdered man's father. The caliph asked Mūsā if he knew the victim. Mūsā's reply was laconic: "Yes, I knew him for his fasting and his praying, and upon him be the curse of God if the man who killed him was better than he."

C. Ibn al-Qūṭiyya, *History of the Conquest of al-Andalus*

Translated from Arabic by Ann Christys

Although Ibn ʿAbd al-Ḥakam provides one of the earliest accounts of the conquest of 711, he was writing far away in the eastern Islamic world. In contrast, Ibn al-Qūṭiyya (d. 977) was an Andalusi author who is said to have been a descendent of Sara, the granddaughter of the last Visigothic king, Witiza (Ibn al-Qūṭiyya's name means "the son of the Gothic woman"). He was born in Seville and later moved to Córdoba where he taught Islamic law and tradition. Ibn al-Qūṭiyya's narrative was written long after the conquest that it describes, and it contains elements not found in other accounts. However, these may record family traditions and reflect an Andalusi perspective of events.[1] (ORC)

The last king of the Goths of al-Andalus, Ghītīsha [Witiza] left on his death three sons: the eldest was called Alamundo, after him came Romulo, then Artubās. Because at the time of the death of their father they were minors, their mother remained in Toledo ruling the kingdom. Rodrigo, who was a general appointed by the former king, left the court, followed by the military men who were under his command, and established himself in Córdoba. . . .

When Ṭāriq ibn Ziyād entered Hispania, in the time of the caliph al-Walīd ibn ʿAbd al-Malik, Rodrigo wrote to the sons of the king, who were already handsome youths and able to manage a horse, inviting them to help him and unite with him against the common enemy. They gathered the frontier troops and marched out, camping in Secunda; they did not dare to enter Córdoba because they did not have complete confidence in Rodrigo: the latter had to leave the city to join up with them.

They set out immediately to meet Ṭāriq, and when the two armies were on the point of joining battle, Alamundo and his brother agreed amongst themselves to betray Rodrigo. The very same night, they sent messengers to Ṭāriq to inform him that Rodrigo was no more than one of their father's vilest vassals, and to ask him for his protection in order that they might cross to his camp on the following morning. They asked him to confirm and assure their possession of the inheritance that their father had held in Hispania. They were three thousand villas, which would later be known as "the royal

English text from Ann Christys, *Christians in Al-Andalus, 711–1000* (Richmond, Surry: Curzon, 2002), pp. 174–75. Reprinted with permission of the publisher.
    1. For a recent translation of Ibn al-Qūṭiyya's whole chronicle, see *Early Islamic Spain: The History of Ibn al-Qutiya*, translated by David L. James (New York: Routledge, 2009).

villas." At dawn they crossed over to Ṭāriq's camp with the troops which they had brought with them. This was the cause of the conquest. . . .

When the three brothers came before Ṭāriq, they said to him, "Are you your own chief or is there a chief over you?" Ṭāriq answered them, "There is a chief over my head and over his another." He permitted them to join Mūsā ibn Nuṣayr in Ifrīqiya so that their relation with him might be confirmed. They requested of Ṭāriq a letter to Mūsā regarding their affairs with Ṭāriq and the pledge that he had given them. Ṭāriq complied. They set out toward Mūsā carrying Ṭāriq's letter explaining their agreement of submission and the conditions granted them. They met Mūsā in his descent toward al-Andalus in the vicinity of the land of the Berbers. Mūsā ibn Nuṣayr sent them to al-Walīd ibn ʿAbd al-Malik. They went to the caliph who ratified for them the pledge of Ṭāriq ibn Ziyād. Along with that he concluded a written contract with each one of them. . . .

The *amīr al-muʾminīn* [prince of the believers] found him to be more prudent than the rest, and treated him with honor. The pact which he had made with ʿAbd al-ʿAzīz a short time before was firmly renewed by him. So he returned to Spain rejoicing and remained secure from then on, so that in no way were these powerful bonds dissolved by succeeding Arab rulers.

7. REGULATIONS FOR NON-MUSLIMS UNDER ISLAMIC RULE

The Pact of 'Umar

Translated from Arabic by Bernard Lewis

The so-called Pact of 'Umar is a fundamental element in Islamic law relating to the protection and toleration of Christians and Jews living in Muslim lands. Although the text takes the form of an agreement between Syrian Christians and the caliph 'Umar ibn al-Khaṭṭāb (d. 644), in practice it was applied equally to both Christians and Jews as a code for regulating the proper conduct of dhimmīs. It is unlikely that the Pact is actually a seventh-century document, and it may be more plausibly associated with the Umayyad caliph 'Umar II (d. 720). Whatever its exact origins, the regulations in the Pact of 'Umar were repeated, with some variations, by many medieval authors all over the Islamic world. This version was recorded by the Andalusi jurist al-Ṭurṭūshī (d. 1126). (ORC)

We heard from 'Abd al-Raḥmān ibn Ghanam [d. 78/697] as follows: When 'Umar ibn al-Khaṭṭāb, may God be pleased with him, accorded a peace to the Christians of Syria, we wrote to him as follows:

In the name of God, the Merciful and Compassionate.

This is a letter to the servant of God 'Umar [ibn al-Khaṭṭāb], Commander of the Faithful, from the Christians of such-and-such a city. When you came against us, we asked you for safe-conduct (*amān*) for ourselves, our descendants, our property, and the people of our community, and we undertook the following obligations toward you:

We shall not build, in our cities or in their neighborhood, new monasteries, churches, convents, or monks' cells, nor shall we repair, by day or by night, such of them as fall in ruins or are situated in the quarters of the Muslims.

We shall keep our gates wide open for passersby and travelers. We shall give board and lodging to all Muslims who pass our way for three days.

We shall not give shelter in our churches or in our dwellings to any spy, nor hide him from the Muslims.

We shall not teach the Qur'ān to our children.

We shall not manifest our religion publicly nor convert anyone to it. We shall not prevent any of our kin from entering Islam if they wish it.

English text from *Islam from the Prophet Muhammad to the Capture of Constantinople*, vol. 2, *Religion and Society*, edited and translated by Bernard Lewis (New York: Oxford University Press, 1974), pp. 217–19. Reprinted with permission of the publisher.

We shall show respect toward the Muslims, and we shall rise from our seats when they wish to sit.

We shall not seek to resemble the Muslims by imitating any of their garments, the *qalansuwa*,[1] the turban, footwear, or the parting of the hair. We shall not speak as they do, nor shall we adopt their *kunyas*.[2]

We shall not mount on saddles, nor shall we gird swords nor bear any kind of arms nor carry them on our persons.

We shall not engrave Arabic inscriptions on our seals.

We shall not sell fermented drinks.

We shall clip the fronts of our heads.

We shall always dress in the same way wherever we may be, and we shall bind the *zunnār*[3] round our waists.

We shall not display our crosses or our books in the roads or markets of the Muslims. We shall only use clappers in our churches very softly. We shall not raise our voices in our church services or in the presence of Muslims, nor shall we raise our voices when following our dead. We shall not show lights on any of the roads of the Muslims or in their markets. We shall not bury our dead near the Muslims.

We shall not take slaves who have been allotted to the Muslims.

We shall not build houses overtopping the houses of the Muslims.

(When I brought the letter to 'Umar, may God be pleased with him, he added, "We shall not strike any Muslim.")

We accept these conditions for ourselves and for the people of our community, and in return we receive safe-conduct.

If we in any way violate these undertakings for which we ourselves stand surety, we forfeit our covenant (*dhimma*), and we become liable to the penalties for contumacy and sedition.

'Umar ibn al-Khaṭṭāb replied: Sign what they ask, but add two clauses and impose them in addition to those which they have undertaken. They are: "They shall not buy anyone made prisoner by the Muslims," and "Whoever strikes a Muslim with deliberate intent shall forfeit the protection of this pact."

---

1. A tall hat.
2. The *kunya* is the part of an Arabic name that indicates that a person is a father or mother (such as Abū Bakr or Umm Fatima). Sometimes this designation is merely honorific.
3. A distinctive belt or sash.

8. A MUSLIM-CHRISTIAN TREATY

The Treaty of Tudmīr (713)

Translated from Arabic by Olivia Remie Constable

There are no contemporary descriptions of the Muslim conquest (the earliest account comes from the Latin Chronicle of 754, translated in Chapter 6), but we do have a record of an Arabic document that appears to date from 713, two years after the first Muslim arrival. This document records a peace treaty between ʿAbd al-ʿAzīz, the son of Mūsā ibn Nuṣair, and Theodemir (called Tudmīr in Arabic), the local ruler of Murcia. In contrast to the accounts of the events of 711 provided by chronicles, which describe a quick and violent military victory, this document suggests that the Muslim conquest of the Iberian Peninsula may have been a more gradual and piecemeal endeavor. In fact, it is possible that two different processes worked to bring the former Visigothic realm under Muslim rule. Some cities, including Toledo, the seat of Visigothic power, appear to have capitulated quickly in the face of military force. Other areas, however, may have been won by more peaceful means, using treaties such as this one to enlist the cooperation of local administrators and inhabitants. This treaty establishes the local Christian population as a protected group under Muslim rule. As with any dhimmī group, they were guaranteed personal safety and allowed to retain their religion in return for their loyalty to the Muslim regime and payment of an annual tax. (ORC)

In the name of God, the merciful and the compassionate.

This is a document [granted] by ʿAbd al-ʿAzīz ibn Mūsā ibn Nuṣair to Tudmīr, son of Ghabdūsh, establishing a treaty of peace and the promise and protection of God and his Prophet (may God bless him and grant him peace). We [ʿAbd al-ʿAzīz] will not set special conditions for him or for any among his men, nor harass him, nor remove him from power. His followers will not be killed or taken prisoner, nor will they be separated from their women and children. They will not be coerced in matters of religion, their churches will not be burned, nor will sacred objects be taken from the realm, [so long as] he [Tudmīr] remains sincere and fulfills the [following] conditions that we have set for him. He has reached a settlement concerning seven towns: Orihuela, Valentilla, Alicante, Mula, Bigastro, Ello, and Lorca. He will not give shelter to fugitives, nor to our enemies, nor encourage any protected person to fear us, nor conceal news of our enemies. He and [each of] his men shall [also] pay one dinar every year, together with four measures of wheat, four measures of barley, four liquid measures of concentrated fruit juice, four

Translated from al-Ḍabbī, *Kitāb bughyāt al-multamis fī taʾrīkh rijāl ahl al-Andalus*, edited by Francisco Codera and Julian Ribera (Madrid: Rūkhas, 1885), p. 259.

liquid measures of vinegar, four of honey, and four of olive oil. Slaves must each pay half of this amount.

Names of four witnesses follow, and the document is dated from the Muslim month of Rajab, in the year 94 of the Hijra (April 713).

9. CHRISTIAN RESISTANCE IN THE NORTH (CA. 718)

Chronicle of Alfonso III (early 880s)
Translated from Latin by Kenneth B. Wolf

Under Alfonso III (r. 866–910), the kingdom of Asturias achieved a political and military stature that expressed itself, among other ways, in the production of historical literature. The Chronicle of Alfonso III *was designed as a continuation of Isidore's* History of the Goths, Vandals, and Suevi. *Its purpose, in narrative terms, was to show, first, how the Catholic Visigothic kings who had united Spain under their rule by the late sixth century lost it all to the Arabs in the early eighth century and, second, how the Christians of Asturias, self-described heirs to the Visigoths, were able to make good their claims to Spain at the expense of the Arabs. The chronicle was apparently written in the early 880s, when the Asturian monarchy under Alfonso III was taking advantage of a period of political instability in the Cordoban emirate and thinking—prematurely, as it turned out—that the days of Arab rule in Spain were numbered. Its author is unknown, although traditionally it has been ascribed to Alfonso III himself.*

The selection below describes the Arab invasion of 711 and Pelayo's rise as a leader of the Christian resistance in Asturias shortly after. The self-confidence and sense of purpose that pervade the text belong more to the late ninth century than to the early eighth. (KBW)

Biblical invokation

But let us return to that time when the Saracens entered Spain on the third day before the Ides of November, era 752 (November 11, 714).

The Arabs, after oppressing the region along with the kingdom, killed many with the sword and subjugated the rest to themselves by mollifying them with a covenant of peace. The city of Toledo, victor over all peoples, succumbed, vanquished by the victories of the Ishmaelites; subjected, it served them. They placed prefects throughout all the provinces of Spain and paid tribute to the Babylonian king[1] for many years until they elected their own king and established for themselves a kingdom in the patrician city of Córdoba.[2] At almost the same time, in this region of the Asturians, there was in the city of Gijón a prefect by the name of Munnuza, a companion of Tariq. While he held the prefecture, a certain Pelayo, the swordbearer of the kings

---

English text from *Conquerors and Chroniclers of Early Medieval Spain*, edited and translated by Kenneth B. Wolf (Liverpool: Liverpool University Press, 1990), pp. 164–68. Reprinted with permission of the publisher.

1. That is, the Umayyad caliph in Damascus.

2. After the Abbasid revolution in 750, one of the few remaining members of the Umayyad family, 'Abd al-Raḥmān, made his way to Spain where he established an independent Umayyad emirate with its capital in Córdoba.

Figure 2. Horseman, possibly a Muslim, depicted in the *Gerona Beatus* (tenth century). Library of the Cathedral of Gerona. Photo credit: Scala/Art Resource, NY.

Figure 3. The scriptorium and the tower of the monastery of Tavara, depicted in Beatus of Liébana's *Commentary on the Apocalypse*, Burgos (dated 1220). Pierpont Morgan Library, New York, MS M. 429, fol. 183. Photo credit: Pierpont Morgan Library/Art Resource, NY.

Witiza and Roderic, oppressed by the dominion of the Ishmaelites, had come to Asturias along with his sister. On account of her, Munnuza sent Pelayo to Córdoba as his envoy. Before Pelayo returned, Munnuza married his sister through some stratagem. When Pelayo returned he by no means consented to it. Since he had already been thinking about the salvation of the church, he hastened to bring this about with all of his courage. Then the evil Tariq sent soldiers to Munnuza, who were to apprehend Pelayo and lead him back to Córdoba, bound in chains. When they came to Asturias, seeking to apprehend him treacherously in a village called Brece,[3] the plan of the Chaldeans was made known to Pelayo by a friend. Seeing that it would be impossible for him to resist the Saracens because they were so numerous, Pelayo escaped from among them, rushed off and came to the edge of the river Piloña.[4] He found it overflowing its banks, but by swimming with the help of the horse upon which he sat, he crossed to the opposite side and climbed a mountain. The Saracens stopped pursuing him. As he was heading into the mountains, Pelayo joined himself to as many people as he found hastening to assemble. He climbed a high mountain called Auseva and headed for a cave on the side of the mountain which he knew to be very safe.[5] From this great cave flows a stream called the Enna. After Pelayo sent an order to all of the Asturians, they gathered together in one group and elected him their leader.[6] Hearing this, the soldiers who had come to apprehend him returned to Córdoba and related everything to their king, saying that Pelayo, as Munnuza had suggested, was clearly a rebel. Hearing this, the king, moved by an insane fury, ordered a very large army from all over Spain to go forth and he placed Alqamah, his companion, in charge of it. He ordered Oppa, a certain bishop of the see of Toledo and son of King Witiza—on account of whose treachery the Goths had perished—to go with Alqamah and the army to Asturias. Alqamah was advised by his colleague Tariq that if Pelayo refused to come to terms with the bishop, he should be taken by force in battle and brought to Córdoba. Coming with an army of almost 187,000 soldiers, they entered Asturias.

Pelayo was on Mt. Auseva with his allies. The army advanced to him and set up countless tents before the mouth of the cave. Bishop Oppa ascended the hill in front of Covadonga and spoke to Pelayo, saying, "Pelayo, Pelayo, where are you?"

Pelayo, responding from an opening, said, "I am here."

The bishop said to him, "I think that it is not unknown to you, brother

3. Location unknown.
4. Near Cangas de Onís.
5. Covadonga, a spot a few miles to the east of Cangas de Onís.
6. Pelayo (r. 718–737).

and son, how all of Spain a short time ago was organized according to one order under the rule of the Goths, and that it outshone all other lands in learning and knowledge. If when the entire army of the Goths was assembled, it was unable to sustain the attack of the Ishmaelites, how much better will you be able to defend yourself on this mountain top? To me it seems difficult. Rather, heed my warning and recall your soul from this decision, so that you may take advantage of many good things and enjoy the partnership of the Chaldeans."

To this Pelayo responded, "Have you not read in the divine scriptures that the church of God is compared to a mustard seed and that it will be raised up again through divine mercy?" (Matt. 17:20). *Deus vult!*

The bishop responded, "It is indeed written thus."

Pelayo said, "Christ is our hope that through this little mountain, which you see, the well-being of Spain and the army of the Gothic people will be restored. I have faith that the promise of the Lord which was spoken through David will be fulfilled in us: 'I will visit their iniquities with the rod and their sins with scourges; but I will not remove my mercy from them' (Ps. 89:32–33). Now, therefore, trusting in the mercy of Jesus Christ, I despise this multitude and am not afraid of it. As for the battle with which you threaten us, we have for ourselves an advocate in the presence of the Father, that is, the Lord Jesus Christ, who is capable of liberating us from these few."

And the bishop turned to the army and said, "Go forth and fight. You heard how he responded to me. I can see by his determination that you will never have a covenant of peace with him unless it be achieved through the vengeance of the sword."

Then Alqamah ordered his men to engage in battle. They took up arms. The catapults were set up. The slings were prepared. Swords flashed. Spears were brandished. Arrows were shot incessantly. But on this occasion the power of the Lord was not absent. For when stones were launched from the catapults and they neared the shrine of the holy virgin Mary, which is inside the cave, they turned back on those who shot them and violently cut down the Chaldeans. And because the Lord does not count spears, but offers the palm of victory to whomsoever he will, when the Asturians came out of the cave to fight, the Chaldeans turned in flight and were divided into two groups. There Bishop Oppa was immediately captured and Alqamah was killed. In that same place 124,000 of the Chaldeans were killed. But the 63,000 who were left alive ascended to the summit of Mt. Auseva and came down to Liébana through Amuesa.[7] But they could not escape the

---

7. The Muslims apparently fled through the heart of the mountainous Picos de Europa region of eastern Asturias and western Cantabria.

vengeance of the Lord. For when they had reached the summit of the mountain, which is over the bank of a river called the Deva, next to a village called Cosgaya, it happened, by a judgment of God, that the mountain, quaking from its very base, hurled the 63,000 men into the river and crushed them all. There even now, when this river fills beyond its limit, it reveals many visible signs of these events. Do not think this to be unfounded or fictitious. Remember that he who parted the waters of the Red Sea so that the children of Israel might cross (Exod. 14:21–22), also crushed, with an immense mass of mountain, the Arabs who were persecuting the church of God.

When Munnuza learned what had happened, he sprang from the same coastal city of Gijón and fled. In a certain village called Olalies he was captured and killed along with his men. Then the country was populated, the church restored, and everyone together gave thanks to God, saying, "Blessed be the name of the Lord who strengthens those who believe in him and destroys wicked peoples." Within a short time, Alfonso, the son of Peter, who was the leader of the Cantabrians and was from the royal line, came to Asturias. He received in marriage the daughter of Pelayo named Ermesinda and he brought about many victories with his father-in-law and also afterward. Finally peace was restored to the land. To the extent that the dignity of the name of Christ grew, the derisive calamity of the Chaldeans wasted away. Pelayo lived as king for nineteen years. His life came to an end with a natural death at Cangas de Onís in the era 775 (737).

Umayyad al-Andalus and the Northern Kingdoms
(Ninth and Tenth Centuries)

10. AN UPRISING AGAINST THE AMĪR AL-ḤAKAM (796–822)

Ibn al-Qūṭiyya, *History of the Conquest of al-Andalus* (late tenth century)

Translated from Arabic by Bernard Lewis

Ibn al-Qūṭiyya (d. 977) was one of the earliest historians of Muslim Spain. His Ta'rīkh iftitāḥ al-Andalus [History of the Conquest of al-Andalus] was probably written down by one of his students in the second half of the tenth century. Ibn al-Qūṭiyya was born in Seville and later settled in Córdoba, where he collected the tales, personal observations, and anecdotes that went into his work. Although he served the Umayyad family, the author's name ("son of the Gothic woman") indicates that he was of Visigothic descent. This selection, describing events in the reign of the amīr al-Ḥakam (r. 796–822), shows some of the difficulties facing the Umayyad rulers in the early period, when factionalism and internal tensions threatened to destroy their new realm. (ORC)

A group of Cordoban chiefs disapproved of certain actions of the amīr,[1] which disquieted them, and tried to depose him. They approached one of his cousins, called Ibn al-Shammās of the line of Mundhir ibn ʿAbd al-Raḥmān ibn Muʿāwiya. They approached him on this and wanted to enthrone him and depose al-Ḥakam. He pretended to agree and said, "Tell me who is with you in this business," and they promised to tell him on a day which they appointed. Then he, himself, went to al-Ḥakam and informed him of this. "You are trying," al-Ḥakam said to him, "to turn me against the chiefs of my city. By God, you will prove this to me or I will cut off your head." "Send me someone you trust on such and such a night," said Ibn al-Shammās, and al-Ḥakam sent his page Vicent and his secretary, Ibn al-Khadā, the ancestor of the Banū'l-Khadā, and Ibn al-Shammās hid them in a place where they would hear what was said between him and them. They came and discussed the matter, and he asked them, "Who is with you in this?" And they gave names, which the secretary, hidden behind the curtain, wrote down. They named so many that the secretary, fearing that he himself would be named, made a noise with his pen on the parchment. The conspirators were startled,

English text from *Islam from the Prophet Muhammad to the Capture of Constantinople*, vol. I, *Politics and War*, edited and translated by Bernard Lewis (Oxford: Oxford University Press, 1974), pp. 120–23. Reprinted with permission of the publisher.
    1. Until 929 Umayyad rulers in Spain did not claim the title caliph but went by the title amīr.

and said, "What have you done, enemy of God?" Those who left at once and fled were saved; those who stayed were captured. Among those who fled were ʿĪsā ibn Dīnār, the chief jurist of Spain, Yaḥyā ibn Yaḥyā, and others. Six prominent men were arrested; of these Yaḥyā ibn Naṣr al-Yaḥsubī, who lived in Secunda, Mūsā ibn Sālim al-Khawlānī, and his son were crucified.

Because of this the people of the suburbs rose in arms and fought against the army [*jund*], but being heavily outnumbered, they cried out that they would submit. Some of the viziers advised him to refuse, while others advised him to accept it, saying that among them there were good as well as bad. He accepted the opinion of those who advised leniency and allowed them to leave Córdoba. . . .

One of those who abetted the rising in the suburbs was Ṭālūt ibn ʿAbd al-Jabbār al-Maʿāfirī, who had studied under Mālik and other great jurists. When the rising failed, he fled from his house, which was in the city near the mosque and ditch which bear his name, and remained hidden for a whole year in the house of a Jew until things became quiet and passions were calmed. There was friendship between him and the vizier, Abu'l-Bassām, the ancestor of the Banū'l-Bassām, the keepers of the granary, and as he was growing weary of his stay in the house of the Jew, he went at nightfall to the house of Abu'l-Bassām the vizier. When he arrived, the vizier asked him where he had been, and Ṭālūt replied, "With a certain Jew." The vizier promised him safety and reassured him and said, "The amīr, may God preserve him, has regretted what happened." Ṭālūt stayed the night with him, and the following morning, having left his guest in safekeeping, the vizier went to al-Ḥakam and said, "What would you say to a fat sheep that has been kept at the manger for a whole year?" "The flesh of a foddered animal is heavy," replied al-Ḥakam. "That of a free-grazing animal is lighter and tastier." "I mean something else," said Abū'l-Bassām. "I have Ṭālūt in my hands." "How did you get hold of him?" asked al-Ḥakam. "I caught him with kindness," replied the vizier.

He was then summoned and given a chair. The old man was brought, overcome with fear. He made obeisance, and al-Ḥakam said, "O Ṭālūt, tell me, if your father or your son had ruled in this palace, could they have shown you more generosity and more honor than I did? Did you ever ask me for anything, for yourself or another, that I did not hasten to grant you? Did I not, when you were sick, go to see you several times? Did I not, when your wife died, go to the door of your house? Did I not walk at her funeral as far as the suburbs and then walk back with you to your own house? Then what happened to you? What is the matter with you, that nothing would content you but to shed my blood, to disgrace and dishonor me?" "At this moment," said Ṭālūt, "I can find nothing that will serve me better than the truth. I hated you for God's sake, and all that you did for me availed you nothing with me."

Al-Ḥakam was shocked into silence and then said, "I sent for you, and there is no punishment on earth which I did not think of in order to inflict it on you. But know that He for whose sake you hated me diverted me from punishing you. Go safe and sound, in God's care! By God, I shall never cease to honor you and treat you as I did before, for the rest of my life, please God. But I wish that what happened, had not happened." "Had it not happened," said Ṭālūt, "it would be better for you."

Then al-Ḥakam asked him, "How did Abū'l-Bassām get hold of you?"

"He did not get hold of me," said Ṭālūt. "I put myself in his hands and sought him because of the friendship between us." "And where have you been all the year?" asked al-Ḥakam. "In the house of a certain Jew," he replied.

Then al-Ḥakam said to the vizier, "O Abū'l-Bassām, a Jew protected him out of respect for his eminence in religion and scholarship and endangered himself, his wife, his possessions, and his children at my hands—and you wanted to involve me again in something which I have already regretted!" Then he said to Abū'l-Bassām, "Leave me! By God, I never want to see your face again!" He gave orders to remove his carpet [i.e., his place in the council] and dismissed him, and his descendants are decayed and degraded to this day. Ṭālūt was honored and respected until he died, as the amīr had undertaken, and al-Ḥakam attended his funeral.

After this, the Caliph[2] was stricken by a long sickness which lasted seven years until he died, in contrition and penitence for what he had done. In sickness he grew gentle, and he spent the nights reading the Qur'ān until he died.

---

2. The author has slipped here, using the title caliph, which was used by the late tenth century when he was writing but not during the reign of al-Ḥakam.

11. A CHRISTIAN ACCOUNT OF THE LIFE OF MUḤAMMAD

History of Muḥammad (ca. 850)

Translated from Latin by Kenneth B. Wolf

The Istoria de Mahomet *[History of Muḥammad] stands as one of the earliest Latin accounts of the life of the Prophet Muḥammad. Its author and date of composition are unknown, but there is evidence that a copy of the text was held at the library of the Leyre monastery, in Navarre, in 850. Although it is not certain, the author was likely Spanish and the text was well suited to an Iberian audience. Possibly the author was a Christian from Muslim-controlled southern Spain who emigrated to the northern peninsula.*

The author of the History of Muḥammad *must have been familiar with the events of Muḥammad's life as they are recorded in Muslim tradition. Many aspects of this "life" reflect events in the canonical version (Muḥammad's youth as an orphan, his marriage to the widow Khadija, the monotheism of Islam and its revelation through the angel Gabriel, the expansion of Muslim armies into Byzantium, even the Prophet's marriage to Zaynab after her divorce from Zayd), but the account has been altered to suit the polemical purposes, or misconceptions, of its Christian author. (ORC)*

The heresiarch Muḥammad rose up in the time of the emperor Heraclius,[1] in the seventh year of his reign. In that time Bishop Isidore of Seville excelled in catholic doctrine and Sisebut held the throne in Toledo. A church in honor of the blessed Euphrasius was built over his tomb in the town of Ildai [Andújar]. Furthermore in Toledo the church of the blessed Leocadia was enlarged with a high roof of wonderful workmanship by order of the aforementioned king. Muḥammad's beginnings were these. As he was an orphan he was put under the charge of a certain widow. When, as an avaricious usurer, he travelled on business, he began assiduously to attend assemblies of Christians, and as a shrewd son of darkness, he began to commit some of the sermons of Christians to memory and became the wisest among the irrational Arabs in all things. Aflame with the fuel of his lust, he was joined to his patroness by some barbaric law. Soon after, the spirit of error appeared to him in the form of a vulture and, exhibiting a golden mouth, said it was the angel Gabriel and ordered Muḥammad to present himself among his people as a prophet.

English text from *Conversion and Continuity: Indigenous Christian Communities in Islamic Lands, Eighth to Eighteenth Centuries*, edited by Michael Gervers and Ramzi Jibran Bizhazi (Toronto: Pontifical Institute of Mediaeval Studies, 1990), pp. 97–99. Reprinted with permission of the publisher.

1. Byzantine emperor Heraclius (r. 610–641).

Swollen with pride, he began to preach to the irrational animals and he made headway as if on the basis of reason so that they retreated from the cult of idols and adored the corporeal God in heaven. He ordered his believers to take up arms on his behalf, and, as if with a new zeal of faith, he ordered them to cut down their adversaries with the sword. God, with his inscrutable judgment (who once said through his prophet: "For behold I will raise up the Chaldeans, a bitter and swift people, wandering over the breadth of the earth, to possess the tents that are not their own, whose horses are swifter than evening wolves, and their appearance like the burning wind, reducing the land to emptiness as a demonstration to the faithful") permitted them to inflict injury. First they killed the brother of the emperor who held dominion over the land and in recognition of the triumph of victory, they established the Syrian city of Damascus as the capital of the kingdom. The same false prophet composed psalms from the mouths of irrational animals, commemorating a red calf. He wove a story of spider webs for catching flies. He composed certain sayings about the hoopoe and the frog so that the stench of the one might belch forth from his mouth and the babbling of the other might never cease from his lips. To season his error he arranged other songs in his own style in honor of Joseph, Zachary and even the mother of the Lord, Mary. And while he sweat in the great error of his prophecy, he lusted after the wife of a certain neighbor of his by the name of Zayd, and subjected her to his lust. Her husband, learning of the sin, shuddered and let her go to his prophet, whom he was not able to gainsay. In fact Muḥummad noted it in his law as if from divine inspiration, saying: "When that woman was displeasing in the eyes of Zayd, and he repudiated her, he gave her to his prophet in marriage, which is an example to the others and to future followers wanting to do it that it be not sinful" (Qur'ān 33:37). After the commission of such a sin, the death of his soul and body approached simultaneously. Sensing his imminent destruction and knowing that he would in no way be resurrected on his own merit, he predicted that he would be revived on the third day by the angel Gabriel, who was in the habit of appearing to him in the guise of a vulture, as Muḥammad himself said. When he gave up his soul to hell, they ordered his body to be guarded with an arduous vigil, anxious about the miracle which he had promised them. When on the third day they saw that he was rotting, and determined that he would not by any means be rising, they said the angels did not come because they were frightened by their presence. Having found sound advice—or so they thought—they left his body unguarded, and immediately instead of angels, dogs followed his stench and devoured his flank. Learning of the deed, they surrendered the rest of his body to the soil. And in vindication of this injury, they ordered dogs to be slaughtered every year so that they, who on his behalf deserved a worthy martyrdom here, might share in his merit there. It was appropriate that a prophet of this kind fill the stomachs of dogs, a prophet who committed not only his own soul, but those of many, to hell. Indeed he accomplished many sins of various kinds which are not recorded in this book. This much is written so that those reading will understand how much might have been written here.

12. CHRISTIANS IN CÓRDOBA

Throughout most of the medieval period, in al-Andalus and other parts of the Islamic world, Christians and Jews were tolerated under Muslim rule provided they did not offend Muslim authorities and followed certain rules (see the Pact of 'Umar, Chapter 7). Nevertheless, between 850 and 859, nearly fifty Christians were executed in Córdoba. According to their chroniclers, Eulogius and Paul Alvarus, many of these men and women intentionally courted death by proclaiming their faith in public, insulting Islam, apostatizing, or proselytizing. Some contemporary Christians supported these actions and saw their coreligionists as martyrs who were following in the footsteps of early Christian counterparts. Thus, the group is usually referred to as "the martyrs of Córdoba." But others in the Mozarab community probably saw them as dangerous fanatics who were disturbing the delicate balance of Muslim-Christian relations. We do not know why these unusual events took place at this time. The martyrs may have been inspired by charismatic preaching, penitential practice, and by the dramatic deaths of others among them. But Christian life in al-Andalus was also under great stress at this time, with increasing conversions to Islam, frequent intermarriage between Muslims and Christians, and rapid assimilation of Arabic and Islamic culture. It is noteworthy that many of the martyrs came from mixed families and had both Muslim and Christian relatives. Both of the selections below were written by Paul Alvarus (d. ca. 861), a layman who was a friend of the Eulogius and an admirer of the martyrs. The first passage is from his treatise Indiculus luminosus *and expresses his concerns about the degree to which many younger Mozarabs had adopted Arabic culture. The second selection, from Alvarus'* Vita Eulogii [Life of Eulogius], *tells the story of the death of one young martyr, Leocritia, and of her mentor Eulogius, in 859. Although this text contains many familiar hagiographic elements and shows a conscious attempt at classical eloquence, it is told in a more personal style than most other biographies of the time. (ORC)*

A. Paul Alvarus, Description of Christian Youth
Translated from Latin by Edward P. Colbert

What trained person, I ask, can be found today among our laity who with a knowledge of Holy Scripture looks into the Latin volumes of any of the doctors? Who is there on fire with evangelical love, with love like that of the prophets, like that of the apostles? Do not all the Christian youths, handsome in appearance, fluent of tongue, conspicuous in their dress and action, distinguished for their knowledge of Gentile[1] lore, highly regarded for their ability

English text from Edward P. Colbert, *The Martyrs of Córdoba (850–859): A Study of the Sources* (Washington, D.C.: Catholic University of America Press, 1962), p. 301. Reprinted with permission of the publisher.

1. In this context, "Gentile" means "Muslim."

to speak Arabic, do they not all eagerly use the volumes of the Chaldeans,[2] read them with the greatest interest, discuss them ardently, and, collecting them with great trouble, make them known with every praise of their tongue, the while they are ignorant of the beauty of the Church and look with disgust upon the Church's rivers of paradise as something vile. Alas! Christians do not know their own law, and Latins do not use their own tongue, so that in all the college of Christ there will hardly be found one man in a thousand who can send correct letters of greeting to a brother. And a manifold crowd without number will be found who give out learnedly long sentences of Chaldean rhetoric. So that from the more sophisticated song of those people they embellish their final clauses metrically and in more polished beauty with the bond of a single letter, according to the demands of that tongue, which closes all phrases and clauses with riming vowels and even, as is possible for them, the various expressions containing the letters of the whole alphabet are all metrically reduced to one ending or to a similar letter.[3] There are many other things which would have shown the reliability of this explanation of ours; that is, which would have brought out into the light the things we are exposing.

B. Paul Alvarus, Eulogius and the Martyrs of Córdoba
Translated from Latin by Carleton M. Sage

At the time when the savage rule of the Arabs miserably laid waste all the land of Spain with deceit and imposture, when King Muḥammad with unbelievable rage and unbridled fury determined to root out the race of Christians, many terrified by fear of the cruel king and hoping to allay his madness, by a cruel use of evil will endeavored to assail Christ's flock with various and ingenious temptations. Many by denying Christ threw themselves into the abyss; others were shaken by severe trials. But others were established and confirmed in flourishing virtue. In his time, as we have said, the martyrdom (or, testimony) of the faithful shone gloriously, and the error of the gainsayers was as shifting as waves (James 1:6). For some who were holding the Christian faith only in secret by God's grace brought out into the open what they had concealed, and without being searched out they sprang forward to martyrdom

---

2. Arabs.

3. Alvarus is aware of the conventions of Arabic poetry.

English text from *Paul Albar of Córdoba: Studies on His Life and Writings*, translated by Carleton M. Sage (Washington, D.C.: Catholic University of America Press, 1943), pp. 201–10. Reprinted with permission of the publisher.

and snatched their crown from the executioners. Among these was blessed Christopher, of an Arab family, the story of whose passion we plan to write in another place. Among them also were blessed Aurelius and holy Felix, who having practiced Christianity in secret, came forward with their wives to the glory of martyrdom. Another of them was the blessed virgin Flora, who indeed flowered with virtues, and despising the transitory pomp of the world won an eternal crown. Our holy doctor Eulogius described the combat of each of these and wrote their lives and acts in a brilliant style.

At this time there was a certain girl named Leocritia, of noble family, but nobler in soul, begotten of the filth of the Muslims and born from the womb of wolves, baptized some time earlier by a Christian nun, Litiosa, who was of her kindred. Secretly she blossomed in the Christian faith she had adopted, and knowledge of her spread abroad as a sweet odor. For as in her childhood she visited the nun as relatives do, and Litiosa daily instructed her as well as she could, at length by divine grace Leocritia received Christian faith and preserved it in her breast with the fire of love. When she came to years of wisdom and attained the lights of knowledge, that faith which she had secretly learned in her earliest childhood, increased by spiritual food day by day, she nourished to still greater growth, at first in secret, then publicly and openly. Her parents gave her earnest warnings, but as this had no effect, they tried to assail her with whipping and beating in order to coerce her by punishment, since she was not to be moved by gentler means. But that flame which Christ sent into the hearts of the faithful cannot yield to any threats. When in this conflict she was beaten day and night, and saw herself attacked with severe punishments and tied with heavy bonds, and fearing that if she did not profess her faith publicly she would be burned in hell for her infidelity, she made her case known through messengers to blessed Eulogius, who was already much esteemed in many such cases, and to his sister, Anulo, a virgin dedicated to God. She explained that she wished to go to safer places among the faithful where she might without fear make her faith known. Thereupon blessed Eulogius recognized his accustomed office, and as he was a zealous partisan of the martyrs, he directed her through the same messengers to leave home secretly. She quickly planned a stratagem, and pretending to yield to her parents, and attacking our faith in words, according to plan she donned all her best ornaments and appeared in the manner of those who are out to please and marry in the world; she set out to change their minds by attiring herself in a way she hated. When she saw that everything was now safe for her, pretending to go to the wedding of some of her kindred which was then being celebrated, beautifully dressed as befitted the occasion, she hurried off to the protection of blessed Eulogius and his sister Anulo. At once they received her with joy, and turned her over to trusted friends to be kept in hiding. Her father and mother awaited her, and when they did not see their daughter, wailing that they had been deceived and torturing themselves into an unheard of rage and grief never before seen, they upset everything, confused everything, running about among friends and strangers, using force and the authority of the judge, they loaded into prisons and chains all whom they suspected; they afflicted with stripes and imprisonment men, women, confessors, priests, nuns, and whom they could, hoping that by these and other measures they might in some way get their daughter back. But the saint unmoved changed her from place to place, taking every precaution that the sheep should not fall into the hands of wolves. Meanwhile she austerely wore down her body, being constant in fasting and vigils, wearing haircloth and sleeping on the ground. The blessed man Eulogius, whose name is to be spoken with reverence, applying himself to nocturnal vigils, and praying prostrate on the ground in the basilica of San Zoylo, spent nights without sleep, beseeching the Lord for help and strength for the maiden, and consecrating her to the Lord by these exercises.

Meanwhile the serene maiden wished to see Eulogius' sister, whom she loved with warm affection, and came by night to their dwelling, moved by a revelation of the Lord and led by her desire of consolation, to spend just one day with them and then return to her usual hiding place. She told them that twice while praying her mouth had been filled with honey, that she had not dared to spit it out but had swallowed it, wondering at the nature of the thick substance. The saint interpreted this to her as a presage that she would enjoy the sweetness of the heavenly kingdom.

The next day when the maiden prepared to go back, it happened that her attendant did not come at the accustomed hour but only when dawn was breaking. She could not set out, for she used to travel at night to avoid being caught. So it was arranged that the virgin of God should stay where she was that day until the sun should put a term to its light for the earth and the shades of night should grant again the desired quietude. It was indeed by human counsel, but really by God's decree that she was held back, in order that he might give her her crown, and bestow the diadem of glory on the blessed Eulogius. For on that day, I know not at whose suggestion nor by whose plottings and betrayal, the hiding-place was made known to the judge, and suddenly their whole dwelling was surrounded by soldiers sent for the purpose. It happened that the elect and predestined martyr was there in person. Bringing Leocritia into Eulogius' presence they arrested both together, and beating them and treating them with disrespect, they brought them to the unjust and infamous judge. The judge at once thought to kill them by scourging, and roused to vehement fury, with truculent face and impatient mind he questioned Eulogius in furious words, and inquired with threatening why he had detained the girl at his house. Eulogius answered him patiently and with good grace, as he commonly spoke, and splendidly made clear the truth of the matter as follows: "Sir, the office of preaching is laid upon us, and it is a part of our faith that we should hold out the light of faith to those seeking it of us, and that we should deny it to no one who is hastening to the highways of life which are holy. This is the duty of priests, true religion demands it, and this also Christ our Lord taught us: that whoever is athirst and wishes to draw from the rivers of faith will find double the drink that he sought. And as this girl asked us for the rule of our holy faith, our purpose necessarily applied itself to her the more gladly as her desire was the more ardent. It was not proper to turn away a person asking this, especially not proper for one who for this purpose was endowed with the office of Christ. Hence as I was able I have enlightened and taught her, and I have shown her that the faith of Christ is the road of the kingdom of heaven. In the same way I should be glad to do it for you, if you should care to ask me." Then the judge with stormy visage commanded rods to be brought in, threatening to put him to death by scourging. The saint said to him: "What do you intend to do with those rods?" He replied: "I mean to put you to death with them." Eulogius said: "Sharpen and prepare the sword with which you may send my soul, released from the bondage of the body, back to Him who gave it. Do not imagine that you will cut my body apart with scourges." And straightway reproaching with clear invective and much eloquence the falseness of their prophet and law, and redoubling what he had said, he was hurried off to the palace and brought before the king's councillors. One of them who was very well known to him addressed him sympathetically: "Even though fools and idiots are borne to this miserable ruin of death, you who are girt with the beauty of wisdom, and famous for your excellent life, what madness drove you to commit yourself to this fatal ruin, forgetting the natural love of life? Please listen to me, and do not rush into this headlong destruction, I beg you. Say only a word in this hour of your need, and afterward practice your faith where you will. We promise not to search for you anywhere." The blessed martyr Eulogius answered him smiling: "If only you could know what things are laid up for those of our faith! Or if I could place in your breast what I possess in my own; then you would not try to hold me back from my purpose, but even more gladly would you yourself think of giving up your worldly position." And he began to offer them the teaching of the everlasting Gospel, and with bold freedom to pour forth the preaching of the Kingdom. But not wishing to hear him, those present ordered him to be put to the sword. While he was being led away, one of the king's eunuchs slapped him. Turning the other

cheek, Eulogius said: "Please strike this too, and make it equal to the other."
When this had been struck, he patiently and meekly turned the first again.
But the soldiers hurried him out to the place of execution, and there kneeling
in prayer and raising his hands to heaven, making the sign of the cross and
saying a few words of prayer silently, he stretched out his neck for the blade,
and, despising the world, by a swift blow he found life. He was martyred in
mid-afternoon of Saturday, the eleventh of March. O blessed and wonderful
man of our age, who in many martyrs sent the fruit of his work ahead of him,
and in the virgin Leocritia left another to follow! Raising in his hands the
standard of victory, and dedicating to the Lord the sheaf of his labor for himself, offering a pure oblation and peaceful sacrifices, and what things he had
taught others, now in himself he presented to Christ the Lord of all things.
As soon as his body was thrown from the upper level onto the river-bank,
a dove of snowy whiteness, gliding through the air, in the sight of all flew
down and sat on the martyr's body. They all tried to drive it away by throwing
stones from all sides, but being nevertheless unable to move it as it sat there,
they sought to put it to flight directly with their hands. But the dove, flutter-
ing rather than flying around the body, came to rest on a tower overlooking
the corpse, with its beak pointed towards the blessed man's body. And I must
not be silent about the miracle that Christ worked for the glory of his name
over the body of the martyr. A native of Écija, while performing with others
his monthly service in the palace and taking his turn with the watch, at night
desiring a drink of water arose and went to the projecting water outlet which
comes to that place. There he saw above Eulogius' body, which lay lower
down, priests glistening white as snow, holding dazzling lamps, and earnestly
reciting psalms. Frightened by thus vision he went back to his station, fleeing
rather than returning. After telling a companion all about it, he decided to
go with him again to the place; but this second time he was unable to see it.
On the next day the effort of the Christians obtained the blessed man's head,
and on the third day they gathered the rest of the body, and buried it in the
church of the blessed martyr San Zoylo.

As for the blessed virgin Leocritia, though they tried to seduce her with
many delights and move her with many promises, she was by God's grace
strengthened in the firmness of faith, and on the fourth day after Eulogius'
martyrdom was herself beheaded and thrown in the Guadalquivir. But she
could not be submerged nor hidden in the water, for moving with body erect
she presented an astonishing sight to all. So she was taken out by the Christians and buried in the basilica of the martyr St. Genesius, which is in the
place called Terzos. Such was the end of the blessed doctor Eulogius, this his
admirable departure, such his crossing over after many labors.

13. THE KINGS OF ASTURIAS (850–883)

Chronicle of Albelda (ca. 883)

Translated from Latin by Kenneth B. Wolf

The Chronicle of Albelda *is generally considered to be the earliest of the surviving Asturian histories, the bulk of it apparently dating from 881 with an additional section that we know was completed in November 883. Its author(s) and place of composition are unknown, but given that the work promoted the legitimacy of the Asturian monarchy we can safely assume its author was connected in some way to the Asturian court.*

The Chronicle of Albelda *has come down to us as part of a broader historical mélange containing geographical information, genealogies, lists of bishops, and curious prophetic materials. The chronicle proper begins with a chronological summary of the reigns of Roman rulers from Romulus to Tiberius III (r. 698–704), followed by a similar outline of the reigns of the Visigothic kings. It ends with entries describing Pelayo and his descendants, the rulers of Asturias. We begin here with the entry for Ordoño I. (KBW)*

[Ordoño I: 850–866]

Ordoño, the son of Ramiro, ruled for seventeen years. He increased the kingdom of the Christians with the help of God. He populated León and Astorga as well as Tuy and Amaya and he garrisoned many other fortresses. Many times he emerged victorious over the Saracens.[1] He took the city of Talamanca in battle and he permitted its king, Mozeror, whom he captured there, to go freely to Peña Santa with his wife, Balkaiz. He likewise stormed the strong city of Albelda. He ambushed its exceedingly powerful king Musa[2] at Mt. Laturce and weakened [Musa's] army with the sword. Musa himself was wounded with a lance, but was saved by a certain friend—who was known to have been one of our [men]—and was carried to a safe place by this friend on horseback. In Ordoño's time, the Northmen came again to the shores of Galicia, where they were killed by a count named Peter. The Moors,[3] coming in their ships, were also defeated on the coasts of Galicia. Such gentleness of soul and mercy

Translated from *Crónicas asturianas*, edited by Juan Gil Fernández, José L. Moralejo, and Juan I. Ruíz de la Peña (Oviedo: Universidad de Oviedo, 1985), pp. 169–81.

1. *Sarraceni* is the most common Latin designation for "Arabs." It is somewhat misleading in the context of Spanish history since the bulk of the original invading force was made up not of Arabs but of Berbers from Morocco

2. Mūsā ibn Mūsā, one of the leaders of the Banū Qasi, a clan of *muwallads* (converts to Islam) that controlled much of the Ebro region in the ninth century. (Arabic names in this text reflect the form in which they appear in the Latin text.)

3. Berbers.

Figure 4. Alfonso III of Asturias-León (866–910) and Queen Jimena making a donation to the Cathedral of Oviedo, from the *Liber testamentorum ecclesiae ovetensis* (twelfth century). Cathedral Archive, Oviedo, MS 1, fol. 18v. Reproduced with the permission of the Metropolitan Chapter of the Cathedral of Oviedo. Photo credit: University of Notre Dame, Rare Books Department.

Figure 5. Four horsemen in a *Beatus* manuscript from the monastery of Santo Domingo de Silos (dated 1109). British Library, Add. MS 11695, fol. 102v. Photo credit: Snark/Art Resource, NY.

[was attributed] to this prince, being so pious to everyone, that he was worthy of being called a father to his people. He died a peaceful death in Oviedo on the sixth day before the Kalends of June [27 May], in the era 904 [866].

[Alfonso III: 866–910]

Alfonso, the son of Ordoño, assumed the kingship in his eighteenth year. In the first flower of his adolescence—in the first year of his kingship and the eighteenth since his birth—he was deprived of his rule as the result of a rebellion by the apostate count of Galicia, Fruela. The king left for Castile. After a short time, this same rebel and unfortunate king, Fruela, was killed by those faithful to our prince [Alfonso] in Oviedo, and the glorious young man was brought back from Castile. He rejoiced, ruling happily from the throne of his father. From the outset of his reign he always enjoyed victory over his enemies. Twice he humiliated and overcame the fierceness of the Basques with his army. During his reign, in a year long past, the Ishmaelite host advanced toward León under the command of Almundar, son of King Abd al-Rahman [II][4] and brother of King Muḥammad [I][5] of Córdoba. No sooner had Almundar arrived than he was impeded [from achieving his goal], for after losing many of his soldiers there, the rest of the army left in flight. Another army approached Bierzo at that time and was completely annihilated. This happened in many regions controlled by the enemy. [Alfonso] took the fortress Deza and then acquired Atienza peacefully. He depopulated Coimbra, which was held by the enemy, and afterward peopled it with Galicians. He subjected many more fortresses to his rule. In his time the church grew and his kingdom increased in size. The cities of Braga, Oporto, Orense, Eminio, Viseo, and Lamego were populated with Christians. By means of yet another victory, he depopulated and destroyed Coria, Idanha, and the rest of the territory of Lusitania[6] all the way to Mérida and the sea, consuming it with the sword as well as hunger. Shortly before that, in the era 915 [877], Abuhalit, the consul of Spain and counselor to King Muḥammad, was captured in battle in the territory of Galicia and was taken to our king in Oviedo. Afterward he redeemed himself, handing over his two brothers, his son, and his nephew [to be held as hostages], until he paid the king 100,000 gold solidi. During that same time in the era 916 [878], Almundar, son of King Muḥammad,[7]

---

4. Amīr of Córdoba (822–852).
5. Amīr of Córdoba (852–886).
6. The old Roman province that corresponds more or less with modern-day Portugal but which also included the cities of Mérida and Salamanca.
7. It is not clear whether this is a different Almundar from the brother (of the same name) of Muḥammad mentioned above or simply an error on the part of the chronicler.

came from Córdoba to Astorga and León with the general Ibn Ganim and an army of Saracens. One contingent of the enemy forces, following opposite the army—a force of 13,000 from Toledo, Talamanca, Guadalajara, and other fortresses—was destroyed by our prince in Polvorosa at the river Orbigo. The [king] knew that Almundar wanted to press on to the fortress of Sublancio because of what happened in Polvorosa. Once Almundar learned that our king was waiting with his entire army to do battle with him in the fortress of Sublancio, he fearfully fled before the light of dawn. At the instigation of Abuhalit, there was a three-year truce between the two kings. Afterward our king, waging war against the Saracens, mobilized his army and entered [Muslim] Spain, in the era 919 [881]. After plundering the castle of Nefza, Alfonso pressed on through the province of Lusitania and, after crossing the Tagus River, advanced to the territory of Mérida. Ten miles outside of Mérida, he crossed the Guadiana River and came to Mt. Oxiferio, which no one before him had ever tried to approach.[8] There he triumphed over enemies with a glorious victory: for more than 15,000 others are known to have been killed at the same mountain. Thus our prince returned to his royal throne in victory. All of the churches of the Lord were restored by this prince and a city was built in Oviedo with a royal palace. He was brilliant in his knowledge and placid in his appearance, dress, and stature. The Lord always inclined [Alfonso's] soul to rule his people piously. After his long rule [*principalis imperium*], he passed from his earthly kingdom to his heavenly one. Amen.

[Continuation]

While this king [Alfonso] was ruling, in the era 920 [882], the above-mentioned Almundar, son of King Muhammad, set out from Córdoba to Zaragoza, accompanied by the general Abuhalit and an army from [Muslim] Spain numbering 80,000. [This was because] Ismail ibn Musa[9] of Zaragoza had become an enemy of the Cordobans. When the army arrived at Zaragoza, it fought there for twenty-two days but won no victory. From there it advanced to Tudela and attacked a fortress held by Fortun ibn Musa,[10] but accomplished nothing. Then Ababdella—also known as Muhammad ibn Lope,[11] who had always been, like his father, a friend to us—made peace with the Cordobans and sent the strongest of his [men] to their army out of envy

8. The success of this long-distance raid in particular seems to have been regarded by the chronicler (and presumably his royal patrons) as a sign that the days of Muslim rule in Spain were numbered. Hence the flurry of self-promoting historical literature produced in Asturias in the 880s.

9. Son of Mūsā ibn Mūsā (a member of the Banū Qasi).

10. Another son of Mūsā ibn Mūsā.

11. A grandson of Mūsā ibn Mūsā.

for his uncles to whom the king [Alfonso] had entrusted his son Ordoño to be reared. Thus the army of the Chaldeans,[12] entering the confines of our kingdom, first attacked the fortress at Cellorigo but accomplished nothing except to lose many of their own men. Vigila Jimenez was the count in Alava at that time. This same army, coming to the frontier of Castile, attacked the fortress called Pancorbo for three days, but won no victory and lost many of its own [men] to the avenging sword. Diego, son of Roderic, was the count in Castile [at that time]. Munio, son of Nuño, left the fortress of Castrojeriz deserted on account of the advance of the Saracens, because it was not yet heavily fortified. Our king, formidably garrisoned in the city of León with his army, waited for the enemy forces so that he might fight them in the suburbs of the city. But when the [Saracen] forces learned that our king was eagerly and daily anticipating their approach to the city, they, on the advice of Abuhalit, who had spied the king's men [in the city], crossed the river Esla fifteen miles from the city and burned a number of garrisoned fortresses. From the plains of Alcoba, [Abuhalit] sent envoys to the Orbigo River to meet our king, asking for the release of his son Abulkazim, whom the king had been holding [as a hostage] up to that time. So Abuhalit sent [as a hostage], for the sake of peace, the son of Ismail ibn Musa, who had been sent to his father from Córdoba, along with Fortun ibn Alazela, whom they had captured by trickery in Tudela. And so, entreating [King Alfonso] and giving him many gifts, [Abuhalit] received his son and made his way across the river Orbigo to Cea. Then he returned to Córdoba. They arrived in Córdoba, whence they had set out the previous March, in September. Later our king handed over the [hostages] from the Banu Qasi—whom he had received from Abuhalit in exchange for his son—to their friends without ransom. The above-mentioned Ababdella, the son of Lope, turned in hate against his uncles and cousins on account of his friendship with the Cordobans, and the question of war arose between them. That winter, on account of the insolence of Ababdella, his uncle Ismail ibn Musa and his cousin Ismail ibn Fortun moved their armies about seven miles wanting to do battle against Ababdella. Ababdella waited for them in rough terrain. Both Ismails, with light escorts, came to the same rugged mountain where they knew him to be, and ascended it with a few men and servants. Ababdella rushed toward them at full speed and, as they broke into flight, Ismail ibn Fortun fell from his horse and was immediately captured. Likewise Ismail ibn Musa was captured as he tried to seize his

---

12. Yet another synonym for Saracens, this one emphasizing the biblical role of the "scourge" Christians often invoked when trying to make sense out of their defeat at the hands of Muslims.

nephew. Many of the nobles of the Banu Qasi were also captured. The rest of the army, which had been waiting in the plain, escaped in flight. Having won a victory, Ababdella transported those whom he had captured, bound in chains, to his fortress called Viguera. From there he proceeded to Zaragoza, and took it in the name of peace without resorting to the sword, thus subjecting it to his authority. He sent messengers to Córdoba at once, acting as if he had done all of this for the sake of the king, so as to appear faithful in all things. But when the Cordoban king requested the city of Zaragoza itself along with the others that Ababdella had captured, and Ababdella would by no means consent to do this, the Cordobans were moved to anger. As a result, [Ababdella and his kinsmen] were reconciled. He released his uncle and received the fortress of Valtierra from him. Likewise Ababdella released his cousin and on account of this received Tudela and the fortress of St. Stephen from him. Ababdella retained (and still holds) Zaragoza, which he had taken before. During this same period, Ababdella sustained many raids and attacks from the counts of Castile and Alava, Diego and Vigila. When he saw that he was hard pressed by them, he immediately sent legates to our king [Alfonso] for the sake of peace and indeed he still sends them, but as yet he has not received any firm peace from the prince. Still he remains friendly toward us and wants to remain that way even if our king does not consent [to a formal peace].

Later, in the era 921 [883], that is, in the present year, the above-mentioned Almundar, son of King Muhammad, was sent along with duke Abuhalit and with the entire army of Spain by his father to Zaragoza. When Almundar arrived he found Ababdella inside. He fought there for no more than two days and tore up trees and fields. He did this not only in Zaragoza but also in all the lands of the Banu Qasi. Almundar then entered part of Degio and plundered it, but took over none of the cities or fortresses. He depopulated Sedia. Later the same army entered the borders of our kingdom where it fought first at the fortress of Cellorigo, sending many of its own men to their deaths in the process. Count Vigila garrisoned this fortress. From there the Cordoban army came to the border of Castile to the fortress of Pancorbo, and spontaneously began to fight, but on the third day it retreated quite beaten. Diego was count [there]. From there the army moved to the garrisoned fortress of Castrojeriz, but it accomplished nothing. In the month of August it arrived at the border of León. But when [Almundar] heard that our king was in the city and learned that he was determined to fight him from the fortress of Sublancio, he crossed the Cea River by night and arrived at the fortress at dawn before our army could arrive. But he found nothing in the fortress except empty houses. The next day our king eagerly awaited the enemy army at the city. But the enemy not only did not come to León, but they did not even follow the route of the previous year nor cross the Esla River, but instead returned again by way of the fortress of Coyanza to Cea and destroyed the church of Saints Facundus and Primitivus to its very foundation. Then they returned to [Muslim] Spain by going back through the pass called Valat Comaltti. While he was within the boundaries of León, the same Abuhalit sent many words of peace to our king. In response to this, our king sent a legate by the name of Dulcidio, a priest of the city of Toledo, with letters to the Cordoban king in the month of September. As of this time, in the month of November, he has not yet returned. The above-mentioned Ababdella has not stopped sending legates seeking peace and the grace of our king. This will come about when it pleases the Lord.

14. ON THE CAMPAIGNS AND DIPLOMACY OF 'ABD AL-RAḤMĀN III (918–939)

The reign of 'Abd al-Raḥmān III (891–961; r. 912–961) has been seen as the zenith of Umayyad power in al-Andalus. In contrast to his predecessors, who had held the title of amīr, 'Abd al-Raḥmān III declared himself caliph in 929. This move may have been motivated by the recent declaration of the Fatimid caliphate in Tunisia, but it also demonstrated the consolidation of Umayyad rule under 'Abd al-Raḥmān III. Although the dynasty had been in difficulty when he came to power, with factionalism within al-Andalus and military challenges from the Christian north, 'Abd al-Raḥmān was able to solidify his control over the realm. Particularly troublesome was the rebellion of Ibn Ḥafṣūn, a muwallad *(Iberian Muslim) who had first raised a revolt in 880. This was centered on the castle of Bobastro (in the mountains near Ronda), and the disturbance continued even after Ibn Ḥafṣūn's death in 917, since his sons (the Banū Ḥafṣūn) continued to hold out in Bobastro until their final defeat in 928. During the late ninth century, Ibn Ḥafṣūn had been a powerful force in promoting factionalism in al-Andalus, driving a wedge between the Arab Muslims and the indigenous Iberian converts to Islam. This situation altered with his conversion to Christianity in 899, at which point he began to draw on Christian support. Only after 928, with the defeat of the Banū Ḥafṣūn, was 'Abd al-Raḥmān III able to solidify his rule throughout al-Andalus. Meanwhile, the caliph was engaged in military skirmishes with Christian armies from the north, while also pursuing more peaceful relations with his northern neighbors through diplomatic channels. These activities are detailed in the following selections from the works of Ibn 'Abd Rabbihi and Ibn Ḥayyān. (ORC)*

A. Ibn 'Abd Rabbihi, *The Unique Necklace* (918–929)

Translated from Arabic by James T. Monroe

Ibn 'Abd Rabbihi, born in Córdoba in 860, was one of the official poets at the Umayyad court during the later reign of Muḥammad I (r. 852–886). He died in 940 during the reign of 'Abd al-Raḥmān III. This selection, taken from his long verse chronicle 'Iqd al-farīd *[The Unique Necklace], describes events in the Islamic years 306–307 (918–920) and 315–316 (927–929). The first passage concerns the campaign of 'Abd al-Raḥmān III against the kings of León and Navarre in retaliation for Christian incursions into the Rioja region. The poet then describes the ongoing struggle with the sons of Ibn Ḥafṣūn and the caliph's eventual victory at Bobastro. (ORC)*

English text from *Hispano-Arabic Poetry*, translated by James T. Monroe (Berkeley: University of California Press, 1974), pp. 88–96, 116–18. Reprinted with permission of the publisher.

Figure 6. Muslim hunter, carved on an Andalusi ivory casket (early eleventh century) in the Museo de Navarra, Pamplona. Reproduced with permission of the Museo de Navarra, Comunidad Foral de Navarra, Pamplona. Photo credit: Sheldan Collins, Metropolitan Museum of Art, New York.

The Year 306/918–919

Then God retaliated against His enemies and decreed victory to His friends:

At the beginning of the year newly commencing, truth filled the soul of the
      hero,

For the purpose of the glorious Imam; the best of those begotten and the
      best begetter was

To take up the defense of the One, the Victorious, and to vent some of his
      anger upon the infidels.

So he mustered soldiers and troops and called together with his trumpet,
      both lord and vassal;

He enrolled [the men] of the borders and frontiers and shunned pleasures
      and good cheer,

Until, when the troops were complete and recruiters and recruits had been
      mustered,

He appointed Badr to command the group, for he was held in great awe.

So he set forth accompanied by troops like the torrent and an army like the
      blackness of night,

Until, when he descended upon Motunia[1] in which the worst of creatures
      was [lurking],

He waged against them an open war that gave off sparks such that fire could
      be kindled from it,

And fighting was intense among them while the foot soldiers surrounded
      them on all sides.

So they waged war all day long, then spent the night with the archers
      banishing their sleep,

So that during the long passage of the night, they were like those fatigued
      whose wounds fester on their limbs.

Then they continued warring against them for a few days until death
      revealed itself to them suddenly and violently.

When they saw the clouds of Fate raining the thunderbolts of misfortune
      down upon them,

The non-Arabs hurriedly made a break for their foreign land and
      reassembled under every star;

So the non-Arab came to their rescue on Thursday in the greatest haste:

In front of him went the foot soldiers and knights, and around him the
      crosses and bells,

For he was hoping to dislodge the army from the side of the fortress that
      had been destroyed,

---

1. Near Calatrava, called Mitonia in Latin sources.

So Badr impeded him with his own men, observing him attentively on his
   march toward him.
Until the right wing of one army met up with the left wing of the other and
   breaths got stuck in the windpipe.
Therefore God's partisans were victorious over the two infidels and the
   familiars of Satan were put to flight.
Thus they were massacred swiftly and dispersed, while the infidel retreated
   with blame and disgrace,
Whereas [our] people set out for Alcolea² and met the enemy on Friday
   morning.
Then the two infidels met together on the road: the Pamplonan and the
   Galician
And agreed to plunder the [Muslim] army, [or else] to die before that
   assembly.
They swore by enchantment and the devil that they would not be put to
   flight before death's encounter.
So they advanced with the greatest body of unbelievers who had covered
   the hills in general with horsemen,
Until [our] people drew near on Saturday, and O, what a moment it was!
For spears were aimed among them and cries of "God is very great!" and
   shouts rose high,
Swords forsook their sheaths, and deaths opened wide their mouths;
Foot soldiers met with foot soldiers and plunged into the thick of the fray
In a place such that glances swerved away from it and in its length lives
   became too short,
And those gifted with patient forbearance and farseeing prudence acted
   with brisk energy, for they rushed upon the nonbelieving enemy,
Until there took place the routing of the Basques as though it were a stain
   of *wars* [a dye plant],
For the eagles and hounds arose and they cried out, calling upon the
   captain of the Galicians:
The eagles of a death that snatches away souls and satiates swords and
   spears.
Thus was the pig put to flight at that time while his shame was revealed in
   that place;
Moreover, they were massacred in every river bottom and [their] heads
   were carried [aloft] on poles,

2. A Muslim fortress under attack by the Christians

And the commander sent forward a thousand heads of the Galicians
   schooled in hardship.
In this way God's favor toward Islam was accomplished while the joy of that
   year embraced us all,
Although the greatest joy that occurred in its course was the death in it of
   Ibn Ḥafṣūn, the pig!
Thus one conquest was added to a second and one victory to another
   granted by the aid of God,
Hence this campaign is called "The Decisive" because after it a great
   calamity was to befall [the enemy].

The Year 307/919–920

For after it, the campaign against Albelda³ took place, carrying off the
   apostates [to their death].
Its beginning occurred when the imām, the elect of God, the most
   trustworthy of earth's inhabitants in matters of justice and in keeping
   promises,
Received news of the way in which the pig had died, and that he had gone
   to hellfire,
[Ibn Ḥafṣūn's] sons wrote to [the Caliph] proffering their submission and
   [announcing] their entry into the [Islamic] community,
And [requesting] that he acknowledge their right to govern in exchange for
   their payment of the land tax and tribute.
Therefore the gracious imām chose [to comply with] that for his thoughts
   were constantly occupied with the granting of favors.
Then Satan turned Ja'far's⁴ head and because of this his nose became
   swollen with pride,
So that he broke the treaties and alliances and adopted discord and apostasy,
Embracing pact-breakers and lawbreakers of the sort who are neither
   reliable nor do they keep their word.
But the Caliph supported [by God] impeded him, for he is the man by
   whom one is reduced to destitution or rendered fortunate;
The man over whom there are guardians watching out for any misfortune;
   guardians who are the [many] eyes of God.
So he mustered troops and companies, appointing commanders and
   squadrons of cavalry,

---

3. Town held by the Banū Ḥafṣūn between Archidona and Bobastro.
4. The oldest son of Ibn Ḥafṣūn. Like his father, he was a convert to Christianity. The
other three sons remained Muslims.

After which he went into campaign with the greater part of [their] number,
   seeking to remain in the pale of [God's] victory and support,
Until, when he reached the fortress of Albelda, he left a commander behind
   as his representative, along with a number [of men],
Forbidding them from dispersing their cavalry and [ordering them] to stand
   guard day and night.
Then he went forth, seeking to descend upon the [other] fortresses, and
   sending out lookouts and scouts.
Until [a messenger] bringing good news from Albelda reached him,
   running with the head of its chief atop a straight lance;
Therefore he led the horsemen swiftly toward it, alighting in it that very day
   by hastening toward it.
Then he surrounded it with horsemen, skilled archers, and all the defenders
   and brave warriors,
While the foot soldiers rushed upon its breaches and the troops thronged
   blindly upon its gates.
Thus it surrendered, though it had never surrendered before, and so an
   infidel [community] was delivered up to a believing one,
While its infidels were led before the sword and massacred for their just
   deserts—not out of injustice.
It all came about because of the good fortune of the imām al-Murtaḍā,[5]
   "the satisfied [with God's decree]," the best of those remaining, the
   best of those who have passed away.
Then, in his wrath he made for Bobastro and left not a single green stalk in
   it,
Breaking down plants and standing corn, and tearing up crops and fields.
So when the dog witnessed what was clearly evident of [the Caliph's] firm
   resolve to countervene his intention,
He humbly submitted to him and requested that he might be spared, with
   his permission,
And that he might be [recognized] governor under his suzerainty, in
   exchange for his payment of the land tax out of the tribute [he
   collected].
Hence the imām bound him by taking hostages, so that he would not
   become blind to his condition,
And the imām accepted his [terms] out of his own graciousness and
   inclination to do good, and departed from him. . . .

5. This was the caliph's official seal name.

The Year 315/927–928

In it he campaigned against Bobastro, resolving to overrun and destroy its
   courtyard.

Then he built [the castle of] Taljīra on the way to it to obstruct the gullet
   [lying] between its two neck veins.

He put [Taljīra] in charge of Ibn Salīm, one fighting hard, tucking up [his
   garment] from his shank to wage war,

Until Hafṣ[6] perceived the path leading to his own right guidance, after
   having exerted himself to the limit,

So that he submitted to the imām, repairing humbly to him and obediently
   surrendering the fortress.

The Year 316/928–929

[That year] he did not campaign, but he went to Bobastro to repair and
   manage it in accordance with his views,

Filling it with power and glory, while also erasing the traces of the Banū
   Hafsūn

By restoring it from the corrupt [state] in which it had lain because of
   them, and purifying [its] tombs by [removing] their bodies,

Until the hollow of every grave was empty of each profoundly disbelieving
   apostate.

[They were all] a party belonging to Satan's sect, hostile to God and the
   Sultan,

Therefore their bodies were violently destroyed whereas their souls roasted
   in hellfire.

B. Ibn Ḥayyān (d. 1076), *Muqtabis*
Translated from Arabic by Paul M. Cobb

*Ibn Ḥayyān (978–1076) was born in Córdoba and he followed his father's profession
working as a secretary at the Cordoban court. Family tradition apparently inspired
his loyalty to the Umayyads, despite the fact that he lived most of his life under Taifa
rule until his death. Ibn Ḥayyān is famous for two works of history: the* Muqtabis
(from which this selection is taken) chronicles Umayyad rule in al-Andalus; the

6. The last surviving son of Ibn Ḥafṣūn

Translated from *Al-Muqtabis V*, edited by Pedro Chalmeta, Federico Corriente, and
Muḥammad Subh (Madrid: Instituto Hispano-Arabe de Cultura; Rabat: Kullīyat al-Adāb, 1979),
pp. 226–31, 241–44, 454–55. There is also a Spanish translation of this text, *Crónica del califa
'Abdarrahmān III an-Nāṣir entre los años 912 y 942*, translated by María Jesús Viguera and Federico Corriente (Zaragoza: Instituto Hispano-Arabe de Cultura, 1981).

Matīn *(now mostly lost) describes events in his own day. The* Muqtabis *is a collection of earlier accounts structured chronologically to form a historical narrative. The passages translated here are an extract from a letter purportedly written by ʿAbd al-Raḥmān III describing the conquest of Bobastro, and a peace treaty negotiated with Christian Barcelona in 939. (ORC)*

The Siege of Bobastro

In the Name of God the Compassionate, the Merciful!

*A lengthy introductory exhortation of praise to God (*taḥmīd*) follows, stressing the following themes: the prophethood of Muḥammad; the role of the caliphs as Successors of the Prophet and upholders of Islam; the virtues of Islam over unbelief; the obligation of struggle against unbelief (*jihād*); the conceit of the infidels; and the historical role of the Umayyad caliphate as warriors for the faith through God's favor.*

Now, the city of Bobastro is a foundation of polytheism, a house of unbelief and falsehood, a center of Christian power, its shelter, refuge, abode, and bastion [made] redoubtable from its flanks and perimeter. Whoever dwells in it is protected and whoever cleaves to it is safe.

This state of affairs was prolonged, and [God's] blessing overtook it. Time aided [God's blessing] by the continuity of the [Umayyad] dynasty and the [steady] succession of those girded with the caliphate, for fifty years. They continued to dominate it in battles while stratagems honed their swords. Thus the allotted period weighed against [Bobastro], and blazing civil strife increased within it. No expectation arrived, nor did any hope ascend to it. It afflicted every town with harm, and its evil has visited upon the people of every district. It emptied every city, carried away every beauty, took possession of every profit, and denied any advantage to [other cities] equal to it, except for paltry trifles and base refuse.

For [the city of Bobastro] is of lofty situation and thick construction, its apex elevated and its upper reaches [located] high on every side; it has no equal nor match comparable to it in the loftiness of [its] construction. Its dwellings on its extremities are crowded by its inhabitants in its residential quarters. The young are raised in it as fighters, and the old go blind in it as auxiliaries.

The lord [of Bobastro], because of the easy confidence and hope in it, and the watch lengthened upon it, fancied that there was no end to [its continued existence], nor decrease in its numbers, nor loosing of its defenses, nor that the hand of Fate would enter into it, nor that one of his misfortunes would overwhelm it.

And so we redoubled our efforts exclusively on [Bobastro], when we saw the walls encircling it, spreading out as far as we spread, extending from [the heights of] the refuges as far as we extended. [However,] we were resolute and advanced toward it, exerting [ourselves] in [our] effort against it, concentrating on besieging it, laboring toward piercing a hole in it and weakening its strength, each great one [among us] finding it a small [task], and making light of it.

Truly, everyone of our people was imposing in the contention with it, aspiring with hope toward it, and advancing in the expectant struggle against it with a resolve that smote the most remote of [our] desired [goals], that arduously cut the necks of [these] lofty sects, so that when they withdrew from [their] nearby fortresses and were isolated from their neighboring stronghold, its power was severed, its brooks dried up, and its wells were blocked up, so that nothing remained except [the city itself] with its spring, [and] a supply of food within.

We made for it in our eagerness and directed our steps toward it in our resolve, so that we had [our] noble cities built against it, and erected the towering fortress above it. We populated these with officers and the troops, multiplying them in number and in supplies. We then advanced toward [the enemy], prolonging the siege of those within [Bobastro], keeping the blockade tight, and [maintaining] the frequent coming and going of the watch, obstructing and cutting off provisions from every side, ceasing to accept pleas from every level, [raising] the sword against any who exited or entered it, and taking captive those of their women and children whose captivity was necessary. For they had violated that [part of] our pact, and [so] had to acquiesce to [this state] by our command.

Those within the city observed renewed tenacity and increased resolve, until the exertion of the siege and the [continued] observation by day and night devoured them. Part of them went to death, others to captivity, witnessing that for which they had neither patience, resolve, nor acceptance. . . .

A passage follows describing how the enemy offered to return to obedience if the Umayyad army would lift the siege and let them be. But they saw through this ploy.

So we dissuaded them from remaining in the aerie of their error, and we permitted them to come down out of it, dispersed from it, so that they hastened to that which we permitted them in compulsion of haste, delivered from the constraint of the siege, and we granted them security. We enjoined the vizier Aḥmad ibn Muḥammad ibn Ḥudayr to order the preparations for their evacuation, to make ready their descent, to complete the pact of safe-conduct for them, and to keep all [violent] hands from them. . . .

The populace dispersed from the city, becoming Umayyad subjects.

Their chief, Ḥafṣ ibn ʿUmar, remained behind them, [his] mind aflut-ter, [his] heart palpitating. He was not delighted to be leaving devoid of strength, nor was he pleased to be fleeing under the pact of safe-conduct. He dreaded every hand that held him and every branch that clung to him. Fear gripped him such that he almost died from it because of his ruin. So the vizier Aḥmad ibn Muḥammad ibn Ḥudayr quieted his grief and assuaged his fear and gave him his full share of our generous pact of safe-conduct as a kindness and a [gesture of] tranquility to rely on. Thus the last of those leaving left and reached those under security.

Thus, by morning his city, that quagmire of error, pulpit of contrariness, mine of deviance, [including] that which surrounded it of walls and houses and dams, and that which was inside it of gardens and buildings, was free of its inhabitants, empty of its tribes as if it had never been filled with residents, as if no inhabitant had settled there. For God reached them from a place whereof they knew not, and cast terror in their hearts (Qurʾān 59:2) because of what they committed. . . .

A passage follows, commenting on how God's punishment could reduce such a popu-lous and healthy city to desolate rubble, quoting Qurʾān 11:102.

At that, we ordered the destruction of the city of Bobastro, reducing its fortifications, pulling down its walls and razing everything standing in it of palaces, dwellings, storehouses, and buildings, returning it to a bare moun-tain, back to [its state] at its first creation and earliest beginning, abolishing it as a place of unbelief of the oppressors, demolishing it as the abode of the haughty polytheists, obliterating it as a house of polytheism, effacing the rub-ble of falsehood: in the morning it was as if it was plucked (Qurʾān 68:20).

Then we summoned the refugee, Ḥafṣ [ibn ʿUmar], to return to what we presented to him of security and strength, and we repeated to him our pardon and guarantee, beginning this through the plain virtue in which God has made us His people. Our doctrine prevailed over his preference, and from this we agreed on that with which he was pleased, and he trusted it, and com-mitted himself to it.

So know this, and take pause upon it, and praise God. Order the read-ing of this, our letter to you, to those Muslims under your authority in the mosque of your place, so that they might praise God—may His countenance be exalted!—for the wonder he has made for them and given to them, and so that they might bring forth thanks to Him—may He be glorified!—for that which He warded off from them. The offering up of prayers of thanks to Him makes His pleasure last—may His countenance be exalted!—and by it obtains an increase in His graces—God willing. For in Him assistance is found.

Written on Thursday, five days elapsed in Dhū al-Ḥijja, the year 315.[1]

Peace with Christian Barcelona

In this year,[2] Ḥasdai ibn Isḥāq the Jewish scribe[3] made a treaty of peace with Sunyer son of Wilfred the Frank, lord of Barcelona and its provinces (r. 914–940), according to only those conditions that al-Nāṣir li-Dīn Allāh[4] approved. He sent Ḥasdai to Barcelona to ratify [the peace] with Sunyer, lord [of Barcelona]. It so happened that the navy set sail from the port of Almería[5] with Ibrāhīm ibn 'Abd al-Raḥmān al-Bajjānī on the last day of Rajab of this year,[6] and set upon the city of Barcelona on Friday, the tenth day elapsed of Shawwāl.[7] So Ḥasdai informed them about the peace with Sunyer, lord [of Barcelona], and he made them refrain from making war on him, and the navy departed from the port of Barcelona right away.

Ḥasdai called upon the nobles of Barcelona to obey al-Nāṣir li-Dīn Allāh and to make peace with him. A group of their kings agreed to this, among them Unjuh,[8] one of their nobles, who had his domain in the land of Arles. So, he sent a delegation to the city to observe for him, and he asked for a guarantee of safety for the various kinds of merchants of his land [traveling] to al-Andalus, and that was agreed upon. The agreement was conveyed to Nāṣir ibn Aḥmad, the commander at Fraxinetum,[9] and to the governors of the Eastern Islands[10] and of the coastal ports of the land of al-Andalus [ordering] safe passage of all foreigners from the land of Unjuh, and any others from that community who capitulated with regard to their life, property, and everything their ships contained. They were free to engage in trade wherever they wished, so that their ships came to al-Andalus from that time on, and the profit increased because of it. Richildis, daughter of Borrell, the sovereign of her people among the Franks, followed the example of Unjuh in this peace with al-Nāṣir li-Dīn Allāh, so she sent Barnāṭ, her Jewish confidant, to him with precious valuables from the various regions of her land. Al-Nāṣir li-Dīn

---

1. 1 February 928.
2. 328 according to the Muslim calendar, or 939–940.
3. Jews often served as diplomats between Muslim and Christian courts.
4. Throne name of 'Abd al-Raḥmān III.
5. Almería was the main Andalusi naval base.
6. 11 May 940.
7. 19 July 940.
8. The identity of this person is not known.
9. A Muslim outpost on the southern French coast.
10. The Balearics.

Allāh received them from her, and returned yet more precious [gifts] to her, and entertained her messenger bountifully.

Then Ḥasdai ibn Isḥāq al-Isrāʾīlī, and with him Gotmar, the messenger of Sunyer, returned to al-Nāṣir li-Dīn Allāh from Barcelona on the last day of Dhū al-Qaʿda of that [year],[11] after having supervised all of [these diplomatic proceedings] according to the conditions that he stipulated: First, that he [Sunyer] terminate assistance to or friendship with all Christians who are not at peace with al-Nāṣir li-Dīn Allāh, that his obedience to him remain incumbent upon him, that he seek his approval, and that he dissolve the relationship that existed between him and García, son of Sancho, the lord of Pamplona (r. 925–971). Sunyer had married his daughter to him [García], so he annulled her marriage contract in obedience to al-Nāṣir li-Dīn Allāh, and guaranteed that all of those who relied upon him from those regions that he ruled would enter with him [in obedience to al-Nāṣir]. Al-Nāṣir li-Dīn Allāh ordered Sunyer to carry out all of that, and sent forth his orders to the governors of the coasts and the commanders of the navy, and he ordered abstinence from his [Sunyer's] provinces and peaceful behavior toward the people of his land. Al-Nāṣir li-Dīn Allāh contracted the safe-conduct and peace with Sunyer according to all of this, together with a peace with Sunifred and both their descendants for two full years. He gave witness to all of this in his assembly chamber on Wednesday, the twelfth day elapsed of Dhū al-Ḥijja of that year.[12]

11. 6 September 940.
12. 18 September 940.

15. DECLARATION OF AN ANDALUSI CALIPHATE

Crónica anónima de 'Abd al-Raḥmān III al-Nāṣir
Translated from Arabic by Paul M. Cobb

After the siege and capture of Bobastro in 928, 'Abd al-Raḥmān III took further steps to solidify and assert his political control in al-Andalus. The most important of these was his declaration of an Andalusi caliphate in 929. Since the earliest Islamic period in the seventh century, it had been understood that there could be only one Muslim caliph at a time, and he would bear the title Amīr al-Mu'minīn (Commander of the Faithful). After the death of the Prophet Muḥammad in 632, the caliphal title was held successively by four of his companions (632–661), and then by rulers from the Umayyad dynasty (ruled in Damascus, 661–750) and the 'Abbasid dynasty (ruled in Baghdad, 749–1258). Even after the arrival in al-Andalus of the refugee Umayyad prince 'Abd al-Raḥmān I, the Spanish branch of the family did not declare a rival caliphate. Instead, for nearly two centuries Andalusi Umayyad rulers used the title amīr, even while they rejected some degree of the 'Abbasid caliph's authority in al-Andalus by refusing to acknowledge his name in Friday prayer services. 'Abd al-Raḥmān III's assumption of the caliphal title in 929 was a strategic assertion of his power and independence in the western Islamic world. However, it was not an un-precedented gesture, since a decade earlier, the ruler of a new Shi'i dynasty in North Africa, the Fatimids, had also declared himself to be caliph. Thus, by the third decade of the tenth century, there were three claimants to the caliphal title in the Muslim world. 'Abd al-Raḥmān III's creation of an Andalusi caliphate was probably more motivated by new political, religious, and territorial rivalries with the Fatimids than by competition with the 'Abbasids. (ORC)[1]

In this year (315/928) on Thursday, the 23rd of Dhū al-Qa'da,[2] Bobastro was conquered by treaty, and the sultan took possession of it.[3] The vizier Aḥmad ibn Muḥammad ibn Ḥudayr entered the city to receive its submission and to grant the treaty to its amīr, Ḥafṣ ibn 'Umar ibn Ḥafṣūn, and to those who were with him in the place. And so Ḥafṣ and those who were affiliated with him came down and handed the city over to the general who was overseeing its siege, Sa'īd ibn al-Mundhir. Sa'īd went up to Bobastro with the sultan's

---

Translated from *Una crónica anónima de 'Abd al-Raḥmān III al-Nāṣir*, edited by E. Lévi-Provençal and E. García Gómez (Madrid and Granada: Consejo Superior de Investigaciones Científicas, 1950), pp. 75–80.

1. There are two good recent studies about the Andalusi caliphate: Janina M. Safran, *The Second Umayyad Caliphate: The Articulation of Caliphal Legitimacy in al-Andalus* (Cambridge, Mass.: Harvard University Press, 2000); and Maribel Fierro, *'Abd al-Rahman III: The First Cordoban Caliph* (Oxford: Oneworld, 2005).
2. This should probably be read as the twenty-first of Dhū al-Qa'da, or 17 January 928.
3. The siege and surrender of Bobastro are also described in Chapter 14.

infantry, raised his banner on its battlements and took possession of it at the beginning of Dhū al-Ḥijja.[4] Aḥmad ibn Muḥammad ibn Ḥudayr then proceeded with Ḥafṣ ibn ʿUmar, his kinsmen, and his companions, to al-Nāṣir li-Dīn Allāh,[5] who endorsed their treaty and prepared fine lodgings for them. Thus did God in His power put an end to the reign of the errant clan of Ḥafṣūn, and stem the floodwaters of discord.[6]

In the year 316 (928–929), al-Nāṣir li-Dīn Allāh went out to the city of Bobastro to direct its affairs and oversee the strengthening of its defenses. Thus were the traces of the tyrants there effaced . . . and its banners broken. He walked to the city's abandoned mosque and prayed in it. God revealed to him the truancy of the accursed Ibn Ḥafṣūn, his wavering while all the time giving the appearance of following Islam, and his return to the faith of the Nazarenes,[7] compelling al-Nāṣir to disinter him from his grave and exhume his remains. For the buried trove of his foul cadaver was uncovered, lying there in the indisputably Nazarene fashion: he was turned, his face to the East, his arms on his chest—many of the people there observed that the cadaver was arranged this way. Thus did God disgrace him and bring to public shame his dark secret.

Al-Nāṣir ordered that the cadaver be brought to the Bāb al-Sudda in Córdoba and raised onto the tallest timber post, as an example from which all watching eyes might take a lesson. Now did his hidden adoption of the Nazarene creed shine clear, and his wicked intentions manifestly appear. And so his cadaver was raised to a spot between the two timbers of his sons Ḥakam and Sulaymān, who had been crucified before him, the two of them hemming him in, while his own post overlooked them.[8] Their timbers remained standing there from the time they were hung on them until the year 331 (942/3), for in that year, the river, swollen to full crest, washed their timbers away. By an amazing coincidence, the crucifixion of ʿUmar ibn Ḥafṣūn and his two sons at the sultan's gate fulfilled the omen made for them by Muqaddam ibn Muʿāfā the poet, a long time before.[9] ʿUmar was at that time in the richest splendor of his error, in the full bloom of his wickedness. During this same time, the poet composed an ode in praise of the

4. 27 January 928.
5. Throne name of ʿAbd al-Raḥmān III.
6. ʿUmar ibn Ḥafṣūn not only rebelled against ʿAbd al-Raḥmān III, but at one point offered allegiance to the Fatimids.
7. Christians. ʿUmar ibn Ḥafṣūn was said to be from a family that had converted to Islam a couple of generations earlier.
8. The crucifixion and public display of dead rebels outside a city's walls was a common practice since Roman times.
9. Muqaddam ibn Muʿāfā al-Qabrī (d. ca. 912) was a famous poet from Cabra, who is, among others, credited with inventing the *muwashshaḥa* form of Andalusian poetry.

commander Aḥmad ibn Muḥammad ibn Abī ʿAbda, while he was besieging ʿUmar at Belda:

> It is as if I can see Ibn Ḥafṣūn on a bare plain between two pillars, undone.
> His two piglets to either side on the road to Arrecife, exposed to the sun.

The invocation to al-Nāṣir li-Dīn Allāh was pronounced in the Congregational Mosque of Bobastro, and prayers and sermons were offered continuously there. Its impoverished mosques were made prosperous, its thriving churches dismantled. For indeed the thriving state and proliferation of these churches while in the clutches of the cursed ʿUmar—and the impoverishment of the mosques there and their continuous neglect—are among the greatest proofs of the apostasy of the cursed ʿUmar, and the most eloquent testimony of his unbelief.

Also in this year, al-Nāṣir li-Dīn Allāh ordered that the invocation in all his decrees, and the invocations to him offered from all the pulpits, should invoke the title of Commander of the Faithful, in accordance with what is only appropriate with this title, which belongs to him by right, and to others than he only by false boasting and empty metaphor. From this time onward, he wore this title as a garment befitting his dignity, as an inheritance [manuscript illegible]. . . .

On Saturday, the second day of Dhū al-Ḥijja of this year,[10] his decree concerning this was sent out to his governors in all the provinces, all based on the same recension. Here is the recension of that decree:

> In the Name of God, the Merciful, the Compassionate. May God send blessings upon His prophet Muḥammad the Noble. Verily he who has received the whole amount of his due is he who is most deserving of it. And he who has recovered the last bit of his fortune, and who wears what God—May He be exalted!—in His generosity has clothed him with, is the most entitled to it. And so it is with us. Now, inasmuch as God has favored us with it, and shown His preference that we have it, and raised our authority toward it, and eased our grasping it, and paved the way for our regime to obtain it; and, inasmuch as He has extended our renown to every horizon, brought our command up to every land, pinned the hopes of all the world on us, made them return from their deviation from us and to rejoice at the protecting shade He has provided for them through our regime—all of this being if God wills, praise be to Him, the Grantor of bounties, which He has granted to us, He who alone is worthy of the favor He has granted to us—we have therefore decided that the invocation should be made to us as "Commander of the Faithful." Let this also be the practice in any letters sent

---

10. 17 January 929.

from us or addressed to us. In consequence, anyone who invokes this title other than us is a fraud and an interloper, a claimant to something to which he has no right. We now see that for us to continue shirking the duty of [using this title] is to give up something that belongs to us by right and to let a firm designation be corrupted. Therefore command the preacher in your location to invoke this title and address your correspondence to us in the same manner, God willing.

The preacher of Córdoba initiated the practice of making his invocation to al-Nāṣir li-Dīn Allāh using the title of Commander of the Faithful . . . ; and that was on the initial day of the month of Dhū al-Ḥijja of this year.[11] And so this was the first Friday sermon in which this title was used, a title that now hung firmly upon him in contrast to the shakiness with which it rested upon others. Afterward it proceeded uninterrupted to the caliphs who were descended from him. God grants His grace to those whom He wills!

Also in this year, al-Nāṣir li-Dīn Allāh founded the mint, and appointed Aḥmad ibn Muḥammad over it; he was the first official appointed over the mint. That was in the middle of Ramadān of this year.[12]

11. 16 January 929.
12. 1 November 928. With the establishment of the new mint, ʿAbd al-Raḥmān authorized the minting of gold coins in al-Andalus. The minting of gold had long been considered a caliphal privilege. The minting of a new Andalusi gold coinage was also made possible by commercial connections between al-Andalus and West Africa and access to the routes of the gold trade.

16. A JEWISH ADMINISTRATOR UNDER CALIPH HISHĀM

Abraham ibn Daud, *Book of Tradition* (1161)
Translated from Hebrew by Gerson D. Cohen

The Sefer ha-Qabbalah *[Book of Tradition] was written by the Andalusi Jewish historian Abraham ibn Daud (ca. 1110–1181) in 1161 to trace and justify rabbinic tradition from biblical times until his own day. The section describing the Iberian rabbinate is a particularly valuable source of information on Jewish life in al-Andalus during the tenth, eleventh, and early twelfth centuries. Very little is known about Abraham ibn Daud himself. He was born in about 1110 and is reported to have died in 1181. In this passage, the author describes the career of Jacob ibn Jau, a Jewish administrator and tax collector appointed in the late tenth century by the chamberlain [ḥājib] al-Manṣūr ibn Abī 'Amīr while he was regent for the young caliph Hishām (r. 976–1013). The passage indicates the precarious nature of court appointments, in which the appointee might hold a position of power one day and find himself in prison the next. This situation held true for both Jewish and Muslim courtiers. (ORC)*

Prior to that,[1] however, the faction opposing the Rabbi, including those who supported Ibn Shatnash, had declined. Among these were two brothers, merchants [and] manufacturers of silk, Jacob ibn Jau and his brother Joseph. They once happened to enter the courtyard of one of the king's eunuchs, who was in charge of the land of Takurunna,[2] at a time when the Muslim elders of the territory under his charge had come to register a complaint against the officer he had appointed over them. They had also brought him a gift of two thousand Ja'afariya[3] gold pieces. No sooner did they begin to speak than the minister issued an order to humiliate them, beat them with clubs, and have them hustled off to prison. Now, in the entrance to the palace there were a number of tortuous recesses into one of which the two thousand gold pieces fell. Although they protested vigorously, no one paid them any attention. However, immediately [afterward], Jacob ibn Jau and his brother

English text from *The Book of Tradition (Sefer ha-Qabbalah)*, translated by Gerson D. Cohen (Philadelphia: Jewish Publication Society of America, 1967), pp. 68–70. Reprinted with permission of the publisher.
　　1. Prior to the death of Ibn Shatnash, a prominent but controversial rabbi, who headed a faction against Rabbi Ḥanok, the leader of the Jewish community in Córdoba. According to Abraham ibn Daud. Ibn Shatnash had been a favorite at the Umayyad court and had translated the Talmud into Arabic for Caliph al-Ḥakam (r. 961–976). Eventually, Rabbi Ḥanok's faction gained the upper hand, and Ibn Shatnash was excommunicated.
　　2. Possibly Tarragona.
　　3. These were gold dinars minted at Medina al-Zahra by Caliph al-Ḥakam between 967 and 970.

Joseph entered [the palace], found the gold pieces and went off. Once they arrived home, they took counsel [on the matter], saying: "[Since] we have discovered this money in the royal palace, let us make a solemn agreement to return it there, coupled with gifts and offerings. Perhaps we shall be able in [that way] to rid ourselves of the abuse of our enemies and gain the support of the King." So they did just that, and they became successful in the silk business, making clothing of high quality and pennants that are placed at the tops of standards of such high quality as was not duplicated in all of Spain. They brought presents to King Hishām and to King al-Manṣūr ibn Abi ʿAmīr, his guardian, with the result that King al-Manṣūr became very fond of Jacob ibn Jau. Accordingly, the former issued him a document placing him in charge of all the Jewish communities from Sijilmasa to the river Duero, which was the border of his realm. [The decree stated] that he was to adjudicate all their litigations, and that he was empowered to appoint over them whomsoever he wished and to exact from them any tax or payment to which they might be subject. Furthermore, he placed at his disposal eighteen of his eunuchs clad in uniform, who conducted him in the carriage of a vicegerent. Then all the members of the community of Córdoba assembled and signed an agreement [certifying] his position as nasi, which stated: "Rule thou over us, both thou, and thy son, and thy son's son also." Upon taking office, he despatched a messenger to the Rabbi, R. Ḥanok, [threatening him] that, should he adjudicate [a litigation] between two people, he would cast him into the sea in a boat without oars. . . .

However, at the end of the first year of his rule as nasi, Ibn Jau was thrown into prison by King al-Manṣūr. The latter had been under the impression that Ibn Jau would produce great profits for him by taking money from Jews in all the communities by fair means or foul and turn it over to him. Since [Ibn Jau] failed to do so, [al-Manṣūr] threw him into prison, where he remained for about one year. Finally, on the day of a Muslim festival, King Hishām happened to pass by the prison on his way from the palace to his house of worship, while Ibn Jau was standing in the entrance to the prison directly in the view of King Hishām. When the latter saw him he asked his guardian al-Manṣūr why he had done this to him. He replied: "Because he does not turn in any tribute from all his domain." Thereupon, King Hishām ordered that he be released and restored to his office. Although this was done, he did not regain quite the same [powers] he previously had.

17. AL-MANṢŪR'S RAID ON
SANTIAGO DE COMPOSTELA (997)

When the caliph al-Ḥakam II died in 976, his heir, Hishām, was only fourteen or fifteen years old and had little political experience. This led to a power struggle at court, from which a powerful courtier named Muḥammad ibn Abī ʿĀmir emerged as victor and regent for the prince. Although he bore the official title of ḥājib (regent or vizier), Muḥammad ibn Abī ʿĀmir became the de facto ruler of al-Andalus until his death in 1002. As a symbol of his power, he adopted the regnal title al-Manṣūr ("the Victorious"), and the period of his rule is often known as the ʿĀmirid period. After his death, his sons tried to assume their father's power, but without success. Other Umayyad claimants also emerged to compete with Hishām, leading to civil war, the end of Umayyad rule, and the emergence of the Taifa states by 1031. Al-Manṣūr was a vigorous military leader as well as a politician, and he launched over fifty campaigns and raids into Christian territory. Because of this, the dreaded figure of "Almanzor" appears prominently in medieval Christian sources. One of al-Manṣūr's most famous raids was made in 997 against the shrine of Santiago de Compostela in Galicia, venerated by Christians as the site of the tomb of St. James. Muslim armies are said to have removed the doors and bells of the church and taken them back to Córdoba, and the military campaign was recorded in both Muslim and Christian sources. (ORC)

A. Ibn Darrāj al-Qasṭallī, Ode in Praise of al-Manṣūr's Victory
Translated from Arabic by Majd Yaser Al-Mallah

Ibn Darrāj al-Qasṭallī (958–1030) is considered one of the most famous classical poets of Muslim Spain. He was nicknamed the "Mutanabbī of al-Andalus," a complimentary title in reference to Arabic's most important poet of the classical period, Abū al-Ṭayyib al-Mutanabbī. Ibn Darrāj joined the court of al-Manṣur ibn Abī ʿĀmir in the year 992, when he composed his first panegyric to the powerful ruler of al-Andalus. He soon became al-Manṣūr's main poet, remaining in the ʿĀmirid court until the death of al-Manṣur's second son ʿAbd al-Raḥmān. These years at the ʿĀmirid court are considered the golden era of Ibn Darrāj, on both the poetic and personal levels. Following ʿAbd al-Raḥmān's death and the beginning of the fitnah, or civil war, in 1009, Ibn Darrāj found it very difficult to achieve stability at a new court and with a new patron. He spent the rest of his life in search of a patron like al-Manṣūr, but to no avail. He died in Denia in the year 1030. Ibn Darrāj's ode, presented to al-Manṣūr in 387/997, praises him and his two sons ʿAbd al-Malik and ʿAbd al-Raḥmān after the Santiago de Compostela battle (called al-Nuniyyah *in Arabic). (MYal-M)*

The translation is based on Ibn Darrāj's *Dīwān*, edited by Maḥmūd ʿAlī Makkī (Beirut: Al-Maktab al-Islāmī, 1970), pp. 314–20.

May your eyes rejoice with the good news,
  and the piercing aims of your two stars.[1]
The two kings of Ḥimyar grew up to be young men,
  adorned with crowns of glory!
They are the chosen ones from the lineage of the exalted Maʿadd;[2]
  they are atop in rank, and the arbitrators of Yaʿrub.[3]
They are the two strong swords on your shoulders,
  and the two lofty mountains that give you pride.
Their high rank in religion and the world is
  like the place of the black pupils of the eyes.
You have devoted them to the victory of God's religion;
  and they have now fulfilled your vow.
And they are still at your service,
  and they will continue to carry the burdens of the Caliphate.
You invented these laws,
  and they[4] were truthful to follow your path.
And they[5] rose in your glorious universe;
  they were light and sun-rise, and they replaced the two luminous stars.
The best protector guarded kingship;
  and power absolved the most fortified strongholds
With the *Ḥājib* of the sun of ʿAbd Shams'[6] state;
  he is God's sword held in its[7] two hands.
He is the state's victor whose arrows
  secured the high frontiers.
You fed them[8] the milk of war,
  until you made them familiar with it.
And they are still nursling from it, whether it's a married woman or a virgin,
  whether they are growing up or already grown men.
Your expectations were not false,
  when they came ahead of others to the height of honors.[9]

1. Reference to al-Manṣūr's two sons, ʿAbd al-Malik and ʿAbd al-Raḥmān.
2. Maʿadd ibn ʿAdnān, whose father was considered the great ancestor of the northern Arabs.
3. Yaʿrub is the name of another of the ancestors of the Arabs.
4. The two sons of al-Manṣūr.
5. His two sons.
6. ʿAbd Shams is the great ancestor of the Umayyads, one of the clan leaders within the tribe of Quraysh. Thus the reference here is to the Ummayad caliphate in al-Andalus and "the *Ḥājib*" refers to the official title of al-Manṣūr ibn Abī ʿAmir, who was the de facto leader at the time, albeit officially still under the umbrella of the Umayyad dynasty.
7. Reference to the state in the previous hemistich.
8. Reference to the two high frontiers in the previous line.
9. Reference to his sons' performance in battle.

And your hopes were not deceived,
>   when they had risen to the high ranks of nobility . . .

*   *   *

And when Islam cried for help,
>   they answered in accordance with your normal habit,
Similar to when you answered the call,
>   when you defended it with the palms of your hand, from the swords of
>   his attackers.
A tradition whose pride you possessed,
>   and one you traced back to your cousins at the battle of Ḥunayn.[10]
And you led its reins, shepherding and guarding it,
>   to the grandsons of your ancestors.[11]
Oh to the pride of the right path, when they rode for the sake of God,
>   without relying on any guardian.
And woe onto their enemies when they were leading,
>   and supported by their troops.
And they had rushed upon the enemy with the best of horses,
>   and they had gone up with the penetrating arrows.
And the victorious soldiers came marching,
>   taking refuge in the shade of noble banners.
Squadrons of cavalry like the darkness of the night;
>   they boast of glory over the night's moon with the gleams of dawn.
He moves forward with each lion who breaks up friends,[12]
>   as if his garment has two manes.[13]
A young man who was born to twins:
>   Nobility and instant death.
His spear-head is like that of a Shiʿī seeking justice,
>   one who embarked on seeking vengeance for Ḥusayn's blood[14]
And every sword, sending forth repeated lightning,
>   with streaks and thin blades.

---

10. A reference to the Prophet Muḥammad's famous battle toward the end of his life, when he was abandoned by most of his followers when they suffered a surprise attack. The Prophet stood firm with only a few of his closest associates, eventually emerging victorious.

11. The two sons of al-Mansūr.

12. The reference is to the soldiers who are like lions, whose killing separates and breaks up friends.

13. His two arms are like two manes.

14. A reference to Ḥusayn ibn ʿAlī, the grandson of the Prophet Muḥammad, who was killed by the Ummayad army at Karbala in the year 680, deepening the rift in the Muslim community and leading eventually to the Sunnī-Shiʿī split.

When the night of war is serving like a soldier,
    they are the flashes of lightning that move quickly into battle.
Alas for these spears and their flashing
    on the day that they received their light from the dawn and the moon.
They brought death to Lamīq's[15] abodes, that were no longer sanctioned,
    and they never strayed from their path.
The armies of death walked through them[16] all night,
    with something greater than torrent and fire.
As if the skies' milky way has encompassed them,[17]
    and they were surrounded by Sirius and Procyon.
The saddles of infidelity had been shackled because of these (armies),
    And sent away on a journey, and the two (princes)[18] were the leaders.
And they rose with blood over its hilltops,
    protecting religion, like the rising of the two stars.
It is the resolve of the two who are righteous and favored (by God),
    and the courage of two victorious and strengthened ones.
They caused the land of Corono and Boga[19] to be swallowed up with their spears,
    at the outset of [their campaign] and on the way back.
The right course[20] had turned the enemy away,
    on the day the two [princes] drew their sword on the side of righteousness.
And infidelity became disgraced by an unlucky day with lightening clouds,
    the [same] day they abased [the enemy] with the soldiers of the truth.
For these are the strongholds of safety that were impossible
    for anyone who is treacherous or untruthful . . .

*   *   *

And everyone who deceives you[21] will not deceive
your sword that cuts the two veins of the neck . . .

*   *   *

15. Lamīq or Lamīqah is a name of a town that al-Manṣūr took during this campaign. See *Dīwān* for more details (p. 317).

16. Reference to abodes in the previous line.

17. Reference to armies in the previous line.

18. Reference to the two sons of al-Manṣūr.

19. These two names are unclear. It seems likely that they refer to the Galician towns of La Coruña and Vigo. In his edition of the *Dīwān*, Makkī notes that they refer to names of small rivers that were on al-Manṣūr's way during the campaign (p. 318).

20. Reference to the true religion.

21. Poet now shifts to addressing al-Manṣūr directly.

A sword whose edges do not leave a soul,
  who has seen himself in the two iron plates.
Your enemy came back with two disappointments:
  false hopes and the loss of life.
Thus infidelity has two causes for disgrace,
  while Islam has one of the two good results:[22]
Earnings that no one can document,
  except the two angels who keep score.[23]
As if earth came to us with the presents
  of Wajrah or the paths of Rāmah,[24]
And every beautiful one with noble eyebrows,
  whose hands were tied with a strong leather strap.
And also a young one, whom you protected with your two swords
  from the wide-mouthed (lion) with the two thick front legs
Oh for the black spears, that are proud and vain,
  that appear white between the two armies.[25]
Oh swords of steel, you cannot be blamed
  for what you accomplished from threads of silver,
Or from the stabbing of noble and generous ones,
  and the striking of glorious and courageous ones.
Pulpits belong to God on the day they boast
  a victory that came on the heels of good news.
If it is called a "conquest" on earth,
  its nickname is the "fulfillment of grace."
[His] conquests filled the world,
  and people's necks, East and West, bowed down in humiliation.
And before them, the cross bowed down in every land,
  lying on the ground before the forehead and the hands.
[These are] the memorable actions of the two ʿAmiriyyayn,[26]
  the ones who build courts of generosity,
And whose resolve competes with previous [claims]

22. The term al-ḥusnayayn ("two good results") refers to victory and martyrdom.
23. Reference to two angels who stand on the right and left of each person and document good and bad deeds (Qur'ān, Surat Qaf, 50:17–18).
24. According to Makkī, Wajra and Rāmah are names of places in the desert, famous for having abundant gazelles. Thus, Ibn Darrāj is describing the abundance of booty brought by al-Manṣūr after this battle.
25. This line appears in the Dīwān with a missing phrase in the second hemistich. The meaning given in the translation is based on Makkī's note (p. 320).
26. Reference to the two sons of al-Manṣūr (here he uses the dual form).

to the inheritance of Tubba'̄'s[27] kingship.
They are the seas of generosity, the lions of every jungle,
     so measure their running against their equals.
Oh, leader of glory, may you be filled with bliss
     that you can enjoy near the Farqadayn.[28]
The consolation of Islam is
     that you retain your sons as your consolation.

B. Latin Account of al-Manṣūr's Raid

Translated from Latin by Colin Smith

This Latin description of al-Manṣūr's raid comes from the Historia Turpini, *an account written in France in the middle of the twelfth century. The text takes its name from the fact that it was once attributed to Archbishop Turpin of Rheims, who lived in the time of Charlemagne (742–814), even though it includes events from after the Carolingian period. The* Historia Turpini *was originally part of a larger manuscript, the* Codex Calixtinus, *which also contains the* Pilgrim's Guide to Santiago de Compostela *(see Chapter 32). Its inclusion reflects the deep interest in Santiago de Compostela and the history of this shrine. (ORC)*

It is our duty to record what happened to the land of Galicia after Charlemagne's death. It remained at peace for a long time after this, but then, by the devil's prompting, there arose in Córdoba a certain Saracen, al-Manṣūr, who proclaimed that he would conquer for himself all the lands of Galicia and Spain which Charlemagne had long ago taken from his predecessors. He gathered all his numerous forces and, ravaging the lands on all sides, eventually reached Compostela, and took as booty all that he found therein. In the same way he shamefully sacked the whole church of the Apostle, removing from it manuscripts and silver tables and bells and other ornaments. The Saracens had lodged themselves and stabled their horses in the church, and this foul people began to digest their meal before the very altar of the

---

27. Tubbac is a "term used by Muslim writers as a dynastic title . . . for the Himyarite rulers who, before the late 3rd century and the early 6th century A.D., controlled the whole of Southwest Arabia"; see A. F. L. Beeston, "Tubbac," in Encyclopaedia of Islam, 2nd ed., edited by P. J. Bearman, Th. Bianquis, C. E. Bosworth, E. van Donzel, and W. P. Heinrichs (Leiden: Brill, 1954–2008), 10:575–76. Ibn Darrāj often drew on al-Manṣūr's lineage, referring to him as a descendant of the Himyarite dynasty.

28. Reference to two stars near the pole.

English text translated from the *Historia Turpini*, in *Christians and Moors in Spain*, vol. 1, *711–1150*, edited and translated by Colin Smith (Warminster: Aris and Phillips, 1988), pp. 76–79. Reprinted with permission of the publisher.

Apostle. By divine retribution, some of them were afflicted by looseness of the bowels, and shot whatever they had in their bellies out through their back passages. Others lost the sight of their eyes and wandered blindly about the church and the city. What next? Al-Manṣūr himself was afflicted with this complaint and, completely blinded, on the advice of one of his prisoners who was a priest of that same church, began to call upon the aid of the God of the Christians with these words: "Oh God of the Christians, God of St. James, of St. Mary, of St. Peter, of St. Martin, of all Christians, if you will restore me to my earlier state of health, I will renounce my god Muḥammad and will not come again to the land of great St. James bent on taking booty. Oh St. James, the Great, if you restore health to my belly and my eyes, I will hand back all that I have stolen from your shrine."[1] After a fortnight, everything having been handed back doubled in value to the church, al-Manṣūr was restored to health and departed from the land of St. James, promising never to return to those parts on expeditions for booty, and proclaiming the greatness of the God of the Christians and of St. James. After that he ravaged other parts of Spain, and coming to a place called Orniz,[2] in which there was a splendid and very beautiful church dedicated to St. Romanus, rich in copes and fine manuscripts and silver crosses, and adorned with hangings worked in gold, this unspeakable al-Manṣūr stripped it of all that he found in it, and likewise destroyed the settlement. While he was lodging in the place with his army, one of his commanders saw, on entering the church, most beautiful stone columns which, covered in gold and silver, held up the church roof. Goaded on by evil and greed, he inserted a metal wedge into the base of one of the pillars. When he drove the wedge in, with mighty blows of a heavy hammer, he tried to make the whole church collapse, but by divine intervention the man was turned to stone. The stone in the shape of a man still stands today in the church, colored in precisely the same way as the Saracen's uniform he was then wearing. Pilgrims who go there to pray say that the stone gives out a stench. When al-Manṣūr saw this, he said to his servants: "The God of the Christians is greatly to be praised, having such followers; for when they have departed from this life they deal justly with the living who offend them, in one case taking away a man's sight, in another turning him into a mute stone. St. James took away my sight; St. Romanus turned a man into stone. But James is more merciful than this Romanus. James in compassion for me

---

1. Rather than being returned, in fact, the bells and other items from Compostela were taken to Córdoba after this raid, and the bells were turned into lamps for the mosque in Córdoba. In the thirteenth century, after Córdoba was conquered by Fernando III, the bells were returned to Compostela.
2. This place has not been identified.

restored my sight, but Romanus refuses to give me back the man he turned to stone. Let us therefore depart quickly from this place."

So the pagan left in confusion with his forces. Afterward it was a long time before he dared to attack St. James' land again. Let those who would disturb that land know that they would be damned for evermore. Those who protect that land from the power of the Saracens will be rewarded with favors in heaven.

The Taifa Period and Early Christian Conquests

(Eleventh Century)

18. ON FORGETTING A BELOVED

Ibn Ḥazm, *The Ring of the Dove*
Translated from Arabic by A. J. Arberry

Ibn Ḥazm was born in 994 in Córdoba, where he had a quiet, comfortable child-hood while his father served as an advisor to the ḥājib al-Manṣūr. The family fell from grace after the demise of their patron, and Ibn Ḥazm's father died shortly afterward in 1012. A year later, as he recounts in this passage, Ibn Ḥazm was forced to flee from Córdoba because of civil war. This selection is taken from Ibn Ḥazm's Ṭawq al-ḥamāma *[The Ring of the Dove], a discourse on love that combines secular anecdotes drawn from his own life and the lives of others with religious and moral reflections. The passage, which provides a rare glimpse into the Andalusi household, describes his youthful passion for a slave girl, followed by his separation from her during exile. When Ibn Ḥazm returned to Córdoba six years later, he found the girl much changed; some have read his tale as an allegory of the changes to Córdoba itself during the period of civil war.* The Ring of the Dove *was the author's only work of elegant literature. Most of his extensive writings (which totaled four hundred works, according to his son) were devoted to theology and law. Ibn Ḥazm died in 1064. (ORC)*

I can tell you with regard to myself, that in my youth I enjoyed the loving friendship of a certain slave-girl who grew up in our house,[1] and who at the time of my story was sixteen years of age. She had an extremely pretty face, and was moreover intelligent, chaste, pure, shy, and of the sweetest disposition; she was not given to jesting, and most sparing of her favors; she had a wonderful complexion, which she always kept closely veiled; in-nocent of every vice, and of very few words, she kept her eyes modestly cast down. Moreover she was extremely cautious, and guiltless of all faults, ever maintaining a serious mien; charming in her withdrawal, she was naturally reserved, and most graceful in repelling unwelcome advances. She seated herself with becoming dignity, and was most sedate in her behavior; the way she fled from masculine attentions like a startled bird was delightful to be-hold. No hopes of easy conquest were to be entertained so far as she was concerned; none could look to succeed in his ambitions if these were aimed in her direction; eager expectation found no resting-place in her. Her lovely

English text from *The Ring of the Dove*, translated by A. J. Arberry (London: Luzac, 1953), pp. 208–14. Reprinted with permission of the publisher.
1. Slavery was an accepted fact in medieval Muslim (also Christian and Jewish) society. Slave women were often taken as concubines by their masters, and if they gave birth to a son they gained special status in the household.

face attracted all hearts, but her manner kept at arm's length all who came seeking her; she was far more glamorous in her refusals and rejections than those other girls, who rely upon easy compliance and the ready lavishing of their favors to make them interesting to men. In short, she was dedicated to earnestness in all matters, and had no desire for amusement of any kind; for all that she played the lute most beautifully. I found myself irresistibly drawn towards her, and loved her with all the violent passion of my youthful heart. For two years or thereabouts I labored to the utmost of my powers to win one syllable of response from her, to hear from her lips a single word, other than the usual kind of banalities that may be heard by everyone; but all my efforts proved in vain.

Now I remember a party that was held in our residence, on one of those occasions that are commonly made the excuse for such festivities in the houses of persons of rank. The ladies of our household and of my brother's also (God have mercy on his soul!) were assembled together, as well as the womenfolk of our retainers and faithful servants, all thoroughly nice and jolly folk. The ladies remained in the house for the earlier part of the day, and then betook themselves to a belvedere that was attached to our mansion, over-looking the garden and giving a magnificent view of the whole of Córdoba; the bays were constructed with large open windows. They passed their time enjoying the panorama through the lattice openings, myself being among them.[2] I recall that I was endeavoring to reach the bay where she was stand-ing, to enjoy her proximity and to sidle up close to her. But no sooner did she observe me in the offing, than she left that bay and sought another, moving with consummate grace. I endeavored to come to the bay to which she had departed, and she repeated her performance and passed on to another.

*   *   *

Then my father the vizier (God rest his soul) moved from our new mansion in Rabad al-Zahira on the eastern side of Córdoba, to our old residence on the western side, in the quarter of Balat Mughith; this was on the third day of the accession of Muḥammad al-Mahdi to the Caliphate. I followed him in February 1009; but the girl did not come with us, for reasons that obliged her to remain behind. Thereafter, when Hishām al-Mu'aiyad succeeded to the throne, we were sufficiently preoccupied with the misfortunes which

2. Muslim houses were built with projecting enclosed balconies, or belvederes, from which the women of the household could look out at the world while remaining hidden from outside observers behind lattice screens.

came upon us, thanks to the hostility of his ministers; we were sorely tried by imprisonment, surveillance and crushing fines, and were finally obliged to go into hiding. Civil war raged far and wide; all classes suffered from its dire effects, and ourselves in particular. At last my father the vizier died (God have mercy on his soul!), our situation being still as I have described, on the afternoon of Saturday, 22 June 1012. Things remained unchanged with us thereafter, until presently the day came when we again had a funeral in the house, one of our relatives having deceased. I saw her standing there amid the clamor of mourning, all among the weeping and wailing women. She revived that passion long buried in my heart, and stirred my now still ardor, reminding me of an ancient troth, an old love, an epoch gone by, a vanished time, departed months, faded memories, periods perished, days forever past, obliterated traces. She renewed my griefs, and reawakened my sorrows; and though upon that day I was afflicted and cast down for many reasons, yet I had indeed not forgotten her; only my anguish was intensified, the fire smoldering in my heart blazed into flame, my unhappiness was exacerbated, my despair was multiplied. Passion drew forth from my breast all that lay hidden within it; my soul answered the call, and I broke out into plaintive rhyme.

> They weep for one now dead,
> High honored in his tomb;
> Those tears were better shed
> For him who lives in gloom.
> O wonder, that they sigh
> For him who is at rest,
> Yet mourn not me, who die
> Most cruelly oppressed.

Then destiny struck its heaviest blows, and we were banished from our loved abodes; the armies of the Berbers triumphed over us. I set forth from Córdoba on 13 July, 1013, and after that one glimpse of her she vanished from my sight for six long years and more. Then I came again into Córdoba in February, 1019, and lodged with one of our womenfolk; and there I saw her. I could scarcely recognize her, until someone said to me, "This is So-and-so"; her charms were so greatly changed. Gone was her radiant beauty, vanished her wondrous loveliness; faded now was that lustrous complexion which once gleamed like a polished sword or an Indian mirror; withered was the bloom on which the eye once gazed transfixed seeking avidly to feast upon its dazzling splendor only to turn away bewildered. Only a fragment of the whole remained, to tell the tale and testify to what the complete picture had been.

All this had come to pass because she took too little care of herself, and had lacked the guardian hand which had nourished her during the days of our prosperity, when our shadow was long in the land; as also because she had been obliged to besmirch herself in those inevitable excursions to which her circumstances had driven her, and from which she had formerly been sheltered and exempted.

For women are as aromatic herbs, which if not well tended soon lose their fragrance; they are as edifices which, if not constantly cared for, quickly fall into ruin. Therefore it has been said that manly beauty is the truer, the more solidly established, and of higher excellence, since it can endure, and that without shelter, onslaughts the merest fraction of which would transform the loveliness of a woman's face beyond recognition: such enemies as the burning heat of the noonday, the scorching wind of the desert, every air of heaven, and all the changing moods of the seasons.

If I had enjoyed the least degree of intimacy with her, if she had been only a little kind to me, I would have been beside myself with happiness; I verily believe that I would have died for joy. But it was her unremitting aloofness which schooled me in patience, and taught me to find consolation. This then was one of those cases in which both parties may excusably forget, and not be blamed for doing so: there has been no firm engagement that should require their loyalty, no covenant has been entered into obliging them to keep faith, no ancient compact exists, no solemn plighting of troths, the breaking and forgetting of which should expose them to justified reproach.

19. ON THE INCONSISTENCIES OF
THE FOUR GOSPELS

Ibn Ḥazm, *Al-Faṣl fī al-milal*

Translated from Arabic by Thomas E. Burman

Ibn Ḥazm of Córdoba (994–1064; see Chapter 18) was among the three or four greatest minds produced by the Islamic civilization of al-Andalus. In the course of a lengthy book describing all the religions and sects known to him, Ibn Ḥazm refuted the Christian and Jewish religions in great detail. His approach in attacking the other religions of the book was to expose the inconsistencies and (what he viewed as obvious) logical errors in the Bible. Like many Muslims, he believed that Christians and Jews had conspired to change their scriptures, removing from them prophecies regarding the coming of Muḥammad and adding heretical teachings. The following excerpt exemplifies his method. (TEB)

In this same chapter [of the Gospel of Matthew] the Messiah said to them, "Do not suppose that I have come in order to introduce peace among the people of the land, but rather the sword; and I have arrived only in order to make division between a man and his spouse and his son, and between a daughter and her mother, and between a daughter-in-law and her mother-in-law, and in order that a man will consider the people of his household enemies" (Matt. 10:34–36).

And in the twelfth chapter of the Gospel of Luke the Messiah said to them, "I have arrived only in order to cast fire upon the earth, and my desire is only the spreading of it, and verily we will plunge all of [the earth] into it. And I am appointed for the completion of this. Do you think that I have come to make peace among the people of the earth? Nay, rather to make division among them. For five men will be divided in a single house, three against two and two against three, the father against the son and the son against the father, the daughter against the mother and the mother against the daughter, the mother-in-law against the daughter-in-law and the daughter-in-law against the mother-in-law" (Luke 12:49–53).

These are the two passages just as you see them.

And in the ninth chapter of the Gospel of Luke the Messiah (upon Him be peace!)[1] said to them, "I was not sent for the destruction of souls but rather for the welfare of them."[2]

Translated from ʿAlī ibn Aḥmad ibn Ḥazm, *Al-Faṣl fī al-milal wa-al-ahwāʾ wa-al-niḥal*, edited by Muḥammad Ibrāhīm Naṣr and ʿAbd al-Raḥmān ʿUmayrah (Jiddah, Saudi Arabia: ʿUkāẓ, 1982), 2:63–64, 73–74.

1. After mentioning Jesus, whom they deem a prophet, Muslim writers typically add the phrase "upon Him be peace."

2. This sentence was added in some ancient manuscripts of the New Testament in the middle of Luke 9:52 (cf. the Vulgate).

And in the tenth chapter of the Gospel of John the Messiah said, "I will not judge him who hears my words but does not keep them, for I did not come in order to judge the world and punish it, but rather in order to preserve the people of the world."[3]

[Ibn Ḥazm's commentary:] These [last] two passages contradict the two passages that preceded them, and each of the meanings [of the respective sets of passages] clearly refutes the other. For if it is said that [Jesus] meant only that He was not sent for the destruction of souls who believed in Him, then we say, [that Jesus] was speaking in general and did not single out [any particular group]. The proof of the falseness of this explanation of yours—that is, that He only meant that He was not sent for the destruction of the souls who believed in Him—is the text of this passage: In the ninth chapter of the Gospel of Luke . . . he says about the Messiah that "He sent before Him messengers and they made their way to Samaria in order to prepare for Him there, but they did not receive Him on account of His wending His way to Jerusalem; but when John and James saw this they said to Him, 'O our Lord, does it suit you if we call out so that fire will descend upon them from heaven and burn all of them just as Elias did?' But He turned to them and scolded them and said, 'The One Who possesses [your] spirits did not send the [Son] of Man for the destruction of souls, but for the salvation of them.' And then they made their way to another city."[4]

. . . Ambiguity disappears, therefore, since it is certain that He did not mean by the souls which He was sent to save some of the souls to the exclusion of others, but rather He meant all the souls, those disbelieving in Him and those believing in Him, for just as you heard, He said this only when His disciples wanted to destroy those who would not accept Him. So the lies of the first statement are manifest. And God forbid that the Messiah (on Him be peace!) should lie; rather the lying without doubt derives from the four iniquitous men who wrote these corrupted, altered gospels. . . .

*   *   *

And in [Matt. 12] the Messiah said to them: "John [the Baptist] came to you and he did not eat or drink and you said, 'He is possessed.' Then the Son of Man came—He means Himself[5]—and you said, 'This man is a glutton

---

3. This verse is in the twelfth chapter of John (v. 47), not the tenth.
4. Luke 9:52–56, the second to last sentence being an addition found in some ancient manuscripts.
5. Ibn Ḥazm adds this phrase for the benefit of his Muslim readers.

and imbiber of wine, a wanton friend of tax collectors and sinners'" (Matt. 11:18–19).

[Ibn Ḥazm's commentary:] In this [passage] there is lying and contradiction [to the teaching] of the Christians. As for the lying, it occurs when he says here that "John did not eat or drink" so that it is said about him that "he is possessed" for that reason. In the first chapter of the Gospel of Mark [it says] that the food of John son of Zachariah[6] (May peace be upon both of them[7]) was locusts and wild honey (Mark 1:6). This is a contradiction; one of the two reports is a lie without doubt. As for the contradiction of the teaching of the Christians, [it occurs when this passage] relates that John did not eat and drink while the Messiah did eat and drink. Now without doubt whoever among mankind God (He is magnified and exalted!) makes able to do without food and drink He has distinguished, and He has raised his status above anyone who cannot do without food and drink. So John [the Baptist in that case] is more virtuous than the Messiah without doubt. . . .

A third narrative [is relevant here] and it is the acknowledgment of Jesus about Himself that He ate and drank, even though among [the Christians] He is considered a god. But how could this god eat and drink? What foolishness is greater than this? For if they say that "the human nature of Him is that which ate and drank," then we say, "and this is a lie on your part in any case, for if the Messiah is considered by you as both a divine nature and a human nature together, then He is two things; now if the human nature alone ate then only one of the combination of the two things ate and not the other." So admit that in that case half the Messiah ate and half the Messiah drank. Otherwise you[8] have lied anyway and your forefathers have lied in their saying "the Messiah ate," and you have attributed to the Messiah falsehood [as well] in His report about Himself that he ate, since only half of Him ate.

[All this shows that] the [Christian] community is altogether vile.

---

6. John the Baptist.

7. On both John and Zachariah; this phrase, of course, is not in the Bible, but rather is Ibn Ḥazm's pious interjection on behalf of these two biblical personages also revered by Muslims.

8. Ibn Ḥazm here resumes addressing Christians in the second rather than the third person.

20. A JEWISH VIZIER DESCRIBES THE BATTLE OF ALFUENTE

Samuel ibn Naghrela, *The Battle of Alfuente* (1038)
Translated from Hebrew by Raymond P. Scheindlin

Samuel ibn Naghrela (993–1056), known in Hebrew as Samuel ha-Nagid and in Arabic as Ismāʿīl ibn Naghrīla, was among the first great poets of the Hebrew Golden Age, a period during which Andalusi Jewish poets began to produce secular lyrics in Hebrew. Samuel often used his poetry to describe the events and passions of his day. Aside from his role as a poet, Samuel was a key figure in the Jewish community in Granada and became vizier to Bādīs ibn Ḥabbūs, the Zirid king of Granada. Samuel's poetry is marked by its blend of two older literary traditions, the Hebrew voice of the psalmist and the voice of the Arabic tribal poet. The latter tradition comes out strongly in this selection, and many elements of the poem, especially descriptions of the battle, draw on Arabic precedents. The poet likewise employs biblical images and references in telling his tale. The battle in question took place in 1038, when Zuhair, ruler of Almería, marched against Bādīs ibn Ḥabbūs, meeting at a place called Alfuente. Zuhair was killed in the battle, and his vizier, Ibn ʿAbbās (who had encouraged Zuhair to attack Granada), was taken prisoner and executed. Samuel was present at the battle and later wrote this poem thanking God for the victory and for the support of his own and the Jewish community's interests in Granada. (ORC)

When Prince Zuhair, whose land was by the sea,[1]
and his vizier, one Ibn ʿAbbās, observed
my status with my king,[2] realized that all
state counsels and affairs were in my hands,
noticed that no decree was ever final
but that the decree had my consent—
they felt resentment over my high rank,
resolved to see me overthrown at once;
for how (they said) can aliens like these
be privileged over Muslim folk
and act like kings legitimate?
So this vizier spread awful things about me,

Translated from *Eloah ʿoz veʾel ayom venora,* from *Diwan shemuel hanagid,* edited by Dov Jarden (Jerusalem: Hebrew Union College Press, 1966), pp. 4–14; H. Jefim Schirmann, *Hashira haʿivrit bisfarad uvprovans,* 2nd ed. (Jerusalem and Tel Aviv: Bialik Institute and Dvir, 1960), pp. 85–92.
 1. I.e., the kingdom of Almería.
 2. Ḥabbūs, the Zirid ruler of Granada.

reckless slanders, brazen, wicked gossip,
had his heinous lies, and plenty of them,
artfully written up as open letters
(but God forbid that I should say a word
that might make anyone think ill of him!).
He circulated these among the towns
to put his slanders in the Muslims' mouths,
inciting them against me with foul words
as Moses' spies[3] used words that caused much grief.
It was not only me he hoped to harm
by framing these malicious, lying words;
his purpose was to wipe out all the Jews,[4]
old, young, men, women, children still unborn.
My master paid no heed to his foul words
(he could not take such nonsense seriously)
but not long after these events he died,
on a day fraught with calamity for me.
Now I was worried. "How," I said, "can I
survive with my protector gone? It's over now!
God has examined me, found out my sin,
and passed on me the sentence I deserve."[5]

*   *   *

Delighted to see the trouble I was in,
my foe, gloating, sent word to all his friends:
"This is the day I have been waiting for;
the only obstacle has been removed.
With Ḥabbūs dead, this Samuel is finished,
and all his hopes are ended, done, and gone."
It angered me: it made God angry too,
made his nostrils rage with the ancient fire.
Then Bādīs, lion of the nations, rose,
succeeded to his father's throne, and ruled.
Losing no time, my enemy now wrote

---

3. The story, in Num. 13–14, served in the rabbinic tradition as an example of the destructive power of slanderous speech.
    4. A conscious allusion to Esther 3:6, another case in which a courtier's enmity toward a single prominent Jew extends to the Jewish people as a whole.
    5. He died in 1038.

strong letters with peremptory demands:
"Are you aware that in our Muslim faith
it is a sin to spare this Samuel's life?
Never will I let you be in peace
as long as any breath is left inside this Jew.
Get rid of him, and that will put an end
to quarreling and strife; come, deal with me.
But if you won't, just know that all the kings
of Andalus have formed a league against you."
Bādīs sent in reply: "If I should do
what you demand, damnation fall on me!
Before I yield my servant to his foes,
I'd see myself a bondsman to my own!"

*   *   *

At this my enemy became enraged,
and furiously increased hostilities,
nor did he rest until his troops were massed,
a league of Slavs[6] and Christians and Arabians
at Alfuente. Here God, when He created
heaven and earth, had laid a trap for him.
He marched his troops at double time, rushing
to battle like a hawk that rides the breeze.
He had designs, but our God had His own;
the Lord's designs cannot be overthrown.
So Av,[7] the month of ancient woes, went out,
And Elul[8] entered, bringing quick relief.
He bivouacked on one side of the pass,
and we took our position facing them.
We chose to ignore his troops, regarding them
as just an ordinary caravan.
But he, on drawing up, harangued my men,
trying to turn them against me with his words.

6. A people largely of Christian descent originally imported from non-Muslim territories in Europe by ʿAbd al-Raḥmān III as slaves or clients; several of the party kingdoms, including Almería, were headed by their descendants.

7. The eleventh month of the Hebrew calendar, corresponding to July–August, the ninth day of which is one of ritual mourning for the destruction of the two temples and other national disasters.

8. The twelfth and final month of the Hebrew calendar.

But seeing that my men were all behind me,
supporting me as one in word and thought,
he tilted lance, drew sword, and leveled spear,
and, closing in, made ready to attack.
He rose to strike; to strike him, God arose—
can creature duel Creator and prevail?
The armies stood arrayed, rank facing rank,
the kind of men who think that death
in raging battle is a boon,
and each has only one desire: to buy renown
although the purchase cost their lives.

*   *   *

And now the earth's foundations heaved and shook,
and overturned like Sodom[9] when God laid it waste.
All glamour now was gone; the soldiers' faces
blackened like the bottom of a pot.
The day was dark with dust-clouds, gloomy, dim;
the sun was black, as black as was my heart;
the din of troops, like Shaddai's[10] thundering,
like ocean's breakers crashing in a storm.
With sunrise, all the earth appeared to melt;
the solid ground was tottering like a toper.
The horses charging, wheeling, backing off,
were serpents darting in and out of their holes.
The flung spears, as they flew, flashed in the sun,
like shafts of lightning, filling the air with blaze.
The arrows as they fell were drops of rain.
The backs of men on whom they fell were sieves.
The bows were twisting in their hands like snakes,
and every snake was spitting out a bee.
The swords were brands, being held aloft,
but when they fell, they put out someone's light.
The blood of men was running on the ground
like rams' blood in the Temple of the Lord.
Then valiant warriors threw away their lives

9. The wicked city overthrown together with Gomorrah, as told in Gen. 19.
10. A name associated with God, sometimes understood as "Almighty."

without a care, for they preferred to die.
Lions of war they were; the wounds that bled
about their heads were crowns to them.
In their faith, dying was a virtue;
living they regarded as a sin.
And I, what could I do?—no place to flee,
no one to trust, and hope a tree uprooted.
The foe was spilling blood like water
on that dreadful day—
                    so I poured prayers
to God Who hurls the villain
into the pit that he himself has dug,
Who turns the wielded sword, the arrows shot
in battle back upon the foe.
I do not say,
            "O grant me victory, Lord,
because I live an upright life;
because my study of Your Law bears fruit,
while sages labor fruitlessly;
because my thoughts untie Your mysteries,
on nights of study, nights when my eyes greet the dawn.
Rather I say,
            "For Your own sake, O Lord,
be my sheltering rock, my wall of fire.
Consume my enemies with your burning rage;
scatter them like chaff before a storm.
Make them like Sisera, me like Barak,
who vanquished him with Deborah's help and Yours.[11]
Break your lightning over them and scatter them;
roar, so that they perish at the roar!
Save me from this fearsome plight
and make my enemy my ransom.
Do not look to my sins, but credit me
with Abraham's and Isaac's righteousness."

                    *   *   *

11. Sisera was a Canaanite general who attacked the Israelites during the time of the
Judges, i.e., the period between the Israelite settlement of the Land of Israel and the first king
(Saul), who ruled from ca. 1000 B.C. He was challenged by the Israelite general Barak but met
his death at the hands of an Israelite woman, Jael. See Judg. 4–5.

And as I prayed like one in labor,
bearing her first child
God heard my prayer.
He blew on them as once He blew
on Pharaoh's troops, swept them away;
they perished in His storm,[12]
and God made manifest His might.
The fire of death consumed them all,
they met their end like wood in a stove.
and all my enemies were turned to dust,
like straw consumed in fire.
The heads of lords lay strewn about the ground,
like figs that sell a thousand for a *fils*.
Fallen princes' bloated corpses lay
like full wine-skins or women big in the womb.
Slaves lay beside their masters, beggars
next to kings, all one in rank,
all turned to dung;
unburied in the field they lay,
they and their king Zuhair.
Not one in ten, one in ten thousand survived,
like grapes unpicked at harvest's end,
and Andalus was rid of Slavs,
the host of Almería crushed, her kingdom gone.

*   *   *

We left them lying on the fields to feed
the jackals, leopards, hyenas, and the boar.
We left them there reclining on the rocks,
lounging on the brambles and the thorns.
We made their flesh a present to the vulture,
a guest-gift to the lion and the wolf.
We gorged the beasts with blood of fresh-killed men,
and meat in quantity, not dainty bowls.
The scavengers thought it odd to find these nobles
stretched out on the ground, and not indoors in shade;
odd that on such a broiling day they hadn't sought

12. The Egyptians pursued the fleeing Israelites into the Red Sea, which had parted for them. But God then reversed the wind, so that the water surged back, engulfing the Egyptians. The story is told in Exod. 14.

their marble halls and cooling upper rooms.
Around the corpses ostriches raise their wail,
and little goats do their macabre dance,
while lions feed upon the fatty flesh,
and the lioness gives portions to her young.
We took possession of their towns and lands,
wreaked our vengeance on their castle walls,
seized their settlements and villages,
took their fortifications by force of arms.
When we returned, we found not one man missing
out of all our troops, not one man lost.

*   *   *

And that vizier who counseled, then decreed
that I be put to death,
who crossed the river to do me harm
(only to be shorn by my hired blade)—
I had him seized and brought in bonds to me,
and shut up in a dungeon, in a keep.
And now I took my pleasure of my foe,
enjoyed my vengeance on his filthy life.
I had made the Torah my mainstay,
dearer to me than any worldly goods;
God paid me back in kind: my enemy
died like a dog on the Torah's festival.[13]
Thus God fulfilled my father Moses' word
to Levi, who served the Lord with scent and song;[14]
and thus the warning Haman's wife[15] pronounced
when he tried to purchase Israel's doom came true.
At last I could take my ease, forget my foes,
enjoy my honors and my increasing sway,
for no one now would dare to slander me,
the end had come to hate and jealousy.

13. The celebration of the conclusion and beginning of the annual cycle of Torah readings. It is also the last festival of the series of holidays that occupies most of Tishri, the first month of the Hebrew year, occurring on the twenty-third of that month.

14. In Moses' song, God promised the tribe of Levi, who were to be priests and Temple singers, that their descendants would be victorious over their enemies. See Deut. 33:11. Like Moses, Ibn Naghrela was a descendant of Levi.

15. See Esther 6:13.

21. TWO JEWISH VIZIERS IN GRANADA

Samuel ibn Naghrela and his son Joseph both served as viziers (wazīrs) to members of the Zirid family, who ruled Granada in the middle of the eleventh century. Samuel, in particular, presents a brilliant example of the "courtier-rabbi," a man who held a prominent position in both the Muslim and Jewish communities of his day. Samuel served under both Ḥabbūs and his successor Bādīs until his death in 1056 (from natural causes, despite his well-grounded fear of enemies at court). Andalusi Muslim rulers often employed Jewish administrators because they posed no political threat. The Jews, in turn, benefited from the rulers' protection. Nevertheless, the relationship was dangerously insecure, since the perceived power of Jewish courtiers could arouse resentment in the Muslim community, and in the absence of a strong royal patron the Jews were in danger. The precariousness of the Jewish position was demonstrated in 1066, when the fall from power of Samuel's son, Joseph ibn Naghrela, resulted in the massacre of Jews in Granada. The following selections demonstrate four different accounts of the careers of Samuel and Joseph, three by Muslim writers and one by a Jewish author. The first two were written by contemporaries of Samuel and Joseph, the last two were recorded about a century later and show the enduring interest in the lives of these two men. The first selection is by ʿAbd Allāh ibn Buluggīn (d. 1090), the last Zirid ruler of Granada and the grandson of Bādīs ibn Ḥabbūs; the second is an angry poem by a Muslim courtier, Abū Isḥaq (d. 1067); the third selection is from the work of Ibn Bassām (d. 1147); the fourth is by the Jewish chronicler Abraham ibn Daud (d. 1181). (ORC)

A. ʿAbd Allāh ibn Buluggīn, *Tibyān* (1095)

Translated from Arabic by Amin T. Tibi

This account is taken from the Tibyān, *a memoir written by ʿAbd Allāh ibn Buluggīn (r. 1073–1090). The book is unusual in its candid autobiographical account of the troubles besetting a minor Muslim ruler in al-Andalus in the late eleventh century. Before detailing events during his own rule, however, the author describes the reign of his grandfather, Bādīs ibn Ḥabbūs (known as al-Muẓaffar), from whom he inherited the throne. The Zirid court was the scene of intense factionalism, with different members of the royal family and their supporters intriguing for power. In this passage, ʿAbd Allāh recounts the plots supported—as he sees them—by Joseph ibn Naghrela, who became his grandfather's Jewish vizier after the death of his father, Samuel. Earlier in the memoir, ʿAbd Allāh always refers to Samuel respectfully, using the name Abū Ibrāhīm, whereas he always calls Joseph "the Jew" or "the swine." Among other things, ʿAbd Allāh blames Joseph for the downfall and murder of his*

English text from *The Tibyān: Memoirs of ʿAbd Allāh ibn Buluggīn, Last Zīrid Amīr of Granada,* translated by Amin T. Tibi (Leiden: Brill, 1986), pp. 62–65, 67–68, 69–71, 74–75. Reprinted with permission of the publisher.

father, Buluggīn ibn Bādīs (known as Sayf al-Dawla), and the disgrace of his uncle, Māksan. He also accuses Joseph of betraying Granada to the ruler of Almería, Ibn Ṣumādiḥ. As well as detailing the charges leveled against them, the passage demonstrates the degree to which Joseph and other Jews were useful to the Zirid family and indicates the dangers inherent in their status. (ORC)

When 'Ali, his brother[1], and the *wazīrs* of the state realised that the Jew[2] had acquired overriding influence with the prince[3] and his son, they were greatly incensed and perturbed, and unanimously decided to sow the seeds of discord between him and my father. The sons of 'Ali and 'Abd Allāh were *wazīrs* and inseparable boon companions of Sayf al-Dawla. Using every device to intrigue against the Jew both independently and with the help of their sons, they said to Sayf al-Dawla, "You have a far better right—and it is your due—to the money which the Jew is gaining and keeping exclusively for himself. The Jew has reduced both yourself and all officers of the state to the status of nobodies. If you did away with him, your father would say nothing to you. What could he do with his own son?" They sought, villains that they were, to do away with their enemy through the agency of the ruler's son so that they could keep their own hand clean of the whole affair. If the prince was to punish anyone, they reasoned, it would be his own son he would punish if he so wished. In this way they would take over the state without running the risk of any reproach from the prince. And so they for ever slandered the Jew and lied about him to Sayf al-Dawla, at the same time lying to the former about things they imputed to the latter. In the end, then, our father, who had scant experience of men and their intrigues, turned against the Jew, who, for his part, also went sour on Sayf al-Dawla. The latter therefore decided to do away with the Jew. He would talk about his intention and openly speak of his secret desire to the *wazīrs* who came to lay complaints against their enemy. But he neither carried out the assassination, nor did he keep the matter to himself. In the long run, then, the Jew found out all about his intentions and decided to anticipate him, once he had seen for himself the change in Sayf al-Dawla's attitude towards him. What happened was that whenever Sayf al-Dawla was on the point of doing away with the Jew and prepared his slaves for the purpose, he would remember his own father's ruthlessness and stay his hand.

Sayf al-Dawla had a young brother called Māksan, a paternal uncle of

---

1. 'Alī ibn Qawarī and his brother 'Abd Allāh ibn Qawarī were other viziers serving Bādīs ibn Ḥabbūs.
2. Joseph ibn Naghrela.
3. Bādīs ibn Ḥabbūs (al-Muẓaffar).

mine who died a martyr at the battle of Badajoz.[4] Now the Jew, swine that he was, put his head together with the Jewish elders and told them of the change in Sayf al-Dawla's attitude towards him. The shrewdest of them said to him, "Don't have high hopes of getting to the top with the death of Bādīs, and don't expect too much from Sayf al-Dawla. You would be well advised to think of some suitable candidate to put on the throne when your ruler dies. If you can think of one, find a way of poisoning Sayf al-Dawla. Now this brother of his, Māksan, is a mere nobody. So, if you were to murder Sayf al-Dawla and set Māksan on the throne he will never forget the service you have rendered him." So the Jew was prompted by his baser self to administer poison to Sayf al-Dawla. He was in a favorable position to execute his plan since my father would often drink with him and visit him regularly at his house.

One day my father, as was his wont, drank at the Jew's home, but no sooner had he left than he vomited all the contents of his stomach and fell to the ground on his back. He was later able to walk home, but only with some great difficulty, and, having spent two more days in agony, he died. . . .

My father's death came as a very great blow to people, for they had been looking forward to obtaining justice under him. Growing restive, they were now bent on assassinating the Jew. Such was the situation that was eventually to culminate in the latter's death. But, as yet, the would-be assassins dreaded the penalty that their ruler might visit upon them. And so the Jew took his intrigues against the Qarawī brothers a step further and created the impression in al-Muzaffar's mind that they had lured his son into the habit of drinking to excess and finally brought about his death. As a result of all this al-Qarawī's sons suffered considerably. They were banished from their homes, and their possessions were seized. A number of *wazīrs* who had been close to my father were put to death because they were suspected of his murder, whereas the true culprit escaped attention. After the death of Sayf al-Dawla, the Jew lorded it in grand style (*tabarmaka*) and worked hard to put my paternal uncle Māksan on the throne.

By this time my grandfather had grown old and more disposed to peace and quiet. With advancing years and the death of his son, he lost all zest for territorial expansion and delegated all powers to the Jew who therefore could exercise just as much authority as he wished. . . .

The Jew tried to establish a connection with my paternal uncle Māksan in the hope of getting his backing. But Māksan in fact treated him worse than anyone else. There was no good counselor in Māksan's entourage to guide him and tell him to take a diplomatic approach. Hence Māksan asked the

4. The battle of Zallāqa, 1086.

Jew outright, "Are you for murdering me as you did my brother?" The Jew was greatly perturbed by this remark. Māksan, however, had a dreadful manner. He was unkind, had an uncouth tongue, and was given to uttering dire threats. He was utterly detested by his father's court, and many a complaint against him was laid before his father.

Māksan's mother avoided having any dealings with the *wazīr*, who tried to curry favor with Māksan, but turned, rather to his maternal uncle, a Jew known as Abū al-Rabīʿ al-Māṭūnī who was the royal bailiff.[5] She was always in touch with this man seeking an advance from him. The *wazīr* accordingly grew jealous and plotted against Māksan, his mother, and his entourage. He lied about them to the Prince, and a group of people at court, who bitterly resented Māksan's behaviour such as I have already described it, came forward to testify to the truth of his allegations. Under such pressures the Prince turned against them and, driven by abhorrence of the evil that he heard attributed to them, he gave orders for Māksan's mother, his nurses, and a certain number of women in their service to be put to death. Because his maternal uncle did not see eye to eye with him on this and other matters, the *wazīr* treacherously murdered him while he was drinking with him at home. Moreover, so that he might not be taken to task by the Prince for the murder, he put himself beyond reproach by paying him a considerable sum of money by way of compensation. The Prince accepted his gift and would have been glad for the *wazīr* to murder a Jew every day if only to draw in the blood money for each one.

Al-Muẓaffar next commanded that his son be sent into exile. The main reason for this measure was as follows. At the time of the troubles with Ibn Ṣumādiḥ, the Prince had gone out to review his troops, and one of their *shaykhs* came up to him and said, "You should not put us under the command of slaves and such people and pass over such a son as you have. Send him with us, and we shall follow him no matter what the venture." He was, of course, referring to Māksan. The remark irritated the father and, as he had already had his anger aroused both by his personal experience of his son's behavior and by reports that he had had of him, he feared lest words such as those just spoken might be followed by deeds designed to overthrow him and put his son on the throne in his stead. The Jew was utterly terrified. "I was sure," he commented, "that that day would see my death." And so he communicated his fears to the Prince, who gave immediate orders for his son's banishment from Granada. To ensure that Māksan would be put beyond all territory under his control,

5. It is clear from this account that the women of the palace were deeply involved in intrigues at court.

he sent one of his slaves to accompany him. The Jew—God curse him!—then instructed the slave to lead Māksan to a certain place named by himself so that without fear of discovery he might strike off his head.

My brother, al-Muʿizz, had been brought up by his grandfather and accordingly succeeded in winning the affection of the princesses who loved him out of regard for Buluggīn. They were all in complete agreement with the Jew that Māksan should be done to death and that al-Muʿizz should become heir to the throne. The reason for this was their fear that Māksan might turn on them and punish them for their love of his nephew and the fact that they had brought him up. These expectations were later borne out in fact.

My paternal uncle left Granada in a most dreadful state. He was alarmed and apprehensive. Some advised that he should be assassinated, while others only favored his banishment from the whole territory. After he had travelled some distance, however, Māksan was relieved of his forebodings by the assassination of the Jew in the circumstances I shall now describe. . . .

The Jew then wrote to Ibn Sumādiḥ to inform him that all likely troublemakers had left the city[6] and that only nonentities remained who could be mown down by his sword if he could but effect an entry. He was ready, he said, to open its gates as soon as he ventured to approach and knock. The only fortresses he bothered about were those of the main towns, and he did not bother to supply garrisons in other fortresses with the required men and provisions, as though he had overlooked the matter, and finally they became abandoned.

Al-Muzaffar, in the meantime, had absolutely no inkling of all this, his only interests being drink and amusement. When the fortresses were abandoned and their occupants were thoroughly convinced that, because they had been neglected and the Prince had not been seen for some time past, he must surely be dead, the word went round from one place to the next and more desertions followed. So Ibn Sumādiḥ's troops seized the opportunity to occupy them and in the long run the only stronghold left to Granada was nearby Cabrera on the way to Guadix.

The Jew immediately sent a message to Ibn Sumādiḥ urging him to march against the city with the assurance that there was nothing to stand in his way. But Ibn Sumādiḥ demurred and took fright at the prospect of tackling a place like Granada. Finally the situation got out of hand and matters went from bad to worse. So the Jew, out of fear of the populace, moved from his house to the citadel (qaṣaba) to await the fulfillment of his hopes, an action which met with strong disapproval. Moreover, it was suspected

6. Joseph had dispatched a number of Granada's military leaders to distant posts outside the city.

that he had built the Alhambra (*al-Ḥamrāʾ*) fortress with a view to taking refuge there with his family when Ibn Ṣumādiḥ entered, and waiting until the trouble had died down. All sections of the population from top to bottom had a detestation of the underhanded ways of the Jews and the widespread changes they had wrought for the worse. Appointments to offices were no longer what they had been used to.

In accordance with God's decree that they should perish on Saturday 10 Ṣafar [459],[7] the Jew decided to carouse that night with some of al-Muẓaffar's leading slaves who had agreed to act in concert with him, although some of them secretly detested him. The Jew then told them about Ibn Ṣumādiḥ and assured them the latter would be coming to their aid and formally assign to them the rights of this and that village in the vega of Granada. One of these slaves who secretly hated him went up to him and said, "We know all about this. Now tell us about the way you've assigned these rights. Is our Master alive or dead?" One of the Jew's entourage gave him an answer and rebuked him for his impudence. The slave immediately took umbrage and ran out blind drunk, shouting, "Hey folks! Have any of you heard about al-Muẓaffar being betrayed by the Jew and that Ibn Ṣumādiḥ's about to enter the city?" Everyone, high or low, heard of it from each other, and dashed in with the intention of killing the Jew. The latter managed to talk al-Muẓaffar into coming out and then declared, "Here's your Prince alive and well!" The Prince tried to calm the mob, but all in vain. It was too late. The Jew turned and fled for his life inside the palace pursued by the populace, who finally ran him down and did him to death. They then turned their swords on every Jew in the city and seized vast quantities of their goods and chattels.

B. Abū Isḥāq of Elvira, *Qaṣīda*
Translated from Arabic by Bernard Lewis

Abū Isḥāq (d. 1067) was born of an Arab family, trained as a jurist, and worked as a scribe and teacher in Granada. He served as a secretary to the chief judge of Granada during the reign of Bādīs ibn Ḥabbūs. At some point in his career, Abū Isḥāq appears to have fallen from grace, either through a conspiracy of other Muslim jurists (as his own writing implies) or through the slander of Jewish enemies (as has been claimed by others). Whatever the original cause, Abū Isḥāq was embittered by this event and

---

7. 30 December 1066.

English text from *Islam in History: Ideas, Men, and Events in the Middle East,* translated by Bernard Lewis (Oxford: Oxford University Press, 1974), pp. 159–61. Reprinted with permission of the translator.

later blamed the Jews for his fall. Before his death in 1067, he composed this poem at-
tacking the Jews of Granada and targeting Joseph ibn Naghrela in particular. His
efforts may have helped to incite the massacre of Jews in Granada. (ORC)

Go, tell all the Ṣanhāja[1]
    the full moons of our time, the lions in their lair
The words of one who bears them love, and is concerned
    and counts it a religious duty to give advice.
Your chief has made a mistake
    which delights malicious gloaters
He has chosen an infidel as his secretary
    when he could, had he wished, have chosen a Believer.
Through him, the Jews have become great and proud
    and arrogant—they, who were among the most abject
And have gained their desires and attained the utmost
    and this happened suddenly, before they even realized it.
And how many a worthy Muslim humbly obeys
    the vilest ape among these miscreants.
And this did not happen through their own efforts
    but through one of our own people who rose as their accomplice.
Oh why did he not deal with them, following
    the example set by worthy and pious leaders?
Put them back where they belong
    and reduce them to the lowest of the low,
Roaming among us, with their little bags,
    with contempt, degradation and scorn as their lot,
Scrabbling in the dunghills for colored rags
    to shroud their dead for burial.
They did not make light of our great ones
    or presume against the righteous,
Those low-born people would not be seated in society
    or paraded along with the intimates of the ruler.
Bādīs! You are a clever man
    and your judgment is sure and accurate.
How can their misdeeds be hidden from you
    when they are trumpeted all over the land?
How can you love this bastard brood
    when they have made you hateful to all the world?

1. The Ṣanhāja were a confederation of Berber tribes with which the Zirids were affiliated.

How can you complete your ascent to greatness
 when they destroy as you build?
How have you been lulled to trust a villain
 and made him your companion—though he is evil company?
God has vouchsafed in His revelations
 a warning against the society of the wicked.[2]
Do not choose a servant from among them
 but leave them to the curse of the accursed!
For the earth cries out against their wickedness
 and is about to heave and swallow us all.
Turn your eyes to other countries
 and you will find the Jews are outcast dogs.
Why should you alone be different and bring them near
 when in all the land they are kept afar?
—You, who are a well-beloved king,
 scion of glorious kings,
And are the first among men
 as your forebears were first in their time.
I came to live in Granada
 and I saw them frolicking there.
They divided up the city and the provinces
 with one of their accursed men everywhere.
They collect all the revenues,
 they munch and they crunch.
They dress in the finest clothes
 while you wear the meanest.
They are the trustees of your secrets
 —yet how can traitors be trusted?
Others eat a dirham's worth, afar,
 while they are near, and dine well.
They challenge you to your God
 and they are not stopped or reproved.
They envelop you with their prayers
 and you neither see nor hear.
They slaughter beasts in our markets
 and you eat their *trefa*[3]
Their chief ape has marbled his house
 and led the finest spring water to it.

---

2. Qur'ān 5:25.
3. Jewish food was sometimes condemned as unfit for Muslims to eat.

Our affairs are now in his hands
    and we stand at his door.
He laughs at us and at our religion
    and we return to our God.
If I said that his wealth is as great
    as yours, I would speak the truth.
Hasten to slaughter him as an offering,
    sacrifice him, for he is a fat ram
And do not spare his people
    for they have amassed every precious thing.
Break loose their grip and take their money
    for you have a better right to what they collect.
Do not consider it a breach of faith to kill them
    —the breach of faith would be to let them carry on.
They have violated our covenant with them
    so how can you be held guilty against violators?[4]
How can they have any pact
    when we are obscure and they are prominent?
Now we are the humble, beside them,
    as if we had done wrong, and they right!
Do not tolerate their misdeeds against us
    for you are surety for what they do.
God watches His own people
    and the people of God will prevail.

C. Ibn Bassām, *Al-Dhakhīra fī maḥāsin ahl al-jazīra*
Translated from Arabic by Ross Brann

Ibn Bassām al-Shantarīnī's (d. 1147) monumental Andalusi Arabic literary miscellany Al-Dhakhīra fī maḥāsin ahl al-jazīra *[The Treasury Concerning the Merits of the People of the [Iberian] Peninsula] devotes two chapters to the Ibn Naghrelas and signals that their intimate involvement in the affairs of a Muslim polity continued*

---

4. This refers to the long-standing tradition of a covenant between Muslims and non-Muslims (Christians and Jews) living under Muslim rule. In return for their protected status, non-Muslims were supposed to abide by certain rules of behavior designed to set them apart from the Muslim community. See Chapter 7.

Hebrew text from Ibn Bassām al-Shantarīnī, *Al-Dhakhīra fī maḥāsin ahl al-jazīra*, edited by Iḥsān ʿAbbās (Beirut: Dār al-thaqāfa, 1979), 2: 761–69. English text from Ross Brann, *Power in the Portrayal: Representations of Jews and Muslims in Eleventh- and Twelfth-Century Islamic Spain* (Princeton, N.J.: Princeton University Press, 2002), pp. 95–96, 103. Reprinted with permission of the author and publisher.

*to occupy the interest of Andalusi and Maghribi Muslim authors in later periods.
The first chapter transmits a rhymed prose epistle in honor of Ismāʿīl (Samuel) and
additional lyrics of fawning panegyric (an example of which is found below) by
the Andalusi Muslim poet Abū Aḥmad ibn Khayra al-Qurṭubī, also known as al-
Munfatil. The second chapter, from which the other selection is taken, is introduced
as a "chapter summarizing what is known of the murder of that Jew." The reader
will note the text's conflation of father and son and its indictment of Ibn Naghrela
for religious as well as political offenses against Islam. (RB)*

Verses by al-Munfatil

A clan from whom Moses and company sprang:
Say of them what you will; you can never describe even a tenth of them.
How numerous are their signs on earth;
How great are their generous deeds among men.
True, you collect the scattered elements of praise
and release incarcerated generosity.
You exceed in generosity the people of east and west
as pure gold exceeds the value of bronze.
If people could distinguish error from truth
they'd kiss naught but your ten fingertips!
They'd embrace your hands like the (Kaʿba's) Black Cornerstone,
your right to theirs, your left to theirs.
I've succeeded in this world and obtained my desire through you;
and through you I hope to attain my aspiration in the Hereafter.
I obey the law of the Sabbath [openly] among you;
among my own people I observe it in secret.
Even Moses was afraid, kept a cautious lookout,
and was in want. But you safeguard from fear and deprivation.

Ibn Bassām's Summary of the Events

Among the extraordinary events of that period of fractious order and tribulations was the elevation of that Jewish scoundrel who upbraided all who ascribed to a revealed religion. Even the Jews, with their accursed religion, did
not heed him nor did they trust him regarding esoteric matters. His father
Yūsuf, a man from the common folk of Jews, had fine manners for one of
them and a favorable character for their like. He was enlisted in Granada by
Bādīs and by his father Ḥabbūs before him to work in the state treasury and
the administration of most of its operations.

His son succeeded him while only a youth and, as people maintained,
just a tender colt. He spellbound those responsible for young men such that

it was said of him: "He's the one; he's the one!" Before long he assumed the reins of administration and had a free hand with the better part of the state funds. A mass of people followed in his footsteps with whom he ran a perverse footrace, making light of the most serious of ugly deeds, he strayed too far and was not mindful of the consequences, such that his hands were awash in kisses and he boasted of his refutation of religion. He composed a treatise in refutation of the aforementioned scholar of religious law Abū Muḥammad ibn Ḥazm in which he openly expressed calumny against Islam. He was not deterred from [writing] this [treatise] by rebuke nor was anyone able to excise it except from one's own mind.

The position in which the government installed him was a source of rage for the Muslims day and night. For that matter the Jews sensed there would be disaster on his account and complained of his tyrannical rule even though he had pulverized rubble for them and paved the way for them in the most difficult matters. Nevertheless, he remained steadfast in his extremist views and turned away from the path of God in his relations with others. He forced his judgments upon the Jews, deposed their leaders, and in accordance with their religious law was named "Nagid," which means "administrator" to them, a position their ancients had regarded with suspicion. Their communal leaders initially treated it (the office) with deference [but] he behaved audaciously with his weak foundation and without regard for his soul.

D. Abraham ibn Daud, *Book of Tradition*
Translated from Hebrew by Gerson D. Cohen

In this passage from the Sefer ha-Qabbalah *[Book of Tradition], written in 1161, Abraham ibn Daud (d. 1181) recounts events that took place in Granada a century earlier. He details the career of Samuel ibn Naghrela (Samuel ha-Nagid), his rise to power at the Zirid court, and his status in the Jewish communities of Córdoba and Granada. He also describes the career of Joseph ibn Naghrela and his downfall. Although the point of view is different, this account overlaps to some degree with Muslim descriptions. Unlike 'Abd Allāh ibn Buluggīn's account, however, this version notes Samuel as a kātib (scribe) and counselor to Ḥabbūs, not a vizier. Abraham's description of Zirid struggles over succession also differs somewhat from those depicted in Arabic sources. The dates used in this passage are cited according to the Jewish calendar. (ORC)*

English text from *The Book of Tradition (Sefer ha-Qabbalah)*, translated by Gerson D. Cohen (Philadelphia: Jewish Publication Society of America, 1967), pp. 71–76. Reprinted with permission of the publisher.

One of his outstanding disciples was R. Samuel ha-Levi the Nagid ibn R. Joseph, surnamed Ibn Naghrela, of the community of Córdoba. Besides being a great scholar and highly cultured person, R. Samuel was highly versed in Arabic literature and style and was, indeed, competent to serve in the king's palace. Nevertheless, he maintained himself in very modest circumstances as a spice-merchant until the time when war broke out in Spain.[1] With the termination of the rule of the house of Ibn Abī 'Amir and the seizure of power by the Berber chiefs, the city of Córdoba dwindled, and its inhabitants were compelled to flee. Some went off to Zaragoza,[2] where their descendants have remained down to the present, while others went to Toledo, where their descendants have retained their identity down to the present.[3]

This R. Samuel, however, fled to Málaga,[4] where he occupied a shop as a spice-merchant. Since his shop happened to adjoin the courtyard of Ibn al-'Arif—who was the *kātib* of king Habbūs ibn Māksan, the Berber king of Granada[5]—the *kātib*'s maidservant would ask him to write letters for her to her master, the vizier Abū al-Qāsim ibn al-'Arif. When the latter received the letters, he was astounded at the learning they reflected. Consequently, when, after a while, this vizier, Ibn al-'Arif, was given leave by his king Habbūs to return to his home in Málaga, he inquired among the people of his household: "Who wrote the letters which I received from you?" They replied: "A certain Jew of the community of Córdoba, who lives next door to your courtyard, used to do the writing for us." The *kātib* thereupon ordered that R. Samuel ha-Levi be brought to him at once, and he said to him: "It does not become you to spend your time in a shop. Henceforth you are to stay at my side." He thus became the scribe and counselor of the counselor to the king. Now the counsel which he gave was as if one consulted the oracle of God, and thanks to his counsel king Habbūs achieved successes and became exceedingly great.

Subsequently, when the *kātib* Ibn al-'Arif took ill and felt his death approaching, king Habbūs paid him a visit and said to him: "What am I going to do? Who will counsel me in the wars which encompass me on every side?" He replied: "I never counseled you out of my own mind, but out of the mind of this Jew, my scribe. Look after him well, and let him be a father and a priest to you. Do whatever he says, and God will help you."

---

1. War broke out in 1009, following the end of 'Amirid rule. Al-Mansūr (Ibn Abī 'Amir), had been *hājib* under the last Umayyad ruler. The war lasted until 1031, after which al-Andalus was divided into Taifa states.

2. At the time of the uprisings, the Muslim governor of Zaragoza defected and established an independent monarchy.

3. In other words, they retained their identity as descendants of the Cordobans.

4. At the time of Ibn Naghrela's flight, Málaga remained in the hands of a pro-Umayyad governor who threw in his lot with 'Alī ibn Hammūd.

5. Habbūs ibn Māksan ruled Granada ca. 1026–1038.

Accordingly, after the death of the *kātib,* king Ḥabbūs brought R. Samuel ha-Levi to his palace and made him *kātib* and counselor. Thus, he entered the king's palace in 4780.

Now the king had two sons, Bādīs the elder and Buluggīn the younger. Although the Berber princes supported the election of the younger, Buluggīn, as king, the people at large supported Bādīs.[6] The Jews also took sides, with three of them, R. Joseph ibn Megash, R. Isaac ibn Leon and R. Nehemiah surnamed Ishkafa, who were among the leading citizens of Granada, supporting Buluggīn. R. Samuel ha-Levi, on the other hand, supported Bādīs. On the day of king Ḥabbūs' death, the Berber princes and nobles formed a line to proclaim his son Buluggīn as king.[7] Thereupon, Buluggīn went and kissed the hand of his older brother Bādīs,[8] thus acknowledging the latter as king. This happened in the year 4787. Buluggīn's supporters turned livid with embarrassment, but in spite of themselves they acknowledged Bādīs as king. Subsequently, his brother Buluggīn regretted his earlier action and tried to lord it over his brother Bādīs. There was nothing, however trivial, that the king would do that Buluggīn would not frustrate. When, after a while, his brother took ill, the king told the physician to withhold medications from his brother, and the physician did just that. Buluggīn then died, and the kingdom was established in the hand of Bādīs. Thereupon, the three leading Jewish citizens mentioned above fled to the city of Seville.[9]

Now R. Samuel was appointed as *nagid* in [4]787.[10] He achieved great good for Israel in Spain, the Maghrib, Ifrīqqiya, Egypt, Sicily, indeed as far as the academy in Babylonia and the Holy City.[11] He provided material benefits out of his own pocket for students of the Torah in all these countries. He also purchased many books—[copies] of the Holy Scriptures as well as of the Mishna and Talmud, which are also among the holy writings. Throughout Spain and the countries just mentioned, whoever wished to devote full time to the study of the Torah found in him a patron. Moreover, he retained scribes who would make copies of the Mishna and Talmud, which he would present to students who were unable to purchase copies themselves, both in the academies of Spain as well as of the other countries we mentioned. These gifts were coupled with annual contributions of olive oil for the synagogues of Jerusalem, which he would dispatch from his own home. He spread Torah

6. This version of the account differs from that of 'Abd Allāh ibn Buluggīn, who reports that the struggle for the throne was between Bādīs and his cousin Yiddīr.
7. They formed a line to perform the ceremony of investiture and give the oath of allegiance.
8. Kissing of hands was part of the ceremony of allegiance.
9. Seville had been the capital of an independent kingdom, hostile to Bādīs, since 1023.
10. The title *nagid* signified a leader or "prince" of the Jewish community.
11. Jerusalem.

abroad and died at a ripe old age after having earned four crowns: the crown
of Torah, the crown of power, the crown of a Levite, and towering over them
all, by dint of good deeds in each of these domains, the crown of a good
name. He passed away in 4815.

His son, R. Joseph ha-Levi the Nagid, succeeded to his post. Of all
the fine qualities which his father possessed he lacked but one. Having been
reared in wealth and never having had to bear a burden [of responsibility] in
his youth, he lacked his father's humility. Indeed, he grew haughty—to his
destruction. The Berber princes became so jealous of him that he was killed
on the Sabbath day, the ninth of Tebet [4]827, along with the community
of Granada and all those who had come from distant lands to see his learning and power. He was mourned in every city and in every town. (Indeed,
a fast had been decreed for the ninth of Tebet as far back as the days of our
ancient rabbis, who composed *Megillat Ta'anit*; but the reason had not been
known. From this [incident] we see that they had pointed prophetically to
this very day.) After his death, his books and treasures were scattered all over
the world. So, too, the disciples he raised became the rabbis of Spain and the
leaders of the following generation.

Does not reconcile with Ibn Bassam's account of Jewish attitudes towards Samuel & Joseph

22. THE CONQUEST OF TOLEDO (1085)

The conquest of Toledo by Alfonso VI of León-Castile in May 1085 is often seen as a watershed in the history of medieval Spain and a turning point in the transition of territory from Muslim to Christian rule. Certainly, the city's capture was seen as a critical event at the time, and it appears to have precipitated the arrival of the Almoravids in the peninsula. Even though Toledo was not as large or important as Córdoba or Seville, it had symbolic weight for both Christians and Muslims as the old Visigothic capital. During the eleventh century, the Taifa of Toledo was ruled by the Dhū al-Nūnid dynasty, who maintained an uneasy truce with their northern Christian neighbors. Alfonso even took refuge at the court of Toledo's ruler, al-Ma'mūn, when he was at war with his brother Sancho. At the time of its conquest, Toledo was home to large numbers of Jews and local Christians (Mozarabs) as well as Muslims. The three texts collected below all relate to Alfonso's conquest and subsequent administration of the city. None are contemporary with the actual conquest. The texts from the Primera crónica general *and Rodrigo Jiménez de Rada both date from the thirteenth century and present very deliberate later narratives of Castilian history; the third text, recording privileges granted to the Mozarabs of Toledo, was issued by Alfonso VI in 1101. (ORC)*

A. Description of the Conquest of Toledo from the *Primera crónica general de España*
Translated from Castilian by John Moscatiello

The Primera crónica general *is also known, perhaps more accurately, as the* Estoria de España. *This chronicle was commissioned by Alfonso X el Sabio (r. 1252–1284) to be an official history of his realms, and the text was completed under his son, Sancho IV (r. 1284–1295). (ORC)*

On How King Alfonso Took the Crops and Fruits Away from Toledo and Populated Extremadura

Almemon [al-Ma'mūn], the king of Toledo, and his son Yssem [Ismā'īl] were killed in the thirteenth year in the reign of King Alfonso [VI]. This was the year 1113 of the Era, which was also the year 1075 of the Incarnation of our Lord and the twenty-seventh year of the reign of the [Holy] Roman Emperor Henry [IV]. After the deaths of Almemon and Yssem, Yahia Alcadirbille [Yahya al-Qādir bi-Allah], who was the son of King Yssem and

Primera crónica general de España, edited by Ramón Menéndez Pidal, Nueva biblioteca de autores españoles 5 (Madrid: Bailly-Bailliere, 1906; reprint, Madrid: Editorial Gredos, 1977), 2: 537–38. The translator wishes to thank Margaret Ringe and Belén Vicéns Sáiz for their assistance and suggestions.

the grandson of Almemon, ascended to the throne.[1] Yahia was an evil and villainous king and far removed from the manners and the customs of his grandfather Almemon and of his father Yssem. He became withdrawn and contemptuous of the best of his Moors and, later, of all his people. He inflicted so much pain and violence on them that everyone longed for his death because they saw that he was an evil and vile man and had no good within him. His grandfather King Almemon gave the lands of Olmos and Canales in the Kingdom of Toledo to King Alfonso; when Alfonso went with Almemon to aid against his Moorish enemies, Alfonso left men there who were sick and weak.

The people of Toledo were being abused by their King Yahia as was said. Because King Yahia did nothing to improve the situation and felt no compassion for the sorrows of his people, even as they were attacked by their enemies on all sides, they joined together and went to him, saying, "King Yahia, it behooves you to defend your people and your land. So we tell you that you must commit yourself entirely to this end or else we will seek another who will defend us." But Yahia, so the story goes, because he was a man of many women and of evil customs, did not heed the advice of his Moors and did not improve anything. Perceiving themselves neglected by their king, his Moors sought help from the king of Badajoz,[2] taking him inside the town in spite of King Yahia. Moreover, because they were in great danger, they secretly sent their messengers to King Alfonso so that he might besiege the town (the terms of the agreement that he made with Yahia's grandfather Almemon had expired).

After that, when they saw that all the people of the city were afflicted with hunger and misery, they advised the starving people to give their city over to King Alfonso. So the people secretly sent their town leaders to tell King Alfonso that they surrendered. When King Alfonso saw the messengers and heard what they had to say, it pleased him and he was very happy. But he was bothered that they had brought the king of Badajoz into the city. This did not stop him, however, from continuing with his plan, and he brought together a great army from all the parts of his kingdom and set

---

1. Al-Ma'mūn, who ruled Toledo from 1043 to 1075, was an ally of Alfonso VI and provided a refuge for Alfonso in Toledo from his older brother Sancho. After al-Ma'mūn's death, his son Ismā'īl survived his father by only a few months, passing rule on to his son (al-Ma'mūn's grandson) Yahya, who took the throne name al-Qādir. Yahya ruled from 1075 to 1080, when Toledo was briefly occupied by the ruler of Badajoz, 'Umar al-Mutawakkil. Yahya's second reign in Toledo lasted from 1081 to 1085, when Alfonso conquered the city and installed Yahya as a puppet ruler in Valencia until his death in 1092. Throughout this passage, the medieval spellings for Arabic names have been retained.

2. 'Umar al-Mutawakkil.

out for Toledo. As soon as he arrived, he took all the crops, the vineyards, and the other fruits away from all the surroundings of Toledo. King Alfonso did this for four years to Toledo and the surrounding towns, one after the other. Although Toledo was better provisioned and more prosperous than all its neighboring towns, it was impossible to maintain its rations because they were taken away year after year. Meanwhile, King Alfonso populated the cities and towns that were uninhabited in Extremadura. The towns he populated were these: Salamanca, Ávila, Medina del Campo, Olmedo, Coca, Iscar, Cuéllar, Segovia, and Sepúlveda. After this King Alfonso returned to León in great honor.

And know this, all of you who hear this history, that El Cid Ruy Diaz agreed with the king in all these things and was honorable in all things. In this thirteenth year [*anno lidio*] of his reign, King Alfonso fought with Abenalhage [Ibn al-Hajj] in Consuegra.[3] After he was defeated in the battle, Alfonso withdrew into the Castle of Consuegra. Diego Ruiz, son of El Cid Ruy Diaz, died.[4] From the thirteenth to the seventeenth festal year [*anno fastal*] of the reign of this king Alfonso, we have nothing to say that pertains to the story, except that in the fourteenth year Abenalhage fought with Álvar Fáñez de Minaya. And according to the testimony of the elders, who are by now quite old and who understand the events of that time better, Álvar Fáñez had fifty knights, whereas Abenalhage had 15,000. But by the grace of God, who desired it to happen, Álvar Fáñez defeated Abenalhage in Almodóvar, south of Córdoba. Others say, however, that Abenalhage defeated Álvar Fáñez and that he even struck him in the face with a sword. In the fifteenth year of his reign, King Alfonso went to Coria, which was still in Moorish hands, and captured it.

This is the history of the great deeds of the king Alfonso in the conquest of Toledo:

On How King Alfonso Won Toledo and All Its Surrounding Towns

Some say it was the nineteenth year, others the twentieth, of the reign of this king Alfonso, which would be the year 1081 of the Incarnation of our Lord and the thirty-third year of the reign of the [Holy] Roman Emperor Henry [IV]. Thus in the year reckoned according to these calculations, King Alfonso gathered together an even greater and larger army and came upon

3. Muḥammad ibn al-Hajj was the Almoravid commander in charge of the Consuegra campaign. The Battle of Consuegra was fought on 15 August 1097. The author appears to be counting Alfonso's reign in festal years, not calendar years.
4. At this time, the Cid was ruling in Valencia, but he sent his son Diego, then twenty-two, to assist Alfonso.

Toledo and, as was his fashion, he encircled and besieged it. Toledo was a strong city: a great part of it was surrounded by hills, the Tagus River ran its course around it, and there were a great number of people dwelling within it. However, when the foodstuffs ran out the people were forced to surrender to King Alfonso. So it was after twenty-four days had passed in the month of May, on the Feast of St. Urban, that Toledo was given over to Alfonso VI.[5] And the Moors gave the city to him under these conditions: that they would remain in the city and retain their houses and estates as they had before and Alfonso would receive the fortress and the orchards beyond the gate that is called Alcántara. The Moors, moreover, would pay to King Alfonso the rents and tributes they were accustomed to give to their Moorish kings. The great mosque would always belong to the Moors. And everything was done according to these terms which Alfonso made with the Moors in his first conquest of Toledo. Once everything was agreed upon and peaceful and he was in control of the town, Alfonso continued on to all of the towns surrounding Toledo.

B. Rodrigo Jiménez de Rada, Conversion of the Mosque of Toledo
Translated from Latin by Colin Smith

Although the original terms of the surrender of Toledo apparently promised that the main mosque would remain in Muslim hands, this situation soon changed. Only a few months after the conquest, in July 1085 while the king was away from the city, the archbishop-elect Bernard de Sédirac and Alfonso's wife Constanza decided to consecrate the building as a Christian church. Although the narrative places all responsibility for this action and the broken promise on the archbishop and queen (both of whom were French), this may have been a convenient fiction. It seems unlikely that the conversion of the mosque would have been undertaken entirely without Alfonso's knowledge or tacit approval. Certainly, it would soon become standard, in other conquered cities, to convert the main mosque immediately into a Christian church. Rodrigo Jiménez de Rada was himself an archbishop of Toledo in the early thirteenth century (his election was confirmed in 1209), a royal chancellor under Alfonso VIII of Castile, and a prolific historian. This selection is taken from his chronicle De rebus Hispaniae. *(ORC)*

---

5. There is some debate about the exact date. See Bernard F. Reilly, *The Kingdom of León-Castilla Under King Alfonso VI* (Princeton, N.J.: Princeton University Press, 1988), p. 171.

English text from *Christians and Moors in Spain*, vol. 1, edited and translated by Colin Smith (Warminster: Aris and Phillips, 1988), pp. 89–91. Reprinted with permission of the publisher.

When Bernard[1] arrived soon after [the city's conquest], he was made Abbot [of Sahagún], in which post he showed himself to be gentle and kindly to all, up to the time when Almighty God restored Toledo to the power of the Christians, and there after a short while he was elected to the archbishopric and primacy. When the King had gone off to León, the Archbishop-elect, with Queen Constanza[2] encouraging him, and with the approval of the Christian troops, entered the chief mosque of Toledo, and having purged it of the filth of Muhammad, set up an altar of the Christian faith, and placed bells in the main tower so that the Christians could be called to worship. When news of this reached the King, he was outraged and deeply grieved, because of the agreement he had made, with the Saracens concerning the mosque, and in three days he traveled from Sahagún to Toledo, proposing to have Bernard the Archbishop-elect and Queen Constanza burned alive. When news of the King's great anger reached the Moors of Toledo, the great and the small together with their wives and children went out to meet the King at Maga. As soon as the King reached the main group of them, he, realizing that they had come to make their protest, said: "This outrage was not done to you, but to me, for up to this point my trustworthiness was unquestioned; now in other matters I shall not be able to boast of that trustworthiness; now it will concern me both to give you satisfaction and to punish the offenders severely." However the Moors, being prudent, raising their voices and on bended knees, sought an audience. Then the King stayed for a while, holding his reins, and the Moors began to address him as follows: "We are fully aware that the Archbishop is the head of your faith, and if we were to be the cause of his death, there might come a day when the Christians out of zeal for their faith would strike at us; and if the Queen should perish on account of us, we shall be forever hateful to her descendants, and after your time they will take a bitter revenge. So we beg you to spare them, and we voluntarily absolve you from the bond of your oath." When he heard this the King's rage turned to joy, since he could have the mosque without any breach of faith, and he went into the royal city where he dealt with all matters of business in a peaceful way.

1. Bernard de Sédirac, a French monk sent from Cluny to the court of Alfonso VI, had been named abbot of the monastery of Sahagún. Bernard was chosen as the first archbishop of Toledo immediately after Alfonso's conquest of the city, and his election was confirmed in 1086.
2. Constanza was the second wife of Alfonso VI. She was a Burgundian princess, and her French point of view may have been similar to that of archbishop-elect Bernard.

C. Privilege Given by Alfonso VI to the
Mozarabs of Toledo (1101)
Translated from Latin by James F. Powers

Alfonso VI issued a charter of privileges to the native Christian inhabitants of Toledo (the Mozarabs) in 1101, a quarter century after the conquest of the city. Earlier, Alfonso had appointed a Mozarab, Sisnando Davídez, as the city's first governor under Castilian rule. Toledo had a very mixed population in the late eleventh and early twelfth centuries, including Mozarabs, Jews, Muslims, new Christian settlers from elsewhere in Alfonso's realms, and foreigners from abroad. Alfonso evidently felt it necessary to confirm the particular privileges granted to the Mozarab community in Toledo. (ORC)

In the name of Christ. I, Alfonso by the grace of God, King of the realm of Toledo, and magnificent conqueror, joined with my most beloved wife Queen Elizabeth,[1] to all the Mozarabs of Toledo, whether nobles or commoners, peace in Christ, and perpetual greeting. With the passing of time there will have been made in Toledo many thorough investigations concerning lands and estates, as much by prior agreement, as by purchase and by conveyance from there to those who may have more, or to those who in fact have little, thus I now seek to make an end to that matter, and I wish that no more be done. For that reason therefore in the month of March I myself have ordered Don Juan *alcalde*, who was prefect and sworn judge of that city, and with the *alguacil* Don Pedro[2] and ten others from the higher ranking of the city's Mozarabs and Castilians, together with them should seek out and equally divide the lands and other holdings beyond the estates among all of them, and what they did with them should remain always undisturbed and enduringly permanent. When all that shall have been done and completed in accordance with my rule, then as now, I, having been asked by the aforementioned investigations and having been favorably moved by their prayers, confirm this charter of stability for all those Mozarabs of Toledo, noble and commoner, that they may have title always for such lands and holdings, whether they hold vineyards and lands held in law in their own right today, and they should not lose anything from that time [to any person] due to any investigation, nor to the advantage

---

Translated from Tomás González, *Colección de privilegios de Simancas* (Madrid: Imprenta real, 1829–1833), vol. 5, no. 8, pp. 28–30.

1. Elizabeth was the fourth wife of Alfonso VI, the mother of his only son, and originally a Muslim princess. It appears that she took the name Elizabeth with her conversion to Christianity, probably at the time of her marriage to Alfonso about 1100. Her Muslim name was Zaida, and she had been the widow of the amīr of Córdoba and daughter-in-law of al-Muʿtamid of Seville. She was already living at Alfonso's court by 1093, when she bore him a son.

2. The *alguacil* was an urban legal officer, or sheriff, in charge of executing the orders of the court.

of any future king, or *zafalmedina*,[3] or count, or military commander, from as much as they hold now, and they have asserted their legal claim by virtue of my judgment, and in perpetuity. And I give to them this freedom so that he who will have been a commoner among them, and will have wished to be noble, and will have the means to be able to do so that he may be noble; in the name of God he may have the power of freely selling, giving, or possessing whatsoever he will have wished to do, at least as regards his property. And if among those some business shall have arisen regarding some judgment, let the settlement be determined in accordance with the opinions in the ancient established *Libro judicum*:[4] and regarding so many false testimonies, they shall have made let them procure the fifth [a fine] solely, as it is contained in the Castilian charter, except for theft and the death of a Jew or Muslim. And concerning all such false accusations I command them to hold to the customary law, such as abides for the Castilians staying in Toledo. And if those who will have been commoners wish to plant or restore vines or other trees, let them thence make a payment of a tenth solely to the palace: this moreover I do for the remedy of my soul, and of my parents, and thus all of you, whether in this city whom I always loved and cherished, or those I have led from other lands to settle [here], may I always have you as loyal and loving subjects. Therefore I absolve you from the dregs of all previously made submissions, and I hand over the prescribed privileges, so that up to the present day and thereafter, neither you, nor your children nor your heirs should withdraw from these prescribed regulations, and in this *fuero* you should always remain steadfast in this enduring time, and through all ages, amen. If, however, that which I believe to be happening to a lesser degree, either I or any man close to me, or a foreigner shall have come to break this deed of mine, whoever he shall have been, who shall have initiated such changes, let him be excommunicated, and freely separated from the freedom of the Christian faith, and with Dathan and Abiram whom the earth swallowed alive (Num. 16:12–15, 25–34), rebels who rose against the command of God, and Judas who betrayed the Lord, because he hanged himself with a noose, and poured forth his life with his entrails, let him drown in the depths of hell to suffer forever from eternal punishment, let this our deed hold full firmness in all situations. Moreover I make this valid charter in [Spanish] era 1139, the fourteenth day before the Kalends of April [19 March 1101]. And let citizen sell to citizens, and neighbor to neighbor, but I do not wish that any of those citizens sell lands or territories to any count or official.

---

3. The *zafalmedina* was an urban prefect charged with civil and judicial powers. The Castilian term is derived from the Arabic *sahib al-madina*.

4. The Visigothic Code, or *Liber iudiciorum*. This law code remained an important source of legal reference for many centuries, and it would be translated into Castilian, as the *Fuero juzgo*, in the thirteenth century.

23. THE BATTLE OF ZALLĀQA (1086)

'Abd al-Wāḥid al-Marrākushī, Account of the Battle of Zallāqa
Translated from Arabic by Charles Melville and Ahmad Ubaydli

After the fall of Toledo to Alfonso VI in 1085, several Taifa rulers, led by al-Mu'tamid of Seville, decided to ask for help from the Almoravids in North Africa. In response to their call, the Almoravid ruler Yūsuf ibn Tāshufīn brought troops to al-Andalus and encountered Alfonso's army at the Battle of Zallāqa (also known as Sagrajas), to the north of Badajoz, in 1086. This resulted in an Almoravid victory, and halted Castilian southward expansion, but did not lead to the Muslim retaking of Toledo. Shortly after the battle, Yūsuf ibn Tāshufīn retired to Morocco with his army, only to return a few years later to establish Almoravid rule in al-Andalus. This account of the Battle of Zallāqa was written by the later Maghribi historian 'Abd al-Wāḥid al-Marrākushī in 1224. (ORC)

When it was 479 (1086), al-Mu'tamid 'ala Allah crossed the sea, heading for Marrakesh, to seek help from Yūsuf ibn Tāshufīn against the Christians. The said Yūsuf gave him a warm welcome and housed him in the finest style, and enquired what he wanted. [Al-Mu'tamid] mentioned that he wished to attack Christian territory and wanted the Amīr al-Muslimīn [Yūsuf] to supply him with horses and men to help him wage war. The Commander of the Muslims hastened to grant his request, and said, "I am the first to be entrusted to come to the assistance of this faith, and none other than I myself will take charge of the matter!"

Al-Mu'tamid returned to al-Andalus happy with the assistance promised him by the Amīr al-Muslimīn; he did not know that his destruction lay in this arrangement. He drew a sword that he thought was for him, and did not know that it was against him. . . .

Yūsuf ibn Tāshufīn, the Commander of the Muslims, began the preparations to cross to the Spanish Peninsula in the month of Jumada I this year (began 14 August). He summoned all the leaders and commanders of the army and the chiefs of the Berber tribes whom he could call upon to fight. About 7,000 horsemen with a large number of infantry assembled and he crossed the sea with a vast army, embarking at the town of Sabta (Ceuta) and landing at the town called al-Jazīrat al-khadra (Algeciras). Al-Mu'tamid met him with the leading men of his state, and displayed more reverence

English translation from *Christians and Moors in Spain*, vol. 3, edited by Charles Melville and Ahmad Ubaydli (Warminster: Aris and Phillips, 1992), pp. 93–99. Reprinted with permission of the publisher.

and deference towards him than the Amīr al-Muslimīn had expected. [Al-Muʿtamid] presented him with kingly gifts, presents and riches such as Yūsuf could not imagine a king possessing. It was this that first kindled a longing for the kingdom of al-Andalus in Yūsuf's heart.

He then set off from Algeciras with his troops, towards the east of al-Andalus. Al-Muʿtamid asked him to enter Seville, his capital, to rest there a few days until the rigors of his journey were soothed and then carry out his intentions. Yūsuf refused, saying, "I have only come with the aim of fighting Holy War against the enemy; wherever he is, I will set off to face him."

Alfonso (VI)—may God curse him!—was giving siege to one of the Muslims' castles, known as al-Līt (Aledo). When he heard that the Berbers had crossed over, he abandoned the siege and returned to his own territories, mobilizing his army to meet the Berbers. . . .

The above-mentioned Yūsuf then reviewed his troops at the fortress of al-Raqqa, and liked what he saw of them. He said to al-Muʿtamid ʿala Allah, "Let's go on the Holy War that we came for, and attack the enemy." He began to grumble about staying in the Spanish Peninsula, and to long for Marrakesh, and to belittle the power of al-Andalus. He was forever saying, "We took the affairs of this Peninsula seriously until we saw it, and now that we have seen it, it has sunk beneath all description." [But] in doing so he was as one "happy to drink the froth."[1] Al-Muʿtamid left him, heading for Toledo.

A mighty army assembled round al-Muʿtamid from different regions of al-Andalus, and the people were summoned to Holy War from other districts. The kings of the Peninsula reinforced Yūsuf and al-Muʿtamid with as many horses, men and arms as they could; the total strength of the Muslims, including volunteers and mercenaries, was about 20,000 men. They and the enemy met where Christian territory began.

Alfonso—may God curse him!—had already called up great and small; there was no one left in the furthest reaches of his territory capable of action whom he had not stirred. He came leading a powerful army, his main intention being to stifle the desire of the Berbers for the Spanish Peninsula and to inspire them with fear. As for the kings of al-Andalus, every one of them was paying him tribute; they were more than contemptible in his eyes and beneath his contemplation.

When the two sides, Muslim and Christian, beheld each other, Yūsuf and his companions were appalled by the enormous size of the enemy numbers, the excellence of their arms and horses and their appearance of strength. He

---

1. I.e., pretending to want only the froth, while actually drinking all the milk.

said to al-Muʿtamid, "I didn't realize that this pig—may God curse him—had grown to such proportions."

Yūsuf and his companions assembled, and he appointed someone to exhort them and preach to them. A sufficient number of them affirmed their vow and their eagerness to fight the Holy War and made light of martyrdom, to gladden Yūsuf and the Muslims.

The two sides made contact on a Thursday, 12 Ramadan (21 December);[2] the envoys were unable to agree on a day for the general advance, so that they could make their preparations. Alfonso said, "Friday is your [Holy Day]. Saturday is the Jews'; they are our ministers and scribes, and make up the majority of the servants in the army and we cannot do without them. Sunday is our [Holy Day]. So Monday would be the best day to begin operations." His intention—God curse him!—was to deceive and mislead the Muslims, but it didn't turn out as he planned. . . .

On the Friday, the Muslims were preparing for the Friday prayers with no sign of [preparation for] a fight. Yūsuf ibn Tāshufīn relied on the belief that kings do not act treacherously, and he and his companions went out dressed for prayers. Al-Muʿtamid took courage and he and his companions rode out armed to the teeth; he said to the Amīr of the Muslims, "Pray at the head of your men; I am ill at ease today. I am here behind you, for I suspect this pig [Alfonso] has a secret design to launch a sudden attack on the Muslims."

Yūsuf and his men began to pray, and when they had performed the first *rakʿa*[3] the Christian cavalry burst into them. Alfonso—may God curse him!—attacked at the head of his men, thinking that he would seize his opportunity, while al-Muʿtamid and his men were behind the Almoravids. That day produced such riches as no one had ever witnessed before. The Almoravids grabbed their weapons and mounted their horses and the two sides became embroiled. Yūsuf ibn Tāshufīn and his men showed a perseverance, heroism and fortitude beyond the calculations of al-Muʿtamid, and God defeated the enemy. The Muslims pursued them, killing them on all sides, but Alfonso—God curse him!—escaped with nine men. This was one of the most celebrated victories in al-Andalus, by which God glorified his religion, elevated his word, and cut off Alfonso's ambitions (may God curse him!) in al-Andalus, after he had been anticipating it coming into his possession and believing that its kings were his servants. All this came about through the pious intentions of the Amīr of the Muslims.

They called this battle al-Zallāqa; the encounter between the Muslims

---

2. The date is incorrect; see note 4.
3. A cycle of the prayer, with bowing and prostration.

and their enemy occurred, as we have mentioned, on Friday 13 Ramadan 480 (12 December 1087).[4] Yūsuf ibn Tāshufīn and his men departed victoriously from the scene, conquered for them and by them, and the men of al-Andalus were delighted with them, and regarded the amīr al-Muslimīn as a good omen and a blessing. Prayers for him multiplied in the mosques and from the pulpits, his praises spread through the Spanish Peninsula in a way that increased his covetousness towards it. This was because al-Andalus, before his arrival, was facing annihilation by the conquests of the Christians and their exaction of tribute from all its kings without exception; and when God overcame the enemy and defeated him at the hands of the Commander of the Muslims, the people proclaimed his glory and love for him grew in their hearts.

4. Al-Marrākushī gives the wrong date. It should be 12 Rajab 479 (23 October 1086).

24. THE POLITICAL DILEMMA OF A GRANADAN RULER

'Abd Allāh ibn Buluggīn, *Tibyān* (1095)

Translated from Arabic by Amin T. Tibi

This passage, like his account of Joseph ibn Naghrela (Chapter 21A), is taken from 'Abd Allāh ibn Buluggīn's memoir, the T̲ibyān. The Tibyān was composed at the end of 'Abd Allāh's life, after he was removed from power by the Almoravids in 1090 and sent to live in exile in Aghmat, a town in southern Morocco. The memoir was written, in part, to describe and justify his actions as ruler of Granada in a time of political difficulty. Although 'Abd Allāh had welcomed the Almoravids when they arrived in al-Andalus in 1086, and had aided them in their victory against Alfonso VI of Castile-León at the Battle of Zallāqa and the siege of Aledo, he soon faced suspicions of double-dealing. According to his account, his chief accuser was al-Mu'tamid, the ruler of the neighboring Taifa kingdom of Seville. While he sought to demonstrate his loyalty to the Muslim cause, 'Abd Allāh was simultaneously threatened by Alfonso and forced to pay tribute money to Castile. His struggle with this dilemma comes through in his memoir. Eventually, Granada was seized by the Almoravids, despite 'Abd Allāh's protestations, and he was sent into exile abroad. (ORC)

When it came for us to leave Aledo, we asked the Amīr of the Muslims[1] to leave troops with us in al-Andalus lest the Christian should come down on us in strength and seek revenge for that and other campaigns. [For if he did] we would find ourselves with no troops to defend us. The Amīr's reply was: "Mend your ways and you'll be able to cope with your enemy." Accordingly, he gave us no troops. We made sure then that the Christian[2] would not lose this opportunity of attacking us. And this was what in fact happened. He soon rallied a large force and then came looking for money and threatening to ravage the territory of those who refused. He concluded a treaty with the prince of Zaragoza and with neighboring princes in the east [i.e., the Spanish Levant] who staved off trouble from him by paying him the sums they owed him.

On receiving this news, I became more anxious than ever and realized that in this business I was like a man on a lion's back. If I surrendered the city [i.e., Granada], when I had no troops at my disposal, it would be

English text from *The Tibyān: Memoirs of 'Abd Allāh ibn Buluggīn, Last Zīrid Amīr of Granada*, translated by Amin T. Tibi (Leiden: Brill, 1986), pp. 130–32, 134–35. Reprinted with permission of the publisher.

1. Here, "Amīr of the Muslims" refers to Almoravid ruler Yūsuf ibn Tāshufīn.
2. Alfonso VI of Castile-León.

ravaged without my being able to get a single dirham back. Yet I would not be excused, and some schemer would not hesitate to say I had lost it out of carelessness or that I had actually led the enemy into it, just as I had seen and heard the same sort of thing held against Ibn Rashīq.[3] Moreover, I would have lost my country into the bargain. I would be unable to provide for the annual campaigns we launched against the Christians and for hospitality extended to the Almoravids. My loss would, therefore, be twofold. But if, on the other hand, I sought to placate the enemy and looked to my own interests, it would be said that I had concluded a treaty with the Christian and be discredited for something I had not done, as indeed happened. And so there was no escape for me from all I had anticipated, for it had been decreed by fate.

Álvar Háñez (*Albar Hānish*)[4] was put in charge of the regions (*jihāt*) of Granada and Almería. It was he who had been entrusted by Alfonso with the implementation of his orders in these two regions whether it was a question of attacking those princes who had failed to meet his demands, or of receiving money or of intervening in anything that might be of advantage to him. Álvar Háñez at first sent a message to me on his own account threatening to enter Guadix and adding that only the payment of a ransom would deter him. I asked myself: "Whose help can I get to protect me from his threat? How can I possibly keep him at bay when no troops have been left to help us defend ourselves? How many Muslim prisoners will he take in this scheme? How much substance will be lost in it? Ten times the amount that will have to be given in tribute, as I know from past experience with these people. O God! What if this should happen and he were to carry out his threat and I were to receive news of Muslim prisoners in their hands. Isn't it better to ransom them with what is precious? It would be worthy of me to do this before the Christians set out on their campaign and thus spare my country the ravages of war. This would earn me the reward of Almighty God who knows the secrets of our hearts. But should I pay out this money quite cheerfully, while I have men to defend me, it would be held against me."

I decided, therefore, to placate Álvar Háñez by making a small payment to him and at the same time concluded an agreement with him whereby he undertook not to come near any of my towns after he had received that

3. Ibn Rashīq had been in control of Murcia, and officially under the suzerainty of al-Muʿtamid, ruler of Seville, but he had angered al-Muʿtamid by trying to declare his independent allegiance to the Almoravids. In response, al-Muʿtamid engineered his arrest and humiliation in the eyes of the Almoravid amīr.

4. Álvar Háñez was a deputy of Alfonso VI to several of the Taifa courts. His name appears in other contemporary sources, including the *Song of the Cid*.

payment. He undertook to abide by these terms but, on receiving the money, he observed: "You're quite safe as far as I'm concerned. But it is more imperative that you placate Alfonso who is preparing to attack you and others. Those who comply with his wishes will be safe, but he will set me on those who do not. I am simply his slave (*'abd*) and am obliged to carry out his wishes and obey his commands. What you have paid me won't be much use if you disobey him. Your payment will only benefit you as far as I'm concerned but it won't get you far with my master (*ra'īs*) if he takes a contrary view." I realized that what he had said was right and reasonable and said to myself: "I can't take the initiative and send an envoy to him [Alfonso]—that would only whet his appetite to devour me. But if and when he sends someone to get to know what has happened, I should apologize to him and he might then accept my request without my having opened any door to him by paying him something that would only whet his appetite. I'll spin out our negotiations as much as I can in the hope that between now and then an army will arrive which can be used to crush him. What he says then won't matter any more. If no help arrives, however, I won't have done him [Alfonso] any wrong for which I shall suffer."

I argued the matter with Álvar Háñez and said I could not afford to pay him [Alfonso] anything. I gave the Almoravids as an excuse and pleaded other expenses which I had had to spend on them. The swine made no comment and, bound as he was to serve his master (*ṣāḥib*) loyally, he sent a messenger to him with a request that he send an envoy to me to demand his tribute (*jizya*).[5] If the envoy returned empty-handed, Álvar Háñez would retaliate by attacking my territories.

Alfonso now prepared for the expedition and sent his envoy ahead of him. When I had confirmed this fact, I was thrown into a state of great anxiety and did not know what to do for the best—whether I should abandon the city for him to ravage or to conciliate him by paying him as much as I could afford. Great panic descended on the people and so terrified was I that I just could not believe that he would accept my money and not remain in occupation of my territory out of sheer spite for the Aledo affair and my agreement with the Almoravids.

I sincerely hoped that his envoy would be satisfied with a small payment, but he said to me: "I've not come for anything of that sort. I am here to demand the payment of tribute (*jizya*) three years in arrears. That amounts to 30,000 [*mithqāls*] net. Unless you pay up, he'll soon be on his way. Then you

---

5. Traditionally, the Arabic term *jizya* referred to tribute paid by Christians and Jews living under Muslim rule.

can do the best you can." I turned the matter over in my mind and came to the conclusion that intransigence would be futile stupidity. "If," I reckoned, "I exact this money from my subjects, there'll be an outcry and a shower of complaints from them and the next thing will be that they'll have a deputation in Marrakesh[6] complaining that I've taken their substance and given it to the Christians. It's at a time like this that a man needs the money he has saved in order to protect his own country and honor. It is only right and proper to disburse the tribute from my privy purse (*bayt mālī*). In this way the country can be saved and at the same time I shall win the gratitude of my subjects by keeping away their enemy without throwing any burden on them and incurring any personal ignominy." So that's what I did. I sent him the 30,000 without causing anyone to lose a single dirham.

Nevertheless, I deemed it necessary to conclude a new agreement with him [Alfonso] whereby he would contract not to molest any town of mine nor play me false. I acted as I did for fear that he might round on me. He agreed to the proposal. "As the money has to be paid," I said to myself, "it is better to have a contractual arrangement. Should I then have need of it I will have it to hand and it can't do any harm. If, on the other hand, there came a time when it's no longer needed, sharp brown lances and fine glittering swords can take its place if only God would be good enough to send me an army to repulse him. All stratagems are fair in war and if you cannot win, at least be crafty." . . .

I then wrote to the Amīr of the Muslims to tell him exactly what had happened and what I had been compelled to do. I said that a man on the spot had a clearer grasp of the situation than a man who was elsewhere. I added that had it been possible to secure the safety of Muslims by delaying even for just so long as it would have taken to obtain his written instructions, I would not have taken any action at all without seeking his advice, as I ought. The pressure was too great for me, however, to think of exposing Muslims to danger and I was confident that, with God's help, they [the Christians] would suffer retaliation at the hands of the Amīr. I had no doubt that I would receive a letter of thanks for my prudent decision, especially as the ransom had come from my own private resources and I had not exacted a single dirham from any Muslim. But I was all the more alarmed when I got his reply reflecting the animosity with which he was filled because of the false picture he had of me [from my enemies]. In his reply, the Amīr said: "I well know your conniving ways and mendacious utterances. I shall soon know just how highly your subjects regard you and your transactions in view of your allegation that

6. Marrakesh was the Almoravid capital in Morocco.

you have served their interests. Do not pin your hopes on the long term. The near future is what matters to you." . . .

I wrote several times to the Amīr of the Muslims explaining to him all that had happened and complaining about the misfortune that had befallen me at the hands of these reprobates but, throughout, the Amīr came back at me relentlessly and believed all they had to say about me. Throughout that whole period, I was in most dreadful plight, not knowing the best thing to do or how to extricate myself.

Moreover, al-Muʿtamid grew suspicious of me because the Christian had entered his territory and left mine alone. He believed this resulted from collusion between us. But, had there in fact been any collusive arrangement, I would have had to pay for it a sum over and above the tribute. In fact they had only mercenaries (*banū 'l-kirā'*) who took orders from no one. The country had already been devastated by the time the Almoravid army arrived at Seville.

Almighty God knows that I gave no help whatever in that affair nor will He hold me responsible for a single word uttered in malice against any Muslim. All the reports reaching the Amīr of the Muslims were unanimous in calling for severe action to be taken against me. Had I, in fact, wanted to cooperate with the Christians and sought to align myself with them, as claimed, the city of Granada would have been full of them before the Almoravids even arrived at Ceuta. I could have done that since I had adequate, even ample, time. However, works are to be judged by their intentions, and those reports were one way of fulfilling the destiny decreed for me. If only people would try to understand my case clearly, it would be found to be unimpeachable and it would become clear that I had never spoken ill of any Muslim nor had I given evidence or entered into a secret agreement or intrigued against any Muslim. How could any of all this be true of me when, in fact, the first sword to be drawn against the Christians was mine at the famous encounter of Nivar (*al-Nībal*)[7] which was under my jurisdiction, when the Christians sought to break through to it by a sudden attack? This [as I have said] coincided with the first irruption of the Almoravids and their arrival at Ceuta. At that time, Alfonso's envoy had arrived to apologize for what had happened but I dismissed him without giving him a hearing so as to have no contact with him, choosing instead to deal with the Amīr of the Muslims. All litigants must face God together [on the Day of Judgment].

7. Nivar, a village near Granada, was unexpectedly attacked by the Castilians in early 1085 and successfully defended by the Zirids.

25. EXILE OF THE CID AND HIS CAPTURE OF VALENCIA (1089–1094)

Song of the Cid

Translated from Castilian by Rita Hamilton

The Cantar de mío Cid *[Song of the Cid] is one of the best-known works of medieval Spanish literature, and its protagonist, Rodrigo Díaz de Vivar, has become a national hero. His honorific title, the Cid, is derived from the Arabic word* sayyid, *meaning lord. Rodrigo Díaz was born around 1043 and made a ward to Prince Sancho, the eldest son of Fernando I of Castile-León, in 1058. Five years later, King Fernando partitioned his kingdom, giving Castile to Sancho and León to his second son, Alfonso (later Alfonso VI). This distribution led to hostility between the two brothers after their father's death in 1065. Rodrigo, a Castilian, remained loyal to Sancho until the latter's death in 1072, at which point the Cid became a vassal to Alfonso. Alfonso was pleased to have the Cid's military prowess at his command, yet he could never bring himself to trust his new vassal completely. The situation was not improved by Rodrigo's tendency to act on his own initiative, though on the king's behalf. In 1081 the Cid launched an attack against the Muslims without Alfonso's permission. As a result, he was banished from Castile and León. The* Cantar *begins with the Cid's banishment in 1089 (included in this selection), then recounts the tale of his further independent campaigns, including the capture of Valencia in 1094 (this city would serve as his stronghold until his death in 1099), and his eventual reconciliation with Alfonso. The story exists in many forms, with the earliest versions dating from shortly after the Cid's death. This version was probably composed in the late twelfth or early thirteenth century. (ORC)*

Tears streamed from his eyes as he turned his head and stood looking at them. He saw doors left open and gates unlocked, empty pegs without fur tunics or cloaks, perches without falcons or molted hawks. The Cid sighed, for he was weighed down with heavy cares. Then he said, with dignity and restraint: "I give Thee thanks, O God, our Father in Heaven. My wicked enemies have contrived this plot against me."

They made ready for the journey and slackened their reins. As they left Vivar a crow flew on the right, and as they entered Burgos they saw it on the left. The Cid shrugged his shoulders and nodded his head: "Good cheer, Álvar Fáñez,[1] for we are banished from this land."

English text from *The Poem of the Cid*, translated by Rita Hamilton (Manchester: Manchester University Press, 1975), pp. 24–29, 35–37, 85–87. Reprinted with permission of the publisher.

1. The nephew and chief companion of Rodrigo Díaz. He was an important figure at King Alfonso's court and was the same as the Álvar Háñez who earlier went to Granada to collect tribute from ʿAbd Allāh ibn Buluggīn (see Chapter 24).

Ruy Díaz[2] entered Burgos with his company of sixty knights. Men and women came out to see him pass, while the burghers and their wives stood at their windows, sorrowfully weeping. With one accord they all said, "What a good vassal. If only he had a good lord!"

They would have offered him hospitality, but no one dared to do so for fear of the King's anger. The King's dispatch had arrived the night before, laying down severe conditions and heavily sealed: no one was to give lodging to the Cid, and anyone who received him into his house should know for a certainty that he would forfeit his wealth and would lose his eyes and furthermore his body and soul as well. All these Christian people were overcome with grief; they hid from the Cid and dared not speak to him. The Campeador[3] made his way to the house where he hoped to lodge, but when he arrived there he found the door locked fast. They had all agreed on this: for fear of King Alfonso, if the Cid did not break in the door, nobody would open it to him. His followers called loudly, but those within returned no answer. The Cid spurred his horse, rode up to the door and, drawing his foot from the stirrup, gave it a kick, but the door did not open, for it was securely locked. A little nine-year-old girl appeared (and said): "Campeador, you were knighted in a fortunate hour. The King has forbidden us (to receive you); his letter came last night, with harsh conditions and heavy seals. We could not possibly dare to open the door or ask you to come in. If we did, we should lose our money and our houses and even the sight of our eyes. Cid, you have nothing to gain by our misfortune. May the Creator protect you with all His holy powers." When the little girl had finished speaking she turned and went back into her house. Then the Cid saw that he had lost the King's favor. He turned away from the door and rode through Burgos. When he came to the Church of Santa María he alighted from his horse, knelt down and prayed from his heart. When his prayer was ended the Cid remounted, rode out by the city gate and crossed the river Arlanzon. Beside the town (of Burgos) he had his tent pitched on the sandy shore and then dismounted. The Cid Ruy Díaz, knighted in a fortunate hour, encamped on the river bank, since no one would give him lodging in his house; with his good band of followers around him he settled there as if he were out in the woods. He had been forbidden to buy any food at all in the town of Burgos, and they did not dare to sell him as much as a pennyworth.

Martín Antolínez, worthy citizen of Burgos, provided the Cid and his companions with bread and wine; he did not buy them, for he had them

2. Ruy is derived from Rodrigo.
3. An honorific title ("Battler") bestowed on the Cid.

already. He supplied them lavishly with provisions for the journey, and the Cid and all those who served him were very well satisfied. Martín Antolínez spoke, and you will hear what he said: "Campeador, born in a fortunate hour, let us rest here tonight and take our departure in the morning, for I shall be accused of having helped you and shall incur the King's anger. If I escape safe and sound with you, sooner or later the King will want me for a friend. Whether or not, I don't care a fig for all that I am leaving behind."

The Cid spoke: "Martín Antolínez, you are a brave and daring fighter. If I survive, I shall double your pay. I have spent the gold and all the silver. As you can very well see, I have no money with me and I shall need some to pay all my followers. I shall do this reluctantly, but otherwise I should have nothing. With your help I shall provide two chests: let us fill them with sand to make them very heavy; they shall be covered with figured leather and finely studded.

The leather will be red and the studs will be fine golden ones. You must go in secret to Rachel and Vidas.[1] (Say) that I am forbidden to trade in Burgos and that the King has banished me; I cannot carry my wealth about with me as it is too heavy, so I intend to pawn it for a reasonable sum. Let them take it away by night so that no one may see it. May the Creator and all His saints see it (and know) there is nothing else I can do, and I do it reluctantly."

Martín Antolínez set off at once, enquiring in haste for Rachel and Vidas; he rode through Burgos and entered the fortifications of the town, making hasty enquiries for Rachel and Vidas.

Rachel and Vidas were sitting together, counting the money they had made. Martín Antolínez, like the shrewd fellow he was, came up and greeted them: "Is that you, my good friends, Rachel and Vidas? I should like a word with you two in private." All three of them went aside at once. "Both of you give me your hands and promise to keep this secret from everyone, Moors and Christians alike, and I shall make your fortune so that you will be rich for life." When the Campeador went to collect the tribute, he received vast sums of money and kept the best part of it. For this reason accusations were brought against him. He has in his possession two chests full of pure gold. The King, as you know, has banished him and he has left his properties, holdings and manors. He cannot carry the chests away with him, for then their existence would be revealed. The Campeador will entrust them to you and you must lend him a suitable amount of money. Take the chests and keep

---

4. The names of these two Jewish moneylenders are both masculine. Rachel may be a form of Raguel, and Vidas (meaning "life" in Spanish) may be a translation of the Hebrew name *Hayyim* (also meaning "life").

them in a safe place, and both of you swear a solemn oath not to look into them for a whole year from now." Rachel and Vidas took counsel together, saying: "We are obliged to make a profit on all our transactions. We know very well that the Cid made his fortune when he went to the land of the Moors and brought back great wealth. A man who carries a large amount of coin about with him cannot sleep without anxiety. Let us take these chests and hide them in a secret place. But tell us, how much will satisfy the Cid and what interest will he give us for the whole of this year?" The shrewd Martín Antolínez replied: "The Cid will ask what is right and just; he will require little of you for the sake of leaving his property in good hands. Needy men are flocking to him from all sides and he will want six hundred marks." Rachel and Vidas answered: "We are quite willing to give them to him." "You see that night is coming on and the Cid is in a hurry. We are in pressing need of these marks." Rachel and Vidas replied: "That is not the way to do business, for taking comes first and then comes giving." Martín Antolínez said: "I am content. Come, both of you, to the illustrious Campeador and we shall help you, as is only right, to bring the chests here and place them, unknown to all, in your safe-keeping." Rachel and Vidas answered: "We are satisfied. Once the chests are here you may have the six hundred marks." Martín Antolínez eagerly rode off at once with Rachel and Vidas. He did not cross over the bridge but forded the river so that no one in Burgos should get wind of what was happening. There they were, then, at the tent of the famous Campeador, and on entering they kissed his hands. The Cid smiled and addressed them: "Well, my friends, Rachel and Vidas, you have forgotten me! Now I am going into banishment, for I have lost the King's favor. It seems to me that you are going to share in my wealth, and as long as you live you will never be the losers." Rachel and Vidas now kissed the Cid's hands (in token of gratitude). Martín Antolínez arranged the conditions of the bargain—that, on the security of those chests, they should give the Cid six hundred marks and that they should keep the chests in safety for a year. They had given their promise and sworn to keep it, so that they would be guilty of perjury if they looked into them before then, and in that case the Cid would refuse to give them a single penny of the interest. Then Martín Antolínez said: "Let the chests be loaded promptly. Take them away, Rachel and Vidas, and put them in your safe-keeping. I shall accompany you to bring back the marks, for the Cid has to set out before cock-crow." How delighted they all were when the chests were loaded up! They could hardly hoist them into place, though they were hefty men. Rachel and Vidas were greatly pleased with the treasure, for they saw themselves rich for the rest of their lives. . . .

The gallant Cid thus took a devout farewell. The riders slackened their reins and rode away. Martín Antolínez said: "I shall go to see my beloved wife, and I must tell those of my household how to behave. I care not a jot if the King wishes to confiscate my property, and I shall rejoin you before the day dawns." Martín Antolínez returned to Burgos, and the Cid spurred on towards San Pedro de Cardeña as speedily as possible.

The cocks crowed betimes and the dawn was about to break when the good Campeador reached San Pedro with the knights who had sworn to serve him faithfully. The Abbot, Don Sancho, a worthy Christian, was saying matins as the day dawned. Doña Jimena[5] was there with five noble ladies, praying to St. Peter and to God the Creator: "Thou who dost rule us all, help (my husband), the Cid Campeador."

They knocked at the gate, and those within learnt that the party had arrived. Heavens, how delighted the Abbot was! The monks poured out into the courtyard with torches and candles, and joyfully received the fortunate Cid. "Thanks be to God," said the Abbot Don Sancho, "that I see you here. You are welcome to stay in the monastery." "Thanks, my lord Abbot" (said the Cid). "I am greatly obliged to you. Here I shall be able to prepare food for the journey for myself and my vassals. As I am leaving the country I shall give you fifty marks, but if I survive I shall double the amount. I do not wish the monastery to be at any loss on my account. Here are one hundred marks that I give you for Doña Jimena, so that you may look after her and her ladies for this year. I am leaving behind my two little daughters; take them under your care. I entrust them to you, my lord Abbot; take care of them and of my wife. If this supply of money should prove insufficient and you should run short, I bid you let them have what they need. For every mark you spend I shall give four to the monastery." The Abbot willingly granted this request. Now here comes Doña Jimena, with her daughters carried along in the arms of two ladies. Doña Jimena knelt down in front of the Campeador, weeping and kissing his hands. "I beg a favor of you, my fortunate Campeador," she said. "You have been driven out of Castile by the wiles of mischief-makers.

I ask a favor, Cid of the flowing beard. Here I am with your daughters, who are still of tender age, and these ladies who attend on me. I see that you are on the eve of departure and we shall be separated. Give us some words of advice, for the love of Holy Mary." The Cid stretched out his hands, took his daughters in his arms and pressed them to his heart, for he loved them dearly. He wept and sighed heavily (saying): "Doña Jimena, my excellent wife, I have always loved you with all my heart, but you see that we must part

5. Jimena Díaz, Rodrigo's wife, may have been related to Alfonso VI.

now, for I am going away while you remain behind. May it please God and Holy Mary that I may be able to give my daughters in marriage with my own hands. With good luck and time on my side I shall provide for you well, my noble wife." . . .

The Cid spent three years taking those towns and conquering Moorish territory, sleeping by day and marching by night.

He had taught the Valencians a severe lesson, and they dared not come out of the town to join him in battle. He cut down their plantations, inflicting great damage on them. Year after year the Cid deprived them of their food. The Valencians lamented loudly, for they were at their wits' end, being cut off from food on all sides. Fathers could not help their sons nor sons their fathers, nor could friends comfort one another. It is indeed a cruel fate for men to be without food and to watch their wives and children dying of hunger. Disaster stared them in the face and there was nothing they could do to help themselves. They sent for aid to the King of Morocco,[6] but he was involved in war with the ruler of the Atlas mountains and could neither relieve them nor come to their assistance. Pleased with this news, the Cid set out one night from Murviedro; he marched all night and dawn found him in the region of Monreal. He sent messengers through Navarre and Aragón and to the land of Castile to proclaim that anyone who was eager to exchange poverty for riches should come to the Cid, who had a mind to ride out to besiege Valencia and restore it to the Christians.

"Whoever wishes to go with me to besiege Valencia, let him come freely and of his own accord, for there is no compulsion. I shall wait three days for him at Cella."

Those were the words of the Cid, the loyal Campeador, who then returned to Murviedro, which he had taken earlier. The proclamation was carried everywhere, and all who scented plunder came in haste. Crowds of good Christians flocked to join him, and the Cid's riches were steadily mounting. When Don Rodrigo saw these crowds assembled he was filled with joy. Without delay he marched against Valencia and began the siege. He encircled the city completely, allowing no one to go in or come out. The Cid's fame had spread through the lands. Great numbers came and few left. He set a certain time limit for them to surrender if no relief came. For nine whole months he besieged them, and when the tenth month came they were forced to surrender. There was great rejoicing in the whole region when the Cid took Valencia and entered the city. Those who had fought on foot were given horses, and as there were untold quantities of

---

6. Presumably Yūsuf ibn Tāshufin, the Almoravid ruler.

gold and silver, all who took part became rich. The Cid commanded his fifth share of the booty to be set apart, and in this there fell to him thirty thousand marks, while the value of the rest in kind was beyond reckoning. The Campeador and his men rejoiced to see his standard flying from the highest point of the citadel.

The Christian North
(Eleventh and Twelfth Centuries)

Map 2. The Iberian Peninsula, 1095.

26. CONCERNING KING SANCHO I OF ARAGÓN AND HIS DEEDS

Chronicle of San Juan de la Peña (ca. 1370)

Translated from Latin by Lynn H. Nelson

The Chronicle of San Juan de la Peña, *compiled about 1370, was a special project of Pedro IV of Aragón (r.1336–1387). Although the work is now less celebrated than the better-known medieval histories of the Crown of Aragón (those of Muntaner and Desclot, together with the autobiographies of Jaume I and Pedro IV), it was the first complete and official history of the kingdom. Pedro IV appears to have commissioned this history both to provide a historical basis for royal authority in the Crown of Aragón and to match the work of Alfonso X (r. 1252–1284), who had instigated the writing of a general history of Castile (*Primera crónica general*).*

Rather than a straight narrative written in one hand, the Chronicle *is a compilation of various materials, tales, and histories. Only part of the text was put together at San Juan de la Peña, and these sections are marked by references to events at the monastery. In this passage, reference is made to the adoption of the Roman liturgy at the monastery in 1071, replacing the Visigothic rite, during the reign of Sancho I of Aragón (r. 1063–1094). This selection also details the complex military and political scenario that played out between the Christian kingdoms of Aragón, Castile, and Navarre and the Muslim states of Zaragoza and Huesca. (ORC)*

After King Ramiro's death, his son Sancho succeeded him at the age of eighteen years. Sancho was later called Sancho Ramírez.

Before we narrate his deeds, we will discuss the king of Navarre. It is known that when King García of Navarre died, he was survived by his two sons, one of whom was called Sancho and the other Ramón. Seduced by unspeakable ambition and fearless of divine retribution, in order that he might rule the kingdom that rightfully belonged to Sancho as their father's eldest-born son, Ramon killed his brother in the Year of Our Lord 1076. Sancho's son, Ramiro, fearing Ramon's malevolence, and suspecting that he might kill him as he already killed his father, fled Navarre and took refuge in Valencia, where the Cid Rodrigo Díaz ruled. The people of the kingdom of Navarre, knowing that no legal heirs could descend from a treasonous lord, and wishing to avoid being subject to such a notorious man, deposed Ramón from the royal dignity which he had improperly and unjustly seized. They elected Sancho Ramírez as king and lord of Navarre. He was then king of Navarre

English text from *The Chronicle of San Juan de la Peña*, translated by Lynn H. Nelson (Philadelphia: University of Pennsylvania Press, 1991), Chapter 17, pp. 18–21. Reprinted with permission of the publisher.

and of Nájera up to Montes de Oca, as well as of Aragón and Sobrarbe. Wishing to erase the name of the traitor in the land, he exiled Ramón and expelled him from his realms and kingdoms.

Sancho Ramírez, eighteen years old when he began to rule, was very brave and able, and open with his knights and subjects. He was neither willing nor able to endure the shame placed upon him by King Sancho of Castile, who had killed his father at Graus for the simple reason that Ramiro had been allied with his cousin, King Sancho of Navarre. Not content with this, Sancho of Castile had seized and occupied a great part of the realms and lands of the king of Navarre. For this reason, Sancho promptly marched against the king of Castile with Aragonese and Navarrese troops. While Sancho was besieging the city of Viana, the king of Castile came with a multitude of armed men, and a great battle took place between them. By the grace of Jesus, Who never abandons those who pursue the truth, the king of Castile was defeated and forced to flee in disgrace upon one of his horses, accompanied by only a few of his men. It is said by some that the horse that he rode in flight was without saddle or bridle, and wore only a halter.[1] Victorious and pouring forth praises of God for such a great victory granted him, Sancho crossed the Ebro, plundering and devastating the lands of his opponents and recovering that which his enemy had occupied of the kingdom of Navarre. He held the Castilians so well at bay that they were unable to find any remedy for his power. The king of Castile then begged ʿAbd al-Raḥmān, king of Huesca,[2] to break the treaties between him and the king of Aragón and to make war against Sancho Ramírez. ʿAbd al-Raḥmān did this, and immediately invaded Aragón.

The king of Huesca did not remain unpunished for violating his treaties, as we shall discuss below when recounting the deeds of King Pedro, son of Sancho. It was understandable that Sancho should at that time conclude a treaty and peace with the king of Castile that he had previously been unwilling to grant. When he learned that the king of Huesca had broken his treaty, he considered it preferable, like a good and Catholic king, to wage war against the Moors rather than against Christians. Also, he made peace only after having obtained victory and honor from the king of Castile. When he had recovered all that the king of Castile had taken from the kingdom

---

1. There is little information on the so-called War of the Three Sanchos. The conflict apparently took place in the summer of 1064, and the Castilians may have made some territorial gains in the course of the hostilities. A curious aspect of the account provided by the *Chronicle* is the description of the disgraceful flight of the king of Castile on a horse equipped only with a halter. This was precisely the same act ascribed by Navarrese chroniclers to Ramiro of Aragón in his defeat by the Navarrese at Tafalla (late 1035 or early 1036).

2. At this time, Huesca was in fact subordinate to the Muslim kingdom of Zaragoza, the ruler of which was Aḥmad ibn Sulaiman al-Muqtadir.

of Navarre and, by the grace of God, had returned that which he had taken from Castile, Sancho Ramírez entered into a treaty of peace with the king of Castile.

He took as wife Lady Felicia,[3] from whom he fathered three sons, Pedro, Alfonso, and Ramiro. Ramiro was a monk of Saint Pons de Thomières. It is known that King Sancho ruled in Aragón for six years before he became king of Navarre.[4]

The Roman liturgy then entered San Juan de la Peña on the eleventh of the calends of April, the second week of Lent, the third feria.[5] The first and third hours were Toledan and the sixth Roman, in the Year of Our Lord 1071. From that time on the Roman rite was observed.

King Sancho Ramírez was a good and virtuous king, which is clearly shown by the following conquests, among other things.[6] In the Year of Our Lord 1080, he took the castle of Corvino and Pratiella, and then the Saracens burned Pina. In the Year of Our Lord 1081, he seized Bolea. In the Year of Our Lord 1083, he took Graus. In the same year, many Christians died in Rueda, he populated Ayerbe, and there was a battle with the Moors at Piedra Pisada on Christmas day.

In the year 1084, the bodies of Saint Indalecio and his disciple Saint James, who succeeded him as bishop of Urtie, which is now called Almería, were transferred with honor to the monastery of San Juan de la Peña by King Sancho Ramírez, his son Pedro, and Abbot Sancho of the monastery, on Maundy Thursday, the nones of April, the fifth feria.[7] On the sixth and after Easter, the king captured Argüedas. On the tenth of the calends of June [23 May], he took Castella and, on the following Saturday [25 May], he fought a battle at Morella.

Recalling that the Cid Rodrigo Díaz had participated with the king of Castile in the death of Sancho's father at Graus, Sancho fought a battle with

3. Felicia was the daughter of influential and well-connected French noble Hilduin of Roucy. Their French relatives would later provide good service to Sancho's sons, Pedro, Alfonso, and Ramiro.

4. Actually from 1063 to 1076.

5. Wednesday, 22 March 1071. The Roman liturgy replaced the Visigothic, or Toledan, rite. The standardization of church liturgy was an important aspect of the Gregorian reform, and Sancho's imposition of it in San Juan de la Peña marked his increasingly close relationship with the papacy. The Visigothic rite was restored on a limited basis in the cathedral of Toledo by Cardinal Francisco Jiménez de Cisneros and is still practiced there.

6. The form and wording of the following passages strongly suggest that the compilers were using a set of annals maintained at San Juan de la Peña. Unfortunately, this source has not survived.

7. Thursday, 5 April 1084. The translation of saints' relics was a particularly solemn event, especially since the acquisition of additional relics increased the prestige and stature of the monastery considerably.

him at that place, and defeated the Cid in the month of May in the Year of Our Lord 1088.[8]

The king built the monastery of Montearagón, and the canonries of Jaca and Fanlo. In the Year of Our Lord 1089, on the day of St. John the Baptist,[9] the king and his son Pedro captured Monzón. In the Year of Our Lord 1090, the city of Huesca paid tribute to the king, and he was present at Toledo supporting King Alfonso of Castile against the Moors.[10] In the same year, he populated Estella and donated many possessions, including churches and other properties in Navarre, to the monastery of San Juan de la Peña.

In the year of the Lord 1091, he built Castellar above Zaragoza. In the Year of Our Lord 1092, he recovered Santa Eulalia. In the Year of Our Lord 1093, he captured Almenar. He populated Luna in the Year of Our Lord 1094.

King Sancho constrained the city of Huesca so tightly that the king of the Moors promised to pay him tribute.[11] But the Moors secretly sent for King Alfonso of Castile, who had conquered Toledo, to come to their aid against the king of Aragón. They promised to give him double tribute and to be subject to him. King Alfonso, forgetting the assistance given him by the king of Aragón, who had taken part with him in the conquest of Toledo, agreed to the Moors' request. He sent Count Sancho with all of his forces to their aid, and the Castilian army moved up to Vitoria.

As soon as the king of Aragón learned of this, he marched against the count with his men and his sons Pedro and Alfonso. The count did not expect him and was forced back into Castile. Sancho moved directly from this action to besiege the city of Huesca with Aragonese and Navarrese troops, in the year 1094.

One day, when he had ridden around the city on horseback looking for a place through which he might gain entry, he saw a part of the exterior of the wall which was much weaker than the rest. He pointed at it with the index finger of his right hand, saying, "It will be possible to gain entrance into the city through that spot." The sleeve of his mail shirt fell open, and the arm

---

8. The Battle of Morella was actually an Aragonese defeat in which a number of important persons fell captive to the Cid.

9. This may be one of two possible feast days, either the birth of Saint John, 24 June, or his martyrdom, 24 September. The first of these was a favorite day of celebration in medieval Spain.

10. Alfonso VI (r. 1065–1109).

11. Sancho Ramírez constructed the castle-monastery of Montearagón a short distance northeast of the city. From this well-protected vantage point, Christian cavalry were able to interdict travel along the main route between Huesca and Lérida and to interrupt at will agricultural work throughout the fertile plain that surrounded the city. Huesca's prosperity was slowly destroyed by these tactics.

which he had raised was laid bare. Seeing this, a Saracen archer who was on that part of the wall struck him in the right side with an arrow that found its mark through the sleeve of his shirt.

Although he realized that he had been hit, the king let no one know, but immediately returned to his tent and ordered his men to take an oath to Pedro as their king. Everyone was quite astonished at this. When this had been done, he had his son Pedro promise that he would not desist from the siege of the city until he had it in his hands, telling him many things that the future held for him.[12] After encouraging his army, he ordered that the arrow be withdrawn from his side, which it had pierced, and gave up his spirit to the Creator.

His son began to rule in such a praiseworthy manner and was so great a comfort to the army that they did not suffer from his dead father's absence.

The body of the king who had ruled for thirty years was carried to Montearagón, where it was kept for six months and fifteen days. This was done because, if a funeral were held, the men of the army would gather for it and it might be noted by the Saracens, who would draw great comfort from what had happened. When this time had elapsed, Sancho's body was solemnly carried to the monastery of San Juan de la Peña where, with the celebration of funeral rites, it was placed in a tomb in front of the altar of Saint John.

12. A curious phrase, suggesting that the dying king had prophetic powers.

27. TWO CHRISTIAN URBAN CHARTERS

Among the best surviving records for the study of urbanism in the Middle Ages are the charters that kings, counts, bishops, and other lords granted to their townspeople. In Spain these charters were often called fueros, *a term derived from the Latin* forum, *meaning marketplace. The* fuero *in this sense was a customary privilege for a community; and, as seen below, each item of a charter was a* fuero. *Charters for villages, like those for towns, make sense in the comprehensive perspective of emancipation from lordship. In the examples below—for Jaca (Aragón, about 1077) and Siurana (Catalonia, 1153)—the reader should consider whether the people of Jaca formed an urban community or a village and how the problems addressed at Jaca differed from those at Siurana. (TNB)*

A. Charter of Jaca (ca. 1077)
Translated from Latin by Thomas N. Bisson.

[Emblem of Christ] In the name of our Lord Jesus Christ and of the undivided Trinity, Father and Son and Holy Spirit, amen. This is a charter of authority and confirmation which I Sancho, by the grace of God king of the Aragonese and Pamplonese, make to you.

Notice to all men who are even in the east and west and north and south that I wish to establish a city [*civitatem*] in my village [*villa*]¹ which is called "Jaca."

1. First, I remit to you all bad *fueros* which you had until this day that I established Jaca to be a city; and so, because I wish it to be well settled, I concede and confirm to you and to all who settle in my city Jaca all the good *fueros* which you have asked of me in order that my city be well settled.
2. And each one may enclose his part as he can.
3. And if it happen that anyone of you comes to dispute and will strike anyone before me or in my palace when I am standing there, let him fine for 1000 s. [solidi] or lose the fight.
4. And if anyone, whether knight or burgher or peasant, should strike another, and not in my presence nor in my palace although I be in Jaca, let him not pay the fine [*calonia*] except according to the *fuero* you have when I am not in the town.

Translated from *Jaca: Documentos municipales, 971–1269*, edited by Antonio Ubieto Arteta (Valencia: Ediciones Anubar, 1975), no. 8.
  1. The word *villa* does not always mean "village" in medieval Latin, but it does often refer to unwalled settlements in Mediterranean Europe.

5. And if it happen that someone be found killed in a robbery in Jaca or its district, you are not obligated to pay homicide.[2]

6. I give and concede to you and your successors with good will that you not go in the army [*hoste*] unless with bread for three days. And this should be in the name of battle in the field [*de lite campale*] or where I or my successors are surrounded by our enemies. And if the lord of the house does not wish to go there, let him substitute one armed footman.

7. And wherever you can buy anything in Jaca or outside of Jaca, or acquire any man's inheritance, you may have it free and unencumbered without any bad cut [*malo cisso*].[3]

8. And after you hold it undisturbed for a year and a day, anyone wishing to disturb them or take it away from you shall give me 60 s., and shall confirm your inheritance.

9. And as far as you can go and return in a day, everywhere, you may have pastures and woods, observing the boundaries of the men living there.

10. And that you should not have duel-war between you, unless agreeable to both; nor with men from elsewhere, unless with consent of the men of Jaca.

11. And that none of you should sit captive giving pledges of your foot [*de vestro pede*].[4]

12. And if any of you commits fornication with any willing woman, except a married one, you shall not pay calumny.[5] And if it happen that he forces her, let him give her a husband or receive her as his wife. And if the raped woman appeals on the first or second day, let her prove by truthful witnesses of Jaca. If she wishes to appeal after three days, it shall avail her nothing.

13. And if any of you goes against his neighbor in anger and armed with lance, sword, club, or knife, let him fine for it 1000 s. or lose the fight.

14. And if anyone kills another let him pay 500 s.

15. And if one strikes another in conflict or grabs him by the hair, let him pay 25 s. for it.

16. And if he falls to the ground, let him pay 250 s.

17. And if anyone enters his neighbor's house in anger, or makes seizures there, let him pay 25 s. to the lord of the house.

18. And that my agent [*merinus*] not receive calumny from any man of Jaca save with the approval of six better men [*vicinis*] of Jaca.

19. And none of all the men of Jaca should go to judgment anywhere but in Jaca.

---

2. That is, the murder fine sometimes imposed by lords on communities.
3. The "cut," like tallage elsewhere, was an arbitrary tax.
4. Meaning unclear.
5. Calumny was a payment exacted for slander.

20. And if anyone has false measure or weight, let him pay 60 s.

21. And that all men should go to mill in mills where they wish, except Jews and those who make bread for sale.

22. And you should not give or sell your honors to the church or to *infanzones*.[6]

23. And if any man is imprisoned for debt, let him who wishes to capture him do so with my agent; and let him put [him] in my palace, and let my jailer guard him; and after three days, he who took him should give him farthing's worth [*obolatam*]; and if he refuse to do [this], my jailer may release him.

24. And if any man seize as pledge the Saracen man or Saracen woman of his neighbor, let him put him in my palace; and the lord of the male and female Saracen shall give him bread and water, because he is a human being [*homo*] and should not starve like a beast.

And whoever wishes to disrupt this charter which I make to the settlers of Jaca, let him be excommunicated and anathematized for his cruelty and wholly separated from all God's faithful, whether he be of my stock or of another. Amen, amen, amen. Let it be done, let it be done, let it be done. The charter made in the year from the Incarnation of our Lord Jesus Christ [. . .], era [II . . .].[7]

I Sancho, by God's grace king of the Aragonese and Pamplonese, have ordered these aforesaid things and I have made this sign [*sign of cross*] of Sancho with my hand.

I Pedro, son of King Sancho of the Aragonese, son of King Ramiro, wished these aforesaid things to be written and I have made this sign [*sign of Pedro I, in Arabic*] with my hand.[8]

B. Charter of Siurana (1153)
Translated from Latin by Thomas N. Bisson

Let it be known to all men that I Ramon Berenguer, count of Barcelona and prince of the kingdom of Aragón and marquis of Lérida and Tortosa, give, assent, and grant to all the settlers and inhabitants of Siurana who are there now or may come in future to live or settle that each one of them should have

---

6. The *infanzones* were the lesser aristocracy of knights in Aragón.

7. The dating clauses are incomplete in the twelfth-century copy on which modern editions are based.

8. The charter has the form of a confirmation by King Pedro I (r. 1094–1104)

Translated from *Cartas de población y franquicia de Cataluña*, edited by José María Font Rius, 3 vols. (Madrid: C.S.I.C., 1969–1983), 1:147–49, no. 94.

and possess wholly and freely, entirely and mightily, his houses and all lands which my knight Bertrand of Castellet, who is in Siurana for me, has given or will give to them as their own free and exempt property. Neither they nor any of their posterity in perpetuity shall pay any rent or custom, except only tithes and first-fruits, to me or anyone else. Moreover, I give to them all pastures and springs and hunting rights and all improvements in the forest and mountains and wood and all things which are used by people, and free exits and access for all of them and all their cattle and animals. And I give them such *fueros* and usages as the inhabitants of Lérida freely have. I retain there in my domain the ovens and mills and my rights of justice, as in Lérida. And in all places of my land where the men of Lérida do not give tolls or usages, the settlers and inhabitants of Siurana shall not give them. And they will always and everywhere in all my land be secure and safe, along with all their property and all their possessions, under my care and protection, just like my sworn men and my own men[1] whom I want at all times to love, to protect, and above all other men in my realm, to honor[2] vigorously. All the aforesaid things I give them with fullness and freedom and good liberty, so that they and all their posterity may be settlers and inhabitants of Siurana for all ages. And let them be my true faithful men in respect of my justice and of my rights, as good men ought to do to their good lord.

S + of Ramon, count.[3]

If anyone try to infringe or disrupt this freedom or establishment let it never succeed and let this charter of donation and franchise remain firm and undisturbed forever.

Which has been done on the third calends of May in the year of Our Lord's Incarnation 1153, in the era 93.[4]

Sig + *num* of William Ramon dapifer. *Sig* + *num* of Ramon of Pugalt. *Sig* + *num* of Arnal of Llers. *Sig* + *num* of Bertrand of Castellet, who by the count's mandate gives and confirms this [act]. *Sig* + *num* of Bernard of Bellog. *Sig* + *num* of William of Castellvell.

Sig + *num* of Ponç, scribe, who wrote this on the day and year aforesaid, with superscript letters in line 3.

---

1. The distinction is between important sworn allies or courtiers and rural tenants (*mei fideles et proprii mei homines*). Men of one or both classes may have done homage as well as fealty and so have been *homines* in the sense of "vassals." But this passage does not say that, and the term "vassal" remained exceptional in Catalonia.

2. The word *honorare* meant both "to honor" and "to enfeoff."

3. *S +* is a scribal abbreviation for *Signum* (meaning sign) plus the cross. The cross would have been made (and its quadrants marked) by the count himself. The subscriptions above are left in Latin form to show how they were normally written.

4. The era is mistaken, although the editor fails to note it. The correct era for the (Christian) year is (11)91.

28. JUSTICE IN CATALONIA

Usatges of Barcelona

Translated from Latin by Donald Kagay

Completed in the mid-twelfth century in the court of Count Ramon Berenguer IV of Barcelona (r. 1131–1162), the Usatges of Barcelona *quickly constituted the fundamental law of Catalonia and became a potent legal force across the Pyrenees into Occitania and among the neighboring realms of the Crown of Aragón. (DK)*

60. Since a land and its inhabitants are ruined for all time by an evil prince who is without both truth and justice, therefore we the oft-mentioned princes R[amon Berenguer][1] and A[lmodis],[2] with the counsel and aid of our nobles, decree and command that all princes who will succeed us in this princely office shall have a sincere and perfect faith and truthful speech for all men, noble and ignoble, kings and princes, magnates and knights, peasants and rustics, traders and merchants, pilgrims and wayfarers, friends and enemies, Christians and Saracens, Jews and heretics, might trust and believe in the princes without any fear or evil suspicion for their persons but also for their cities and castles, fiefs and property, wives and children, and for anything they possess. And all men, noble and ignoble, magnates, knights, and footmen, sailors, privateers, and minters, who are remaining in their land or coming from elsewhere, should help the aforesaid princes maintain, guard, and govern their faith and true speech in all cases great and small with a righteous faith and without deceit, evil intent, or bad counsel. And among other matters, let the peace and promise not to take violent action which the princes should give to Spain and the Saracens on land and sea be maintained by them.

64. Indeed if in any case the prince should be besieged, hold his enemies under siege, or hear that a certain king or prince is coming against him to wage war and he warns his land by both letters and messengers or by the

---

Translated from *Usatges de Barcelona: El codi a mitjan segle XII*, edited by Joan Bastardis i Parera (Barcelona: Fundació Noguera, 1984); English text from *The Usatges of Barcelona: The Fundamental Law of Catalonia*, translated by Donald Kagay (Philadelphia: University of Pennsylvania Press, 1994), pp. 78, 90–91. Reprinted with permission of the publisher. Some passages vary from the printed version.

1. Ramon Berenguer I, count of Barcelona (r. 1035–1076), who widened the base of his sovereignty by defeating his rebellious nobles and supporting the war on the Muslim Taifa states that bordered Catalonia.

2. Almodis de la Marche, southern French noblewoman who in 1052 repudiated her first husband, Count Pons of Toulouse, in favor of Ramon Berenguer I, to whom she bore two sons. She incurred the wrath of her stepson Pere Ramon, who murdered her on 16 October 1071.

Figure 7. Alfonso II of Aragón (1162–1196) presented with documents by his royal archivist Ramon de Caldes; frontispiece to the *Liber feudorum maior* (late twelfth century). Archivo de la Corona de Aragón, Barcelona. Photo credit: Scala/Art Resource, NY.

Figure 8. A noble marriage in the Crown of Aragón, from the *Liber feudorum maior* (late twelfth century). Archivo de la Corona de Aragón, Barcelona. Photo credit: Scala/Art Resource, NY.

usual customs of warning the land—namely, by bonfires—that it must come
to his aid, then let all men, knights and footmen alike, who are old and strong
enough to fight come to his aid as quickly as they can immediately after they
hear or see the signal. And if one is derelict in giving the prince that which
he might render him in this regard, he must lose everything which he holds
from him. And he who does not hold a fief from him must make compensation to him for this dereliction of duty and dishonor which he committed
against him with his own property and by swearing an oath with his own
hands since no man must fail the ruler in such a great matter and crisis.

70.[3] If anyone lures a baptized Jew or Saracen back to his religion or calls
him "turncoat" or "renegade" or if anyone within our city walls or burghs is
the first to draw a sword against another or calls him "cuckold," let him pay
a fine of twenty golden ounces of Valencia[4] to the prince because of his ban.
And if he hears or suffers any wrong there, let no compensation be made him
for this and afterward let him await the legal action of his adversary.

73. Indeed, let none of the magnates—namely, the viscounts, *comitores*,[5]
or *vasvassores*[6]—hereafter presume in any way either to punish criminals (that
is, to hang them for justice) or to build a new castle against the prince, or to
hold his fortification under siege or wage war with siege engines which are
vulgarly called *fundibula, goza,* and *gata*[7] since this is a great dishonor to the
rulers. But if a person does this, let him abandon or destroy the castle or give
it back to the prince without any lessening of its value if he had captured it,
immediately after being so demanded by the prince. And by the distraint of
the prince, let him make double compensation for all offenses he has committed there to the person against whom he committed them. And if he captures
knights and other vassals there, let him release and return them to the prince.
Indeed, let him afterwards make compensation to him for the dishonor which
he has done him in this matter with his property or fief by swearing an oath
with his own hands but he is not bound to make any further compensation
to him. Thus the exercise of this distraint is conceded to none but the rulers.

---

3. This article is similar to a portion of the municipal law code of Tortosa that deals with
the uttering of insults between townsmen. It also influenced a law of Jaume I of 1242 that forbade anyone from calling a Jew converted to Christianity *renegat*, "renegade," *tornadiz*, "turncoat," or *tresallit*, "apostate."

4. The *uncia auri cocti* (Catalan *onces d'aur cuyt*) was a Muslim coin of the late tenth
century minted in Córdoba but circulated in all the Christian realms of the peninsula.

5. *Comitor* (Catalan *comdor*) was a rank of nobility in service to the Catalan counts during the period of Spanish March.

6. A middle-grade noble who served as the "vassal of a vassal." In Catalonia *vasvassor* was
a term that generally referred to castellans.

7. The *fundibula* and *goza* were catapults of various sizes and designs. The *gata* was a
battering ram.

Since the rendering of justice in regard to criminals—namely, concerning murderers, adulterers, sorcerers, robbers, rapists, traitors, and other men—is granted only to the rulers, thus let them render justice as it seems fit to them: by cutting off hands and feet, putting out eyes, keeping men in prison for a long time and, ultimately in hanging their bodies if necessary.

In regard to women, let the rulers render justice: by cutting off their noses, lips, ears, and breasts, and by burning them at the stake if necessary. And since a land cannot live without justice, therefore it is granted to the rulers to render justice. And just as it is granted to them to render justice, thus it is permissible for them to release and pardon whomever they please.

85. If anyone violently rapes a virgin, either let him marry her if she and her parents are willing and let them give her dowry[8] to him, or let him give her a husband equal to his rank. If one violently ravishes a woman who is not a virgin and makes her pregnant, let him do the same.

89. Husbands can accuse their wives of adultery, or even of the suspicion of it, and then they [the wives] must clear themselves by their affirmation on oath and by judicial battle[9] if there are clear indications and evident signs in these. Moreover, wives of knights should do so by oath and likewise by judicial battle between knights. Wives of townsmen and burghers and noble bailiffs, by judicial battle between foot champions. Wives of peasants, by their own hands through the ordeal of boiling water. If the wife is victorious, let her husband honorably keep her and make compensation to her for all expenses which her retainers have incurred in this suit and judicial battle. But if she is defeated, let her come into the custody of her husband with everything she has.

103. Indeed, the above-mentioned princes issued another noble, honorable, and useful rule of customary law which they observed and commanded their successors to observe in perpetuity—namely, that they shall maintain a court and a great household, form a band of retainers, give them soldier's fees,[10] grant redress, render justice, judge according to the law, support the

8. The *exovar* had become one of the most prevalent dotarial forms in Catalonia during the period of the *Usatges* compilation. It derived from the Arabic *al-ashwwar*, the bride's household furniture and cooking implements, but by the end of the twelfth century the *exovar* had become synonymous with the Latin *dos* (dowry) in describing grants exchanged between a betrothed couple or from the parents of the bride to their future son-in-law.

9. *Bataia* (Catalan *batala*) was a judicial procedure like the ordeal that decided the adjudication of disputes by combat. Depending on their rank, women were represented in such struggles by either knights or foot soldiers.

10. The *sollata* (var. *solidata*) was a royal grant, usually of money, not unlike the northern European fief rent. This stipend, originally of no more than one sou, compensated vassals who were forced to spend more than the customary term in the sovereign's host or those in the martial employ of lords other than their own.

oppressed, and come to the aid of the besieged. And that whenever the princes want to eat, they should have the horn blown so the nobles and commoners will come to dine and there the princes should distribute fine garments which they have among the magnates and within their own household, and there summon military expeditions[11] with whom they set out to destroy Spain,[12] and there make new knights.

11. A *hoste* (Catalan *ost*) was any sizable military expedition that involved summoning vassals for military service.
12. Hispania was the name used by Christian Spain for the territory of the peninsula controlled by the Muslims.

29. REDEEMING A CAPTIVE JEWISH WOMAN

Judah ha-Levi, Two Letters from the Cairo Geniza (ca. 1125)

Translated from Judeo-Arabic and Hebrew by S. D. Goitein

Judah ha-Levi (d. 1141) is most famous as a medieval philosopher and a poet, but he was also a physician and an influential figure in the Andalusi Jewish community during the first half of the twelfth century. Born in Tudela in 1075, Judah later lived in Granada, Toledo, Córdoba, and elsewhere. Although he stayed in the peninsula for most of his life, Judah had many friends in the eastern Mediterranean and traveled eastward in 1140. He died on the way from Egypt to the Holy Land in 1141. The two letters here show Judah in his capacity as a community leader, working to raise money to ransom a Jewish woman held captive in Toledo. Both were probably written during the summer of 1125 and were addressed to an Egyptian friend. It is likely that the "wicked woman" to whom Judah ha-Levi refers in the first letter is Queen Urraca, who ruled Toledo from 1109 to 1126. The standard ransom was thirty-three and one-third dinars, but Judah mentions only thirty-two. He presumably had contributed the balance of the payment himself. These letters and others by Judah ha-Levi have been preserved in the Cairo Geniza collection, a cache of medieval Jewish documents discovered in a synagogue in Cairo at the end of the nineteenth century. (ORC)

1. Report About the Progress of the Collection

My lord and master, may God make your honored position permanent.

I received this letter from our master and teacher Judah b. Ghiyāth, lord of mine and admirer of yours, may God elevate you both, and decided to rush it to you so that you may enjoy it—may God let me enjoy your company.

In my previous letter I thanked you for your efforts in the matter of the captive woman. [The girl probably was traveling in a caravan in Muslim territory when it was overtaken by raiders from Christian Toledo.] Kindly alert her father to come to us, for her affair is nearing a satisfactory solution: We here in the town pay 10 *mithqāls*; the Turks, the Ghuzz have sent 4 or so; and then the *mithqāl* donated by you. From Málaga we expect 6, and when he [her father] will bring 10 from Lucena, the matter will be settled and we may get his daughter out before the holidays. For that wicked woman has changed her mind and does not permit us any longer to take the girl out of the prison on Sabbaths and holidays. If he [her father] prefers to send us what has been collected thus far and to go to Granada in order to secure what might still be missing from the 32, let him do so. But I believe the best thing

English text from S. D. Goitein, *A Mediterranean Society* (Berkeley: University of California Press, 1988), 5:463–64. Reprinted with permission of the publisher.

is to obtain her release as quickly as possible. God may guide us to whatever may be the best. The final term agreed with the wicked woman is the end of Tishri, and she does not grant us even one hour more.

Kindly let me know how you are in body and soul, may God shelter them in his grace. And Peace!

[*Verso. Address*]

To the illustrious scholar, the noble leader, our m[aster and] te[acher] Ḥalfōn ha-Levi, may the All [merciful] pre[serve him], son of his honor, our m[aster and] t[eacher] Nethanel ha-Levi m[ay he rest in] E[den].

2. Bid for Speeding up the Collection and Other Requests

My lord and master, [may God] unite [us] soon under desirable circumstances.

You have strained my yearnings. Please [mend] soon what you have impaired.

May I ask you a favor? Kindly approach your uncle and your paternal aunt and also the Head of the Police Abū Ibrāhīm Ibn Barōn, who values you very much and who is my support—may God make his honored position permanent—that they should talk to Ibn al-Shayyānī with regard to the balance of the pledge made for the imprisoned woman. For we are in trouble with regard to the small balance remaining as we had been with regard to the large sum.

The bearer of this letter of mine—may God restore his health—asks you to kindly recommend him to someone who could be of help to him. For he was a man of means and has become the opposite; on top of this, he has lost his health and eyesight and is far away from his family and native country. And God may let you be the originator of every charity and good work.

And Peace upon my lord and God's mercy.

[*Verso. Address: same as in preceding letter*]
[*Postscript, written upside down*]

Convey my highest regards to the illustrious Master [Rāv], the Light of Israel, may the All merciful preserve him, and substitute for me in asking him to reply to the people of Toledo. They rely on me in this matter, and I cannot say that my requests find no friendly response with the Master, may his Rock protect him.

And peace upon my lord.

30. DECLARATION OF A LEONESE EMPIRE

Chronica Adefonsi Imperatoris

Translated from Latin by Olivia Remie Constable

As its name implies, the Chronica Adefonsi Imperatoris *chronicles the reign of Alfonso VII, who ruled the kingdom—and then the empire—of León from 1126 to 1157. He was the grandson of Alfonso VI, who had forcibly reunified the realms of his father (León, Castile, and Galicia) and then gone on to conquer Toledo. Many of the same themes continue in this chronicle, which not only details the ongoing political competition and warfare between the different Christian kingdoms in Spain (including the newly created kingdom of Portugal, ruled by Alfonso VII's first cousin, Afonso Henriques) but also the pressing defensive campaigns against the Almoravids. In 1135, Alfonso VII declared himself an emperor, but this move did little to lessen the tensions with his Christian and Muslim neighbors. The* Chronica Adefonsi Imperatoris *was written by an anonymous author in the middle of the twelfth century and is thus almost contemporary with the events that it narrates. It is generally considered accurate, though biased in favor of Alfonso VII, and most of its information can be confirmed in other sources.*

After this, in the era 1173 [1135 C.E.], the king declared a day, the fourth of the nones of June [June 2], the Feast of the Holy Spirit, for celebrating a council in the royal city of León, with all the archbishops, bishops, abbots, counts, princes, dukes, and judges in the kingdom in attendance. On the stated day, the king came with his wife and queen, the lady Berengaria, and his sister, the princess lady Sancha, and along with them king García [Ramírez of Navarre] from Pamplona. And just as the king had ordered, they all met together in León. Along with them came a great multitude of monks and clerics also, and innumerable common people, all hoping to see, or hear, or speak the word of God.

On the first day of the council, all the great and lowly people were gathered together in the Church of Santa Maria, along with the king, and there they considered whatever was suggested by the beneficence of our lord Jesus Christ, and whatever was fitting for the salvation of the souls of all the faithful. On the second day, when the coming of the Holy Spirit to the apostles is celebrated, the archbishops, bishops, abbots, all the nobles, non-nobles, and all the commoners came together in the Church of the Blessed Maria, along with king García and the king's sister. Accepting the council of God, they declared the king to be an emperor, because king García and king Zafadola

Text from *Chronica Hispana saeculi XII: Pars I*, edited by Emma Falque, Juan Gil, and Antonio Maya, CCCM 71 (Turnholt: Brepols, 1990), chaps. 69–81, pp. 181–88.

of the Saracens,[1] and count Raymond of Barcelona,[2] and count Alfonso of Toulouse,[3] and many other counts and dukes in Gascony and France, all owed homage to him. The king was attired in a cloak of the most marvelous workmanship, and they placed a crown of gold and precious jewels on his head, and a scepter in his hands. King García held his right arm and Arias [González], the bishop of León, his left, and they led him before the altar of Santa Maria, along with the bishops and abbots, singing the *Te Deum* all the way through to the end, and then saying "Long live Emperor Alfonso!" Having pronounced the blessing over him, they celebrated mass in the manner of a feast day. Thereafter, they all returned to their quarters. [Alfonso] then ordered a great feast to be held at the royal palace, with all the counts and princes and dukes serving at the royal table. The emperor likewise ordered that generous stipends be given to the bishops and abbots and all others, and he made large donations of food and clothing to the poor.

On the third day of the event, the emperor and all the others came together in the royal palace, as they were accustomed, to discuss things pertaining to the welfare of the whole Spanish kingdom. The emperor then gave out customs and laws for his entire realm, just as had happened in the days of his grandfather, the lord king Alfonso [VI]. And he ordered that [property] should be restored to all the churches, heirs, and families who had lost it without [recourse to] trial or justice, and he decreed that villages and lands which had been desecrated by warfare should be resettled and replanted with vines and all kinds of fruit trees. He likewise ordered that all judges should work to eradicate crime among those men who were found to be against justice and against the decrees of the king, prince, state, and judges. Of those, he ordered some to be hanged, and others to have their hands or feet cut off. Likewise, [judges] should not judge the rich with more leniency than the poor, but they should give justice to each according to his guilt. Moreover, he ordered that evildoing should not be tolerated to any degree, for as God said to Moses: "Do not tolerate the wicked." And in the sight of all assembled, some criminals that had been caught were hanged.

[The emperor] ordered that the governor [*alcaydis*] of Toledo and all of the people living along the frontiers were to be assiduously prepared in military matters and ready to make war against the infidel Saracens every

---

1. Sayf al-Dawla would have been the ruler of Zaragoza, but he was displaced by the Almoravids in 1110. He became an ally of Alfonso I of Aragón, and assisted in his conquest of Zaragoza in 1118. Later, Sayf al-Dawla changed his allegiance and became a vassal of Alfonso VII. See Bernard F. Reilly, *The Kingdom of León-Castilla Under King Alfonso VII* (Philadelphia: University of Pennsylvania Press, 1998), p. 38.

2. Ramon Berenguer IV.

3. Alfonso Jordan, Count of Toulouse, was a cousin of Alfonso VII.

year. They were not to spare Muslim cities or towns, and should avenge all [challenges] to God and Christian law. Having settled all of these matters, the council ended. . . .

After a year had passed in complete peace according to these agreements, king García of Navarre began to create a disturbance, and he came with his warriors against the lands of the emperor. At the same time, a similar thing was happening with Afonso [Henriques], the king of Portugal, the son of count Henry [of Burgundy] and queen Teresa. Teresa was the daughter of the lord king Alfonso [IV], but not legitimate, for she was born to the king's beloved mistress, whose name was Jimena Muñoz. Because the king loved [Teresa] and wanted to treat her honorably, he gave her in marriage to Count Henry and endowed her with the lands of Portugal in perpetuity. After the death of Count Henry, the Portuguese named her their queen, and when she died, they honored her by naming her son as king after her.

Thus, these two kings noted above launched aggressive actions against the emperor at the same time. Each prepared for war from his own kingdom, king García on [the borders of] Castile and the king of Portugal on [the borders of] Galicia. Next, the king of Portugal came into Galicia and captured the city of Tuy and other castles. The count Gómez Nuñez, who held many castles and land in the region of Toroño, and the count Rodrigo Pérez Velloso, who held the castle at Limia as a fief from the emperor, both proved themselves unfaithful to their lord the emperor and they surrendered their castles and fiefs to the king of Portugal. . . .

When the emperor heard of this, he gathered a large army from Galicia and León, and his many soldiers made haste to Limia and besieged the castle of Celmes. A few days later he launched an attack against it. He captured many of the noble knights of the palace who were serving the king of Portugal, and he held them under guard for many days. This caused intolerable misery at the court of the Portuguese king, because nothing had turned out as he had intended. The emperor, however, was delighted that the whole region of Limia had reverted to his control, and having fortified the castle of Celmes, he returned home to León. . . .[4]

Once again, the king of Portugal gathered a group of his followers and marched on Limia [where he this time defeated Galician troops]. . . . After this victory, the king [Afonso] immediately returned to the land of Portugal in order to rescue those of his people who were in a castle called Erena. This had been built across from another castle, which was held by the Moors, [in

4. The chronicler notes here that in fact the campaign to Limia had taken place before the declaration of the Leonese Empire.

the place called] called Santarém, which had been built for attacking Santarém, Lisbon, and Cintra, along with other Saracen strongholds in the same region.

At the same time, the Moabites and the Hagarenes[5] launched an attack on the aforesaid castle of Leiria, and captured it in a fierce fight, and all of the fighting men, more than two hundred and fifty Christians, and some of the nobles close to the king, were put to the sword. This caused great sadness and perturbation at the court of the king of Portugal.

While all this was happening [in Portugal], the emperor was on campaign in the lands of king García. He seized a number of fortified castles, and captured count Latro Jiménez, the most illustrious of all the nobles at the court of king García.[6] He destroyed his lands, plundering, burning, and cutting down vineyards and orchards. [In the face of this], Latro Jiménez gave the emperor his oath of loyalty, and served him for many years. Nevertheless, even after this peace was made between the emperor and count Latro Jiménez, war continued for several more years between king García and the emperor. However, the strength of king García against the emperor was minimal and ineffective.

Meanwhile, in Portugal, Fernando Yañez, the commander of Limia, continued to wage constant attacks against the king [Afonso Henriques], along with others who were faithful to the emperor, and he fought this war bravely. The king was even wounded by a lance, which one of the foot soldiers of Fernando Yañez had courageously thrown. He suffered for many days until he was cured by his doctors. During the war, the aforesaid Fernando seized property from the nobles of the realm and despoiled their great riches.

After all these events had taken place, the emperor ordered that the counts of Castile (that is, Rodrigo Gómez, Lop López), together with duke Guter Fernández and the other nobles, should outfit themselves for daily attacks against king García. Meanwhile, the emperor himself mobilized a large army from the lands of León and went to Portugal, where he seized fortified castles and left a wake of great plunder and destruction throughout the land. In response, the king of Portugal gathered his army and came out to fight a few soldiers who had stupidly become separated from the emperor's forces. After this, he came upon Count Ramiro,[7] who was conquering his lands [on

5. The author is probably making a distinction here between the North African forces of the Almoravids and those of Andalusi Muslims.

6. The text calls this Basque count "Ladrón Navarro," but Bernard Reilly identifies him as Latro Jiménez. This nobleman swore loyalty to Alfonso VII in 1136 (Reilly, *Kingdom of León-Castilla*, p. 55).

7. Ramiro Froílaz.

behalf of the emperor], and they engaged in battle together. Count Ramiro was defeated and captured by the king.

The emperor established his camp across from the castle which is called Peña de la Reina [Penna de Regina], in a place which is called Portella de Vez. The king of Portugal pitched his tents facing the camp of the emperor, but on higher and more uneven ground, with a valley lying between the two of them. But without the permission of the emperor, many of his nobles and soldiers went down into the valley, as did many soldiers from the camp of the king, and they began to fight with each other. And many from both sides fell off their horses onto the ground and were captured.

Seeing this battle, the senior nobles among the Portuguese said to their king: "My lord king, it seems to us neither good nor useful to wage war against the emperor, nor can we resist his forces much longer because they are so much greater and stronger. There will be no tomorrow for us unless we act today. If there had been peace between us, then all of our brothers who died at the hands of the Saracens at the castle of Leiria would not have perished. We must ensure that the Moabites and Hagarenes to not come again to attack our towns and castles on the other side of the Dauro River, in which case the situation would be worse than ever. Therefore, send several of us to petition the emperor to make peace with us. We will give back all of his castles that we hold, and in return he should restore to us everything that his knights have taken from us. It will be much better for all of us to have peace rather than war."

Having listened to the advice of his nobles, the king was pleased with their idea. He sent some of the nobles of his court as messengers to the emperor, to whom they relayed the aforementioned words of peace from the king. After giving them audience, the emperor was likewise pleased with the proposal. After this, the king's messengers received pledges from [Alfonso's] nobles that there would be a truce between them until the aforementioned peace treaty was concluded or—if God were to look unfavorably upon it—rescinded. Then, somewhat later, the nobles of the emperor went down to the camp of the king and similarly accepted pledges of truce from the Portuguese nobles, who likewise gave them.

The next day, the nobles of the emperor met together with those of the king, and they negotiated a peace treaty between the emperor and the king. This was not to be of eternal duration, but rather for a set number of years. And they swore again that peace would be firmly enforced, so long as this treaty endured, and both sides were pleased with this agreement. All of the castles that the Portuguese king had captured in Galicia were returned to representatives of the emperor, and the same thing occurred with respect to [the castles] of the king, which soldiers of the emperor had taken from him during the war. Then count Ramiro was released, and all of the other soldiers who had been taken captive on both sides were also set free.

Peaceful relations continued between them for many years, and this was very helpful for the Christian cause. The king [of Portugal] also rejected count Rodrigo [Pérez] and count Gómez Nuñez from his service because they had sown discord between himself and the emperor. Count Gómez Nuñez acknowledged the charge against him, and was shamed. He fled across the Pyrenees, because there was no place where he was welcome to live [in Spain], and he became a monk at the monastery of Cluny. However, the emperor was moved to pity in the case of count Rodrigo, so he ordered him to attend his court at the palace, and he gave [Rodrigo] a stipend in gold and silver, just as though he were one of the [other] nobles who assisted at his court.

31. THE SIEGE OF LISBON

The Conquest of Lisbon (1147)

Translated from Latin by Charles Wendell David

The anonymous chronicle De expugnatione Lyxbonensi *[The Conquest of Lisbon] records the siege and capture of Lisbon from the Muslims in 1147. At the same time that Alfonso VII of Castile and Ramon Berenguer of Catalonia were pushing their borders southward into Muslim-held areas, King Afonso Henriques of Portugal was expanding his Portuguese territories. In March 1147, Afonso Henriques took the city of Santarém, north of Lisbon, and then laid siege to Lisbon. He was assisted by the fortuitous arrival of a fleet carrying crusaders from England, Germany, Flanders, and Normandy on their way to the Holy Land for the Second Crusade. In return for their help, Afonso promised that the crusaders could plunder Lisbon. The city endured a long and grueling siege, during which the Muslim defenders received no help from outside, despite their pleas to fellow Muslims for aid. Lisbon eventually capitulated in October, and the city was sacked and looted. Although the Muslim inhabitants had been promised safe-conduct while they left the city, many were killed. The author of the work is not known, but it is clear that he was present at the siege and probably wrote his account shortly after the event. (ORC)*

But finally, when we had been besieging the city for six weeks and it had been learned that the enemy were rather hard pressed by hunger, while an untold abundance of bread and wine and fruits was at hand for our forces, they gradually plucked up their spirits. They drew the ships up on dry land, lowered the masts, and put the cordage under the hatches, as a sign that they were spending the winter. But the men of Cologne five times began to dig mines for the purpose of overturning the wall and were as many times overwhelmed. Hence our forces again had cause for deep discouragement, and, murmuring much among themselves, they were making such complaints as that they might have been better employed elsewhere, when, after some days, there came to us by the determination of divine mercy no small consolation.

For in the evening ten Moors entered a skiff beneath the wall and rowed away in the direction of the castle of Palmela. But our men pursued them so closely that they abandoned the skiff in desperation, and everything they were carrying in it. Letters were found in it, directed to several parties and written in the Arabic language. An example of one, as I got it from an interpreter, is as follows:

English text from *De expugnatione Lyxbonensi* (*The Conquest of Lisbon*), translated by Charles Wendell David (New York: Columbia University Press, 1936), pp. 137–47. Reprinted with permission of the publisher.

"To Abū Muḥammad, king of Évora, the unfortunate people of Lisbon: may he maintain his kingdom in safety. What great and terrible and unexpected disasters have come upon us, the desolate ruin of our city and the great effusion of noble blood—memorials, alas, of our everlasting grief—proclaim. Already the second moon has almost passed since the fleet of the Franks, which has been borne hither to our borders with the aid of heaven and earth and sea, has kept us shut within the circuit of this close-drawn wall. And what is to be hoped for amid this sum of woes is more than doubtful, except only to look for succor by means of ransom. But with our cooperation we doubt not that you will liberate the city and the country from the barbarians. For they are not so very numerous or warlike, as their tower and engines which we have burned with force and arms bear witness. Otherwise, let your prudence beware, for the same outcome of events and evils awaits you."

And the other letters besought the same things from parents and other relatives and friends, and from debtors; and besides, they besought them to pray for them to Allah, that is, God, that, at the least, he would not permit them at the moment of death to be cheated of that eternal retreat in which his beloved Muḥammad dwells in glory. They also gave information concerning their supply of bread and other foodstuffs. When our men learned of these things, their spirits were greatly encouraged to continue the attack against the enemy for some days longer. After a short time the corpse of a man who had been drowned was found beneath our ships; and on an arm a letter was tied, of which the tenor was as follows:

"The king of Évora to the men of Lisbon, liberty of action. Having long since entered into a truce with the king of the Portuguese, I cannot break faith and wage war upon him and his people. For the rest, take heed in good time. Buy safety with your money, lest that prove a cause of your hurt which ought to be a cause of your well-being. Farewell. Give something worthwhile to this our messenger."

So, finally, as the Moors' last hope of relief was destroyed, our men kept watch the more vigilantly. A part of our army returned from the castle of Cintra with a great quantity of booty; for the nature of the site prevented them from attempting an assault upon the castle or a siege.

While we were carrying on the foregoing operations, the king dismissed all of his own forces except a small number of knights and the officers of his household, having either sold his provisions or sent them to Santarém. Only the bishop of Oporto remained constantly with us until the surrender of the city. Meanwhile, the Moors being hard pressed by hunger, whenever any of their poor were able to do so secretly, they gave themselves up to our men.

And so it soon came about that the acts and plans of the enemy could be but little concealed from us. . . .

Then our men, attending more strictly to the siege, began to dig a subterranean mine between the tower and the Porta do Ferro in order that they might bring down the wall. When this had been discovered, for it was quite accessible to the enemy, it proved greatly to our detriment after the investment of the city, for many days were consumed in its vain defense. Besides, two Balearic mangonels were set up by our forces—one on the river bank which was operated by seamen, the other in front of the Porta do Ferro, which was operated by the knights and their table companions. All these men having been divided into groups of one hundred, on a given signal the first hundred retired and another took their places, so that within the space of ten hours five thousand stones were hurled. And the enemy were greatly harassed by this action. Again the Normans and the English and those who were with them began the erection of a movable tower eighty-three feet in height. Once more, with a view to bringing down the wall, the men of Cologne and the Flemings began to dig a mine beneath the wall of the stronghold higher up—a mine which, marvelous to relate, had five entrances and extended inside to a depth of forty cubits from the front; and they completed it within a month.

Meanwhile, hunger and the stench of corpses greatly tormented the enemy, for there was no burial space within the city. And for food they collected the refuse which was thrown out from our ships and borne up by the waves beneath their walls. A ridiculous incident occurred as a result of their hunger when some of the Flemings, while keeping guard among the ruins of houses, were eating figs and, having had enough, left some lying about unconsumed. When this was discovered by four of the Moors, they came up stealthily and cautiously like birds approaching food. And when the Flemings observed this, they frequently scattered refuse of this sort about in order that they might lure them on with bait. And, finally, having set snares in the accustomed places, they caught three of the Moors in them and thereby caused enormous merriment among us.

When the wall had been undermined and inflammable material had been placed within the mine and lighted, the same night at cockcrow about thirty cubits of the wall crumbled to the ground. Then the Moors who were guarding the wall were heard to cry out in their anguish that they might now make an end of their long labors and that this very day would be their last and that it would have to be divided with death, and that this would be their greatest consolation for death, if, without fearing it, they might exchange their lives for ours. For it was necessary to go yonder whence there was no need of returning; and, if a life were well ended, it would nowhere be said to have been cut short. For what mattered was not how long but how well a life had been lived; and a life would have lasted as long as it should, even though not as long as it naturally could, provided it closed in a fitting end. And so the Moors gathered from all sides for the defense of the breach in the wall, placing against it a barrier of beams. Accordingly, when the men of Cologne and the Flemings went out to attempt an entrance, they were repulsed. For, although the wall had collapsed, the nature of the situation [on the steep hillside] prevented an entry merely by the heap [of ruins]. But when they failed to overcome the defenders in a hand-to-hand encounter, they attacked them furiously from a distance with arrows, so that they looked like hedgehogs as, bristling with bolts, they stood immovably at the defense and endured as if unharmed. Thus the defense was maintained against the onslaught of the attackers until the first hour of the day, when the latter retired to camp. The Normans and the English came under arms to take up the struggle in place of their associates, supposing that an entrance would be easy now that the enemy were wounded and exhausted. But they were prevented by the leaders of the Flemings and the men of Cologne, who assailed them with insults and demanded that we attempt an entrance in any way it might be accomplished with our own engines; for they said that they had prepared the breach which now stood open for themselves, not for us. And so for several days they were altogether repelled from the breach.

32. THE PILGRIMAGE TO SANTIAGO

The Pilgrim's Guide to Santiago de Compostela (ca. 1140)
Translated from Latin by Paula Gerson, Annie Shaver-Crandell, and Alison Stones

The Pilgrim's Guide to Santiago de Compostela *was probably written by a Frenchman who traveled there around 1135 and wrote between 1137 and the mid-1140s, not by Pope Calixtus or Aymericus the Chancellor, whose names have been attached to some chapters. The* Guide *is part of a larger compilation of texts related to the Cult of St. James (Santiago).*

The relics of the apostle James the Greater were allegedly discovered in the northwest corner of Spain during the first half of the ninth century by a hermit, Pelayo, and Theodomir (d. 847), bishop of Iria Flavia. A chapel was built over the site by Alfonso II (r. 791–842), and a cult was documented by 859. The date of the earliest pilgrimage is not known, but the first named pilgrim was Bishop Godescalc of Le Puy (traveling 950–951). By the eleventh century, the reconquista had politicized St. James and his shrine, and by the end of the twelfth century, Santiago Matamoros (St. James, slayer of Moors) had become the patron saint of many of the Spanish kingdoms. The pilgrimage to Santiago de Compostela reached its apogee in the twelfth and thirteenth centuries, rivaling the pilgrimages to the Holy Land and Rome. Although less popular in modern times, the call of St. James's shrine remains strong. Today, one can travel the pilgrims' route in summer and meet many devotees on their way to the Cathedral of Santiago de Compostela to celebrate the Feast of St. James (25 July).

The Pilgrim's Guide *begins with details of the routes to travel, with special emphasis given to Spanish towns (chapters 1–3). This is followed by information on where the pilgrim should and should not drink water in Spain (chapter 6, first selection). Chapter 7, from which the second selection is drawn, concerns the land and people the pilgrim may encounter during his trip. In two chapters, the prejudices of a Frenchman against Gascons, Navarrese, Basques, and Spaniards are clearly voiced. Chapter 8 is devoted to sanctuaries the pilgrim should visit while en route. Chapter 9 contains a long description of the Cathedral of Santiago de Compostela (begun in the 1070s) as it looked around 1135; the third selection is from this chapter. The guide concludes with cautionary words about the proper treatment of pilgrims.* (PG)

Chapter VI. The Good and Bad Rivers Found on the Road to Santiago (Pope Calixtus)

These are the rivers between the Port de Cize, the Somport and Santiago. From the Somport pass flows a pure river by the name of Aragón which

English text from *The Pilgrim's Guide to Santiago de Compostela. A Gazetteer with 580 Illustrations.* Paula Gerson, Annie Shaver-Crandell, and Alison Stones (London: Harvey Miller, 1995) pp. 67–68, 72–74, 94. Reprinted with permission of the publisher.

waters Spain. From the Port de Cize, indeed, comes forth a pure river which is called by many the Runa and which runs through Pamplona. The Arga runs along with the Runa to Puente la Reina. At a place called Lorca, in the eastern part [i.e., of Spain], runs a river called the Salty Brook. Be careful not to let it touch your lips or allow your horse to drink there, for this river is deadly! On its bank, while we were going to Santiago, we met two men of Navarre sitting sharpening their knives; they are in the habit of skinning the mounts of pilgrims who drink that water and die. When questioned by us, these liars said that it was safe to drink. We therefore watered our horses, and immediately two of them died, which these people skinned on the spot. At Estella runs the Ega; this water is fresh, pure and excellent. Through the town called Los Arcos runs a death-carrying river, and beyond Los Arcos towards the first hospice—that is, between Los Arcos and that hospice—runs a river fatal to beasts and men who drink it. At a town called Torres del Río, in Navarrese territory, runs a river fatal to beasts and men who drink it. After that, at a town called Cuevas, runs a river that is similarly fatal. At Logroño runs an enormous river, called the Ebro, which is pure and abounds in fish. All the rivers between Estella and Logroño have water that is dangerous for men and beasts to drink, and the fish from them are poisonous to eat. Whether it be the fish commonly called red mullet or that which the Poitevins call *alose* and the Italians *clipia*, or the eel or the tench, should you eat any of them in any part of Spain or Galicia, you will undoubtedly die shortly afterwards or at least fall ill. And if by chance someone ate some and did not get sick, it is because he was healthier than others or because he has remained for a long time in that country. All the fish, beef and pork of the whole of Spain and Galicia cause illnesses to foreigners.

In truth, the rivers that are fresh and safe to drink from are popularly known as the Pisuerga, the river that runs to the bridge of Itero del Castillo; the Carrión, which runs to Carrión de los Condes; the Cea at Sahagún; the Esla at Mansilla; the Porma, across which is a certain huge bridge between Mansilla and León; the Torio, which runs near León below Castro de los Judíos; the Bernesga, which flows near the same city, from the other side— that is, towards Astorga; the Sil at Ponferrada in Valverde; the Cúa at Cacabelos; the Burbia, which runs to the bridge of Villafranca; the Valcarce, which runs in its valley [i.e., the Valcarce]; the Miño, which flows to Puertomarín; and a certain river two miles from the city of Santiago, in a wooded place which is called Lavacolla, because in it French people making the pilgrimage to Santiago are in the habit, out of love of the Apostle, to wash not just their genitals, but to remove the dirt from their entire bodies, having taken off their clothes. The Sar River, which runs between the Monte del Gozo and the city of Santiago, is considered to be pure; similarly the Sarela River, which flows from the other side of the city towards the west, is said to be pure.

I have described thus these rivers, so that pilgrims starting out for Santiago may be careful to avoid drinking those which are fatal and may choose those which are safe for them and their mounts.

Chapter VII. The Names of the Lands and the Characteristics of the Peoples on the Road to Santiago

And also in the Basque country, there is on the way of Saint James a most excellent mountain which is called the Port de Cize, either because the gateway to Spain is there, or because it is by this mountain that necessary things are transported from one country to the other. The ascent of it is eight miles, and the descent is similarly eight. For the height of the mountain is so great that it seems to reach the sky. To him who ascends it, it seems that he can touch the sky with his own hand. From its summit can be seen the Sea of Brittany and the Western Ocean, and also the territories of three regions—that is, Castile, Aragón and France.

In truth, at the summit of this mountain is a place which is called the Cross of Charlemagne because it is here that with axes and picks and spades and other implements Charlemagne, going to Spain with his armies, once made a road, and he raised on it the sign of the cross of the Lord. And then, kneeling facing Galicia, he poured out his prayer to God and Saint James. On account of this, the pilgrims, bending the knee towards the land of Saint James, are accustomed to pray, and each one plants his own standard of the cross of the Lord. About a thousand crosses are to be found there. That is why that place is considered the first station of prayer to Saint James. On the same mountain, before Christianity was widespread within Spanish territories, the impious Navarrese and Basques not only robbed the pilgrims going to Santiago but also were wont to ride them like donkeys and to slay them.

Near this mountain, that is, towards the north, is a valley called Valcarlos, in which Charlemagne was encamped with his armies while the warriors were being killed at Roncesvalles. Indeed, through there pass many pilgrims travelling to Santiago who do not wish to climb the mountain.

Finally in truth, on the way down from that same mountain, are found a hospice and the church which contains the rock that Roland, that most powerful hero, split through the middle from top to bottom with a triple blow of his sword. Then comes Roncesvalles, the very place where the great battle was once fought in which King Marsile, and Roland and Oliver and other warriors died, together with forty thousand Christians and Saracens.

After this valley is found the land of Navarre, which abounds in bread and wine, milk and cattle. The Navarrese and Basques are held to be exactly alike in their food, their clothing and their language, but the Basques are held to be of whiter complexion than the Navarrese. The Navarrese wear short black garments extending just down to the knee, like the Scots, and they wear sandals which they call *lavarcas* made of raw hide with the hair on and are bound around the foot with thongs, covering only the soles of the feet and leaving the upper foot bare. In truth, they wear black woollen hooded and fringed capes, reaching to their elbows, which they call *saias*. These people, in truth, are repulsively dressed, and they eat and drink repulsively. For in fact all those who dwell in the household of a Navarrese, servant as well as master, maid as well as mistress, are accustomed to eat all their food mixed together from one pot, not with spoons but with their own hands, and they drink with one cup. If you saw them eat you would think them dogs or pigs. If you heard them speak, you would be reminded of the barking of dogs. For their speech is utterly barbarous. They call God *Urcia*, the Mother of God *Andrea María*, bread *orgui*, wine *ardum*, meat *aragui*, fish *araign*, house *echea*, the master of a house *iaona*, the mistress *andrea*, church *elicera*, a priest *belaterra*, which means "fair earth," grain *gari*, water *uric*, a king *ereguia*, Saint James *Ioana domne Iacue*.

This is a barbarous race unlike all other races in customs and in character, full of malice, swarthy in color, evil of face, depraved, perverse, perfidious, empty of faith and corrupt, libidinous, drunken, experienced in all violence, ferocious and wild, dishonest and reprobate, impious and harsh, cruel and contentious, unversed in anything good, well-trained in all vices and iniquities, like the Geats and Saracens in malice, in everything inimical to our French people. For a mere *nummus*, a Navarrese or a Basque will kill, if he can, a Frenchman.

In certain regions of their country, that is, in Biscay and Álava, when the Navarrese are warming themselves, a man will show a woman and woman a man their private parts. The Navarrese even practice unchaste fornication with animals. For the Navarrese is said to hang a padlock behind his mule and his mare, so that none may come near her but himself. He even offers libidinous kisses to the vulva of woman and mule. That is why the Navarrese are to be rebuked by all experienced people.

However, they are considered good on the battlefield, bad at assaulting fortresses, regular in giving tithes, accustomed to making offerings for altars. For, each day, when the Navarrese goes to church, he makes God an offering of bread or wine or wheat or some other substance. Wherever the Navarrese or Basque goes, he hangs a horn around his neck like a hunter, and he habitually holds in his hand two or three javelins which he calls *auconas*. And when he enters or comes back to his house, he whistles like a kite and when in secret places or skulking alone in ambush, he wishes to call his comrades without words, he either hoots like a horned owl or howls like a wolf. Those people are commonly said to be descended from the race of the Scots because they are similar to them in customs and appearance.

Julius Caesar, so it is said, sent three peoples—namely the Nubians, the Scots and the Cornish people with tails—to Spain to conquer the Spanish peoples who did not wish to render him tribute, directing them to slay by the sword all of the masculine sex and to spare the lives of women only. When these people had come by sea to that land and had broken up their boats, they laid it waste by fire and the sword from the city of Barcelona to Zaragoza and from the city of Bayonne to the Montes de Oca. They were not able to advance beyond that boundary because the Castilians united to drive the attackers out of their territory. They, however, fled to the coastal mountains which are between Nájera and Pamplona and Bayonne, towards the ocean, in the land of Biscay and Álava, where they settled and built many fortresses; they killed all the males, whose wives they carried off by force for themselves, by whom they begat sons who later came to be called Navarrese; this accounts for "Navarrese" being interpreted as *non verus*—that is, not begotten as the true offspring of a legitimate race. And also the Navarrese first took their name from a certain city called Naddaver, which is in that territory from which they came originally. Indeed, the blessed Matthew, Apostle and Evangelist, in early times converted that city to the Lord by his preaching.

After the land of these people, once past the Montes de Oca, towards Burgos, the land of Spain continues with Castile and Campos. This country is full of riches, gold and silver, blessed with fodder and very strong horses, well-provided with bread, wine, meat, fish, milk and honey; however, it is devoid of wood and full of wicked and vicious people.

Then comes Galicia, after crossing the region of León and the passes of Mount Irago and Mount Cebrero; this is wooded and has rivers and is well-provided with meadows and excellent orchards, with equally good fruits and very clear springs; there are few cities, towns or cornfields. It is short of wheaten bread and wine, bountiful in rye bread and cider, well-stocked with cattle and horses, milk and honey, ocean fish both gigantic and small, and wealthy in gold, silver, fabrics, and furs of forest animals and other riches, as well as Saracen treasures. The Galicians, in truth, more than all the other uncultivated Spanish peoples, are those who most closely resemble our French race by their manners, but they are alleged to be irascible and very litigious.

Chapter IX. The Characteristics of the City and the Basilica of Saint James the Apostle of Galicia

The Master Stonemasons of the Church, and the Beginning and End of Its Construction

. . . The master stonemasons who first constructed the basilica of the blessed James were called Master Bernard the Elder, a marvellous master, and Robert, who, with about fifty other stonemasons, worked there actively when the most faithful lord Wicart and the lord canon of the chapter, Segeredo, and the lord abbot Gundesindo were in office, in the reign of Alfonso, King of Spain, and in the episcopacy of Dom Diego I, most valiant knight and generous man.

The church, however, was begun in the year 1116 of the Spanish era [A.D. 1078]. Indeed, from the year it was begun up to the demise of Alfonso, most valiant and famous King of Aragón, there are fifty-nine years, and up to the decease of Henry, King of the English, sixty-two years, and up to the death of Louis the Fat, King of the French, sixty-three; and since the first stone of its foundation was laid up to that in which the last was put in place there were forty-four years [A.D. 1122].

From the time when it was begun up to the present day, this church is renewed by the light of the miracles of the blessed James. In it, indeed, health is given to the sick, sight restored to the blind, the tongue of the mute is loosened, hearing is given to the deaf, soundness of limb is granted to cripples, the possessed are delivered, and what is more, the prayers of the faithful are heard, their vows are accepted, the bonds of sin are broken, heaven is opened to those who knock, consolation is given to the grieving, and all the people of foreign nations, flocking from all parts of the world, come together here in crowds bearing with them gifts of praise to the Lord.

33. TWO ARGUMENTS IN SUPPORT OF CHRISTIAN FAITH

A. Mozarabic Refutation of Islam (ca. 1140)

Translated from Arabic by Thomas E. Burman

Sometime in the 1140s an anonymous Mozarabic (Arabic-speaking) Christian priest wrote the following brief refutation of Islam in Arabic. The priest is identified only as min al-qūṭ—*one of the Goths—a reference to the fact that his distant ancestors were (probably) Visigoths. The text also reveals that he is from Toledo, which makes perfect sense: Toledo in the twelfth century was the center of the Mozarabic community. Like the anonymous defense of the Trinity translated below this treatise has been preserved only in the pages of a much longer Muslim refutation of it, and it possibly was abridged or edited by the second author. That, at any rate, would account for the awkward choppiness of the work as it stands—and for the fact that some of the purported quotations of the Bible are spurious. The reader will perhaps be surprised to find this Christian priest quoting the Qurʾān to justify Christian beliefs; this was a common argumentative strategy in the Middle Ages, adopted because the contents of the Qurʾān and the Bible are very similar at many points. Jesus, for example, figures in an important way in the Qurʾān, where he is portrayed as both a prophet and an extremely holy man (though not, as in the Christian tradition, as the divine Son of God). What better way to argue than to contend that one's adversaries' scriptures confirm one's own view?*

The longer Muslim work in which this refutation of Islam is preserved is by Aḥmad ibn ʿAbd al-Ṣamad al-Khazrajī and is called Maqāmiʿ al-Ṣulbān/Hammers for (Breaking) the Crosses *]. The Mozarabic priest's comments comprise paragraphs 2–10; certain repetitive and unessential passages have been left out of this translation. (TEB)*

In the name of the Father and the Son and the Holy Spirit, one God.[1] May peace be upon you . . . and the grace of God and His blessing.

[On Belief in Jesus as the Messiah][2]

Praise be to God who guided us to His religion and helped us with His right hand and favored us with His Son and His beloved, and extended over us His Mercy, the Crucified One, Jesus the Messiah our God, "who created the heavens and the earth and what is between them"[3] and who redeemed us by

---

Translated from Aḥmad ibn ʿAbd al-Ṣamad al-Khazrajī, *Maqāmiʿ al-Ṣulbān*, edited by ʿAbd al-Majīd al-Sharfī (Tunis: Al-Jamiʿah al-Tūnisiyah, 1976), pp. 30–39.
1. Like many Christian authors who lived within Islamic society, this author consciously echoes the manner in which Muslim writers customarily begin their works: "In the name of God, the merciful, the compassionate." (Muslims, in turn, do this in imitation of the Qurʾān.)
2. Subtitles in square brackets have been added by the translator to clarify the text.
3. The Christian author is here quoting the Qurʾān knowingly or unknowingly, for in several places the Qurʾān describes God as "He who created the heavens and the earth and what

His holy blood, and from the suffering of Gehenna[4] He protected us; and He lifted from our necks the sin which was on the necks of the sons of Adam because of his [Adam's] eating from the tree from which he was prohibited. For the Messiah saved us with His blood and redeemed us and protected us from the suffering of Gehenna. He shed His blood in satisfaction for all of the children of Adam. . . .

If you desire that God protect you with His grace and that you attain His paradise,[5] then believe in God and confess that "the Messiah is the son of God who is God," and believe in the Holy Spirit: three persons yet one person,[6] and then you will prosper and be rightly guided.

Have you not heard what is in the book which the author of your law [Muḥammad] brought, that He [Jesus] is the Spirit of God and His Word,[7] and that He was "eminent in this world and the next and one of those brought close to God"? (Qur'ān 3:45). And who is more eminent in this world and the next than the Messiah, the Son of God?

And in the book which the author of your law brought [it is written] that He [Jesus] gives life to the dead and this suffices as evidence that He is God.[8] Then [it says] that He endowed some of his disciples with the power of raising the dead so that they raised the dead just as did the Messiah. And the Messiah sent them to all nations and ordered them to spread His authority after He Himself had granted to them His laws. And the people saw Him with their eyes, and He behaved humbly so that it was incumbent upon them that they act just as they saw their Creator act. For verily when He (May He be exalted and sublime!)[9] addressed the world through the tongues of His prophets He made them His messengers and mediators to His creation to the end that they would teach [mankind] to acknowledge His lordship. [The prophets] legislated to [mankind] that they should leave their idols and images which were diffusing their aberrance in all the earth. Then He

---

is between them" (cf. Qur'ān 43:39, 50:39). To describe Jesus in particular this way was quite common among Arabic-speaking Christians in Spain.

4. Hell. The Arabic word used here—*jahannam*—was borrowed from the same Hebrew word from which we get the English "*Gehenna*."

5. The Christian author here uses the typically Islamic word for heaven or paradise, *al-jannah*, which literally means "the garden."

6. The author here demonstrates that he is probably not all that well educated in theology; the proper formula for the Trinity would be something like "three persons in one substance," not "three persons in one person."

7. Jesus is identified in the Qur'ān as being in some sense the Spirit and Word of God (cf. 4:171).

8. The Qur'ān attributes several miracles to Jesus, including giving life to the dead. See, for example, 3:49 and 5:110.

9. The Christian author here follows the Islamic tradition of including such interjections as these after the mention of God's name; by doing so he is implicitly asserting Jesus' divinity.

descended (praise be upon Him!) after this from heaven to address mankind Himself in order that they have no argument [which excused their unbelief to use] against Him, and that their argument should be [immediately] cut off because He spoke to them Himself, not through a mediator between them and Himself. . . . He descended therefore personally from heaven and was made flesh in the womb of Mary the Maid, the Virgin Mother of the Light. So He took on a [fleshly] veil from her just as He anticipated in His eternal wisdom because "in the beginning was the Word and the Word was God (John 1:1)." And He was created with respect to the body and Creator with respect to the spirit. . . . And He was God the Perfect One.

It is part of His perfect mercy toward mankind that He was willing to shed His blood on the wood of the cross. . . . The accursed Jews crucified Him. And the Jews affirm that they crucified Him, whereas you [Muslims] deny this on your side. But for us the denial of the crucifixion is unbelief,[10] so everyone who denies it is an unbeliever. Nevertheless you exalt the Messiah, and on account of this I hope that God will guide you to the truth.

[The Superiority of Christianity]

And all your beliefs are nothing but good. And there is among you much justice and general goodness at the root of your religion. So if you were to believe in the Messiah and affirm that He is God, the Creator of the heavens and the earth, your belief would be perfected. And there is no doubt that you read the Torah and the Psalms and the Books of the Prophets; take heed [of them], for in these are evidences of all of this [that I have said]. . . .

God has given into the hands of the bishops what He has not placed in the hand of any [one else], and this in order that everything which they do on earth God does in Heaven. So when we sin they are the ones who receive penances and forgive sins, and in their hands is the well-being of the living and the dead.

And as for your religion, many of our bishops have written books discrediting it and in refutation of it. They tell of the author of your law and they describe things in such a way that we see that you do not follow the truth; but rather the truth is with us, and there is no [further] profit in your religious law because we find that the [basic] ordinances of religious law are two. The first is from the Torah: "Whoever strikes you, strike him."[11] The

---

10. The Qur'ān and Islamic tradition both deny that Jesus was crucified.

11. The Hebrew Bible, of course, does not use these words, but the Christian author seems to have had in mind the standard of justice outlined in Exod. 21:24, where injustice is to be repaid "life for life, eye for eye, tooth for tooth, hand for hand, foot for foot, burn for burn, wound for wound, stroke for stroke" (Jerusalem Bible). Part of this verse is quoted in Matt. 5:38, which immediately precedes the verse the Christian author is about to cite.

second is from the Gospel and is this: "Whoever strikes your right cheek, present him your left (Matt. 5:39)." You see that this second is superior to the first, and you will not find any other third ordinance except such as are really included in these two.

And what evidence is more convincing of the fact that do you not follow the truth than what it is written in your book: "Marry those women who are agreeable to you, two and three and four (Qur'ān 4:4)." Yet God said in the Gospel: "A man should not marry more than one woman, just as was [the case with] Adam and his wife."[12] And it is written in your book that when a man makes the divorce proclamation [the required] three times, "she is not [legally] available again to him until she marries a husband other than him [and then divorces that second husband] (Qur'ān 2:229)."[13] Yet God said in the Torah, "Whoever divorces his wife and then wants to return to her again, well she is [legally] available for him as long as no other man has touched her." . . . [14]

[The Errors of the Qur'ān]

There is matter for wonder in his [Muḥammad's] saying about Mary the mother of the Messiah, "And Mary is the daughter of 'Imrān who guarded her chastity (Qur'ān 66:12)." And he said about her in another passage, "Oh sister of Hārūn [Aaron], your father was not a man of iniquity and your mother was not a whore (Qur'ān 19:28)." But the mother of the Messiah was not the sister of Hārūn and was not the daughter of 'Imrān . . . who was the sister of Mūsā [Moses] and Hārūn.

And he said also in your book, about Iblīs [Satan], that God cast him to earth when he refused to worship Adam (cf. Qur'ān 7:11) even though He said in the Torah that He cast Iblīs from heaven before He created Adam because he wanted to make himself the equal of God. He tried to exalt himself above the angels and said to them, "I am made of fire and I have no creator, so make for me a throne upon which I will be the [very] likeness of the Most High."[15] But his words were not finished before God cast him from heaven into the disgrace of the here below, him and all his followers. . . .

---

12. This verse attributed to the Christian Scriptures is wholly spurious.

13. This complicated stricture is indeed part of the Islamic law of divorce. See "Ṭalāk," in *Encyclopedia of Islam*, 2nd ed., edited by P. J. Bearman, T. H. Bianquis, C. E. Bosworth, E. van Donzel, and W. P. Heinrichs (Leiden: Brill, 1954–2008), 10: 151–57.

14. This passage attributed to the Hebrew Bible is wholly spurious.

15. The author seems to imply that this statement attributed to Satan is from the Bible. It is certainly not, though it is reminiscent of certain statements in the Qur'ān (cf. 15:28).

[The False Teachings of Islam]

And you say in the Torah and the Gospel and the Psalms and the Prophetic Books there is abundant confusion and that we have added things to them and taken other things [from them]. But this is part of your unbelief and you have no evidence of this, nor is it written in the book which the author of your religious law produced. . . .[16]

And you say that in Paradise there are food and drink and sexual relations and all these things are recorded in the book which the author of your law brought, and we deny all of this. . . . [However] when we are gathered together on the day of resurrection we *will* come together with our bodies and souls, but we will not eat or drink.[17]

And the religion of the cross has spread throughout the earth without the sword and without coercion. But your religion triumphed by the sword and coercion on the earth. And the author of your way fought nations and conquered them. . . . And the Arabs entered our cities and uprooted our abodes. . . . The Messiah son of Mary, on the other hand, came humbly and in weakness and did not fight anyone. And He was crucified in propitiation for us. He was our God and our Creator and our Provider and the one who causes us to die and the one who gives life to us;[18] and He (may He be magnified and exalted!) by His grace forgives our sins and protects us by His mercy.

B. In Support of the Trinity (mid-twelfth century)
Translated from Arabic by Thomas E. Burman

A Spanish Christian, probably a convert from Judaism, wrote the following defense of the Trinity sometime between about 1130 and 1200. He was a man of some learning, familiar with the Latin-Christian intellectual tradition and with medieval Islamic

16. Islamic tradition holds that Christians and Jews "corrupted" their Holy Scriptures by removing from them prophecies of the coming of Muḥammad and adding to them heretical doctrines such as the Trinity. This brief paragraph is a refutation of that idea.

17. In this paragraph the author refutes the Islamic belief that the blessed will enjoy food, drink, and sex in paradise—another Islamic teaching that seemed to medieval Christians to be clear proof of the weak morals of Islam.

18. The Christian author (like other Arabic-speaking Christian writers in the Middle Ages) is here using very Islamic language to describe Jesus: in Islamic tradition God is frequently described as—among other things—the Creator, the Provider, the Giver of death, and the Giver of life.

Translated from *Al-I'lām bi-mā fī dīn al-naṣārā min al-fasād wa-awhām wa-izhār maḥāsin dīn al-islām wa-ithbāt nubuwwat nabīyinā Muḥammad ʿalayhi al-ṣalāt wa-al-salām*, edited by Aḥmad Ḥijāzī al-Saqqā (Cairo: Dār al-Turāth al-ʿArabī, 1980), pp. 47, 57, 63, 71, 77.

and Judaic thought, and his demonstration of the Trinity reflects these aspects. When he argues that the faculties of power, knowledge, and will belong especially to the Father, Son, and Holy Spirit respectively, he is borrowing directly from contemporary twelfth-century Latin theology. But when he explains all this in Arabic he uses philosophical terminology drawn directly from Muslim and Jewish philosophical discussions in Arabic on the nature of God. In particular, the argument presented here appears to be a direct refutation of the strict and highly rationalist monotheism of the Almohads (cf. the ʿAqīda, an Almohad statement of faith translated in Chapter 44). The section that follows is the first of the three parts of his defense of Christianity called Tathlīth al-waḥdānīyah, a title that might best be translated as "Trinitizing the Unity of God," or "Demonstrating the Triune Nature of the Divine Unity." This Christian apology written in Arabic probably would have been lost had it not been preserved in the pages of a much longer Muslim rebuttal of it written in the early thirteenth century and attributed to a certain al-Qurṭubī, "The Cordoban." This Muslim work is called Al-Iʿlām bi-mā fī dīn al-naṣārā min al-fasād wa-awhām wa-iẓhār maḥāsin dīn al-islām wa-ithbāt nubuwwat nabīyinā Muḥammad ʿalayhi al-ṣalāt wa-al-salām, which might be translated as "A Statement of the Corruption and Delusions to Be Found in the Religion of the Christians, and a Manifestation of the Merits of the Religion of Islam, and a Proof of the Prophethood of Our Prophet Muḥammad." (TEB)

Praise be to God, who gave generously of the faculties with which He endows us, and who commands us to praise Him; so we praise and we give thanks to Him and we glorify Him in the way we have become accustomed to praise, give thanks to, and glorify our kings and those people of whom we stand in awe among us who possess governing authority: that is, as a religious duty to Him, as those giving thanks, praising, and glorifying but not comprehending His essence or apprehending any part of it. Rather we know only the names of His acts in His creation and in His sustaining [of His creation] through His lordship.

It is now necessary that I ask you,[1] in connection with the matter of the Trinity, about God's creation of everything He created. Did He create these things through power, knowledge, and will, or did He create them otherwise? Now since this question has forced you to recognize [these faculties], I will ask you: Are these names for the essence of God? Or are they names for His acts? If you say "they are names for His essence," then you have contradicted yourself and made them names for His essence and fallen into something you must deny: that God has a body. And if you say "they are some of the names of His acts on account of which He is known as the Omnipotent, the Knowing, and the Willing," then this is the Trinity which He commanded us to confess.

---

1. The author is speaking to Muslim (or perhaps Jewish) readers in general.

But if you say, "Why do you not say, 'In the name of the Omnipotent, the Knowing, and the Willing,' when you say, 'In the name of the Father and the Son and the Holy Spirit?'" know that when the Messiah sent the Disciples unto all the nations he said to them, "Those among them who believe, baptize them in the name of the Father and the Son and the Holy Spirit" [cf. Matt. 28:19]. And he spoke to us merely in accordance with our understanding, for he laid down these names [threefold—and they are the names of the acts—with various names]² according to the diversity of the causes³ of the acts. . . .

Now the first cause is God's creation of everything by [His] hand; [the Messiah] called it "Father" and attributed it to the [faculty of] power. He attributed the cause of the Messiah's exhortation of mankind to the [faculty of] knowledge, and He called it "Son" because knowledge cannot be comprehended until it is born as speech. He attributed the cause of the annihilation of all of the temporal world and the reward of its people for their actions to the [faculty of] will, and he called it the Holy Spirit. [God, therefore,] is the Powerful, the Knowing, and the Willing—names for the One who is not multiplied.

At this point the author responds to a Muslim (or Jewish) objection to his argument so far:

"Now if you believe in the Trinity [only] because it is [an expression] for the names of the actions of God, then [we object that] the names of His actions are more than three: so believe in them just as you believe in the Trinity. For [God is also called] the Mighty, the Powerful, the Victorious, the Hearing, the Conqueror, the Seeing, the Forgiving, the Indulgent, the Wrathful, the Punisher,⁴ and other names derived from His acts: so profess them all just as you profess the Trinity." But I say to you that these names we have recounted are the origins of all other naming [of God] and from them [the other names] emanate and within them they are incorporated. The

---

2. The portion in brackets is not in the first quotation of the work by al-Qurṭubī on p. 63, but on pp. 68–69 he quotes this section with this portion—which is essential to the meaning.

3. I have used "causes" here to translate the Arabic *qadaya,* which normally does not have quite this meaning, because I believe that the Christian author had in mind the Latin word *causi,* as it was used by twelfth-century Latin theologians in contexts just like this (cf. Peter Abelard, *Theologia christiana* I.I, CCCM 12:72, ll. 1–15). Normally *qadaya* means "causes" only in a legal sense.

4. These are all among the so-called Most Beautiful Names of God that Islamic tradition ascribes to God and which are very important in Islamic piety. See L. Gardet, "al-Asmā'al-ḥusnā'" in *Encyclopedia of Islam,* 2nd ed., edited by H. A. R. Gibb, J. H. Kramers, E. Lévi-Provençal, and J. Schacht (Leiden: Brill, 1954–2008), 1: 714–17.

origin of [the names] "the Mighty," "the Powerful," "the Victorious," "the Conqueror," and others similar to these is power, and from it they emanate and in it they are incorporated. The origin of [the names] "the Forgiving," "the Merciful," "the Indulgent," "the Wrathful," and "the Punisher" is will, and from it they emanate and in it they are incorporated. [And likewise for knowledge.]

If you say, "but [the names] 'the Eternal' and 'the Living' do not emanate from [those three] and are not incorporated in them, so believe in a 'quintinity,'" I say to you that "the Eternal" and "the Living" are names of [God's] essence and not names of [His] acts. Every name pertaining to [God's] essence only conveys one meaning by negation of its opposite— "eternal" by negation of "temporal," "living" by negation of "dead," "lord" by negation of "dominated," and "god" by negation of "subject to god."[5] But each of these names—power, knowledge, and will—which are names of acts are three [names] applied to one essence, and there are no more. Just as [we] understand that no action in the soul of a man can come to be without these same three things—if one of them is lacking, then an action cannot be completed for him, and if a fourth is added to them, it will not happen—in the same way we understand about our Creator that His governance of us [arises out of these] three . . . (that is, power, knowledge, and will with no fourth among them). If one of them is ineffective, then the act will not be completed for Him by the remaining two. If He knows and wills and is not able, then He will be incapable [of the act]; and if He is able and knows how, but does not will it, no act will be complete for Him without will; and if he is able and does not know how, no act will be complete for Him in ignorance. The [Holy] Scriptures, therefore, have given us an approximate knowledge of the Creator through His creation of [all things, and this knowledge] is in accordance with our conventional understanding of our selves: for power, knowledge, and will are self-sustaining properties which are the completers of [each] act for us, and they are [nevertheless] one essence. Just so is the Trinity one in God.

If some opponent were to say, "what is the evidence of the veracity of what you claim about the Trinity and the unity of God? and how is it possible that three things be one and one three when you started out saying and affirming that [God] is one and eternal?" then we would say to him the following: That three is one and one is three is—upon my life!—something which

---

5. The view expressed here regarding what sorts of names can be properly used to describe God—that is, those arising either from God's actions with respect to creation or essential attributes ascribed to God negatively (by negation of their opposites)—is almost exactly that held by the great medieval Jewish philosopher of Spanish birth and education Moses Maimonides.

cannot be. Rather we say that [God] is an eternal substance always existing in three eternal persons, whose substances do not differ among themselves and are unseparated in the [one] eternal substance which is undivided and unpartitioned in itself and its perfection. So He is not three things—since the three things are the persons—in the same sense that He is one; and He is not one in the same sense in which He is three. By this I mean that He is not one person but rather three persons. This, then, is our teaching about the triune nature of the oneness of the Creator.

34. TALES OF INSTRUCTION FOR LIFE

Petrus Alfonsi, *Disciplina clericalis* (early twelfth century)
Translated from Latin by P. R. Quarrie

Petrus Alfonsi (1062–ca. 1110) was the name adopted by a Jewish rabbi from the Aragonese town of Huesca at the time of his conversion to Christianity in 1106. Rabbi Moses Sefardi, as he was originally called, had been trained as a theologian, doctor, and man of letters. His wide learning is demonstrated in the Disciplina clericalis, *one of the most important collections of medieval exemplary tales. The "disciplina" of the title refers to the Hebrew genre of tales providing instructions for life. Although the book was written after Petrus Alfonsi's conversion, his writing reflects his religious and linguistic background. The stories in his collection were designed to entertain, instruct, and improve the reader and were drawn from a long and broad heritage. They include proverbs, verses, fables, and anecdotes adopted from classical Greek, Hebrew, and Arabic traditions. Petrus Alfonsi's collection of tales became well known throughout medieval Europe and provided inspiration for preachers, moralists, and later authors including Chaucer and Boccaccio. The following selection is taken from the very beginning of the* Disciplina clericalis. *(ORC)*

These are the words of Petrus Alfonsi, a servant of Jesus Christ, who has written this book:

I give thanks to God who is first without beginning, from whom all good things have their beginning, who is the end without end, and the fulfiller of all good, who is wise and brings wisdom and reason to mankind, who has breathed into us his wisdom and led us into the light with the marvelous clarity of his teaching and who, by the multiform grace of his holy spirit, has enriched us. Therefore because God has designed to clothe me in his many-sided wisdom, although I am a sinner, in order that the light given to me should not be hid under a bushel, and at the prompting of that same holy spirit, I have been moved to write this book. And I beseech Him that He may adjoin to this the beginning of my little book a good conclusion, and that He may guard me, lest anything should be there said that might displease His will. Amen.

Therefore may God be my help in this undertaking. He, who has compelled me to write this book and translate it into Latin. For while I toiled to learn the causes of man's creation by every means and by frequent ponderings, I have found that the human spirit has been set down for this very

English text from *The "Disciplina clericalis" of Petrus Alfonsi*, translated by P. R. Quarrie (London: Routledge and Kegan Paul; Berkeley: University of California Press, 1977), pp. 103–6. Reprinted with permission of the publisher.

purpose by the precept of the creator, that so long as it is in the world it may study and busy itself with holy philosophy, to have thereby a better and greater knowledge of its creator, to live in moderation and continency and to learn to protect itself in the midst of the supporters of ungodliness, and to follow that path in the world which will lead it to the kingdom of heaven. When a man has lived according to the aforementioned rules of holy "discipline," he has indeed fulfilled that for which he was created, and deserves to be called perfect. I have also considered the infirmity of man's physical nature which makes it necessary to break up instruction into small sections so that boredom does not set in. Also I have been mindful of the fact that in order to facilitate remembrance of what has been learnt, the pill must be softened and sweetened by various means, because man is by nature forgetful and has need of many tricks which will remind him again of those things he has forgotten. For that reason, then, have I put together this book, partly from the sayings of wise men and their advice, partly from Arab proverbs, counsels, fables and poems, and partly from bird and animal similes. So, I have thought out a way so that if perchance I should have to write more these writings should not be a labor to the reader but rather a help, so that both readers and hearers should have both the desire and opportunity for learning. The learned shall remember what they have forgotten through those things contained in this book, to which I have given a title, *Disciplina clericalis,* a name that well describes the contents, for it renders the educated man well versed in knowledge. On the other hand, I decided that, within the capabilities of my senses, everything must be avoided in this book that might be found contrary to our beliefs or different from our faith. To do which may Almighty God to whom I dedicate myself, help me. Amen.

If, however, anyone should flick through this work with a human and therefore superficial eye, and see something in it where human nature has not been sufficiently on its guard, I advise him to re-read it again and again, and I propose that he, and all others who are perfect in the Catholic faith, correct what is wrong. For in anything invented by man, there is no perfection, as the philosopher says.

Fear of God

The philosopher Enoch, called Edris in Arabic, said to his son: "Let the fear of the Lord be your business, and you shall have wealth without toil." Another sage said: "He who fears God, is feared by everything, but he who does not fear God, himself fears everything," and another philosopher said: "Who fears God, loves him; who loves God, obeys him." An Arab poet said: "You do not obey God, yet you pretend to love him, and that is unbelievable, for if you really loved him, you would obey him. For he who loves, obeys."

Hypocrisy

Socrates said to his followers: "Watch that you be not obedient and disobedient towards God at the same time." And they said: "Explain to us what you mean," and he said: "Put aside hypocrisy. For it is hypocrisy to pretend in men's presence to obey God, but in secret really not to believe." One of his pupils asked him: "Is there any other type of hypocrisy of which man must beware?" Socrates said to him: "Imagine a man who both openly and secretly shows himself as obedient to God, that he may be considered holy by men, and thereby be more honored by them. Another man more subtle than the first disregards this type of hypocrisy in order that he may be aided in a greater, for when he fasts or gives alms, and is asked if he has done this, he answers: 'God knows!' or rather: 'No,' in order that he may be viewed with greater reverence, and that it may be said of him that he is no hypocrite, because he does not wish to brag about what he has done before people. Also I believe that there are few who do not share in this hypocrisy in some way. See to it, therefore, that you be not led astray by this and deprived of the reward for your exertions. To prevent this happening, do everything with a pure heart, lest you seek to gain glory." Another sage said: "When you lean firmly on God, wherever you go everything shall be favorable."

The Ant, the Cock, and the Dog

Balaam, who in Arabic is called Lukaman, said to his son: "My son, let not the ant be wiser than you for it collects in summer what it will live on in winter. My son, let not the cock be more watchful than you, for he is vigilant in the mornings when you sleep. My son, let not the cock be stronger than you, for he keeps his ten wives strictly in check, when you cannot even chastise one. My son, let not the dog be nobler of heart than you, for he forgets not those who have done him kindnesses, whereas you forget your benefactors. My son, do not think that one friend is too few, and do not imagine that a thousand friends is too many; for I tell you the following."

The Half Friend

An Arab who was about to die called his son to him and said: "Tell me, my son, how many friends have you gained during my life?" The son answered: "A hundred friends, I think, I have gained." The father said: "A philosopher says that a man should not count a man as a friend, until he has proved his friendship. I am much older than you and I have with difficulty obtained only half of one man as a friend. How is it that you have gained one hundred? Go, then, and put all of them to the test, that you may know who of all of them is a real, true friend." The son asked: "How do you advise me to put them to the test?" The father explained: "Kill a calf, cut it into pieces and put it in a sack; but let the bag be smeared with blood on the outside. When you come to a friend, say to him: 'My dear friend, I have, even as you see, killed a man. I entreat you bury him in secret, for no one will suspect you, and in this manner you can save me.'"

The son did as the father ordered. But the first friend to whom he came answered him: "Put the body on your back and go. If you have committed evil, you must suffer the consequences. You shall never from this day forth enter my house."

One by one he went round all his friends, and received the same response from all. Then finally he returned to his father and told him what had happened to him. The father said: "What the philosopher meant when he said: 'Many are a man's friends, when he counts them, but few when he has need of them,' has happened to you. Now go to the half a friend that I have, and see what he says to you."

The son went to this man and addressed him in exactly the same words as the others. He said: "Come in. This is no secret that one should withhold from neighbors." He sent his wife out and with all his servants he dug the grave. When the son saw everything ready, he told him the entire truth and thanked him. Then he told his father of what he had done. The father said: "It is of such a friend that the sage speaks when he says: 'He is in truth a friend who helps you when the world has deserted you.'"

35. GRANTS TO CHRISTIAN MILITARY ORDERS

Military confraternities, like formally organized military orders, were created during the twelfth century in both Spain and Palestine to provide troops for the war against Islam. The first document (A) refers to the Confraternity of Belchite, one of several semireligious confraternities founded by Alfonso I of Aragón (r. 1104–1134) in the aftermath of his conquest of Zaragoza (1118). Its purpose—and of those similarly established at Daroca, Monreal del Campo, and Zaragoza itself—was to defend the area south of the Ebro, the population of which remained mostly Muslim, from counterattack by the Almoravids. Although founded around 1122, the confraternity is known to us only through an 1136 privilege issued by Alfonso VII of León-Castile in the aftermath of Ramiro II of Aragón's surrender to him of the territory of Zaragoza.

The second and third documents (B, C) deal with the foundation of the specifically Spanish military orders. Document B records the act by which Sancho III of Castile (r. 1157–1158) replaced the Templar garrison at the key fortress of Old Calatrava, above the important Muradal pass, with a religious military confraternity. This had been organized by the abbot of the Navarrese Cistercian monastery of Fitero and soon developed into the first Hispanic military order, that of Calatrava. Document C marks a stage in the evolution of these military groups from essentially local units into more broadly based orders. This shows the confraternity or "Brothers" of Avila joining forces with the new military order of Santiago, forging bonds of cooperation that seem to stop just short of full union at a time when Spain was being harassed by the Almohad caliph Abū Yaʻqūb Yūsuf I (r. 1163–1184). (JWB)

A. Privilege to the Confraternity of Belchite (1136)
Translated from Latin by James W. Brodman

In the name of Our Lord, Jesus Christ, Amen. I, Alfonso, by the grace of God emperor of Spain, along with my wife, Queen Berengaria, with the advice and agreement of the archbishops, bishops, abbots, leading men, and counts of my entire realm, grant and confirm this charter for the service of God and for the military confraternity of Zaragoza, just as it is written below. We show our gratitude for the great and boundless merit of the entire Trinity, which has visited us with a clarity and sharpness of vision, and which through its mercy and heart has sent us from on high a messenger with its counsel. Indeed, the innermost core of our humility has been excited by the oppression of the Christian brethren who are cast down much too much by the vain and insolent superstition of the unbelievers. These people deride and ridicule in their mind the sacred mysteries of our faith, holding in complete contempt

Translated from Peter Rassow, "La Cofradía de Belchite," *Anuario de Historia del Derecho Español* 3 (1926): 220–22.

the venerable sacraments of Christ's cross; and, moreover, they destroy some of our people with the unbearable punishment of captivity until death. Some they have fatally cut to pieces with a blow from a killing sword; others, whose bodies have been mutilated, they scatter over fields without compassion. Therefore, having been touched by divine grace, for my salvation and that of my parents, for the preservation, defense, and expansion of Christian people, and for the suppression and destruction of the arrogance and aggression of the faithless pagans, we have determined and established through our imperial authority a Christian knighthood and a brotherly army of Christians in Christ, in Spain at the castle, which is called Belchite, or in another place beyond Zaragoza that is pleasing to the confreres, just as it seems better to them and to us, so that they may serve God there, and thereafter for all the days of their lives subdue the pagans. Nevertheless, over this army and these knights of Christ, I make myself in God's name the principal brother and protector; below me, I establish and confirm there as chief and rector Lupo Sancho, so that he may govern and protect and lead that army of God and those knights of Christ, and so that they, who are about to serve me above and beyond [other] Christians, themselves remain exempt from a service obligation to me.[1] Let all who wish to serve God there for their entire life also share in that same privilege. In addition, whatever money or possessions they will have been able to acquire then and in the future from the pagans, and whatever wasteland, wherever it is, they will have been able to populate, I assign and concede all of it to them, in such fashion that they may have and hold those possessions from God, and from there serve God. Let them never render any fifth[2] to me, but instead I wish and grant that the above-mentioned leader of the confraternity himself may receive it and distribute it to those serving God there, just as it seems best to him. Furthermore, let them have in their entirety and possess freely the towns, castles, settlements, and everything else they will have been able to acquire through their labor and talent. I also command and establish that they have two merchants in their service who, in my entire realm, will pay no toll or customs. Let the brothers themselves never

---

1. Settlers along the frontier normally owed the king defensive military service whenever their towns were threatened as well as offensive military service (*fossatum* or *fonsado*) when summoned by the king. Exemptions from or limitations on the latter were often granted to categories such as new settlers or even newlyweds. Here, Alfonso, eager to provide for the security of this district, evidently does not want his other military activities to detract from the work of this confraternity. On requirements for military service, see James F. Powers, *A Society Organized for War: The Iberian Municipal Militias in the Central Middle Ages, 1000–1284* (Berkeley: University of California Press, 1988), pp. 14–39.

2. The *quinto*, a 20 percent royal levy on spoils of war, a custom Christian rulers had taken over from the Muslim practice of reserving a portion of the proceeds of a jihad for God (see Powers, p. 163).

make peace with the pagans, but let them strive for all their days to harass and assault them, except for those who are under the lordship of Christians, in such fashion that Christians themselves hold them in their own hands and peacefully control the principal places of the towns, castles, or settlements in which they live. But if any of the aforementioned confreres have injured anyone else, we command and establish that, before he be punished or disturbed in any fashion, he be summoned before all of the aforementioned confreres at that place where they are together, and judged according to their verdict. But if the one accused will have refused to appear, let him be expelled from their community and defended by them no longer. Moreover, if anyone will have dared to arrest for debt or harass in any other fashion one of those confreres, let him pay 5,000 morabatins of the purest gold and set things right and be held by all to be a thief and defiler. Furthermore, I donate or will donate the greatest part of my possessions and patrimony to this confraternity of God, and wish and pray that all, bishops as well as the counts and great men of my realm, and all upright men, clerics and laics, will do the same with a generous hand.

I, Alfonso the emperor, confirm this charter which I have ordered to be made, and I have validated it with my hand in the second year that I first received the crown of the empire in León.

The charter was made at Burgos, on the fourth day before the nones of October [October 4], in the year of the era [of Spain] 1174 [1136], with Alfonso the emperor reigning in Toledo, Zaragoza, Nájera, Castile, León, and Galicia.

All the archbishops, bishops, counts, leading men, who were present at the council that Lord Guido, the cardinal and legate of the apostolic see, celebrated at Burgos, are witnesses to the charter of this confraternity.

B. Donation of Calatrava (1158)
Translated from Latin by James W. Brodman

In the name of the holy and individual Trinity, Father, Son and Holy Spirit, who together are worshipped and adored by all the faithful. Because the mercy of the royal dignity ought always to be firmly directed to this end, that it be able to please almighty God (in whose hand the hearts of kings are discerned to be), and strive to serve Him with a pious intention, without which the kingdom is not able to gain earthly things or attain those of everlasting life, therefore, I, King Sancho, by God's grace, son of Lord Alfonso of

Translated from *Bullarium ordinis militiae de Calatrava,* edited by Ignacio de Ortega y Cotes (Madrid, 1761), p. 2.

fond memory, the illustrious emperor of the Spains, inspired by divine favor, make this charter of donation and this written text of perpetual validity for God and Blessed Mary and the Holy Congregation of Cîteaux, and for you Lord Raymond, abbot of the Church of St. Mary of Fitero, and for all your Brothers, present and future, from the villa that they call Calatrava, so that you may have and possess it as a donation, free and safe, by hereditary right and so on for ever, and that you may defend it from the pagan enemies of the Cross of Christ, with His and with our assistance. Thus, I say, I give it to you, and concede it along with its adjoining territory, its woodlands, lands, waters, and pastures, with its entrances and exits, and with all the levies belonging to this locality, that you may have and possess it as hereditary property (as we have said), you and all your posterity, whoever will be members of your Order and wish to serve God there forever. And I do this for you out of the love of God, and for the salvation of my soul and of my parents, and that God may be honored through you, so that the Christian religion may be spread, and that our Realm may receive through your service augmentation and protection, being very grateful to almighty God. If anyone, in a brazen crime, wish to infringe upon this act and donation of mine, initiated by divine favor, may he be cursed and excommunicated and damned in hell along with Judas, the knave of the Lord, and may my act always be firmly maintained.

This charter was done at Almanzán in the year of the era [of Spain] 1196 [1158], in the month of January, the year in which the Lord Alfonso, the very renowned emperor of the Spains, died, with King Sancho of Navarre acting as vassal of the Lord King. I King Sancho confirm this charter, that I have ordered to be made, with my own hand. King Sancho of Navarre confirms it. Count Manrico confirms it. Count Lope, the alférez[3] of the king, confirms it. Count Vela of Navarre confirms it.

C. The Brothers of Avila and the Order of Santiago (1172)
Translated from Latin by James W. Brodman

In the name of the Father, the Son and the Holy Spirit. Amen. Whenever the zeal of the faithful desires something to be accomplished for the salvation of souls, it is fitting that it be committed to the permanence of writing lest it

---

3. The *alférez*, or royal standard-bearer, was a noble of high rank who commanded the royal armies.

Translated from José Luis Martín, *Orígenes de la Orden Militar de Santiago (1170–1195)* (Barcelona: C.S.I.C., 1974), pp. 226–28, no. 53.

disappear by some accident from the memory of mortals. Accordingly, with this charter it is recorded that, with the inspiration of divine mercy, several residents of Avila, drawn from the leading citizens of the same city, being concerned for the conversion of the present life with its acknowledged worries and unfruitful labors and seeking to become fulfilled under the habit and sign of the Military Order of Santiago, have elected to serve God and, just as the Military Order itself, to fight without cease in defense of the Church against the enemies of the Cross of Christ. They have promised to obey the Lord Pedro Fernández, the first master of the same Military Order, and his successors, and to live according to the provisions of its Rule, namely in such a way that the Brothers of Avila will hold and preserve faithfully the property that they now have or which, in the future, they gain or will have gained for the profit of their brothers and the growth of their house. They are not to be forced to give any of their property to anyone unless they do wish to do so, and the master does not have to give anything to them unless he wishes to do so. Let those drawn from their own community provide for themselves and administer the necessities of life.

If, God willing and with the master present, they acquire any personal property or a town or castle in the land of the Saracens, after reimbursement has been made for horses and arms lost there, let a fifth part and the lordship of the town or castle be given to the master. If he shall have acquired what we said before with the master not present (but with his brothers), let the tenth part of all personal property be given to the master, and let the lordship of the town or castle that is acquired be assigned to the same master; let the rest, and those properties that they will be able to populate, belong to the Brothers of Avila. If by chance they will have taken a town or a castle or anything else with the master and his brothers not present, let them give a tenth part from it to the master and not anything else.

When the master should demand their aid and his succor on an expedition, they will hasten to lend it to him according to their ability, as is proper; the master will in return not abandon them, but let all in similar fashion render that aid according to their ability. Likewise, when it is necessary, let the other brothers aid one another as brothers should even when the master is not present.

But if it happens that, with the Saracens expelled from Spain beyond the sea, the master and chapter should propose to go into the land of the Moroccans, they will not refrain from aiding them like brothers. Likewise, and if it be necessary, to Jerusalem.

Let the master confirm the very same one that they select as preceptor for themselves; if, by chance, he should have to be changed and the greater and wiser part of the chapter should have consented to his deposition, let him be deposed and another whom the master and chapter select hold the place of that one.

Let no one except with the general direction of the chapter be received into their society; no one from those already accepted shall be separated from their society unless, after the faults are examined, he shall have been found to be unworthy of such a religious community.

If any one of those should appeal to the Supreme Pontiff or if they should be summoned by others, in as much as it will be necessary, let the master act for them just as for other brothers.

Let those who have been summoned to the chapter of the master come, having let go of all other things.

Let them be compelled by the master to do nothing else, or let the master out of duty do nothing else, unless it is contained written in this charter.

This charter was made in [the year of the Spanish] era 1214 [1172], on the ides of May [12 May], during the reign of King Fernando of León, Galicia, Asturias, and Extremadura and his wife, the Lady Queen Urraca, and with his son King Alfonso, and during the reign of King Alfonso in Castile, Toledo, and Nájera along with his wife, Queen Eleanor.

36. PLANNING FOR CHRISTIAN EXPANSION

The Treaty of Cazola (1178)

Translated from Latin by James W. Brodman

One of two treaties signed in 1178 between Alfonso II of Aragón and Alfonso VIII of Castile (the other called for a partition of the kingdom of Navarre), this engagement set the approximate boundary that would emerge in the thirteenth-century between the realms of Castile and Aragón. In effect, by limiting Catalan-Aragonese expansion to Valencia, it reserved Murcia for Castile, an agreement that Jaume I (the Conqueror) would observe despite the difficulties of his son-in-law, Alfonso X, in winning and holding this region. Although later condemned by Catalans for giving up too much, the accords at Cazola released Alfonso II from the obligation of vassalage for the kingdom of Zaragoza that Ramon Berenguer IV had conceded to Alfonso VII. Likewise, and unlike the earlier agreement of Tudellen (1151), Cazola freed the count-kings from any feudal subordination to Castile for the territory to be gained from the Moors. In return, the Aragonese for the first time recognized Murcia as belonging to Castile's sphere of expansion. (JWB)

In the name of Christ, Amen. This is the understanding faithfully made between the illustrious Alfonso, king of Castile, and Alfonso, king of Aragón, count of Barcelona, and marquis of Provence, over the division of the land of Spain. For they are dividing the land of Spain between themselves according to this manner.

Indeed the said Alfonso, king of Castile, approves, concedes, and ordains for himself and for his successors forever to the said Alfonso, king of Aragón and to his successors, that they might acquire for themselves, and have and possess in perpetuity, freely, securely, and absolutely, without any contrary interference from one to the other, Valencia and the entire kingdom of Valencia with all of its territories, inhabited and uninhabited, which belong to it or ought to belong to it. Similarly, he approves, concedes, and ordains, to the same and to his successors in perpetuity, Játiva and all its inhabited and uninhabited territories; and Biar with its populated and unpopulated districts, and all the inhabited and uninhabited land at the pass beyond Biar called the pass of Biar, just as it looks back toward Valencia and Játiva; and Denia and the entire kingdom of Denia with all of its inhabited and uninhabited zones just as the port runs and leads all the way to the sea and goes all the way to Calpe. He also approves and ordains in perpetuity on behalf of himself and

Translated from *El reino de Castilla en la época de Alfonso VIII*, edited by Julio González (Madrid: C.S.I.C., 1960), 2: 528–30, no. 319.

his successors to the said Alfonso, king of Aragón and his successors all castles and settlements, inhabited and uninhabited, with all their appurtenances which are or will be within the said realms and said boundaries.

Likewise the said Alfonso, king of Aragón, count of Barcelona and marquis of Provence approves, concedes and in perpetuity ordains through himself and his successors to the already mentioned Alfonso, king of Castile, and his successors that they may acquire for themselves and have and possess forever, freely, securely and absolutely, all the land of Spain, populated and unpopulated, beyond the said mountain pass, that is beyond Biar, which is called the pass of Biar, with all the castles, and populated and unpopulated settlements, and with all appurtenances which are or which will be beyond the said pass, without any contrary interference from one to the other.

Therefore, the said kings make this division, and concession and definition between themselves and their successors in good faith and without any fraud and deceit, with a willing mind and a free will, to endure and be valid forever. And they agree between themselves that neither one of them would carry off for himself or reduce anything from the assigned portion, or that one would maliciously scheme against the other over the said division.

The charter was made at Cazola, since the said kings had a meeting there, in the year of the Lord 1178, in the era [of Spain] 1217, 13 days before the Kalends of April [20 March].

The seal of Alfonso, king of Castile.

The seal of Alfonso, king of Aragón, count of Barcelona, and marquis of Provence.

37. TOWARD A NEW ORDER OF POWER

The statutes of 1188 in León and Catalonia are of great comparative interest. Those of León are famous for their prescription of consultation in a form that would be institutionalized as the cortes. Those of Girona (in old Catalonia), though much less studied, lie at the origins of the Catalonian corts. The texts should be studied in two comparative dimensions. First, they tell us of legislative concerns in León and Catalonia in the later twelfth century and point to characteristic problems in these societies. Second, they tell us about parliamentary behavior—although the texts inform us very differently. In contrast to the more explicit statutes of León, almost everything about the assembly at Girona has to be read between the lines. It is helpful to bear in mind that the peace and truce in Catalonia were a legal order of security imposed by the lord-king and his bishops on barons and knights who resented it as an intrusion on their lordship over peasants. In 1173 the king had imposed statutes on the nobles much like the present ones, but without mention of vicarial enforcement. In 1192, the king held a poorly attended assembly in a borderland town of Aragón during which he admitted that the peace and truce had been rejected entirely by the barons in a tumultuous assembly held at Barcelona (in about 1190?) of which no other record survives. We can only infer what happened at Girona in 1188. (SD & TNB)

A. Statutes of León (1188)
Translated from Latin by Simon Doubleday

In the name of God. I, lord Alfonso, king of León and Galicia, when I was holding court at León with the archbishop and the bishops and the magnates of my kingdom, and with the citizens chosen from every city, decreed and declared under oath that I would observe toward all people, both clerical and lay, the good customs that have been decreed by my predecessors.

I have also decreed and sworn that if anyone makes an accusation [*mez-clam*] about someone, I will without delay present the accuser to the accused, and if he cannot prove the accusation he made, in my court, he shall suffer the same punishment that the accused ought to suffer if the accusation had been proved. I have also sworn that I will never punish nor do harm to anyone on account of an accusation made to me or some evil that is said of him, either to his person or his property, until I summon him by my letter to come to my court to do right according to the orders of my court, and if it is not proved, the man who has made the accusation shall suffer the

Translated from *Alfonso IX*, edited by Julio González (Madrid: C.S.I.C. 1944), 2: 23–26, no. 11.

aforesaid punishment, and shall in addition pay the expenses of the accused in coming and going.

I have also promised that I will not make war or peace or alliance [*placitum*] without the counsel of the bishops, nobles, and men of good standing [*boni homines*] through whose counsel I should rule.

I have decreed in addition that neither I nor anyone else in my kingdom shall destroy or seize or cut down the vines or trees of another man, but anyone who has a grudge against someone shall complain to me or the lord of the land or the justices who have been established on my authority or that of the bishop or the lord of the land. If the man about whom he complains wants to give surety or pledges of goods, he shall suffer no punishment if he acts according to the procedure, following his *fuero*; but if he does not want to do so, the lord of the land or the justices shall prosecute him as shall be just. If the lord of the land or the justices do not want to do this, they shall make a denunciation to me with the testimony of the bishop and the *boni homines*, and I will do him justice.

I also firmly prohibit anyone to fail to go on military forays, for he shall seek justice before me, as said above. Therefore, if anyone does this, he should pay double the damages occasioned thereby, and lose my love, and benefice, and the land he held of right.

I have also decreed that no one should dare to seize by violence any movable or immovable thing which another man has in his possession. Therefore, if he has made this thing his own, he shall restore it twofold to the man who suffered the violence.

I have also decreed that no one shall take pledges of goods except through the justices or *alcaldes* who are established on my authority. They and the lords of the land in the towns and districts [*alfoces*] shall faithfully do right to all who seek it. Therefore, if anyone has taken pledges of goods in another way, he shall be punished as if he were a violent intruder. Similarly, anyone who has taken pledges of oxen, or cattle for plowing, or the property a serf [*rusticus*] had with him in the field, or the person of the serf; so if anyone has taken pledges or seized something, he should be punished as is said above and should in addition be excommunicated. If, however, he denies that he has committed any violence, in order to avoid the aforesaid punishment, he shall give surety according to the *fuero* and the prior customs of his land, and there should be an inquiry as to whether he did this violence or not, and according to the outcome of that inquiry he should be made to give satisfaction by means of the giving of surety. The investigators should be those agreed upon by the complainant and the man being complained against, and if they do not agree they should be from among those whom you have put on the land.[1] If they have set up justices and *alcaldes* through the counsel of the aforesaid men or whoever is holding my land, they shall have seals to warn the people to come to redress the wrongs of those who had complained against them and testify to me which of the people's claims are true and which not.

I have also declared that if anyone denies justice to a man who complains to the justices or defers it maliciously and denies him right for three days, the plaintiff shall bring forward witnesses before any of the aforesaid justices, through whose testimony the truth of the matter may be ascertained and the justice should be compelled to pay the plaintiff double for both the claim and the expenses. If it happens that all the justices of that land deny justice to a claimant, he shall bring forward witnesses of the *boni homines* through whom he would prove his case, and—without cavil[2]—witnesses of the pledges for the justices and the *alcaldes* both of the petition and of the expenses, so that the justices themselves should pay double and in addition the justices shall pay double the loss which would have resulted for the man from whom pledge was taken.

I also added that nobody shall challenge the justices or seize pledges when he wishes to proceed against someone. If he does so he shall pay double for the penalty and the plea and the expenses, and in addition should pay the justices sixty solidi; and if any of the justices appeals to any of the people entrusted with administering justice and neglect to help him, they shall be held to the aforesaid penalty and in addition shall pay the lord of the land and the justices one hundred maravedis, and if the defendant or debtor does not have the necessary resources, the justices and *alcaldes* shall seize his person and everything he has without cavil and hand him and all his things over to the claimant, and if necessary take him into safekeeping, and if anyone should abduct him by force the abductor shall be punished as severely as a violent intruder. If any loss occurs to any of the justices in the administering of justice, all the men of the realm shall recover it for him, and if by chance he who occasioned the loss does not have the wherewithal to render it to him, and if by chance—heaven forbid!—anyone should kill him, he shall be regarded as a traitor and betrayer [*alevosus*].

I have also decreed that if anyone is called by a letter from the justices and neglects to come to the plea before the justices, he shall pay the justices sixty solidi if it is proven against him by *boni homines*. If anyone is accused of

---

1. This sentence is both obscure and odd in that it contains the only second person plural in the entire text.
2. "Without cavil" is a modern legal term meaning, in effect, "without any funny business."

theft or unlawful deed and the accuser has called him before the *boni homines* so that he come to do right before the justices, and he has failed to come for nine days, if the claim is proved, he shall be an outlaw; and if he is a noble, he shall lose five hundred solidi, and whoever takes him without cavil shall do justice to him, and if it happens that the noble at some time has made amends and has satisfied all those complaining against him, he shall recover his noble status and shall have the five hundred solidi as he previously had.

I also swore that neither I nor anyone else shall go against the gift of anyone by force, or cause any harm to it or to his inheritance, and if anyone does so, he should pay double the loss to the master of the house and in addition should pay nine times the loss to the lord of the land if he has not promised right as is written. If he happens to kill the lord or lady of the house, he shall be a traitor and betrayer. If the lord or lady or any of those who helped to defend their house should kill any of them for homicide, he should not be punished and should never respond for any harm which he does to them.

I have decreed that if someone wants to do justice to a man because he had a grievance against him, and the aggrieved party does not want to accept the legal action from him according to the terms stated above, he shall do no harm to him, and if he does so he shall pay him double; and if he also happens to kill him he shall be a traitor.

I have also decreed that if anyone is passing from one city to another or from one town to another or from one land to another, and someone with a sealed letter from the justices comes to the justices of that land in order that they capture him and bring him to justice, they shall not hesitate to capture and arrest him immediately and without delay, and if they do not do this the justices shall suffer the penalty which the outlaw should suffer.

I also forbid any man who has property under my authority from giving it to a religious order.

I have also ordered that nobody shall go for the justice of my court or the justice of León except on account of these reasons, for which they should go in accordance with their *fueros*.

All the bishops promised, and all the soldiers and citizens swore under oath that they were faithful in my council to upholding justice and promoting peace in my kingdom.

B. Statutes of Girona (1188)

Translated from Latin by Thomas N. Bisson

Because to no one more suitably than the prince is known to pertain the preservation of things divine and human and nothing should be so fitting for a good and upright prince than to avert wrongs, to stop wars, to establish and organize peace, and, once made, to hand it over to the care of his subjects, so that it may not improperly be said of him and proclaimed what was said by the Prince of kings: "through me kings reign and the powerful write justice,"[1] therefore, in the year of the Lord's Incarnation 1188, on the ides of August, having upon this [matter] discussion and deliberation at Girona with the venerable Berenguer[2] archbishop of Tarragona and with some of his suffragans and with all magnates and barons of our land, to whom it seemed unanimously just and fair and expedient to common utility that in all our land from Salses to Tortosa and Lleida with their borderlands [that] a peace and truce be instituted and the wicked audacity of brigands and robbers be exterminated, We who are known to rule by God's grace in the kingdom of Aragón[3] and the county of Barcelona and Provence, with the assent and will of all the aforesaid, providing for the public utility and wishing to care for the health of [our] soul and of those of our forebears, have undertaken to secure with the guard of our protection and perpetually to fortify all churches and religious persons with all their property. Accordingly, we order all, both clergy and laypeople who are known to live in our said land, to hold and inviolably preserve the truce and peace according to the form placed and prescribed below, and we oblige and bind ourselves to observe this even to the point of punishing them who may violate it.

1. First, then, following the examples of our ancestors, with the counsel and will of the aforesaid men, we constitute all churches and their cemeteries under perpetual peace and security because by the special judgment of men they are understood to be the property of God; so that no one of any status may presume to attack or violate them or their cemeteries or the sanctuaries established on the grounds of any church or try to take anything away, the violators of this statute to be struck by the penalty of sacrilege to be imposed

---

Translated from *Les constitutions de pau i treva de Catalunya. (segles XI–XIII)*, edited by Gener Gonzalvo i Bou, Textos Jurídics Catalans, Lleis i Costums II/3 (Barcelona: Generalitat de Catalunya, 1994), pp. 92–100, no. 17.

1. Cf. Prov. 8:15.
2. Berenguer de Vilademuls, archbishop of Tarragona (1174–1194).
3. The Latin is *Aragonum* ("of Aragóns"), a plural probably derived from a misread abbreviation.

by the local bishop and with a double satisfaction of the injury that they have caused to be paid to him who has suffered.

2. We also constitute fortified churches to be under the security of this peace and truce. Therefore let no one gather booty or [do] other offenses in these churches or make war from there. If anyone do otherwise, complaint should be brought to the bishop in whose diocese the offense was committed and to us or to our bailiff, and then by our authority and that of the bishop either what has been done should be corrected or the aforesaid church should be set apart from the peace.

3. We constitute the demesnes[4] of bishops and canons and monasteries and all clergy and their goods under the same security of the peace, with the penalty of double restitution for those who presume to violate them or cause harm. And we place clerks, monks, nuns, and widows, and all their goods under the same defense of the peace, so that no one may seize them or do them any injury unless they be discovered in misdeeds.

4. If anyone should lay violent hands on any of them or take anything from them, let him restore double what was taken and moreover let him make satisfaction for the deed by judgment of the bishop in whose diocese it took place; and moreover let him pay the amend of sacrilege to the bishop.

5. Moreover, the immunities of the Temple and Hospital of Jerusalem, and of the Holy Sepulcher,[5] and also of other venerable places, as well as the venerable brothers of these same places with all their goods we place under the same defense of the peace, with equal threat of punishment as for clerks and their goods and the churches.

6. We constitute under the security of the peace and truce peasants, male and female, and all their goods movable and mobile, that is, cattle, he- and she-asses, horses and mares, sheep and pigs, and other animals, whether suitable for plowing or not. Let no one of any status seize them or otherwise cause harm to them bodily or in respect of their movables, unless they are discovered in misdeeds, or unless they go on cavalcades with their lords or with others, or go forth armed against someone. But when they shall have returned from their cavalcades we shall provide protection for them, if in these cavalcades they did harm to one who by his own fault was excluded from the truce.

7. Likewise we establish that no one may destroy or burn the dwellings of peasants or start fires with malicious intent or burn the olive groves.

4. The demesne (here *dominicatura*) was landed lordship exploited directly, not granted out in fief.
5. These were new religious orders of monk-knights endowed to support pilgrims and warriors against Muslims.

8. Let plowshares and other plowing implements be in the same peace, and let him or her who plows with the aforesaid animals or leads them, together with all the things they carry with them or own, be protected by the same peace. Let no man presume to take or seize these plowing animals for pledge or for other reason, with the exception of peasants who are debtors or guarantors for those other than their lords, as is stated below. If anyone violates this constitution, he may simply restore for the misdeed with 15 days from the time of summons by the bishop and the lord-king's vicar, with no other punishment added, except for the 60 *s.* which he fines for the broken truce [and] unless the deed was such as to entail another penalty according to the tenor of written custom to be offered besides.

9. But if he refuses to make restitution for that wrongdoing within 15 days, as is stated just above, he must offer single or double compensation, in consideration of the nature of the misdeed according to the tenor of written custom, along with a fine likewise of 15 *s.* But if [he is] admonished [and] he refuses to do either, [then] the malefactor and his accomplices are to be understood as set outside the aforesaid truce, so that if any harm should come to them on account of this, it is not considered that the peace and truce are broken, as long as the peace of plowing animals and their implements and of fire is preserved. If the malefactor or his accomplices shall have harmed the aforesaid plaintiff, restitution for the broken peace shall be made. Moreover, we establish that if two or three or more men of any knight or any lord anywhere fight among themselves, whatever harm they do each other, and for whatever reason they dispute, the quarrel should be heard and settled by their lords. But if they have different lords, we establish that they should show the plenitude of justice toward each other, and by the judgment of their lords the said case should be rightfully settled. Nevertheless, if within 20 days their lords refuse to show the plenitude of justice among themselves, the aforesaid men may after those 20 days have elapsed bring their complaint to the bishop and the king's vicar; and through them, as established above, the punishment of the peace and truce shall be exacted.

10. Likewise, no peasant may work on lands placed in dispute when it appears to the ordinary judge[6] that the possessors are unwilling to stand trial. But if after two or three warnings the peasant works the lands and is thereby harmed, there will be no case of broken peace, except in the case of death or injury, and saving the peace of animals given for use in labor and [the peace of] fire. We do not want plowing animals to be seized, attacked, or destroyed on account of the complaint of peasants.

6. I.e., the count-king or his vicar.

11. If any debtor or guarantor does not take care to satisfy his creditor, let him be distrained of his own property, and not be held liable for the broken peace, saving however the peace of beasts given for use in labor and of fire, namely in such case where someone is guarantor for his own lord.

12. Likewise, we decree that no one of any status should have license to distrain any peasant or bailiff from the service of his lord, as was stated just above, under the penalty of the broken peace against him who does otherwise, unless he is a debtor or guarantor of his own lord, except those bailiffs who are of knightly status according to written usage, unless he is a debtor or guarantor of his own lord.

13. Likewise, since it is our intention to preserve everyone's right and as much as possible put down the malignities of some, those who, summoned by anyone and legitimately cited in law concerning injuries and possessions detained by them, fail to respond, having first been excluded as contumacious and separated from the truce and aforesaid security and then excommunicated by the bishop, in these two cases we give license to these parties of distraining and receiving their property, even of their peasants, saving however [the peace of] plowing animals and of fire. We exclude and except from this peace or security not only those with their men and their honors but also their accomplices who refuse to establish their innocence according to written custom of charges to betray or deceive their lords.

14. We also place and constitute under the aforesaid peace and security the safe places of all our land, both new ones and those of ancient foundation.

15. We exclude from the aforesaid peace and security thieves and brigands and those who harbor them if they refuse to right the wrongs they have committed and scorn to do right.

16. Likewise, we establish that if a malefactor admonished by the bishop or the lord-king's vicar, assuming the bond of excommunication, refuses to make satisfaction in the aforesaid way, the bishop together with the lord-king's vicar should assemble an army of all his diocese in this way, that one man from each manse goes in the army so that a suitable penalty may be inflicted on the malefactor. But if the inhabitant of the manse refuses to send a man to the mustering of the army, let him be excommunicated by the bishop and be subject to the fetter of excommunication until he makes satisfaction to the bishop and the vicar, according to their will.

17. Furthermore, we establish that if a bishop neglects to exercise his justice against malefactors, either out of love or fear of them, neither he nor his men will be able to seek justice in our courts or among our vicars so long as he fails to make amend for his negligence. The vicar may [then] exclude that malefactor from the aforesaid peace.

18. Likewise, we establish that if a malefactor admonished by the bishop and the king's vicar refuses to remedy his wrong, as indicated above, and for his contumacy his bishop and the vicar shall bring cavalcades to impose a penalty and there the bishop and the vicar should incur expenses or suffer other damages thereby, then expenses and other damages should be restored by estimate of the bishop and the vicar.

19. Likewise, I place and constitute public ways, roads, and highways in such security that no one shall attack travelers covered by the peace bodily or in their possessions or cause them any injury or harm. If anyone does otherwise, let him restore double the loss and pay a penalty of 60 s.

20. Moreover, we have decided this to be constituted and firmly observed under the same truce and peace: Sundays, festivals of all the apostles, the Lord's Advent to the octaves of Circumcision, Lent to the octaves of Easter, also the day of the Lord's Ascension, also holy Pentecost and its octaves, the three festivals of the Blessed Mary, and the festival of Saint John Baptist and of Saint Michael and of All Saints and of Saint Felix of Girona. And moreover let it be known that the aforesaid penalty of 60 s. should be divided equally between us and the bishop, with half of the double [restitution]. The other half of the latter should be given to him who suffered loss.

21. Likewise, we wish that there be no derogation from written usage on account of this constitution, that is, [concerning] the giving power of castles by vassals to their lords, or the restitution of vassals, or all others.[7]

22. Likewise, we establish that if anyone presume to go against written custom, if he or his supporters suffer any loss, there shall be no summons or amend of the broken peace.

23. Likewise, we establish that if sheep or oxen or any other animals are led away or shut away in favor of the pasturage of cattle, there shall be no summons or amend for the broken peace.

24. Likewise, let it be manifest to all that we promise henceforth that we shall exact nothing by reason of *bovaticum* or of the constituted peace[8] from any men settled from Salses to Lleida and Tortosa and in their borderlands.

25. We promise that we shall not appoint any vicar other than a Catalan in the whole aforesaid land.

In order that all the foregoing might be better and more strictly observed, I, Alfonso, by the grace of God count-king of Aragón, count of

7. Here is a clear reference to the *Usatges of Barcelona*; compare especially *usatges* 29, 30, 42, 71.

8. That is, there will be no tax either by reason of the written establishment of peace or of the protectorate of cattle (*bovaticum*; Catalan *bavatge*). *Bovaticum* referred ambiguously to the protection tax and to the "peace of beasts," often mentioned in these statutes.

Barcelona, and marquis of Provence, in Vilafranca del Penedès, swear, physically touching the holy gospels, that I shall comply with all the foregoing in
good faith and see that they are complied with, so help me God and these
holy gospels.

   Sig + *num* of Alfonso, king of Aragón, count of Barcelona, and marquis
of Provence.

38. MUNICIPAL LAW ON THE CASTILIAN FRONTIER

Fuero de Cuenca

Translated from Latin by James F. Powers

As Muslim towns were conquered by Christian rulers, it became common to grant them municipal law codes that governed legal, economic, and social matters within the town, regulated relations between urban authorities and the king, and gave privileges and protections to the town's residents. These law codes, or fueros, were useful in attracting Christian settlers to newly conquered territories, and they helped to solidify legal and social relations in these new frontier communities. The town of Cuenca was taken by Alfonso VIII of Castile in 1177, shortly after the capture of nearby Teruel by Alfonso II of Aragón in 1171. Within the next two decades, both towns received fueros from their kings. The Fuero de Cuenca *(Forum Conche) and the* Fuero de Teruel *(Forum Turoli) were both lengthy and comprehensive, and these documents would provide important models for later* fueros *in both Castile and Aragón. These two* fueros *had much in common, and they were undoubtedly created in competition as each ruler sought to populate, solidify, and defend his new lands. No copy of the original* Fuero de Cuenca *survives, but we possess thirteenth-century copies in both Latin and early Romance, as well as numerous copies made for other towns in Castilian Extremadura, La Mancha, Andalusia, and Leonese Extremadura. There are other selections from the* Fuero de Cuenca, *having to do with urban defense, in Chapter 52. (ORC)*

I.8. Only the king and the bishop may possess palaces

I command that there be in Cuenca no more than two palaces; namely, that of the King and the Bishop. All other houses, rich and poor, noble and commoner, have the same rights and same obligations.

I.10. Privilege of the settlers

I likewise grant to all settlers this prerogative: whoever may come to live in Cuenca, whatever condition he may be, whether Christian, Moor, or Jew, free or servile, should come in safety. He need not answer to anyone by reason of enmity, debt, bond, inheritance, *mayordomia*, *merindadico*,[1] or any other thing he may have done before the conquest of Cuenca. But if he had an enemy before the conquest of Cuenca, and he encounters his enemy while living here, both parties should designate bondsmen, according to the code

English text from *The Code of Cuenca: Municipal Law on the Twelfth-Century Castilian Frontier*, translated by James F. Powers (Philadelphia: University of Pennsylvania Press, 2000), 31, 35, 40, 52, 67, 79, 81, 83, 92, 114, 132, 162, 198, 214. Reprinted with permission of the publisher.

1. Both of these were special taxes paid to the royal officials.

of Cuenca, so that they remain in peace. He who does not want to designate a bondsman should leave the city and its district.

II.2. No sale of real estate to monks

No one is permitted to give or sell real estate to monks or to those who have renounced the world. Since their order forbids them to give or sell real estate to us, so the code and custom forbid us to do the same for them.

II.31. Ovens and bakers

The baker should heat the oven, place the bread in it, and, when it is cooked, remove it. The ovens should cook up to thirty-two loaves of bread. The baker has the right to one-fourth of the rent of the oven. If the baker, male or female, does not arise every morning to heat the oven, he or she should pay double the damage that ensues for this reason, according to the judgment of the owner of the oven. . . .

V.10. Those who destroy another's fence

Whoever breaks another's enclosure should pay five *aurei* [gold coins] and double the damage that ensues from this, if it can be proved; but if not, he should swear with two citizens and he should be believed.

X.4. Children are under the power of their parents

Children should be under the power of their parents and are family members until they should contract marriage. And until that moment, everything the children acquire or obtain should belong entirely to their parents; the children holding nothing against their parents' will.

XI.13. Those who form a gang in the city

Whoever forms a gang in the city against the council should pay double the pecuniary penalties of the crimes that it [the gang] commits, both he and all his collaborators; and equally, if someone takes up illegal weapons, he should pay twenty *aurei*; if he injures someone, forty; if he causes him wounds, sixty; if he kills him, four hundred. . . .

XI.14. Those who kill a guest

Anyone who invites someone to his house to eat or to drink or calls him to consult and kills him should be buried alive below the dead person. This same penalty should apply to the one who kills his master whose bread he eats and whose order he obeys, or who puts him [the master] in the hands of his enemies so that they do with him what they please.

XI.23. He who has a child with another's Moorish woman

If someone has a child with another's Moorish woman, this child should be the servant of the *señor*[2] of the Moorish woman, until his father redeems him. Also, we say that such a child should not divide with his siblings that which corresponds to the patrimony of their father, while he remains in servitude. Later should he become free, he should take a share of the goods of his father.

XI.36. The bigamist who has two women simultaneously

Anyone who has a legitimate wife in another place and gets married to another in Cuenca while the first woman still lives, let him be hurled from the city cliffs. If a woman has a husband in another place and gets married to another in Cuenca, she should be burned alive; if she is taken by a man as a concubine, she should be whipped in the square and in all the streets of the city and expelled from this place.

XIII.4. He who sells food to the Muslims

Whoever sells or gives weapons or food to the Muslims let him be hurled from the city cliffs, if it can be proved; but if not, he should clear himself with twelve citizens and should be believed; or he should swear alone and respond to the challenge by judicial combat, the one which pleases the council more. We call food bread, cheese, and everything which one can eat, except for living livestock.

XVI.27. The office of *notarius*

The *notarius*[3] should be honest in the reading of the Book [in this case, the *padrón*, the census and tax list for the city], in the accounts of the council and in the polling list of the council, in such a manner as to preserve it always as he had written it with the sworn witnesses. He should also guard against erasing or writing something in the Book without the order of the king or of all the council. He should keep accounts of the *iudex* and of the *alcaldi*[4] faithfully, so that he should commit nothing fraudulent with them.

XX.12. Which witnesses are competent

The code and also the statutes of law [passed in addition to the code] establish that the citizens of the city and the children of citizens of the city may

---

2. *Señor*: The male head of a family or household or an owner, employer, or master.
3. *notarius*: Clerk of records, kept the census list and the city's tax records.
4. The *iudex* was the chief elected civil officer in the city, both a mayor and a justice at the first level of appeal in court; *alcaldi*: Elected alderman and judge in a parish.

swear and testify against a citizen of the city or against the son of a citizen of the city, and not any other. All those who are designated citizens of the city, as much of the city as of the villages, who are inscribed in the census list: *attemplantes*, tenant farmers, *milites*,[5] and prebendal clergymen. All these should testify against a citizen and against any other man; but only a resident should testify against a resident.

XXIX.17. The oath of the Jew and of the Christian

For all claims, should they be Christian, should they be Jewish, up to a value of four *menkales*,[6] the Christian should swear without the cross and the Jew without the Torah. If the claim is worth four *menkales* or more, the Christian should swear on the cross and the Jew on the Torah. And if the Jew or the Christian does not want to swear, he should lose the case.

XXXVIII.1. The loyalty of all wage earners and servants

Every salaried servant, be he a herder, swineherd, or gardener, ought to keep this loyalty to his *señor*, to know that he should be faithful to him in all that is entrusted to him and given to him in deposit and as a secret. He should be faithful in keeping all his goods, so that he does not cause damage to them nor consent that someone else might do it. And he should not have relations with the wife of his *señor*, nor with his daughter, nor with the wet nurse, nor with the housekeeper.

XLIII.2. How the houses of the city ought to be covered

He who has a house in the city covered by straw should cover it with tile; if [he fails to do so], he should pay all his taxes as if he does not dwell in the town. And if there is someone so obstinate that he will not cover his house with tiles, he should give it to another settler who will cover it with tile; and the former owner should pay his taxes before everyone. This should be done from the tower of Malvecino up to the new work on the wall of the Arrabal, in such a way that it should enclose the wall on the side of the Júcar and the wall on the side of the Huécar.

---

5. *Attemplantes* were a resident class lacking full citizenship; *milites* (plural of *miles*) were horse owners who rendered combat on horseback, the bottom rank of the nobility, roughly equivalent to the term "knights."

6. A *menkal* was a coin of copper or copper and silver mixed, valued at about one-fourth of an *aureus*.

Al-Andalus Under the Almoravids and Almohads
(Twelfth and Thirteenth Centuries)

Map 3. The Iberian Peninsula, 1212.

39. MARKET REGULATIONS IN MUSLIM SEVILLE

Ibn 'Abdūn, *Ḥisba* Manual (early twelfth century)
Translated from Arabic by Bernard Lewis

For much of the medieval period, Muslim Spain was more urbanized than the Christian north. Andalusi cities such as Seville, Córdoba, and Almería were busy hubs of population, commerce, and learning at a time when the northern kingdoms had few urban centers. By the twelfth century, this situation was changing as towns began to develop in Castile and Aragón, but Muslim cities in the south remained dominant in terms of their size, importance, and economic organization.

Little is known about the author of this piece, who was either a judge [qāḍī] or a market inspector [muḥtasib] in Seville during the late eleventh and early twelfth centuries. The text is a classic example of the genre known as ḥisba, a handbook for market inspectors that laid out the proper economic and moral administration of the city. Technically, a muḥtasib's duty was "to promote good and prevent evil," and this encompassed a wide range of powers. One aspect of the job, demonstrated in this excerpt, involved the supervision of markets, including surveillance of product quality, prices, weights and measures, and business practices. Another task was to enforce the proper relationship between Muslims, Christians, and Jews. The market inspector was likewise responsible for the moral conduct of the city's inhabitants, public decency, segregation of the sexes, and regular attendance at mosques. The instructions presented in ḥisba manuals are prescriptive, and it is difficult to know to what extent they reflect actual practice. Nevertheless, there is sufficient incidental detail in Ibn 'Abdūn's text to suggest that his description of Seville's markets was accurate and specific. (ORC)

The *muḥtasib* must arrange the crafts in order, putting like with like in fixed places. This is the best and most orderly way.

There must be no sellers of olive oil around the mosque, nor of dirty products, nor of anything from which an irremovable stain can be feared.

Rabbits and poultry should not be allowed around the mosque, but should have a fixed place. Partridges and slaughtered barnyard birds should only be sold with the crop plucked, so that the bad and rotten can be distinguished from the good ones. Rabbits should only be sold skinned, so that the bad ones may be seen. If they are left lying in their skins, they go bad.

Egg sellers must have bowls of water in front of them, so that bad eggs may be recognized.

English text from *Islam from the Prophet Muḥammad to the Capture of Constantinople*, translated and edited by Bernard Lewis (Oxford: Oxford University Press, 1974), 2: 157–65. Reprinted with permission of the publisher.

Truffles should not be sold around the mosque, for this is a delicacy of the dissolute.[1]

Bread should only be sold by weight. Both the baking and the crumbs must be supervised, as it is often "dressed up." By this I mean that they take a small quantity of good dough and use it to "dress up" the front of the bread which is made with bad flour. A large loaf should not be made up out of the *poya*[2] rolls. These should be baked separately and as they are.

The glaziers must be forbidden to make fine goblets for wine; likewise the potters.

The *raṭl* weights for meat and fish and *harīsa*[3] and fritters and bread should be made of iron only, with a visible seal on them. The *raṭl* weights of the shopkeepers should always be inspected, for they are bad people.

The cheese which comes from al-Madāʾin[4] should not be sold, for it is the foul residue of the curds, of no value. If people saw how it is made, no one would ever eat it. Cheese should only be sold in small leather bottles, which can be washed and cleaned every day. That which is in bowls cannot be secured from worms and mold.

Mixed meats should not be sold on one stall, nor should fat and lean meat be sold on one stall. Tripe should only be sold dry on boards, for water both spoils it and increases its weight. The entrails of sheep must be taken out, so that they should not be sold with the meat and at the same price, which would be a fraud. The heads of sheep should not be skinned, except for the young. The guts must always be removed from the bodies of animals, except lambs, and should not be left there, for this too would be an occasion for fraud.

No slaughtering should take place in the market, except in the closed slaughterhouses, and the blood and refuse should be taken outside the market. Animals should be slaughtered only with a long knife. All slaughtering knives should be of this kind. No animal which is good for field work may be slaughtered, and a trustworthy and incorruptible commissioner should go to the slaughterhouse every day to make sure of this; the only exception is an animal with a defect. Nor should a female still capable of producing young be slaughtered. No animal should be sold in the market which has been brought already slaughtered, until its owner establishes that it is not stolen. The entrails should not be sold together with the meat and at the same price.

---

1. Eating truffles was supposedly a sign by which a dissolute person could be recognized.
2. A roll given to the baker as payment for the use of his oven.
3. A dish made of meat, cracked wheat, and sour milk.
4. A region on the Guadalquivir River south of Seville

A lamb weighing six *ratls* with its offal shall not be sold at the same price as a lamb the meat of which alone is of that weight.

Fish, whether salt or fresh, shall not be washed in water for this makes it go bad. Nor should salted fish be soaked in water, for this also spoils and rots it.

[Word missing in text] should only be sold cut into small pieces and with the bones removed. Jerked meat should not be sold, for it is prepared with bad and rotten meat. There is no goodness in it, and it is a deadly poison.

Left-over and rotten fish should not be sold.

Sausages and grilled rissoles should only be made with fresh meat and not with meat coming from a sick animal and bought for its cheapness.

Flour should not be mixed with the cheese used for fritters. This is fraud, and the *muhtasib* must watch out for it.

Women should not sit by the river bank in the summer if men appear there.

No barber may remain alone with a woman in his booth. He should work in the open market in a place where he can be seen and observed.

The cupper. He should only let blood into a special jar with graduation marks, so that he can see how much blood he has let. He should not let blood at his discretion, for this can lead to sickness and death.

The water wheel. Most of the holes for the spindles should be wedged, as this is best for its working.

No one may be allowed to claim knowledge of a matter in which he is not competent, especially in the craft of medicine, for this can lead to loss of life. The error of a physician is hidden by the earth. Likewise a joiner. Each should keep to his own trade and not claim any skill of which he is not an acknowledged master—especially with women, since ignorance and error are greater among them.

Only a skilled physician should sell potions and electuaries and mix drugs. These things should not be bought from the grocer or the apothecary whose only concern is to take money without knowledge; they spoil the prescriptions and kill the sick, for they mix medicines which are unknown and of contrary effect.

The sale of tame pigeons must be prohibited, for they are used only by thieves and people of no religion. The sale of cats should also be banned. Any broker who is known to be treacherous and dishonest should be excluded from the market, for he is a thief. He must be watched and not employed.

The lime stores and [other] empty places must be forbidden, because men go there to be alone with women.

Only good and trustworthy men, known as such among people, may be allowed to have dealings with women in buying and in selling. The trades-people must watch over this carefully. The women who weave brocades must be banned from the market, for they are nothing but harlots.

On festival days men and women shall not walk on the same path when they go to cross the river.

Graves should be slightly lengthened and widened. I saw a corpse which was exhumed from the grave three times; graves should allow for this. I saw another which had to be forced into the grave. The first concern of the *muḥtasib* should be to demolish buildings erected in the cemetery and to watch over this for reasons I have already explained above.[5]

Paper should be of somewhat larger format, with more glazing.

Raw bricks should be thicker and smoother.

The basins in the public baths should be covered. If they are left uncovered, they cannot be protected from pollution, yet this is a place of purity. The bath attendant, the masseur, and the barber should not walk about in the baths without a loincloth or drawers.

A Muslim must not massage a Jew or a Christian nor throw away his refuse nor clean his latrines. The Jew and the Christian are better fitted for such trades, since they are the trades of those who are vile. A Muslim should not attend to the animal of a Jew or of a Christian, nor serve him as a muleteer, nor hold his stirrup. If any Muslim is known to do this, he should be denounced.

Muslim women shall be prevented from entering their abominable churches, for the priests are evil-doers, fornicators, and sodomites. Frankish[6] women must be forbidden to enter the church except on days of religious services or festivals, for it is their habit to eat and drink and fornicate with the priests, among whom there is not one who has not two or more women with whom he sleeps. This has become a custom among them, for they have permitted what is forbidden and forbidden what is permitted. The priests should be ordered to marry, as they do in the eastern lands. If they wanted to, they would.

No women may be allowed in the house of a priest, neither an old woman nor any other, if he refuses marriage. They should be compelled to submit to circumcision, as was done to them by al-Muʿtaḍid ʿAbbād.[7] They claim to follow the rules of Jesus, may God bless and save him. Now Jesus was circumcised, and they celebrate the day of his circumcision as a festival, yet they themselves do not practice this.

5. Ibn ʿAbdūn includes an entire section on cemeteries elsewhere in his book.
6. Christians from Christian Spain and other areas of Europe were called Franks in Arabic.
7. Ruler of Seville (1040–1069).

A garment belonging to a sick man,[8] a Jew, or a Christian must not be sold without indicating its origin; likewise, the garment of a debauchee. Dough must not be taken from a sick man for baking his bread. Neither eggs nor chickens nor milk nor any other foodstuff should be bought from him. They should only buy and sell among themselves.

The sewer men must be forbidden to dig holes in the streets, as this harms them and causes injury to people, except when they are cleaning the entire street.

Itinerant fortune-tellers must be forbidden to go from house to house, as they are thieves and fornicators.

A drunkard must not be flogged until he is sober again.

Prostitutes must be forbidden to stand bareheaded outside the houses. Decent women must not bedeck themselves to resemble them. They must be stopped from coquetry and party making among themselves, even if they have been permitted to do this [by their husbands]. Dancing girls must be forbidden to bare their heads.

No contractor, policeman, Jew, or Christian may be allowed to dress in the costume of people of position, of a jurist, or of a worthy man. They must on the contrary be abhorred and shunned and should not be greeted with the formula, "Peace be with you," for the devil has gained mastery over them and has made them forget the name of God. They are the devil's party, "and indeed the devil's party are the losers" [Qur'ān 57:22]. They must have a distinguishing sign by which they are recognized to their shame.

Catamites must be driven out of the city and punished wherever any one of them is found. They should not be allowed to move around among the Muslims nor to participate in festivities, for they are debauchees accursed by God and man alike.

8. Probably a leper.

40. TRADE AND INDUSTRY IN A MUSLIM PORT

Al-Idrīsī, Description of Almería

Translated from Arabic by Olivia Remie Constable

Almería was founded in the tenth century as the main Umayyad naval base under ʿAbd al-Raḥmān III, and it subsequently grew into a major center for Andalusi shipping, commerce, and industry. It was especially known for its production of luxury textiles. During the eleventh century it was the capital of a Taifa kingdom before coming under Almoravid rule. In 1147, Almería was captured by the forces of Alfonso VII of Castile and Ramon Berenguer IV of Barcelona, with the aid of Genoa and Pisa (both of these Italian cities were interested in Almería because of its strategic location for shipping and trade). Ten years later, in 1157, Almería was taken by the Almohads, and it remained in Muslim hands until the end of the fifteenth century. The author of this passage, the geographer Muḥammad al-Idrīsī, was born in Morocco in 1100 and was educated in Córdoba. He later moved to Norman Sicily, where he completed his famous treatise on world geography, the Kitāb al-nuzhat, *which is often called the* Book of Roger *because it was written under the patronage of King Roger II, in 1154. (ORC)*

During the Almoravid period,[1] Almería was an Islamic town in which there were all kinds of industry and wonderful things, including eight hundred workshops for silk manufacture. Here they made all kinds of silk products: fine thread, fancy fabrics and brocades [*dībāj* and *siqlāṭūn*], silks in the style of Isfahān and Jurjān, silk curtains and netting, clothing and coverings, striped silks [*ʿattābī*] and knotted silks [*muʿājar*], and all other categories and types of silk.

Before the present day, Almería was [also] famous for the manufacture of many kinds of items made of copper and iron, and there was no regulation or limit to the circulation of these manufactured goods. The valley near the city produced many different kinds of fruit that were inexpensive to buy. This valley links Almería to Pechina, and it is four miles long. There were gardens and orchards and mills in this area, and all of the livestock and fruits produced here were brought to Almería, [and because of this] Almería was a destination for ships coming from Alexandria and Syria. There was nowhere else in al-Andalus where all the people were more prosperous and wealthy, nor anyone more commercialized in regard to the many different kinds of merchant activity, sales, and accumulation of goods.

Text from Muḥammad al-Idrīsī, *Kitāb al-nuzhat al-mushtāq fī ikhtirāq al-āfāq (Opus geographicum)*, ed. Enrico Cerulli (Naples, 1970; reprint, Beirut: ʿĀlam al-kutub, 1989), pp. 562–63.

1. Al-Idrīsī refers to the Almoravids as *al-mulaththam* ("the veiled ones") because Almoravid men covered the lower half of their faces with a veil (*lithām*).

Physically, Almería is formed by two hills with a populated low-lying area between them. On one hill there is a citadel which is famous for its fortifications, and on the second hill there is a suburb called Jabal Laham. A wall surrounds both the city and the suburb, and it has a number of gates in it. On the western side there was a large and prosperous suburb known as the suburb of the reservoir. This suburb had its own wall, and it was filled with markets, houses, *funduqs*,[2] and bathhouses. In sum, Almería was a large city, visited by many merchants and travelers. Its inhabitants were prosperous, and there were no people in all of al-Andalus who were more civilized. Its people had ready money and they were wide-ranging in their interests. There were 970 *funduqs* where duties on wine were taken, and as we have already mentioned, there were a large number of workshops for silk.

Almería is encircled on all sides by piles of boulders and rocks that are hard and jagged. There is no arable soil in this area, as if its earth had been sifted for soil and nothing was left in the place but rocks.

At the current time, when I am writing my book, Almería has fallen into the hands of the Christians [*Rūm*]. Its beauties have been ravaged, its people have been taken as captives, its houses have been destroyed, its lofty buildings have been demolished, and nothing remains of it.

2. A *funduq* was a commercial facility where merchants could stay and store their merchandise. Goods stored in a *funduq* could conveniently be assessed for taxation. They were also often sites for drinking and socializing.

41. HISPANO-ARABIC POETRY

Examples of *Zajal and Muwashshaḥa* (twelfth century)
Translated from Arabic by James T. Monroe

Andalusi poets wrote in many styles, but two forms of Hispano-Arabic poetry, the muwashshaḥa *and the* zajal, *were invented in al-Andalus. Both are marked by the combination of colloquial Arabic and Romance within the structure of the poem. In the* zajal *example below, written by Ibn Quzmān (d. 1160), the text is in colloquial Arabic interspersed with Romance words (though these are written out in Arabic script). In contrast, the* muwashshaḥa *was written in classical Arabic with a final section (called a* kharja, *or "exit") in either colloquial Arabic or Romance. Typically, there is a striking contrast between the elegant style of the main poem and that of the earthier vernacular* kharja. *In the selected example, composed by al-Aʿmā at-Tuṭīlī (d. 1126), the* kharja *is in Romance, although it includes an Arabic word. Clearly the audience for these poems must have been comfortable in both Arabic and a version of medieval Spanish. The romantic themes characteristic of* zajal *and* muwashshaḥa *poetry have led to considerable speculation regarding their relationship to troubadour poetry in southern Europe. (ORC)*

Ibn Quzmān

My life is spent in dissipation and wantonness!
O joy, I have begun to be a real profligate!
Indeed, it is absurd for me to repent
When my survival without a wee drink would be certain death.
Vino, vino![1] And spare me what is said;
Verily, I go mad when I lose my restraint!
My slave will be freed, my money irretrievably lost
On the day I am deprived of the cup.
Should I be poured a double measure or a fivefold one,
I would most certainly empty it; if not, fill then the *jarrón*![2]
Ho! Clink the glasses with us!
Drunkenness, drunkenness! What care we for proper conduct?
And when you wish to quaff a morning drink,
Awaken me before the *volcón*![3]

English text from *Hispano-Arabic Poetry*, translated by James T. Monroe (Berkeley: University of California Press, 1974), pp. 248–50, 260–72. Reprinted with permission of the publisher.

1. Spanish for "wine." Wine, of course, was forbidden in Islamic law.
2. Spanish for "jug."
3. Spanish for "the emptying of cups."

Take my money and squander it on drink;
My clothes, too, and divide them up among the whores,
And assure me that my reasoning is correct.
I am never deceived in this occupation!
And when I die, let me be buried thus:
Let me sleep in a vineyard, among the vinestocks;
Spread [its] leaves over me in lieu of a shroud,
And let there be a turban of vine tendrils on my head!
Let my companion persevere in immorality, to be followed by every beloved
    one.
And remember me continuously as you go about it.
As for the grapes, let whomsoever eats a bunch,
Plant the [leftover] stalk on my grave!
I will offer a toast to your health with the large cup;
Take your bottle, lift it high and empty it!
What a wonderful toast you have been honored by.
Let whatever you decree against me come to pass!
By God, were it not for a trick done to me in a matter concerning a woman,
I would have won bliss. She said [to me]: "There is a certain desire which
I will not grant you, it being a question of my honor."
Alas! The price of that was paid out later!
I, by God, was seated, when there came to me with a garland on her head,
A Berber girl; what a beauty of a *conejo*!
"Whoa!" [Said I, "she] is not a *sera* of *cardacho*,
But don't pounce [on her] for neither is she a *grañón*!"[4]
"Milady, say, are you fine, white flour or what?"
"I am going to bed." "By God; you do well!"
I said: "Enter." She replied: "No, you enter first, by God."
(Let us cuckold the man who is her husband.)
Hardly had I beheld that leg
And those two lively, lively eyes,
When my penis arose in my trousers like a pavilion,
And made a tent out of my clothes.
And since I observed that a certain "son of Adam" was dilated,
The chick wished to hide in the nest.
"Where are you taking that *pollo*,[5] for an immoral purpose?"

---

4. *Conejo*, Spanish for "rabbit"; *sera*, "basket"; *cardacho*, "thistle"; *grañón*, "boiled wheat porridge."
    5. From Latin *pullus* for "young animal" (probably not from Spanish *pollo*, "chicken").

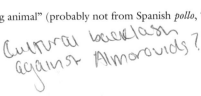

Here we have a man to whom they say: 'O what shamelessness!' "
I, by God, immediately set to work:
Either it came out, or it went in,
While I thrust away sweetly, sweet as honey,
And [my] breath came out hotly between her legs.
It would have been wonderful, had it not been for the insults that were
       exchanged next day,
For they began to squabble and to brawl:
"Remove your hand from my beard, O ass!"
"You, throw the frying pan for the *tostón*!"[6]
One claws at an eyelid, the other slaps;
One tears clothes to shreds, the other floors his adversary;
No matter where I throw green quinces,
I get hit only on the head by the *bastón*![7]
That is the way the world is! Not that it is my style,
Yet in this way they managed to humiliate me.
As for me, O people, although it was a light [punishment],
Never have I suffered such shame as at present.
Indeed, my opinion is as follows: You are viewed by the eye of reproof;
No place in this city is big enough for you to hide.
Where are the means [of departure] for one such as Ibn Quzmān?
In my opinion nothing is more certain than that [I shall get them].
O my hope and my well-watched star;
My life and my beloved one:
I desire largesse and it is from you that it is desired!
I am your guarantor for your glory will be guaranteed!
Your hands have an eminent right to dispose of me,
And in your honor do I go and stop,
While your virtues are too excellent for me to describe.
Drops of water are not to be compared with bursting rain clouds.
You have shown me a path to prosperity;
You have adorned me before my enemy and my friend;
For in you my hand has been attached to a firm rope;
You who are such that all others are withheld from me.
O, Abū Isḥāq, O lord among viziers,
Bright flower of this world and lord among emirs!
The like of you gives new life to poetry for poets,

6. Spanish for "toast fried in olive oil."
7. Spanish for "cudgel."

Elite - composition + recitation
of poetry

While you make public a generosity that was hidden [before your arrival]!
May you remain happy, achieving your aspirations,
And may you witness high rank and nobility with affability,
As long as darkness changes [to light] and the new moon shines,
And as long as a plant still grows green and branches rise high!

Al-A'mā al-Ṭuṭīlī

Tears that are shed and a breast that is burned
   Water and fire!
Things never joined save for matters of moment!
     By my life, it is harsh, what the censor has said,
     For life is but short while love's toils are long.
     O, for the sighs that betray one who loves!
     And O, for the tears that flow like a stream!
Sleep is taboo, visitation is far;
   No peace and quiet!
I would fly, yet I find no place to take flight!
     O Ka'ba to which all hearts journey forth
     Torn by passion that calls and answering love,
     You called on a sinner returning to you;
     Here I am! I heed not the words of the spy!
Allow me to travel and worship therein;
   Make no excuse!
My heart is the gift and my tears are the stones.
     Welcome is he, though he expose me to death;
     One supple of waist and languid of eye.
     O hardness of heart which love sees as soft,
     You have caused me to learn that thoughts can think ill!
Since he made off from those nights which were short
   My tears gush forth
As though in my lids were sharp-pointed swords!
     I've chosen a lord who unjustly condemns;
     To him I allude not revealing his name;
     My justice is wondrous in view of his wrong!
     Him you may ask for the tryst and refusal.
He tore from a passion well proven my share
   Of obedience,
Though shunned. Joy after him may choose whom it wills.
     I cannot resist him on any condition;
     A lord who accuses, treats harshly, delays;

Who left me in pledge to despair and disease,
   Then sang with an air between boldness and love:
"Meu l-ḥabīb enfermo de meu amar.
   ¿Que no ha d'estar?
¿Non ves a mibe que s'ha de no llegar?"[8]

8. The Romance words mean: "My beloved is sick for love of me. / How can he not be so? Do you not see that he is not allowed near me?"

42. IBN TUMART AND THE RISE OF THE ALMOHADS

'Abd al-Wāḥid al-Marrākushī, *The Admirable in Abridgment of the News of the West* (1224)

Translated from Arabic by John A. Williams

Like the Almoravids, the Almohads came into existence in the Maghrib (northwest Africa), where they expanded their territories with Berber support before extending their rule into al-Andalus. Their movement began in the early twelfth century with the appearance in Morocco of a charismatic leader called Ibn Tumart. Ibn Tumart was born in the Atlas Mountains in about 1082 and traveled to the Near East to study Islamic theology and philosophy. During this period, he elaborated a new form of Muslim belief that placed particular emphasis on the unity of God. This central assertion of unity (Arabic tawḥīd) led his followers to be called al-Muwaḥḥidūn ("those who emphasize unity") or Almohads. Although the Almoravids' movement also had a religious basis, the Almohads projected a clearer and more coherent vision for the reform of Islam.

When Ibn Tumart returned to Morocco in about 1118, he joined forces with a man called 'Abd al-Mu'min, who would become his student and eventually succeed him as ruler of the Almohads. In 1121, Ibn Tumart proclaimed himself to be the Mahdi, a divinely inspired leader who would restore the purity of Islam and guide his followers to salvation. Ibn Tumart provided both spiritual and military leadership for the Almohad movement until his death in 1130. With the support of the Maṣmūda confederation of Berber tribes, the Almohads took over Almoravid domains in North Africa and captured Marrākesh, the Almoravid capital, in 1147. The same year, they moved into al-Andalus, where they slowly consolidated their rule and established an Almohad capital in Seville. By 1160, their domains stretched as far east as Tunisia. Almohad rule in Spain disintegrated after 1223, when the caliph died without an heir. The historian al-Marrākushī wrote this account shortly thereafter. The Almohad movement died out in North Africa by the middle of the thirteenth century. (ORC)

In the year 515 (A.D. 1121), there arose in the Sūs district (of the Atlas) one Muḥammad ibn 'Abdallāh ibn Tumart, in the guise of one who commands to do good and rejects the reprehensible. This man Muḥammad was a native of Sūs, born in the village known as Ijilī (in the territory of the Banū) Wārghan, of the tribe named the Ḥargha, of the people known as the Isarghinan, which signifies "high-born," in the language of the Maṣmūda Berbers. A genealogy has been found for him, written in his own hand, tracing his descent from

English text from *Themes of Islamic Civilization*, edited and translated by John A. Williams (Berkeley: University of California Press, 1971), pp. 210–14. Reprinted with permission of the translator.

al-Ḥasan ibn al-Ḥasan, son of ʿAlī. He had traveled in the course of the year
501 (A.D. 1107–1108) to the Orient to study, and went as far as Baghdad.
There he met Abū Bakr al-Shāshī (d. A.H. 507; noted Shāfiʿī scholar),[1] from
whom he learned something of the principles of law and theology; he heard
ḥadīth from Mubārak ibn ʿAbd al-Jabbār and others like him, and it is said that
in Damascus he met al-Ghazālī at the time he was living as an ascetic there,
but as to that, God knows best. . . .[2]

    He returned by way of Alexandria, where he attended the lectures of
the jurist Abū Bakr al-Ṭurṭushī (d. A.H. 520). The call he made in that city
to order the good and reject what is reprehensible led to incidents following
which he took ship. I am told that he continued his habit of commanding
and reprehending until the crew threw him into the sea, but for more than
half a day he swam in the wake of the ship without incident, and when they
perceived this they took him out, and he became great in their sight. They
continued to treat him with consideration until he disembarked at Bijāya
(Bougie) in North Africa. There he openly began to teach and preach, and
people gathered to him and became sympathetic to him. When the prince
of Bijāya became fearful of his influence, he ordered him to depart, and he
departed toward the West, stopping in a village called Malāla, about one
farsakh[3] from Bijāya, where he met one ʿAbd al-Muʾmin ibn ʿAlī, who was
on his way to the Orient to study (and persuaded him to accompany him).
Ibn Tumart stayed in Malāla some months, and then traveled to the West,
accompanied by one of the inhabitants, a man named ʿAbd al-Wāḥid, known
to the Maṣmūda as ʿAbd al-Wāḥid the Easterner, who was the first to follow
him after ʿAbd al-Muʾmin, until they came to Tlemcen where (Ibn Tumart)
stayed at a mosque outside it, known as al-ʿUbbād. (There he was) active in
his usual way, and did not leave until all the inhabitants, ruler and subject,
venerated him, so that he departed having attracted the notables and won
their hearts. From there he came to the city of Fez, where he exposed and developed the doctrines of the Ashʿarīya school. Now we have already remarked
that the people of the Maghrib had tasted little of this sort of knowledge, and
they followed with great eagerness one who could expound it to them. The
governor of the city then organized a debate between him and the [Mālikī]
fuqahāʾ,[4] in which he won the victory, for he had found a virgin field, and a

---

    1. The Shāfiʿī school was one of the four main branches of Islamic law.
    2. It is still debated whether Ibn Tumart actually met the famous Muslim scholar
al-Ghazālī during his travels. It seems clear, however, that his thinking was influenced by al-
Ghazālī's philosophy.
    3. A unit of distance.
    4. Scholars of the Mālikī school of Islamic law, another of the four main branches. Fol-
lowers of the Mālikī school predominated among scholars in the Maghrib and al-Andalus.

people deprived of all speculative knowledge or anything but the application of legal rulings.

When the *fuqahā'* had heard his theology, they advised the governor of the city to exile him, lest he corrupt the minds of the common people. Exiled, he went to Marrākesh. . . .

When (a learned Andalusian) Mālik ibn Wuhayb heard Ibn Tumart, he counseled 'Alī ibn Yūsuf, the [Murābit or Almoravid] Commander of the Muslims,[5] to kill him, saying, "If he gets abroad in the land of the Masmūda with this, much evil will befall us from it." The Murābit ruler hesitated to kill him, for religious scruples. He was in fact a virtuous man, but weak and devoid of energy, and in the latter part of his reign appeared a number of reprehensible things and hateful scandals, produced by the intrusion of women into affairs and the authority they assumed. . . .

Then Mālik counseled him to imprison Ibn Tumart for life, but he said "How shall we take one of the Muslims and imprison him without just cause?" Thus he and his companions went out and turned their steps to the Sūs, where he settled in a locality known as Tīnmal.

From this place he began his propaganda, and he is buried there. When he had settled, the notables of the Masmūda gathered around him and he began to teach them religious knowledge and invite them to good deeds, without however disclosing to them his goals or his thirst for power. He composed for them a treatise on the articles of faith in their own tongue, in which he was one of the most eloquent men of his time, and when they understood the refinements of this treatise, their veneration for him was much increased: their hearts were filled with love of him, and their bodies with obedience to him.

When he felt sure of them, he summoned them either to stand with him or not, in the guise of ordering the good and rejecting the reprehensible, and he absolutely forbade them to shed blood (in feuds). After some time of this, he charged those men whose minds he judged were ready for it to preach his mission and conciliate the chiefs of the tribes. He began to mention the Mahdī and make them desire his coming, and to gather the traditions which speak of him in the collections.

When he had fully impressed on them the excellence, the genealogy, and the qualities of the Mahdī, he claimed the title for himself, and said that he was Muhammad ibn 'Abdallāh, and openly declared that he was the sinless Mahdī. They took the oath of allegiance to him, and he said that he

---

5. 'Alī ibn Yūsuf was the Almoravid ruler from 1106 to 1143. In Arabic, the Almoravids are called al-Murābitūn (or Murābits).

undertook the same engagements to them that the Prophet undertook to his companions.

Afterward he wrote several treatises on religious knowledge for them, among these the book called *A'izz mā Yuṭlab*, and statements of belief in the principles of religion.

The obedience of the Maṣmūda to Ibn Tumart kept increasing; their enchantment with him grew, their respect for him was confirmed, so that at last they came to the point where if he had ordered one of them to murder his own father or brother or son, he would have hastened to do so without the least hesitation. This would have been facilitated by the natural lightness with which these people shed blood; this is a thing which is one of the inborn traits of their nature, and to which the climate of their region predisposes them . . . as to the alacrity with which they shed blood, I myself during my stay in the Sūs saw some astonishing examples.

In 517, he raised a considerable army of Maṣmūda, composed of men of Tīnmal and their allies from the Sūs, and told them: "March against these heretics and perverters of religion who call themselves the al-Murābiṭs, and call them to put away their evil habits, reform their morals, renounce heresy, and acknowledge the sinless Imām Mahdī. If they respond to your call, then they are your brothers; what they have will be yours, and what you owe they will owe. And if they do not, then fight them, for the Sunna makes it lawful for you."

He gave them as commander 'Abd al-Mu'min, saying "You are the Believers, and this is your Commander." The army then marched on Marrākesh, and the Murābiṭs met them not far from them at al-Buḥayra with a strong army of warriors of the Lamtūna.[6] The battle took place, and the Maṣmūda were defeated with many losses. . . . When the news was brought to Ibn Tumart, he said "Did 'Abd al-Mu'min escape?" When they told him yes, he said "Then it is as if no one had fallen!"

After this, the Maṣmūda began raids on the territory of Marrākesh, cutting off provisions and communications, killing and pillaging without sparing anyone. A great number of people recognized their authority and joined them. Ibn Tumart thereupon gave himself over more and more to asceticism and simplicity, giving the appearance of a saint, and strictly applying the full provisions of the Law, following the first Muslim practice. . . .

All this strengthened their uprising and their veneration for him, as well as predictions he made which came true. Such was the case, favorable for him and his companions, since the affairs of the Murābiṭs were in decline, as we

6. The Lamtūna were the original Murābiṭ tribe.

have mentioned earlier, and the dissolution of their empire was gaining, until Ibn Tumart died in A.H. 524/A.D. 1130, having laid the foundations of their affairs, organized the administration, and traced for them the path to follow.

After the death of Ibn Tumart, 'Abd al-Mu'min continued to conquer province after province and to subject the land, so that its people accepted his rule.

His last conquest of the lands of the Murābits was the city of Marrākesh, their capital (where he put to death the young ruler) and when all the provinces of Morocco were submissive to 'Abd al-Mu'min, he turned his armies to the (eastern areas of North Africa, and then to Spain.)

43. THE DOCTRINE OF DIVINE UNITY

The Almohad Creed (1183)

Translated from Arabic by Madeleine Fletcher

The Almohad Creed, or 'Aqīda, provides an important piece of evidence for the immense debt European scholasticism of the thirteenth and fourteenth centuries owed the Almohad renaissance of the second half of the twelfth century in Islamic Spain.[1] This is when the integration of Aristotle into the western European religious worldview helped determine the future intellectual personality of western Europe. The insertion of Aristotelian rationalism into the intellectual tissue of Latin Christianity prepared western Europe for later rationalist developments in both science and enlightenment philosophy.

The person most responsible for transmitting an understanding of Aristotle to the West was the Spanish Muslim scholar Averroes (Ibn Rushd in Arabic). Averroes was a close advisor to the Almohad ruler Yūsuf in 1183 at the time the text of the Creed was set down; a number of internal reasons suggest that Averroes was its author. First, the philosophical propositions about God (Chapters 2–11) are largely those of Aristotle in his Metaphysics, *and it is known that Averroes's principal life work was the editing and commentary of Aristotle's works. Second, other elements in the Creed find parallels in the work of the eastern Muslim scholar al-Ghazālī. Al-Ghazālī was a basic ideological referent for the Almohad dynasty because Ibn Tumart, the founder of the Almohad movement, claimed to have been his student. The circumstances in which the Almohad Creed was first set down make it part of an official government document of the Almohad dynasty. This conjunction of religion and politics was quite normal in the medieval Islamic world. Thus, for a member of the Almohad ruling group faced with the task of writing a creedal document for the dynasty, the most normal thing would have been to borrow elements from al-Ghazālī, and Averroes was very familiar with his works. In addition, the subtlety with which the creed is written, threading its way between doctrinal pitfalls, bespeaks a very intelligent author—although of course no point of the doctrine is original.*

Statements in the Almohad Creed can be tested against the reader's own logic and personal experience and in this it differs noticeably from previous Islamic creeds.

Translated from *Le livre de Mohammad Ibn Toumert,* edited by Jean Dominique Luciani (Algiers: Pierre Fontana, 1903), pp. 229–39. This is a disparate collection of texts assembled and copied down at the end of the reign of the Almohad caliph Yūsuf ibn 'Abd al-Mu'min. The manuscript (Paris B.N. arabe 1451) is dated A.H. 579/A.D. 1183. The Almohad Creed contains twenty-seven chapters in its entirety.

1. Recognition of this legacy began with Ernest Renan's *Averroes et l'Averroisme* (1861), followed by works by Miguel Asín Palacios such as "El averroismo teológico de Santo Tomas de Aquino" in *Homenaje a D. Francisco Codera* (Zaragoza: Escar, 1904), or his introduction and notes to his translation of a work on theology by al-Ghazālī, *El justo medio en la creencia* (Al-iqtiṣād) (Madrid: Instituto de Valencia de don Juan, 1929). In both studies, Asín provides the translation of the passage from Averroes or al-Ghazālī and then quotes parallel texts from Saint Thomas Aquinas in notes at the bottom of the page so that the texts speak for themselves.

The revolutionary statement of the first sentence of Chapter 2 declares reason to be a criterion of religious truth: "It is by the necessity of reason that the existence of God, Praise to Him, is known." At the end of each chapter a Qur'anic verse making a similar point buttresses the proposition first deduced by logic.

Because its method is based on appealing to the reader's intelligence, the Almohad Creed seeks to find a common ground on which to establish its faith propositions. The first recourse is to the laws of reason, the axioms of Greek logic in use among the philosophers of the time. When this is not appropriate, the argument is based on Islamic law. Deductive reasoning is used in Chapters 2–11 to prove certain basic theological points, using as premises logical formulas such as the impossibility of overturning truths, or what leads to the absurd is itself absurd, for example.

The Almohad Creed is of particular interest to students of thirteenth-century Europe, because we have a Latin translation completed in 1213.² The lines of communication from Muslim Spain in this period were kept current as clerics in Paris awaited the latest word from Seville by way of the translators in Toledo. This same route was traversed by Averroes's well-known commentaries on Aristotle, as well as important scientific works on chemistry, pharmacology, medicine, mathematics, astronomy, and agronomy. (MF)

Chapter 1. On the Merit of the Divine Unity and Its Incumbency and It Is the First Thing About Which Knowledge Should Be Acquired³

There is a *ḥadīth* according to Ḥumrān, a client of 'Uthmān ibn 'Affān who had it from 'Uthmān ibn Affān:

The Messenger of God said "He who dies knowing that there is no God but God enters paradise."

Another *ḥadīth*: According to Ibn 'Umr, the Prophet said, "Islam is according to five things: That God is One; performing prayer; giving alms; fasting during Ramadan; and the pilgrimage."

Another *ḥadīth* according to Ibn 'Abbās:

It happened that the Messenger of God sent Mu'ādh to Yemen and he said, "Direct yourself to the people of the Book and let the first thing you call them to be the worship of God. And if they confess God, obligate them with the five prayers in day and night and if they perform them, then tell them that God obligates them to give alms taken from their wealth and given to their poor, and if they obey then take from them but avoid taking their best

---

2. Georges Vajda and Marie-Thérèse d'Alverny, "Marc de Tolède, traducteur d'Ibn Tumart," *Al-Andalus* 16 (1951): 1–56. Marcos of Toledo, a canon who translated the Qur'ān in 1209–1210, also translated the Almohad Creed.

3. The Arabic word for "one" is *wāḥid*. The founder of the Almohad movement, the Mahdi Ibn Tumart, gave his followers a name based on the same root: Muwaḥḥidūn. Thus the al-Muwaḥḥidūn, or Almohads, are those who proclaim the oneness of God. Chapter 1 of the Almohad Creed uses three *ḥadīths* to demonstrate that in the Prophet Muḥammad's mind, the notion of God's unity was the first and most fundamental element of religion.

animals." In another version of this same tradition it adds, "Fear the prayer of the oppressed for there is no veil between him and God."

And it is proved by this that worship is not correctly performed except through faith and sincerity. Faith and sincerity are achieved through knowledge, and knowledge through study, and study through the will, and the will through desire and terror, and desire and terror through the promise and the threat, and the promise and the threat from Revelation, and Revelation through the credibility of the Messenger, and the credibility of the Messenger through the appearance of the miracle, and the appearance of the miracle through the permission of God, Praise to Him.

Chapter 2

It is by the necessity of reason that the existence of God, Praise to Him, is known. Necessity is what is not open to doubt and what no reasonable man can deny. And this necessity is of three kinds: what is necessarily true, what is necessarily possible, and what is necessarily impossible. And what is necessarily true is that for which there is no way out of its existing, as, for example, the need for an action to have a doer. And the necessarily possible is that which might exist and also might not exist such as rain falling. And the necessarily impossible is that whose existence is impossible as the simultaneous affirmation of a thing and its negation.

This necessity is independently present in the minds of all who are endowed with reason. Thus it is independently evident in their minds that an action must have a doer and that the existence of the doer is by necessity not in doubt. And for that reason God, may He be Blessed and Exalted, calls attention to this in His Book, saying, "And is there doubt as to God, the Creator of the Heavens and the Earth?" [Qur'ān 14:11]. Thus the Exalted One informs us that the Creator of Heaven and Earth's existence is not to be doubted. And that for which doubt is denied is necessarily true. Thus we have proved by this that the Creator, Praise to Him, is known by the necessity of reason.

Chapter 3

From the fact of his own creation man knows the existence of his Creator, since he knows of his own existence after having been nonexistent. As the Exalted One says, "I created you from a previous state when you were nothing" [Qur'ān 19:10]. And also because he knows he was created from lowly water, as the Exalted One says, "Let man consider what he was created from; he was created from water spurting forth" [Qur'ān 6:5]. And man knows by necessity that the water from which he was created is of one nature, not differentiated as to composition, form, bone, flesh, hearing, or seeing. Then later all of these characteristics are found in it after being absent from it. And when he knows of their creation, he knows that they must be from a Creator who created them, as the Exalted said, "And We created man from a concentration of mud, then We put him, a sperm drop, in a solid receptacle, then We created a clot from the drop and of the clot a piece of tissue, and of the tissue bones, and clothed the bones in flesh, and then brought him forth as another creation. Blessed be God the best of creators" [Qur'ān 23:12].

Chapter 4

By the first act the existence of the Creator is known, Praise to Him, and in the same way the second and the third all the way to limitlessness. The existence of the Creator is known, Praise to Him, by the heavens and the earth and all created beings. Similarly, His existence is known by the creation of the first movement, since it needs to have been done by the agency of someone and it is impossible that it should exist without such an agent. And what is true of the first movement as to its needing an agent is true of all acts where it is recognized that something existing after having not existed necessitates its having been created. Necessarily one knows of the creation of night and day, people and animals, beasts and birds, wild animals and predators and other species that exist after not having existed. And if the creation of the first body is known, the creation of all the other bodies is known since they are the same in extension in space, mutability, positioning, particularity, adventitiousness and need for a creator, and God draws attention to their creation in His Book when He says, "Surely in the creation of the heavens and the earth and the alteration of night and day and the ships that ply the sea with profit to men and the water God sends down from heaven by which He revives the earth after it is dead and scatters in it all sorts of animals—in the loosening of the wind and cloud between heaven and earth—surely there are signs for people of understanding" [Qur'ān 2:159].

Chapter 5

And if it is known that these things exist after having not existed, then it is known that what is created is not able to be a creator, since created things arc in three categories: reasoning animate beings, irrational animate beings, and inanimate objects, and it is understood that if one got together all the animate reasoning beings to put back a single finger after it had disappeared, they would not be able to do so. And if the animate rational beings are unable, so must the irrational beings be unable and if these two cannot, the inanimate objects are even farther from it. And by this it is understood that

God is the Creator of everything according to His divine word, "God is the Creator of all things and the Guardian of all things" [Qur'ān 39:63].

Chapter 6

And if God is known to be the Creator of all things it is known that He is not like anything else, since nothing resembles anything except something of its kind. And the Creator, Praise to Him, if He were of the kind of created things, then He would be incapable as they are incapable, and if He were incapable as they are, the existence of His acts would be impossible, and we have witnessed incontrovertibly the existence of His acts, so to deny them while affirming them is necessarily impossible. By this it is known that the Creator does not resemble His creation as God, Blessed and Exalted, said, "Is He who creates like he who does not create? Will you not remember?" [Qur'ān 16:17].

Chapter 7

And to understand the denial of the similarity between Creator and created is to understand the absolute existence of the Creator, since everything that has a beginning, an end, delimitation, and specialization must also have an extension in space, mutability, a position in space, particularity, adventitiousness, and a creator. The Creator has no beginning since everything that has a beginning has a period before it existed, and everything that has a period before it existed has a period after its existence, and everything that has a period after its existence has a limit, and everything that has a limit is created, and everything that is created needs a creator. And the Creator, Praise to Him, is the First and the Last, the Outward and the Inward. He knows everything: the First without a beginning, the Last without an end. The Outward without delimitation, the Inward without particularization, existing in an absolute existence without similarity or modality. If all minds brought together as one attempted to understand the modality of created sight, hearing or intelligence, they could not, even though it is a matter of created things. And if they are incapable of understanding the modality of created things, then they must be even more incapable of understanding what has no similarity to created things nor analogy to what can be understood. There is nothing like Him which can be used as a term of comparison, as the Most High says: "There is nothing like Him, He is the All-hearing, the All-seeing" [Qur'ān 42:9]. The imagination does not touch Him, and the mind does not grasp His modality and for that reason the Prophet, may God pray for him and grant him peace, said, "I do not consider praising You as You have praised Yourself," calling attention to the prohibition of comparison and modality (an explanation of particular circumstances), and acknowledging in the matter of Him who needs no praise because of His glory and majesty, a limit to human understanding.

Chapter 8[4]

Minds have a limit at which they stop and which they do not exceed, and that is the inability to assign modality and past this limit [human reasoning] has no sphere and application except anthropomorphism (assigning God a body) and *ta'ṭīl* (denying God His attributes). And those who know [modality] know it by its actions, and they deny modality concerning God because it leads to anthropomorphism and *ta'ṭīl*, which is absurd, and everything that leads to the absurd is absurd from the witness of actions as to the existence of a Creator who is alone in being able to do them.

And as for the sacred texts that cause people spuriously to imagine comparison and modality such as the verse of the Qur'ān about God's sitting Himself upon the throne [Qur'ān 20:4] or the *ḥadīth* about the descent and other misleading texts in the law, it is incumbent to believe them as they stand while rejecting comparison and modality. Only one with a deviant heart will follow the misleading passages in the law. In the words of Almighty God: "As for those in whose hearts there is a deviance, they follow the ambiguous part, desiring dissention and desiring its interpretation; and none knows its interpretation save only God. And those firmly rooted in knowledge say 'we believe in it; all is from our Lord'" [Qur'ān 3:5]. The Most High tells us that the deviant hearts follow what is ambiguous in it desiring dissention and desiring its interpretation, and He blames them for that, and He tells us that the firmly rooted in wisdom say, "we believe in it, all is from our Lord" and He praises them for that. And the Messenger of God also warns against those who follow what is ambiguous in the Qur'ān in the following words transmitted by 'Aisha. "God's Messenger was asked about the verse, 'It is God

---

4. Chapter 8 deals with anti-anthropomorphism, a central tenet of Almohad ideology and of political importance. The Almohads accused their opponents, the Almoravids, of being *mujassimūn,* or anthropomorphists. As the name implies, anthropomorphism is the notion that God can be compared to man. In the earlier eastern history of this controversy, the Qur'ān verses that made it seem that God had the form of a man "sitting on the throne" needed explanation. The Ash'arite school of theology proposed an allegorical interpretation of these verses (or *ta'wīl*), opposed by the Hanbalites. Tempers rose to the point that there were street scuffles in Baghdad over this issue.

The author of the Almohad Creed takes an unusually independent view of this controversy. He shows the faultiness of both sides' basic premises and provides a third perspective from which the polemic is rendered meaningless, saying that the limitation of human perspectives makes a logically incoherent picture of God inevitable. Rejected as self-evidently absurd is any idea leading to *tajsim* (giving God a human form, as the Almoravids were accused of doing) or *ta'ṭīl* (stripping God of His qualities, a Mu'tazilite doctrine).

who revealed to you the book containing clear verses that are the essence of the Book and other ambiguous verses.' As for those in whose hearts there is a deviance, they follow the ambiguous part, desiring dissention and desiring its interpretation; and none knows its interpretation save only God. And those firmly rooted in knowledge say 'we believe in it; all is from our Lord'" [Qur'ān 3:5]. And the Messenger of God, may God pray for him and grant him peace, said, "If you should see those who follow what is ambiguous, those are the ones God named and so beware of them."

The human imagination can only conceive of someone who is restricted to the ten following terms: before and after in time, underneath and above, right and left, in front of and behind, whole and part; at the same time, all who are restricted to these terms are necessarily created and in need of a creator, and the Creator, Praise to Him, is He who has no need, the Benign.

Chapter 9[5]

And if His absolute existence is known, then it is also known that He has no other with Him in His power since if there were anyone sharing with Him, then He would necessarily be constrained by the limits of the created things from the necessity that the other independent being exist separately. And the Creator, Praise to Him, is not joined to anything or separated from anything. If He were characterized by being joined or separated, then He would necessarily be created. And the Creator being created is impossible, through the impossibility of overturning truths. And it is known by this that He is One God and there is not a second with Him in His power, in the words of the Highest, "Do not take two Gods Because He is One God So fear Me" [Qur'ān 16:53].

Chapter 10

And if it is known that God is alone in His oneness according to what is necessary for Him in power and glory, then the impossibility of imperfection in Him is known also because of the Creator's being Living, Knowing, All-Powerful, Willing, Hearing, Seeing, and Speaking; all this without imagining the modality of it. If He were characterized by imperfections then the existence of His actions would be impossible, because it is impossible for someone who is ignorant and weak and sleeps and dies to be a creator. The entire world testifies to the One who has no need, the Benign, because of what is in it: specialization, figuration, accord, disaccord, capacities, organization, rules,

---

5. Chapter 9 seems to be directed against the Christian idea of the Incarnation and the Trinity in denying the possibility of God's being associated with anything.

and certainties to the point that He, the Blessed, the Most High, is capable of all He wishes, "Accomplisher of what He plans" [Qur'ān 11:109], "The Living, the Everlasting, who neither slumbers nor sleeps" [Qur'ān 2:256]; "He knows the unseen as well as the visible" [Qur'ān 6:73]; "From God nothing whatever is hidden in earth and heaven" [Qur'ān 14:41]; "He knows what is in land and sea; not a leaf falls but He knows it" [Qur'ān 6:59]; "Not so much as the weight of an atom in heaven and earth escapes Him, nor anything smaller than that or greater" [Qur'ān 34:3]; "God encompasses everything in knowledge" [Qur'ān 65:12]; "He has numbered everything in numbers" [Qur'ān 72:28]; "Shall He not know who created? He is the Subtle, the Aware" [Qur'ān 67:14].

Chapter 11

And if the necessity of His existence in His eternity is known, then the impossibility of His changing from what is necessary for Him, of His glory and His majesty, is also known because of the impossibility of overturning established truths, since if the necessary were to be overturned into the possible, and the possible into the impossible, then what is universally accepted as true would be reversed. And by this it is learned that God must necessarily endure, that He has not ceased and will not cease knowing all created beings according to the specifics of their characteristics and the divisions of their species and their times and their complete number before their actual existence. And what is predestined for them is known by the All-Knowing in His eternity and it takes place according to His knowledge in a way that is incalculable and with an organization that cannot be puzzled out.

44. A TALE OF ROMANCE AND ELEGANT SOCIETY

Ḥadīth Bayāḍ wa Riyāḍ

Translated from Arabic by Cynthia Robinson

The Ḥadīth Bayāḍ wa Riyāḍ *recounts the passionate love between an Andalusi slave girl, Riyāḍ, and Bayāḍ, a Syrian merchant's son, in an unidentified but almost certainly Andalusi city. One afternoon, Bayāḍ spots a beautiful girl (Riyāḍ) and falls hopelessly in love with her. Due to the damaged state of the manuscript containing the story, there is a gap in the narrative, but it appears that Bayāḍ then seeks out the help of an Old Woman (ʿajouz), to serve as his counselor and go-between. The story is told in the Old Woman's voice. The narrative plays on the conflicting passions of lovesickness and the social requirements of proper behavior and self-control. Rather than communicating directly with each other, Bayāḍ's actions are mediated by the advice and help of the Old Woman, and Riyāḍ remains under the oversight and control of her mistress, the* Sayyida. *The Old Woman arranges for Bayāḍ to attend a gathering* (majlis) *in the* Sayyida's *garden, where he will be able to see Riyāḍ. The* majlis *is elegant, enlivened with wine, poetry, and music. Bayāḍ delights the* Sayyida *and her slave girls with his verses, finishing with a thinly veiled description of Riyāḍ's beauty. His impassioned words cause Riyāḍ to exceed the boundaries of good taste by singing a series of love songs, thus revealing her passion. Words that should have been pronounced playfully, as part of a genteel party game, are sung with a sincerity that throws Riyāḍ's good character into question. The* Sayyida *is furious at her emotional display, and punishes Riyāḍ. Meanwhile, the Old Woman hustles Bayāḍ away. The rest of the story consists of the trials and tribulations of the lovers. Unusually for Arabic love stories, this tale has a happy ending with a reunion of the lovers sanctioned by the very social forces with which they have been in conflict. Thus, although many elements of the story are drawn from Arabic literary conventions, this particular tale is also suggestive of contact with European romance traditions. Both the story and its unusual illustrations provide insights into the internal life and pursuits of a wealthy Andalusi household.*

This text exists in a single manuscript, written in Maghribi script and generously illustrated with miniatures showing events in the story. Details in the images and the script suggest that the manuscript dates between 1180 and 1240, contemporary with the Almohad presence in al-Andalus, and it may have been made in Valencia or Seville. However, the frivolous subject matter of the story and the nature of the illustrations make it unlikely that the manuscript was produced under official Almohad patronage. Likewise, the pedestrian quality of both prose and verse would appear to rule out any connection to the royal dīwān, *or scriptorium. Possible patrons include educated members of a middle or merchant class, as well as members of one of the anti-Almohad courts, such as that of Ibn Mardanīsh. (CR & ORC)*

Arabic poetry influences European poetry first

Figure 9. Bayāḍ playing the lute and reciting poetry for Riyāḍ, the *Sayyīda*, and others. From the *Ḥadīth Bayāḍ wa Riyāḍ*, an Arabic manuscript probably from Seville or Valencia, early thirteenth century. Vatican Library, MS Ar. Ris. 368, fol. 10r. Permission and photo credit: Biblioteca Apostolica Vaticana © 2009.

[After Bayāḍ and Riyāḍ had seen each other from a distance and fallen in love, the Old Woman came to tell Bayāḍ that Riyāḍ was the favorite slave girl of a rich man, a powerful courtier or ḥājib. The Old Woman speaks:]

He [Bayāḍ] stood and he sat, and he sat and he stood, and then finally he sat down and stayed still until I was sorry I had even told him the news. I thought he was going mad, and I didn't speak to him [lacuna; probably "until he had calmed down"] . . . Then he said to me: "And what else?" And I said to him: "What more do you want than that?! I told you the news, and you became pale and speechless, and you got all worked up, and you stood up and sat down, and if you had a bit more sense, you wouldn't have done what you've done! By God, you've got a feeble brain, and the proof of your feeble brain is that you fell in love with the *ḥājib*'s favorite, in the *ḥājib*'s own house, knowing his power and his high position and the greatness of his influence and his great love for Riyāḍ and her importance to him, and you being a foreigner, and obviously not from around here. You were really way off base there!" . . .

He said to me: "Oh, mother, what is the solution to this?!" And I said to him, "Oh, my son, Love without misfortune and shame is only possible through secrecy; indeed, from what we know of great lovers . . . listing all of them would take forever—they were all put to the test through speaking of their beloveds in poetry, through divulging secrets and making themselves notorious, and they fell into madness and fainting, following the wrong road until they lost all possibility of being pardoned, while of those who conceal their secrets, and veil them, not one thing is known of them! There is no mention of them—a lot of people fall in love but the only ones we know about are the ones who disclose their secrets and make them known."

The Old Woman said: And he said to me, "Oh, mother, what can I say to you, since you have told the truth? But Love is the invited guest of the honorable, and the ornament of the educated, and the companion of the elegant!" And I said to him, "But what are you going to do? By God, you saw that Riyāḍ is just as weak as you are, and firmly devoted to you. She's showing all the symptoms of love and conviction. Her Mistress[1] is fond of those who might please her in refinements and pleasures. She requests your attendance for the betterment of her *majlis*, and we have a *rendez-vous* for Friday, God

---

Translation of *Ḥadīth Bayāḍ wa Riyāḍ*, Vatican Ar. Ris. 368; English text from Cynthia Robinson, *Medieval Andalusian Courtly Culture in the Mediterranean* (London: Routledge, 2007), pp. 16–20, 25–26, 31, 33–35. Reprinted with permission of the publisher.
   1. The *Sayyida*, daughter of the *ḥājib*.

willing. If you attend, control yourself and govern your soul, like one who is owner of his reason, and if you look at anyone, let your gaze be toward the Lady, or at me, as though nothing at all were going on, for the best men are those who measure before cutting, those who plan before acting. If you see that your beloved Riyāḍ is possessed of gravity and silence, and gentleness and discretion, like someone who knows how to control herself, you may have hope of her, but if you see her behaving in a frivolous, flirtatious manner, forget about her and turn your heart from her, for reason is the best of God's creations and the best of God's gifts to his servants. Remember my counsel, oh, Bayāḍ!" . . .

The Old Woman said: And he said to me, "Oh, mother, may God reward you! Do you think you can find out if the meeting will truly take place, and what has happened in the palace since you were last there, and find out the truth about these matters?" I said, "Yes," and then I went to the palace and asked for permission to enter and was granted it. Then, once I was inside the palace, out came Riyāḍ, looking just like a star shining in the blackness of the night, wearing a thin green tunic and wrapped in a shawl of colored stripes over green, so slender I was afraid she'd break right in two, and the girl just about [lacuna] . . . as she moved first left and then right, getting everything ready for the *majlis,* with the slave girls there in front of her with flasks of perfume and wine, and different sorts of sweets. She had a cane in her hand, and she was using it to order the other girls around, half serious and half joking. I took her by the hand and drew her aside . . . and said to her, "Oh, Riyāḍ, Bayāḍ sends you his greetings . . . for love of you, so tell me, what ruse shall we use and how shall it be?" And she said, "Who is Bayāḍ?" And I said, "The young man, a very literary sort—you know, the poet you saw from atop the tree . . . you two had a *rendez-vous* for Friday!"

The Old Woman said: And when I told her that, she fainted dead away, and the slave girls hurried up, saying, "What has happened to our friend, Riyāḍ? By God, our lives will be dark and all hope will have fled if anything serious has happened to her!" Then they brought rosewater and camphor and splashed her face with it. . . .

The Old Woman said: And I put my confidence in her and left her presence and the castle; and I went to him [Bayāḍ] and told him the news, and we passed that night. And so the next morning we went toward the appointed meeting place. I walked ahead a ways, and let him walk toward the river, to the garden I mentioned earlier. I saw that he had brought a lute of very good quality, and I hadn't realized that he was a lutenist. When I reached the garden [lacuna] . . . I found [lacuna] . . . carpets, cushions, stools, and different types of delicacies, food and drink . . . as befits women of their class . . .

and I sat down for a moment, and the whole group of girls approached me and laid out silken beds and furnishings . . . worldly and young and by God I thought the garden [lacuna]. . . . from what I saw of their beauty and their astonishing appearance and their splendor and magnificence and . . . the painful wooing of his two cheeks . . . after that the Lady said to them, "Be seated!" . . . Then they sat down, and excellent food was brought, and different kinds of fruit were offered, all of which were astonishing, then she ordered more of all of that . . . and the male slaves stood guard at the garden gate. Then pleasure made its rounds, and the playing and singing began. . . .

Then the Lady said to one of her slave girls named Ṭarūb: "Oh, Ṭarūb, take the lute and sing something for our guest!" She said, "Yes, I'd be honored to!" Then she took the lute and tuned it and jumped in and started to sing the one that goes like this:

The arrows of a glance split my entrails;
 My patience was exhausted and my body was weakened.
And sleep fled me and love kept me awake,
 With the pains of grief and sadness.
What ails me is terrible, and I see no one
 Who might help me, in all of Creation.
Leave off your criticizing, then, I beg you, for God's sake!
 For it is the greatest of torments to me!

(And the Old Woman said:) And when the slave girl had finished with her poem, she kissed the ground before Bayāḍ, and placed the lute in his lap and said to him, "Do, my Lord, that which I know you to be capable of doing!" Bayāḍ took the lute and jumped in and began to sing these verses, where it is said . . .

Because of passion, flaming fires of love burn in my chest,
 And desire slips furtively to the furthest reaches of my heart.
Love holds absolute power over my soul,
 A power that would make the hardest iron melt.
Nevertheless, I consent to make Love my intimate companion,
 Even though it makes my entrails burn!
Its terrible power breaks me to pieces through desire,
 Causing me pain and tears!

(And the Old Woman said:) And when his paroxysm had passed, he kissed the lute and he put in on the carpet, saying, "That's the extent of my knowledge of singing," and the *Sayyida* said to him, "It was beautiful—you offered us something truly marvelous . . . true *badī*!² It's no wonder your name is Bayāḍ!³ Tell me something about yourself, whose son you are and all that . . ."

"I am Bayāḍ ibn Husain ibn Muḥammad ibn Idrīs,⁴ from the city of Damascus, in the *bilād al-shām*.⁵ I was traveling with my father until we reached your country, because of business, and my father left to go and work. He left me alone to enjoy myself, and I was amusing myself greatly here at the shore of this river, consoling myself and delighting my eyes in the views and the scenery, when, at some moment during the day, there appeared to me from among the trees a girl, and I have not been able to see her again since that day, since that moment."

And the *Sayyida* said, "Well, come here to us each Friday, because we are always here," and then she said, "Oh, Bayāḍ, would you recognize the young girl with whom you spoke if you saw her?" and he said, "No, by your life." The *Sayyida* said to him, "Well, this is the one, my good sir!" and pointed to Riyāḍ, Bayāḍ looked at her, and said, "Without a doubt, this is the one." Then the *Sayyida* said to him, "By God, is she not beautiful?" And he said to her, "Oh, *Sayyida,* truly the moon and the stars shine because of her light!" and the *Sayyida* said to him, "By your merit, and the truth of your affection and the superiority of your origins and the acuteness of your intellect, keep secret all that you see here, and don't go making yourself all hoarse about it— do the right thing, and the proper thing!" Bayāḍ said: "Oh, *Sayyida*, nothing at all will be said about this, for your servant is of the ones who accept wise counsel and allow themselves to be taught; I trust in God and in his Prophet to preserve me from such an error!" . . .

Then the *Sayyida* said, "Oh, Bayāḍ, you are a true poet and a proficient man of letters⁶— we only recite what we have learned or memorized and that which we know by heart, and that which we have heard from others, but you say that which you find within yourself, may God bless you and protect you, and reward you with the goodness of happiness, and all of us beg you to lend to us awhile your intellect and your being and your presence and your knowledge of poetry. . . .

Bayāḍ said to her, "Order me to say whatever I might, by means of my

2. The term *badī* probably has to do with eloquence, referring to a specific style of complex poetry, filled with metaphor and language play.

3. "Bayāḍ" can connote the possession of a fine character or a good reputation.

4. These are all the names of prophets, and at least two of them have Shi'ite associations.

5. Name for the region of the Islamic world (approx. modern Syria) where Damascus is located.

6. *Adīb.*

capabilities and the eloquence of my tongue, and my intellect; and with luck, my words will not offend." The *Sayyida* said to him, "Say whatever you wish; truly I have learned that you are not lacking in strength in what you say." Bayāḍ responded, "Yes." And then he sighed deeply and composed, saying:

Oh, you of the languid glances, genteel and of soft skin,
    Moon of the night and more resplendent than the sun
Delicate of complexion and slim!
    Her tunic of silk and her mantle are the very embodiment of beauty,
White skin, of a fresh, patent loveliness!
    She shoots a glance and her eyes wound all mortals.
In her cheeks is a most pleasant garden of beauty,
    And in her neck there is charm, how beautiful it is!
If she looked at the heart of an indifferent one, she would shoot into it
    Arrows of death, and he would never love another!

Or if she touched a hard stone, water would flow from it!
    Or if she spoke to a dead man, he would say to her, "Here I am!"
Beauty is resplendent in the rays which shine from her forehead,
    And from her wafts a breeze of camphor and musk.
She deprived me of the forces of my patience and I do not hope
    For remedy for my love in this world, if it come not from her.

(The Old Woman said:) And when he finished the somewhat troubled recitation of his poem, Riyāḍ and the *Sayyida* and the slave girls said, "That was truly beautiful, by God, oh, Bayāḍ; we loved it!" Bayāḍ said, "By God, there is nothing further left concerning this matter!" But Riyāḍ said, on hearing this, "Oh, ʿItāb, bring me the lute," and she took up the lute and tuned it and began rashly to sing these verses, where it says:

Truly the fires of love have burned in my heart
    And melted my body from the pains of love—
I was left without my soul, and I spent the night sleepless,
    Trying to contain the tears caused by the ardor of love.
There is an amorous passion in my soul, whose flames never go out,
    And my patience has betrayed me, as did my good sense.
Sorrows torment me with burning sighs,
    Together with a love lodged between my breast and my heart.
There is no one to help me in the torment of my love,
    Except tears that flow from my eyes like rain.

What consolation, what patience, can I expect for my passion,

Since there is no remedy which can free my heart from the torment of love?
Why is he whom I love distant and far?

And why is there no possibility of reunion? What ruse must the lover employ?

Then she began to cry, and her eyes filled with tears, and the entire *majlis* fell silent, right down to the last one. . . .

(The Old Woman said:) And when she finished her poem, the *Sayyida* said to her, "By God, in what have I not aided you, Oh, Riyāḍ? And what have you ever asked of me which I have not given to you? By God, I have sought your favor and your pleasure, even to the point of uniting you here with your beloved, the two of you here together in one *majlis*, with me present! I even took pleasure in the matter, just as if nothing at all were going on, and I said to myself, may God judge, may his will be done, for only He knows the length of my time, or of hers. And my father has asked me to give you to him, but I couldn't bring myself to do that, but by God, now I'll sell you in the market for nothing!" Then she tore her gown and stood up, enraged, and behaved in a most violent manner. The slave girls fled toward the interior of the garden. But they couldn't find the way out, and they were afraid of betrayal and shame. Riyāḍ came over to me and said, "My Lady, I have made a grave mistake, and now will come the rumors, and the disclosing [of the secrets]!"

The Old Woman said: And I said to her, "You did not do right by us . . . you ruined the *majlis* and the loveliness of the day," then I took Bayāḍ and examined him closely, and I took his lute with me and left with him, as though he were one of the slave girls. The guards didn't realize what had happened in the garden, and Riyāḍ stayed there crying, sad and sorry for what she had done. We arrived home without further incident, and Bayāḍ said, "Do you see, Oh, my Mother, what has been God's will, may the glory be his?" I said, "Yes, I see." And he said to me, "And what now?" and I said to him, "I don't know," and thus we spent that perfidious night.

45. JEWISH LISTENERS AND AN ARAB ASTROLOGER

Judah al-Harizi, *The Book of Tahkemoni*
Translated from Hebrew by David S. Segal

The Book of Tahkemoni of Judah al-Harizi (1170–1235) follows the model of the Arab al-Harīrī's rhymed prose Maqamat: in fifty independent episodes a frequently roguish wandering rhetor (Hever the Kenite) reencountered by the narrator (Heman the Ezrahite) displays poetic prowess, preaches or instructs, gulls innocents, or performs a combination of these.

Gate (or chapter) 22 of Tahkemoni centers on Jewish collective fate and astrology. From talmudic times through the Middle Ages, most Jewish sages and philosophers believed in the vital role the stars exerted on human destiny.[1] They differed primarily on the degree to which Jews and the Jewish nation were subsumed under this general rule. There were few outright opponents of star readers' claims (foremost among them was Maimonides); indeed several Jewish astrologers made names for themselves in Islamic lands.

In this tale of turnabout, a popular astrologer making outrageous claims, rather than a legitimate court astrologer, displays extraordinary powers. Telepathically he reveals and enlarges upon an undeclared question—when Jewry's redemption will come. In his restatement and expansion of the query he emphasizes Jewish vulnerability and persecution; that and his rousing the populace, combined with the Jews' hair's-breadth escape from death, make for a dramatization of the very predicament encapsuled in the original query—and an apt fictional mirroring of the ultimately precarious situation of the Jews of Spain. (DSS)

Gate 22: Of Fate's Rack and the Zodiac

Thus spoke Heman the Ezrahite:

When dawn [*zarah*] shown bright and I rode fresh and light, when the stars veered right and left at my command, when, on every hand, I grazed on ripe red flowers [Song of Sol. 2:16] in leafy bowers, lolled in shady nooks by gurgling brooks, took my ease in every myrrh-steeped breeze and did whatever I might please, even on such a day I made my way through field and plain and came, at last, upon a fellow weary and downcast, near disconsolate, at the city gate whom, at closer sight, I recognized as Hever the Kenite.

Haveri, my friend, what befell you?

Patience; I will tell you.

English translation from David S. Segal, *The Book of Tahkemoni* (London: Littman Library of Jewish Civilization, 2001), pp. 205–9. Reprinted with permission of the publisher.

1. For an overview of astrology in Jewish civilization, see *Encyclopaedia Judaica.*

Yesterday I was with Hebrew friends. At the city's outskirts we saw a large melee, a swirling tide, men pushing in from every side. Curious, my Hebrew friends and I hurried toward this stir, this dusty blur, to find that an Arab savant had arrived at the city gate, an intimate, we were told, of stars and fate, one who unrobed the future before it came, revealing mysteries that bore no name.

My companions ventured, Well, now, let us look into this prophet's schemes and see what shall become of his dreams [Gen. 37:20].

Advancing into the crowd we saw the sage, an imposing figure advanced in age, a broad instrument in his hands and thereon a net of crisscrossed copper bands wherewith he gauged the circuits of the sun, when and where her race had begun, wherein she spun, where her course would run and when be done, declaring the while to observers of the scene, Ask me what all upper portents mean—these I can explain, yes, read you heaven's hieroglyphic plain; but ask earth's mysteries and nothing gain: I have not spoken in secret, I said not, Seek ye me in vain [Isa. 45:19]. With me commune to learn the secret laws of sun and moon, the heaven's highroads, the five planets' thoroughfares and byroads: all, all, are *my* roads. I know all the planets' zodiacal stations, their towns and castles and habitations, their ascensions and declinations, twelve princes according to their nations [Gen. 25:16], who, though they in heaven reign, habit my brain, bound fast in my thought's thick chain.

Saturn's ills I know, know Jupiter and all the good his to bestow, and warrior Mars of the blood-red glow. I hold the sun in his might, Venus with her delight, Mercury, wise and bright, and the moon of silvered light. I know where the zodiac wends, where one house begins and the other ends.

If Fortune be a throne, I be its legs; if a tent, its pegs. I snap my fingers, the Ram turns lamb; I yoke the Bull and bid him pull; Pollox and Castor call me master; I am the lancer who skewers Cancer; I lift my brows and Leo meows; Virgo, sweet maid, is by me unmade; my mind's fierce flail o'erturns the Scale; the tramp of my feet sounds Scorpio's retreat; I shoot—the Archer makes swift departure; I cut the throat of the bleating Goat; frown, and Aquarius drown; I carve the Fish on a serving dish.

Swiftly, sprightly, quickly, lightly, I probe the stars' secrets and judge them rightly.[2] I bring them under the yoke of my law and mend their every flaw. Men bend their ears to me to hear my prophecy: I tell each man where fate will call him and what shall befall him from his first-drawn breath until his death. I say if his life shall be honey-sweet or he shall taste defeat; shall he root

2. Ps. 9:9 and others.

or roam, die at sea, in desert, or at home. I read his planet's flight, its risings and settings, its plain and hidden light, all the acts of its power and its might [Esther 10:2]. His least duress to his mightiest success are incised, through my art, on the tables of my heart.

Then, waxing poetic he sang:
Mine is the heart with a thousand eyes
    unciph'ring Time's scrawled mysteries.
Tomorrow bows to kiss my hand;
    Yesterday falls upon its knees.
Ask: Seer, shall I falter, stoop, or rise?
    Ask: shall I stride, or limping go?
Shall so-and-so prosper? Such-and-such beg,
    bear sons or daughters? I know, I know!
Say, son of man,[3] shall you win hoar hairs?
    Shall your life be the flight of the bumblebee?
Shall your feet root you out of your native soil?
    Shall your fingers stroke silver like winds the sea?
To each I unveil what the heart hath hid—
    and who can contend with the heart's hid power?
I disclose to each seeker what lies him in store—
    season by season, hour by hour.
Ask what you will, step forward and see—
    see that Time has engendered no other like me.

Said the teller of the tale: Hearing these wonders, the assemblage, thoroughly cowed, bowed low, then rushed like waves shoreward to learn how Time would bear them forward. They pleaded one by one: What will become of me or my son? Or my wife? Shall I have long life? Health? Wealth?

When he had done answering—or, shall I say, guessing?—each man rewarded him according to his blessing [Deut. 12:15].

Now I, ill-fated and star-led, turned to my friends and said, Shall we believe him or deny him? Let us try him, explore his strange hold, and cull his dross from his gold.

Yes, they answered, let us confirm him or undo him by putting one question to him: when shall salvation come to the sons of our scattered nation? Let us ask, of one accord, When shall the Fallen One[4] be restored?

So we came before him and declared, Bare your swift sword: tell us our question and win your reward.

---

3. Ezra 2:6 and many others.
4. I.e., Israel, Amos 5:2.

He answered, Set you each man his hand upon the sand and I will split Holiness' domain from that of the profane [Ezek. 42:20].

We did as he asked. Then he drew on the sand myriad dots and signs and crisscrossed many lines. Once done these intricate designs he made many a calculation, lifting an astrolabe before his face and fixing the sun in its station; then, with lines for borders and partition, he fixed the ascending planet in its exact position until each star nearly fell from its berth to bow before him to the earth [Gen. 37:10]. Long he sat in strange surmise, then raised his eyes to stare.

I swear, he said, by Him who fashioned earth and air, moon, and sun, the planets every one, who set the Zodiac turning and the whirling constellations burning, yes, who put each star in place: you be not of us nor do you the Nazarene embrace; no—you are of the accursed Jewish race.

Jews we be, said we.

Thereat the old man raised a cry: I lift my hand to God Most High [Gen. 14:22], who probes men's hearts with His all-seeing eye, who teaches His servant to understand the secrets of stars and sand, who divides the holy from the profane [Ezek. 42:20]; you ask me to explain deep mysteries and fathom thick-veiled future histories.

You ask, Shall a lost sheep walk through lions' dens and rise from the feast of a seventy-toothed beast?[5] What power, you ask, can raise a fallen tower, seize the helm of a sinking ship and wrest its voyagers from the maelstrom's grip? You ask if a scattered folk, laughed to scorn, can be ingathered in a world reborn? You seek the dead's rejuvenation and the nations' devastation; by God and His revelation, you ask earth's ruination! Sons of death [1 Sam. 26:16], you would see our kingdom destroyed; you would hurl us to the void! Said the teller of the tale:

After the old man had roundly disowned us, the entire congregation would have stoned us [Num. 14:10]. They spat on us, hooted us, booted us, dragged us hands and feet through street after street until, battered and blood-spattered, we were flung at the gate of the city's magistrate.

Spilling us in the dirt, our captors shouted, These dogs seek the king's hurt!

Now this righteous Gentile, before whom we had been brought, could, at a glance, discern a man's most secret thought. At once, he took us to a private place and bade us tell him what had taken place—the which we did. Thereat he said, Peace be with you, do not fear [Gen. 43:23]: no harm shall come you

---

5. Literally, "shall it escape the lions' teeth," the reference being to the nations of the world.

here. He called loud to a servant, Put these sons of perversity [1 Sam. 20:30] under lock and key! And so we passed the night in prison. But shortly after the sun had risen and the crowd had long gone, he bade us travel on.

God in his clemency had sent an angel to set us free [Num. 20:16]. And now that we have escaped that mob's wide jaws and raking claws, I say, Blessed be the Lord in heaven above and on earth beneath,[6] who gave us not as prey unto their teeth [Ps. 124:6].

6. Exod. 17:14; Deut. 4:39, and others.

46. JEWISH LAMENT IN THE WAKE OF ALMOHAD PERSECUTIONS

Abraham ibn 'Ezra', Poem

Translated from Hebrew by Ross Brann

Abraham ibn 'Ezra' (ca. 1089–1164) is often regarded as the last Hebrew poet of the Andalusi Jewish "Golden Age." Ibn 'Ezra' was very much a polymath: he was a Neoplatonic philosopher, astrologer, astronomer, Hebrew grammarian, seminal biblical commentator, and prolific liturgical as well as social Hebrew poet who famously served as a transitional religious and literary intellectual transmitting the learning and values of al-Andalus to the Jews of the Christian Iberian kingdoms and Latin Europe. This poem ("Ahah yarad' al sefarad") is a strophic lyric comprising four strophes of ten monorhyming lines each (the last lines in each strophe are linked by a common rhyme) except for the final strophe, which has eleven. It is written in a syllabic meter common in Andalusi devotional poetry rather than in the Arabic-style quantitative meter characteristic of Andalusi Hebrew social verse. The poet, who had already left al-Andalus and was not an eyewitness to the scenes depicted in the lyric, appears to be speaking as the personified voice of the exiled Jewish communities of al-Andalus and the Maghrib in the wake of Almohad persecutions there. In some respects this lament anticipates some of the images and themes found in Abū al-Baqā' al-Rundī's famous Arabic lament for the fall of Seville (Chapter 51B). (RB)

O woe! Misfortune from heaven has fallen upon Sefarad!
My eyes, my eyes flow with tears!
My eyes weep like ostriches on account of Lucena!
The Exile dwelt there blamelessly in safety
Without interruption for a thousand and seventy years.
But the day came when her people were banished and she became like a
    widow,
Without Torah study or biblical recitation, the Mishnah sealed shut,
The Talmud as though desolate, all its glory vanished.
With murderers and mourners this way and that,
The place of prayer and praise reduced to ill-repute.
That is why I weep and beat my hands, laments forever on my lips;
I cannot remain silent. Would that my head were a spring of water.

Hebrew text published in *Abraham ibn 'Ezra' Reader*, edited by Israel Levin (New York and Tel Aviv: Israel Matz Hebrew Classics and Edward I. Kiev Library, 1985), pp. 101–3. English text from Ross Brann, *Power in the Portrayal: Representations of Jews and Muslims in Eleventh- and Twelfth-Century Islamic Spain* (Princeton, N.J.: Princeton University Press, 2002), pp. 121–22. Reprinted with permission of the publisher.

I shave my head and weep bitterly for the exile of Seville—
For its nobles are corpses and their sons captives,
Their elegant daughters handed over to a foreign religion.
How was Córdoba plundered and become like the desolate sea?
There sages and great men died in famine and
Not a Jew besides me is left in Jaén or Almería.
Mallorca and Málaga are without sustenance
And the Jews who remained received a festering blow.
That is why I mourn, learn to wail bitterly, and utter so grievous a lament!
My howls in my anguish—let them melt away like water.

Woe, like a woman in labor I cry out for the community of Sijilmasa,[1]
A city of eminent scholars and sages whose brilliance eclipsed the darkness.
The Talmud's pillar bent, its structure destroyed,
The Mishnah subjected to scorn and trampled underfoot.
The enemy's eye took no pity on precious ones run through.
O woe! The entire community of Fez is naught
Where is the protection of the community of Tlemcen, its glory melted
          away?
I raise a bitter wail for Ceuta and Meknes
And rent my clothing over Derʿa earlier seized
One Sabbath day, its sons' and daughters' blood shed like water.

What can I maintain? On account of my sin all this has happened
And disaster has overcome me from my God, the Rock of my strength.
For whom can I hope? What can I say? I have done it all by my own hand!
My heart is enraged within me for my soul has been perverse
And from its land, its chosen territory, it has been exiled to an unclean soil,
Too shamed and dumb, too weak to relate its catastrophes.
With pain in her heart she hopes for the kindness of her Rock
To ordain redemption from enslavement while she seeks refuge in the
          shadow of His wings.
Ever imprisoned, she comes alive when she mentions His Name.
Tears on her cheeks, she is held by a maidservant who
Fires a bow directly at her until the Lord looks down from heaven.

1. The preceding verse refers to communities in Andalusi cities; in this verse the poet laments communities in Maghribi cities.

47. THE LIFE OF AN ANDALUSI MYSTIC

Ibn al-'Arabī, *Sufis of Andalusia* (1203–1204)
Translated from Arabic by R. W. J. Austin

Ibn al-'Arabī was born in Murcia in 1165 and moved with his family to Seville when he was eight. He lived in this city until 1194, and it was here that he was first exposed to Sufism, a form of Islamic mysticism. One of his early teachers was the Sufi Abū Ja'far al-'Uryanī; Ibn al-'Arabī's biography of his teacher is included here. This selection, written in 1203–1204, is set in the anecdotal form characteristic of much Arabic biographical writing. The passage not only details the life of a traveling mystic but also provides insights into Muslim Andalusi life. Ibn al-'Arabī became one of the most famous mystics in Islam, traveling to Mecca and the Near East before his death in Damascus in 1240. (ORC)

Abū Ja'far al-'Uryanī of Loule

This master came to Seville when I was just beginning to acquire knowledge of the Way. I was one of those who visited him. When I met him for the first time I found him to be one devoted to the practice of Invocation. He knew, immediately he met me, the spiritual need that had brought me to see him.

He asked me, "Are you firmly resolved to follow God's Way?" I replied, "The servant may resolve, but it is God Who decides the issue." Then he said to me, "If you will shut out the world from you, sever all ties and take the Bounteous alone as your companion, He will speak with you without the need for any intermediary." I then pursued this course until I had succeeded.

Although he was an illiterate countryman, unable to write or use figures, one had only to hear his expositions on the doctrine of Unity to appreciate his spiritual standing. By means of his power of Concentration he was able to control men's thoughts, and by his words he could overcome the obstacles of existence. He was always to be found in a state of ritual purity, his face towards the *qiblah*[1] and continuously invoking God's Names.

Once he was taken captive, along with others, by the Christians. He knew that this would happen before it took place and he accordingly warned the members of the caravan in which he was travelling that they would all be taken captive on the next day. The very next morning, as he had said, the enemy ambushed them and captured every last man of them. To him,

English text from *Sufis of Andalusia*, translated by R. W. J. Austin (London: Allen and Unwin; Berkeley: University of California Press, 1971), pp. 63–67. Reprinted with permission of HarperCollins Publishers.

1. Both ritual purity and facing the *qiblah* (Mecca) are necessary conditions for proper performance of the prayer rite.

however, they showed great respect and provided comfortable quarters and servants for him. After a short time he arranged his release from the foreigners for the sum of five hundred dinars and traveled to our part of the country.

When he had arrived it was suggested to him that the money be collected for him from two or three persons. To this he replied, "No! I would only want it from as many people as possible; indeed, were it possible I would obtain it from everyone in small amounts, for God has told me that in every soul weighed in the balance on the Last Day there is something worth saving from the fire. In this way I would take the good in every man for the nation of Muḥammad."

It is also told of him that, while he was still in Seville, someone came and informed him that the people living in the fortress of Kutāmah[2] were in desperate need of rain, begging him to go there and pray for them, so that God might bring them rain.

Although there lay between us and the fortress the sea and an eight-day journey overland, he set off with a disciple of his named Muḥammad. Before they set off someone suggested to him that it would be enough for him to pray for them without travelling to the fortress. He replied that God had commanded him to go to them in person.

When they had finally reached the fortress they found themselves barred from entering it. Nevertheless, unknown to them, he prayed for rain for them and God sent them rain within the hour. On his return he came to see us before going into the city. His disciple Muḥammad later told us that when God had sent the rain it had fallen on all sides of them but that not a drop of it had touched them. When he expressed his surprise to the master that the mercy of God did not descend upon him also, the master replied that it would have done so if only he had remembered when they were at the fortress.

One day, while I was sitting with him, a man brought his son to the master. He greeted him and told his son to do the same. By this time our master had lost his sight. The man informed him that his son was one who carried the whole of the Qur'ān in his memory. On hearing this the master's whole demeanor changed as a spiritual state came upon him. Then he said to the man, "It is the Eternal which carries the transient. Thus it is the Qur'ān which both supports and preserves us and your son." This incident is an example of his states of spiritual Presence.[3]

He was staunch in the religion of God and in all things blameless.

2. Al-Qaṣr al-Kabīr.
3. Absorption of the inner consciousness of the heart in the contemplation of God and its abstraction from the world of forms.

Whenever I went to see him he would greet me with the words, "Welcome to a filial son,[4] for all my children have betrayed me and spurned my blessings except you who have always acknowledged and recognized them; God will not forget that."

Once I enquired of him how his spiritual life had been in the early days. He told me that his family's food allowance for a year had been eight sack-loads of figs, and that when he was in spiritual retreat his wife would shout at him and abuse him, telling him to stir himself and do something to support his family for the year. At this he would become confused and would pray, "O my Lord, this business is beginning to come between You and me, for she persists in scolding me. Therefore, if You would have me continue in worship, relieve me of her attentions; if not tell me so." One day God called him inwardly, saying, "O Aḥmad, continue in your worship and rest assured that before this day is over I will bring you twenty loads of figs, enough to last you two and a half years." He went on to tell me that before another hour had passed a man called at his house with a gift of a sack-load of figs. When this arrived God indicated to him that this was the first of the twenty loads. In this way twenty loads had been deposited with him before the sun set. At this his wife was most grateful and his family well content.

The Shaikh was much given to meditation and in his spiritual states generally experienced great joy and hope.[5]

On my last visit to him, may God have mercy on his soul, I was with a company of my fellows. We entered his house to find him sitting and we greeted him. It happened that one of our company was intending to ask him a question on some matter or other, but as soon as we had entered, he raised his head to us and said, "Let us all consider a point which I have previously put to you, O Abū Bakr (meaning me), for I have always wondered at the saying of Abū al-'Abbās ibn al-'Arīf,[6] 'That which never was passes away, while He Who ever is subsists.' We all know that that which never was passes away and that He Who ever is subsists, so what does he mean by it?" None of the others in our company were prepared to answer him so he offered the question to me. As for me, though I was well able to deal with the question, I did not do so, being very restrained in speaking out. This the Shaikh knew and he did not repeat the question.

When he retired for sleep he did not remove his clothes and when he

---

4. This was a spiritual relationship.

5. The spiritual state (ḥāl) is the temporary action of a spiritual grace bestowed upon the Sufi in accordance with his condition and aspiration.

6. A celebrated Andalusi Sufi who died in 1141.

experienced Audition[7] he did not become disturbed, but when he heard the
Qur'ān being recited his restraint broke down and he became very agitated.[8]
One day I was praying with him at the house of my friend Abū 'Abdallāh
Muḥammad al-Khayyāṭ, known as the starcher (al-'Assād), and his brother
Abū al-'Abbās Aḥmad al-Ḥarīrī, when the Imām was reciting the chapter of
the Qur'ān entitled "The Tiding" [Qur'ān 78]. When he came to the place
where God says, "Have we not made the earth a resting place and the mountains for supports . . . " [Qur'ān 78:6]. I became abstracted from the Imām
and his recitation and saw inwardly our Shaikh, Abū Ja'far, saying to me,
"The resting place is the world and the supports are the believers; the resting
place is the community of the believers and the supports are the gnostics; the
gnostics are the resting place and the prophets are the supports; the prophets
are the resting place and the apostles are the supports; the apostles are the
resting place and then what?" He also uttered other spiritual truths, after
which my attention returned once more to the reading of the Imām as he was
reciting, ". . . and He speaks aright. That is the true day." [Qur'ān 78:38–39].

After the prayer I asked him about what I had seen and found that his
thoughts concerning the verse had been the same as I had heard him express
in my vision.

One day a man rushed upon him, knife in hand, to kill him, at which the
Shaikh calmly offered his neck to the man. The Shaikh's companions tried to
seize the fellow, but the Shaikh told them to leave him alone to do what he
had been urged to do. No sooner had he raised the knife to cut the Shaikh's
throat than God caused the knife to twist about in the man's hand so that
he took fright and threw the knife to the ground. Then he fell down at the
Shaikh's feet full of remorse.

Were it not for the lack of space I would have related much more concerning this man, of his amazing aphorisms and the discussions we had on
spiritual questions.

---

7. Audition as a general principle is the awakening of inner spiritual states through the
inner force of some external sound. More specifically, it is listening to music or poetry to induce
such states, as is practiced by certain Sufi orders.
8. Regarded as the Word of God, the Qur'ān must necessarily evoke responses of this
kind in properly receptive listeners.

Christian Conquest and Settlement

(Thirteenth Century)

48. THE CHRISTIAN CONQUEST
OF VALENCIA (1238)

Jaume I of Aragón, *Book of Deeds*
Translated from Catalan by Damian J. Smith and Helena Buffery

The Catalan Llibre dels Fets *(called in English the* Book of Deeds*) is a lively first-person description of the life of Jaume I of Aragón, who ruled from 1213 to 1276. The chronicle has often been called an autobiography, but it is doubtful that it was actually written down by Jaume himself, although he oversaw its creation. This passage describes final negotiations for the surrender of Valencia in 1238, after a long campaign, from its Muslim ruler Zayyān ibn Mardanish. Jaume's conquests in the eastern peninsula, may have been motivated in part by the desire of his second wife, Violante, to obtain the territories of Mallorca and Valencia for her children (at this point, the older kingdoms of Aragón and Catalonia were to go to Jaume's son by his first wife). It is not surprising, therefore, that the queen figures prominently in this part of the chronicle. After the conquest of Valencia, houses and land in and around the city were distributed among the Christians, while the Muslim inhabitants were allowed to leave in safety or remain under the king's protection. (ORC)*

When the third day arrived, he [the Rais Abū al-Hamlat][1] sent us a message to say that if we would grant him safe-conduct, he would come to us. And we sent him one of our nobles, and he came to our presence as soon as the noble had gone there. He said to us that the king of Valencia, Zaén,[2] understanding that the town could not be defended in the long term, and so that nobody suffered more harm than they had already received from us, had agreed that he would surrender it to us, on the condition that the Saracen men and women could take all their belongings, and that nobody should search or maltreat them, and that both they and he would be accompanied under our protection to Cullera.[3] For, as God willed that we should have Valencia, he, too, had to accept it.

We said to him that we would consult with the queen alone, who was

English text from Damian J. Smith and Helena Buffery, *The Book of Deeds of James I of Aragón: A Translation of the Medieval Catalan* Llibre dels Fets (Aldershot: Ashgate, 2003), pp. 228–31. Reprinted with permission of the publisher.

1. "Rais" (also spelled "Rays" in this text) is from the Arabic *ra'īs*, meaning person of authority, governor, or military commander. Abū al-Hamlat, son of King Zayyān's sister, was a very powerful man and his uncle's closest confidant, but little is known about him. The *Llibre dels Fets* provides a number of variant spellings of his name (Abulhamelet, Abulfamalet, etc.), but it was probably Abū al-Hamlat in Arabic. For more on this name, see Robert I. Burns, *Islam Under the Crusaders* (Princeton, N.J.: Princeton University Press, 1973).
2. Zayyān ibn Mardanish.
3. Coastal town south of Valencia.

Figure 10. Fresco, perhaps by a Muslim artist, showing the military camp of Jaume I during the Mallorca campaign (1229). From the Palacio Berenguer de Aguilar, now in the Museu d'Arte de Cataluna, Barcelona. Photo credit: Werner Forman/ Art Resource, NY.

in that council. And he said that he considered that a good idea and he left our chamber. We remained there with the queen and we asked her what she thought. And she said that if it seemed good to us, we should accept the agreement, because it seemed a good idea to her, as he who could have Valencia from one day to the next should by no means leave it to chance.

We recognized that she had advised us well, and we told her that we agreed with the advice she had given us, but that we wished to add one thing, and that, having added it, we would consider the advice good: If the town was taken by force, it would be difficult to avoid great disputes between the men of the army and us over vile assets or belongings, and we ought not delay that which our lineage had always desired to have and to take. Moreover, if we were wounded or became ill during the period of delay until the town was taken by force, all could be lost. For a deed such as that should not be left to chance, and it was necessary to make good haste to have it.

Figure 11. Jaume I of Aragón (1213–1276) commissions the bishop of Huesca Vidal de Canellas to compile a collection of Aragonese law. From the *Vidal Mayor*, J. Paul Getty Museum, MS 83.MQ.165, fol. 1r. Permission and photo credit: J. Paul Getty Museum, Los Angeles.

With these words, we sent for the *Rais* Abulfamalet[4] and replied to him as follows: "*Rais*, you are well aware that we have spent a great deal on this deed, but despite the money our men and we have spent, and the harm we have suffered here, we shall not give up fulfilling this deal, and we will protect you as far as Cullera, with all the belongings that the Saracen men and women carry there and can carry there. And out of love for the king and you, who have come here, we wish to do this grace: that the people may leave safely and securely, with their belongings and with what they can and want to carry."[5]

Now it pleased him, when he heard it, and he said that he thanked us very much, although they would lose much by it. Even so, he thanked us very much for the mercy we had shown him. And after a while we asked him on what day it should be. And he said that they would need ten days grace. But we said to him that he asked for too much, and that the army had been calm for a long time and it greatly troubled them to do nothing, and that it was not in our interests or theirs. So, after much discussion, we agreed that they would surrender the town on the fifth day, and begin to leave.[6]

When this pact was agreed between him and us, we said to him that he should keep it a secret until we had spoken with the archbishop of Narbonne, the bishops and with our noble men. And he said that he would do so. And we said to him that we would speak of it that evening, ordering that from that hour forward nobody should do them harm.

When that was done, and we had eaten and drunk and slept in a tent that was near our quarters, we sent for the archbishop of Narbonne, and he came. And when everybody was in our presence, we told them how Our Lord had conceded to us many favors and, among them, now he had conceded one to us for which they and we should thank Him greatly. And as they had a great share in this good fortune of ours, we wished to let them know it, so that they should rejoice in it: Valencia was ours.

When we had said these words, Don Nunó, Don Jimeno de Urrea, Don Pedro Fernández de Azagra, and Don Pedro Cornel went pale, as if somebody had wounded them straight to the heart.[7] And except for the arch-

4. Abū al-Hamlat again.
5. The Muslims were allowed to remain in Valencia under Jaume's protection. Those who wished to leave were to do so within eight days with what they could carry. Those who remained would have to guarantee to live alongside the new arrivals. There was a seven-year truce with Zayyān. The city would be ruled by King Jaume and his men, who swore to observe the pact. Zayyān was to deliver to Jaume all the towns found to the north of the Júcar (Xúquer in Catalan) excepting the castles of Dénia and Cullera, within twenty days.
6. 28 September 1238.
7. The nobles were furious because Jaume had taken the city without their help, without an opportunity for battle or plunder, increasing his own power at their expense.

bishop and some bishops,[8] who said that they thanked the Lord for this good and this mercy that He had done us, none of them began to praise it or thank God for it, nor held it for something good.

But Don Nunó and Don Pedro Fernández de Azagra asked us how that could be and in what manner. So we said that we had assured the king of Valencia and all the Saracens who lived at the town, men and women, that they could go under our protection to Cullera and Dénia, and that in this way they would surrender the town on the fifth day.

And they said that it seemed reasonable to them, since we had done it. And the archbishop of Tarragona said: "This is the work of God, and I do not believe that of these three things, one of them is not to be found in you at all times: either you have served God, or now you serve him, or you shall serve him."

Then Ramon Berenguer d'Ager said: "We must greatly thank Our Lord for the love that He has shown you. As that which your line and you have desired has now been fulfilled through you, we have to thank Our Lord."

When the next day came, at the hour of vespers, we sent word to the king and to *Rais* Abulhamelet that, in order that the Christians might know that Valencia was ours, and thus not harm them in any way, we would place our standard on the tower that now belongs to the Templars. They said that that was agreeable to them. And we were then between the gully and the camp and the tower. When we saw our standard upon the tower, we dismounted and we turned towards the East, tears falling from our eyes, and kissed the ground for the great mercy God had done us.

Meanwhile, the Saracens hurried to leave, inside the five days they had agreed with us, and by the third day all were prepared to depart. With knights and armed men near us, we brought them all outside, to the fields between Russafa[9] and the town. As we did so, we were forced to wound fatally men who wished to rob the belongings of the Saracens and seize some Saracen women and children. Thus, even though such a great multitude of people departed from Valencia, in which there were some fifty thousand men and women,[10] by the mercy of God they did not lose a thousand sous in value, so well did we protect them and did we have them protected until Cullera.

When we had done that, we entered the town.[11] And when the third day came we began to divide the houses with the archbishop of Narbonne, the

---

8. The archbishops of Narbonne and Tarragona were both present, as were the bishops of Barcelona, Zaragoza, Huesca, Tarazona, Segorbe, Tortosa, and Vic. All witnessed the surrender.

9. Ruzafa, a southern suburb of Valencia.

10. Burns puts the number at fifteen thousand (*Islam Under the Crusaders*, p. 76).

11. 9 October 1238.

bishops and the nobles who had been with us, and with the knights who had been given inheritances in that district. We also gave portions to the corporations of the cities, each according to the company and the men-at-arms they had sent there.[12]

Later on, some three weeks having passed,[13] we appointed partitioners to divide up the land of the district of Valencia; and we examined the charters detailing the donations we had made, and we found that there were more documents than there was land in the district, because of the donations that we had made to some men. There were other men, too, who had said they wanted very little, but afterwards it would be found that it was two or three times as much. Because of the trickery they had done to us, and because there was not enough to meet the donations in the documents, we took land from those who held too much, and redistributed it fairly, so that all had adequate land there. And in this way the land was divided.

12. See selections from the *Repartimiento* of Valencia, recording these divisions, Chapter 53.

13. Late October–early November 1238.

49. THREE CHARTERS FROM THE KINGDOM OF VALENCIA (1238–1259)

Translated from Latin by Robert I. Burns

A. Surrender Agreement (28 September 1238)

Valencia held out against King Jaume's crusaders so long that hardly any chance remained for a negotiated surrender. In this brief surrender agreement, the Muslims keep only their lives and movable property; they must abandon the city itself, and may remain on their farms only as renters. A seven-year truce stalls the crusade. The severity here contrasts with the usual Valencian surrenders in place. (RIB)

We Jaume by the grace of God king of the Aragonese and of the kingdom of the Mallorcas [Balearic Islands], and count of Barcelona and Urgell and lord of Montpellier, promise to you King Zayyān, grandson of King Lūb and son of Mudāfiʿ, that you and all the Moors, both men and women, who wish to go away from Valencia, may travel and leave safe and secure with their weapons and all their movable belongings that they wish to take and carry with them, under Our protection and safeguard from this present day when they are outside the city, up through twenty following consecutive days.

We wish and concede besides that all those Moors who wish to stay in the district of Valencia city may remain under Our protection safe and secure, and that they may make [rental] agreements with the [Christian] landlords who will own the properties.

Besides, We give security and solid truce, for Us and all Our vassals, that henceforth for seven years We shall not do any damage, harm, or war by land or sea, nor shall We permit any to be done in Dénia or Cullera or their districts. And if perhaps any of Our vassals and men shall do so, We shall make amends fully according to the amount of the said damage.

The more firmly to attend, fulfill, and observe these conditions, We in Our own person swear, and cause [the following] to swear . . . [the names of two princes and eighteen barons are here]. Besides, We Pere by the grace of God [bishop] of Narbonne and Pere archbishop of Tarragona, and Berenguer [bishop] of Barcelona, Bernardo bishop of Zaragoza, Vidal bishop of Huesca, García bishop of Tarazona, Ximèn bishop of Segorbe, Ponç bishop of Tortosa, and Bernat bishop of Vic, promise to observe all the aforesaid and to have it observed as far as in Us lies or as We shall in good faith be able.

Translated from Archive of the Crown of Aragón, Barcelona, Cancillería Real, Pergaminos de Jaume I, 734.

And I Zayyān, the aforesaid king, promise you Jaume, by the grace of God king of the Aragonese, that I shall hand over and surrender to you all the castles and towns that are and that I hold above the Júcar River, within the aforesaid twenty days, keeping out and retaining for myself those two castles, namely Dénia and Cullera.

Given in Ruzafa, in the siege of Valencia, on the fourth kalends of October, in the [Aragonese] era 1276 [1238].

The [notarial] sign of Guillem Escrivá who wrote this charter by order of the lord king for the lord Berenguer bishop of Barcelona his chancellor, in the place, date, and era placed above.

B. Surrender Constitution (29 May 1242)

During the thirteenth-century conquest of eastern Islamic Spain (the kingdom of Valencia) by Jaume the Conqueror, most places surrendered by timely negotiations. Here is a typical surrender constitution, given to a cluster of six small places around defense towers and setting up the Muslim community as a kind of state-within-a-state. As with most such treaties, the Arabic version is now lost; this copy is from the Latin (adjustments have been made to the obviously incorrect transcription).

This is a charter of favor and protection that Jaume, by the grace of God king of the Aragonese, the Mallorcas, and Valencia, count of Barcelona and Urgell, and lord of Montpellier, makes to the entire community [*aljama*] of Saracens who are in Eslida and in Ahín, in Veo, in Senquier, in Pelmes and Sueras, who placed themselves in his power and became his vassals.

Therefore he granted them that they may keep their homes and possessions in all their villages with all their districts, income, and profits, in [both] dry-farming and irrigated lands, cultivated and unworked, and all their farms and plantings.

And they may make use of waters just as was the custom in the time of the Saracens, and may divide the water as was customary among them.

And they may pasture their stock in all their districts as was customary in the time of the pagans [Muslims].

And Christians or anyone of another Law [religio-ethnic group] are not to be sent to settle in their districts without their permission.

Nor may anyone bother their pasturage or stock. And they are to be safe and secure in their persons and things. And they can travel over all their districts, for tending to their affairs, without Christian [interference].

Translated from Archive of the Kingdom of Valencia, Bailiff General, Real Patrimonio, fol. 238 (F. Fernández y González, *Mudéjares,* doc. XVII).

And the castellans of the castles, or the bailiffs, may not demand castle-provisioning [*azofres*] of wood and pack animals and water or any service for the castles. Nor are [Christians] to bother them in their houses or vineyards and trees and produce.

Nor may they forbid preaching in the mosques or prayer being made on Fridays and on their feasts and other days; but they [the Muslims] are to carry on according to their religion. And they can teach students the Qur'ān and all the books of the *ḥadīth* [Muhammad's authenticated example]; and the mosque endowments are to belong to the mosques.

And they are to judge legal cases under the control of their *qāḍī* for those Saracens who are in Eslida, about marriages, and inheritance shares, and purchases and all other cases, according to their Law.

And Saracens who are now outside the villages of the said castles, whenever they come back, can recover their properties forever. And Saracens who want to go away from there can sell their properties and other things to Saracens living there, and the bailiffs cannot stop them; nor are they to pay any fee for that purpose to the castellan of the castle.

And they are to be secure in going about by land or sea, in person and possessions and family and children. And they are not to pay any military exemption fee, or army substitute, or tally upon their properties except the [civil or rental] tenth on wheat, barley, panic grass, millet, flax, and vegetables; and the tenth is to be paid on the threshing floor. And they are to give from mills, public ovens, shops, merchants' inns, [and] baths that portion which they used to give in the time of the pagans.

And when they wish, they can go visit relatives, wherever they may be.

And the dead may be buried in their cemeteries, without interference or fee. And fines are to be given according to their Law.

And they are not to pay on any produce, such as onions, cucumbers, or other fruits of the land except the aforesaid. On trees and their fruits and on climbing vines they are not to give a tenth, but they give a tenth on vineyards and they give the *zakāt* [Islamic alms tax] on livestock according as they are accustomed.

And Christians may not be housed in their homes and properties unless the Saracens wish. And Christians are not to bring charges against Saracens except with a proper Saracen witness.

And the Saracens of the said castle are to recover their properties, wherever they may be [in the kingdom] except in Valencia city and Burriana.

And on beehives and domestic animals they are not to have anything except what has been said.

And if a Saracen dies, his heirs are to inherit the property. And if he does not have heirs, then the *aljama* takes over his property. And Saracens who want to marry [*contrahere*] outside their village may do so, without opposition from the castellan or a fee.

And those of Eslida, Ahín, Veo, Pelmes, and Senquier are tax-free on all things from the day on which the lord king granted this charter up through one year. And when that year is finished, they are to discharge the services as above. And the lord king receives them and theirs under his protection and safeguard.

Done at Artana, on the fourth kalends of June, in the year of our Lord 1242.

Witnesses to this matter are the Master of the Templars; the Master of the Hospitallers; Guillem d'Entença; Ximèn de Foces; Lladró; Ximèn Periç; the commander of Alcañiz; Fray Garcés.

The sign of Jaume, by the grace of God king of the Aragonese, of the Mallorcas, and of Valencia, count of Barcelona and Urgell, and lord of Montpellier, who approves and grants the aforesaid as contained above.

I, Guillemó, scribe of the lord king, by his mandate transcribed this in the place, day, and year affixed.

C. Confirmation of Holdings (2 October 1259)

Thousands of land grants went to Christians in the conquered kingdom of Valencia; each generated paperwork. Arnau de Romaní, bailiff of Valencia in 1257 and justiciar in 1258, received the village of Beniparrell and later the valley of Villalonga. Here the king's notary enters a general confirmation of Arnau's holdings to date, with the typical prolixity and formulas of a lawyer (notaries were a kind of public lawyer for contracts).

By Us and Ours We approve, give, concede, and confirm to you, Our beloved Arnau de Romaní knight and to yours forever, all purchases that you made from any persons up until this day in the city and kingdom of Valencia: of buildings, farms, vineyards, fields, properties, and whatsoever other possessions up until this day, both from Our royal holdings and from whatsoever other holdings; in such wise that all buildings, farms, vineyards, fields, properties, and whatsoever other possessions you and yours may have, hold, possess, and exploit in perpetuity, just as the other knights of the kingdom of Valencia have and hold the properties and possessions given and granted

Translated from Archive of the Crown of Aragón, Barcelona, Reg. Jaume I, doc. 261, Reg. 11, fol. 152v; Robert I. Burns, ed., *Diplomatarium* (Princeton, N.J.: Princeton University Press, 1986).

by Us to them [to be held] for giving away, selling, pledging, alienating, and using for all your purposes to whomever you wish, free and clear forever, without any retention by Us and Ours or any other person whatsoever; notwithstanding any point of the laws or customs of Valencia, or conditions required in any charters [saying] that the aforesaid buildings, farms, vineyards, fields, estates, and possessions not be sold or otherwise alienated to knights; and notwithstanding any other reasons, claims, laws, or customs by which We or Ours might be able to contravene [this]. But if you buy from Our royal holdings or servitors any possessions from now on, from this day forward on which this letter is written, as was said, you and yours are to serve Us and Ours for those which you buy from now on from this day forward.

Given at Castielfabib, the sixth nones of October, in the year of the Lord 1259.

50. A TREATY ON THE VALENCIAN FRONTIER

The Treaty of al-Azraq (1245)
Translated from Castilian and Arabic by
Robert I. Burns and Paul Chevedden

Abū ʿAbd Allāh ibn Hudhayl (known as al-Azraq) controlled a number of castles in the mountainous region inland from Dénia, and he was the last of the Muslim leaders in eastern Spain to surrender to Jaume I. His treaty with Jaume was drawn up in the name of Jaume's son, Prince Alfonso, and it exists in both a Castilian version and an Arabic version, written together in alternating lines on the same piece of parchment. It seems likely that both texts were written by scribes in Prince Alfonso's chancery, but the two versions are slightly different. For example, the Castilian text names al-Azraq as a vassal, whereas the Arabic version merely speaks of a three-year truce. The documents also bear different dates, but the Castilian date of 1244 appears to be an error, while the Arabic date of Dhū al-Qaʿda, A.H. 642 (15 April 1245) is correct.[1] Both leaders probably entered into this treaty in order to buy time in an ongoing conflict, and the differences in the wording may reflect their different needs. In fact, the treaty only lasted until 1247, and it would take Jaume several more years to definitively conquer the region south of Játiva. Al-Azraq was exiled, but later returned to participate in the Valencian revolt of 1276, during which he lost his life. King Jaume I died in the same year. (ORC)

Christian Version of the Treaty

Let it be known to all present and future: that I Abū ʿAbd Allāh ibn Hudhayl, vizier and lord of Alcalá, make myself your vassal, lord Don Alfonso the elder ˙ son of the king of Aragón, and I give you eight castles—one called Pop and the other Tárbena, and Margarida, Cheroles, Castell, Alcalá, Gallinera, and Perpunchent.

These aforesaid castles I give you with their villages, and with districts, and with pastures, and with as much as belongs to them. And of the aforesaid castles, I give you lord Don Alfonso two castles immediately, Pop and Tárbena; and I retain for myself Alcalá and Perpunchent, as an estate for me and for my children and for my family-line, to do with them entirely according to my will. And the other four castles—Margarida, Cheroles, Castell, and Gallinera—these I keep for three years in such accord that you lord Don Alfonso have half the revenues and I the other half; and those three years having

English text from Robert Burns and Paul Chevedden, *Negotiating Cultures: Bilingual Surrender Treaties in Muslim-Crusader Spain* (Leiden: Brill, 1999), pp. 36–37, 49–50. Reprinted with permission of the publisher.

1. See Burns and Chevedden, *Negotiating Cultures*, pp. 15-17.

passed, that I give you the castles free and quit, without any litigation, with all their districts and with all their rights just as is said above.

And besides, I make this agreement with you, lord: that of as many castles as I can win from here on through the three years, I give you half the revenues; and the three years having passed, that I give you the castles that I will gain, along with the other four, just as is said above.

And I Don Alfonso by the grace of God prince, elder son of the king of Aragón, receive you Abū 'Abd Allāh ibn Hudhayl vizier and lord of Alcalá as my cherished and much esteemed and very honored and loyal vassal. And I grant and give you two castles, Alcalá and Perpunchent, as an estate for you and all your family-line, to give, sell, pledge, or use entirely according to your will.

And I give you the revenues of the two villages Ebo and Tollos for those three years, and after the three years that you release to me those two villages, with the other castles.

Furthermore I swear and contract and grant that all these agreements hold, just as is written above, but in such wise that you be my vassal for the castle of Alcalá and for that which I give you.

Given at Pouet, the sixteenth day of April, in the era 1282 [1244].

Witnesses of this event:

the lord William Hugo

the lord Gonbald, knight

the lord Peter Maza

the lord Peter Sánchez Gurren

the lord Raimon de Montpellier

Sign of Prince Alfonso, first-born of the illustrious king of Aragón.

I . . . , by order of the same, wrote this charter and put my [notarial] sign, at the place [and on the] day and era recorded above.

Muslim Version of the Treaty

In the name of God, the Merciful, the Compassionate. May God bless our Lord Muḥammad and his family!

This is a noble decree, enjoined by the Exalted Prince [al-malik], the Heroic, the Most Fortunate, [he whose beneficence is] hoped for [and] sought, the Infante Don Alfonso, son of the Exalted King, the Divinely Assisted, the ruler of Aragón, upon the Most Illustrious Wazīr, the Noble, the Highest, the Most Eminent, the Most Exalted Abū 'Abd Allāh ibn Hudhayl—may God honor him! [Wherefore] the abovementioned Exalted Prince makes an agreement with him for three years from the present date, which is stated at the end of the decree, that his [the Wazīr's] property and retainer[s] shall remain in his castles, and that the abovementioned Wazīr shall give to the abovementioned Exalted Prince two castles, namely Pop and Tárbena, which he shall now hand over to him. The rest of the castles shall remain in the possession of the abovementioned Wazīr, namely Castell, Cheroles, Margarida, Alcalá, Perpunchent, and Gallinera, until the end of three years. But the abovementioned Wazīr shall hand them over to the abovementioned Prince when the three years have expired, except for the castle of Alcalá with its revenues and the revenues of the villages of Perpunchent, which shall remain henceforth in the perpetual possession of the abovementioned Wazīr and his descendant for the duration of the reign of the Exalted Prince. [Furthermore], the Exalted Prince shall give to the abovementioned Wazīr the revenues of Ebo and Tollos for the duration of the three years. When he [the Wazīr] hands over to him [the Prince] the abovementioned castles, namely Margarida, Castell, Cheroles, and Gallinera, he [the Wazīr] shall [also] hand over to him [the Prince] Ebo and Tollos. The Exalted Prince [also agrees] to give to the *qāʾid* Abū Yaḥyā ibn Abū Isḥāq, the ruler of Castell, the village[s] of Espel·la and Petracos to be his perpetually for the duration of the reign of the Prince, [both] for himself and his descendant. It is further agreed that the Wazīr shall give to the Exalted Prince from the four castles, which he shall hand over to him when three years have elapsed [i.e., Margarida, Castell, Cheroles, and Gallinera], half the tithe (*al-ʿushr*); and whatever castles the Wazīr obtains for the ruler of Aragón, either by force or by capitulation, the Wazīr shall have half of the revenue [from these castles] for the duration of the three years. But when the three years expire, he [the Wazīr] shall hand them [i.e., the castles which he has obtained] over to him [the Prince] along with the four [other] castles [i.e., Margarida, Castell, Cheroles, and Gallinera]. Written on the fifteenth of the month of Dhū al-Qaʿda in the year 642 [15 April 1245].

51. THE CHRISTIAN CONQUEST OF SEVILLE (1248)

A. *Primera crónica general de España*

Translated from Castilian by Simon Doubleday

The Primera crónica general de España *was commissioned by Alfonso X (r. 1252–1284) to chronicle the history of Spain and, more particularly, to celebrate the history of his own kingdom, Castile. The history begins in ancient times and proceeds chronologically until the reign of Alfonso's father, Fernando III (r. 1217–1252). This selection describing the Christian conquest of Seville in 1248 comes at the end of the chronicle. (ORC)*

On the Magnificence and the Wealth of the Army at Seville

The army [camp] that King Fernando had near Seville had the appearance of a great city, noble and very rich. It was filled with all kinds of things, and all the splendors befitting the opulence of a replete and wealthy city. It had streets and squares, and areas for all necessities, one right next to another. One street had rag-and bone dealers and money changers; another had grocers, and apothecaries for the medicines the wounded and those in pain needed; another had armorers and bridle-sellers; another had butchers and fishermen; and so on for every need that can exist in the world. All had their separate streets, all of which, by order, were measured and neat and well arranged. So a man who saw that army could very well say that he had never seen a city so rich or organized, that there was no army with more people or greater power than this, or one so full of noble and marvelous things. It was so abundant with food and all kinds of merchandise that no rich city could outdo it. The people had settled down with animals and with their property, wives, and children as if they were always going to be there; because the king had laid down and promised that from now on he would never leave in all the days of his life, until he had the city [of Seville]; and so God wished, and he fulfilled his will and what he wanted. This certainty of having it made people come from everywhere and take root as deeply as we tell you.

On How Long Seville Was Besieged, and on the Fine Appearance of Its Splendors

The blessed King Fernando had the noble city of Seville besieged for sixteen months, and he did not do so for any other reason than to strive hard for it,

Translated from *Primera crónica general de España,* edited by Ramón Menéndez Pidal, Nueva biblioteca de autores españoles 5 (Madrid: Bailly-Bailliere, 1906; reprint, Madrid: Editorial Gredos, 1977), 2:768–270.

for it was noble. It is a greater city besieged than any other to be found or
seen this side of the ocean or overseas, since it is so harmonious; and its walls
are extremely high and strong and very wide; high and well-spaced towers,
large and made with great labor; however well besieged it was, they had another town in its barbican alone. Even the Tower of Gold, how it was built in
the sea and so evenly constructed and by hard work made so delicate and so
marvelous, and how much it cost the king who ordered it built—who could
it be that could know or guess how much it would be? Then all the glories of
the Tower of St. Mary, and how great are its beauty and height and nobility:
its roof is sixty fathoms wide, and its height is four times that much; so wide
and so smooth and with such mastery was it made, and so fine is the staircase
by which they go up to the tower, that kings and queens and important men
who want to go up there on horseback can go up to the top when they wish.
On top of the tower there is another tower, which is eight fathoms high,
made most marvelously. On top of this there are four spheres placed one on
top of the other; they are made so large and with such great labor and with
such great nobility that in the whole world there cannot be any so noble, or
any equal. The one on top is the smallest of them all, and then the second
which is beneath it is greater, and the third much greater. But the fourth,
which is such a large and such an extraordinary piece of work that it is difficult for someone who has not seen it to believe, cannot be described: it is
made with channels, and there are twelve of these channels, and each of these
channels is five ordinary palms in width. When they brought it into the city,
it would not fit through the gate, and they had to pull down the gates and
widen the entrance; and when the sun strikes it, it shines like very bright rays
for more than a day. It has many other great splendors, quite apart from those
we have mentioned; there is no such well-situated and harmonious city in the
world, a city to which a ship comes by river every day; for ships and galleys
and other seagoing vessels bring, even within the city walls, all the merchandise of the world: of Tangier, of Ceuta, of Tunis, of Bougie, of Alexandria,
of Genoa, of Portugal, of England, of Pisa, of Lombardy, of Bordeaux, of
Bayonne, of Sicily, of Gascony, of Catalonia, of Aragón, and even of France,
and of many other overseas places, of Christian and Moorish lands, and often
many other places. For how can a city so finished and so complete, and which
has such an abundance of goods, as there are here, not be very fine and very
precious? Its olive oil alone supplies the whole world by sea and by land,
not to mention all the other bounties and the other riches there are, which
would be a difficult thing to tell someone who wanted to cover everything.
On its hinterland [*Ajarafe*] there were a hundred thousand farmhouses, not
to mention the taxes from which great, limitless rents come. According to

the source of this account, this was one of the greatest and most honorable conquests that has ever been seen or carried out in the world, to have been done in so short a time; because no one could understand how he could be lord of it and have and win it in so short a time, except that it was the will of the Lord, whose servant he was, to honor him and give him good fortune, so that he should have such a noble and perfect lordship, and furthermore, the flower of the ultimate of all honors: the great loyalty of the vassals he had. For there was no king in the world who had better vassals or so many by right, for we know that throughout the world the Castilians have always had this honor over all the other peoples there are, and are greater servants of their lord, and more long-suffering in any task. Thenceforth, God promotes his great prestige, for his honor and his birthright.

On the Year in Which the Noble City of Seville Was Won, and How King Fernando Populated It

The noble city of Seville was won in 1286 [Spanish era], when it was the year 1248 of the Incarnation of our Lord, on St. Clement's Day, twenty-three days of the month of November having passed. This King Fernando expanded his kingdom with great lands he did not previously have, and put them under his servitude, and kings and kingdoms recognized his lordship and entered into his vassalage. From them he levied taxes and tributes and had seigneurial rents; everything in the land that was under Moorish law was placed under his lordship and came to pledge allegiance to his will. As soon as the noble king Fernando was established in his city and had overcome his complete joy at the great feat God had granted as a reward for his work, he began to restore, to the honor and praise of God and Holy Mary his mother, the archiepiscopal see, which had been deserted and vacant for a very long time and was deprived of the pastor it deserved. A highly honorable canonry was created there, to the honor of Holy Mary, whose name that noble and holy church bears; and the noble King Fernando endowed it with good and landed properties—towns and castles and very wealthy places, and many other great riches. He then gave the archbishopric to Don Raimundo, who was the first archbishop of Seville after King Fernando had won it. After King Fernando had ordered all this, he also organized his city very well and nobly; he settled it with very good people, he allowed it to be shared, he gave property to the military orders and many good knights, and he also endowed princes and nobles, and he gave them great estates and many very rich homes there. For others, masters and skilled people, so that they would be able to live well there for the whole of their lives, he had streets and roads established, arranged with great elegance, as many as one might imagine would befit the

grandeur of a rich and noble and thriving city. He also partitioned the hinterland and had it settled and worked by many people who came from all parts
of the land to settle because of the fame of the great splendors of Seville. He
gave privileges wisely to his city, and gave it great liberties and freedoms, to
give honor and reward to the people who were there and who participated in
his conquest, and to pay them for the afflictions and hardships they endured,
and to compensate them for the great service they had done him there.

B. Abū al-Baqā' al-Rundī, Lament for the Fall of Seville (1267)
Translated from Arabic by James T. Monroe

*Little is known of Abū al-Baqā' al-Rundī, a poet from Ronda who died in 1285. This
poem was written in the hope of gaining aid from Muslims in North Africa to help
battle Christian armies. Although the fall of Seville is its theme, the text was actually
written in 1267, after the Naṣrid ruler Muḥammad ibn al-Aḥmar surrendered several
cities to Alfonso X. The poet refers to events in ancient Arabian and Persian history
as well as to the capture of Seville in his attempt to inspire military support. (ORC)*

Everything declines after reaching perfection, therefore let no man be
    beguiled by the sweetness of a pleasant life.
As you have observed, these are the decrees that are inconstant: he whom
    a single moment has made happy, has been harmed by many other
    moments;
And this is the abode that will show pity for no man, nor will any condition
    remain in its state for it.
Fate irrevocably destroys every ample coat of mail when Mashrifi swords
    and spears glance off without effect;[1]
It unsheaths each sword only to destroy it even if it be an Ibn Dhī Yazan
    and the scabbard Ghumdān.[2]
Where are the crowned kings of Yemen and where are their jewel-studded
    diadems and crowns?
Where are [the buildings] Shaddād raised in Iram[3] and where [the empire]
    the Sassanians ruled in Persia?

English text from *Hispano-Arabic Poetry*, translated by James T. Monroe (Berkeley: University of California Press, 1974), pp. 332–34. Reprinted with permission of the publisher. For
additional commentary, see Charles Melville and Ahmad Ubaydli, *Christians and Moors in Spain*
(Warminster: Aris and Phillips, 1992), 3: 145.
    1. Mashrifi swords were proverbial for their excellence.
    2. Saif ibn Dhī Yazan was a pre-Islamic Yemenite king and Ghumdān was his castle.
    3. Shaddād was a king of the legendary people of 'Ad of Hadramaut, who built a city called
"many-columned Iram" (cf. Qur'ān 89:6).

Where is the gold Qārūn[4] once possessed; where are ʿĀd and Shaddād and
Qaḥṭān?[5]

An irrevocable decree overcame them all so that they passed away and the
people came to be as though they had never existed.

The kingdoms and kings that had been came to be like what a sleeper has
told about [his] dream vision.

Fate turned against Darius as well as his slayer,[6] and as for Chosroes,[7] no
vaulted palace offered him protection.

It is as if no cause had ever made the hard easy to bear, and as if Solomon
had never ruled the world.

The misfortunes brought on by Fate are of many different kinds, while
Time has causes of joy and of sorrow.

For the accidents [of fortune] there is a consolation that makes them easy
to bear, yet there is no consolation for what has befallen Islam.

An event which cannot be endured has overtaken the peninsula; one such
that Uḥud has collapsed because of it and Thahlān has crumbled![8]

The evil eye has struck [the peninsula][9] in its Islam so that [the land]
decreased until whole regions and districts were despoiled of [the faith].

Therefore ask Valencia what is the state of Murcia; and where is Játiva, and
where is Jaén?

Where is Córdoba, the home of the sciences, and many a scholar whose
rank was once lofty in it?

Where is Seville and the pleasures it contains, as well as its sweet river
overflowing and brimming full?

[They are] capitals which were the pillars of the land, yet when the pillars
are gone, it may no longer endure!

The tap of the white ablution fount weeps in despair, like a passionate lover
weeping at the departure of the beloved,

Over dwellings emptied of Islam that were first vacated and are now
inhabited by unbelief;

In which the mosques have become churches wherein only bells and crosses
may be found.

Even the mihrabs weep though they are solid; even the pulpits mourn
though they are wooden!

4. Cf. Qurʾān 28:76.
5. Qaḥṭān was the ancestor of the South Arabians.
6. The slayer of Darius was Alexander the Great.
7. The Shah of Persia.
8. Uḥud and Thahlān are mountains near Mecca.
9. Al-Andalus.

O you who remain heedless though you have a warning in Fate: if you are
asleep, Fate is always awake!

And you who walk forth cheerfully while your homeland diverts you [from
cares], can a homeland beguile any man after [the loss of] Seville?

This misfortune has caused those that preceded it to be forgotten, nor can
it ever be forgotten for the length of all time!

O you who ride lean, thoroughbred steeds which seem like eagles in the
racecourse;

And you who carry slender, Indian blades which seem like fires in the
darkness caused by the dust cloud [of war],

And you who are living in luxury beyond the sea enjoying life, you who
have strength and power in your homelands,

Have you no news of the people of Andalus, for riders have carried forth
what men have said [about them]?

How often have the weak, who were being killed and captured while no
man stirred, asked our help?

What means this severing of the bonds of Islam on your behalf, when you,
O worshipers of God, are [our] brethren?

Are there no heroic souls with lofty ambitions; are there no helpers and
defenders of righteousness?

O, who will redress the humiliation of a people who were once powerful, a
people whose condition injustice and tyrants have changed?

Yesterday they were kings in their own homes, but today they are slaves in
the land of the infidel!

Thus, were you to see them perplexed, with no one to guide them, wearing
the cloth of shame in its different shades,

And were you to behold their weeping when they are sold, the matter
would strike fear into your heart, and sorrow would seize you.

Alas, many a mother and child have been parted as souls and bodies are
separated!

And many a maiden fair as the sun when it rises, as though she were rubies
and pearls,

Is led off to abomination by a barbarian against her will, while her eye is in
tears and her heart is stunned.

The heart melts with sorrow at such [sights], if there is any Islam or belief
in that heart!

52. ADMINISTRATION OF AN URBAN MILITIA

A. *Fuero de Cuenca* (ca. 1190)

Translated from Latin by James F. Powers

The Fuero de Cuenca *[Code of Cuenca; Latin* Forum Conche*] is an extraordinary document, constituting one of the earliest fully developed municipal codes in European history. In all probability the code was granted to Cuenca by Alfonso VIII in 1189–1190, and it formalized a considerable amount of regional urban tradition into an extensive municipal code. This law was born of frontier challenges from both Muslims and nearby Aragón, and the royal need to settle conquered lands in the maintenance of a permanent hold on the newly gained territories. These selections are intended to provide a glimpse of the pressing military needs that this life on the frontier engendered. Other selections from the* Fuero of Cuenca *are translated in Chapter 38. (JFP & ORC)*

XXX.1. The government of the military expedition and the guarding of the city

When the council wants to make a military expedition [*exercitus*] against the enemy, before it departs, watchmen should be placed in each parish who should guard and keep watch over the city day and night. There should remain also two sworn *alcadi*[1] together with an acting *iudex*,[2] whom the annual *iudex* leaves in his place. And these *alcadi* together with this *iudex* should concern themselves with protecting the city, as has been said. Also it remains established in the code that once the council has departed [on expedition], all strangers should be expelled from the city. After sunset, if the guards find anyone walking in the streets without carrying a light, they should seize all his belongings and put him in confinement until the following morning. In the morning, he should be brought before the [acting] council, and if he was a citizen or a son of a citizen, he should be absolved;[3] but if he was a stranger, let him be hurled from the city cliffs. The guards abovesaid should guard the city against fire, warning the house-dwellers that they should be careful of fire and if, God forbid, a fire happens, everyone should hasten first to the gates and secure them, and only then should [they] return to extinguish the

English text from *The Code of Cuenca: Municipal Law on the Twelfth-Century Castilian Frontier*, translated by James F. Powers (Philadelphia: University of Pennsylvania Press, 2000), pp. 165–66. Reprinted with permission of the publisher.

1. Parish representatives.
2. Romance *juez*; chief executive, drawn from judicial functions he exercised.
3. The Romance version notes that he is to be stripped and beaten.

fire. This is stated because on many occasions some, wanting to betray the city, set a fire so that, while everyone was trying to extinguish the blaze, they were free to open the gates and receive the enemy. Furthermore, if someone is suspected of potentially endangering the town, the acting *iudex* together with the *alcadi* should expel him from the city or hold him captive until the council returns. The same precautions should be taken to guard the city at harvest-time.

XXX.2. The pay of the guards of the city

Those [compelled to] remain in the town by the council [during a military expedition] should nonetheless have the same share of booty taken by the militia which is granted to any horseman [who did serve]. We establish this because those required to stay behind by the council's order had no opportunity to take any booty.

XXX.3. He who stays behind from the military expedition without the command of the council

All horsemen, whether from the city or the villages, who stay behind from the military expedition without the mandate of the council should pay two *aurei*. Also, foot soldiers[4] in the same circumstance should pay an *aureus*, unless they were ill or absent from the district of Cuenca.

XXX.4. The *señor* of each house should go on the military expedition

The *señor* of each house should go on the military expedition and no other in his place. But if the *señor* of the house is old, he may send in his place his son or nephew who represents his house, and he should not be a salaried worker. Wage earners should not excuse their masters from going on the military expedition.

XXX.5. What arms are borne on campaign, and shares their bearers have

The horseman serving in the militia expeditions who fails to bring a shield, land, and sword should receive only one-half of his normal booty share. A foot soldier who failed to bring a light lance and a dagger or a club should receive no share. A foot archer bringing a crossbow with two bow strings and one hundred arrows should receive a half-share of the booty for them; any substitution for this equipment should receive nothing. The horseman archer, trained in that skill, who brings a crossbow with two bowstrings and

---

4. Latin *pedites*, Romance *peones*. A non-noble fighter without a horse is clearly meant.

two hundred arrows should receive a full share of booty [for that equipment]; any substitution for this equipment should receive nothing. A person wearing a long-sleeved mail jacket with a helmet should receive a full booty share for them, as does a person with a short-sleeved or sleeveless mail jacket with a helmet. Mail jackets worn alone should receive a half-share of booty. Persons wearing only a helmet should receive a quarter-share. Persons who bring chains with twelve collars [for holding prisoners] should receive a full share. The share should be reduced proportionately for a chain with fewer collars.

XXX.6. Children and women should be prohibited from the military campaign

Women and children should not go on campaign with the town's militia, nor receive any shares of booty.

B. Charter to the Non-Noble Knights of Burgos (1256)
Translated from Castilian by Teofilo Ruiz

The document below is a translation of the privilege granted by Alfonso X (r. 1252–1284) to the city of Burgos and its non-noble knights on 27 July 1256. From the mid-twelfth century to the last decades of the thirteenth century, the kings of Castile-León granted the Fuero real *(a Roman-based code of urban law) to Castilian municipalities in an attempt to create a uniform system of law in their realms. These royal charters also included extensive financial privileges to the non-noble knights, that is, to those citizens with a house within the town's walls, a horse, and weapons. These concessions, which varied very slightly from location to location, followed more than a century of royal privileges to the towns' mounted militias and transformed the political structure of the realm. The king gained the support of the non-noble knights against an unruly and powerful nobility, and, in return, the non-noble knights, through these and similar concessions, gained a monopoly of the economic, political, and social life of Castilian cities. (TR)*

Christus, Alpha and Omega. Let it be known to all the men who would read this letter, how I, Don Alfonso, by the grace of God, king of Castile, of Toledo, of León, of Galicia, of Seville, of Córdoba, of Murcia, and of Jaén, found that the noble city of Burgos, which is the head of Castile [*cabeça de Castilla*],[1] did not have a complete statute [*fuero*], so that they [the citizens

---

Translated from Burgos, Municipal Archive of Burgos, clasificación 115 (27 July 1256).

1. Burgos, among the cities in the realm, had the right to speak first at the meetings of the cortes.

of Burgos] would have judgments as they should, and for this reason [that Burgos did not have a *fuero*] there were many doubts, many disputes, and many enmities, and justice was not exercised as it should have been. I, the aforementioned king Don Alfonso, wishing to put an end to these problems, together with the Queen Doña Yolant[e], my wife, and with my son, the Infante Don Fernando, give and grant to the city council of Burgos, to those of the town as well as of the hamlets, the *fuero* [*Fuero real*] that I drew with the counsel of my court, written into a book and sealed with my lead seal, so that they [the citizens of Burgos] be judged by it [the *Fuero real*] in all things for ever more, they and those who come from them. And [I] also [grant this law] to do them good and mercy and to reward them for the many services that they did to the most noble, and most high, and most honored king Don Alfonso [VIII], my great-grandfather, and to the most noble, and most high, and most honored king Don Fernando [III], my father, and to me before and after the beginning of my rule. I give and grant these privileges that are written in the charter.

And I order that the knights[2] who have the great houses in the town with their wives and children, and those [knights] who do not have wives with the company they have, and who inhabit [these houses] from eight days before Christmas until eight days after Quinquagesima Sunday[3] and who have horses and weapons: the horse of a value of over thirty *maravedís* (*mrs.*) shield, lance, an iron helmet, sword, coat of mail, armor, and quilted under waistcoat that they be excused from taxes. And for other properties which they may own in other towns of my realm, let them [also] be exempted. Their servants, plowmen, millers, gardeners, sheepherders—who keep their mares and cattle—and the nannies, [let them be also] exempted from taxes. These exempted servants and retainers are to be excused from taxes if their properties and goods are valued under 100 *mrs.,* but if over 100 *mrs.,* let them pay taxes to the king.

And when the knight dies, and his wife remains alive, I order that she retains this privilege while she is a widow. If she marries a knight with horse and weapon let her have the privilege of a knight as knights do. And if she marries a taxpayer [*pechero*] let her pay. If the widow had children under age, let them be excused from taxes until the age of sixteen. When they come of age, if they have horses and weapons and do their obligations as other knights [do], let

2. These are non-noble knights. In Burgos and other Castilian cities, they derived their income from trade, artisanal activities, and land rents. In other places, such as Segovia and Sepúlveda, the non-noble knights were landholders and engaged in transhumance.

3. The Sunday before the beginning of Lent or the seventh Sunday before Easter in the Catholic liturgical calendar.

them have this honor and exemption from taxes and if not, let them pay the taxes. . . . [The charter continues granting the council of Burgos rights of pasture and other exemptions.] Moreover, I grant that the knights can fence pasture lands for their cattle in their properties, and that these pasture lands be fenced in a manner that will not damage [the well-being] of nearby villages. In addition, I grant them [the knights] that the year that the [militia] of the city of Burgos joins the army by order of the king, that those serving will be exempted from *marzadga*.[4] And I order that no one should dare to go against, break, or lessen this privilege under a penalty of 10,000 *mrs.* and double that amount to [be paid] to the council of Burgos.

The charter had a lead seal and was drawn in Segovia by order of the king on 27 July era of 1294 (1256). A long list of princes, magnates, and ecclesiastics witnessing and confirming the charter follows underneath.

4. A territorial tax paid throughout Castile in March.

53. RESETTLEMENT AND REDISTRIBUTION OF LAND

Libros de repartimiento (1238–1491)

Translated from Castilian and Catalan by Thomas F. Glick

The Libros de repartimiento *were the legal instruments that recorded the transformation of the landscape of al-Andalus into new Christian kingdoms. They contain two kinds of information. First, they can be read for indications of the preexisting Islamic landscape. In general, we can perceive a pattern of rural settlement in eastern Spain, Granada, and Almería of hamlets* (alcarías *or* alquerías), *originally settled by tribal segments or clans and where land was held and cultivated collectively, and of private estates called* rahals, *generally owned by important persons.* Alquerías *were normally irrigated. The Christians preserved the* rahals *more or less the way they were and settled* alquerías *as if they were European hamlets, which entailed the establishment of metes and bounds where none had existed previously. In general, although the roster of crops tilted toward the Christian preference for cereal grains (on which the feudal agrarian tax system was based), patterns of irrigation were typically preserved intact. The urban landscape of al-Andalus is also revealed: when houses were granted in a town, a settler almost always received more than one. The standard* casas moriscas *were so small that Christians either joined two or more together or tore them down for stables or to rebuild in a larger format. Muslim mosques and shops were also converted into domestic space.*

The second kind of information has to do with the social structure of the newly implanted colonial society. Knights, footsoldiers, burghers, and peasants were all awarded grants of land and houses in accord with their social status. The Repartimiento *of Valencia in particular displays the varied provenance of settlers: archers, troubadours, royal officials, women, married couples, and Jews (one of whom is granted the house of another Jew who had lived there before the conquest). The* Repartimientos *contain a wealth of other data, covering everything from the number and kind of trees planted on each parcel to arrangements ensuring the continuation of the Muslims' irrigation systems. They generally record grants of urban and suburban land. Rural parcels with the Muslim population intact were not recorded nor were large, rural feudal grants.* (TFG)

Translated from *Llibre del Repartiment de Valencia*, edited by Antoni Ferrando i Francés (Valencia: Vicent Garcia, 1979); *Repartimiento de Murcia*, edited by Juan Torres Fontes (Madrid: Academia Alfonso x el Sabio de Murcia, 1960), pp. 140–46; *Repartimiento de Orihuela*, edited by Juan Torres Fontes (Murcia: Academia Alfonso x el Sabio de Murcia, 1988), p. 51; *Repartimiento de Sevilla*, edited by Julio González (Madrid: C.S.I.C., 1951), 2:13; *Libro de los repartimientos de Loja I*, edited by Manuel Barrios Aguilera (Granada: Universidad de Granada, 1988), p. 53; *El libro de repartimiento de Almería*, edited by Cristina Segura Graiño (Madrid: Universidad Complutense de Madrid, 1982), pp. 77–78.

Repartimiento of Valencia, 1238–1249 (issued by Jaume I)

To Pere Roiç, majordomo of the queen, the alqueria of Arriola and the houses of the wife of Urat Caçim, the silversmith, without ovens or mills.

To Entensi, the archer, some houses in Valencia and three jovates in Beniferri.

To Guillem Romeu and his wife Jordana, some houses in Valencia and two jovates in Campanar.

Teresa Gil, the houses of Abdela Avincenna and the orchard of Alhatiealquefen and five jovates in Albalat.

Jafuda Albala, Jew, the houses of Alcohen, Jew, and two houses in Mizlata.

To Abraham, moneychanger, Jew, the houses of Jucef Amnalcayt (near the estate) in Rusafa, of Sanç de Loriz.

To Cresques, Jew of Bellcaire, the houses of Faraix Abinçcoyde, Jew, in the Jewish quarter, and one orchard of two fanecates.

To Bernat de Tornerons, that mosque in the city of Valencia, for houses, and the dwelling called Alabida, in the Jewish quarter, with other houses belonging to that mosque, in Çabaçcalanum.

To Bernat de Terol, the mill with five sets [of] millstones that belonged to Amahomet Zayp Albacet, and a field adjoining it, property of Mahomat Abenhomar, which are between the Xarca and Açachar gates. We retain each year in perpetuity, one third of all the benefits of the mill and one-fourth of the harvest of the mentioned field, having first deducted the share and work of the millers.

To Guillem of Avignon, singer [*joglar*], and his wife Guasqueta, some houses in Morvedre, quit and free, and four jovates of land in the same district and four fanecates of grapevines; for two sous per jovate.

Repartimiento of Murcia, 1266 (issued by Alfonso X)

This is [the grant of] the great knight [*caballero mayor*]: Pero Monçon has twelve alfabas. He has three tahullas[1] of irrigated land in Carabaixa, worth one alfaba and three-eighths. He has a tahulla in Aduffa worth four-eighths. He has ten alfabas[2] less an eighth in Beniuiuas[3] and half an alfaba of unirrigated land. This totals twenty-four and one-quarter alfabas, including four tahullas of irrigated land.

---

1. From Arabic *taḥwila*, measure of agriculture land.
2. From Arabic *al-ḥabba*, unit of account for evaluating agricultural land.
3. Beniuiuas, like most other place-names beginning with Beni- ("sons of"), was an *alquería* originally settled by a tribal segment or clan.

These are middling knights [*caballeros medianos*]: Pasqual García has four and one-half alfabas in San Pedro.

These are the greater footsoldiers [*peones mayors*] of the Beniuiuas grant: Nicholas de Belchit has five and one-eighth alfabas of groves of trees and cereal fields [*alvar*] in Beniuiuas.

These are the middling footsoldiers: García Pérez de Calant has four alfabas in Beniuiuas and five-eighths of trees.

These are the lesser footsoldiers of Beniuiuas: Lop de Belmont has two and three-eighths alfabas in Beniuiuas and two and a half eighths of cereal fields.

Repartimiento of Orihuela, 1272 (issued first by Jaume I, then in this version by Alfonso X)

[It is ordered] that all the property owners of Orihuela, not only those who have grants, but also the other residents, be made to clean and repair the drainage ditches and the large and small irrigation canals of the territory of Orihuela, so that the water might flow without impediment just as it flowed in the time of the Moors. And let them apportion the water by tahullas to each one as he had it, just as they lawfully had in the time of the Moors. We order them to seize the properties of those who do not wish to obey and give them to whoever will uphold custom and neighborly duty. And if any should force the irrigation officers [*acequieros*] to give them water, let them forfeit their persons and everything they have to the king.

Furthermore we order that no one dare to plant grapevine in those irrigated places that were for cereals. Those who so plant let it be taken for the king.

Repartimiento of Seville, 1291 (begun under Fernando III and Alfonso X, issued by Sancho IV)

Don Alfonso . . . in order to populate and pacify the noble city of Seville, must know how many alcarías and estates there are, how many fig and olive groves, huertas, vineyards, and grain fields, and [he was informed of all this] by Ruy López de Mendoza, Gonçalo García de Torquemada, Ferrán Servicial, and Pedro Blanco the Scout [*adalid*], who went throughout the entire territory and found out how much there was. And according to the account they gave of what was in each place, the king ordered in this fashion, as it is written down in this book. They accounted for everything by measure of land and by measure of feet in the proportion of 50 feet to the acre. The king made grants by measure of feet, which was more precise than the land measures. And he made very good and great donations, and he apportioned them in this fashion: first he settled estates upon his uncle the prince don Alfonso de Molina, and his brothers, the queens and their nobles, the bishops and Orders, monasteries, his hidalgos . . . and on those of his company and many other men. And he took estates for his galley and for his wine steward and for his larder, and he gave grants to two hundred knights in Seville and he gave them estates apart, and every other estate which he acquired he gave to the town of Seville as is written and ordered in this book.

        This is the estate the king gave to his uncle, prince Alfonso de Molina in Seville: he gave him the village [*aldea*] that in the time of the Moors was called Corconia: and they said it used to have 30,000 feet of olive grove, and measured 15,000 feet, and 120 units [*almarrales*] of vineyards, and they included 80 units, and fig trees for 1,000 baskets of figs. And there were 150 of the best houses. And there were twelve olive oil mills, three in good condition; and eight huertas with their wells barren. The entire village measured 600 acres.

Repartimiento of Loja, 1486 (issued by Fernando and Isabel)

Know that in order that the city of Loja which I [King Fernando] conquered from the Moors, enemies of our holy Catholic faith, be more ennobled and honored, I ordered it be populated with settlers, wherefore it is my wish that houses, fields, vineyards, huertas, and other estates be apportioned among them. I order you to . . . inform yourselves of all the houses there are in the said city and its citadel and in Alfaguara and Joafin, that you make up deeds for all of them, and then apportion them to the knights and other persons who reside or may come to live here, following the order, instruction, and memorial which so authorizes you, with my signed mark, by my accountants. I further order that you inform yourselves by whatever way you best can where the bounds are, what lands there are, and in what quantity and manner, and likewise, the huertas, vineyards, olive groves, and other properties, cultivated fields, plots, and irrigated fields that there may be in this city, its surroundings, and district. Of all this make a book and a copy of it. Bring surveyors who shall measure and apportion the lands in this manner: fields, by units [*cavallerias*] of twenty fanecates of wheat each, and the vineyards and huertas by acres [*aranzadas*], just the way in which they are measured in Andalusia. Make me a copy of these and send it to me so that I can read it.

Repartimiento of Almería, 1491 (issued by Fernando and Isabel)

The form in which one may have residence in the city of Almería is the following: there will be five kinds of residents. Squires and farmers—to these go the estates preferentially. Then, married artillerymen. Then merchants and officials, to whom should be assigned huertas. . . . All the above must be married and thus should have a house, and those who are not should be given neither estates nor huertas. The rest who are married should be admitted as settlers, no matter what their class may be, giving them only a house with no estate. This is said because . . . the others who might come to settle here would be content with houses or with something more, if anything remains.

They should include the following persons: the squires with their arms. . . . And each one of the merchants and officials and cultivators who are to work, who have a helmet, cuirass, large shield, dagger, lance and sword and crossbow, or a musket instead of a crossbow. But if unable to have the aforementioned, they must at least own a crossbow or musket, with its appurtenances, and a lance and sword for a specified time until they are able to be fully equipped.

And inasmuch as some of the estates are too far away to come and go in one day, and all the others they wish, they can put there the senders they wish, whether Moor or Christian . . . And the Moors, wherever they come from, should not be rowdies, nor persons of low habits, but honest cultivators, examined by the alcalde, the surveyor and two Moors from Almería who know them.

54. A CHRISTIAN ALLIANCE AGAINST GRANADA
(1309–1310)

Ramon Muntaner (d. 1336), *Chronicle* (1325–1328)
Translated from Catalan by Anna Goodenough

The Chronicle *of Ramon Muntaner (d. 1336) is one of the best known and most interesting works of Catalan history, and it is marked by its author's abiding love for Catalonia. The author was a Catalan nobleman who witnessed many of the later events described in his book, which spans the period from the birth of Jaume I in 1208 to the coronation of Alfonso IV in 1327. The selection below relates to events in 1309–1310, when the rulers of Castile and Aragón made an unusual alliance against Muslim Granada. Whereas earlier treaties had reserved all Granadan conquests for Castile, this agreement promised the port city of Almería to Aragón. In the end, the Aragonese did not succeed in taking Almería, and the only Christian victory of the campaign was the Castilian capture of Gibraltar in 1309. Muntaner's account is particularly interesting for what it demonstrates of relations between Castile and Aragón. The treaty was sealed by a marriage between the two royal families, but this barely concealed the long-held distrust and frequent enmity between their kingdoms. The author's Catalan and Aragonese loyalties come through clearly in this passage. (ORC)*

When the Lord King of Aragón [Jaume II] had taken the Kingdom of Murcia from King En Fernando [Fernando IV] of Castile and had devastated much of his territory, the Lord Infante En Pedro of Castile and others of Castile saw that the war with Aragón did them no good and they, and in particular Don Enrique who was very old and wise, negotiated a peace with the Lord King of Aragón; so that peace was made in this manner; that the eldest son of the King of Aragón, called the Infante En Jaume,[1] was to take to wife the daughter of King En Fernando as soon as she was old enough; and they delivered her at once to the Lord King of Aragón, who had her brought up in Aragón. And the Lord King of Aragón gave up the Kingdom of Murcia to King Don Fernando, except what was of his conquest, which the Lord King En Jaume, his grandfather, had given as a dower with one of his daughters to Don Manuel, brother of King Don Alfonso [Alfonso X] of Castile; and, as that lady had died childless, the territory should have gone back to the Lord King of Aragón. And because of the great friendship between the Lord

English text from *The Chronicle of Muntaner,* translated by Anna Goodenough, Hakluyt Society Works 2nd ser. 50 (London: Hakluyt Society, 1920–1921), 2:587–593. Reprinted with permission of the publisher.
    1. He eventually became a monk.

King En Jaume and King Don Alfonso, his son-in-law, and between him and the Infante Don Manuel, the Lord King now wished to recover this territory and with good reason and right. So, in that peace, he recovered it, and it is Alicante and Elche, and Aspe, and Petrel, and the valley of Elda and Novelda and Mola and Crivillente, and Abanilla and Callosa and Orihuela and Guardamar.

*   *   *

And when he had signed the peace, the Lord King of Aragón thought that, as he was at peace with all peoples, he would attack the Saracens, namely the King of Granada, who had broken the truce when the King of Castile had left him; therefore he wished to take a complete revenge for this.

And he arranged with the King of Castile that they should march resolutely against the King of Granada in this manner, that the King of Castile, with all his power, should go and besiege Algeciras de Alhadra, and the Lord King of Aragón should go and besiege the city of Almería. And so it was ordained and promised by both Kings, that this should be done on a fixed day, and that neither should abandon the war nor his siege without the leave of the other. And this was wisely ordained in order that the King of Granada should be obliged to divide his followers in two parts. And so it was done; the King of Castile went to besiege Algeciras and the Lord King of Aragón, Almería, which is a very fine city. And the siege lasted full nine months; the Lord King conducted it with catapults and with mangonels and with all the apparel belonging to a siege. The Lord King of Aragón came to it very powerfully apparelled, with many Catalan and Aragonese *richs homens* and barons. And amongst others came the Lord Infante En Ferrando, son of the Lord King of Mallorca, very richly apparelled with a hundred armed horses and with many men afoot and with galleys and lenys[2] which brought the horses and victuals and companies and catapults. For the Lord King of Mallorca wished him to come to the assistance of the Lord King of Aragón well arrayed at all points, as one who was himself one of the most accomplished knights of the world. And this was well apparent in all the feats which fell to his share in the siege, for, amongst other affairs, he had three times encounters with the Moors and he carried off the palm of chivalry from all men.

*   *   *

2. A type of ship.

It happened one day, on the eve of Saint Bartholomew, that the Moors had all got ready, all there were in the Kingdom of Granada, against the Lord King of Aragón, through the fault of the King of Castile, who raised the siege he was conducting without letting the Lord King of Aragón know anything about it. And it was a great crime of the King of Castile not to let the Lord King of Aragón know that he was raising the siege, for it put the Lord King of Aragón into great hazard; he was surprised by so many people who came upon him, a thing he had not expected. And so all the power of Granada came, on the eve of Saint Bartholomew, upon the host of the Lord King of Aragón. And he, when he saw this great power, marvelled much; but he was nothing dismayed by it, but ordained that the Lord Infante En Ferrando should stay with his company near the city, at a place called the esperonte[3] of Almería, in order that if anyone should attempt to issue from the city to attack the besiegers whilst he was fighting with the Saracens, the Lord Infante should prevent it. And I wish you to know that it was the most threatened point there was, and therefore the Lord Infante chose it, otherwise he would not have remained there. What shall I tell you? When the Lord King was ready with all his host to attack the host of the Saracens, there came out of Almería by the esperonte, a son of the King of Guadix with full three hundred horsemen and many afoot, wading through the sea, with water up to the horses' girths. And the cry of alarm arose in the tents of the Lord Infante. And he, very handsomely arrayed, with his company, issued forth with all his chivalry in very good order. And when the Moors had passed the esperonte, this son of the Moorish King, who was an expert knight and one of the handsomest of the world, came on first with a javelin in his hand, crying:—"Ani be ha Soltan!"[4] No other words issued from his mouth. And the Lord Infante asked "What is he saying?" And the interpreters who were near him said:— "My Lord, he says that he is a King's son." Said the Lord Infante:—"He is a King's son, and so, too, am I." And the Lord Infante rushed towards him and before he could get near him, he had killed more than six knights with his own hand and had broken his lance; and then he seized his sword and, sword in hand, made room for himself, until he came to him who was shouting that he was a King's son. And he, seeing him come and knowing that he was the Infante, came towards him and gave him such a blow with his sword that the last quarter of the Infante's shield fell to the ground (and it was a most marvellous blow) and he cried:—"Ani be ha Soltan!" But the Lord Infante gave him such a blow with his sword on the head that he cut it open to the teeth,

3. A projecting angle in front of a door or gate.
4. "I am the son of the Sultan!"

and he fell dead to the ground. And at once the Saracens were discomfited and those who could return by the esperonte saved their lives, but the others all died and so the Lord Infante overcame those of the city.

And whilst this clamour at the esperonte was going on, the Moors of the host were preparing to attack, and the Lord King wished to attack, but En Guillem de Anglesola and En Asberto de Mediona dismounted and seizing the King's bridle said:—"My Lord, what is this? On no account do this; there are those already in the van who will attack and do it well." The Lord King was so desirous of attacking that his heart was nearly broken. And I tell you that if he had not had those *richs homens* and other honorable men to hold him back, he would not have refrained, but he could not help himself. And so the van attacked amongst the Moors and vanquished them; and, assuredly, the Moors would have lost all their chivalry on that day, had it not been that the pursuit had to stop, for fear that others might come and attack the besiegers from another side. Nevertheless innumerable Moors died that day, horse and foot; it was the greatest feat ever done and the greatest victory. From that day the Moors so feared the Christians that they dared not resist them. What shall I tell you? The Lord King returned with all his followers, with great joy and gladness, to the tents where they found that the Lord Infante En Ferrando had performed as many feats of arms as Roland could have done, had he been there.[5] And on the following day they celebrated worthily the feast of the blessed Saint Bartholomew, apostle.

And when the King of Granada saw the marvellous deed performed by the Lord King of Aragón and his followers, he held himself for lost, for he had not thought at all that there was so much strenuousness and so much valor in them. And so he chose his messengers, whom he sent to the Lord King of Aragón to tell him that he begged him to raise the siege, for winter was coming upon him; and that he might see well that he was working for people in whom he would find no merit; that the Castilians had raised the siege of Algeciras in order that the King of Aragón and his followers should be killed; that this conquest was not worthy of him; and so he begged him to be pleased to make a truce with him. And he offered always to support him in war against all the men in the world, and again that, for love of him, he would liberate all the Christian captives he had, which was a considerable matter.

And when the Lord King had heard the message, he called his council together and put before them what the King of Granada had sent to tell him. And in the end the advice was that, for three reasons especially, he should

---

5. Roland was reputed to have been the bravest of Charlemagne's knights and was the hero of the epic poem *The Song of Roland*. In this tale, he is killed by Muslims.

return to his country. The first reason was that winter was coming upon him; the other was the great ingratitude the Castilians had shown him; and the third was the surrendering of the Christian captives, which was a greater thing than if he had taken two cities of Almería. And so it was agreed and the truce confirmed.

And so the Lord King had all his followers collected with all their property. And when they were collected the Lord King, with all his followers and all their property, returned, some by sea and some by land to the Kingdom of Valencia. And so you may understand whether the Lord King of Aragón is desirous of increasing and multiplying the Holy Catholic faith, when he went to conduct a siege in a conquest which was none of his. You may all be certain that, if the Kingdom of Granada had been of his conquest, it would long ago have belonged to the Christians.

Society Under Christian Rule
(Twelfth to Fourteenth Centuries)

Map 4. The Iberian Peninsula, 1264–1492.

55. EVERYDAY LIFE IN THE CROWN OF ARAGÓN

This selection of documents from Vic, Huesca, and Mallorca spans the period from 1101 to 1269. The texts demonstrate the variety of situations and personal relationships in which written documents were used in the Crown of Aragón, including arrangements for inheritance, landholding, protection, manumission, and legal disputes. (ORC)

A. Three Documents from Vic (1101–1269)
Translated from Latin by Paul Freedman

The three charters translated below show relations between lords and peasants in twelfth- and thirteenth-century Catalonia. They are from the cathedral archives of Vic, which lies about thirty miles north of Barcelona. Until the late eleventh century, most peasants were tenants, that is, they held their land from a lord, but the rent paid was usually not burdensome, and they were not subject to that lord by any personal bond. This began to change in the late eleventh and twelfth centuries as lords imposed harsher forms of control and tenants became serfs—unfree peasants bound to their lord by more than the simple payment of rent.

In Arxiu Capitular, calaix 6, 2213, a free peasant, Arbert, is willing to dispute the seigneurial rights claimed by the powerful local baron, Ramon Bermund of Taradell, by undergoing the ordeal of boiling water. Ramon Bermund and his supporters refuse to accept the result even before the ordeal is to take place, and a "compromise" is worked out whereby Arbert is compelled to acknowledge the unwanted lordship of Ramon Bermund.

The two thirteenth-century charters show a more routine form of seigneurial control over peasants. Pere de Comalada recognizes that his body and property belong to the canon-provost of the cathedral chapter of Vic. In many documents of this type, the tenant bound not only himself but his posterity to the lord. Arxiu Capitular, calaix 7, 223, is an example of the freeing of a dependent tenant in return for money. Ermessendis is redeemed from the lordship of Berenguer along with her offspring. (PF)

Vic, Arxiu Capitular, calaix 6, 2213, 27 April 1101 (copy made in 1172)

Ramon Bermund de Taradell and his followers claim rights over land held by Arbert Salamó. Arbert is willing to prove his claim by ordeal but a compromise is arranged whereby he will make an annual payment in return for protection.

Let it be known to all men now and in the future that I, Ramon Bermund, along with my castellans Bernat Berenguer and Bernat Guillem, argued a legal dispute with Arbert Salamó and his heirs before the entrance to the church of Santa Eugenia in the presence of many clerics, knights, and rustics. I, Ramon Bermund, and my castellans claimed rights of protection and jurisdiction [*baiulia*] over the manse of Serra. Arbert and his heirs responded that we never had this right, nor anyone of our family before us. Judging this case Guillem Borrell d'Eures and Pere Miró de Muntanyola decided that Ramon Bermund and his castellans should prove that this right of protection and jurisdiction had been exercised in the past by the lords of Taradell, for which they could supply no evidence. And afterwards Arbert was ready to prove [his claim] by his body. When mass had been said and Arbert was about to place his hand in the cauldron that boiled in front of the church of Santa Eugenia, those above-mentioned [opponents of his] cried that they would not accept this decision. After this, with the counsel of Guillem Ramon de Taradell, Guillem Borrell, Bernat Ermengol, and Dalmau, brothers, and Pere Miró, Berenguer Amalric, Pere Sumar, Ramon Guifre, Bernat Guillem, and Amat Salamó and many other men who were present, it was decided that Arbert and his heirs should give 3 *quarters* of feed-grain and 3 hens to Ramon Bermund and his castellans. And for this annual payment [*censum*] that they received, they would defend Arbert and his progeny, their bodies, wealth, and property everywhere against all men and women and if they failed in this, they should not receive the payments. And if they defended faithfully as described above, they should receive the above-mentioned payments, and it is acknowledged that they should not extort anything, nor receive anything beyond this annual payment. Done 5 kalends of May in the 40th year of the reign of King Philip [Philip I of France]. Signed: Ramon Bermund, Bernat Berenguer, Bernat Guillem: we who praise, define and confirm as written above. Signed Pere Sumer, Ramon Gaufred, Amat Salamó, Bernat Guillem.

Guillem, priest, wrote this on the day and in the year given above. Ramon, priest, faithfully transcribed this on 15 kalends of July, in the 25th year of reign of King Louis the Younger [Louis VII of France].

Vic, Arxiu Capitular, Liber dotationum antiquarum, folio 146v, 18 March 1212

Pere de Comalada recognizes that he and his possessions belong to Gilabert de Muntral, canon of Vic and provost for the month of October. Gilabert promises to protect Pere.

Be it known to all that I, Pere de Comalada, son of Bonadona of Pradel, recognize my body and all my things, movable and immovable, to belong to you Gilabert de Muntral, canon of Vic and provost for the month of October, in perpetuity. And that therefore I may not claim any lord other than you and your successors as provost. For greater security, I agree to give to you, as was customary to give your predecessor provosts, for the rest of my life, annually on the kalends of October, one pair of pullets or four deniers, whichever I shall elect. And I, Gilabert, provost, agree with you Pere de Comalada, for myself and for the Church of Vic, to maintain and defend you and yours wherever as our own possessions. Done on the 15 kalends of April in the year of the Lord 1211. Signed Pere de Comalada. Signed Vidal de Santa Cecília, bailiff. Signed Bernat Coqui. Signed Bernat de Prat Santa Cecília. Signum Bernat de Soler. I, Gilabert de Muntral, provost for the month of October, sign.

Peter, priest, who wrote this on the day and in the year as above.

Vic, Arxiu Capitular, calaix 7, 223, 23 December 1269

Berenguer de Sentfores manumits Ermessenda and her children and possessions for eleven ternal sous of Barcelona.

Be it known to all that I, Berenguer de Sentfores, for myself and my successors, by this public instrument absolve and release [*diffinio*] without any reservation on my part or by any of mine you, Ermessenda, daughter of Pere Foget, deceased, and his wife María of the parish of Sentfores, along with all your children and all your and their possessions, movable and immovable, which you now or shall have. Such that, moreover, I affirm that neither I nor any successor of mine nor anyone acting for me or in my name shall nor can demand or require anything of you, your children or possessions by reason of lordship wherever you are or wherever you dwell. By reason of this release made by me to you, I acknowledge receipt of eleven Barcelona sous of ternal coinage,[1] renouncing any exception by reason of uncounted money. Done 10 kalends of January in the year of the Lord 1269. Signed Berenguer de Sentfores, the aforesaid who enacts and signs this. Witnesses in this matter are Arnau de Soler, Simon de Benencasa. Signed B. de Senfores who signs this. Pere de Vilar de Pau, bailiff, who signs this.

Signed Pere d'Avreis, canon of Vic and notary public of the town of Vic.

Signed Pere de Alibergo, sworn scribe who wrote and closed this by order of Pere d'Avreis, notary of Vic, on the day and in the year as above.

---

1. From *de terno,* a measure of silver content of coins, three-twelfths fine, instituted by a coinage reform of Jaume I in 1258.

B. Three Documents from Huesca (1158–1207)
Translated from Latin by Lynn H. Nelson

Muslim Huesca was a city with a population of between five thousand and eight thousand when it was conquered in 1096, after a long siege and decisive battle, by the Aragonese King Pedro I (r. 1094–1104). The city was pleasantly situated, surrounded by orchards and gardens irrigated from the river Isuela that flowed nearby. It ceased to be the royal capital after the capture of Zaragoza in 1118, and most of its noble inhabitants sold their property in Huesca and moved. Although this city regained its status as royal capital by 1138, few nobles moved back. Huesca thus became predominantly a city of merchants and artisans. However, since the district had little in the way of natural resources or raw materials and was not located on any major active trade routes, it also lost its attraction for merchants. For this reason the artisan class, most particularly the shoemakers and butchers, became the leading citizens of the city, sharing eminence with royal officials and the personnel of the cathedral.

The following three documents, selected from more than one thousand surviving from the period, are representative of the social and economic milieu of the times. In their pursuit of wealth, the middle-class inhabitants of Huesca turned their hands to many different enterprises at once. They were simultaneously artisans, retailers, bankers, agricultural entrepreneurs, real estate dealers, and processors and wholesalers of agricultural commodities. (LHN)

Mortgage Contract (CHDU no. 227, dated August 1158)

María, a widow, mortgages a field to don Jofre Isaac and his wife María. Jofre Isaac was a shoemaker, but also one of the more important moneylenders in the city. This particular type of contract served some important functions. The lender received any rents, renders, or portions of the harvest that were due from the land until such time as the full amount of the loan was repaid, and thus managed to lend money at interest in spite of the opposition of the Church to such a practice. The mortgage could be redeemed at any time after payment was due, but borrowers frequently had no intention of repaying the loan. The mortgage was, in fact, a circumvention of a customary law of inheritance that did not allow alienation of property. The ownership of mortgaged lands, together with the debt, was passed on to one's heirs, although this practice was generally discouraged.

In the name of God.

This is the charter of mortgage that I, doña María, who was the wife of García Santas Masas, make.

It pleases me with the best spirit and good will that I place under mortgage to you, don Jofre, and your wife, doña María, a field that is in [the district of] Almeriz. And it has these adjacencies: on the east, the irrigation canal

Translated from the *Colección diplomática de Catedral de Huesca*, edited by Antonio Durán Gudiol (Zaragoza: C.S.I.C., 1969), 2:646–47, 657–58.

that passes through Almeriz; on the south, the field of doña Poncia of Jaca. And you loan me on this field twenty-six solidi of the money of Jaca, of four deniers to the solidus, which have been given into my hand, and nothing of these moneys remains with you, don Jofre, or with you, doña María. And the term of this mortgage is the feast of Santa María in the middle of August in three years. And if the money is changed or diminished you, doña María, will return to us morabetins *aiars et lopis,* good by weight and law, at the rate of seven solidi and two deniers to the morabetin.[1]

And I give you as guarantor of title according to the law of the land, Domenec Alberrec.[2] Stephan, felt-maker, and don Rabin, shoemaker, and don Pere Cavaller are witnesses. This charter was done in the month of August, in the era 1196 [1158]. And I, Simón, son of Calbet of Illo Alguinio, who wrote this charter.

Court Case (CDHU 683, dated March 1207)

Pere Tallator and wife Boneta take Aquelmes Boclón to court seeking either payment of an alleged one hundred solidi or release of the security to them. Guillem Boclón had been a teacher in the cathedral school of Huesca. Some twelve years after his death, his favorite niece and her husband claimed that Guillem had promised his niece one hundred solidi. Since he did not have the money, he wrote her a mortgage on some property in the amount that he wished her to receive. Aquelmes Boclón, Guillem's brother and executor of his estate, refused to give the niece either the money or the property, and the two brought Aquelmes into court to force him to agree to the terms of the document they possessed.

The case is particularly intriguing because it occurred at a time when middle-class authority was not yet fully established in the city. The case was argued before an assembly of eminent citizens under the presidency of the justiciar, a royal appointee who administered the law in the city in the king's name. The justiciar decided the case in council with the citizens [probi homines]. Later, however, the justiciar convened a royal court, consisting of the chief of police and six district representatives, in the king's palace in order to review the case and confirm his judgment. A few years later, middle-class authority was ascendant, and such confirmation was not necessary.

Let it be known by all that Pere Tallator for himself and for his wife Boneta demanded of don Aquelmes that he should give him the hundred solidi that

---

1. Apparently the lender feared the coinage would be devalued and provided for payment in gold dinars of Lope, Almoravid king of Murcia. A solidus of four deniers meant the coin was one-third silver; the solidus was in fact devalued shortly after to three deniers, one-fourth silver.

2. The "guarantor of title according to the law of the land" was pledged to defend the title to the property against all other claimants and, if he failed to sustain the claim, to provide the contractor with other property of equal value.

Master Guillem Boclón agreed to give his niece Boneta, wife of the afore-said Pere Tallator, or that he should confirm them in the possession of the security, to wit two fields and a vineyard, which the aforesaid Master Guillem placed in pledge to the aforesaid Boneta, as is contained in a document which he made to her concerning the aforesaid fields and vineyards.

Pere Tallator and friends of don Aquelmes came before Pere de Sarvisé, justiciar, and in the presence of many *probi homines* in council concerning this matter. When the arguments for each side had been spoken, Pedro de Sarvisé, justiciar, accepted a charter from Pere Tallator. Having taken council with the *probi homines*, he adjudged that, in conformity with don Aquelmes, he did not find the aforesaid Boneta or her husband in tenancy of the aforesaid fields and vineyard, that Aquelmes should not confirm them in possession of this pledge, nor respond concerning the hundred solidi.

Justiciar Pere de Sarvisé rendered this judgment on the last Wednesday of March, in council, in the presence of Juan Peitavin; Pere Cuende; Sancho of Huesca, son of Pere Frontín; Mateo del Mas, zalmedina; Domingo Lois, Lorenzo del Collet; and Pere d'Avenna, who was advocate on behalf of don Aquelmes, and Sancho of Lavata, who was advocate on behalf of Pere Talla-tor; and in the presence of many other *probi homines*.

Moreover, the following sixth feria (Saturday), Justiciar Pere de Sarvisé confirmed this same judgment in the royal palace, in the presence of these *iuratos* [sworn witnesses] to wit, Mateo del Mas, zalmedina; Pere d'Avenna; Pere of Valle; Guillem of Briva; Pere Gil; Ramon de doña Blancha; and Juan Carbonel.

I, Pere of Novales, by order of Justiciar don Pere de Sarvisé; Mateo del Mas, zalmedina; and the *probi homines* written above, wrote this charter in the month of March, in the era 1245 [1207].

The Custom of Inheritance (CDHU 671, dated June 1206)

The following is an agreement between Pedro Maza and his wife, Constanza, re-garding the division of their goods. The Mazas were one of the richer and more powerful Aragonese noble families and one of the few aristocratic clans to keep their seat in the city of Huesca. According to legend, their ancestor had been an exiled noble who came, together with all of his kinsmen, to aid King Pedro I in the climactic battle of Alcoraz (1095) that sealed the fate of Muslim Huesca. As a reward, he was taken back into royal favor and enriched with extensive properties in and about the city. This is the only document of this series involving aristocrats; it was chosen for its detailed description of the customary law of inheritance. The inheritance customs outlined in this document were typical of both the nobility and middle class of the time and display the basically Germanic foundations of custom-ary law in the region.

In the name of God and His grace. This is the charter that I, don Pere Maza, and my wife, doña Constanza, jointly made. It pleased us both, united in good will and in the presence of *boni homines*, that we should make this agreement and concord between us; namely, that we should give to our sons and daughters what we possess today and will possess in the future.

We should give and concede all those properties that we have today and whatever we shall acquire jointly, so that after the end of both of us, our aforementioned sons and daughters may have and hold all that written above as their own property.

But in our lifetimes, if we wish, it shall be permissible for us jointly to give wherever we wish or to advance one of our sons and daughters above the others from our property or goods. Likewise, if, in our lifetimes, we both wish to give for whatever reason, for our souls or [those] of our family, we may give. Even at our death, if either of us wishes, we may give to a religious foundation as much as we want of our property, each one from his or her grandparental inheritance or from our personal goods. But let us not have the power in our lifetimes of selling, or mortgaging, or alienating those properties that we have now or others that we shall jointly acquire.

Moreover, if it happens that one of us should die and the survivor shall wish to take a wife, or the wife a husband, and he or she shall have other sons and daughters in addition to those whom we both have or shall have, let the survivor have neither the license nor the power to give properties or goods that we have or shall acquire jointly in our lifetimes. Let the survivor not have the power to give except to the sons and daughters of we who are written above.

And so that we may attend in good faith to that which is written above, I, don Pere Maza, give to you, my wife, doña Constanza, as guarantors that I will thus comply and attend to you, doña Constanza, and your sons and daughters, as it is written above, don Ramon of Pueyo, son of don Ramon of Pueyo, and don Guillem of Pueyo, son of don Juan de Maza, and myself pledged jointly with them.

Likewise, I, doña Constanza, with a good will, wish and grant all that is written above, and so that I will attend in good faith as it is named [*sic*] to you, don Pere Maza, my husband, as guarantors to you and your sons and daughters as it is written above, don Ramon of Pueyo, son of don Ramon of Pueyo, and don Guillem of Pueyo, son of don Juan Maza, and myself, pledged jointly with them.

Witnesses of that written above are don Juan Maza, son of don Juan Maza and don García Galur and don Domingo Luís.

This charter was enacted in the month of June, in the era 1244 [1206].

I, Ramon, abbot of Bandaliés, wrote this charter [and] made this sign with my [own] hand.

C. Will of Pere Calafat, Mallorca (1267)
Translated from Latin by Larry J. Simon

Wills offer insight into popular piety and religious practices, inheritance and family structure, and, among numerous other items, personal lifestyle and finances. Where other documentation has not survived, wills have been utilized to trace the history of hospitals and suppressed religious orders, and where wills have survived in abundance, historians have used computer analysis to chart demographic replacement ratios, per capita debt, epidemic disease, and fundamental shifts in religious ideology. Readers will readily note the long-winded, legal language of the genre, but an amazing and concrete view of medieval life emerges from testamentary documents.

In his last will and testament, dated 18 August 1267, Pere [Peter] Calafat acknowledges his serious illness and proceeds to order the disposition of his earthly goods. Pere arranges for burial in his parish cemetery in Valldemossa, disburses numerous pious and personal legacies, frees his baptized slaves Pere and Romia, returns to his wife her dowry, and, having no surviving children, names his nephew Bartomeu as his main testamentary heir. Particularly noteworthy are not only the lengthy list of nieces and nephews, or perhaps cousins, to which Pere leaves legacies, but the special concern, having been appointed guardian, he has for the minor children of a niece or aunt Pelegrina. This is one of the very few published testaments extant for thirteenth-century Mallorca. (LJS)

The chosen must always fear the end. Therefore, I, Pere Calafat, dwelling in Valldemossa, restrained by serious illness, concerning which I am reluctant to die, fearing the pains of hell and desiring to reach the much sought after joys of Paradise, in good sense and understanding, and with steady speech and sound memory, in the name of God, I make, order, and compose my will, in which I choose my executors, without any harm to themselves or their affairs, that is, Guillem Cerdan and Berenguer of Podio Maluerio. Whom I beg, by way of request, that, if it should happen that I die before I am permitted to draw up another will, they should distribute, divide, seek, sell, receive, order, and demand all my goods, both movable and immovable, just as they shall find it written and ordered here below. Moreover, I desire, order, and direct that all my debts and legacies and my manifest injuries be paid before all my

Translated from *Diplomatari del Monestir de Santa Maria, de la Real de Mallorca,* vol. 1, *1232–1360,* edited by Pau Mora and Lorenzo Andrinal (Palma: Imprenta Monàstica, 1982), pp. 310–13.

goods be restored, and I give my executors full power of selling and dissolving as much of my goods, movable and immovable, as they require to pay my debts and legacies and to fully make restitution for my manifest injuries. And I grant also to the said executors full power of bequeathing to the buyer or buyers all my goods, movable and immovable, without eviction, if they should possess or buy any of my aforementioned goods.

First, I direct that my body be buried in the cemetery of Santa María of Valldemossa, and I take, for my soul, from my aforementioned goods six hundred royal sous of Valencia, of which I leave five sous for the work of the said church, and for the altar of Sant Bartomeu, which has been built in the same church, two sous, and to the rector of the same church six sous.

Item, I leave for the work of the See of Blessed María of Mallorca two sous. Item, I desire that a certain image of wax, weighing one pound, be given to the said See. Item, I leave to the chapel at the cove of Sant Martí of Pollença about a pound of wax, as I promised to give there. Item, I leave to the table of the Franciscans [fratrum Minorum] and the table of the Dominicans [fratrum Predicatorum] two sous, to each, and to the table of the Friars of Penitence and the table of Santa Clara and the table of Santa Margarida eighteen dinars each. Item, I leave to each of the hospitals of the poor of Mallorca eighteen dinars and eighteen dinars for the ransoming of captives. Item, I desire that a measure of grain be paid to the Hospital of Santa María Magdalena of Mallorca, which I owe there. Item, I leave for the work of the monastery of Santa María la Real, twenty sous. Item, I leave to each of my said executors, fifty royal sous of Valencia, that they may be mindful of my soul and my testament. Item, I leave, for my burial, in the aforementioned church of Santa María of Valldemossa, fifteen sous.

Item, I leave to Joan Calafat and Pere Calafat, my nephews, sixty royal sous of Valencia, to each, for all, that is, which the said nephews may be able to claim among my goods. Item, I leave to Romia, daughter of my late niece [neptis, sometimes "aunt"] Pelegrina, fifty royal sous of Valencia, which may be given her as soon as she takes a husband, and if it happens that she does not take a husband, or that she die without legitimate offspring, I desire that the said fifty sous be given, for the love of God, on behalf of my soul. Item, I leave twenty sous to Richerona, the daughter of Richer. Item, I leave to the daughter of Guillem, the baptized, my goddaughter, two sous. Item, I leave to the daughter of En Rovira, who lives at the alquería [or "farm hamlet"] of Na Matona, two sous. Item, I leave to Guillema, daughter of my nephew Bartomeu, thirty Valencian sous. Item, I leave to Romia, daughter of the said Bartomeu, twenty sous. Item, I leave to Miquel, son of the said Bartomeu, another twenty sous, and to Pere, son of the same Bartomeu, another twenty sous. And I desire and bid that all the aforementioned bequests, which I make to the women above, be paid to the same women at the time of their marriages.

Item, I call, make, and designate Pere the Baptized, and Romia the Baptized, sister of the same Pere the Baptized, my slaves, free, liberated, quit, and freed, so that they can go, stay, and remain wherever they desire without bond, restriction, and objection of me or mine any person. Moreover, I leave to the said Pere the Baptized ten sous, and to the said Romia the Baptized twenty sous. Item, I leave to the son of Ramon of Sant Jordi, my godson, twenty sous. Item, I leave to Guillem Arnau twenty sous. All of which aforementioned bequests are to be paid out of the six hundred sous, and of that which might remain let there be made for my need a tomb of stone. The remainder of the said six hundred sous, when my aforementioned bequests have been paid and my tomb has been built, for the knowledge of my said executors, I desire to be given to the poor of Christ for the salvation of my soul.

Moreover, I praise, grant, and confirm to my lady and wife, her dowry, which she possesses over my goods, which gift is two hundred royal sous of Valencia. And as long as my wife shall desire to stay and remain in my goods and not desire to request for my heir, appointed by me below, the two hundred sous, I desire that she possess, from my goods and throughout her life, food and clothing according to her pleasure.

Item, I leave from the remainder of my goods two quarts of grain to Ollaría, always, for every year throughout her entire life.

And I leave in the power of God and of my said executors the children of Pelegrina, my late niece [*neptis*], of whom I am guardian, granting to my said executors full power and right and even all my estate portions that they [the executors], in the love of God and in the sense of true piety, should nourish, direct, defend, govern and serve these young ones and their goods, and thereby do all other things whatsoever which testamentary guardians can and must do, or just as in the manner I can do.

Item, I leave to Guillemona, my niece [*neptis*], wife of Guillem Muntaner, to satisfy all her desires, a certain share of land, as it has been assigned and decided by me in my alquería, which I hold and ought to possess in Valldemossa, and which I hold from the monastery of Santa María la Real, as clearly divides rocky points of olives, which points appear from the homes of the same alquería and descend from the said rock along a wide border, which border returns to the stream, which is toward the east and which descends to the sea. So the said Guillemona is obliged to give from this, for the next ten years to come, to my heir, designated by me below, that is, in each year of the ten years, thirty royal sous of Valencia, from the harvests which shall come from the said divided land, appointing the said Guillemona, for the said divided land which I leave to her, my legitimate testamentary heir.

Truly all my other remaining goods, movable and immovable, belonging to me or owed to me, by whatever right, cause, or reason, once my debts and legacies have been paid and restitution made for my injuries and my burial done, I leave to Bartomeu Calafat, my nephew, appointing the said Bartomeu Calafat, my nephew, my legitimate testamentary heir. Concerning the paying of the aforementioned legacies, my said heir should not be constrained for half of the year to come. This, moreover, is my last will, which I desire to be valid by right of testament or by right of my last will, which, if it is not valid by right of testament or by right of my last will, at least let it be valid by right of codicil or of any other right.

This was made on the fifteenth kalends of September, the year of our Lord one thousand two hundred sixty-seven. Signature of Pere Calafat, aforementioned testator, who praises and confirms this testament and asks that it be confirmed by my executors.

Signature of Guillem Cerdan, signature of Berenguer of Podio Maluerio, the aforementioned executors, who praise and confirm these things, without harm to ourselves or danger to our affairs. Witnesses to this testament are Ferrar de Balneis, Albert Lombard, Vital Dominic, Arnau Bartomeu, Pere Guisbert and Joan Reya. Signature of Bernat Rotland, rector of the church of Santa María of Valldemossa, who had this testament written and concluded.

56. SHIPPING IN BARCELONA

Barcelona Maritime Code of 1258

Translated from Latin by Roy C. Cave and Herbert H. Coulson

During the thirteenth century, Barcelona became one of the most important ports in the Mediterranean and a rival to Genoa and Venice. Barcelona's naval and commercial strength would be critical for the territorial expansion of the Crown of Aragón to Sicily and southern Italy, and into the eastern Mediterranean. Maritime law was also developing at this time, with cities such as Barcelona, Tortosa, and Marseille establishing codes of sea law that codified earlier usage and tradition. Maritime law codes regulated all aspects of shipping, including safety and security, loading and unloading, provisions and supplies, relations between passengers, merchants, and crew, and the role of the king in regulating maritime affairs. (ORC)

Be it known to all that we, Jaume, by the grace of God, King of Aragón, of Mallorca, and of Valencia, Count of Barcelona and Urgel, and Lord of Montpellier, hearing the ordinances written below, which you, Jaume Gruny, our faithful servant, have made at our wish and command and with our consent, and which you have drawn up with the advice of the honest water-men of Barcelona and based upon the ordinance of the same, having heard, seen, and understood that the said ordinances were to be made in our honor, and for the use and welfare of the water-men and the citizens of Barcelona, having confirmed the document by the authentic application of our seal, we grant, approve, and confirm all and each of the undermentioned ordinances, made by you and the said honest men on our authority. Wishing that the said ordinances may endure and be observed as long as it shall please us and the said honest water-men of Barcelona, by commanding our mayors, and bailiffs, both present and future, that they observe each and all of the undermentioned regulations, firmly and strictly, if they hope confidently for our grace and affection, and that they see that they are observed inviolably, so that they do not allow them to be disturbed by any one.

1. In the first place: we ordain, wish, and command, that the captain of a ship or vessel[1] of any kind and the sailors and mariners shall not leave or depart from the ship or vessel in which they arrived, until all the merchandise, which is on the ship or vessel, be discharged on land, and until that same ship

---

English text from *A Source Book for Medieval Economic History*, edited and translated by Roy C. Cave and Herbert H. Coulson (New York: Biblio and Tannen, 1965), pp. 161–68. Reprinted with permission of the copyright holder.
    1. The word vessel throughout this document means a small ship with covered deck or decks.

or vessel be emptied of ballast and moored. But the captain of that ship or vessel will be able to go on land with his clerk when he begins to discharge the cargo, if the sea be calm; and if perhaps the weather be such that he cannot discharge the cargo the said captain, if he be on land, shall immediately repair to the said ship or vessel, and if he cannot so repair by reason of the weather, his crew shall have full power and permission to depart with the ship or vessel from the place at which it arrived, and to go to the harbor or put out to sea. Nevertheless, if the said captain be unwilling to go to his ship, his merchants shall be able to order and command him firmly, on behalf of the Lord King and the said Jaume Gruny, to repair to the said ship or vessel and to place upon him such penalty as the said Jaume Gruny is empowered to place upon him. Moreover, the said captain of the ship shall not dare to stay on land until all merchandise which came in the ship or vessel be discharged. And if the merchants wish to disembark from the ship or vessel and a storm should arise after their disembarkation, the captain of the ship or vessel, if he be there, or his crew, shall have permission to withdraw from the place in which he was with that ship or vessel and with the merchandise contained therein, and of going to sea or putting in to harbor. But if the mariners should not have done this let each one incur a penalty of ten solidi of the money of Barcelona, and the captain of a ship fifty solidi, and the captain of a vessel thirty solidi; and over and above the said penalty the captains of ships and vessels shall be condemned to repair all the damage which the said merchants suffered through their fault. But of the penalties, both foregoing and those written below, the King will receive half, and the other half will go to the Order of Water-men of Barcelona. Moreover, these penalties and all those written below shall be paid as long as it be the will of the honest water-men of Barcelona.

2. Also: we order that every ship and vessel shall have a sworn clerk on every voyage, which clerk shall not write anything in the contract book of that ship or vessel unless both parties are present, namely the captain and the merchants, or the captain and his mariners; and the said clerk shall be a good and lawful man, and shall make out the expenses truly and lawfully, and all the mariners shall be expected to swear to the captains of the ships and vessels that to the best of their ability they will save, protect, and defend the captain and all his goods, and his ship or vessel, and its rigging and equipment, and all the merchants going with it, and all their goods and merchandise, by sea and land, in good faith and without fraud. Moreover, the said clerk shall be at least of the age of twenty years, and if the captains of the said ships or vessels do not wish to have the said clerk they shall not leave Barcelona or any other place in which they may be, until they have another clerk, if they can find one.

3. Also: we command that on every ship which loads at sea, so that it

is loaded with merchandise worth 2000 solidi, half the mariners of the ship with one officer shall be obliged to remain one night with their arms on the ship; and after any vessel has loaded at sea with merchandise worth 1000 solidi, half the mariners of that vessel with one officer shall be obliged to stay on their vessel for one night with their arms. Also we command that the captain of a ship or vessel shall have food in his ship or vessel sufficient for fifteen days; namely, bread, wine, salt meat, vegetables, oil, water, and two packets of candles. And if the said captain of ship or vessel be unwilling to do this, let him incur a penalty of twenty solidi, and each of the mariners and crew incur a penalty of five solidi. . . .

5. Also: we command that no boat shall load for a voyage nor send away any living merchandise and if it loads with heavy goods, it shall not dare to load except as far as the middle of the deck, and the captain of the boat shall take his boat, manned and with its rigging, just as is understood between the captain and the merchants whose merchandise it is; and if the said merchants fear they will be held as hostages in any place, the captain of the boat shall not enter with his boat nor go into the place suspected of holding them without the consent of the merchants. Moreover every boat shall be expected to carry two *ballistae*[2] with their equipment, and a hundred spears and two shields; and every sailor is expected to bear a lance and a sword or bill. And if the captains of the boats should not observe this rule they shall incur a penalty of ten solidi. . . .

7. Also: we command that every ship's mariner who is expected to do the work of a *ballistarius*, shall carry two *ballistae* of two feet, and one scaling ladder, and three hundred spears, and a helmet, and a breast-plate or corselet, and a straight or curved sword. Likewise, the *ballistarii* of the other vessels shall be expected to carry the same weapons; but the other mariners on ships shall be expected to bear a breast-plate, and an iron helmet, or *cofa maresa*, and a shield, and two lances, and a straight or a curved sword. But mariners on vessels shall be expected to carry a breast-plate or corselet, shield, iron helmet, or *cofa maresa*, and two lances, and a straight or a curved sword. And if the said mariners do not have the said arms, the captains of the ships or vessels shall not take them; and if they do take them they shall pay as a penalty fifty solidi for each mariner. . . .

9. Also: we command that captains of barges and those who discharge cargoes shall discharge well and in good order from ships, vessels, and boats, all merchandise with their barges and boats, and they shall not load their

---

2. A *ballista* was a weapon, like a large crossbow, for defense of a ship. A *ballistarius* operated a *ballista*.

barges or boats excessively; and if they do load them excessively, let them be in the jurisdiction and command of two honest men whom Jaume Gruny or his *locum tenens* with the advice of his counsellors shall have appointed; and if the said captains of barges transgress the command and jurisdiction of the two honest men, let them repair all damage which the merchandise has suffered, in the knowledge of the said two honest men.

10. Also: we command that every captain of a barge or boat shall not dare to take ashore any mariner of a ship or vessel or boat until the said vessel or ship be discharged and emptied of ballast, or until the said boat be discharged; and if they do contrary to this they shall be expected to pay five solidi as a penalty for every mariner they take from the ship or vessel.

11. Also: we command that every co-proprietor of a ship or vessel, and every merchant, and every pilot of a ship or vessel who accepts wages from that ship or vessel shall be expected to take an oath to the captain of the ship, just as the other mariners who are not partners, or pilots, or merchants, and this by an oath taken by them to us.

12. Also: we command that a vessel with a covered deck shall not take away any merchandise upon the covered deck, except only the sea-chests of the mariners and merchants, and the wine and water which are necessary to the mariners and merchants; and if the said vessel have store-rooms, it shall not take away any merchandise in those store-rooms, except only its arms and those of the mariners and merchants, and the rigging of the vessel, if they wish to place them there. Moreover every vessel with a covered deck shall take four shields and twelve lances, besides the arms of the mariners and merchants who sail in the vessel above mentioned; and if any merchandise be carried in the said store-room, it shall pay a fine for the merchandise, which fine shall be divided between the Lord King and the Society of Water-men.

13. Also: we command that a vessel with two covered decks shall not send or carry away any merchandise between the mainmast and the poop, except only its boat with its rigging and the company of the merchants; and if it wishes to have merchandise in the same place, it may do this with the consent of the merchants, and without their consent it shall not dare to place any merchandise in the said place. But in the cabin of the poop of the vessel it shall carry its company and that of the merchants. Moreover, on the higher deck of the said vessel it shall not dare to carry water or wine, or other merchandise, except only its sea-chests and those of the mariners and merchants, and in the store-rooms of that same vessel it shall not carry any merchandise, except only the arms going in that vessel, and the rigging if it can place any there, except it do so with the consent of the majority of the merchants, and

if it carry any merchandise in the said places, it shall pay the fine incurred just as is contained in the preceding paragraph.

14. Also: we command that every captain of a ship or vessel, of whatever kind it be, shall free his ship or vessel and the rudders from all tolls in whatever dominion or lordship it be, whether of Christians or Arabs, without any expense or payment from the merchants. In the same way the merchants shall free all their merchandise, in whatever dominion or lordship it be, without any expense to the captains of the vessels or ships, and if the said lordship should chance to make other tolls, let them stand in the pledge of two honest men, whom they have elected in the said ship or vessel.

15. Also: we command that every merchant and mariner who takes of his own accord or in company with his friends anything in common to Barbary [Morocco] or to other parts, before he departs from Barcelona shall come to an agreement with three or four or more of his partners, according as he be able to gather several of the said company together, and when the expenses of the purchase have been made with the deliberation of that same company, the said merchant or company carrying the goods shall not accept any merchandise from the said partners except according as they agreed on that day on which it was pledged, and this under pain of an oath to be taken by them to us and the honest men before mentioned.

16. Also: we command that merchants or mariners or other persons carrying the company to any parts shall not take their wages or fare nor shall they be given to them until they return to Barcelona, and then when they have made an agreement with the partners of the company they shall have and take their wages and fare with the knowledge of their partners with whom they made the agreement about the company above mentioned. And if the said merchant be not a mariner or do not perform the office of mariner, he shall not take his wages or fare. . . .

18. Also: we command that all men who have submitted to this ordinance, in whatever parts they be, shall love each other, and protect and help each other, both in their persons and in their goods against all other persons, just as if they were the special goods of each one; and they shall do this in good faith and without any fraud, by virtue of an oath taken to us and to the honest water-men of Barcelona.

19. Also: we command that if any ship or vessel should have stopped at the quays of Barcelona so that it could not straightway sail, that all captains of ships and vessels of that society with their mariners, although their ships or vessels are prepared to sail, shall help the said ship or vessel to sail or put to sea and they shall not leave that ship or vessel which is detained until it have sailed, and if they are unwilling to do this the captain of the ship or vessel shall incur a penalty of fifty solidi and the mariners of five solidi.

20. Also: we command that if any mariner should die in the service of any ship or vessel, from the time when that ship or vessel moved from the quay or river bank, or from any port, the said mariner shall have all his wages, just as was written in the contract book of that ship or vessel. And if any mariner be sick or be injured in his legs from the time when the ship or vessel put to sea, the captain of the ship or vessel shall give to the said mariner his needs in food for the whole voyage, if the mariner make the voyage, and the mariner shall have all his wages. But if the mariner be unwilling to go on the voyage, he shall not have any wages. But if the mariner has accepted such free victuals for doing work on the said ship or vessel, so that he cannot go on the said voyage to the knowledge of two honest men of the society, he shall have only half his wages; and if the captain of the said ship or vessel shall have paid all the wages to the mariner, he shall not be expected to put another mariner in the place of the one who remained ashore. And if the said captain shall have paid half the wages to the mariner who remained, the captain shall be expected to put another mariner in his place, and to give him the remaining half of the wages which he did not pay. And the merchants will be expected to give the other half of the wages to the mariner placed in the position of the other who did not go. . . .

*   *   *

Given at Barcelona on the twenty-sixth of August, in the year 1258. Seal of Jaume, by the grace of God, King of Aragón, etc.

57. THE BARCELONA DISPUTATION OF 1263

Medieval Christians had a long tradition of debating theological points with Jews, or at least of imagining arguments that could potentially be deployed to win such debates. Interfaith theological controversy took an unexpected turn in the mid-thirteenth century, however, as a new generation of intellectuals—including mendicant friars with Hebrew training, some of whom were converts from Judaism—reacted to formal condemnation and then burnings of the Talmud at Paris. Official Church toleration of Judaism continued in Iberia for another two and a half centuries, but a general deterioration in Christian-Jewish relations soon led to expulsions from England (1290) and France (1306).

It was in this charged atmosphere that a Provençal Jew turned Dominican friar named Paul Christiani was invited to debate with the venerable rabbi Moses ben Nahman (Nahmanides, also known as Ramban) in the Crown of Aragón. The meeting took place under royal auspices at Barcelona in the summer of 1263, with a variety of traditional biblical and more innovative Talmudic proof texts being advanced. Many of the arguments centered on proofs for the identity and understanding of the Messiah. One of the issues reflected in these documents is a struggle between Jewish and Christian leaders to demonstrate control over the sources and practice of Judaism. Both claimed superior understanding of the sources and practices of Judaism. The documents reflect this struggle for control in both the tone and the structure of the arguments presented. Rabbi Moses was promised freedom of speech by the king. So much can be gleaned from two extant accounts of the debate. The first of these is a brief Latin summary, the second is Nahmanides' Hebrew account of the debate.

The Latin account was registered by an anonymous scribe, with near-identical copies going to both the Aragonese royal archive and the episcopal archive at Girona (rabbi Moses' home town) shortly after the event. Other details are uncertain, including the scribe's claim of Christian victory, which is at odds with Nahmanides' account. Friar Paul remained active in the Crown of Aragón for some months after the Disputation had concluded, seeking to force Jewish attendance at conversionary sermons. He also led a team of friars dedicated to the censorship and expurgation of Jewish books, including theological works of Maimonides as well as the Talmud. His work was carried on in later years by the notorious anti-Jewish polemicist Raymond Martini.

The Hebrew account was written by Nahmanides in response to the Latin version of events. Rabbi Moses was a celebrated legal scholar, theologian, physician, and philosopher; he was born in Girona in 1194 and later served as a community leader in that city. According to his account, he won the debate with Paul Christiani, and his victory was recognized by a monetary reward from the king. However, in writing down his version of the debate, Nahmanides seems to have overstepped the freedom of speech granted during the event itself. He was condemned for the arguments in his text and exiled from the lands of Aragón. Although this was not originally intended as a permanent exile, Nahmanides never returned to his homeland and he died in the Holy Land in about 1270. (RV, NC, & ORC)[1]

---

1. Special thanks to Robin Vose and Nina Caputo for their work on this chapter.

A. Christian Account of the Disputation
Translated from Latin by Hyam Maccoby

In the year of the Lord 1263, on the 20th of July, in the presence of the lord King of Aragón, and many others, barons, prelates, and religious and military persons in the palace of the lord King at Barcelona, when Moses, called Master, a Jew, had been summoned from Gerona by the lord King himself at the instance of the Preaching Friars, and was present in that same place together with many other Jews who seemed and were believed by the other Jews to be experts, Brother Paul after discussion with the lord King and certain Friars of the Preaching and Minorite Orders who were present (not in order that the faith in the Lord Jesus Christ, which because of its certitude should not be put into dispute, should be drawn into the arena with the Jews as if it were a matter of doubt, but that the truth of that faith should become manifest in order to destroy the errors of the Jews and remove the confident faith of many Jews who, though they could not themselves defend their errors, said that the said Jewish Master could sufficiently reply to each and every point which was put to them) proposed to the said Jewish Master that he would prove, with the help of God, through writings accepted and authoritative among the Jews, the following things in order, namely: that the Messiah (of which the interpretation is "Christ") whom the Jews expect, has undoubtedly come; further, that the Messiah himself, as had been prophesied, must be both God and man; further, that he truly suffered and died for the salvation of the human race; further, that legal or ceremonial matters ceased and had to cease after the coming of the said Messiah. When therefore, the said Moses had been questioned whether he wished to reply to the aforesaid matters, he said and firmly asserted, "Yes," and that he would remain, if necessary, for this reason, in Barcelona for a day or a week or a month or even a year. And when it was proved to him that he ought not to be called "Master," because no Jew ought to be called by this name since the time of the passion of Christ, he conceded this at least, that it was true for the last 800 years. Eventually it was put to him that when Brother Paul had come to Gerona to discuss with him matters which are relevant to salvation, and expounded diligently, among other things, the belief in the Holy Trinity, both as to the Unity of the Divine essence, and as to the Trinity of the Persons, as held by Christians, he [Moses] conceded that if Christians believed what had been expounded to him, they believed what in truth ought to be so held. And

Latin text edited by Y. Baer, *Tarbiz* 2 (1930–31): 185–87. English translation from *Judaism on Trial*, edited and translated by Hyam Maccoby (1982; reprint Oxford: Littman Library of Jewish Civilization, 1993), pp. 147–50. Reprinted with permission of the publisher.

when this was repeated in the presence of the lord King, he did not deny it, but was silent, and so, by his silence, assented. Then in the palace of the lord King the said Jew was asked whether the Messiah who is called Christ had come; and when he answered with the assertion, "No," and added that Messiah and Christ are the same, and if it could be proved to him that the Messiah had come, then this ought to be believed about no other than him, to wit Jesus Christ, in whom Christians believe, since no other had come who dared to usurp this name, or had been believed to be the Christ, it was proved to him clearly both by the authority of the Law and the Prophets and by the Talmud, that Christ had in truth come, as Christians believe and preach. To this he was not able to reply. And defeated by irrefutable proofs and authorities, he conceded that Christ, or Messiah, was born 1,000 years ago in Bethlehem and later appeared to some people in Rome. And when he was asked where that Messiah is, whom the Jews declared to have been born and to have appeared at Rome, he said that he did not know. Afterwards, however, he said that he lived in the earthly Paradise with Elijah. But he said that though he had been born, nevertheless he had not yet come, because the Messiah is said to have come only when he assumes dominion over the Jews and frees them and the Jews follow him. Against this reply the authority of the Talmud was adduced, which says plainly that the Messiah will come to them even today, if they listen to his voice and do not harden their hearts, as it says in the Psalm: "Today if you listen to his voice" [Ps. 95:7]. It was added, too, that for the Messiah to have been born among men is the same thing as for him to have come amongst men, and it cannot be otherwise understood. And to these things he was able to make no reply. Further, among the proofs put forward for the advent of the Messiah was adduced that one from Genesis: "The scepter shall not pass away from Judah" [Gen. 49:10]. Since, therefore, it is certain that in Judah there is neither scepter nor leader, it is certain that the Messiah who was to be sent has come. To this he replied that the scepter has not been taken away but is merely discontinued, as it also was in the time of the Babylonian Captivity. And it was proved to him that in Babylon they had the heads of the captivity with jurisdiction, but after the death of Christ they had neither leader nor prince nor the heads of captivity such as those attested by the prophet Daniel, nor prophet nor any kind of rule, as is manifestly plain today. By this, it is certain, that the Messiah has come to them. He, however, said that he would prove that they had the aforesaid heads after Christ, but he could show nothing about the aforesaid, and indeed admitted that they had not had the aforesaid heads for the last 850 years. Therefore it is plain that the Messiah has come, since authority cannot lie. Further, when the said Moses said that Jesus Christ ought not to be called

Messiah, because the Messiah, as he said, should not die, as it is said in the psalm, "he asked for life from you and you granted it to him" [Ps. 21:4], but he ought to live for ever, both he and those whom he will liberate, he was asked whether the chapter of Isaiah, 53, "Lord, who would have believed . . ." (which according to the Hebrews, begins at the end of chapter 52, where it says, "Behold my servant will understand . . .") speaks about the Messiah. He firmly asserted that it does not speak of the Messiah at all, but it was proved to him by many authorities from the Talmud, which speak of the passion of Christ and his death, which they prove from the said chapter, that the said chapter of Isaiah is understood of the Christ, and in it the death of Christ and his passion and burial and resurrection are plainly contained. He however, compelled at length by the authorities, admitted that it is understood and explained in reference to Christ. From this it is plain that the Messiah had to suffer and die. Further, since he was unwilling to admit the truth unless compelled by the authorities, when he could not explain the authorities, he said publicly that he did not believe in the authorities which were cited against him, though they were in ancient, authoritative books of the Jews, because, as he said, they were sermons, in which their teachers, for the sake of exhorting the people, often lied. For this reason, he dismissed both the teachers and the scriptures of the Jews. Further, he first denied all, or nearly all, the things which he had previously admitted and which had been proved to him, and then, having been refuted again through authorities and defeated, he was compelled to admit them again. Further, since he could not reply and had been defeated many times in public, and both Jews and Christians were treating him with scorn, he said obstinately in front of everyone that he would not reply at all, because the Jews had told him not to, and some Christians, namely Brother P. de Janua and some respectable citizens had sent to him to advise him not to reply at all. This lie was publicly refuted by the said Brother P. and the respectable citizens. From this it is plain that he was trying to escape from the Disputation by lies. Further, though he had promised in the presence of the lord King and many others that he would answer questions on his faith and law to a small gathering, when the lord King was away from the state he secretly fled away and departed. From this it is plain that he does not dare and is not able to defend his erroneous creed. [We, Jaume, by the grace of God king of Aragón, Mallorca, and Valencia, count of Barcelona and Urgel, and lord of Montpellier, truly confess and recognise that each and every one of the words and deeds in our presence and of many others were as is contained above in this present writing. In testimony of this we have caused our seal to be appended in perpetual commemoration.]

B. Moses Nahmanides, Account of the Disputation
Translated from Hebrew by Nina Caputo

Our lord the king commanded me to debate with Frai Pul[1] before him and his council in his palace in Barcelona. I answered and said: I will do as you command, my lord king, if you give me permission to speak as I please. And I request in this matter the permission of the king and of Frai Ramon de Peña Fort[2] and his colleagues who are here.

Frai Ramon [de Peña Forte] replied: "Only if you do not speak contemptuously."

I replied to them: "I do not want to subject myself to your judgment on this; I must speak as I please during the disputation just as you may say what you wish. As for me, I have [sufficient] wisdom to speak discreetly. But I must speak as I wish." They all granted me freedom to speak freely.

Then I answered and said: "Disputations between the gentiles and the Jews have focused on many matters of tradition on which principles of belief do not rely. However, I do not want to debate in this exalted court anything but matters on which the entire controversy hinges."

All of them answered, saying: "You have spoken well. Now, we have agreed to open with the matter of whether the Messiah has already come, as the Christians believe, or if he will come in the future, as the Jews believe. After that, we will discuss the question of whether the Messiah is substantially divine or fully human, born of a man and a woman. And after that, we will address the question of whether the Jews or the Christians observe the true law [*torah*]"

Then Frai Pul said that he would argue, based on our Talmud, that the Messiah announced by the prophets had already arrived.

I replied: "Before we dispute this question, I request that he instruct me and explain to me how this is possible. I heard that he (Frai Pul) previously went about Provence and many other places saying such things to the Jews, and I am very surprised. He will answer me, wanting to suggest that the sages of the Talmud believed that Jesus was the Messiah and that he was fundamentally human *and* truly divine, as the Christians believe. Is it not a known fact that in truth the case of Jesus took place [during the time of] the Second Temple and Jesus was born and died before the destruction of the Temple?

Translated from *Kitveh Rabbenu Moshe ben Nahman*, edited by Hayim Dov Chavel (Jerusalem: Mosad ha-Rav Kook, 1963), pp. 302–9, 316, 319–20.

1. The name is transliterated from the Hebrew spelling. Most English scholarship refers to the friar as "Friar Paul Christiani" or "Pablo Christiani."
2. The Hebrew is written out in two words.

The sages of the Talmud, such as Rabbi Akiva and his circle, lived after the destruction [of the Temple]. And the same people who taught the Mishnah of Rabbi [Yehudah ha-Nasi] and Rav Nathan lived many years after the destruction. Indeed, Rav Ashi, who assembled and recorded the Talmud, lived some 400 years after the destruction. If these wise men believed in the messianic nature of Jesus, and [believed] that he was a true [Messiah] and that his faith and religion were true, and if these words from which Frai Pul argues were written as he says, how then did the [rabbis] stand by the religion of the Jews and their traditions, for they [the rabbis] were Jews and remained in the faith of the Jews throughout their days and as Jews. They and their sons and their students who heard all of their words from their mouths lived and died as Jews, just as we do today. (And why would they along with their students who accepted the Torah from their mouths not have become apostates and returned to the religion of Jesus as Frai Pul did, since he understood from their words that the faith of the Christians was correct—God forbid—and apostatized on account of their words.) And it was they who taught us the faith of Moses and Judaism, since all our actions today are a product of the Talmud and what we saw that the sages of the Talmud who were our leaders do from the day of its [the Talmud's] composition until today. For is not the whole Talmud [intended] to teach us the traditions of the Torah and the Commandments and how our fathers [in the time of the Temple] conducted themselves according to the words of the prophets and Moses, on him may there be peace? If they believed in Jesus and his faith, how could they not have done as Frai Pul has done, who believes their words even more than they do themselves."

Frai Pul answered (and said [to me]): "These long words are intended to put a stop to the disputation. Nevertheless, you must hear what I am saying."

I said to them: "This is clear evidence that he will not speak words of substance. [However,] I will listen to them because you, our lord King, wish so."

He began, saying: "Here, it says in the Scriptures *the staff shall not pass from the tribe of Judah . . . until Shiloh has come* [Gen. 49:10], and he [Shiloh] is the Messiah. If so, then the prophet [Jacob, speaking in Gen. 49:10] says that Judah will always have power until the Messiah who comes from him. Thus, today, since you have neither a single tribe nor a ruler's staff, the Messiah, who is from his [Judah's] descendants has already come, and he holds rule of government."

I answered and said: "It was not the intention of the prophet to say that there would be no break in the rule of Judah at all during any time; rather, he said that it would not end and completely depart from him [Judah]. The

intent [of this verse] is that at every time that there is kingship for Israel, it
will reside with Judah. And if their kingship shall cease due to sin, it will return to Judah. The proof of my words is that for a long period of time[3] before
Jesus, kingship had been removed from Judah and not from Israel, and for
a long time it was also removed from both Israel and Judah. Surely, during
the seventy years of exile in Babel there was no royal government in Judah
or in Israel at all. . . . And certainly now, as the nation is in exile [*galut*] then
there is no king."

Frai Pul answered: "During all of those same times, even though you
had no kings, you did have a [legitimate] government. So they explained in
the Talmud [Sanhedrin 5, 1]: *the staff shall not pass from Judah*, [refers to] the
leaders[4] during the Babylonian exile who ruled the nation with a scepter
(harshly), and *and the scepter from between his feet*, this refers to the sons and
disciples of Rabbi Hillel, who taught Torah to the multitudes. But today you
do not have a recognized ordination in accordance with the Talmud, so also
that form of government has ceased for you. Thus, there is no one among
you who can properly be called 'Rabbi.' The title you apply to yourselves
today, *Maestri*, is mistaken and you fraudulently lead by that title."

I answered him with scorn: "This is outside of the [parameters defined
for the] disputation, but you are not speaking the truth. [The title] 'Rabbi'
is not the same as *Maestri*; rather, a 'Rav' is a *maestri*, and one does not need
ordination to be called 'Rav' according to the Talmud. Nevertheless, I concede that I am neither a *maestri* nor a *talmid tov* [a good student/scholar]."
I said this by way of instruction. I then returned [to the matter at hand] and
said to him: "I will show you that our rabbis of blessed memory did not mean
to interpret the verse as referring to anything other than real kingship. However, you have understood neither our justice nor our law, you know only a
few homilies [*haggadot*] with which you have familiarized yourself . . . it is
not the opinion of the Sages of the Talmud that Judah would always control
a staff and scepter, but rather the prophet assured Judah that when there is a
kingdom, Judah would rule. Nevertheless, kingship was suspended for many
years, as I mentioned, because during the time of the Babylonian Exile they
had neither staff nor scepter. Also, during the Second Temple, when there
was a kingship of priests and their servants, Judah held no staff except of
government. There was neither an Exilarch [*Rosh Galut*] nor a Prince [*Nasi*],
because leadership and the powers of prince were held by the kings among

3. Literally, "many days." The language in this statement foreshadows a later point in
the disputation (not included here) about under what circumstances it is acceptable to interpret
yom (day) as "year."
4. I.e., the Exilarchs.

the priests and their judges and ministers, and those who were pleasing in their eyes." . . .

*   *   *

Frai Pul . . . argued that in the Talmud they said that the Messiah already came, and he brought with him a *haggadah* that is in *Midrash 'Aykha*, which states "a man was plowing, and his cow lowed, an Arab passerby said to him, bar Yehudai, bar Yehudai, untie your cow, untie your plow, untie your plowshare, for your Temple has been destroyed. He untied his cow, untied his plow, and untied his plowshare. [The cow] lowed a second time. [The Arab] said to him, tie up your cow, tie up your plow, tie up your plowshare, for your Messiah was born" [Midrash Lamentations, 1:51].

I replied, saying "I do not believe in the homily at all, although it is proof for my words."

Then the same man shouted: "Here is proof that he denies [the authority of] their books!"

I said: "It is true that I do not believe that the Messiah was born on the day of the destruction [of the Temple], and this *haggadah* is either not true or it has an alternative interpretation from the secrets of the sages. But I can ascertain this meaning in the literal interpretation you cited, for it is proof for me. Thus, the *haggadah* says that on the day of the destruction after the Temple was razed, at that same time, the Messiah was born. If this is so, then Jesus was not the Messiah, you have said, because he was born and died before the destruction. In truth, he was born more than two hundred years prior to the destruction. And according to your calculations, 73 years before." Thus, the man was silenced.

Maestri Gilliam, the king's judge, answered: "This disputation is not about Jesus. Rather, the question is whether or not the Messiah has come. You said that he has not come, and this book of yours says that he has."

I said to him: "As is your custom, you chose to answer in a deceitful manner. Nevertheless, I will answer you on this matter. The sages did not say that he came; they said that he was born. On the day that Moses our teacher (may he be blessed) was born he did not come,[5] he was not yet a redeemer, but when he came to Pharaoh as was God's command and said to him *so says the Lord: send forth my people* . . . [Exod. 8:1], then he came [as Moses the prophet]. So too the Messiah, when he will come to the pope and say to him according to the command of God *send forth my people*, then he will have

---

5. I.e., he did not make himself known as Israel's leader.

come. And know that as of today, he has not come [as the redeemer], and we do not yet have a messiah[6] at all. David the King was not king and was not anointed on the day of his birth, but when Samuel anointed him he became a messiah [an anointed one]. And on the day that Elijah will anoint the Messiah in accordance with God's command, he will be called Messiah. And after that day, he will come to the Pope and redeem us and then it will be said that the redeemer has come." . . .

*   *   *

Then our lord the king answered: "If he was born on the day of the destruction of the Second Temple and that was more than one thousand years and he hasn't come again, when will he come, because it is not in man's nature to live one thousand years."

I said to him: "There were conditions [stating] that I would not debate with you, so I will not answer in the debate. Suffice it to say that among the first men there were already those, like Adam and Methuselah, who lived for one thousand years. And Elijah and Enoch lived longer than that, for life is from God."

He said: "Then where is he today?"

I said: "This is not among the prescribed topics of the disputation so I will not answer you. Perhaps you will find him at the gates of Toledo, if you send a man there from your team of couriers." I said this by way of a joke.

Then they stood and the king gave the time for the disputation on the following Monday.

On that day the king went to the cloisters in the city and gathered there all of the people of the city, gentiles and Jews. And the bishop and all of the priests and the Franciscan masters and preachers, and that same man [Frai Pul] rose to speak.

I said to our lord the king: "My lord, please hear me." And he said to me: "He should begin and speak first, for he is the prosecutor."

I said: "Permit me to explain my views in the matter of the messiah, then he will be able to respond to the matter with clarity."

I rose, saying: *Hear me, all people* [Micazh 1:2]. Frai Pul asked me if the messiah that the prophets talk about had already come, and I said he had not come. He brought a book of homilies [*sefer haggadah*] that says that he was born on the very day that the Temple was destroyed. And I said that I did

---

6. He is making the point that there are two types of messiah—one who is an anointed leader, like David, and one who will be sent as a redeemer.

not believe that, but that it was proof of my argument. Now I will explain to you why I said I did not believe that. [You should] know that we have three types of books. The first is the *biblia*[7] and all of us believe it in its entirety. The second is called the Talmud, and it explains the commandments of the Torah, for the Torah contains 613 commandments and not one of those is not explained in the Talmud. We accept it as an explanation of the commandments. Finally, we have a third body of literature that is called Midrash, that is to say, *sermones*.[8] It is as if the bishop were to stand and give a sermon, and one of the audience found it pleasing and wrote it down. If one believes the content of this literature, then all the better; if one does not believe it, then no harm is done. So, we do have sages who wrote that the Messiah would not be born until the time of the end is near, then he will come to bring us from the *galut* [exile]. Thus, I do not believe in the statement in the book that the Messiah was born on the day of the destruction. Moreover, we call this book *Sefer Haggadah*, which means *Rasionamiento*. That is to say, it is simply sayings that one person tells his friend. But I accept the simple meaning of the *aggadah* (homily) according to your wish, because it demonstrates with clarity that your Jesus is not the Messiah. . . .

*   *   *

On the next day, the sixth day (of the week) they made arrangements to meet in the palace, and *the king sat on his seat, from time to time on his seat near the wall* [1 Sam. 20:25]. The bishop and many of his ministers, and Giles De'Sergon, and Pere Barga, and many knights, and all those who are shunned from the city and the poor of the nation were there.

Speaking to the king: "I do not wish to dispute any longer."

The king said: "Why not?"

I said: "Now many from the [Jewish] community are here, and they all have detained me and begged me, for they are very afraid of these people, of the preachers, who impose themselves and strike terror on the whole world. Also, the great priests and honorable men among them sent [word] to me not to continue. And many knights from your household, my lord king, told me that I am doing great harm to speak before them against their faith. Frai Pere of Girona, a Franciscan scholar, told me that the matter [i.e., outcome]

---

7. Here Nahmanides transliterates the vernacular term, rather than using the customary Hebrew term *Tanakh*, an acronym for sections of the Hebrew Bible: *Torah*, Pentateuch, *Neviim*, prophets, and *Ketuvim*, writings.

8. I.e., sermons. Again, Nahmanides presents a transliteration of the vernacular to introduce this body of commentary.

is not good. And the people of the city said to the Jews that I should not continue." And indeed, that was the case, but when they saw that it was the king's wish [to continue], they hesitated and all stated that I would continue. The discussion among us was extended on this matter.[9] In the end, I said I would continue the debate. However, the judge permitted that for one day, I would ask the questions and Frai Pul would answer me, since he had asked me and I answered for three days. . . .

*   *   *

This is an account of all of the disputations. To my knowledge, I did not change a word. Afterwards, on the same day [that the debate ended] I stood before our lord the king, who said: "Let the disputation stand,[10] for I have never seen a man who does not have justice on his side who argued his case so well." That is, as I did. And I heard in the court that the king wanted the preachers [friars] to come to the synagogue on Shabbat, so I remained in the city for eight more days. And they arrived there on the following Shabbat. I answered the king in proper order, for he preached with zeal, saying that Jesus was the Messiah . . . [a short account of Nahmanides's reply follows].

Our lord the king stood and descended from the Ark of the Law and they left. The next day, I stood before our lord the king and he said to me: "Return to your city and live there in peace." Then he gave me three hundred *dinarim* and I departed from him with great love. May the Lord make me worthy of life in the World to Come. Amen.

9. I.e., among the Jewish community.
10. In other words, let it stop here.

58. JEWISH COURT DOCUMENTS FROM BARCELONA

A. A Jewish Widow and Her Daughter (1261–1262)
Translated from Hebrew by Elka Klein

For matters relating to Jewish law and internal affairs, Jewish communities in Barcelona and elsewhere had recourse to their own Jewish courts of law. In March 1261, a Jewish woman named Cruxia (pronounced Crusha), widow of an important scholar, Shmuel (Samuel) HaSardi, appealed to the Jewish court in Barcelona on behalf of her daughter. She claimed that her daughter's inheritance was being dissipated due to neglect by her guardians. Cruxia was concerned that since her brother, one of the guardians, had married and moved to Tortosa three years previously, the other two guardians were not fulfilling their duties. In response to her appeal, the court wrote the following document. (EK)

We, the undersigned court [testify] that it so happened that the Lady Cruxia, widow of R. Shmuel ibn R. Yitzhak HaSardi, appeared before us and said, "It has been some time since the death of my lord and husband, R. Shmuel . . . who left a minor daughter, named Reina; after her father, my husband, died, the court appointed three guardians to supervise the legacy which my husband left my orphaned daughter,[1] and they are my brother Don Bonsenyor of Gerona, R. Yehuda ibn R. Shmuel, and Don Zark Malet. As of now, it has been nearly three years since my brother Don Bonsenyor went to Tortosa, having married a woman there, and the two other guardians, R. Yehuda and Don Zark Malet, who remain in the city do not wish to exert themselves and to make an effort in the affairs of my orphaned daughter, because the third guardian is not with them. I fear that the property may go to the royal treasury for several reasons: first that the interest is consuming it on account of the debts which she [Reina] owes; also that the officials appointed for tax collection are pressuring and pressing me and requesting the taxes owed on the estate of her father; also my orphaned daughter needs food and there is no one who is making an effort to provide for her from her property and to pay her taxes and her debts. Now, please summon the two guardians, R. Yehuda and Don Zark Malet and persuade them to fulfill their role as guardians, and to make an effort in the affairs of my orphaned daughter."

And we the court saw that her words had merit and deserved attention,

These documents are found in the Arxiu Capitular de Barcelona and were published in facsimile by J. M. Millas i Vallicrosa, *Documents hebraics de jueus catalans* (Barcelona: Institut d'Estudis Catalans, 1927), nos. 16, 18, 21. Translation reproduced with permission of the family of the translator.
    1. Reina, having lost her father, was considered an orphan.

Figure 12. Passover scene from the Barcelona Haggadah (ca. 1350). British Library, MS Add. 14761, fol. 28v. Permission and photo credit: British Library, London, © The British Library Board.

על הבית נע ביונו שאומרים ההודה

Figure 13. Synagogue scene from the Sister Haggadah (ca. 1350). British Library, MS Or 2884, fol. 17v. Photo credit: HIP/Art Resource, NY.

and we investigated the matter of whether Don Bonsenyor and R. Yehuda and Don Zark Malet had been appointed [to deal with] the property of the orphan, and the matter remained unclear. Since the property of the orphan was being wasted because there was no one to take care of it, and we saw that R. Yehuda ibn R. Shmuel and Don Zark Malet were trustworthy, affluent, and fit to appoint as guardians for the orphan, we made them agents of the court and appointed them and Don Bonsenyor guardians for the property

of the orphan, with the stipulation that whenever all three of them should
be in this city, they shall do whatever needs to be done in the affairs of the
orphan by agreement of the three of them, and whenever Don Bonsenyor
is not in this city, we have given full power and authority to R. Yehuda and
Don Zark Malet to do business, the two of them alone, with the property of
the orphan. . . .

*The rest of the document specifies the powers of the guardians, and concludes with
standard formulas. It is dated Nisan, 5061. Fifteen months later, in Elul 5062, Cruxia
was back in court. This time, she wanted to collect her* ketubbah *(marriage settlement), which was still owed her by her daughter. The court wrote:*

We the undersigned court were obliged [to act] in the matter of the
honored lady Cruxia, the widow of R. Shmuel ibn R. Yitzhak HaSardi, who
delayed the prayers in the synagogue for many days to have her *ketubbah* and
the gift which her husband . . . made to her collected for her; the [Jewish]
officials in charge of justice in this city ordered us, the undersigned court, to
take care of her needs . . . to collect her *ketubbah* and her gift from the estate
of her husband.

The court proceeded to verify all aspects of her claim. They first examined her ketubbah *and the deed of gift from her husband, recording the amounts of money involved,
the dates, and the witnesses to the two documents and validating the signatures of
the witnesses. The sum owed her came to 400 gold coins. The court then summoned
Reina's guardians to ask if there was any evidence that she might have been paid
already. When the guardians confirmed that there was no such evidence, the court
required Cruxia to swear that she had not received any part of the money which she
was claiming. Finally, they examined Reina's property to determine what would be
best to sell in order to pay Cruxia. They recorded that only one pair of buyers was
found; the rest of the document is a bill of sale selling the designated land to the two
buyers, Moshe de Tolosa and Avraham Ascandrani, who were also buying some land
from Cruxia herself.*
     *Another document dated the same month describes the actual transfer of both
plots of land, the one sold by the guardians and the one sold by Cruxia herself.*

We the undersigned witnesses [testify that] we were present together
when R. Moshe and R. Avraham took possession of that land . . . which was
R. Shmuel HaSardi's . . . and the guardians of the orphan Reina, daughter
of R. Shmuel HaSardi and Don Perfet Bonafos [acting] for Cruxia . . . were
present, and in our presence the guardians and Don Perfet for Cruxia said
to them, "go and take possession and buy that land" . . . and R. Moshe and
R. Avraham asked us to write this memorial of testimony to be a proof for

them that they took possession with the authorization of the aforementioned guardians and with their [referent unclear] authorization and with the authorization of the lady Cruxia by the agency of Don Perfet.

B. Opinions Concerning a Daughter's Inheritance (1293)
Translated from Hebrew by Elka Klein

Court Record of Bonadona's Claim

The following document was produced in 1293 by the Jewish court in Barcelona at the request of Bonadona, daughter of Samuel (Astrug) Ascandrani. The document is simply an official copy of a document produced by a different court a year earlier. (EK)

We the undersigned court [state]: the Lady Bonadona, the wife of R. Judah ibn R. Jucifia Saporta, came before us and said to us, "please make an official copy of this record of a legal decision for Estevan deSpelugis, monk of Santa Anna, since he bought from me a vineyard which is mentioned in the record, since the purchaser did not want to give me the money until I hand over to him the official copy of this decision which was handed down about this vineyard, along with the rest of my property." We saw her words [to be reasonable] and heard her request [lit. voice] and we made an official copy of it for the aforementioned monk and this is the copy, letter for letter and word for word, without addition or subtraction:

"We the undersigned court [state]: it happened that Lady Bonadona, the wife of R. Judah ibn R. Jucifia Saporta, came before us and said to us, "since my father, R. Samuel ibn R. Abraham Ascandrani made a will concerning his possessions at the time of his death and he had no heir but me and he gave me as his heir the houses which I live in today in the Jewish quarter, and a vineyard at the edge of this city [Barcelona] near Mogoria, and a seat in the synagogue in the courtyard of the Israelites [i.e., in the men's section of the synagogue] in this city and he said at that time that if (heaven forbid) I should die without children then the aforementioned property should revert to a charitable trust; now I need to sell [the property] in order to support myself and I am afraid that I will not find a buyer since everyone knows that this property is mortgaged to the charitable trust because of my father's will.

The first text (Court Record) is translated from Joaquim Miret y Sans and Moise Schwab, "Documents sur les juifs catalans aux XIe, XIIe, et XIIIe siècles," *Revue des Etudes Juives* 68 (1914), document 36; the second text (Letter) is from the *responsa* of Solomon ibn Abraham Adret, *Teshuvot sheelot leha-Rashba* (Jerusalem: Hots'at bet ha-sefarim ha-le'umi veha-'universita'i, 1976), vol. 1, no. 704. English translations reproduced with permission of the family of the translator.

Please consider the laws and examine my father's will and determine for me whether my father's words giving the possessions after my death, are valid or not. We looked in her eyes and heard her voice [request] and we took the will of her father from her and went over it in detail and discussed what was written in it, and all three of us were of one mind after we went over it about the law, and with the agreement and advice of our teacher and rabbi, R. Solomon ibn R. Abraham ben Adret we made a judgment about the law that the charitable trust has no right to any of the aforementioned possessions, even if the Lady Bonadona should die without children, since her father ordered that she should have title to the possessions as an heir all the days of her life, and even though he ordered that they should return to the charitable trust after her death if she should die without children, he did not have the power to make such a condition since inheritance has no interruption [an heir's possession of his inheritance cannot be interrupted by the wishes of the person who bequeathed the property]. In order for Lady Bonadona to have it as a proof, we signed our names here in the month of Elul, in the year 5052 since the creation of the world [15 August–12 September 1292], as we reckon it here in Barcelona, and it is valid and binding: Judah ibn R. Solomon (may God protect him); Samuel ibn R. Joseph (may his Rock and Redeemer protect him); Judah ibn R. Yeshua (may he rest in peace)."

      This is the record of the legal decision and the court which signed it which we copied for the aforementioned monk on the orders of the Lady Bonadona; we examined the signatures of the court and we know that these are their signatures and we have written and signed and given it to the aforementioned monk to be evidence of his purchase and it is valid and binding: Hosea ibn R. Joseph (may he be remembered for the life of the world to come); Hiyya ibn R. Solomon (may his Rock and Redeemer protect him); Solomon ibn R. Samuel Saporta [not apparently a close relation to Bonadona's husband].

Letter About the Case from Solomon ibn Abraham Adret

The following is an abridgment of the letter from Solomon ibn Abraham Adret (1235-1310) to the Barcelona court about Bonadona's problem. Barcelona rabbi Solomon Adret was a student of Nahmanides (see Chapter 57) and was one of the most respected scholars of his day.

Question: You asked [about] a person on his deathbed who made his will in gentile script [i.e., Latin], namely he ordered that his words be written as a will by X and Y in [both] Hebrew and Latin so that it would be effective. Does it matter that they wrote them as a will after his death? Do we say that these people are the agents of the dying man, given that an agent cannot act after death [of the one who empowered him] or shall we say that he is only like one who conveys his intentions to them, to carry them out as long as they wish, even after his death? If you say that they can write them, tell us about his instruction that it should be effective in Hebrew and Latin: should [we take it] literally so that if their language is sufficient in Hebrew (for complete fulfillment of what he said), would they be forbidden from writing it in Latin; or perhaps he meant only that it should be effective, even if it is not effective in Latin?

Moreover, your brother also asked in your name about the substance of the will which the dying man made: he bequeathed what he had to his daughter and he even went so far as to specify that if she should die with no surviving child that some of the property should revert to his brother(s) and some to a charitable trust and moreover, even if the daughter gave [her bequest] as a gift [he stipulated] that none of it should come to her husband, nor income from it, nor income from its income—is this provision valid or not?

Answer: First of all, I will discuss general principles and afterwards, I will deal with the particulars. Even though [the sages] said that "the words of a dying man are as if they were written and conveyed,"[1] they only intended this to apply to the words which he said, not to add to his words or take away from them in order to put them into effect, even though he revealed his intentions [i.e., if what he ordered could have legal effect, we do it, but we do not modify his requests even when it is clear what he wanted to achieve by them]. . . . Now I will explain the specifics which emerge from these principles. Consider that since the dying man intended for his daughter to inherit all the property from him, it immediately became hers by biblical law as it says in scripture, "and on the day that he wills to his sons" [Deut. 21:16]. So long as he does not recover and revoke the gift, it is entirely the property of the heir and if he makes any conditions about it afterwards, he is making conditions about the property of the heir [over which he has no control]. . . . Thus the reservation which he made in the daughter's bequest that the husband would have no share in the property is meaningless, as we learn in the Talmud, "if she only receives what she consumes [her husband gets nothing]," but here he did not say so. Moreover, I already said that we never reduce his gift, so that she only gets some small part of the property in order to fulfill his purpose and his orders; especially since the daughter alone inherits all the property left by the father, anything left her as a [mere] gift comes to

---

1. Baba Batra 151a, 175a; Gittin 13a, 15a. This refers to two tractates (Baba Batra and Gittin) in the Talmud.

her with the force of inheritance, . . . therefore there is no vestige of support for what he ordered and bequeathed, including all of those reservations and conditions which he made. . . . It is clear that after his death no one can add to or subtract from [what he said], and everything [else] he said would be of no effect, even if he were still alive, [since] he insisted on this exact language and ordered thus, even though this is a deathbed bequest. Especially since if he said, "write and seal and give it" [i.e., he gave specific instructions about the writing] we worry lest the acquisition can only be completed in a document, and one cannot issue a document after death, as it says in Baba Batra chapter 8 and chapter 9. Especially in the case of this man who commanded that his words be put in an effective document perhaps it was the document which he wanted.

59. THE KING AND THE CORTES

A. Rulings of the Cortes of Castile-León (1258–1325)

Translated from Castilian by Joseph F. O'Callaghan

The Cortes of Castile-León typified the development of representative parliamentary institutions in western Europe during the High Middle Ages. The origins of the Cortes as a parliamentary assembly of the estates of the kingdoms of Castile and León gathered at the king's command date to the late twelfth century (Chapter 37). By the second half of the thirteenth century the Cortes had emerged as a body consisting of the three estates of bishops, nobles, and representatives of the towns. The king summoned the Cortes most often to obtain consent for taxation, but the urban representatives (and sometimes the prelates and nobles) took advantage of these meetings to present petitions to the king; if he approved them, they became the law of the land. Ordinances drawn up by the royal council were also promulgated in the Cortes. The selections below are intended to illustrate the composition of the Cortes and some of its principal functions. (JFO'C)

Alfonso X Enacts Laws Concerning the Royal Court, Food, Lodging, Dress, and the Protection of the Environment in the Cortes of Valladolid, 17 January 1258

Don Alfonso, by the grace of God, king of Castile, Toledo, León, Galicia, Seville, Córdoba, Murcia, and Jaén, to all the magnates, knights, and nobles, and all the good men of the [military] orders, and to all the [municipal] councils of the kingdom of León who may see this my charter, health and grace. Know that I had counsel and agreement with my brothers, the archbishops and bishops, the magnates of Castile and León, with good men of the towns of Castile, Extremadura, and the kingdom of León, who were with me in Valladolid, concerning many objectionable matters that were done to the damage of myself and of my whole realm, and they agree to remove them and to set down specific and certain things so that you might live. And what they set down I consented to hold and to cause it to be held and observed by all my realms. And they also swore and promised to observe it and hold it and the archbishops and bishops imposed the sentence of excommunication on all those who would not hold it. And the matters are these. . . .

 3. The king shall command the men who live with him to eat more

 Translated from *Cortes de los antiguos reinos de León y de Castilla*, edited by Real Academia de la Historia (Madrid: M. Rivadeneyra, 1861–1903), 1:54–63, 130–33, 142–45, 187, 236–37, 372–89.

moderately and not to go to such great expense as they do. The expense that they shall incur shall be only as much as the king commands. . . .

8. They think it right that each [municipal] council that has a suit before the king shall send two good men [as representatives] and no more [to the court]. . . .

9. The king commands that all litigants who come to his court shall go before the judges and if the plea is one that the judges can hear and adjudicate, let them adjudicate it at once; if the plea is one for the king, let them bring it to him. . . .

42. The king commands that they shall not set fire to the woods and the one who is found doing so is to be thrown into it. . . .

43. The king commands that no one shall throw into streams herbs or lime or other things that might kill the fish. . . .

And I the aforesaid King Don Alfonso order you to hold and to observe all the aforesaid agreements. . . .

Given at Valladolid, as the king ordered, the seventeenth day of January in the era 1296 [1258].

Fernando IV Confirms the Laws and Customs of the Towns in the Cortes of Valladolid, 8 August 1295

In the name of God, the Father, Son, and Holy Spirit, who are three persons and one God, and of the Virgin Holy Mary, his mother, whom we take for our lady and advocate in all our affairs, we want those who are now and will be in future to know by this our privilege, how we Don Fernando, by the grace of God, king of Castile, León, Galicia, Seville, Córdoba, Murcia, Jaén, and the Algarve, and lord of Molina, while in the cortes in the town of Valladolid, having summoned to it prelates, magnates, masters of knighthoods [military orders] and all the others of our realms, so that we might know what is to the service of God and ourselves and the very great benefit of all the people of our realms, and the improvement of the estate of our whole realm; and having the desire to do good and favor to all the councils of our realms, with the counsel of the queen Doña María, our mother, and with the consent of Infante Don Enrique, our uncle and our guardian, and with the counsel of Roy Perez, master of Calatrava, our tutor, and of Don Juan Osorez, master of the knighthood of Santiago, and of the prelates and magnates and other good men who were there with us, we ordain and we grant and we confirm these things for ever more.

1. First, that we will preserve for them [the municipal councils] their laws, privileges, charters, franchises, liberties, usages, and customs that they had in the time of the emperor [Alfonso VII, r. 1126–1157] and of King Don

Alfonso [VIII, r. 1158–1214], who won the battle of Úbeda, and of King Don
Alfonso [IX, r. 1188–1230], who won the battle of Mérida, and of his son
King Don Fernando [III, r. 1217–1252], and of the other kings whence we are
descended. . . .

Twelve other articles follow.

And we the aforesaid King Don Fernando . . . promise and pledge to
hold and preserve all the aforesaid things and not to contravene them at any
time. And for greater stability in all this Infante Don Enrique, our uncle and
our guardian, as guardian swore for us, on the Gospel and on the cross, and
he pledged homage and fealty that we would maintain and preserve this for
all time as it has been said. And we order this privilege sealed with our seal of
lead to be given to the council of Burgos, the head of Castile and our chamber. Given at Valladolid, the eighth day of August, in the era 1333 [1295].

Fernando IV Receives the Petitions of the Towns of León in the Cortes of Valladolid, 15 April 1299

Don Fernando, by the grace of God, king of Castile, León, Toledo, Galicia,
Seville, Córdoba, Murcia, Jaén, and the Algarve, and lord of Molina, to the
council of Cáceres, greeting and favor. I make known to you that in the cortes that I now ordered to be held in Valladolid, the good men of the towns
and places of the kingdom of León who were there with me presented their
petitions to me and asked my favor to grant them and confirm them and to
order them to be preserved. Because I have a great desire to do much good
and much favor to all those of my realm I think it right.

1. First of all they asked me to go at once through the realm and to make
arrangements concerning the business of the war. To this I say that after
taking counsel with the good men who are here with me I will do with my
council what will be best for my service and the benefit of the realm.

2. They also asked me to command that the customs and privileges that
they have from the kings from whom I am descended and from me, shall be
preserved . . . [they also asked] that if any one violates them or tries to violate
them in the future, I should order the judges and magistrates in every place to
arrest them . . . and . . . hold them to impose whatever [penalty] I may order.

3. They also asked my favor to order that justice be done on those who
merit it . . . and that no persons shall be arrested or killed or their goods
taken without their being heard by law and the custom of the place where
they are; and this shall be guarded better than it has been guarded up to now.
To this I say to you that I think it right and I will do so in the future. . . .

And I ordered this charter sealed with my pendant wax seal to be given to you. Given at Valladolid the fifteenth day of April in the era 1337 [1299].

Fernando IV Assures the Cortes of Valladolid That He Will Not Levy Extraordinary Tributes Without Obtaining Consent, 29 June 1307

6. Because the realm is deserted and very poor and because, thanks be to God, there is no war, they asked me, as a favor, that I should try to settle and foster the people of my realm, and that I should try to determine how much my kingdoms render in customary revenues and in my other rights, and that I should take therefrom what I think best for myself, and that I should apportion the rest among magnates, barons, and knights, as my favor may decide, so that I should not impose taxes or illegal tributes on the realm. To this I say, that I think it right, but if it should happen that I have need of any tributes, I will have to ask for them, and I will not impose any tributes on the realm in any other manner.

Queen Mother María de Molina and Her Son Infante Pedro, Regents for King Alfonso XI, Promise the Cortes of Palencia That They Will Hold the Cortes Every Two Years, 15 June 1313

11. Also they [the cortes] ordained that from now on we shall always be bound to cause the general cortes to be summoned every two years between Michaelmas [September 29] and All Saints Day [November 1] in a convenient place in order to know how we have labored in the previous period; and if perchance we do not want to summon the cortes, the prelates and counselors in the name of the king shall cause the cortes to be summoned and we shall be bound by their summons or that of anyone of them to come to the cortes . . . .We think it right and we grant it.

Alfonso XI, on Coming of Age, Dismisses His Guardians, Summons the Cortes to Valladolid, and Responds to the Petitions of the Municipal Procurators, 12 December 1325

In the name of God, amen. Let all those who see this booklet know that I, Don Alfonso, by the grace of God, king of Castile, Toledo, León, Galicia, Seville, Córdoba, Murcia, Jaén, the Algarve, and lord of Molina, while in Valladolid following the feast of Saint Hippolytus on which I completed my fifteenth year and ought no [longer] to have a guardian, I took power for myself to use it in my realms as I ought, and I decided to send my letters to summon to the cortes here in Valladolid all those of my realms to ordain and to do many things that are to my service and benefit and the preservation of my dominion. There were here with me, Infante Don Felipe, Don Juan, son of Infante Don Manuel, and Don Juan, son of Infante Don Juan, and prelates, and magnates, masters of the [military] orders, the prior of the Hospital of St. John, barons, and knights, my vassals, and knights and good men, procurators of the cities and towns and places of my kingdoms. I sent my letters to summon here the procurators of the cities and towns and places of my kingdoms of Castile, León, Toledo, and the Extremaduras. In the name of the councils whose procurators they were, they presented their petitions to me, seeing that it was to my great service and benefit and the preservation of all the people of my realm. The petitions are those that follow, and I granted them and swore to observe them, according as they follow in this booklet. [*Forty-two petitions follow.*]

I ordered this booklet sealed with my pendant seal of wax to be given to the council of Mula. Given at Valladolid, the twelfth day of December in the era 1363 [1325].

B. Rulings of the Cortes of Portugal (1372)
Translated from Portuguese by Rita Costa Gomes

Towns have increasing amount of power

Like those of Castile-León, the rulings of the Cortes of Portugal were a source of law. Since the Cortes of Leiria (1254), in Portugal the participation of the delegates of the towns became the norm. But it was only with the government of king Afonso IV (r. 1325–1357) that the meetings resulted in written petitions (capítulos or artigos). These were systematically sent back to the towns in royal charters containing also the king's answers (respostas), documents which are the main source of information on the matters discussed in each meeting. The "golden age" of the Cortes in Portugal was the later medieval period. The meetings became more frequent, going from once every five to ten years between 1320 and 1360 to one meeting every two to three years in the last decades of the 1300s, and even every twelve to eighteen months in the first half of the fifteenth century. By then, the Cortes had become an important instrument of governance and a generator of political consensus in a more structured political society.

During the sixteen years of the reign of Fernando I, nine meetings of the Cortes are documented. The war policy of this monarch, siding with the opponents of the new rulers of the Trastámara family in Castile and as an ally to the English and the Aragonese, led to two successive devaluations of money (in 1369 and 1373), and to painful destruction of many areas of the kingdom invaded by Castilian armies. The refuge given to exiled noblemen from other regions of Iberia soon became unpopular. All these matters were to be discussed in the Cortes, where the cities repeatedly

Translated from *Cortes portuguesas: Reinado de D. Fernando I (1367–1383)*, edited by A. H. de Oliveira Marques and Nuno José Pizarro Pinto Dias (Lisbon: Instituto Nacional de Investigação Científica, Centro de Estudos Históricos da Universidade Nova de Lisboa, 1990), pp. 81–87.

criticized the king's policies in a tone of rising exasperation. After the <u>death of king</u> Fernando, the Cortes of Coimbra in 1385 <u>refused to accept as queen of Portugal his</u> <u>daughter Beatriz</u>, who was <u>married to Juan I of Castile</u>, and instead elected as the new king the master of Avis João. (RCG)

The Cortes of Porto, July 1372

In the name of God, Amen. We Dom Fernando by the grace of God king of Portugal and the Algarve, to whoever sees this charter we make known that, as we consider how our royal state was given to us by God to govern the said kingdoms and to maintain our people within law and justice and good customs, such as it is proper for each king to do, with the help of God we took the task of ruling the said kingdoms. And since God's service and ours would be to have good governance of the kingdoms, in such ways that the people would be bettered and would prosper, each person living safely as he should within right and justice, thus we summoned our Cortes in the city of Porto. And we had two good men (*homens-bons*) from each city and town of our kingdoms sent to the Cortes with the purpose of having good counsel and agreement with them, not only about the coinage that we had made but also about taxation and other matters which were in the service of God and ours, and of benefit to our people, so that they would see and consider how and in which manner the governance of the said kingdoms could be corrected and improved and how we could redress any evil or damage done, and also that they would tell us of any abuses which they may have received from us or from our officials or other powerful people, so that we could correct those according to what is right and proper, and so that we would grant them favor, as it pertains to us.

And so the good men [*homens-bons*], citizens and other people under our lordship appeared in our presence in the said Cortes and gave us in writing the record of those matters that they judged should be done for the service of God and ours, and the common good of the said kingdoms, and by which our governance of the kingdoms could be improved, and also those things that the people claimed as abuses made to them. . . .

And as we saw what they said and showed, taking the counsel of those who are with us at the royal court and other numerous and good men of law from our land, we answered to each petition as follows:

In response to the first petition which said that we waged <u>war against</u> <u>the kingdom of Castile</u>, <u>and that</u> was cause for great damage and the rise of prices all over the land, for many reasons that would be long to narrate. And the people are aggrieved because they were not called to be a part of this decision, as they rightfully should since they had their share in it. And

(handwritten margin note: towns before waging war to think ?)

because the damage caused by the war could not be repaired unless there were peace.

Therefore, the people were asking in our mercy that we make all effort possible to have peace (may God give it to us) with all the kings who are Christian. And if by any chance in the future it may happen that we consider being in our honor to engage in war, then we should first summon our people and hear their counsel.

To this we respond that we now have peace, God willing, with all Christian kings. And if it happens that some king will want to make war against us, we will take the counsel of the better men of the kingdom and we will make agreement with them regarding the honor and guard and defense of our kingdoms.

Item to what they said in the second article, that one of the things they thought caused damage to our land was because of the coinage that we had made. Because from ancient times it was established between the kings our predecessors and the people that if [the king] wanted to make coins, those should be from the new type of coin as it circulated before the aforementioned war. And [the agreement was] that new coin should be struck only in one year during our lifetime, and issued twice and no more. But we are now going against that which was established, to great detriment of our kingdoms and people, and we had many diverse types of coins made, with different alloy composition. And such coins we had put in very high and unreasonable prices for the bullion that was used in them, for which reasons men, for lack of knowledge of these new coins, squandered much gold and silver and other things they had, believing that they were selling for good money, but the price soon turned to naught in these new coins. And to add to this damage we then had the money devalued, thus making those who had it lose half of what they had and more. And for this the people suffered more than they should, for it would be fair that we should have been charged with the loss, since we had the profit from the new money. And if we wanted to lower the value of the money, we should have had the new coins first taken for ourselves, by the same price that we gave it to our people. And much other damage ensued by reason of this coinage, which would be too long to tell.

And it seemed to our people that all the damage that came from it could not be amended unless we stopped making more coins, and if the new coins already made were not returned to their fair value, according to the quantity of their metals. Nor would the land return to its previous state, because nobody wants to either receive these coins or sell anything accepting them. For this would be too much for them, while getting paid with such money those who had it were losing much wealth, and the loss should be ours and not theirs as it is said before. But since we could not endure it without loss of our service, and since they hoped that this would be amended by us together with other matters and it would be our mercy that they would receive this damage.

So they asked us in our mercy that no more coins are made, neither by ourselves nor by others in our kingdoms. And that the coins that were already made are returned to the fair prices they should have in comparison with the coinage that circulated before the war, and have the coins thus run all throughout the kingdom. For they believed that the land could return to its state, and if not, then the land would be at risk of total loss.

To this the city of Lisbon contradicted the part about the devaluation of the money. And they asked about the new coin named *coroados*, which was debased in comparison to the one called *graves*, that its value should be converted to the same alloy of the *graves*, and let it circulate that way as long as we do not make more coinage. And that we should make the decision of no future changes in it. And the cities of Elvas, Olivença, Monforte, Portalegre, and Sabugal agreed with Lisbon.

To this article we say that the towns have their answers in separate charters.

Item to what they say in the third petition, that we bring damage to our people and our land because it was the custom that everybody living under our lordship could sell freely their bread, and the wine, and the cattle, and the other things they had, without any imposed fixed prices [*almotaçaria*]. But now against the said custom we had certain prices fixed and established for all things to be sold in our territories, and we ordained that things be sold for such small prices that their owners were in great loss, most of all because of the bad coinage. Because the things that we ordained should be sold at the value of 20 *soldos* did sell only for 2 *soldos* or little more, as we were told by those who had the knowledge of the said coins. So it happened that the lamb that we ordered be sold for 10 *soldos* was sold for 4 *soldos*, and the yard of cloth which we ordered should be valued at 36 *soldos* was sold for 3 and a half, and this way of all the other things. And to make things worse, that we ruled that even if the owners of the things did not want to sell them, they would be forced to do so, and by the prices that we had decided. And these orders were not respected with equality, nor are they followed to this day, because the great lords and noblemen and prelates of our land took the things from the small people following the said rule and paid for those things almost nothing. And we ourselves did so, since when we saw things becoming so cheap we took what we needed for us, as shall be declared later on. And so we ordered that some of those things be given to some other people, thus acting as if "from the bread of his father we give a great piece to our godson."[1] [In the meantime], all that we and they had was kept hoarded. So it was that this taxation of prices [*almotaçaria*] was not respected, except by those who did not own *tabardos*.[2] And, if needed, proof would be presented that there were some great lords who took the things from the humble people, and proceeded to resell those for a sum that was sevenfold the price of cost. And in the meantime they kept hoarded quantities of bread and wine and other things, which they did not want to sell, neither were they forced to do so. Instead, the humble people who sold theirs were lacking, for they were and still are dispossessed each day, as already told here. And therefore, our land, which before this used to be the most abundant that could be found in the world, is now one in which no necessities can be found for sale. And further-more, because of the said taxation we lost a great part of our tax rights in the transactions of cloth and iron and bread and many other things which ceased to come to our land because of it, and were greatly needed. And if this is not corrected, then our land would be in a state of ruin.

For this reason our people were asking let it be our mercy that we should lift this taxation of prices [*almotaçaria*] and that each person could sell that which was his on his own volition and the way he wanted, keeping the prac-tice of taxation only to the municipalities, free and exempt as they always were. And we were asked that our royal officers, judges and *corregedores* and *ouvidores*, should not judge on the conflicts arising from this [municipal *al-motaçaria*], either in first instance or by appeal. And we should order the great lords of our land to sell the bread and wine that they had hoarded, since so far they have eaten and they eat from what is not theirs. And since there were many men who did not want to give what was theirs by the taxed price, they were denounced and had to run away, and some of them were im-prisoned. To repress such evil, [the people] asked that we pardon those who disregarded such taxation of prices, even if they were already imprisoned and condemned because of it.

To this article we respond and order, because we want to award mercy and grace to our people, that the taxation of prices that was made by us be lifted, as long as this will be made according to what is decided in the answer to the second petition, and contained in the letters that were sent to the towns. And we also pardon all those who disrespected such taxation up to

1. This sentence seems to use a popular expression ("dando grande pedaço de pão de nosso compadre a nosso afilhado") equivalent to the English "robbing Peter to pay Paul."
2. The *tabardo* was an expensive piece of apparel, a rich cape often doubled with fur. Therefore, with this expression "those who did not own *tabardos*," the text uses a euphemism to say "those who were not rich."

this point, and let those who were imprisoned and convicted for this reason be freed.

Item to what they say in the fourth article that we oppress our people and damage our land because of the great donations of towns and villages and other places which we gave to our vassals, both those from our land as well as those who are from abroad. And these [donations] were done against our service and in damage of our land because we used to have good rent from the said places which were thus given, from which we used to sustain all the expense of the kingdom, and we used to have depositories of bread which were much needed for [purveyance of] our fleet and castles. Hence the land has been and is destroyed, because those to whom we gave it took refuge there with numerous followers who wasted any single thing they found, so that the inhabitants of the said places could not have any sustenance and received many debasements and injuries, for those people would dishonor their wives and daughters and made many more insufferable insults to them, for instance, they would launch money penalties, which were never used in our land, and some of them even claimed that since the king gave them the lands, they could sell those or give them in mortgage as if theirs entirely. Therefore, the said inhabitants claimed they would rather be in the power of Moors than of these people, since their situation would not be as bad. And for such reason many of the said places were on the verge of being deserted. And another reason for this was that we also donated the rights of justice and of high and low jurisdiction [*imperium merum et mixtum*] to many of the lords, and this we could not and should not have done because our person was chosen by God so that in his name we increase justice in the land and give to each person what he deserves and is right, and when any such function is thus determined, it could not be committed to anyone else. And it would be fair that if the person who had any privilege or right, and used those in ways that he should not have, then he should lose them. And, furthermore, since such donations were made against the law, for this reason they should not be valid, and it pertains to each one to revoke that which he should not have done, and this will be counted for great wisdom.

Therefore, our people asked us let it be our mercy to be willing to revoke such donations, and that we return all the lands and rights and jurisdictions and justices to our possession, and return to the towns the territories which we took from their counties' jurisdictions. And since there is no doubt that the said vassals of ours were worthy of all our mercy, that it would be good for us to share our rents and treasury with them, in such a way that they would be willing to serve us.

To this article we answer that it is our intention to put some temperance

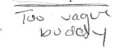

in this and in the part of the jurisdictions as well, in such a way that our service will be guarded as well as the good of the kingdom, and we have all the purpose of doing it so.

Item to what they say in the fifth petition that one of the things that our people find to be most needed to our service as a king is to have a treasury, from which derives much profit. Among other good things that derive from it, it is there in times of need even if the king has little power, since he can consequently gather much more power from his treasury. And since the one who has small income from rents and great expenses cannot generate a treasury, therefore our people asked us let it be our mercy to look after the rents we have, and according to such rents control the expenses of our household and of the queen's household and that of our brothers, and equally the money fiefs that we give to our vassals, and the payments given to those in our mercy. Because of the high prices in our land and the weak value of the money, we had raised their payments and rents, but if we now return the money to its value, since God had given us peace, then things would return to what they once were, and there would be no reason not to return their payments and rents to what they used to be. And [our people asked] that we should regulate all this in such a way that we should set apart each year a certain sum for our treasury, for they thought this would be greatly in our service.

To this article we answer and say that until now we could not prevent such great expenses, in our household as well as in the payments made to those in our mercy, because of the high prices of the things they needed to sustain themselves. But since we think that from now on things will return to their right prices due to the devaluation of the money that we now have determined, we shall look into this, as it is our duty, and we will regulate it the way it should be done.

60. TALES OF MARIAN MIRACLES

Five Stories from the *Cantigas de Santa María*
Translated from Galician-Portuguese by Kathleen Kulp-Hill

The manuscript of the Cantigas de Santa María *brings together an extensive collection of songs and stories in praise of the Virgin Mary. Each tale, written in Galician-Portuguese, recounts a miracle performed by Mary, and the text is accompanied by musical notation and a facing folio of six illustrations depicting its narrative. The luxurious manuscript was commissioned in two volumes by Alfonso X of Castile in the third quarter of the thirteenth century, and some of the songs may have been written by the king himself. Both volumes survive, but they have been separated. The first volume is held in the Escorial Library near Madrid, the second (which was never finished) is in Florence, Italy. Most of the tales in the* Cantigas de Santa María *relate to events in the Iberian Peninsula, but some stories are based on narratives from elsewhere in Europe. Many different kinds of people appear in these miracle stories: Christians, Muslims, and Jews; laypeople and religious; inhabitants of urban and rural areas; rich and poor; men and women; and people from all walks of medieval life (including Alfonso X himself). A number of stories, including two presented here, relate to miracles involving animals. These stories, and especially the detailed illustrations that accompany them, provide precious insights into daily life and thought in medieval Castile. (ORC)*

94

This is how Holy Mary served in place of the nun who left the convent.[1]

The Virgin Mary ever strives to protect us from shame and sin and error.

She protects us from sin and shields us even when we lapse into error. Then She makes us repent and atone for the sins we commit. Concerning this, the Peerless Holy Queen who guides us performed a miracle in an abbey.

There was a lady there who, as I learned, was young and beautiful. Furthermore, she observed the rules of the order so scrupulously that there was no one as diligent as she in turning everything to good account. Therefore, they made her treasurer. However, the devil, who was displeased by this, made her love a knight passionately and gave her no peace until he caused her to

English text from *Songs of Holy Mary of Alfonso X, the Wise: A Translation of the Cantigas de Santa Maria*, translated by Kathleen Kulp-Hill (Tempe: Arizona Center for Medieval and Renaissance Studies, 2000), pp. 118-19, 133-34, 177, 204, 214-15. Reprinted with permission of the publisher.

[1] This is a version of the legend of Sister Beatrice, of which the oldest written account is "De Beatrice custode," in the *Dialogus miraculorum* of 1223 by Caesarius von Heisterbach, a Cistercian monk in the Rhineland. The legend spread throughout western Europe in Latin and the modern languages.

Figure 14. The Story of How Holy Mary Served in Place of the Nun Who Left the Convent, *Cantigas de Santa María*, number 94. Biblioteca Real del Escorial, Codex T.I.I, fol. 136v. Reproduced with permission from the Patrimonio Nacional, Madrid. Photo credit: University of Notre Dame, Rare Books Department.

Figure 15. The Story of How Holy Mary Saved from Death the Jewess Who
Was Thrown over a Cliff in Segovia, *Cantigas de Santa María*, number 107.
Biblioteca Real del Escorial, Codex T.I.1, fol. 154r. Reproduced with permission
from the Patrimonio Nacional, Madrid. Photo credit: University of Notre Dame,
Rare Books Department.

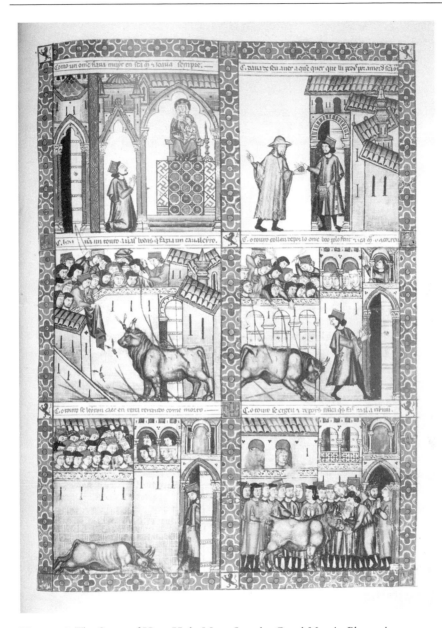

Figure 16. The Story of How Holy Mary Saved a Good Man in Plasencia from Death by a Bull, *Cantigas de Santa María*, number 144. Biblioteca Real del Escorial, Codex T.I.1, fol. 200r. Reproduced with permission from the Patrimonio Nacional, Madrid. Photo credit: University of Notre Dame, Rare Books Department.

Figure 17. The Story of a Miracle Which Holy Mary Performed for a Church of Hers in La Arrijaca, *Cantigas de Santa María*, number 169. Biblioteca Real del Escorial, Codex T.I.I, fol. 226v. Reproduced with permission from the Patrimonio Nacional, Madrid. Photo credit: University of Notre Dame, Rare Books Department.

Figure 18. The Story of a Little Boy of Alcarraz Whose Father Had Given Him a Little She-Mule and It Died, *Cantigas de Santa María*, number 178. Biblioteca Real del Escorial, Codex T.I.1, fol. 237r. Reproduced with permission from the Patrimonio Nacional, Madrid. Photo credit: University of Notre Dame, Rare Books Department.

leave the convent. Before she departed, she left the keys she wore at her belt in front of the altar of the One in whom she believed. "Oh, Mother of God," she then prayed, "I leave you this charge and commend myself to you with all my heart." Then she went away to do as she would with the man she loved more than herself. She lived a long time with him in sin. After the knight took her off with him, he had sons and daughters by her. However, the Benevolent Virgin, who never condoned willfulness, performed a miracle and caused the girl to miss the life she formerly led and long to return to the cloister where she used to live. Moreover, while the girl lived her wayward life, the Virgin took good care of everything she had left in Her charge, for She assumed her place and performed all her duties and was remiss in nothing, according to the opinion of all who saw Her. As soon as the nun repented, she left the knight and neither ate nor slept until she saw the convent. She entered fearfully and began to inquire of those she knew about the conditions of the place, for she was very concerned. They told her frankly: "We have a most excellent abbess, prioress and treasurer who do us great service and have no faults." When she heard this, she began to cross herself, because she heard them speak of her this way. In great alarm, trembling and pale, she went to the church. The Mother of the Lord showed her such great love—for which may She be blessed—that she found the keys where she had placed them and picked up the clothes she had formerly worn. At once, without hesitation or shame, she joined the other nuns and told them the great favor which the One who has the world in Her command did for her. To prove to them all that she told them, she had her lover called in to tell it to them also. The nuns of the convent thought it a very great miracle when they saw it to be a proven thing and swore by Saint John that none so beautiful had ever been told to them before. They began to sing joyfully: "May God save you, Star of the Sea, Light of Day."

107

How Holy Mary saved from death the Jewess who was thrown over a cliff in Segovia.[2] Because she commended herself to Holy Mary, she did not die nor suffer harm.

2. This story is based on an event which took place in 1237 and is still commemorated in Segovia. A Jewess, known popularly as Marisaltos ("Leaping Mary"), was thrown from the promontory Cerro de los Hoyos as punishment for an alleged crime, perhaps adultery or sympathy with the Christian faith. She survived unharmed and was cleared of her guilt. She is entombed in a niche in the cloister of the cathedral of Segovia, and a picture representing a scene from the incident is painted on the wall. The Virgin Mary is revered as protectress of Segovia. See John Esten Keller, "Daily Living as Presented in the *Canticles* of Alfonso the Learned," *Speculum* 33 (1958): 484–98; and "Miracle of the Jewess Thrown from a High Cliff': Number 107 of the *Cantigas de Santa Maria*," *Xavier Review* 2 (1982): 62–67.

The Holy Virgin will aid those in distress if they believe in Her.

Concerning this, the Mother of Mercy performed a miracle, in all truth, in the city of Segovia, as this song will relate. It was for a Jewess who was caught in a crime and arrested and taken to be hurled from a high and rugged cliff in that place. She said: "Oh, woe is me, how can anyone who falls from here remain alive unless it be by God's will? But you, Queen Mary, in whom Christians believe, if it is true, as I have heard, that you succor the unfortunate women who are commended to you, among all the other guilty women, come to my aid, for I have great need. If I remain alive and well, I will, without fail, become a Christian at once, before another day dawns." The Jews who led her, dressed only in her shift, let go of her and pushed her over the cliff, shouting: "There she goes!" But when she fell from there, the Virgin came to her aid. Therefore, she did not perish but fell clear of the rocks right at the foot of a fig tree. She sprang up nimbly and went on her way, saying: "May the Glorious One, Precious Mother of God, who was so merciful to me, be ever praised. Who will not serve Her?" She arrived at the church of Her who should always be blessed, where she saw a great crowd of people, and she said: "Come at once and baptize me, then you will hear a miracle which will astound you and all who hear it." Those people baptized her without delay, and she was henceforth always a devoted believer in the One who prays to Her glorious Son for us, that He have mercy on us on the fearful day when He will come to judge us.

144

How Holy Mary saved a good man in Plasencia[3] from death by a bull which came at him to kill him.

It is only right that the beasts have great fear of the Mother of that Lord Who has power over all things.

Concerning this, Holy Mary, the Peerless Virgin, performed a great miracle in Plasencia, as I heard it told by good and reliable men. They recount this miracle thus: a good man lived there who loved this Lady above all things, as I learned. Whenever anyone came to ask him something for Her sake, he at once granted it to him without fail, with no hesitation or deceit, for he would not go back on his word for anything. He fasted faithfully on the eve of all Her feast days and never failed to hear Her holy hours, for his only thought was of how to please Her. Then a knight from that city was married, and he had bulls brought for his wedding. He selected the fiercest of them and set it running in a large square which is there in front of the house of the good

3. This is a town in the province of Cáceres, Spain.

man I have mentioned to you. However, the latter had not the least desire to go there to watch it. This man had a *compadre*[4] who was a priest, Matthew by name, who sent for him, as I learned, because he wished to discuss some things with him. So the man went out to go there, and the bull lunged at him to wound him treacherously by thrusting its horns through his back. The priest, when he saw this from a window, asked mercy of Holy Mary, and She did not fail the man, for She came to his aid at once. She aided him in such a way that the bull fell down on the ground and stretched out all four legs, as though it were about to die. It lay in this manner until the man was at the entrance of the house of his *compadre,* who received him warmly and took him into the house. The bull got up, and from then on never did it harm anyone, because of the power of the Peerless Lady, who will not let Her servants come to grief.

169

This is about a miracle which Holy Mary performed for a church of Hers in La Arrijaca[5] of Murcia and tells how Moors had decided to destroy it and never succeeded.

It is no wonder that She whom God made Mother and Daughter in order to save us wishes to be honored by us.

Concerning this, I shall tell a great miracle, which I saw when God granted me Murcia.[6] I also heard it told by many Moors who formerly lived there and held the territory, to our dismay, and who often remembered this. The miracle happened to an ancient church of the Peerless Queen which stood there in the district of La Arrijaca. The Genoese, Pisans, and others from Sicily went there to pray, and they made their offerings. If they prayed with all their hearts to the Virgin, their prayer was heard at once, and She always protected them from mishap and harm, for whoever She takes under Her protection is protected. Therefore the Moors had no power to do any harm whatever in that holy place, nor to remove the church from there, although it lay in their domain. Although many times they begged me to have the church removed, showing me that it would be a good thing if I did so, and their request was granted, it availed them nothing. Then some time ago it happened again, when the king of Aragón, the worthy don Jaume, made the cathedral out of the great mosque, that the Moors rebelled from Murcia

4. This is the relationship of the godfather of a child to the child's parents and god-mother; it indicates close friendship.
5. This is the Moorish section of the city of Murcia, which was first conquered by Jaume I of Aragón, then taken by Alfonso X in 1266.
6. This story is told in the voice of Alfonso X.

to Seville. The Moorish community came to him to ask that that church in La Arrijaca be destroyed. Although he consented to it, they could not touch a single nail of it. After this, it happened that I went to Murcia,[7] and most of the Moorish community asked me to remove the church from their midst, but I was loath to do so, for it had been freshly painted. However, very reluctantly, I granted their request, and all the Moorish community went to the Moorish king to ask him to have it done, but he said: "I will not, for Mariame deals severely with those who displease Her." Later, when Aboyuçaf, lord of Salé, passed by with a great army,[8] it is true that the Moors thought to take Murcia by trickery, in order to exalt their faith. However, the Holy Virgin undid their treacherous plot, for She drove them out of there and left very few of them in La Arrijaca. Thus She freed Her church from them, for in that way She banishes those She despises. Therefore, Her church is now free, for never can Muḥammad hold power there because She conquered it, and furthermore, She will conquer Spain and Morocco, and Ceuta and Asilah.[9]

178

This is about a little boy of Alcarraz[10] whose father had given him a little she-mule, and it died. He commended it to Holy Mary of Salas,[11] and it got up alive and well.

She who surely makes the dead man rise can well make other creatures live.

Concerning this, the Mother of the Savior performed a very great miracle for a little boy who was the son of a farmer. When you hear it, you will take great pleasure in it and will praise the Virgin who always befriends us. A pretty little she-mule was born to the farmer in his house which he at once gave to his son. Caressing the boy tenderly, he said: "Let this mule be a gift to you, and I shall give you barley and straw for it." The boy accepted this and was pleased with that gift and took as good care of the mule as he could from then on. However, one night it died. On account of that, the father took his son to the field where he was working so that he would not find out about it. However, the mother, who stayed at home, at once took that dead mule and called a servant of hers and ordered it to be skinned, planning to

---

7. This was probably in 1271.

8. Marinid sultan of Morocco Abū Yūsuf Yaʿqūb ruled from 1258 to 1286. This reference is probably to the Marinid campaign of 1264–1265.

9. Ceuta and Asilah are cities in Morocco.

10. This may refer to Alcarraz (also spelled Alcarrás) in the province of Lérida, Alcaraz in the province of Albacete, or Alquézar in the province of Huesca.

11. The Virgin of Salas was especially renowned for miracles of healing. Several other stories in the *Cantigas* also relate to her miracles and veneration.

get five *soldos* and a *mealha*[12] for the hide. While they were about this, the farmer came back from the field, and the boy saw his mule being skinned. He cried out loudly: "Let my mule be, for I have already given it to Holy Mary of Salas, and I am sure She will help me." Both hind legs of the mule had already been skinned, and the mother said to her son: "You are acting just like a silly child, for you give a dead thing to the Virgin, and that is the same as giving Her nothing." The boy paid no attention to anything she said but took off his belt and carefully measured the mule. He made a long candle by the measurement to light before the One who has persuasion with God for the guilty and enmity with the devil. Once the candle had been presented, the mule came back to life. When the boy saw this, he was delighted and gave it something to eat, and the mule ate while all praised the Virgin, whom God put above all the other saints. Hence let us pray to Her to preserve us in this world from misfortune and other perils and to give us spiritual life in the other world and to destroy the devil who always is our enemy.

12. The *soldo* and *mealha* were both small coins.

61. THE MIRACLES OF A FARMER SAINT

Life of San Isidro

Translated from Latin and Castilian by Kenneth B. Wolf

*This anonymous Life of Isidro [Isidore] of Madrid, who died pre-1192, represents a
rare medieval effort to justify the sanctification of a non-noble layman, in this case,
a tenant farmer. Note how the author does this, in part, by depicting Isidro as a man
who made a virtue out of the curse inflicted on Adam ("You will earn your bread
from the labor of your hands and the sweat of your brow," Genesis 3:19) by embracing
the life of an agricultural laborer. Isidro was famous for his piety and charity and
worked miracles during his lifetime. After his death, however, people continued to
come to his tomb, seeking healing from many ailments, especially blindness and diseases of the eyes, and he also worked other miracles. A number of entries are carefully
dated. The final entry, added in Castilian in the early fifteenth century, indicates
the ongoing veneration of Isidro and is notable for its inclusion of personal names.
Isidro was canonized in 1622, along with Ignatius Loyola, Francis Xavier, Teresa of
Ávila, and Philip Neri. Shortly thereafter, Isidro became the patron saint of Madrid. (KBW & ORC)*

1. In Madrid[1] [lives] the memory of blessed Isidro,[2] most glorious confessor of our Lord Jesus Christ, who, while he was [only] a simple farmer,[3] was
seen to be devoted to God and a friend to man. And being a diligent—by
no means negligent—imitator of Holy Scriptures, he placed spiritual matters
before temporal ones, not temporal before spiritual. For each day (as we have
learned from the reports of reliable men) at the break of dawn, he would put
off his farming duties and frequent the thresholds of many holy churches of
God with the intention of praying. He persisted for the better part of the
day in prayer, while his neighbors applied themselves to their labors, and was
the last one [to report to work]. Yet marvelously enough, he energetically

---

Text from *Leyenda de San Isidro por Juan Diácono*, ed. Fidel Fita, *Boletín de Biblioteca
de la Real Academia de Historia* 9 (1886): 97–157. The full English translation is available at
http://canilup.googlepages.com/san_isidro. Selections published here with permission of the
translator.

1. The author uses "Maioritum" for Madrid, suggesting that he was steering away from
the more obvious Arabic forms (Magerit, Magerid, Maidrit, Madrit, Magerito, Maiarid, Mag-
erritum, etc.) that appear in the earliest Madrid-related documents, conveniently collected by
Fidel Fita.

2. Some commentators have speculated that he was named after St. Isidore of Seville (d.
636), suggesting that perhaps he was born on 4 April (Isidore's feast day) or that his parents were
influenced in their choice of name by the translation of Isidore's remains from Seville to León in
1053.). However, Isidorus was a common name in Spain.

3. Peasant saints are rare but not unheard of. However, Isidro seems to have been the
only one who spent his entire life as a farmer.

performed the labor that he owed and, with the assistance of the Lord, sur-
passed the work of the others. . . . Ignited with the grace of charity, [Isidro]
burned with divine love, and although he was not rich, having nothing and
yet possessing everything [that really mattered], he put out food not only for
men but also for birds, laboring in their hunger and in the cold. In fact one
winter day, when the land was covered with snow, Isidro was making his way
to the mill, in the company of his young son[4] to grind his grain, when he
saw a flock of doves sitting together on the branch of a tree. Realizing that
the birds had been suffering for a long time and were in danger of starving,
he was moved by pity toward them. He brushed [the snow away from] the
ground with his feet and hands and placed there for the birds a good amount
of the very grain that he had intended for his own needs. Seeing this, a certain acquaintance of his was irritated and mocked blessed Isidro, treating
him as if he were stupid for wasting the grain. But when they arrived at the
mill, they discovered that there was no less grain in his sack [than there had
been before]. Indeed, marvelous to behold, the [amount of] flour [that was
produced from his grain] actually increased to such an extent that the bags of
both [men], which had been half empty, were abundantly filled.

2. A second prodigy that divine providence deigned to work through
Isidro, the man of God, one that stood out among all the rest and is by no
means worthy of omission. With the judgment of divine providence and in
accordance with what was said to the first human couple—"You will earn
your bread from the labor of your hands and the sweat of your brow"[5]—he
rightly dedicated himself to the same. Assuming no other life, he chose to
seek his food from the labor of his hands. So, making himself obedient to the
Lord's command with regard to the first couple, he made himself a humble
tenant of a knight of the counsel[6] from Madrid [working for] a yearly wage.
When, in this capacity, he was placed in a field near the city,[7] Isidro married[8] and led a life of labor, thus rendering to God the things that were
God's [Mark 12:17] and to his neighbors, the fraternal [obligations] that he
owed. But certain ones from the adjoining fields spoke to the knight—whose

4. Previous translators have shied away from identifying Isidro's companion here as his
son, preferring to interpret *filiolus* as a hired hand or apprentice of some sort. But there is no
compelling reason why it would not be his son.
5. Gen. 3:19. Here we see a would-be saint turning the curse directed against fallen man
into his own kind of spiritual discipline.
6. This would have made Isidro's lord a *caballero villano*, from the lowest level of the
nobility.
7. These fields are commonly identified as those in which the hermitage and cemetery
of San Isidro are currently located.
8. Note that even Isidro's marriage is treated implicitly as an imitation of Adam, who
needed an "Eve."

land he worked for a set wage—about Isidro, accusing him in the following manner: "Venerable Lord, we profess ourselves to be truly subject to you. In the interests of your well-being, we do not wish to be silent about that which causes injury to you. May you know for certain that Isidro, whom you chose to labor in your field so that he might work your farm for an annual wage, rises at the break of dawn, abandons the farm work that he is supposed to do, and heads off in the manner of a pilgrim to visit all the churches of Madrid under the pretense of prayer. Because he only returns to his work in the evening, when the day has passed, he does not even complete half of the work that he owes. With regard to this matter, do not think us malicious or hateful. We have simply been frank with you about what is useful and profitable for your household." Having heard these things, the knight was deeply disturbed. Moved with anger, thinking that what they had told him was true, he set out the next day and, approaching the blessed man, upbraided him harshly. But blessed Isidro, already educated in the patience of Christ, responded modestly with words of this kind: "O most dear and venerable man, under whose dominion I am placed, I admit to you faithfully that I do not wish nor am I able to be separated by any means from the King of kings and [his] flock of saints, and their service. If you fear that on account of my tardiness in beginning my work that the anticipated yield of your harvest is threatened, according to the judgment of my neighbors, may it please you that I restore, from my own [crops] whatever there may be in the way of a loss. I beseech your honor that, as long as I carry out the service of my Lord without depriving you of the use [of my labor], you will hold nothing serious against me." Hearing these words, the upright knight, modestly restoring him to his grace, returned to his own home, though somewhat dubious about what he had just heard. . . .

The aforementioned knight, to whose dominion Isidro was subject, wondering how he might find out what the man of God was really up to, rose at dawn on a particular work day and, heading out along the road, hid himself in a certain vantage point so that he might see with his own eyes what the man of God was doing. When he spied the servant of God returning even later from his usual pilgrimage, he grew angry as he watched, thinking that he was being negligent about putting his hand to the plow. Disturbed by this, he began to make his way to him so that he might sternly discuss this matter with him. But because, in accordance with the prophetic word, "Who knew the meaning of the Lord, who was his advisor?" [Isa. 40:13] as the knight was making his way down the road, deeply irritated with the servant of God, suddenly—as the result of divine power—he saw in the same field given over to farming, two yoke of oxen—not his own—white in color and plowing quickly and heartily alongside the man of God. Astonished by this vision and marveling at it, he stopped on the road and stood there. Deeply stunned, he tried to figure out what this could mean. Finally coming to the conclusion that he was benefiting from no human help, he was forced to accept the fact that this man of God enjoyed divine assistance in his labors. Rejoicing and marveling, he approached [Isidro] so that he might understand [better]. As he drew near to him to ask what it was [that he was seeing], the knight glanced elsewhere and when he returned his gaze to the cultivation of his field, he saw no one except the man of God, Isidro. . . .

Then the knight, pierced in his heart and illuminated from on high by the things that he had seen, realized that divine grace adhered to the servant of God. So, as he was about to depart, he said to him: "Whatever the envious and the whisperers have said to me in order to disparage you, I do not believe. In fact whatever I own in this farm I place under your power and whatever is to be done I leave to your discretion." Having done this, the knight returned home and reported to many of his neighbors what had happened to him. This miracle, among all the rest, has been pressed into the memories of many up to this very day. . . .

5. It happened, in accordance with divine providence, that, as is the custom in various regions, Isidro was a member of a certain confraternity. On one particular day, when everyone [in the confraternity] had gathered to celebrate a meal together, Isidro, the so-called "man of God," was late arriving since he was accustomed to going to the churches for the sake of devout prayer. When he finally did arrive—mercifully bringing with him certain alms-seeking poor people whom he had found at the door of the house where the feast was being held—the celebration was already over. Seeing this, one of the members offered him a word of this type: "Good man of God, it is marvelous that you have brought these poor men with you, but there is nothing left except the portion that we saved for you." The man of God, bearing the words with patience, responded: "Let us all share equally from the portion of God which was given to us." When the servers went to the pot on the table so that they might give him the portion that had been saved, they found the pot filled to overflowing with meat. Seeing this prodigy, they were suddenly and marvelously stunned and fell silent for a time. Waiting for an opportune moment to proclaim [the miracle], they served, with joy and happiness, the excellent meal to the man of God and to the poor people that he had let in, satisfying them all. The amount of food was in fact so great that they [were able] to give the leftovers to other poor people. . . .

6. As long as he was able with good humor to do so, he managed his household well and legitimately had a wife and a son. Thus leading a

praiseworthy life, he deserved to receive an even more praiseworthy death, thanks to the mercy of God. When the time came in which the Lord Jesus Christ, a just judge, resolved to reward most piously his assiduous labor, Isidro collapsed in his bed. When he realized that the end his life had arrived, he was given the last rites, disposed of his temporal goods—however few they were—and admonished his family to follow the Lord as was appropriate. Stricken in the chest, with his hands clenched and his eyes closed, he consigned himself to his Maker, his Redeemer, to whom he had dedicated himself— having doubled the gift of the talents [Matt. 25:14–23]—and gave up his humble spirit to Christ, ready to receive from Him the eternal wages of his life on earth. . . . He was buried in the cemetery of the blessed apostle Andrew, from whose church he used to withdraw, in the time of his assiduous pilgrimage and prayer, finally returning to his labors at the estate. There his body lay for a long time, that is, forty years, visited by virtually no one . . . [but the Lord] allowed neither the hair nor the skin of his faithful servant to deteriorate in the least.[9]

7. It happened by divine mercy that [Isidro] appeared by night to a certain friend who was in the aforementioned church, admonishing him to tell the men of that church's parish that his body ought, by God's command, to be taken out of that grave and be placed in the church of blessed Andrew. But that friend of his, mindful of his own humble life and being truly full of doubt, refused to make public the admonition which he had experienced. As a result of this, he was struck with an illness that lasted until the day that [Isidro's body] was finally translated. By divine disposition, [Isidro] appeared to a second person, a certain matron of good faith, telling her through a vision one night, the same thing: that he ought to be moved into the church. This matron, in good faith, communicated this [message] to the people, some of whom were unaware of his just and decent life. When they had heard this [from her], they all together most diligently dug up the grave of the man of God. They found [the body] whole and unharmed, with healthy-looking, undamaged skin and the sweet odor of incense. With great joy and praises of gratitude, they . . . placed, with appropriate honor, the body of the blessed man in the church of the aforementioned apostle next to the altars of the blessed apostles in a new mausoleum. . . .

9. It would not be right to pass over that which it pleased the divine dignity to be miraculously done. For upon the elevation of the holy body, for the sake of taking it into the church of San Andrés, the Lord deigned to reveal

9. Luke 21:18 is the Gospel basis for the traditional idea that natural processes of decomposition do not apply to the bodies of saints.

the following prodigy. All of the bells of this church began to ring altogether, as if they had been shaken by human hands, yet in fact moving of their own accord, without the help of any hand or artifice, until the body was laid in the sepulcher. On account of which both those present at the time and those who came after, recognizing it to be a divine prodigy, ascribed the title of saint to the man of God, at least as far as faith is concerned, even without pastoral authority. As a result from then on he was generally called "Saint Isidro" by men and women alike, thus fulfilling that scripture which is laudably recited in church: the Lord our God "made him his saint for his faith and his meekness and chose him out of all flesh and glorified him in the presence of kings" [Sirach 45:3–4]. It should not be omitted that certain poor people, crippled and blind, begging on the public roads, dwelling at the manor nearby, having heard the news of such a prodigy, rejoiced out of their faith and, gathering at the gravesite, collected dirt from the hole and rubbing it on their own limbs, received the grace of health, thanks to divine mercy, for the sake of testifying to his faithful servant. . . .

15. Nor should one be reticent about another miraculous thing that happened. In this time of pestilence, when the faithful as well as infidels persisted in praying for rain, and the hands of the Lord delayed the giving of rain, a certain Moor, by the name of García, vowed the following vow in the presence of certain Moors as well as of many Christians: "I promise God and the Christian faithful that if the Lord, in this time of drought, deigns to bestow rain, for the sake of which the Christians extracted St. Isidro from his mausoleum in order to bring about rain, I will not delay in becoming a Christian. If I have not become a Christian within eight days [of the rainfall], may I not be able to evade an awful death." When God, after this period of drought, finally deigned to release abundant rain, on account of the merits of his saint, and the holy man was closed back up in his tomb, the aforementioned García, a miserable man, spurned the fulfillment of the vow which he had sworn, and before the end of the eighth day, at night, as the rainfall stopped, he was consumed by a horrible death, being killed by the blades of swordsmen. . . .

17. In the era 1303 [1265 C.E.], in the month of July, during the reign of King Alfonso [X], the Lord similarly deigned to reveal another miracle in conjunction with a certain boy through the same blessed Isidro. There was a certain man who, with his wife, had a young son whose eyes were so afflicted with disease that they were as red as fire. On account of this malady, the boy, almost four years old, was unable to see. Seeing him this way [his parents] claimed that he was practically blind. Finally his parents, encouraged by good men, made a vow that they would take him to the sepulcher of happy Isidro for an uninterrupted vigil lasting nine nights, hoping that God would have

mercy on this boy just as he had been merciful toward many others who were oppressed with various diseases. It happened that on a particular day in accordance with her vow, the mother brought him to the sepulcher in which the venerable corpse had been deposited. And there, while she poured forth prayers, a certain cleric began to touch the [infected eyes] of this boy with the handkerchief in which the most blessed body had been wrapped in the tomb. And, with divine mercy, that small boy began to call out, claiming that he could see! His mother began to respond with great joy, asking: "who cured you, my son?" The boy responded: "Blessed Isidro." And the boy was healed from that hour on, so that he returned on foot to his house without any guide, even though he had not been able to come to the church without being led by someone. The Lord deigned to work this miracle through his servant and to visibly demonstrate [it] to everyone standing there. . . .

22. In the year 1308 [1270 C.E.], a certain upright man by the name of John Dominic, an inhabitant and citizen of the city of Córdoba, had advanced along with other Christians into frontier areas, fighting in military campaigns against the Saracens. As a result of their sins, he and his companions were surrounded by the infidels and overcome by the power of their forces. Bitterly vanquished, they were taken into captivity. The aforementioned John Dominic, on account of the sufferings under which he labored so bitterly, assiduously beseeched his Lord with all his heart to free him mercifully from the hand of his enemy through one of his saints. Looking down on him with great mercy, the Lord sent the holy man Isidro to him by night, disguised as a Madrileño,[10] and offering words of this sort: "Give thanks to God, who mercifully heard you, I have been sent to you so that I might free you from the hand of the enemy." Immediately released from his chains, he led him to a place from which he would be able to leave safely. And so, liberated by the servant of God, he returned to his own home. Though he had made a promise with regard to this prodigy to go to the tomb of the man of God with an oblation, he did not fulfill the promise which he had made to the saint because his friends did not believe what had happened and disparaged the story. Not long after that, he was once again led into captivity. Recognizing the extent of his guilt, he asked God, crying and wailing, that, in his great mercy, he release him from the power of the enemy a second time—just as he had deigned to do the first time—through his holy servant. Wondrously at that very moment, divine mercy was fulfilled. Liberated by such a prodigy, he returned to his home and told his relatives and friends and many others what had miraculously happened. . . .With great haste he made the necessary

10. A man from Madrid.

preparations and, with candles and the oblations, made the journey, quickly arrived in Madrid with the greatest desire to visit the tomb of the holy man. There, fulfilling his vow in a heartfelt manner, with candles and oblations, once the divine offices were celebrated and copious thanks were offered to divine mercy and his servant, he returned home joyful and unharmed. We have had it inscribed here exactly what the aforementioned man reported to us. . . .

44. A certain man from the outskirts of Madrid was laboring in his vineyard, tried to strike a certain log with his tool but hit his own eye instead, cutting it in half, so that half of it hung outside his eye socket. When, in the midst of such desperate danger, he had given up hope of ever being cured by men, he promised to fast during the feast of St. Isidro if he would succor him. Immediately the saint restored the eye to its proper place and rejoined the divided eye that he had struck and adorned him with his former sight so that no traces of any injury remained. . . .

68. [*In Castilian*] Sunday, with four days left in the month of May in the year of our Lord 1421. On this day in the church of San Andrés in Madrid, were gathered first the lord archdeacon of Madrid, Martin Sánchez—his benefice being from the same church—and Juan Álvarez, a priest from the same church; and Diego Gutierrez, a priest from Santiago; and Alfonso Martínez, a cleric from Canillas;[11] and . . . [*there follows a long list of clerics and local laypeople of various professions*]. The holy body of the lord St. Isidro was taken out, which was seen by all the witnesses mentioned above. And the body was returned to the place where it was before. But first the archdeacon of Madrid performed the office along with the other lord clerics mentioned above. And I, Juan Álvarez, priest of this church, being there present, recorded what is contained here about this event so it would be remembered, and recorded those who donated money for the fabric of this church. Therefore I put my name in the record book which belongs to the holy body, on the day and year mentioned above. Juan Álvarez, priest of this church.

11. A village just northeast of Madrid.

62. THE PROPER QUALITIES OF A KING

Siete partidas (early fourteenth century)
Translated from Castilian by S. P. Scott

As its name implies, the Siete partidas *is a law code composed of seven sections detailing a vast corpus of medieval legal thought and heavily influenced by Roman law. The seven* partidas *cover (1) canon law, (2) public law on government and administration, (3) procedure and property, (4) domestic relations, (5) obligations and maritime law, (6) succession and inheritance, and (7) criminal law. The original compilation of the* Siete partidas *was begun at the instigation of Alfonso X of Castile (r. 1252–1284), but it was not completed until the early fourteenth century. It was formally adopted as law by Alfonso XI in 1348. The code has been called "a unique monument to the legal development of medieval Europe . . . not only does it cover the entire body of law, it also provides philosophical and theological justification and explanation for specific problems of law."[1]*

This passage on the ideal qualities of a king is taken from the second partida; *the full list of royal virtues is much longer than the selections given here. Some of the qualities described in the text may, in fact, describe Alfonso X himself, since he was famous for his interest in the sciences and in games such as chess, as well as for more traditional royal occupations. His intellectual achievements gained him the title Alfonso el Sabio (Alfonso the Wise). (ORC)*

A King Should Perform His Actions with a Good Demeanor

Not only should the king observe caution in the two kinds of action which relate to the interior of his body, as we have shown in the preceding laws, but he should also be careful in regard to the other two, which are exterior, and relate to daily intercourse with men. The first of what we desire to speak now, is his demeanor: for, in this the king should be very correct, while walking, as well as standing; also while sitting, and riding on horseback; as well as when he eats or drinks, and when he lies down, or even when he gives a reason for anything; and as to his gait, it should not be too rapid, nor should it be loitering. He should not stand long, except in church while hearing the service, or on account of something else which he cannot avoid. Moreover, it does not become him to remain for a long time in one position, or to change his seat

English text from *Las siete partidas,* translated by Samuel Parsons Scott (Chicago: Commerce Clearing House, 1931; reprint Philadelphia: University of Pennsylvania Press, 2001), pp. 287–90, 294–97. Reprinted with permission of the publisher.

1. Joseph F. O'Callaghan, *A History of Medieval Spain* (Ithaca, N.Y.: Cornell University Press, 1975), p. 451.

frequently, sitting down in one place, and then in another. When he rises up, he should not appear very straight nor very bent, this also should be the case while he is on horseback; and he should not ride too fast through a town, or linger too long on the way.

In eating and drinking he should be careful to do so in a well-bred manner, because this is something in which men cannot readily restrain themselves, on account of their great eagerness; and, for this reason, the king should be very circumspect, in order that he may not eat and drink too fast, or, on the other hand, too slowly: and he should be careful not to sleep too much, nor, when he retires, should he lie drawn up, nor across the bed, like some do who do not know where to keep their heads or their feet. Moreover, he should take care to assume a good mien when he speaks, especially as regards his mouth, his head, and his hands, which are members that are constantly employed by men in conversation. He should also be careful rather to

Figure 19. Alfonso X of Castile (1252–1284) and Musicians; *Cantigas de Santa María*, number 1. Biblioteca Real del Escorial, Codex T.I.1. Photo credit: Bridgeman-Giraudon/Art Resource, New York.

explain by words, than by gestures, what he desires to say. The ancient sages, who considered everything minutely, showed that kings should observe all this which we have mentioned, in order that they may act with propriety; and this is the case because they are more accustomed to it, and more noble, for it is something which is especially suitable for them, as men imitate their example in what they see them do. With regard to this, the ancient sages said of them, that they resemble a mirror, in which men view their images, whether they display elegance, or its opposite. And, for another similar reason, they should be solicitous not to act improperly in these matters which we have mentioned; and this is because it appears worse in them than it does in other men, and they will be the more readily censured on that account. Moreover, God will not fail to punish them in the next world as being persons who should be polite and noble, because of the surpassing elegance and nobleness of their master whose place they occupy; while, on the other hand, they make themselves vile, and afford an example to others to be so.

A King Should Dress with Great Elegance

Dress has much to do with causing men to be recognized either as noble, or servile. The ancient sages established the rule that kings should wear garments of silk, adorned with gold and jewels, in order that men might know them as soon as they saw them, without inquiring for them; and the bridles and saddles with which they ride, should be ornamented with gold, silver, and precious stones. Moreover, on grand holidays, when they assemble their Cortes, they should wear crowns of gold, richly decorated with magnificent jewels. There are two reasons for this; first, in order to indicate the splendor of Our Lord God, whose position they occupy on earth; second, that men may recognize them, as we have stated above, so as to approach them to serve and honor them, and ask favors of them, when it is necessary. All these honorable decorations, which we have mentioned above, should be worn by them at proper times and used by them in an elegant manner; and no one else should attempt to make use of them, or wear them; and he who does this in order to compare himself with the king, and occupy his position, should lose his life and all his property; as being a person who dares to usurp the honor and place of his master, without having the right to do so. Where a king consents that anyone may do this—leaving out of consideration the great degradation he would be guilty of on account of his bad behavior in this world—God will require an account of him for it in the next; as being a vassal who did not value the honor which his lord conferred upon him, or make use of it as he should have done. Where anyone, however, through presumption or want of understanding, acts contrary to what is stated in this law, the king should inflict such punishment upon him as he thinks he deserves.

A King Should Be Gentle, and What Distinctions Exist Between Habits and Manners

A king should have very good habits and manners. For, although he may be well-bred in his demeanor and his dress, if his habits and manners are not good, he will display much incongruity in his actions, for the reason that he will be greatly deficient in nobility and elegance. And because men hold that habits and manners are one and the same thing, since they originate from the same source, so far as they refer to the actions of men; we desire to show that there is a distinction between them, as the ancient sages have declared. For habits are excellent qualities which man has in himself, and obtains through long practice: manners are things which man performs by his own exertions through natural knowledge. These two virtues are very becoming to a king— and much more so than to another man—in order that he may know how to live properly and honorably; and also in order to govern his people well, by pointing out to them excellent examples, and showing them ways by means of which they may do good: for he cannot know God, or how to fear or love Him; or how to keep a watch upon his heart, or his words, or his actions, as we have stated above in other laws; or how to govern his people well; if his own habits and manners are not good. . . .

A King Should Be Eager to Learn to Read and to Know What He Can of the Sciences

A king should be eager to learn the sciences, for, by means of them, he will understand the affairs of sovereigns and will better know how to act with regard to them. Moreover, by knowing how to read, he will be better able to keep his secrets, and be master of them, which, under other circumstances, he could not well do. For, by want of familiarity with these things, he would necessarily have to admit someone else into his confidence, in order that he might know them, and there might happen to him what King Solomon said, namely: "He who places his secret in the power of another, becomes his slave; and he who knows how to keep it, is the master of his own heart, which is very becoming to a king." And, even without this, by means of the Scriptures he will the better understand the Faith, and will know more perfectly how to pray to God. By reading, he can become acquainted with the remarkable events that transpire, from which he will learn many good habits and examples. Not only did the wise men of the ancients deem it proper that a king should know how to read, but also that he should study all the sciences in order to be able to profit by them. On this subject King David, while giving advice to kings, said, that they should be learned and wise, since they had to judge the earth. King Solomon, his son, also said that kings should learn the sciences and should not forget them, for by means of them they would have to judge and protect their people. And Boetius, who was a very wise knight, declared that it was not fitting for any other man to be acquainted with the beneficial sciences, as it was for the king, for the reason that his wisdom was very profitable to his people, since through it they were to be maintained in justice. For undoubtedly a great action of this kind can be accomplished by no man, unless by one of good understanding and great wisdom. Wherefore a king who treats knowledge of the sciences with contempt, will also despise God from whom they all proceed, for King Solomon said that all science comes from God, and abides with him forever. He would even treat himself with contempt, for, since God desires that the intelligence of men should be distinguished from that of beasts, by means of wisdom, so far as man is concerned, the less he has of it the smaller distinction will exist between him and animals. And to a king who acted in this way, there would happen what King David said, namely: "When a man occupies an honorable position and does not understand its responsibilities, he causes himself to resemble the beasts, and is such as they are." . . .

A King Should Be Dexterous

In addition to the practices which we have mentioned in preceding laws, a king should become familiar with others that are very suitable for him. These are of two kinds: first, those which relate to arms, that he may have recourse to them when it is necessary; and second, those from which he may derive enjoyment and pleasure, and by means of which he may the better be able to endure labors and afflictions when they come upon him. For it is proper for him to understand whatever relates to chivalry, in order the better to protect his own property, and conquer that of his enemies. For this reason he should know how to ride well, and make use of all kinds of arms, not only those which he should wear to protect his body, but others by means of which he should defend himself. Those which are for the purpose of protection he should wear and make use of, in order to be able the better to endure them when it becomes necessary, so that he may incur neither danger nor shame from their annoying him. With regard to such arms as are used in battle, as, for instance, the lance, the sword, and the club, and the others with which men fight with all their power, in the management of these he should be very dexterous, so as to be able to inflict wounds with them.

It is also necessary that he should handle all these arms which we have mentioned, those which he must wear as well as the others, in such a way that he will be master of them, and not they of him. In former times, kings were taught to shoot with the bow, and the cross-bow; to mount quickly on horseback; to swim; and all other things which promote activity and valor; and this was done for two reasons. First, that they might know how to protect themselves by this means, when it became necessary; second, that men might take a good example from them, and desire to do and practice these exercises. Wherefore, if the king does not accustom himself to the practice of arms, as we stated above, leaving out of consideration the injury which will result to him, for the reason that his people will abandon the use of weapons on his account, he himself will be liable to danger, because he will lose the use of his body, and incur great shame.

A King Should Be Skillful in Hunting

A king should be skillful in, and acquainted with, other things from which pleasure and joy are derived, so as to be the better able to endure great trials and afflictions, when they come upon him, as stated in the preceding law. For this purpose one of the things which wise men found to be of most benefit is hunting of every kind, for it contributes much to diminish serious thoughts and vexations, and is more necessary for a king than for any other man; and without considering this, it confers health, as the exertion which is employed in it, when it is done in moderation, causes a man to eat and sleep well, which is the principal thing in life. The pleasure which is derived from it is, moreover, a great source of joy; as, for instance, the obtaining possession of birds and wild beasts, and causing them to obey and serve man, by bringing others into his hands. Wherefore the ancients considered that it was more suitable for a king than for other men, and that this was the case for three reasons. First, to lengthen his life and his health, increase his understanding, and remove from him cares and griefs, which are things that greatly obscure the intellect: and all men of good sense should practice this in order the better to carry their acts to completion. And, on this subject, Cato the Wise said, that every man should, at times, mingle joy and pleasure with his cares, for anything which does not rest occasionally does not last long. Second, because hunting is an art, and imparts knowledge of war and conquest, with which kings should be thoroughly familiar. Third, because kings are more abundantly qualified to practice it than other men.

Nevertheless, they should not make it so expensive as to cause loss in what they have to accomplish, and they should not engage in it so frequently as to hinder them from doing other things which it is their duty to do: and where kings practice hunting in any other way than those we have mentioned above, they should be considered as deficient in understanding, on account of their neglecting, for hunting, other great deeds which they should perform. And, without taking this into consideration, the joy which they should receive from the sport will inevitably be turned into distress, for which reason serious illness will come upon them instead of health: and, moreover, God with great justice will take vengeance upon them, because they made use of the things which He created in this world in a way that they should not have done.

Concerning the Pleasures Which a King Should Have Recourse to Occasionally, in Order to Take Comfort in Affliction and Care

There are other pleasures, in addition to those we mentioned in the preceding laws, which have been devised in order that a man may take comfort when oppressed with care and affliction. These are listening to songs and musical instruments, and playing chess, draughts, or other similar games. We also include histories, romances, and other books, which treat of those matters from which men derive joy and pleasure. And, although each of these has been found to be beneficial, yet men should not make use of them, except at suitable times, and in a way that may be productive of benefit, and not of injury. This is more proper for kings than for other men, for they should perform their acts in a very orderly way, and according to reason. Referring to this subject, King Solomon said, that there are appointed seasons for everything, which are proper for it and for nothing else; as, for instance, to sing at marriages, and to weep at funerals. For songs should not be sung except for joy, so that persons may derive pleasure from them, and forget their cares. Wherefore, if anyone makes use of them to excess, he will remove joy from its proper place, and transform it into a kind of insanity. We declare that this is also true concerning musical sounds and instruments. But with regard to the other games which we have mentioned above, they should not be practiced except to drive away care, and to receive joy from them, and not through a desire for gain thereby; for any gain which is obtained from them, can neither be great nor very profitable.

Whoever practices these games in any other way, will receive therefrom great distress, instead of pleasure, and they will be exchanged for a kind of a gambling, which is something from which great injury and evil is derived, and greatly grieves both God and men, for the reason that it is opposed to all excellence. Wherefore a king who does not know how to practice these things skillfully, as we stated above, in addition to the sin and impropriety of which he will be guilty on this account, will also suffer great injury, which will degrade his actions, on account of his abandoning great and good things for those which are vile.

63. POSITIONS AT THE ROYAL COURT

Don Juan Manuel (1282–1348), *Libro de los estados* (1326–1329)
Translated from Castilian by Simon Doubleday

The Libro de los estados, *composed between 1326 and 1329, was the work of Don Juan Manuel, one of the most colorful and influential figures on the fourteenth-century stage. Don Juan (1282–1348) was a nephew of Alfonso X of Castile, and in his prolific literary output he proved himself a true heir to the tradition of the Alfonsine court; among his other well-known works was* El conde Lucanor. *The* Libro de los estados *is an inventive expression of Don Juan's aspirations for the moral ordering of society: an examination of the proper role of the different social estates and of the individual within them. Don Juan's key fictional device is his use of the voice of "Julio," a Castilian cleric appointed to instruct the pagan prince, as an instrument for the expression of his ideas. The author's overwhelming concern is with the upper echelons of the social hierarchy—a logical preoccupation in view of the increasing social predominance of the Castilian aristocracy to which Don Juan belonged. Noble houses such as the Laras and Haros had soared to astronomical heights of influence. Don Juan allied himself to the House of Lara in 1320 by marrying the sister of Juan Núñez III of Lara. Alongside Juan Núñez, Don Juan Manuel orchestrated a prolonged civil war against Alfonso XI. He epitomized the proud insubordination of the "old nobility"—the constellation of noble houses that predated the violent change of dynasty in 1369. The account in the following passage of the human interior of an aristocratic household is central to the history of Castile in the fourteenth century. (SD)*

xcv. The ninety-fifth chapter talks of how Julio told the Prince [*infante*] that those who raise the children of lords, just as they may do good in raising and punishing them, may also be lacking or may err in what they carry out

Besides, those who raise the children of lords, just as they can do much good in raising them and punishing them so that they are good and well brought up, may also err if they fail to do this in some situation, flattering their charges so that they have a better relationship with them, or sheltering them or praising them when in some situation they don't do what they should; for as a result of what they allow them to do then, the children are greatly damaged in the future, as regards their bodies and their actions and the people they have to support. So it is a great danger to the souls of those who raise the children of lords if in their position of power they err from what they should do in raising the children.

Translated from *Libro de los estados*, edited by Robert Brian Tate and Ian Richard Macpherson (Oxford: Clarendon Press, 1974), pp. 198–205.

Now, my lord Prince, I have told you all the dangers which I understand can befall some of the defenders of the realm in the offices which they must hold."

"Julio," said the Prince, "I have well understood all that you have told me of the estates of the offices which the noble defenders of the realm must hold from the lords, and of the dangers which [*words missing from manuscript*] and for the saving of their souls. And since you have spoken to me fully of this, I beg you to tell me what you understand of the other offices."

"My lord Prince," said Julio, "as you so wish, I must tell you from now onward of the dangers which I know for the saving of souls in the offices which lords give to men in their household.

My lord Prince, the most honorable and most valuable office, and which necessarily involves most knowledge of the lord's business and secrets, is the chancellor, for the role of the chancellor is that he must have the lord's seals and have all his public documents made, orders as well as transactions and letters of thanks and replies, and documents for collecting the lord's rents and monies, and judicial documents and documents of payment. He must necessarily have recorded all the documents that there are. Finally, to wrap everything up for you, it is advisable that all the documents that come to the lord, or that the lord sends in any way, should come into the hands and the power of the chancellor. For, since there cannot be a document without a seal, the lord cannot have anything done without the chancellor knowing and without it coming into his hands and his power.

Because of all these reasons for which the chancellor should know all the lord's business, it is best for him to be his confidant and counselor. And because all these things cannot be avoided, lords always choose such chancellors as have been their charges, or their fathers', and who are greatly indebted to them so that they will serve them, and who will be loyal and have good understanding. If the chancellor has more good qualities than these, so much the better; but if he is lacking any of this, the lord who has such a chancellor will be putting all his business in great jeopardy.

Furthermore, the chancellor must collect his dues for the documents, from some more and from others less, according to which are the most profitable for the people that receive them, and according to how the dues are organized in the household of the lord whose chancellor he is.

If the chancellor performs his office well and loyally and works as he should, he does a great service to the lord and benefits the people greatly, and can very well save his soul by proving his value and his honor in this world. But if the chancellor is greedy, or malicious and ill-intentioned, he can do many evil things, because while pretending to serve the lord he can hide many things that are the lord's by right, through greed for what he can gain thereby. Moreover, while pretending he is acting for the benefit of the lord, he is all too prepared to do harm to whomever he wishes. Besides, he can hide many of his mistakes from whomever he wants to keep away. Furthermore, he can have time to extricate himself or undo whatever he wants, whether he is right or wrong, and can extend or shorten hours and take from people whatever he wants. What more shall I say? You may rightly believe that neither the lord himself nor anyone in his household is so prepared to do deeds so evil and so deceitful—while having it understood that he is doing the right thing—as the chancellor, if he wants to do evil and is greedy or malicious. And because he can err in so many things and is so ready to conceal his mistakes and his greed, his office is very dangerous for the saving of his soul.

xcvi. The ninety-sixth chapter talks of how Julio told the Prince about the estate of the physicians of the household of great lords, for in part it was great and in part it was not

Moreover, the physicians of the lords' households have a very strange office, which in part is greater than all others and in part is not as great. For in that the lord has to entrust to him his body and his own life and that of his wife and children and all his household, it is the most important office, in which is needed greater loyalty and greater understanding than in all the other offices. But in that it is in the nature of his practice not to have dealings with the lord, nor involve himself in his business, he does not have so much power as the other officials.

All the ability of the physicians to have great power and great intimacy with the lords—apart from what they have to do in medicine—lies in what understanding and what manners and what habits they have by nature, and not in their knowledge of things said by sciences, which they will merely have learned. For if the man does not naturally have good understanding, and what he understands is only through the sciences which he knows, at the time when he has to go beyond what he has read, he will have as little wisdom as if he had never read it. So, for the physician to have the confidence of the lord, apart from medicine, it is best that he have good understanding which will make him loyal, and good deportment and good habits. Since the physician necessarily has to talk often and on many occasions with the lord, if the lord finds in him the above-mentioned things, he inevitably has a great role in his confidence and his counsel.

If the physician works well in medicine and in the confidence of the lord—if he receives it—he can do many good things and may very well save his soul, if he is a Christian. But if the physician is greedy or ill-intentioned, he may secretly do many evil things; for he can demand from the sick such a great amount to care for them that it can be a greater affliction than the pain that they have. Likewise, by prolonging illnesses and raising the cost of medicines, or by making people think, through a kind of swindling, that he is doing something better or more subtle than is the truth; or in many other ways in which he can err, understanding it or not understanding it as he should. Or if, through his ill fortune, through greed or ill will, he is lacking in the loyalty he should keep toward those who put themselves in his power, or reveal the hidden maladies people have and show to their physicians, trusting in them that they will guard them from—and will not expose them to—the nasty or hidden or shameful illnesses that they have.

Because physicians have many ways to gain money from people, not doing such things because they need to be done, and have a great willingness to conceal a bad deed when they do it—giving one to believe that they were doing it well—for all these reasons the office of physicians is very dangerous for the saving of their souls.

The lords also have in their households another official whom they cannot do without, who is called the chamberlain. He has to keep and guard the lord's jewels, which are of gold and silver and precious stones and cloth, and all the things that are befitting for the decoration and adornment of the lord's chamber. He must gather and hold all the monies which the lord has to carry with him to give and distribute. He has to have his dues, which also come from the monies the lord orders to be given out, as with other things, according to the way it is arranged in the household of the lord whose chamberlain he is. His men must sleep in the chamber where the lord sleeps, and he must guard the door of the chamber once the lord has entered through it. They have to dress and undress the lord and know all the hidden secrets which other people must not know.

Because of the great intimacy the chamberlain has with the lord, if he has good understanding and is loyal and has good discretion and good manners and good habits, he inevitably plays a very large role in the confidence and the counsel of the lord. If he performs his office as he should and does good works, he does a great service to the lord and benefits the people greatly, and can very well save his soul. But if the chamberlain is greedy or malicious, because of the many good and desirable things which he has in his power, he is more willing than any other man to do what he should not do, out of greed. Furthermore, in all the ways which I previously said that the chancellor and physician could do evil deeds in the guise of good ones, in the same ways, and in more, the chamberlain can do evil deeds if he wishes. Because of the great willingness that he has to do evil and deceitful deeds, his office is very dangerous for the saving of his soul.

xcvii. The ninety-seventh chapter talks of how Julio told the Prince about the office of the steward, and how he has to buy victuals for the household

The steward is another official who has to do much in the lord's household, because he has to buy and gather all the victuals necessary for the lord's household, and he has to divide and distribute them, both those that are eaten in the house and those that are given as rations. The steward has to provide all the officers what each one has to provide in performing his office. He has to collect the letters of receipt from the officers, for the victuals they are given, and he gives his own receipt for everything. He has to keep an account of the officers every day, and often has to collect money. He has in his power much money which the lord has given to him for his store of provisions. He has power over all the officers to punish or impose a penalty on them according to the errors into which each one has fallen.

For all these reasons, the steward has very great power in the lord's household. If the lord finds that he is of good understanding, and loyal, and has a good soul, and that he wants his service without delay, because of the great intimacy he has with the lord (if over a long period of time the lord finds him to be what is said), he inevitably comes to trust him and involve him in many aspects of his business that are much more than provisioning. So if the steward is such that he looks after everything as he should, he can do a great service to the lord and greatly benefit the people who live in the household, and even some others where the lord has to go. By doing all of this well and directly, he will do all these good things that have been said and that may very well save his soul.

But if the steward is covetous or has an evil soul or is ill-intentioned, he can do many evil things. For because he does not have any certain income from his office, and everything the lord distributes and much of what he gives has to pass through his hands, greed grows in him because he sees that it is in his power—and furthermore, because many people have to go to eat with him, because he is the steward, and ask for a loan from him, and something of his own.

For these reasons, and because he has many ways to conceal what he does not do as he should, he ventures to do what is not appropriate. To do it deceitfully he conspires with the officers and covers up the errors they make so that they pay him something and so that they will also keep quiet and cover up what he does. Moreover, he can be deceitful in buying and purchasing, putting the price for what they buy and purchase higher than it really is, taking more of the lord's victuals than is his share, and claiming to be given and distributed things that have not been given or distributed; and among other various ways that they know, to attempt to take what is the lord's deceitfully and with revolting skill.

Because he needs much more than what he should rightfully have from the office, and because it seems to them strange to see that they are giving to everyone and are not taking anything for themselves, and because all men want to get rich quickly, and because they have many ways to take things that can enrich them, and can do it secretly, and because all these ways are deceitful and sinful, as a result of these ways the office of the steward is very dangerous for the saving of his soul.

xcviii. The ninety-eighth chapter talks of how after the offices of the physician and steward there are many other officers in the household of the great lords

After the physician and the steward there are many other officials in the households of the emperors and the kings and the other lords, such as the cupbearers and the table-clearers and the pastry-makers and the stable-boys and the falconers and the doormen and the messengers and the cooks, and many other lesser officers whom it seems better to keep quiet about than to put in a book such as this. All the above-mentioned officers, carrying out their duties well and loyally and not deceiving the lord nor the people of his household nor of the land, can very well save their souls. But because each one of them has a very great willingness to err, through greed or through ill intention, their estates are very dangerous for the saving of their souls."

"Julio," said the Prince, "I am very satisfied with what you have told me about these estates. And I beg you if you know of other estates to tell me what you know about them."

"My lord infante," said Julio, "after these estates which are in the lords' households, there are other people in the towns and in the country whom they call artisans. And these are of many estates, such as shopkeepers and tailors and goldsmiths and carpenters and blacksmiths, and master builders of towers and houses and walls, and shoemakers and bridle-makers and saddlers and veterinarians and leather-dressers and weavers, and other artisans who need not all be written down in this book.

All these kinds of artisans, and even the workers who work for themselves—like farmers or plowmen or shepherds or gardeners or millers, or others of lesser estates—may very well save their souls, by doing what they should do loyally and without greed. But if because of the willingness that they have not to do everything as well as possible, and because many of them are lacking in understanding, so that in stupidity they could fall into grave errors without understanding, their estates are very dangerous for the saving of their souls."

64. JEWISH PRAISE OF A CHRISTIAN KING

Todros ben Judah Abulafia, Two Poems in Honor of Alfonso X el Sabio

Translated from Hebrew by Raymond P. Scheindlin

Todros ben Judah Abulafia, who was born in Toledo in 1247 and lived at least until 1298, was the most productive and versatile of the Hebrew poets of Christian Spain. He wrote Hebrew panegyrics for powerful Jewish courtiers of Alfonxo X, and Todros himself held some unknown position at court. Alfonso's interest in the literary heritage of Arabs and Jews is well known; he undoubtedly found in Todros's Hebrew encomiums delightful curiosities in line with his own cultural interests. (RPS)

Poem I

This epigram, like most of Todros's poems, was composed using the system of quantitative meters that Jewish poets had adopted from Arabic two centuries earlier. The poem is built on the conceit that Alfonso is God and Todros is a pilgrim bearing the obligatory pilgrimage gift to the Temple in fulfillment of the rule enunciated in Deuteronomy 16:16–17; by climaxing with the witty use of a quotation from the Bible, Todros gestures toward the biblical heritage he and Alfonso shared.

When I went to the king to enter his service I gave him a finely crafted goblet engraved with this inscription:

Truth beheld revenge on falsehood
    when Alfonso became our king.
To wait on you I come; a cup
    engraved with Hebrew verse I bring.
For thus the Lord bade: "Every pilgrim
    must bear Me an offering."

Poem II: A Hebrew Canzone

Since virtually all the Hebrew poetry written in Christian Spain continued to make use of forms adopted from Arabic, this canzone-like poem is an exceedingly rare case of a Hebrew poem from Spain that uses a literary form originating in a Romance literature. (In Italy, Romance forms had greater success in Hebrew.) It thus hints at a replacing of the old Hebrew-Arabic synthesis with a Hebrew-Romance synthesis; but though other hints of this new synthesis exist, especially in the sphere of narrative,

Text translated from Todros Halevi Abulafia, *Gan ha-meshalim vehaḥidot*, edited by David Yellin, 3 vols. (Jerusalem, n.p., 1932–36).

it never achieved full flowering, and Iberian Hebrew poetry remained bound to Arabic models until the expulsion.

How good it is to serve the King!
Don Alfonso crushes all rebellion.
Whatever he decrees is done.
Nothing evil in him, no good lacking.
No single person could tell all his praises.[1]

No hymn or song does justice to his praises.
Who could number all the qualities God put in him,
all he has accomplished in a man's short life?[2]
If all mankind together tried to tell it all, they would fail.
He has no like on earth, none to compare him with.
His only sin is that he killed off poverty.[3]
His kindness sets the poor on thrones.

A warrior, with justice as his armor—
When he rides out on the day of battle,
he belies the proverb, "God, not stallions, makes for victory."[4]
He only longs for money to distribute it.
He knows no "no" to prince or beggar,
wants only to say "yes" and "yes" again.
His kindness shines like the sun, like dawn light.

His rank is like the sun's for elevation.
His fame flies to the four directions;
Liberality has lent it wings to soar.
Other kings are merely stars that orbit him, a sun
not shaded by the clouds or darkened by eclipses.
He has no night, nor does a thing escape his sunlike gaze.
He shines, yet rains his bounty over every passer-by.

---

1. Two lines are unfortunately missing between lines 3 and 4 in this stanza.

2. This line employs a familiar Hebrew proverb: "The day is short, the tasks are many" (Mishna, Avot 2:15).

3. This line employs a figure of speech according to which praise is expressed in the style of blame.

4. This saying is not exactly a proverb, but a verse from Psalms used proverbially (Ps. 33:17).

65. SLAVERY IN CASTILE

Siete partidas (early fourteenth century)
Translated from Castilian by S. P. Scott

Slavery was a fact of life in the medieval Mediterranean world, not only in Iberia, but also elsewhere in southern Europe, Byzantium, and the Islamic world. In most cases, medieval people owned slaves who were very different from themselves: men and women who came originally from other regions and/or who were of another religion. Often, these unfortunate men and women had been captured in war or in raiding expeditions. For example, several years after the Christian conquest of Valencia in 1238, Muslim slaves from Valencia began to appear in sale documents from northern Italy. Likewise, Christian slaves from Spain were captured and sold in North Africa. But not all slaves had been captured, since some people were born into slavery, while others were enslaved for crimes committed by themselves or by their parents or lost their freedom in other ways. Most medieval slaves were not used for agricultural labor. Instead, they were often put to work as domestic servants or as laborers in urban industries. Ramon Llull bought a Muslim slave to instruct him in Arabic (see Chapter 67). Slaves frequently converted to the religion of their master, but conversion did not necessarily bring freedom. These chapters taken from sixth and seventh partidas of the Siete partidas, *the massive law code commissioned by Alfonso X (see Chapter 62), outline some aspects of legal thinking on slavery in Castile during the thirteenth and fourteenth centuries. (ORC)*

Concerning Slaves

Slaves are another kind of men who are under obligations to those to whom they belong, by reason of the authority they have over them. Wherefore, since in the preceding Title, we spoke of the retainers that a man brings up in his house, who are free, we intend to speak here of slaves because they belong to the household. In the first place we shall explain what servitude is; where it originated and how many kinds there are; under what circumstances a slave is bound to protect his master from injury; and what authority masters have over their slaves.

What Servitude Is, Whence It Derived Its Name, and How Many Kinds There Are

Servitude is an agreement and regulation which people established in ancient times, by means of which men who were originally free became slaves and

English text from *Las siete partidas*, translated by Samuel Parsons Scott (Chicago: Commerce Clearing House, 1931; Philadelphia: University of Pennsylvania Press, 2001), 977–80, 1389–90, 1436. Reprinted with permission of the publisher.

were subjected to the authority of others, contrary to natural reason. The slave derived his name from a word called in Latin, *servare*, which means, in Castilian, to preserve. This preservation was established by the emperors, for, in ancient times, all captives were put to death. The emperors, however, considered it proper, and ordered that they should not be killed, but that they should be preserved, and use made of them.

There are three kinds of slaves, the first is those taken captive in war who are enemies of the faith; the second, those born of female slaves; the third, when a person is free and allows himself to be sold. Five things are necessary, in the case of the third. First, the party must voluntarily consent to be sold; second, he must receive a part of the price; third, he must know that he is free; fourth, the party who purchases him must believe that he is a slave; fifth, he who permits himself to be sold must be more than twenty years of age.

To What Conditions Those Belong Who Are Born of a Female Slave and a Freeman

Persons born of a father who is free and a mother who is a slave are slaves, because they follow the condition of the mother, as respects both slavery and freedom. But where a woman of this kind, while pregnant, is set free, her child will be free also, although the said child may be born only an hour, or even less, after she was liberated. And, even if the mother should be subsequently returned to slavery, her child will always remain free, on account of the time during which his mother bore him after she was liberated, whether this be much, or little. Children born of a free mother and a father who is a slave are free, because they always follow the condition of the mother, as aforesaid. Although we stated above that children follow the condition of the mother, nevertheless, children who are born of a father and mother who are free, should follow the condition of the father, so far as secular honors and *fueros* are concerned.

The Sons of Priests, Who Are in Sacred Orders, Should Be Slaves of the Church

There are certain contingencies and reasons on account of which persons who are born of a father and mother who are free, become slaves, and one of these is where a priest who has received Holy Orders marries a free woman, in the same manner as laymen should marry according to law; for children born to women of this kind will be slaves of the church in which the priests who contracted such a marriage has a benefice. Slaves of this kind should not, however, be sold like other slaves, but are always bound to serve that church. Children of this kind labor under still another impediment on account of the fault which their father committed in marrying in this way, for they cannot inherit the property of their father, although they have a right to inherit that of their mother.

Christians Who Provide the Enemies of the Faith with Iron, Wood, Arms, or Ships, Become Slaves by Reason of Such Acts

There are some wicked Christians who give assistance or advice to the Moors, who are the enemies of the faith; as, for instance, when they give, or sell them arms of wood and iron, or galleys or ships already built, or the materials with which to build them; and this also includes those who pilot or navigate their ships in order to inflict injury upon Christians; and those who give or sell them wood for the purpose of making battering-rams or other engines. And, for the reason that such persons are guilty of great wickedness, the Holy Church deemed it proper that whoever could seize individuals guilty of acts of this kind, might reduce them to slavery, and sell them if they desired to do so, or make use of them as they would of their own slaves. In addition to this, such persons are excommunicated solely on account of their deeds, as stated in the Title concerning Excommunications, and they should lose everything they have, and become the property of the king.

Under What Circumstances a Slave Is Bound to Protect His Master from Injury

Every slave is bound to protect his master from injury and dishonor, as far as he can, or knows how to do so, and he is obliged to obey him, and contribute to his honor and advantage in every way. Not only is a slave under obligations—with respect to the matters aforesaid—to his master, but also to the wife and children of the latter; and if they have need of his help, where anyone desires to kill or dishonor them, he should run to their assistance, and give up his life for them to prevent them from suffering death or disgrace. A slave should do this well and faithfully, and he cannot excuse himself in any way for not doing so, if he has the power, except when he is ill so that he cannot perform his duty; or where he has been taken captive, or is imprisoned, or is so distant from the place that he cannot by any means go and render assistance. Where a slave wounds or kills anyone while defending his master from danger of death, he should not be liable to any penalty.

What Authority Masters Have over Their Slaves

A master has complete authority over his slave to dispose of him as he pleases. Nevertheless, he should not kill or wound him, although he may give him cause for it, except by order of the judge of the district; nor should he strike him in a way contrary to natural reason, or put him to death by starvation; except where he finds him with his wife or his daughter, or where he commits some other offense of this kind, for then he has certainly a right to kill him. We also decree that, where a man is so cruel to his slaves as to kill them by starvation, or to wound or injure them so seriously that they cannot endure it, in cases of this kind said slaves can complain to the judge; and the latter in the discharge of his official duty should investigate and ascertain whether the charge is true, and if he finds that it is, he should sell the slaves, and give the price of them to their master; and he should do this in such a way that they never can be again placed in the power, or under the authority of the party through whose fault they were sold.

Any Profits Obtained by Slaves Will Belong to Their Masters

All the earnings obtained by a slave, no matter how he obtains them, will belong to his master. We also decree that any property left by will to a slave can also be claimed by his master, just as if it had been bequeathed to himself. Moreover, we decree that where anyone places his slave in a shop, a ship, or in any other place, ordering him to follow a trade or conduct a business, all contracts entered into by such a slave, no matter with whom he makes them, which relate to the trade or business in which his master establishes him, the latter is bound to keep and perform, just as if he himself had made them.

Neither a Jew nor a Moor Can Hold a Christian as a Slave

Neither a Jew, a Moor, a heretic, nor anyone else who does not acknowledge our religion, can hold a Christian as a slave. Anyone who violates this law, by knowingly holding a Christian in servitude, shall lose his life on that account, and forfeit all his property to the king. We also decree that if any of the persons aforesaid has a slave that does not acknowledge our religion, and said slave becomes a Christian, the latter will be free for that reason, as soon as he is baptized and accepts our faith; nor will he be required to pay anything for himself to the party to whom he belonged before he became a Christian; and even though the party who was his master may subsequently become a Christian, he will retain no rights in said person who was his slave and became a Christian before he did.

This is understood to apply where a Jew, or a Moor purchases a slave who becomes a Christian, with the intention of making use of his services and not for the purpose of disposing of him in trade. If, however, he buys him with the intention of selling him, he should do so within three months; and if, before the said three months have expired, and while his master was making an attempt to sell him, he should become a Christian, the said Jew or Moor should not, for that reason, lose all the price he paid for him, but we decree that the slave shall be required to pay for himself, or the party who caused him to become a Christian should pay for him, twelve *maravedis* of the money current in that locality; and where he has not the means to pay them, he should give his services instead of them, not as a slave but as a freeman, until he is entitled to that amount. If he should not be sold within the three months aforesaid, the party who was his master will retain no rights in him, even though he may subsequently become a Christian. . . .

What Penalty Those Deserve Who Steal or Kidnap the Children or the Slaves of Others

Robbers entice away, or steal the children or the slaves of others, with the intention of taking them for sale into the enemy's country, or in order to make use of them as slaves; and for the reason that persons of this kind are guilty of great wickedness they deserve punishment. Wherefore, we decree that whoever commits a larceny of this kind, (if the thief is a person of noble birth) shall be placed in irons and be condemned for life to labor on the royal works; and if he is not a man of noble birth, he shall be put to death for his crime; and if he is a slave, he shall be thrown to wild beasts that they may kill him. The same penalty shall be indicted upon all those who give away or sell a freeman, and on those who knowingly purchase, or accept as a gift a person of this kind, with the intention of either making use of him as a slave, or selling him.

Concerning Slaves Who Escape, or Who Steal Themselves

Slaves steal themselves when they escape from their masters with the intention of not returning to them; but a slave who escapes in this way, cannot be lost by his lord through lapse of time, for whenever he finds him he can bring suit for him in court and return him to slavery; except where the slave escapes to the country of the Moors, and after he has been there in safety and freedom he afterwards returns, of his own free will, to the country of the Christians, coming in the character of a peaceful Moor, and as an emancipated slave; for then, although his master may find him, he cannot return him to slavery because the ownership which he had in him was lost as soon as he reached the country of the Moors, and recovered the freedom which he enjoyed before he was taken captive. We decree that the same rule shall apply where a slave has been a fugitive, for thirty years, in the country of the Christians, his master having lost possession of him during that time; for after that, even though he finds him, he cannot institute legal proceedings to return him to slavery.

We also decree that where a slave has been brought up from childhood in his master's house, and has gone about for twenty years in good faith as a freeman, thinking all the time that he was free, although he was a slave; and no claim is made for him within the said twenty years; and afterwards an attempt is made to claim him as a slave, this cannot be done; but we decree that he is free and has obtained his liberty by this lapse of time; as we stated in the Title concerning property which is acquired or lost by lapse of time, in the laws which treat of this subject. . . .

What Penalty Jews Deserve Who Hold Christians as Slaves

A Jew shall not purchase, or keep as a slave a Christian man or woman, and if anyone violates this law the Christian shall be restored to freedom and shall not pay any portion of the price given for him, although the Jew may not have been aware when he bought him, that he was a Christian; but if he knew that he was such when he purchased him, and makes use of him afterwards as a slave, he shall be put to death for doing so. Moreover, we forbid any Jew to convert a captive to his religion, even though said captive may be a Moor, or belong to some other barbarous race. If anyone violates this law we order that the said slave who has become a Jew shall be set at liberty, and removed from the control of the party to whom he or she belonged. If any Moors who are the captives of Jews become Christians, they shall at once be freed, as is explained in the Fourth Partida of this book, in the Title concerning Liberty, in the laws which treat of this subject.

66. THE LEGAL STATUS OF JEWS AND MUSLIMS IN CASTILE

Siete partidas (early fourteenth century)
Translated from Castilian by S. P. Scott

Visigothic law codes regularly included legislation relating to Jews, and such regula-
tions continued to concern Christian rulers and jurists in the later Middle Ages.
By the thirteenth century, however, Jews were not the only religious minority living
under Christian rule, and law codes began to include laws pertaining to Muslim
subjects. This selection is taken from the seventh partida *of the* Siete partidas *of Al-*
fonso X of Castile (see introduction to Chapter 62). These passages demonstrate that
conversion was of particular concern, as were sexual relations between Christians
and non-Christians. Both religious minorities were entitled to certain protections
under law, and both were closely regulated, but legal rulings indicate that Jews
and Muslims were not viewed equally. In particular, regulations on conversion and
places of worship indicate a greater fear and antipathy on the part of Christians
toward Mudejars. This differentiation may stem from the fact that Jews had long
lived within Christian society, whereas Muslims in Castile had only recently shifted
from being enemies to being subjects.[1] *(ORC)*

In What Way Jews Should Pass Their Lives Among Christians; What Things They Should Not Make Use of or Practice, According to Our Religion; and What Penalty Those Deserve Who Act Contrary to Its Ordinances

Jews should pass their lives among Christians quietly and without disorder, practicing their own religious rites, and not speaking ill of the faith of Our Lord Jesus Christ, which Christians acknowledge. Moreover, a Jew should be very careful to avoid preaching to, or converting any Christian, to the end that he may become a Jew, by exalting his own belief and disparaging ours. Whoever violates this law shall be put to death and lose all his property. And because we have heard it said that in some places Jews celebrated, and still celebrate Good Friday, which commemorates the Passion of Our Lord Jesus Christ, by way of contempt; stealing children and fastening them to crosses, and making images of wax and crucifying them, when they cannot obtain children; we order that, hereafter, if in any part of our dominions anything

English text from *Las siete partidas,* translated by Samuel Parsons Scott (Chicago: Commerce Clearing House, 1931; Philadelphia: University of Pennsylvania Press, 2001), pp. 1433–42. Reprinted with permission of the publisher.

1. For more details, see Dwayne E. Carpenter, "Minorities in Medieval Spain: The Legal Status of Jews and Muslims in the *Siete Partidas,*" *Romance Quarterly* 33 (1986): 275–87.

like this is done, and can be proved, all persons who were present when the act was committed shall be seized, arrested and brought before the king; and after the king ascertains that they are guilty, he shall cause them to be put to death in a disgraceful manner, no matter how many there may be.

We also forbid any Jew to dare to leave his house or his quarter on Good Friday, but they must all remain shut up until Saturday morning; and if they violate this regulation, we decree that they shall not be entitled to reparation for any injury or dishonor inflicted on them by Christians. . . .

How Jews Can Have a Synagogue Among Christians

A synagogue is a place where the Jews pray, and a new building of this kind cannot be erected in any part of our dominions, except by our order. Where, however, those which formerly existed there are torn down, they can be built in the same spot where they originally stood; but they cannot be made any larger or raised to any greater height, or be painted. A synagogue constructed in any other manner shall be lost by the Jews, and shall belong to the principal church of the locality where it is built. And for the reason that a synagogue is a place where the name of God is praised, we forbid any Christian to deface it, or remove anything from it, or take anything out of it by force; except where some malefactor takes refuge there; for they have a right to remove him by force in order to bring him before the judge. Moreover, we forbid Christians to put any animal into a synagogue, or loiter in it, or place any hindrance in the way of the Jews while they are there performing their devotions according to their religion.

No Compulsion Shall Be Brought to Bear upon the Jews on Saturday, and What Jews Can Be Subject to Compulsion

Saturday is the day on which Jews perform their devotions, and remain quiet in their lodgings, and do not make contracts or transact any business; and for the reason that they are obliged by their religion, to keep it, no one should on that day summon them or bring them into court. Wherefore we order that no judge shall employ force or any constraint upon Jews on Saturday, in order to bring them into court on account of their debts; or arrest them; or cause them any other annoyance; for the remaining days of the week are sufficient for the purpose of employing compulsion against them, and for making demands for things which can be demanded of them, according to law. Jews are not bound to obey a summons served upon them on that day; and, moreover, we decree that any decision rendered against them on Saturday shall not be valid; but if a Jew should wound, kill, rob, steal, or commit any other offence like these for which he can be punished in person and property, then the judge can arrest him on Saturday.

We also decree that all claims that Christians have against Jews, and Jews against Christians, shall be decided and determined by our judges in the district where they reside, and not by their old men. And as we forbid Christians to bring Jews into court or annoy them on Saturday; so we also decree that Jews, neither in person, nor by their attorneys, shall have the right to bring Christians into court, or annoy them on this day. And in addition to this, we forbid any Christian, on his own responsibility, to arrest or wrong any Jew either in his person or property, but where he has any complaint against him he must bring it before our judges; and if anyone should be so bold as to use violence against the Jews, or rob them of anything, he shall return them double the value of the same.

Jews Who Become Christians Shall Not Be Subject to Compulsion; What Advantage a Jew Has Who Becomes a Christian; and What Penalty Other Jews Deserve Who Do Him Harm

No force or compulsion shall be employed in any way against a Jew to induce him to become a Christian; but Christians should convert him to the faith of Our Lord Jesus Christ by means of the texts of the Holy Scriptures, and by kind words, for no one can love or appreciate a service which is done him by compulsion. We also decree that if any Jew or Jewess should voluntarily desire to become a Christian, the other Jews shall not interfere with this in any way, and if they stone, wound, or kill any such person, because they wish to become Christians, or after they have been baptized, and this can be proved; we order that all the murderers, or the abettors of said murder or attack, shall be burned. But where the party was not killed, but wounded, or dishonored; we order that the judges of the neighborhood where this took place shall compel those guilty of the attack, or who caused the dishonor, to make amends to him for the same; and also that they be punished for the offence which they committed, as they think they deserve; and we also order that, after any Jews become Christians, all persons in our dominions shall honor them; and that no one shall dare to reproach them or their descendants, by way of insult, with having been Jews; and that they shall possess all their property, sharing the same with their brothers, and inheriting it from their fathers and mothers and other relatives, just as if they were Jews; and that they can hold all offices and dignities which other Christians can do.

What Penalty a Christian Deserves Who Becomes a Jew

Where a Christian is so unfortunate as to become a Jew, we order that he shall be put to death just as if he had become a heretic; and we decree that his property shall be disposed of in the same way that we stated should be done with that of heretics.

No Christian, Man or Woman, Shall Live with a Jew

We forbid any Jew to keep Christian men or women in his house, to be served by them; although he may have them to cultivate and take care of his lands, or protect him on the way when he is compelled to go to some dangerous place. Moreover, we forbid any Christian man or woman to invite a Jew or a Jewess, or to accept an invitation from them, to eat or drink together, or to drink any wine made by their hands. We also order that no Jews shall dare to bathe in company with Christians, and that no Christian shall take any medicine or cathartic made by a Jew; but he can take it by the advice of some intelligent person, only where it is made by a Christian, who knows and is familiar with its ingredients.

What Penalty a Jew Deserves Who Has Intercourse with a Christian Woman

Jews who live with Christian women are guilty of great insolence and boldness, for which reason we decree that all Jews who, hereafter, may be convicted of having done such a thing shall be put to death. For if Christians who commit adultery with married women deserve death on that account, much more do Jews who have sexual intercourse with Christian women, who are spiritually the wives of Our Lord Jesus Christ because of the faith and the baptism which they receive in His name; nor do we consider it proper that a Christian woman who commits an offense of this kind shall escape without punishment. Wherefore we order that, whether she be a virgin, a married woman, a widow, or a common prostitute who gives herself to all men, she shall suffer the same penalty which we mentioned in the last law in the Title concerning the Moors, to which a Christian woman is liable who has carnal intercourse with a Moor. . . .

Jews Shall Bear Certain Marks in Order That They May Be Known

Many crimes and outrageous things occur between Christians and Jews because they live together in cities, and dress alike; and in order to avoid the offenses and evils which take place for this reason, we deem it proper, and we order that all Jews male and female living in our dominions shall bear some distinguishing mark upon their heads so that people may plainly recognize a Jew, or a Jewess; and any Jew who does not bear such a mark, shall pay for each time he is found without it ten *maravedis* of gold; and if he has not the means to do this he shall publicly receive ten lashes for his offence. . . .

Concerning the Moors

. . . We decree that Moors shall live among Christians in the same way that we mentioned in the preceding Title that Jews shall do, by observing their own law and not insulting ours. Moors, however, shall not have mosques in Christian towns, or make their sacrifices publicly in the presence of men. The mosques which they formerly possessed shall belong to the king; and he can give them to whomsoever he wishes. Although the Moors do not acknowledge a good religion, so long as they live among Christians with their assurance of security, their property shall not be stolen from them or taken by force; and we order that whoever violates this law shall pay a sum equal to double the value of what he took.

Christians Should Convert the Moors by Kind Words, and Not by Compulsion

Christians should endeavor to convert the Moors by causing them to believe in our religion, and bring them into it by kind words and suitable discourses, and not by violence or compulsion; for if it should be the will of Our Lord to bring them into it and to make them believe by force, He can use compulsion against them if He so desires, since He has full power to do so; but He is not pleased with the service which men perform through fear, but with that which they do voluntarily and without coercion, and as He does not wish to restrain them or employ violence, we forbid anyone to do so for this purpose; and if the wish to become Christians should arise among them, we forbid anyone to refuse assent to it, or oppose it in any way whatsoever. Whoever violates this law shall receive the penalty we mentioned in the preceding Title, which treats of how Jews who interfere with, or kill those belonging to their religion who afterwards become Christians, shall be punished.

What Punishment Those Deserve Who Insult Converts

Many men live and die in strange beliefs, who would love to be Christians if it were not for the vilification and dishonor which they see others who become converted endure by being called turncoats, and calumniated and insulted in many evil ways; and we hold that those who do this wickedly offend, and that they should honor persons of this kind for many reasons, and not show them disrespect. One of these is because they renounce the religion in which they and their families were born; and another is because, after they have understanding, they acknowledge the superiority of our religion and accept it, separating from their parents and their relatives, and abandoning the life which they have been accustomed to live, and all other things from which they derive pleasure. There are some of them who, on account of the dishonor inflicted upon them after they have adopted our Faith, and become Christians, repent and desert it, closing their hearts against it on account of the insults and reproaches to which they are subjected; and for this reason we order all Christians, of both sexes, in our dominions to show honor and kindness, in every way they can, to persons of other or strange beliefs, who embrace our religion; just as they would do to any of their own parents or grandparents, who had embraced the faith or become Christians; and we forbid anyone to dishonor them by word or deed, or do them any wrong, injury, or harm in any way whatever. If anyone violates this law we order that he be punished for it, as seems best to the judges of the district; and that the punishment be more severe than if the injury had been committed against another man or woman whose entire line of ancestors had been Christians.

What Punishment a Christian Deserves Who Becomes a Moor

Men sometimes become insane and lose their prudence and understanding, as, for instance, where unfortunate persons, and those who despair of everything, renounce the faith of Our Lord Jesus Christ, and become Moors; and there are some of them who are induced to do this through the desire to live according to their customs, or on account of the loss of relatives who have been killed or died; or because they have lost their property and become poor; or because of unlawful acts which they commit, dreading the punishment which they deserve on account of them; and when they are induced to do a thing of this kind for any of the reasons aforesaid, or others similar to them, they are guilty of very great wickedness and treason, for on account of no loss or affliction which may come upon them, nor for any profit, riches, good fortune, or pleasure which they may expect to obtain in this world, should they renounce the faith of Our Lord Jesus Christ by which they will be saved and have everlasting life.

Wherefore we order that all those who are guilty of this wickedness shall lose all their possessions, and have no right to any portion of them, but that all shall belong to their children (if they have any) who remain steadfast in our Faith and do not renounce it; and if they have no children, their property shall belong to their nearest relatives within the tenth degree, who remain steadfast in the belief of the Christians; and if they have neither children nor relatives, all their possessions shall be forfeited to the royal treasury; and, in addition to this, we order that if any person who has committed such an offense shall be found in any part of our dominions he shall be put to death. . . .

What Penalty a Moor and a Christian Woman Deserve Who Have Intercourse with One Another

If a Moor has sexual intercourse with a Christian virgin, we order that he shall be stoned, and that she, for the first offense, shall lose half of her property, and that her father, mother, or grandfather shall have it, and if she has no such relatives, that it shall belong to the king. For the second offense, she shall lose all her property, and the heirs aforesaid, if she has any, shall obtain it, and if she has none, the king shall be entitled to it, and she shall be put to death. We decree and order that the same rule shall apply to a widow who commits this crime. If a Moor has sexual intercourse with a Christian married woman, he shall be stoned to death, and she shall be placed in the power of her husband who may burn her to death, or release her, or do what he pleases with her. If a Moor has intercourse with a common woman who abandons herself to everyone, for the first offense, they shall be scourged together through the town, and for the second, they shall be put to death.

67. THE EARLY CAREER OF RAMON LLULL

A Life of Ramon Llull (ca. 1311)

Translated from Latin by Anthony Bonner

This selection is the first part of a Latin biography of Mallorcan poet-philosopher Ramon Llull (ca. 1232–1316), the Vita coaetanea, *probably composed in 1311, five years before Llull's death. The work is written in the third person by an author other than Llull, yet it is said to be based on Llull's dictated account of his life. Llull was a remarkable philosopher and theologian, as well as a poet, mystic, and preacher. Born to a rich family around 1232, he spent his early life at the Aragonese court, where he lived a secular life until visions of Christ convinced him to adopt an ascetic religious life inspired by the example of Saint Francis. He became committed to the idea of converting Muslims to Christianity through preaching, and to this end he learned Arabic and urged other Christians to study the language. Llull undertook several missions to Muslim lands and taught at the universities of Paris, Montpellier, and Naples. He also found time for pilgrimages and visits to Rome seeking the pope's assistance in his effort to promote Arabic studies. Meanwhile, he continued to produce a vast number of written works on a wide range of subjects. (ORC)*

To the honor, praise, and love of our only Lord God Jesus Christ, Ramon, at the instance of certain monks who were friends of his, recounted and allowed to be put down in writing what follows concerning his conversion to penitence and other deeds of his.

Ramon, while still a young man and seneschal to the king of Mallorca, was very given to composing worthless songs and poems and to doing other licentious things. One night he was sitting beside his bed, about to compose and write in his vulgar tongue a song to a lady whom he loved with a foolish love; and as he began to write this song, he looked to his right and saw our Lord Jesus Christ on the cross, as if suspended in midair. This sight filled him with fear; and, leaving what he was doing, he retired to bed and went to sleep.

Upon arising the next day, he returned to his usual vanities without giving the vision a further thought. It was not until almost a week later, however, in the same place as before, and at almost exactly the same hour, when he was again preparing to work on and finish the aforementioned song, that our Lord appeared to him on the cross, just as before. He was even more

English text from *Selected Works of Ramon Llull*, edited and translated by Anthony Bonner (Princeton, N.J.: Princeton University Press, 1985), pp. 13–18, 21–22. Reprinted with permission of the publisher.

Figure 20. Ramon Llull and his Muslim slave, from the *Breviculum*, commissioned by Thomas le Myésier (ca. 1325). Badische Landesbibliothek, Karlsruhe, St. Peter perg. 92, fol. 3v. Permission and photo credit: Badische Landesbibliothek, Karlsruhe.

frightened than the first time, and retired to bed and fell asleep as he had done before.

Again on the next day, paying no attention to the vision he had seen, he continued his licentious ways. Indeed, soon afterwards he was again trying to finish the song he had begun when our Savior appeared to him, always in the same form, a third and then a fourth time, with several days in between.

On the fourth occasion—or, as is more commonly believed, the fifth—when this vision appeared to him, he was absolutely terrified and retired to bed and spent the entire night trying to understand what these so often repeated visions were meant to signify. On the one hand, his conscience told him that they could only mean that he should abandon the world at once and from then on dedicate himself totally to the service of our Lord Jesus Christ. On the other hand, his conscience reminded him of the guilt of his former life and his unworthiness to serve Christ. Thus, alternately debating these points with himself and fervently praying to God, he spent the night without sleeping.

At last, as a gift of the Father of lights, he thought about the gentleness, patience, and mercy which Christ showed and shows toward all sorts of sinners. And thus at last he understood with certainty that God wanted him, Ramon, to leave the world and dedicate himself totally to the service of Christ.

He therefore began to turn over in his mind what service would be most pleasing to God, and it seemed to him that no one could offer a better or greater service to Christ than to give up his life and soul for the sake of His love and honor; and to accomplish this by carrying out the task of converting to His worship and service the Saracens who in such numbers surrounded the Christians on all sides.

Coming back to himself, however, he realized that he had none of the knowledge necessary for such an undertaking, since he had scarcely learned more than a bare minimum of grammar. This thought worried him, and he began to feel very sad.

While turning over these doleful thoughts in his mind, suddenly—he himself did not know how; these are things only God knows—a certain impetuous and all-encompassing notion entered his heart: that later on he would have to write a book, the best in the world, against the errors of unbelievers. Since, however, he could conceive neither the form nor manner of writing such a book, he was most amazed. Nevertheless, the greater and more frequent was his wonder, the more strongly the inspiration or notion of writing the aforementioned book grew in him.

However, thinking again, he realized that, even though in the course of time God might bestow on him the grace for writing such a book, he could still do little or nothing alone, especially since he was totally ignorant of the Arabic language, which was that of the Saracens.

It then occurred to him that he should go to the pope, to kings, and to Christian princes to incite them and get them to institute, in whatever kingdoms and provinces might be appropriate, monasteries in which selected monks and others fit for the task would be brought together to learn the languages of the Saracens and other unbelievers, so that, from among those properly instructed in such a place, one could always find the right people ready to be sent out to preach and demonstrate to the Saracens and other unbelievers the holy truth of the Catholic faith, which is that of Christ.

Having therefore firmly made up his mind about these three intentions, that is to say: to accept dying for Christ in converting the unbelievers to His service; to write the above-mentioned book, if God granted him the ability to do so; and to procure the establishment of monasteries where various languages could be learned, as is explained above—early the next day he went to a church that was not far from there and, amid tears of devotion, fervently begged our Lord Jesus Christ to deign to bring about in a way pleasing to Him those three things which He himself had mercifully inspired in his heart.

After that he returned to his own affairs. Since he was still too imbued with his worldly life and licentiousness, he was quite lukewarm and remiss in carrying out the above-mentioned three projects for the next three months, that is, until the feast day of Saint Francis. Then on that feast day, a certain bishop preached in the Franciscan convent, explaining how Saint Francis had abandoned and rejected everything so as to be more firmly united to Christ and to Christ alone, etc. Ramon, incited by the example of Saint Francis, soon sold his possessions, reserving a small portion for the support of his wife and children; and, in order to ask the Lord and His saints for guidance in the three things the Lord had placed in his heart, he set out for the shrines of Saint María of Rocamadour, Santiago, and other holy places, intending never to return.

Having carried out these pilgrimages, he prepared to set out for Paris, for the sake of learning grammar there and acquiring other knowledge required for his tasks. But he was dissuaded from making this trip by the arguments and advice of his relatives and friends and most of all of Brother Ramon[1] of the Dominicans, who had formerly compiled the *Decretals* for Pope Gregory IX, and those counsels made him return to his own city, that is, to Mallorca.

When he arrived there he left the grand style of life he had previously led

---

1. Ramon de Penyafort (ca. 1185–1275).

and put on a lowly habit of the coarsest cloth he could find. And in that same city he then studied a bit of grammar, and having bought himself a Saracen, he learned the Arabic language from him.

Nine years later it happened that, while Ramon was away, his Saracen slave blasphemed the name of Christ. Upon returning and finding out about it from those who had heard the blasphemy, Ramon, impelled by a great zeal for the Faith, hit the Saracen on the mouth, on the forehead, and on the face. As a result the Saracen became extremely embittered, and he began plotting the death of his master.

He secretly got hold of a sword, and one day, when he saw his master sitting alone, he suddenly rushed at him, striking him with the sword and shouting with a terrible roar: "You're dead!" But even though Ramon was able, as it pleased God, to deflect his attacker's sword arm a bit, the blow nonetheless wounded him seriously, although not fatally, in the stomach. By means of his strength, however, he managed to overcome the Saracen, knock him down, and forcibly take the sword away from him.

When the servants came running to the scene, Ramon kept them from killing him, but allowed them to tie him up and put him in jail until he, Ramon, decided what would be the best thing to do. For it seemed harsh to kill the person by whose teaching he now knew the language he had so wanted to learn, that is, Arabic; on the other hand, he was afraid to set him free or to keep him longer, knowing that from then on he would not cease plotting his death.

Perplexed as to what to do, he went up to a certain abbey near there, where for three days he prayed fervently to God about this matter. When the three days were over, astonished that the same perplexity still remained in his heart and that God, or so it seemed to him, had in no way listened to his prayers, he returned home full of sorrow.

When on the way back he made a slight detour to the prison to visit his captive, he found that he had hanged himself with the rope with which he had been bound. Ramon therefore joyfully gave thanks to God not only for keeping his hands innocent of the death of this Saracen, but also for freeing him from that terrible perplexity concerning which he had just recently so anxiously asked Him for guidance.

68. ON PREACHING AND CONVERSION

Ramon Llull, *Blanquerna* (ca. 1285)
Translated from Catalan by E. A. Peers

The Mallorcan poet-philosopher Ramon Llull produced an astonishing number of works, in several languages, devoted to the subjects of mission and conversion. Llull was convinced that the conversion of Muslims to the Christian faith could be best achieved through preaching and reasoned argument rather than force. To this end, Llull believed it was crucial for Christian preachers be fluent in Arabic, and he argued passionately for the importance of establishing schools to teach Arabic to missionaries. Many of his books and pamphlets expand on this theme. Blanquerna *was written between 1282 and 1287 while Ramon was in Montpellier, and it has become one of the author's most famous works. Ostensibly a novel,* Blanquerna *combines elements of romance, polemic, allegory, and even autobiography. The story traces the life of a man, Blanquerna, devoted to reforming and improving the world as he rises through the clerical ranks to become pope and then returns to the life of a simple hermit. Llull uses the tale of Blanquerna's career as a vehicle for the presentation of his own values and beliefs. Selections from chapter 80 are translated below. (ORC)*

The Pope Blanquerna went into the Consistory with the Cardinals to the end that through their good works glory might be given to God in the Heavens; and the Pope said to the Cardinals that he prayed them that they would assist him to use his office to the glory of God, in such wise that they might be able to bring men back to the first intent of the offices and the sciences, namely, that glory might be given to God; for the world has come to such a sinful state, that there is scarce any man who has his intent directed toward that thing for the which he was created, nor for the which he holds the office which is his. While the Pope spake thus with the Cardinals, a Saracen messenger came before him and the Cardinals, and presented to him a letter from the Sultan of Babylon. In that letter were written many things, and among them the Sultan said to the Pope that he marvelled greatly concerning him, and concerning all the kings and princes of the Christians, that in conquering the Holy Land beyond the seas they acted according to the manner of the prophet Muḥammad, who held by force of arms the lands which he conquered. He marvelled that the Pope and the Christians worked not after the manner of Jesus Christ and of the Apostles, who through preaching and through martyrdom converted the world, and that they followed not

English text from Ramon Llull, *Blanquerna*, translated by E. A. Peers (London: Dedalus, 1987), pp. 322–31. Reprinted with permission of the publisher.

the manner of those who preceded them in conquering other countries; for this cause, he said, God willed not that they should possess the Holy Land beyond the seas. These letters the Saracen brought to the Holy Apostolic Father, and like letters brought he to the kings and princes of the Christians. Deeply thought the Pope and the Cardinals upon the words which the Sultan had written to them. . . .

After these words, the Pope and the Cardinals and the religious, to honor the glory of God, ordained that to all monks that had learning there should be assigned friars to teach divers languages, and that throughout the world there should be builded divers houses, which for their needs should be sufficiently provided and endowed, according to the manner of the monastery of Miramar, which is in the Island of Mallorca. Right good seemed this ordinance to the Pope and to all the rest, and the Pope sent messengers through all the lands of the unbelievers to bring back certain of them to learn their language and that they at Rome might learn the tongues of these unbelievers, and that certain men should return with them to preach to the others in these lands, and that to those unbelievers that learned Latin, and gained a knowledge of the Holy Catholic Faith, should be given money and garments and palfreys, that they might praise the Christians, who when they had returned to their own lands would continue to assist and maintain them.

Of the whole world the Pope made twelve parts, and appointed to represent him twelve men, who should go each one throughout his part and learn of its estate, to the end that the Pope might know the estate of the whole world. It came to pass that those who went to the unbelievers brought from Alexandria and from Georgia and from India and Greece Christians who were monks, that they might dwell among us, and that their will might be united with the will of our monks, and that during this union and relationship they might be instructed in divers manners concerning certain errors against the faith, and should then go and instruct those that were in their country. Wherefore the Pope sent also some of our monks to the monks aforesaid, and ordered that each year they should send to him a certain number of their friars, that they might dwell with us, and, while they dwelt among us, learn our language.

"Beloved sons!" said the Pope to the monks: "Jews and Saracens are among us who believe in error, and disbelieve and despise the Holy Faith whereby we are bound to honor the glory of God. I desire and ask that to these Jews and Saracens who are in the lands of the Christians there be assigned certain persons to teach them Latin and to expound the Scriptures, and that within a certain time they shall learn these, and if they have not done so, that there shall follow punishment; and while they learn let them be provided for from the possessions of Holy Church; and after they have learned let them be made free men and honored above all others, and then will they convert their fellows and be the better fitted to understand the truth and to convert these others."

When the Pope had spoken these words, the Chamberlain said that, if the Pope made this establishment, the Jews and the Saracens that are among the Christians would take flight to other lands and the income of Holy Church would be diminished. But Ramon the Fool said to the Chamberlain: "Once on a time a man loved a woman, and said to her that he loved her more than any woman beside, and the woman inquired of him wherefore he loved her more than any other woman, and he replied that it was because she was fairer than any. The woman made sign with her hand in a certain direction, saying that in that direction there was a woman that was fairer; and when the man turned and looked in that direction the woman said that if there were another woman that was fairer, he would love her more, and this signified that his love to her was not perfect." The Jester of Valor said that if there were another thing better than God the Chamberlain would love it more than God; so there was question among them which thing was the more contrary to the glory of God and to Valor, whether the diminution of the income of Holy Church or the dishonor which the Jews and the Saracens show to the glory of God and to Valor.

As the Pope desired, even so was it ordained. After this the Pope enquired of the Masters of the Temple and of the Hospital what part they would take in honoring the glory of God, and both these Masters answered and said that they were already in the Holy Land beyond the seas to defend that land and to give example of the Catholic Faith. The Jester enquired of Ramon the Fool if the love which he had to his Beloved was growing in proportion as his Beloved gave him greater pleasures. The Fool answered: "If I could love Him more, it would follow that I should love Him less if He diminished the pleasures which He gives me." And he said likewise that, since he could not do other than love his Beloved, neither could he increase the love which he bore to Him; but the trials which he suffered grew daily, and the greater they were, the more were the joys increased which he had in loving his Beloved." The Holy Apostolic Father said to the two Masters that from that which was signified by the aforesaid words, it followed that to honor the glory of God both the Masters should make ordinance whereby an Order should be created, that the Jester of Valor should not cry out upon the dishonor which is done to Valor by disputes concerning that wherein there would be agreement if they made an Order. He said furthermore that they should use their houses and masterships to make schools and places of study, wherein their knights should learn certain brief arguments, by means of the *Brief Art of Finding Truth*,[1] that they might prove the articles of the Holy Faith and give counsel to Masters, princes and prelates through the art aforesaid; and that they might learn divers languages, and go to kings and princes of the unbelievers that one knight might challenge another to maintain, by feats of arms or by learning, the honor and truth which beseem the valor that is in the Holy Catholic Faith. The ordinance aforementioned was granted to the Pope by the two Masters and by all the friars of their Order, and Ramon the Fool spake these words: "Humility conquered Pride, and the Lover said to his Beloved: 'If Thou, Beloved, wert to die, I should go to weep upon Thy tomb.' And the Beloved answered: 'Weep before the Cross, which is My monument.' The Lover wept bitterly, and said that through over much weeping the sight of his eyes was blinded and knowledge became clear to the eyes of his understanding. Wherefore the Order did all that it could to honor the glory of God." . . .

Throughout all the world went forth the fame of the holy life of the Pope and the great good which he did, and daily was valor increased and dishonor diminished. The good which came from the ordinance which the Pope had established illumined the whole world, and brought devotion to them that heard the ordinance recounted; and throughout all the world was sent in writing an account of the process of the making thereof. It chanced one day that the Pope had sent to a Saracen king a knight who was also a priest, and of the Order of Science and Chivalry. This knight by force of arms vanquished ten knights one after the other on different days, and after this he vanquished all the wise men of that land by his arguments, and proved to all that the Holy Catholic Faith was true. By messengers of such singular talent, and by many more, did the ordinance aforementioned, which was established by the Holy Apostolic Father, illumine the world. . . .

In a certain land there were studying ten Jews and ten Saracens together with ten friars of religion; and when they had learned our holy law and our letters, the half of them were converted to our law, and they preached our law to other Jews, and to Saracens our holy Christian faith, in the presence of many that had not yet been converted, and thus did they daily and continually. And because the Papal Court did all that was in its power, and through the continuance of the disputation, and because truth has power over falsehood, God gave grace to all the Jews and Saracens of that country so that they were converted and baptized, and preached to others the Holy Faith. Wherefore the good and the honor which, through the Pope Blanquerna, was done to the Christian Faith, can in no wise be recounted.

---

1. Llull's *Ars compendiosa inveniendi veritatem* (ca. 1274)

69. FOUNDATION OF A CONVENT OF FRIARS

Establishment of Puigcerdà (1320)

Translated from Latin by Jill R. Webster

Founded in 1320, Puigcerdà was one of the second group of Franciscan houses to be founded in the Crown of Aragón. The order made rapid growth in the Iberian Peninsula after the first friars established communities in the 1220s. Before a religious house could be founded in the fourteenth century the friars had first of all to make themselves known in the area and secure the economic support of their contemporaries. They then would approach the municipal government and enlist their help in writing to the king. Royal permission was essential and the crown saw in the friars a group who would serve its own political interests.

Puigcerdà was in many ways unique. In the early fourteenth century it was an important and prosperous commercial center on the north-south trade route; positioned close to the French border, it was in an ideal location for merchants from both France and the kingdoms south of the Pyrenees. The Franciscan house reflected this unusual situation and shared in the town's prosperity and decline. The house belonged to the custody of Narbonne within the Franciscan province of Provence and seems to have had little contact with members of the order to the north, and even less with those in the rest of the province of Gerona in which the town was situated. Its quasi-independent existence made it vulnerable to the problems that beset both church and society from the end of the fourteenth century and it was unable to survive long after the changes that came about with the Reformation. (JRW)

Let it be known by all that the lord Sancho, by the grace of God king of Mallorca and count of Roussillon and Cerdanya, and lord of Montpellier, has decreed that a convent of the Order of Friars Minor be newly built and established in Puigcerdà, in the service and honor of God, and in praise of blessed Francis, with the least inconvenience to the said town. So that it should be adequate and fitting to the town and to the friars of the Order of Saint Francis coming to it and serving the Lord in it, the king sent Pere de Bardoli, his procurator, to be present personally in the town of Puigcerdà. The town convoked the consuls and jurates in his presence and made them appear in person, as the king had willed and ordained. By this decree, the consuls of the king and his procurator, acting on his behalf, are to choose a site large enough to accommodate the friars and not inconvenience the town. They are to bring the friars to establish and build the monastery conceded to the friars by his royal majesty.

Adapted from Jill R. Webster, "El desconocido convento de Puigcerdà," *Archivo Ibero-Americano* (Madrid) 49 (1989): 188–90.

The aforesaid consuls and jurates after two days, having deliberated with due solemnity among themselves and diligently consulted and taken the advice of other good citizens specially convoked by them, first taking an oath, informed and indicated to the procurator when he so requested, that the site described below was as adequate and large as any for the building of their house or monastery or convent; that there might be another site, sites, house or patios within or without the walls of the town of Puigcerdà, of equal value to other sites within or without the walls, with the least inconvenience to the town, since the site mentioned is not inhabited. That not having done so, the said Pere de Bardoli, the procurator, immediately wrote letters and told the king all the above-mentioned and the king ordered through master Pere de Bardoli that the aforesaid monastery or convent should be established in the place indicated below and that he should have the friars brought there and the place estimated by good citizens and all this and more is contained in the king's letter which reads as follows:

Sancho, by the grace of God, king of Mallorca, count of Roussillon and Cerdanya and lord of Montpellier, to his faithful procurator, Pere de Bardoli, greetings. We received your letter in which you explained to us at length what you had done with the consuls, jurates and good citizens of the town of Puigcerdà, in regard to the assigning of a place in that city for the Friars Minor. Since your letter indicates that you and the above men are in full agreement that a monastery should be built on the site containing the house and workshop of the late Bernat de Mornach, and which extends to the gate of the town or to the walls in the direction of Querol; that you agree that the garden outside the walls is adequate and that it should be assigned to the friars. In view of the fact that you and the consuls, jurates and good citizens are in agreement, we are satisfied and wish the monastery to be established in the place mentioned. You should have the site valued on behalf of the friars by the good citizens who should take an oath at our court to the effect that they will make a good and accurate assessment of the value of the site. Once they have been chosen and constituted and you have estimated the price and completed assessment to see whether they are appropriate and have paid for them on the friars' behalf, you should take counsel about the establishment and building of the monastery to see that it goes forward. In regard to all these matters we wish you to carry them out with diligence and loyalty and in the usual way hand the site over to the monastery. Perpignan, 4 kalends May, 1320.

The Assessment completed, the friars take possession of the site

The said Pere de Bardoli, before sending the letters and having consulted diligently about the matter, chose four good citizens from the town of

Puigcerdà, to value and faithfully estimate the value of the site mentioned, to wit Joan Blanc, Arnau Guillem de Lora, Guillem de Ager and Pere Thon of Puigcerdà. The above are themselves to evaluate the site, the house and patio as is detailed below. The valuation made by them is to be transcribed in the same way by the aforesaid procurator, Pere de Bardoli, and when the latter arrives, we should immediately return to the town of Puigcerdà, and go to the said site and there personally bring together the friars named below, that is Fr. Francesc Raynaud, guardian of the convent of Friars Minor, Perpignan, Fr. Ramon Talló, guardian-elect of the Puigcerdà convent, Fr. Guillem Catllar and many other friars of the said convent. The above-mentioned Fr. Ramon Talló and Fr. Guillem Catllar, in their own name and in that of the other friars chosen for the convent of Friars Minor in Puigcerdà, the said sites having been evaluated by the above-mentioned, were given full possession and the sites handed over to them in person, and as a true and irrevocable sign of their possession of the site, the keys of the house or hospice brought to them, the entrance of the hospice being opened and closed, as is customary with the friars both in that and other places. It was also agreed by the said procurator that the friars could not live in or make their home in the said hospice and patios until they had approved of them or agreed otherwise and with the possessions in that place, Pere de Bardoli, the procurator, ordered the aforementioned evaluators that they should assess the site which was designated as the convent garden, and the procurator handed over the property to the above-mentioned friars. The lord procurator ordered all the above matters to be written down by a public notary, as a perpetual record. Witness Jaume Bocanova of Perpignan.

70. LEGENDARY ORIGINS OF NOBLE FAMILIES

Livro de Linhagens do Conde Dom Pedro

Translated from Portuguese by Rita Costa Gomes

*The Portuguese genealogical literature consists of compilations of lists of names or-
dered by lines of succession from noble families settled in the western areas of the
Iberian Peninsula (Portugal and Galicia). It contains also genealogies from other
regions of Iberia, thus reflecting the movement and resettlement of noble families
that occurred with the Christian Reconquest. The oldest works are the* Livro Velho
de Linhagens *(ca. 1286–1290) and the* Livro do Deão *(ca. 1342). The most complete
is the* Livro de Linhagens do Conde Dom Pedro, *composed between 1340 and 1344
by the Count of Barcelos, an illegitimate son of King Dinis of Portugal (r. 1279–1325).
This text attempts to trace the ancestry of each noble family as far back as possible
and to position the Portuguese genealogies in an Iberian and even a universal context. In general terms, the historical exactitude of the information reported by the*
Livro de Linhagens do Conde Dom Pedro *is remarkable, in particular for the
families of the high nobility and for the generations that came after the emergence
of the kingdom of Portugal. The* Livros de Linhagens *often narrate historical circumstances surrounding the foundation of noble families, other times they attribute
to them legendary and mythical origins. The two legends below recount the origins of
the family of Haro, from the Basque country, and that of the Marinhos from Galicia.
They illustrate one specific type of narrative organized around a female figure. In
both cases, we can detect a supernatural origin for the female ancestor at the origins
of the family, and even of its name in the case of the Marinho family. These legends
are variants of the famous tale of "Melusina," the female ancestor of the French
lineage of Lusignan, and they have been likewise dated from the thirteenth century.[1]
The union of a noble knight with a woman coming from the forest, or from the sea
would evoke his courage and ambition as the founder of the family. His charisma
would be related to a pact with the occult and demonized forces of nature achieved
through the sexual union with a female figure bearing the attributes of the devil
(a goat's foot) or nonhuman attributes such as the mute lady coming from the sea.
In the genealogy of the Haros, the lady with the goat's foot continues to protect her
son, even after she returned to the forest, and the family thrives with a reputation
of magical powers. As for Dona Marinha, it is only after her animal attributes are
transcended by the human love she expresses for her progeny that the sacramental
marriage can take place. (RCG)*

Translated from *Narrativas dos livros de linhagens,* edited by José Mattoso (Lisbon: Im-
prensa Nacional-Casa da Moeda, 1983), pp. 70, 72–73. Introductory information derived from
Mattoso's commentary on the same edition, pp. 65–68.
    1. For more details, see Jacques Le Goff, "Melusina: Mother and Pioneer" in his *Time,
Work, and Culture in the Middle Ages* (Chicago: University of Chicago Press, 1982), pp. 205–22.

The Lady with a Goat's Foot (Chapter on the Family of Haro)

This Diogo Lopes was a very good hunter, and one day as he was in the forest waiting for the wild boar to appear he heard loud singing by a woman on the top of a boulder. He went there and saw that she was very beautiful and very well dressed, and he fell strongly in love with her, and he asked her who she was. She said to him that she was a woman of very high lineage. And he said to her that since she was a woman of high birth he would marry her if she wanted, since he was the lord of all that land. She then said that she would do so, if he promised that he would never make the sign of the cross. He conceded that to her, and she went with him right away. This lady was very beautiful with a well-proportioned body, only she had one hoofed foot as the goats do. They lived for a long time together and had two children, one by the name of Enheguez Guerra and the other a female by the name of Dona [name missing].

When Dom Diogo Lopes and his wife ate together, he sat with their son by his side, and she sat with the daughter on the other side. One day he went hunting and killed a very big boar, and he brought it to his house and put it in front of the table where he sat eating with his wife and children. As they threw a bone from the table, two of the dogs, a male alaunt[2] and a female running-hound, were fighting for it, in such a way that the female caught the alaunt at the neck and killed it. Dom Diogo Lopes, as he saw this, considered it a miracle, and he made the sign of the cross saying: "Holy Mary, who ever saw such a thing!" And his wife, as soon as she saw him make the sign of the cross, reached for the son and the daughter, and Dom Diogo Lopes held on to the son and did not let go of him. And she escaped with the daughter out of one window of the palace to the mountains, in such a way that nobody ever saw her again nor the daughter.

Dona Marinha (Chapter on the Family of Marinho)

The first [of this lineage] was a good knight who went by the name of Don Froiam, and he was good in hunting and venery. One day, when he was in a hunt riding his horse by the seashore, he found a woman from the sea asleep by the shore. He had three of his squires with him, so when she noticed them and wanted to take refuge at the sea, they went forcefully after her until they captured her, before she could escape to the ocean. And after the knight took her from those who had captured her, he had her put on a mount, and took her to his house.

She was very beautiful, and he had her baptized. No name seemed as

2. A large dog used to hunt wild animals.

appropriate as that of "Marinha" because she came from the sea.[3] He had two sons with her, and one of them went by the name of Joham Froiaz Marinho.

This Dona Marinha never said a word. Dom Froiam loved her dearly, and regardless of all the things that he could do to her, he never got her to speak. One day he had a great fire made in his palace, and she was coming in from the outside bringing her son with her, whom she loved with all her heart. And Dom Froiam caught that son who was his and hers, and pretended that he wanted to toss him into the fire. With the rage that came over her on account of the son, she made an effort to scream, and with her shout came out her mouth a piece of meat, and henceforth she spoke. And Dom Froiam received her as his wife and married her.

3. In Portuguese and Galician, *mar*.

71. THE EVILS OF MONEY AND DRINK

Juan Ruíz, *Libro de buen amor*
Translated from Castilian by Jill R. Webster

Juan Ruíz (d. ca. 1351), archpriest of Hita, whose exact dates are still a cause for specu-lation, is traditionally thought to have written the Libro de buen amor *sometime during the first half of the fourteenth century. It is a didactic treatise on the pitfalls of immorality and excess in daily life, overcome only through* buen amor, *or the love of God, although some have interpreted it as a textbook on how to engage in* loco amor, *or sexuality. By criticizing contemporary society and pointing out the church's flaws, Juan Ruíz provides a useful commentary on fourteenth-century Castilian customs.*

The excerpts chosen illustrate two of the common ills associated with immoder-ate behavior and the dangers of sin for the cleric: money is seen as the root of all evil; drink leads to lack of control and worldliness. Juan Ruíz emphasizes the cleric's inability to respect his calling and reject the overall desire for power that motivates much human behavior. He regards the corruption he sees among clerics and laity alike as symptomatic of the breakdown in social mores, which may support a late fourteenth-century date for the Libro de buen amor *when both church and society were troubled by schism and change. (JRW)*

Juan Ruiz, Archpriest of Hita, Describes the Effects Money and Drink Have on Social Behavior, Especially on Those Who Have Dedicated Their Lives to God's Service

The Power of Money

Money works miracles and is to be greatly cherished for it makes the man of slow wit respectable and competent. It makes the lame run and the dumb speak and the man without hands eager to grasp it.

If a man is ignorant and a rough farmer, money makes him noble and knowledgeable. The more he has, the more important he becomes and if he lacks money, he has no power either.

If you have money, you will have comfort, pleasure and happiness and will be important to the Pope. You will be able to buy Paradise and gain salva-tion, for where there is much money, there is great blessing.

In the Roman Court where His Holiness resides, I saw that everyone present did obeisance to money. They all honored it with due solemnity and bowed down before it as if to His Majesty.

Money was responsible for the creation of priors, bishops, abbots,

Translated from Juan Ruíz, *Libro de buen amor*, edited by G. B. Gybbon-Monypenny (Madrid: Clásicos Castalia, 1988), pp. 210–13, stanzas 490–510.

archbishops, doctors, patriarchs and potentates in abundance and to many clerics it conferred positions of dignity, converting truth into falsehood and falsehood into truth.

It was responsible for creating clerics and ordained men, monks and nuns, and an abundance of holy religious. It gave them good results in their examinations while the poor were told that they were not literate.

Money was responsible for many a judgment and bad decision, upheld by lawyers who conducted bad lawsuits and brought them to conclusion. In the end the power of money bought repentance.

Money breaks the thickest bonds; it opens doors and bars and gains access to impenetrable prisons. A man who has none finds himself placed in bondage. Money works wonders wherever it is found.

I saw wonders worked where it was held in abundance. Many deserved to die and it gave them life; others were innocent and it had them killed; it caused the loss of many souls and was the salvation of many others.

It makes the poor man lose his house, vineyards, furniture and all his roots, casting everything into disarray. The whole world is plagued by its curse and where money prevails many things are overlooked.

I saw the role of money in the best dwellings, tall and costly and beautifully painted; in castles, family properties and villas with turrets; all of them bought with and in the service of money.

It partook of many foods of different kinds; it was attired in noble cloths and vestments of gold; it wore precious jewels in the pursuit of entertainment and vice, strange adornments and noble mounts.

I saw many monks curse money and its temptations in their sermons and finally grant pardons in exchange for money, thereby giving up fasting and prayer for money.

But although the monks curse it in public, they hoard it in cups and glasses in the monastery. How much better are they than crows and vultures when they use money to complete their work and their mission?

As friars do not handle money they are well remunerated when they hold positions and they borrow money from their procurators, so what do they mean when they say they are poor?

Monks, friars and clerics who love to serve God, if they suspect that the rich man is about to die and hear the clink of his money, which of them will dare to admonish him?

They are all there waiting to see who will get the largest share and he is not even dead when they say the *Pater noster* like an evil omen. Like crows on an ass as they devour his skin, they say tomorrow is our turn and it is right for us to have it.

Wherever women are found and ladies of high estate, they pay out money and great riches. I never saw beauty desirous of poverty for where there is much money, there is great nobility.

Money is both mayor and judge, highly lauded as counselor, skillful advocate, policeman and guard, resourceful and powerful in all positions where it holds sway.

All in all, I advise you to take advantage of it, for where there is money, mountains are moved. It turns the servant into the master, the master into the servant and all things everywhere obey its call.

The Evils of Drink and How It Led the Hermit Astray

You must always have good habits. Take care not to drink too much wine for wine made Lot turn back with his daughter to the great shame of the world and it made him incur God's wrath.

It made a hermit lose body and soul for he had never tasted it before. He tried it to his great harm. The Devil tempted him with his cunning tricks and made him drink the wine. Listen to this strange example.

There was once a hermit who for forty years had served God in the desert and throughout his life had abstained from drinking wine. He drank of holiness, fasting and prayer.

The Devil was very sad about this and thought how he could take him away from his pious works. He came one day with a cunning proposal: "May God keep you, good man," he said to him in a simple way.

The monk was surprised and said, "To God I commit myself. Tell me who you are for I do not understand you. I have been serving God here for a long time and I never saw a human being. I protect myself with the Cross."

The Devil could not reach his person and being forced backwards he began to tempt him, saying: "That body of God which you wish to taste, I will show you how you can take it.

"You must not doubt that the wine becomes the true blood of God; in it is a very holy sacrament; try it if you will." The Devil looked for a way to ensnare the monk.

The hermit said: "I don't know what wine is like." The Devil quickly replied with what he had come for and said: "Those publicans who go along the highway will give you plenty of it; hurry up and get some."

He made him go for the wine and when he returned said: "Bless it and drink of it since you have fetched it. Try a little of it and when you have drunk it, you will see that my advice to you is good."

The hermit drank a lot of the wine without caution and as it was strong and pure, it made him lose consciousness. When the Devil saw that he had secured a base, he turned his temptations to building upon it and adorning it.

"My friend," he said, "you know not what time of day or night it is, nor how the world is ruled; get a cock to show you the hours of the day and with it a hen, as with a female it will breed better."

The hermit believed his bad advice for he had partaken of the wine; and being inebriated, he saw how the cock and the hens lay down together, and he took delight in them. From the time he became inebriated, he wanted to fornicate.

He was filled with greed, the root of all evils, lust and pride, all three mortal sins, then homicide—for wine brings these sins to the immoderate.

He went from the hermitage, raped a woman who, even though she screamed as loudly as she could, was unable to defend herself from him. After he had sinned with her, he was afraid of what would happen and killed her, thereby setting out on the road to perdition.

In the words of the proverb, it is true that evil comes to him who evil thinks. His bad behavior was discovered and from this moment the monk was taken prisoner.

He discovered how much evil he had done when inebriated; he was then sentenced, as was appropriate, and the poor misled man lost both his body and soul. Drink is the root of all evil.

It sends one blind and shortens one's life; it saps one's strength if it is taken without moderation; it makes the muscles tremble and all common sense is forgotten. Where there is a lot of wine, all is lost.

It makes the breath smell which is a very bad sign, the mouth smells bad and there is nothing worthwhile; it burns the intestines and penetrates the liver. If you want to love ladies, wine is of no use to you.

Drunken men get old sooner; they lose their color, wither and waste away. They commit many shameful acts, everyone abhors them and they sin greatly against God, losing their reputation in the world.

Where wine rises above the center of the marrow, the intestines make a noise like pigs and crows, and deaths, fights and conflicts ensue. A lot of wine is good in buckets and containers.

Wine, if it is taken in moderation, is very good in itself for it has many good properties. He who drinks too much loses his senses and in the world engages in all kinds of wrongdoing and every kind of madness.

For that reason flee from wine.

72. LOVE LYRICS BY A CATALAN QUEEN

Queen Violant, *E-z ieu am tal que es bo e bell*
(mid-fourteenth century)
Translated from Catalan by James J. Wilhelm

The sole extant manuscript of this poem attributes it to "The Queen of Mallorca,"
traditionally identified as Constance (d. 1346), wife of Jaume III, last king of the
Catalan-speaking island kingdom of Mallorca. However, the poet is more likely Vio-
lant, who married Jaume in 1347. Jaume's business in France included selling his
domain of Montpellier to France to finance his unsuccessful attempt to regain posses-
sion of Mallorca. (ORC)

I love one who's good and handsome;
I'm as happy as the white bird
Who, for love, bursts out in song;
I am a sovereign lady,
And let him I love make no appeal,
Because I love more than any other woman,
Since I have chosen him of greatest worth,
The best in the world; I love him so
That in my mind I think I see him
    And hold him close;
    But this is not true,
And great despair sweeps over me
    When I realize he's away in France.

*　　*　　*

My longing and the great desire
I have for you have all but killed me,
My sweet, beloved lord;
I could easily die ere long
Because of you whom I love and want so much,
If I don't see you soon return:
I'm so impatient for our kisses,
    Our intimate talks,
    And all the rest.

English text from *Lyrics of the Middle Ages: An Anthology*, edited by James J. Wilhelm
(New York: Garland, 1990), p. 259. Reprinted with permission of the publisher.

When I think of how you went away
    And haven't come back
    And how far away you are,
My despairing heart barely beats:
    I'm as good as dead
    If I'm not cured fast!

*   *   *

Have pity, husband; in pain I endure
The sufferings you give me: please return!
    No treasure
    Is worth a heart
    That dies for you
    With loving thought.

73. MEMOIRS OF A CASTILIAN NOBLEWOMAN

Leonor López de Córdoba, *Memorias*

Translated from Castilian by Kathleen Lacey

*Leonor López de Córdoba (ca. 1362–ca. 1412) was born in about 1362 into a noble Cas-
tilian family, supporters of King Pedro I (r. 1350–1369). She was also a descendant of
Juan Manuel, author of the* Libro de los estados *(Chapter 63). After King Pedro's
death at the hands of his half brother, Enrique de Trastámara (thereafter Enrique
II, r. 1369–1379), on the field of Montiel, Leonor's father, Martín, continued to hold out
against the new king from his fortress at Carmona, near Seville. From Carmona,
where he held custody of King Pedro's daughters and much of the Castilian treasury,
Martín López de Córdoba encouraged the claims of Fernando of Portugal to invade
Castile and take over the throne from Enrique II. His efforts were thwarted, however,
by a treaty between Portugal and Castile in 1371. A few months later, Martín surrendered Carmona to Enrique on the condition that his family and Pedro's children be
allowed to leave the country in safety. This agreement was not honored; Martín was
beheaded and his family was imprisoned until 1379. Even after her release, Leonor continued to meet with hardships. Among these was the plague, which persisted in Europe
during the later fourteenth century after its devastating outbreak in 1348. (ORC)*

Therefore, may whoever reads this document know that I am Doña Leonor
López de Córdoba, the daughter of my lord, Master Don Martín López de
Córdoba, and Doña Sancha Carrillo, to whom God gave glory and paradise.
I swear, by the meaning of the cross that I adore, that all that is written here
is true, that I saw it, and it happened to me. I write it for the honor and glory
of my Lord Jesus Christ, and of the Virgin, St. Mary his mother, who gave
birth to him, so that all creatures that were in tribulation may be secure—as
I put my faith in her mercy—that if they commend their hearts to the Virgin
St. Mary, she will console and succor them, as she consoled me. And so that
whoever hears this knows the story of the deeds and miracles the Virgin St.
Mary showed me, and as it is my intention that these deeds and miracles be
remembered, I ordered this to be written, as you see.

I am the daughter of the said master who was Lord of Calatrava in the
time of King Pedro. The king did my father the honor of giving him the
commission of Alcántara, which is in the city of Seville. The king then made
him master of Alcántara and, in the end, of Calatrava. This master, my father,
was a descendant of the house of Aguilar, and the great-nephew of Don Juan

English text from *Medieval Women's Visionary Literature*, edited by Elizabeth A. Petroff
(New York: Oxford University Press, 1985), pp. 329–34. Reprinted with permission of the
translator.

Manuel, son of his niece who was the daughter of his brother. He rose to a very high estate, as can be discovered in the chronicles of Spain. And as I have said, I am the daughter of Doña Sancha Carrillo, niece and ward of King Alfonso of most illustrious memory, to whom God granted paradise, who was the father of King Pedro.

My mother died very early, and so my father married me at seven years old to Ruy Gutierrez de Henestrosa. He was the son of Juan Fernández de Henestrosa, King Pedro's head valet, his chancellor of the royal seal, and head majordomo of Queen Blanca his wife; Juan Fernández married Doña María de Haro, mistress of Haro and the Cameros. To my husband were left many of his father's goods and several estates. He received three hundred mounted soldiers of his own, and forty strands of pearls as fat as chick-peas, and five hundred Moorish servants, and silver tableware worth two thousand marks. The jewels and gems of his house could not be written on two sheets of paper. All this came to him from his father and mother because they had no other son and heir. My father gave me twenty thousand *doblas* as a dowry; we lived in Carmona with King Pedro's daughters, my husband and I, along with my brothers-in-law, my sisters' husbands, and with one brother of mine, who was named Don Lope López de Córdoba Carrillo. My brothers-in-law were named Fernán Rodríguez de Aza, Lord of Aza and Villalobos, and Ruy García de Aza, and Lope Rodríguez de Aza. They were the sons of Álvaro Rodríguez de Aza and Doña Costanza de Villalobos.

That was how things stood when King Pedro was besieged at the castle of Montiel by his brother, King Enrique. My father went down to Andalusia to bring people to aid King Pedro, and on the way he discovered that the king was dead at the hands of his brother. Seeing this disgrace, he took the road to Carmona where the princesses were, King Pedro's daughters, who were very close relatives of my husband, and of myself through my mother. King Enrique, becoming King of Castile, came to Seville and surrounded Carmona. As it is such a strong town, it was surrounded for many months.

But by chance my father had left Carmona, and those of King Enrique's camp knew how he was gone, and that it would not remain so well protected. Twelve knights volunteered to scale the town, and they climbed the wall. They were captured, and then my father was informed of what had happened. He came to Carmona then, and ordered them to be beheaded for their audacity. King Enrique observed this, and because he could not enter Carmona by force of arms to satisfy himself about this deed, he ordered the constable of Castile to discuss terms with my father.

The terms that my father put forward were two. First, King Enrique's party was to free the princesses and their treasure to leave for England, before he would surrender the town to the King. (And so it was done. He ordered certain noblemen, his kinsmen and natives of Córdoba bearing his family name, to accompany the princesses and the rest of the people who intended to leave with them.) The second condition was that my father, his children, his guard, and those in the town who had obeyed his orders would be pardoned by the king, and that they and their estates would be considered loyal. And so it was granted him, signed by the constable in the king's name. Having achieved this, my father surrendered the town to the constable in King Enrique's name, and he left there—with his children and the rest of the people—to kiss the king's hand. King Enrique ordered them to be arrested and put in the dungeon of Seville. The constable, who saw that King Enrique had not fulfilled the promise he had made in his name to this master (my father), left the court and never returned to it.

The king ordered my father to be beheaded in the Plaza de San Francisco in Seville, and his goods confiscated, as well as those of his son-in-law, guardsmen, and servants. While he was on his way to be decapitated, my father encountered Mosen Beltran de Clequin, a French knight, the knight, in fact, whom King Pedro had trusted and who had freed him when he was trapped in the castle of Montiel, but who had not fulfilled his promise, and instead surrendered him to King Enrique to be killed. As Mosen Beltran met with my father, he said to him, "Master, didn't I tell you that your travels would end in this?" And my father replied, "Better to die loyal, as I have done, than to live as you live, having been a traitor."

The rest of us remained in prison for nine years, until King Enrique died. Our husbands each had seventy pounds of iron on their feet, and my brother, Don Lope López, had a chain between the irons in which there were seventy links. He was a boy of thirteen years, the most beautiful creature in the world. My husband especially was made to go hungry. For six or seven days he neither ate nor drank because he was the cousin of the princesses, the daughters of King Pedro.

A plague came into the prison, and so my brothers and all of my brothers-in-law and thirteen knights from my father's house all died. Sancho Miñez de Villendra, my father's head valet, said to my brothers and sisters and me, "Children of my lord, pray to God that I live for your sakes, for if I do, you will never die poor." It was God's will that he died the third day without speaking. After they were dead they took them all out to the smith to have their chains taken off, like Moors.

My poor brother, Don Lope López, asked the mayor who had us in his charge to tell Gonzalo Ruíz Bolante that much charity was shown to us, and much honor, for the love of God. "Lord Mayor, it would be merciful of you

to take off my irons before my soul departs, and not to take me to the smith."
The mayor replied to him as if to a Moor, "If it were up to me, I would do
it." At this, my brother's soul departed while he was in my arms. He was a
year older than I. They took him away on a slab to the smith, like a Moor,
and they buried him with my brothers and my sisters and my brothers-in-law
in the church of San Francisco of Seville.

Each of my brothers-in-law used to wear a gold necklace around his
throat, for they were five brothers. They put on those necklaces in Santa
María de Guadalupe, and they vowed not to take them off until all five lay
themselves down in Santa María. Because of their sins, one died in Seville,
and another in Lisbon, and another in England, and so they died scattered.
They ordered that they be buried with the gold necklaces, but the monks,
after burying them, greedily removed the necklaces.

No one from the house of my father, Master Don Martín López, remained in the dungeon except my husband and myself. At this time, the most
high and illustrious King Enrique, of very sainted and illustrious memory,
died; he ordered in his will that we were to be taken out of prison, and that
all that was ours be returned. I stayed in the house of my lady aunt, Doña
María García Carrillo, and my husband went to demand his goods. Those
who held them paid him little attention, because he had no rank or means
to demand their return. You already know how rights depend on one's petition being granted. So my husband disappeared, and wandered through the
world for seven years, a wretch, and never discovered relative nor friend who
would do him a good turn or take pity on him. After I had spent seven years
in the household of my aunt, Doña María García Carrillo, they told my husband, who was in Badajoz with his uncle Lope Fernández de Padilla in the
Portuguese War, that I was in good health and that my relatives had treated
me very well. He mounted his mule, which was worth very little money, and
the clothes he wore didn't amount to thirty *maravedis,* and he appeared at
my aunt's door.

Not having known that my husband was wandering lost through the
world, I requested my lady aunt, my lady mother's sister, to speak with Doña
Teresa Fernández Carrillo, who was a member of the Order of Guadalajara,
which my great grandparents founded; they have given an endowment to
support forty wealthy women of their lineage who should join the order.
I sent my aunt to petition that Doña Teresa would wish to receive me into
that order, for through my sins my husband and I were lost. She, and all
the order, agreed to this, for my lady mother had been brought up in their
monasteries. King Pedro had taken her from there and had given her to my
father in marriage because she was the sister of Gonzalo Díaz Carrillo and

of Diego Carrillo, sons of Don Juan Fernández Carrillo and Doña Sancha de Rojas. Because these uncles of mine were afraid of King Pedro, who had killed and exiled many of his lineage and had demolished my grandfather's houses and given his property to others, these uncles of mine left there, in order to serve King Enrique when he was count, because of this outrage. I was born in Calatayud, in the king's house. The lady princesses, his daughters, were my godmothers, and they brought me with them to the fortress of Segovia, along with my lady mother, who died there. I was of such an age that I never knew her.

And after my husband arrived, as I said, I left the house of my lady aunt, which was in Córdoba next to San Ipólito, and my husband and I were received into some houses there, next to hers, and we came there with little rest.

For thirty days I prayed to the Virgin St. Mary of Bethlehem. Each night on my knees I said three hundred Ave Marias, in order to reach the heart of my lady aunt so she would consent to open a postern to her houses. Two days before my praying ended, I demanded of my lady aunt that she allow me to open that private entrance, so that we wouldn't walk through the street, past so many nobles that there were in Córdoba, to come eat at her table. In her mercy she responded to me and granted it, and I was greatly consoled. Another day, when I wanted to open the postern, her servants had changed her heart and she would not do it. I was so disconsolate that I lost patience, and she that had caused me the most trouble with my lady aunt died at my hands, eating her tongue.

Another day, when only one day remained to complete my prayer, a Saturday, I dreamed I was passing through San Ipólito touching the alb. I saw in the wall of the courtyard an arch, very large and very tall. I entered through it and gathered flowers from the earth, and saw a very great heaven. At this I awoke, and I was hopeful that my Virgin St. Mary would give me a home.

At this time there was a robbery in the Jewish quarter, and I took in an orphan boy who was there, so that he would be instructed in the faith. I had him baptized so that he would be instructed in the faith.

One day, coming with my lady aunt from mass at San Ipólito, I saw being distributed among the clerics of San Ipólito those grounds where I had dreamed there was the great arch. I implored my lady aunt, Doña Mencía Carrillo, to purchase that site for me, since I had been her companion for seventeen years, and she bought it for me. She gave these grounds to me with the condition—which she indicated—that I build a chapel (erected over the houses) for the soul of King Alfonso, who built that church in the name of San Ipólito because he was born on that saint's day. These chaplains have another six or seven chapels built by Don Gonzalo Fernández, my lady aunt's husband, and Don Alfonso Fernández, lord of Aguilar, and by the children of the marshal. Then, when I had done this favor, I raised my eyes to God and to the Virgin Mary, giving them thanks.

There came to me a servant of Master Don Martín López, my lord and father, who lives with Martín Fernández, mayor of the doncels [young women], who was there hearing mass. I sent a request with this servant to Don Martín Fernández that, as a kinsman, he thank my lady aunt for the kindness she had shown me. He was greatly pleased, and so he did it well, saying that he received her kindness to me as if it were shown to him.

Now that possession of these grounds had been given to me, I opened a door on the very place where I had seen the arch which the Virgin Mary showed me. It grieved the abbots to hand over that site to me, for I was of a great lineage, and my children would be great. They were abbots, and had no need of great knights so near them. This I heard from a reliable voice, and I told them to hope in God that it would be so. I made myself so agreeable to them that I opened the door in the place that I wanted. God helped me by giving me that beginning of a house because of the charity I performed in raising the orphan in the faith of Jesus Christ. For thirty days before this, I had gone at Matins to the image of St. Mary the Fainting, which is in the Order of San Pablo of Córdoba, barefoot and with tears and sighs, and I prayed to her the prayer that follows sixty-three times, with sixty-six Ave Marias, in reverence for the sixty-six years that she lived with bitterness in this world, so that she would give me a home, and she gave me a home, and houses better than I deserved, out of her mercy. Here begins the prayer: "Mother St. Mary, your well-taught son took on great pain for you. You saw him tormented with great tribulation; your heart fainted after his tribulation. He gave you consolation; Lady, you who know my pain, give the same to me." It was the Virgin St. Mary's will that with the help of my lady aunt, and by the labor of my hands, I built in that yard two mansions, and an orchard, and another two or three houses for servants.

In this period of time a very cruel plague came. My lady aunt did not want to leave the city; I requested of her the kindness to permit me to flee with my children so that they would not die. She was not pleased but she gave me leave. I left Córdoba and went to Santa Ella with my children. The orphan that I raised lived in Santa Ella, and he lodged me in his house. All of the neighbors of the town were delighted by my coming. They received me with warm welcome, for they had been servants of the lord my father, and so they gave me the best house there was in that place, which was that belonging to Fernando Alonso Mediabarba. Being without suspicion, my lady aunt came there with her daughters, and I withdrew to a small room.

Her daughters, my cousins, never got on well with me because of all the good their mother had done me. I suffered so much bitterness from them that it cannot be written.

The plague came there, so my lady left with her people for Aguilar, and she took me with her as one of her own daughters, for she loved me greatly and said great things of me. I had sent the orphan that I raised to Ezija. The night that we arrived in Aguilar, the boy came from Ezija with two small tumors in his throat and three carbuncles on his face, and with a high fever. In that house there were Don Alonso Fernández, my cousin, and his wife and all of his household. Though all of the girls were my nieces and my friends, knowing that my servant came in such a condition, they came to me and said, "Your servant, Alonso, comes with the plague, and if Don Alonso Fernández sees it he will be furious at his being here with such an illness."

And the pain that reached my heart anyone who hears this history can well understand. I became worldly wise and bitter. Thinking that through me such great sorrow had entered that house, I had Miguel de Santa Ella called to me. He had been a servant of the master, my lord and father, and I begged him to take that boy to his house. The wretched man was afraid, and he said, "Lady, how can I take him with the plague, which will kill me?" And I said to him, "Son, God would not want that." Shamed by me, he took the boy; and through my sins, thirteen persons who watched over him by night all died.

I made a prayer which I had heard, which a nun said before a crucifix. It seems that she was a great devotee of Jesus Christ, and she says that after she had heard Matins she came before a crucifix. On her knees she prayed seven thousand times "Pious Son of the Virgin, may piety conquer you." One night, when the nun was near that place, she heard that the crucifix answered her, and it said, "Pious you called me, and pious I will be for you." I found great devotion in these words. I prayed this prayer each night, begging God to free me and my children, and if he had to take someone, let it be the eldest, for he was very sick.

One night it was God's will that there was no one to watch over that sorrowful boy, for all who had until then watched over him had died. My son, who was called Juan Fernández de Henestrosa like his grandfather, and who was twelve years and four months old, came to me and said, "Lady, is there no one to watch over Alonso tonight?" And I told him, "You watch over him, for the love of God." He replied to me, "Lady, now that the others have all died, do you want to kill me?" I said to him, "For my charity, God will take pity on me." And my son, so as not to disobey me, went to keep vigil. Through my sins, that night he was given the pestilence, and another day I buried him. The sick one lived after all the others had died.

Doña Teresa, the wife of my cousin Don Alonso Fernández, became very angry because my son was dying in her house at that time. She ordered that he be removed from the house on account of his illness. I was so transfixed by grief that I could not speak for the shame that those words caused me. My poor son said, "Tell my lady Doña Teresa not to cast me away, for my soul will leave now for heaven." He died that night. He was buried in Santa María la Coronada, which is in the same town. Because Doña Teresa felt very hostile to me, and I did not know why, she ordered that he not be buried within the town. When they took him to be buried, I went with him. As I went through the streets with my son, people came out, making a great hue and cry, ashamed for me. They said, "Come out, lords, and see the most unfortunate, forsaken, and accursed woman in the world!" with shouts that trespassed the heavens. Like those of that place, all who were there in that crowd were servants of the lord my father, and had been brought up by him. Although they knew that it grieved their present lords, they made a great lament with me as if I were their lady.

This same night, after I came from burying my son, they told me to return to Córdoba. I went to my lady aunt to see if she had ordered this. She said to me, "Lady niece, I cannot fail to do it, for I have promised my daughter-in-law and my daughters, for they are acting as one. In the meantime, it distresses me to have you leave, although I have granted permission. I do not know what annoyance you have caused my daughter-in-law Doña Teresa, that makes her so hostile to you."

I said to her with many tears, "Lady, if I have deserved this, may God not save me." And so I returned to my house in Córdoba.

The Christian Kingdoms and Muslim Granada

(Fifteenth Century)

74. THE CONVENT AND THE WORLD

Letters to and About Teresa de Ayala and María de Ayala
Translated from Castilian by Heath Dillard

The following selections are excerpts from letters collected by Teresa de Ayala (1353–1424) and her daughter María de Ayala (1367–1424), prioress and nun of the Dominican convent of Santo Domingo el Real de Toledo. Doña María, who became a nun in 1392 at age twenty-five, was the illegitimate daughter of King Pedro I of Castile, murdered in 1369 in a fratricidal civil war with his illegitimate half brother Enrique II. Doña Teresa, long since widowed by the man she had married after her youthful encounter with King Pedro, followed her daughter into the convent and soon became prioress. By that time Enrique II, the usurper and first king of Castile in the Trastámara dynasty, had been succeeded by his son, Juan I, and then by Juan's son Enrique III, both of whom corresponded with the convent. So, too, did Enrique III's wife, Queen Catalina, daughter of one of Pedro I's daughters and the English duke of Lancaster and thus doña María's paternal niece. Included here are letters from Enrique III; Juan II, son and heir of Enrique III and Catalina; his sister María de Castilla, queen of Aragón; and doña Juana de Mendoza, wife of the admiral of Castile and a friend of Toledo's Dominican convent, in whose uncataloged archive the letters survive. The rise of the Trastámara dynasty is the single most important political fact of late fourteenth-century peninsular history. Although some of the nuns' correspondents, who dictated their letters to scribes, were players on the political stage, the texts are interesting to us perhaps chiefly as an informal record of interpersonal relations, details, and preoccupations of daily life, especially among women—secular and religious—of the late medieval Castilian aristocracy. (HD)

3 September 1404, Madrid. Enrique III to His Subjects

I, by the grace of God, King of Castile . . . Greetings and grace. You are all hereby notified that doña Teresa de Ayala, prioress of the monastery of Santo Domingo el Real de Toledo, and doña María, her daughter, are traveling through various parts of my kingdom. I therefore order you all and each one of you to receive them, and any persons who may be with them, whenever and at whatever places of yours they may appear. You are to welcome them and provide them with decent lodgings, not unsuitable inns. You are to supply them with food and anything else they may require, for which they have money to pay. See to it that no one is permitted either to harm them or to attempt to injure or disturb them in any way. And let anyone who does, or

Translated from Verardo García Rey, "La famosa priora doña Teresa de Ayala: Su correspondencia íntima con los monarcas de su tiempo," *Boletín de la Real Academia de la Historia* 96 (1930): 733–73, Colección Salazar, Madrid, Real Academia de la Historia, Manuscript N-43, 132v; M-21.

tries to do so, be punished in a manner appropriate to the evil deed intended. I command you also that, should they express to you a need for mules, beasts of burden, or other animals, you are to furnish whatever they request, for which they will pay you a rental fee, within reasonable limits. If, by chance, they are encountered along a dangerous road or at any other such place, you are to accompany them and take responsibility for their safety, going with them from one place to another and from one village to another. Let no one of you do them any harm whatsoever, on penalty of my curse, and that of God. . . . I, the King

3 September 1404, Segovia. Enrique III to Queen Catalina

I send you warm greetings, as to the one I love as well as my own heart, and notify you that, considering the condition you are in at present and so that you may have with you persons who will give you pleasure and free you of your cares, I have arranged to send for doña Teresa de Ayala, prioress of the monastery of Santo Domingo el Real de Toledo, and to send her to you so that she can keep you company. She, more than any other, is just the sort of person you will enjoy having with you, and she will perform for us whatever service and pleasure she possibly can. She cannot leave the monastery, however, without permission from her superiors, but I am told you have written authority from the provincial of the [Dominican] order in the event that I or you should require the presence of the said prioress, or of doña María, your aunt, and that you are thereby enabled to give them permission to leave the monastery and go wherever we command. I ask you, therefore, immediately upon receipt of my letter, that you send me your letter for the said prioress, giving the permission allowing her to leave the said monastery and to come here whence I shall send her on to you so she can be with you as the time draws near. You should send me the written authority you have from the said provincial and, as soon as it is shown to the said prioress, I will send it back to you. . . . I, the King

26 February [1405], Casa de la Rivera, Segovia. Enrique III to Doña Teresa and the Marshal

I, the King, send warm greetings to you, Sister doña Teresa, prioress of Santo Domingo el Real de Toledo, and to Diego Fernández, my marshal, as persons in whom I greatly trust. I hereby notify you that I have seen the letter you sent me and have considered what you wrote on the subject of the wet nurses you are to investigate. Know that you would perform my service in this matter by investigating the twenty candidates named in your letter, making certain that they satisfy the following conditions. First, they should be between twenty and thirty years old and have clear skin, good color, and full figures. They must also have given birth from two to four months previously and should be women of blooming appearance, if at all possible. Also, their own nurslings must be well cared for and well developed, and they must have milk that is excellent in quantity, color, and quality. They must be of the best sort and condition of women, preferably noblewomen, and none should be the wife of a foreigner. As soon as you have investigated and selected them, you should immediately send me the names of their husbands and tell me where they are from so that I can instruct you how to proceed from there. . . . I, the King

13 March [1405], Coria. Enrique III to Doña Teresa and Doña María

I, the King, send warm greetings to you, doña Teresa de Ayala and Sister doña María, as persons for whom I wish much honor and good fortune. I hereby notify you that I have been led to understand that the queen has chosen and appointed several women around the prince, my son [Juan II, born at Segovia, 6 March], as ladies-in-waiting, women to watch over him, and other such offices. I am greatly amazed by what she has done since it is I who ought to make arrangements for all such officials and see to all matters pertaining to the chamber of the said prince. I therefore request and require you, if you would please me and perform my service, to tell the queen not to meddle in any of these things. Leave her with no doubt that I am extremely annoyed by what she has done, and I will in no wise tolerate it. Moreover, for whatever reason she bethought herself to have acted properly, quite the opposite is the case since it is not appropriate that these officials, nor any others, be named in the household of the prince. Whoever thinks she ought to have done these things has done great injury and harm to themselves. . . . I, the King

3 September 1422, Ocaña. Juan II to Doña María

I, the King, send warm greetings to you, Sister doña María, my aunt. I write to tell you that, inasmuch as my wife the queen is about to give birth, she ought to have persons of rank and respectability in her company at such a time. For this reason, and in consideration of you personally, I have decided that you should be there, for I am certain that you will take care to perform whatever my service requires. I therefore ask you, if you desire to please me, to leave that place immediately, go to the town of Illescas where the queen is residing, and stay there with her through her delivery. I also request and order that Sister doña Teresa go there. It is our pleasure, therefore, to command you both to go to be with the queen, as I have said, and in so doing you carry out my pleasure and perform my service. . . . I, the King

12 October [1422], Alcalá de Henares. Juan II to Doña María

I, the King, send cordial greetings to you, doña María, my aunt, as one I love deeply. I write to tell you that the queen, my wife, has informed me that you have been there with her up to the present and, now that her delivery is past, you say you would like to return to your religious community and ask me kindly to grant you license to go. Be assured of my deep appreciation, for I consider it a great service that you have been there. Since it is your pleasure to return to your community, I give you license to do so whenever it would seem to you a good time to leave. I ask only that I be remembered in your prayers and holy devotions. . . . I, the King

12 May 1423, Barcelona. Doña María de Castilla, Queen of Aragón, to Doña María

Dearest aunt. We have received the bolster and the cushions which please us immensely, for they are very beautiful and well executed. We ask you now to send us valances for the foot of a bed, three palms wide, done in the same work as the bolster, and we are writing to Bernal de Gallaque to pay the expenses. We thank you enormously for the great care you have given to the bolster and the cushions. May the Holy Trinity, whom It may please to keep us in Its service, keep you under Its special protection. . . . I, the Queen

6 March s.a., n.p. Doña Juana de Mendoza to Doña Teresa

My lady cousin. I, doña Juana de Mendoza, wife of the admiral of Castile, commend myself into your grace, as a person whose life and good health may it please God always to prosper with much consolation for your heart. My lady cousin, I have seen the letter you sent me and take great pleasure in learning of the good health of my niece doña María and yours. As for the admiral's, my own, and my children's health, I can inform you that we are all well, thanks be to God, and I write to tell you this, for I am certain that it will be pleasing to a person of your noble nature, lady, to be told of it. Know that I am sending you my man with this and 2,000 *mrs.* for the coverlets I requested. I beg your grace to send them in a large basket, just as you send glazed tiles, and that you wrap them in a sheet so that they will be well protected. Also, dear lady, I ask your grace to have bought for me 800 tiles as follows: 300 white ones, 250 black, and 250 green, and that you put them together with the 200 yellow ones which are still there. I am sending you the money for these 800 tiles at 400 *mrs.* per thousand, the price I paid for the ones sent me last summer. Lady, the admiral commends himself into the mercy of his cousin and into yours, and my children kiss your hands and commend themselves into your mercy. Also, lady cousin, I ask your grace to have made for me now yet another 3,000 tiles: 300 yellow, 1,000 white, and the remaining 1,700 half black and half green. Let me know how much these will cost and when they might be sent. The builders must come to me from Seville now, and I do not have any tiles here for them to work with. . . . May God maintain you. . . . doña Juana

29 September s.a., Cabañas, near Yepes. Juan II to Doña Teresa

I, the King, send warm greetings to you, doña Teresa de Ayala, prioress of Santo Domingo el Real, and may God grant you great honor and good fortune. I write to say that I have been told that doña Mencía, daughter of Pedro Carrillo, my chief constable of Toledo, has decided firmly to become a nun. I would be particularly dismayed if this occurred, especially since the said Pedro Carrillo has no children other than the said doña Mencía. It would therefore not be in my service for the said doña Mencía to enter a religious order. Rather she ought to marry, and she should take as her husband Ferrand Álvarez, lord of Valdecorneja, who, I am told, made an attractive proposal to Pedro Carrillo, saying he wished to marry his said daughter. I therefore request and command, if you would please me and perform my service, that you go to doña Mencía and approach her in such a way as to convince her to accept this husband and to do as her father has ordered in the matter. In this you will be carrying out my pleasure and performing enormous service. . . . I, the King

75. THE WEDDING OF KING JOÃO I
OF PORTUGAL (1387)

Fernão Lopes, *Chronicle of Dom João* (ca. 1434)

Translated from Portuguese by Derek W. Lomax and R. J. Oakley

The circumstances of the marriage between King João I of Portugal and the English princess Philippa, daughter of John of Gaunt, reflect the tangled web of political hostilities, alliances, and ambitions in the Iberian Peninsula in the late fourteenth century. The passage selected here also demonstrates the critical role of dynastic marriages in solidifying political aspirations, and it is noteworthy for its description of ceremonial and the royal household.

João, illegitimate son of King Pedro of Portugal (r. 1357–1367), claimed the throne after the death of his half-brother, King Fernando, in 1383. João's succession was supported in Portugal, where he was crowned in 1385, but it was disputed by the Castilian king, Juan I, who claimed the Portuguese throne for himself through his marriage to Beatriz, Fernando's daughter. To back up this claim, Juan invaded Portugal in 1385, but he was defeated by João at the Battle of Aljubarrota, south of Leiria. This battle fully established Portuguese independence, and the defeat of Castile encouraged the English duke, John of Gaunt, to continue his quest for the Castilian throne (on the basis of his marriage to Constanza, eldest daughter of Pedro I of Castile). England and Portugal entered into alliance against Castile in 1386 and solidified their ties through the marriage of King João and Philippa. English and Portuguese forces invaded Castile in 1387, but their campaign came to nothing, and a truce was declared between England, Portugal, and Castile in 1389. At this point, John of Gaunt gave up his own aspirations to the Castilian crown, and another dynastic marriage was arranged between Philippa's sister Catalina and Enrique, oldest son of Juan I and heir to the throne of Castile.

Little is known of the life of Fernão Lopes (b. ca. 1380), author of this chronicle. He worked at the Portuguese court from at least 1418, when he was appointed keeper of the royal archives; in 1434 he was commissioned to write a chronicle of the kings of Portugal from Afonso Henriques until his own day. Although we do not know his date of birth, it is possible that as a child he witnessed the events described in this passage. (ORC)

Princess Philippa was brought to the city of Oporto in a most honorable manner on the orders of her father, and as we said it had been agreed. There she was welcomed with great celebration and joy. Her large escort of Englishmen and Portuguese included Sir John Holland, the Duke's constable;

English text from Fernão Lopes, *The English in Portugal, 1367–87*, translated by Derek W. Lomax and R. J. Oakley (Warminster: Aris and Phillips, 1988), pp. 227–37. Reprinted with permission of the publisher.

Thomas Percy, Admiral of the fleet; Richard Burley, his marshal; Juan Gutiér-rez, Bishop of Dax; and the Archbishop of Braga, Vasco Martins de Melo and João Rodrigues de Sá, as well as certain others who went with them. The Princess was lodged in the Bishop's palace which is situated close to the cathedral of that city. The King [João I] left Evora accompanied by the Constable, and when he arrived in Oporto, he found his bride-to-be, Princess Philippa, already there. The next day, he went to see the Princess whom he had still not set eyes upon, and talked with her for some considerable time in the presence of the Bishop. Then he took his leave and went off to supper. When the King had eaten, he sent jewels to the Princess and she sent some to him. Among the presents the King gave her was a brooch with a cock-erel on it, studded with precious stones and mother-of-pearl, and exquisitely made. She gave him another one on which there was a pin well studded with the costliest gems. The King stayed only a few days before proceeding to Guimarães, but he left Gonçalo Peres, who was at the time overseer of his finances, with instructions to provide anything that she or her attendants might need.

How the King Prepared to Set up His Matrimonial Household and How He Wrote to the City Councils of His Kingdom

While the King was in that city directing preparations for the campaign, there was some discussion concerning his marriage. It was felt that if it were not to receive the blessing of the Church on the following day, this might not be possible for a long time because it was the beginning of Lent, when Church custom forbids such celebrations.[1] So with everyone's agreement the King then wrote to the Bishop of Oporto asking him to have everything made ready the following day for the blessing; and the Bishop did so. The King rode out on the afternoon of the same day and travelled all night so that he arrived in the city in the early morning, having completed a journey of eight leagues.

Dom João was already prepared, dressed in his episcopal robes, and with his clerics arrayed in the appropriate manner. The Princess was escorted with pomp and ceremony from the palace where she had been staying to the ca-thedral; and there, in the presence of everyone, in the name of the Lord God, the King received her as his lawfully wedded wife. The ceremony was

---

1. In the later Middle Ages, Christians normally got married in two successive ceremo-nies, the betrothal and the wedding, which might be separated by weeks or even years, but both of which ought normally to be celebrated publicly in church. Since neither was normally allowed during Lent, a time of sorrow and penance, João I tried to hold both ceremonies as quickly as possible before Lent began on Wednesday, 20 February 1387.

conducted with the utmost solemnity. This took place on 2 February, the Feast of the Purification of the Blessed Virgin, when the King was twenty-nine years old and the Princess his wife, twenty-eight.

The ceremony of the blessing over, the King ordered the wedding and the establishment of his household eight days after the following Thursday, and wrote letters to the cities and towns throughout his kingdom, declaring it to be his pleasure that they should send representatives to his wedding festivities. The summary of the letters he sent to all of them was in the following form:

"To the most noble council and good citizens of our town or city of such and such a place.

"We, the King, send you greetings. We believe you are well aware of how we have sworn and promised to wed the Princess Philippa, daughter of the King of Castile and Duke of Lancaster [John of Gaunt]. Now, finding ourselves in Guimarães on the point of departure for a destination with which you are acquainted, her father, the aforesaid King of Castile, requested us to take her as our wife before we left this country, as we had agreed with him. He said that he would have it so for the sake of God, his honor, and the advancement of his and our own interests. In view of the fact that our lord Pope had given us a dispensation to marry, we took counsel on the matter, and it was agreed that we should get married before we left this region. For this reason, we came there and then to the city of Oporto and received together the Church's blessing this very day, the Feast of the Purification of St. Mary. This is because if it were not done on this day, it could not be done until eight days after Easter, according to the ordinances of Holy Church. We intend, God willing, to set up house together in a manner fitting our rank and station eight days after the Thursday of this week, which will be the fourteenth of February. We would have you know that it would please us greatly that some of you should be present at this ceremony and at all others that might be conducted in our honor. However, given the need we have to proceed immediately with our military campaign, we are cutting short the time devoted to this matter. Because we know that you may not be able to come for whatever reason, we are making all this news known to you, because we are certain that it will please you. Written, etc."

How the King Had His Marriage with His Wife in the City of Oporto

Despite the fact that time was short for the making of arrangements, all the more at that period when elaborate celebrations were customary, nevertheless, he issued instructions to certain members of his household and officials in the city concerning their respective duties regarding the celebrations.

Whether their job was to clear the squares and streets through which the procession was to pass, or to organize games, toys and night revels, each one endeavoured to dispatch the task assigned to him by the King with diligence and good sense. A great open space was hastily cleared in the area between São Domingos and the Souto Street, which was mostly taken up by gardens. Here, great nobles and knights took part in jousts and tourneys, but only ones expert in the art, and not others. In this way, the whole city was engaged in the many different tasks relating to the celebrations.

Once everything was made ready, on the Wednesday, the King departed from where he was staying and repaired to the Bishop's palace where the Princess was staying. On the Thursday, the citizens came together in various groups for games and dances in all the squares. There they enjoyed many amusements and indulged in other delights. All the main streets through which the procession was to come were strewn with a variety of green and aromatic plants. The King rode out of the palace, mounted on a white horse, royally dressed in gold cloth. The Queen rode on another, dressed in an equally royal fashion. They wore on their heads gold crowns richly studded with costly gems and mother-of-pearl. Neither of them took precedence but rather they rode in complete equality. The grooms, on foot and elaborately dressed, led the steeds of the most high-ranking people that were there; and the Archbishop led the Queen by the rein. Ahead of them went so many pipes, trumpets and other instruments, that nothing else could be heard. As is customary at weddings, noblewomen and citizens' daughters came along at the back, singing.

So great was the crush and so small the space between palace and church that it was impossible to control and marshal the huge crowds.

In these conditions they arrived at the cathedral door which was very near there. Here, Dom Rodrigo, Bishop of Ciudad Rodrigo, was awaiting them in his pontifical vestments, together with the clergy. He took the couple by the hand and instructed them to say the words ordained by Holy Church to be uttered in this sacrament. Then he said mass and preached. When he had performed his task, the King and Queen returned with similar rejoicing to the palace from which they had come and where they were to eat. The tables were already laid out with everything necessary; and not only the table at which the newly wedded couple were to sit, but also the tables reserved for the bishops and other persons of rank, nobles and local merchants as well as ladies and maidens from the palace and the city.

The master of ceremonies was Nun'Alvares Pereira, Constable of Portugal. The napkin- and cup-bearers and other attendants were high-ranking nobles and knights. There were sufficient dishes of all manner of different foods.

For the duration of the meal, men skillful in certain games performed for all to see: balancing on a tightrope, chasing round tables, acrobatic jumping and other enjoyable games. When these were over, everyone rose and began to dance while the ladies stood around in a group, singing joyfully. Meanwhile, the King went to his chamber: and after supper, in the evening, the archbishop and other prelates with many burning torches, blessed his bed with those benedictions that the Church has ordained for such occasions. Then the King remained with his wife, and the others all went to their lodgings.

Neither the Queen's father nor the Duchess witnessed these wedding celebrations because all their attention was taken up with the task of meeting together with their forces in the place where they had agreed with the King to make their incursion into enemy territory.

How the King Gave the Queen a Household and an Income for Her Expenses

For the space of fifteen days, before and after, feasts and royal tournaments in honor of the wedding took place as we have been describing; and festivities and revels were held, not only in that place, but in all the towns and cities of the realm, according to the capacity of each, as was normal at that period.

The King established a household for the Queen and a certain income for her expenses until such times as he could give her, as promised, lands for the maintenance of her status. He assigned officials to serve her, appointing Lopo Dias de Sousa, Master of the Order of Christ in Portugal as her chief steward, Lourenço Eanes Fogaça as manager of her finances, Afonso Martins, who later became Prior of Santa Cruz, as overseer of her household, Gonçalo Vasques Coutinho as her head butler and as his deputy Rodrigo Eanes, the King's own servant, and Fernão Lopes de Abreu as head of the stores. Also, there were to be officers to take charge of cutlery and table-linen and the pantry, together with other necessary officials; and also the Grand Chaplain and the Confessor and other ministers of the divine office; and squires, as many as were necessary, to attend upon the Queen.

The women appointed to attend and serve her were Beatriz Gonçalves de Moura, the wife of Vasco Fernandes Coutinho, who was to be her housekeeper. Her maids of honor were Dona Beatriz de Castro, daughter of Dom Alvaro Peres; Teresa Vasques Coutinho, daughter of Beatriz Gonçalves, the Queen's chief lady-in-waiting and wife of Dom Martinho, son of Count Gonçalo; Leonor Vasques, her sister, who later married Dom Fernando whom they called Fernando de Bragança; Berengeira Nunes Pereira, daughter of Rui Pereira who died in the sea-battle in front of Lisbon and wife of Afonso Vasques Correa; Beatriz Pereira, daughter of Alvaro Pereira the Marshal (already deceased) and wife of Martim Vasques de Resende; and Leonor Pereira, her legitimate sister who was married to Gomes Freire. As well as these, there were other maidens and waiting-women to a number appropriate for one of the Queen's rank.

The King ordered that until she had lands of her own, the Queen should receive, in order to meet her expenses, the income from customs-duties and port-duties together with the palace of Madeira, from which the income amounted to easily twenty thousand *dobras* which were all at her disposal if she wanted to spend them all.

Of Some of the Ways and Virtues of Queen Philippa

This Queen Philippa, daughter of a noble father and mother, had been praised when a princess for all the virtues that are appropriate to a high-born woman, and the same was true and indeed even more so after she was married and raised to royal estate. Moreover, God granted her a husband to her taste, and their union produced a fine generation of virtuous and successful sons, as you shall hear later on. For this reason, it would have been for us a most pleasurable task to praise her virtues, if we had been capable of doing so; but because we lack the necessary skill, we must content ourselves with describing these virtues only briefly.

If in her youth this blessed queen was devout and had a good knowledge of the divine liturgy, later she was even more so once she assumed responsibility for her own household and organized the services as she wished. She always prayed the canonical hours according to the Use of Sarum[2] and although this observance was by no means easy to arrange, she was so keen on this that she taught it to her chaplains and other worthy persons. Every Friday it was her custom to read the Book of Psalms and she would speak to no one until she had quite finished it. When she was prevented from doing so through illness or through giving birth, somebody would read to her all that she was wont to read on that particular day; and she would listen devoutly and without interruption. There is no need to speak at length about fasting or the practice of reading the Holy Scriptures at convenient times; for all this was a regular part of her life and ordered so wisely that idleness could gain no foothold in her imagination.

She cared for the poor and needy, giving alms most liberally to churches and monasteries. She loved the noblest of husbands most faithfully. She made

---

2. The Use of Sarum was a local modification of the Roman liturgy used in Salisbury, compiled there in the early thirteenth century and gradually adopted in the next two centuries by most churches in England, Wales, and Ireland.

great efforts never to annoy him, and set great store by the education and sound upbringing of her children. Nothing she did was done out of rancor or hatred. On the contrary, all her actions were dictated by love of God and of her neighbor.

Her conversation was plain, and often helpful without showing any pride in her royal rank; and her way of speaking was sweet, gracious and most pleasing to all who heard her. In order not to appear too cut off from others, she delighted sometimes in relaxing with her maidens in those lawful games in which no trickery could be involved and which were seemly for any honest person. So if the perfect manner in which she lived could be recorded in detail, any woman could study it with profit, no matter how high her rank.

76. PAGEANTS AND FESTIVITIES IN CASTILE

A. Preparations for a Royal Wedding (1440)
Translated from Castilian by Teofilo Ruiz

In 1440 the infanta Doña Blanca, accompanied by her mother, the queen of Na-
varre, came to Castile to marry her cousin, the infante Don Enrique, heir to the
throne of Castile. In the Castilian cities and towns along the road to Valladolid,
where the wedding was to take place, great festivities were organized in the bride's
honor. The following account describes her reception at Briviesca, a small town in
the lordship of the count of Haro. The chronicle provides a detailed rendering of the
feasts, reflecting the fantastic and theatrical nature of fifteenth-century Castilian
court life. As an added historical note, in spite of the displays and expenses of her re-
ception, the marriage was not consummated. The infante Don Enrique was unable
or unwilling to perform his conjugal duties—and the infanta returned to Navarre
after the marriage was annulled. (TR)

While the king [Juan II] was at Valladolid, there was an agreement reached
that since the prince [infante] Don Enrique and the princess [infanta] Doña
Blanca, daughter of Don Juan, king of Navarre, were of age to marry that
[therefore] Doña Blanca should come into Castile. Don Pedro de Velasco,
count of Haro, Iñigo López de Mendoza, lord of Hita and Buitrago, and
Don Alonso de Cartagena, bishop of Burgos, were chosen to welcome her
[into the kingdom], and they traveled to Logroño for this purpose.

One day after the arrival of the Castilian envoys to Logroño, the princess
Doña Blanca, her mother, the queen, her brother, the prince Don Carlos
(who after accompanying them returned to Navarre), and a retinue of ecclesiastical dignitaries and knights from the kingdoms of Aragón and Navarre
also arrived at Logroño, where they were given a great welcome.

From Logroño they continued on their way to Belorado, a village of
the count of Haro, who had arranged for an appropriate reception for all
those coming, foreigners as well as Castilians. From there they all proceeded
to Briviesca, where the count of Haro had arranged for the greatest, most
original [*mas nueva*], and strangest festivities that had been seen in Spain in
our time. They were celebrated in this fashion:

Before the ladies [the princess and the queen] reached Briviesca, two
leagues outside the town, the count had one hundred men-at-arms, their
horses covered with cloth, their helmets adorned with plumes, waiting for

Translated from Fernán Pérez de Guzmán, "Crónica de Juan II," in *Crónicas de los reyes
de Castilla* II, Biblioteca de Autores Espanoles 68 (Madrid: M. Rivadeneyra, 1875), pp. 565–66.

them. Fifty of the knights, their horses' covers in white, stood on one side [of the road?], the other fifty, their horses with red covers, stood on the other side. [Upon seeing the cortege], they began to fight [those in red against those in white] with their lances. Once their lances were broken, the knights took to their swords and began wounding each other as it is done in tournaments. After a while had passed, the count ordered them to stop their fight; each of the knights returned to his original location.

From there the ladies, the queen and the princess, continued on their way to Briviesca, where festivities were prepared for them and where all [the inhabitants] of the town welcomed them with much solemnity. The guilds [*oficios*] all came out with their banners and theatrical skits [*entremeses*], in the best possible fashion; and with great dances, great enjoyment, and happiness. Following them [the artisans] came the Jews with the Torah and the Moors with the Qur'ān [dancing] in the manner usually reserved for [the entry of] kings who come to rule a foreign country. There were also many trumpets, tambourines, drums, and flute players [*ministriles*] which made such great noise that it seemed as if a very large host was coming. In arriving to the town all together, they [the nobles, artisans, Jews, and Moors] accompanied the queen and the princess to the count's palace. There the important people dismounted and repaired to a place where a collation was prepared, supplied with such a diversity of poultry, meats, fish, delicacies, and fruits that it was a marvelous thing to see. The tables and servers were set in a fashion becoming such great ladies. And they [the ladies] were served by knights and gentlemen [*gentiles hombres*] and by richly dressed pages from the count's household.

At the queen's table only the princess and the countess of Haro (who had been commanded by the queen to join her) ate. The other duennas [*dueñas,* married ladies] and maids [*doncellas*] who were in the queen's retinue sat in this fashion: a knight sat between two *doncellas* or *dueñas*. A[nother] tent was set, covered with an elegant [*gentil*] tapestry, and there were also tables and servers for Don Alonso, bishop of Burgos, the prelates, and foreign clergymen. They were also offered as many and diverse delicacies as had been served to the queen and the princess. And these victuals were given to them all the while they remained there. The others were [also] fed abundantly in other tents. The feast lasted for four days.

During these festivities, the count of Haro ordered a town crier to proclaim that nothing should be sold in town to anyone, whether Castilian or foreigner, coming to Briviesca for the feast. Instead these visitors were to come to his palace for their meals and to ask for and be given whatever they wished. In a chamber on the first floor of the palace there was a silver fountain pouring out wine, and people took as much wine as they wanted. During the three days [of the feast] the knights and the gentlemen danced at the palace; there were also mummers, running of bulls, and jousts. On the fourth day, the count had an immense room built in a large fenced meadow behind his palace. In this artificial hall, a very high stage was built, requiring twenty steps to ascend to the top. It was covered with grass to look like a natural mound. There sat the queen, the princess and the countess of Haro on rich scarlet brocade, as befitted such great ladies. Below them in lower artificial mounds covered with grass and rich tapestries sat the ladies and knights in the fashion of previous days.

On one side of the meadow, there was a list for a joust with twenty knights and gentlemen. On the other side there was a pond which had been specially stocked for the feast with large trout and barbels. As each fish was caught, it was brought to the princess. And in another part of the meadow, there was a beautiful copse of trees [*un bosque*], which the count had ordered to be stocked with bears, boars, and deer. The wood was surrounded by almost fifty huntsmen with "gentle" [*gentiles*] mastiffs, greyhounds, and hounds [*sabuesos*] in such manner that no animal was able to escape. Unleashing the dogs, the huntsmen pursued and killed the beasts and brought them to the princess. And it seemed a very strange thing that in a house [the artificially created great hall] so many different sports could be carried out at the same time. . . .

After the joust, the hunt, and the fishing had concluded, the dancing began and lasted almost all day. Everything was lit so well that it seemed to be illuminated by the midday sun. Once the dance finished, a collation was served as befitted such great ladies, prelates, and knights as were there. And when the collation ended, the count generously distributed money to the trumpeters and minstrels from two large bags of coins. To the princess, he gave a rich small jewel [*joyel*], and to each of the ladies accompanying the princess rings with diamonds, rubies, spinel rubies, and emeralds in such manner that no one was left without a jewel. To the foreign [lords] and knights, he gave mules to some, brocade to others, and to the gentlemen different types of silk cloth.

That way the feast ended and all went to sleep for the few hours of the night that were left. And the next day at the hour of Terce, the queen and the princess left for Burgos where they [also] received a very notable welcome.

B. Christmas Festivities in Jaén (1462)
Translated from Castilian by Ronald Surtz

Miguel Lucas de Iranzo was of low birth—his father was reputed to be a farmer—but he was elevated to the nobility by King Enrique IV, who named him constable of Castile in 1458. Court intrigues forced his retirement to Jaén, where he made himself master of the city, winning the support of the upper bourgeoisie by according them the rank and privileges of knights. The old aristocracy became his dire enemy, and, in time, his protection of converted Jews made him unpopular with the lower classes. In 1473 he was assassinated by a commoner as he prayed in the cathedral of Jaén.

The chronicle devoted to his life and exploits highlights his activities in defense of the frontier with Muslim Spain and recounts in great detail the yearly festivities with which his court marked the principal feasts of the liturgical calendar. Perhaps the constable's particular interest in such pageantry can be attributed to his desire to show himself worthy of a noble estate to which he had not been born. Such displays of pomp and circumstance constituted an opportunity to demonstrate his liberality, martial prowess, and material splendor.

The Epiphany festivities for 1462 included a cavalcade, chivalric entertainment, banquets, gift giving, performance of a play, and social dancing. With regard to the Epiphany play, the constable begins as a spectator of the Holy Family's entrance into his palace, but he is soon incorporated into the dramatic action as he assumes the role of one of the Magi. Patristic tradition turned the wise men of Matthew 2:2 into kings. Thus, in the pageant the "king" of Jaén is typecast in the role of biblical king. The Holy Family flatter the constable by their presence; he honors them by seating them among his own relatives, thus creating an extended Holy Family. (RS)

When the feast of the Nativity of Our Lord and Savior Jesus Christ of the year 1462 arrived, after ordering his entire household to be dressed in silks and wools, as was his custom, on Christmas Eve he [the constable] had fresh fish, both breaded and in kegs, brought from Seville and distributed to the knights and ladies and monasteries of the city.

And because it has already been told how the aforementioned lord constable comported himself on similar holidays—both in his dress and in dancing as well as in hearing Matins and the hours, and playing dice, and offering and distributing many gifts and alms to all those who came from all over, drawn by his reputation for largesse—there is no reason to elaborate. Except that on the first Sunday after Christmas, after ordering all the dignitaries of the cathedral and the clerks of the university to eat supper with him, on Epiphany he likewise invited all the aldermen, magistrates, knights and squires, and some ladies of said city to dine and sup with him.

Translated from *Hechos del condestable don Miguel Lucas de Iranzo*, edited by Juan de Mata Carriazo (Madrid: Espasa-Calpe, 1940), pp. 69–72.

And before dinner, in front of his palace, he had an iron ring set up. And the lady countess [his wife] and the ladies Doña Guiomar Carrillo, his mother, and Doña Juana, his sister, with many other married and unmarried ladies, were watching from the highest tower in his palace, and many other people on horseback and on foot, along the streets and in windows, on walls [and] rooftops. And with [so] many torches and lanterns [lighting his path] that, because the light was so intense, it seemed as at midday, said lord constable left the palace of Fernando de Berrio, a city councilman, which is by [the plaza of] the Magdalene, where he prepared [his cavalcade] for departure, and he crossed nearly the entire city in the following manner.

He came on a very attractive and spirited speckled horse, riding long in the saddle, with very fine gear both in front and in back. He wore a gold-plated doublet, over it a jerkin whose *blaones* [gussets?] were trimmed with fine yellow wool, black embroidered hose, and on his head a finely wrought royal crown with a mask. And in his hand [was] a naked sword, resting firmly on his saddle, as befits a gallant knight.

Two identically dressed pages preceded him, about fifteen years in age, wearing yellow wool jackets over brocade doublets, and bearing his two lances. And in front of them [the pages] were twelve gentleman knights on very well appointed horses, with lances in their hands. And in front of everyone was another knight, riding a huge horse, who carried a banner. All were dressed in that [same] livery, with masks and crowns on their heads in memory of the three kings, whose feast they were celebrating.

And in this fashion he arrived at the place where the iron ring was set up, accompanied by many knights, and [musicians playing] trumpets and drums and shawms, and musketeers [firing their weapons], and yells and shouts and many torches; [in short], amid the most extreme clamor and noise imaginable. And as soon as he arrived, they immediately removed their masks.

And he ordered two brocade doublets [as a prize] for the first knights who should thrust their lance through the iron ring, and four yards of silk to each of the others who from that moment on should hit the mark. And out of the desire to win said doublets, all the knights made many passes [at the target], and many of them managed to thrust their lances through said ring.

But among all of them said lord constable surely bore himself most worthily, not only because he was riding a fine and swift horse, but also because he was a comely and confident rider. And every time he made a pass, if he missed the ring, he would break his lance against the barriers. And thus he broke five or six lances, all with extreme grace and dexterity.

And after they had spent two or three hours in this activity, he dismounted at his palace, where the tables and sideboards were all ready, both for him and for all the aldermen, magistrates, knights, squires and some married and unmarried ladies of said city, who supped that night with him, as has been said.

And as soon as they had eaten dinner and the tables were cleared, a woman entered the hall, riding a small donkey, with a child in her arms. She was pretending to be Our Lady the Virgin Mary with her blessed and glorious Son, and Joseph was with her. And with great reverence, the aforementioned lord constable welcomed her and brought her up to the chair where he had been sitting. And he seated her between the aforementioned lady countess and his mother, lady Doña Guiomar Carrillo, and his sister lady Doña Juana, and the other women and young girls who were there.

And the aforementioned lord retired to a chamber that was at the other end of the hall, and in a little while he came out of said chamber with two very well dressed pages, with masks and crowns on their heads in the manner of the three wise men. And each one carried a vessel [containing] his gifts. And thus he advanced very slowly through the hall, with a very comely mien, keeping his eyes on the star that was guiding them, which moved along a rope that was [stretched] across said hall. And in this fashion they reached the other end of the hall, where the Virgin and her Child were [seated], and he offered his gifts, amid a great clamor of trumpets and drums and other instruments.

And when this was over, he retired to the aforementioned chamber, from which he emerged dressed in a different fashion. And then [musicians] played their shawms, and he began to dance with the lady countess and with lady Juana his sister. And afterward other gentlemen and pages and young girls [danced]. And after they danced both popular and courtly dances, a light snack was served and he retired to sleep.

77. LETTER CONCERNING REFORM AND GOOD GOVERNMENT IN PORTUGAL

Translated from Portuguese by Rita Costa Gomes

Political matters were often discussed at the Portuguese court in epistolary form. The monarchs would solicit advice from the princes of the royal family and other great nobles, who would express their opinions in writing, for example, about proposed military expeditions to Morocco. During the last years of the reign of João I (r. 1385–1433), his son and heir to the throne, Duarte, was assigned to some tasks of government. In the summer of 1425 Pedro, second son of the Portuguese king, departed for a long journey that took him to England, Flanders, and Germany, where he entered the service of Emperor Sigismund and fought the Turks on the Hungarian frontier. From there he went in 1428 to visit Venice, Florence, and Rome, stopping on his return to Portugal in Barcelona and Valencia, as well as several Castilian cities. Duarte and Pedro were very close. Several extant letters attest to their common interests and the influence of humanist ideas in their use of epistles as means of reflection and communication. This particular letter was written from Bruges in 1426. Both wrote long treatises, for instance, on the art of governing and on technical disciplines such as horse riding, and they commissioned or translated classical authors from Latin. In this letter, Pedro gives his view of the major problems of the kingdom of Portugal and recommends potential solutions to his brother, who would become king a few years later, in 1433 (RCG).

Letter That the Infante Dom Pedro Sent from Bruges

Most high and honored Prince and beloved Lord,

You ordered me in your written instruction that when I would be in this land I should write a text of counsel such as the other one which you gave to me.[1] And it seems to me, my lord, that three obstacles stand in the way of my doing so, the first being the authority of lordship that you have upon me, the second your seniority, and the third your higher standing in goodness and reasoning. However, since I am taught by that doctor whose teachings never fail that obedience is better than sacrifice, to obey your command, and sailing against these obstacles as well as the occupations and great worries which I at present have, I will write my opinion here. Yet I consider in you, my lord, a double person. The first is you as a singular person, and the second is our lord the king, and you, taken together with the whole community of your land. As for the singular person, my lord, I know not what to write, because since the

---

Translated from *Livro dos Conselhos de El-Rei Dom Duarte (Livro da Cartuxa)*, edited by J. J. Alves Dias and A. H. Oliveira Marques (Lisbon: Estampa, 1982), 27–39.

1. This letter of Duarte to Pedro probably corresponds to the text "Conselho do infante pera seu irmão o Infante Dom Pedro quando se partiu pera Hungria" included in the same compilation known as *Livro dos Conselhos* (Book of Counsel).

time of my departure I hope in God that you will have always improved, and I saw then more reasons to marvel and to follow you than things to correct and amend. As for the common good, Sir, I will write some things which I already addressed in conversation with you before my departure, as well as others that came to me after I left.

Most high and honored prince and beloved lord, since the whole world confesses that all mercy and reward comes to us from God, and no lord repays his servant as a result of his own will as much as for the need to requite the service done, hence, my lord, in order to get God's reward by addressing all your actions, you must take special care of those which are His. And those are the people who belong to the church or to the clergy. And since the goodness of the prelates greatly amends the subjects, and they are made in your land by your consent and authority only, it seems to me, Sir, that you should make way for the existence of good ones in your land, ordained as they should. And the ways I think this should be done I already left in a written document which I did under your command. It seems to me, my lord, that by ordering this matter the right way you will make great service to God, a service which will not remain unrewarded. I have no doubt that you have great displeasure because in spite of your past efforts in this matter some people obey you less and acknowledge you little. But this, Sir, I do not write looking at the past as much as by way of warning of what is to come.

Because you know, my lord, how little service it is to God and how much it goes against your justice that there would be so many clergymen with minor orders. Both with the current prelates as well as the future ones, you should make it that the orders would not be given except to the man who wants to become a cleric, making certain before he takes the minor orders that he would proceed to take the sacred orders. And if the prelates would not agree on doing this, at least let them take pains not to give orders to any person who does not know Latin. Because for what I have seen and heard, outside of the lands of Spain this is considered a great defect, and those who are worthy should be the ones ordained. And to avoid the excuse of the prelates that for lack of Latinate candidates they would not be able to follow this rule, it seems to me that the university in your land should be reformed, and the manner to do it I will write here, following what I heard from someone who had more knowledge on this matter than I do.

First, let there be at the said university ten or more colleges, in which poor students would be maintained, together with some rich ones at their own expense, living together under a master who would be in charge of the college. In the city of Lisbon and its district, where the university has five or six churches, in each of these churches one such college could be made, and

each would have its own vicar to administer the sacraments, and his maintenance would be paid from the rents of the church, the remainder being used
for the students placed in that college. And these should sleep in one single
residence that would have cells, and they would eat together in one single
place, and would be cloistered in one single cloister. And these, Sir, after
two years attending the lectures in the university would graduate, and they
would become readers under oath. Having such good breeding with the help
of God they would become well-costumed ecclesiastics. And the bishops in
their chapters could each of them make such colleges for their people and the
black monks [Benedictines] the same, and the regular canons theirs, and the
same for the white monks [Cistercians], and they would have them organized
the way this is done in Oxford and Paris. This way the scholars and the sciences would prosper, and the noble lords would find honest and competent
chaplains to take in their service, and when they would promote them they
would not be contradicted. Besides, another consequence would be that you
would find scholars to become officers of royal justice, and whenever those
would displease you there would be others you could take at your service,
and they would be afraid of the consequences, therefore they would serve
you better and more diligently. And from these would come good beneficia-
ries who could become good electors, as well as good prelates, bishops, and
so forth, for this would be a good start to get good reformers. It seems to
me, my lord, that if your mercy would be to order this, there would be much
honor and profit to the land, because knowledge should always be cherished,
since it took and takes many [persons] from doing bad deeds. And the reformers of the university should be good men of good customs who were
once in it, or you should order someone to write for you the regulations of
the said colleges.

It seems to me, Sir, that from the authority and power given to you by
God you have the capacity to donate the administration of many chapels and
charitable foundations, and you should give them to such people who would
administer them in the service of God, since I understand that you will do
more service to Him by governing and managing well under your power that
which was given by those who passed away, than to give anew what you cannot give at present. But contrary to this rule, in your land it is usual to give
those to whoever will destroy them. Furthermore, in any locality where you
travel where such hospitals or houses of God exist, they will use them as your
court jail, and the prisoners and others will destroy the clothing and anything
else that is in that house, in such a way that it will be too late to amend things
and put them in the correct order as they were before.

My lord, you should not forget the main part of the spirituality that consists of the religious people, for whom you can be even more of a prelate than to the other clergymen. If they are not working toward becoming knowledgeable, honest, and serious, you can call upon their superiors and say so. And if you see that the case is conveyed upward and nothing is done, then you would remove the prelate and say to the provincial or the minister that you will do the same to him, and that you are taking such care of them because of the great affection that you have for them. I think you will do this correction well.

As for the friars, you should order that none of them will eat in their chamber, if not by noticeable necessity, and that none will sleep but in a common dormitory, and thus of the other things of which you could be well informed. Among friars, none is to become a prelate unless he is elected, and if he is designated by a [papal] letter, let it be accepted only if it pleases his brethren. Always among the prelates it seems to me, Sir, that the elder should be more esteemed who have lived well for a long time, rather than the younger ones even if they are honest enough, because often the sun in its early brightness brings rain, and the less clear sunshine lasts all day. Among the friars, idleness should be much avoided, since the canonical hours are not so long and to the young ones it should not suffice to pray, they can write and occupy themselves in other things, in such a way that this life should not be followed by those who do not serve their duties.

My lord, I would not give such counsel of having as much authority over these things of the Church if you did this in a tyrannical way or out of temporal greed, and I would judge it wrong if anyone would give similar counsel. But if you do this with the intention of serving God, and with the agreement of the prelates and other men of good judgment who in your opinion are men of sane conscience, I believe that He will reward you well for this.

Speaking now of the temporal things, it seems to me that the good government of all the land comes from the four cardinal virtues and some of these I judge not to be in your kingdom in good perfection.

First, speaking of Fortitude through which the kingdoms are defended and augmented, it seems to me that in yours there is not much care of it, on the contrary there are many reasons for its lack. Second, Fortitude resides only to the help of God and the good hearts of the people, in the multitude of men and their good command. And you yourself may judge clearly the many ways in which the men from your land are attracted to go [serve] elsewhere, and those who are away are made to have very little desire to return to it. You can also judge on how many occasions your vassals and servicemen have been ill ordered.

And briefly, Sir, the manner in which I see this could be amended would be, first of all, to prevent the depopulation of the land, by avoiding the dangers and efforts and hardships that the people suffer unnecessarily and with great damage. This would be done by eliminating some of the laws and ordinances that cause grievance to them and are not of great advantage to the land, nor of much service to the lord our king or to you.

Better that anyone else, you yourself were the first person I heard reasoning about the harm and obstacles caused by the existence of an inordinate multitude of vassals. So it seems to me, Sir, that you should order a certain quantity of them to be distributed across the different districts of your kingdom, according to the need determined by you. And this number should not be augmented, regardless of requests or petitions. Because, my lord, they used to have two benefits: one was that they had privileges, and the other that they received the money fiefs [*contias*].[2] And thus they had two duties: the first was to have weapons, and the second was to maintain their horses. It seems to me that for each profit there should be a corresponding charge. And since your land was greatly lacking in horses when I left, a problem that I think has not yet improved, I believe that it will be less of a charge for you to respect their privileges than to pay them their *contias*. In my opinion you should order that all the vassals who are not noblemen, or who did not serve in past wars, if they want to have privileges they must have horses, and if you give them *contias* they must have weapons. And you should find a way to make them have the *contias*, something that would be of great service and defense of the land, and it seems to me that you should maintain this good order decreed by your ancestors and extant for so long until now, for it would be a great loss of your authority if it were to fail. . . .

Another part of Fortitude lies in the repair and provisioning of towns and castles, and the careful guarding of armories and of the provisions that are in them. But the general rule that I saw being followed in your kingdom was that the necessary repairs were often forgotten, and the improvements became a heavy charge on the population and a major expense. Sir, it seems to me that the mandated work that the people have to execute would be less of a pain to them if it were reasonable. There are many works that are being made all over the land, for which they have to serve one day a month, but even if they had to serve two days, if those works were of great necessity and were required in the proper way, the people would not take it as a grievance to give two or three days of work for things that are in their interest and for their defense. But the major part of the complaints results from the

2. The word can designate both money fief and indenture, that is, either the military service that results from feudal homage or a simple contract for military service.

disordered requests and demands of your officers. And the same thing I said of the military services, I say of the fortification works and the way they are done: you should put in charge a good man of sane authority who would decide the smaller cases and report to you the bigger ones, so that you could decide about those as you would judge it to be your service.

As for the armories, I believe that for the last few years many more were made than had existed before. I have no doubt that, in some of the fortresses where weapons were apportioned, for lack of three or four wood planks out of which to make a closet to store them, or to avoid similar small expense, a lot of them might now be lost. And the remedy for this and many other things would be to enforce the respect of the regulations given to the *corregedores*,[3] or better named *danadores* [destroyers], of the districts. As I heard the story once told by our lord the king, he saw Gonçalo Peres keep in a coffer the written instruction given to him, and he never took it from the said coffer all the time till he had finished what he was ordered to do. Another great advantage to all the matters of your land would be for you to visit each district every year, or at least every two years, and you should journey with good people, and not too numerous company. This would be, it seems to me, great recreation to you and those of your court, and it would be to the benefit and pleasure of the good people of your kingdom as well as a punishment and fright to the evildoers, and all the good things that would result from this would be too long for me to write here.

Justice, Sir, is the other virtue which does not seem to reign in the hearts of those who are in charge of judging in your land, except for our lord the king and yourself, and if there are others I do not know for certain. And it also seems to me, my lord, that this justice that lies in your heart does not come out as it should, because you should want not only to preserve the rights of all people, but also to order how this should be done. And it should be ordained that the ones in charge of your justice should be good, more fearful of God than they are of you, and more afraid of losing your favor than eager to gain other affections or material advantage. Whenever these men serve as they should, they should receive rewards, and those who do the opposite, if you can be sure this thing is so (as you did recently of certain people), then they should not go without punishment. For you know well, Sir, that you are put in the world by authority of the apostle for praise of the good and avengement of the evildoers, and if you use this well I know of no other rule that would be sufficient for the improvement of all those whom

---

3. The *corregedor* was a royal officer put in charge of justice and administration in every major district or *comarca*. There were six such districts in the whole kingdom, and the duties of the *corregedor* had been regulated in successive written *regimentos* in 1332, 1340, 1361, and 1418.

you govern. It seems to me, my lord, that Justice has two parts: one consists of giving to each one what is rightfully his, and the other is to do so without delay. And even if I think that they are both missing in your land, I am especially certain that the latter is lacking, which causes great damage to the land because those cases which are delayed are lost. For I see in your court a great multitude of justicial officers, but by all of these few cases are solved, and from them and the great multitude of courtiers (of which I will write later on) it seems that one can confirm the saying of Isaiah, "Thou hast multiplied the nation, but not increased the joy."[4] I believe, Sir, that six of them who were diligent in their office and willing to solve the cases would be able to do more than forty who do not care. And for the expedition of the cases it will be very useful to follow the abbreviation of the Bartolus[5] ordered by our lord the king, as long as the book is well written and corrected by two good doctors of law besides the one who copied it. Similarly the ordinances and laws of the kingdom must be compiled under separate titles, each according to its content, and if some will be found among them which are revoked, let them be eliminated since they are no longer in use, and the good ordinances be kept on the things about which they are made.

Of the virtue of Temperance and all that is done against it, I will leave the charge for the preachers and confessors to address it. Yet it seems to me that, compared to many other lands which I have seen, Temperance is in better shape in yours than in any other. Against a major virtue such as Prudence I see in the land many different errors, of which I will write but a few. One of the main ones is the lack of order which creates many inconveniences in the land and could well be corrected, as it consists of the many people that the king, yourself, and your brothers take into your household service without any measure, and following this practice all the other lords of the kingdom. And all the evils that ensue from this I could not write about, but I will touch briefly on a few.

The king our lord, you, and all the other aforementioned incur for this matter great expenses which cannot be supported by the land, and because of these new fines and taxes are launched which waste the land even more. Another [consequence] is that in any town or city in which you are residing the people lose their houses and clothes in order to lodge your followers, in such ways that they can no longer recover them, and thus in many places your [court] cannot find good accommodation for all. Yet another [evil] is the loss of the animals of the peasants, since a lot of them are required for this reason whenever you are traveling throughout the land. Another [evil]

---

4. Isa. 9:3: *Multiplicasti gentem, sed non magnificasti leticiam.*
5. Bartolus of Saxoferrato (d. 1357) was a very influential Italian jurist and legal scholar.

is that the country and all the noblemen in it are so badly served, because it is no longer enough for people to learn the office that their father had, nor do they want to serve other lords, but all want to come to the royal court in the hope of becoming squires of the king, or yours, or of each of your brothers. And because of this I have often seen the lord our king and yourself so overspent that even if you wanted to be generous to others to whom you are obliged, or if you wanted to do some other good deed, you would not have the resources to do so. . . .

Of the matters of Ceuta[6] I have already reasoned many times with you about how I feel. The conclusion is that while the city is thus ordained as it stands now, it will be a cause for the loss of many of your people, weapons, and money. And for what I have heard from good men of authority from here [Bruges] and from England, people are no longer talking of the honor and good fame that comes from its possession, but they refer to the lack of discretion that consists of maintaining it with such great loss and destruction of the land. And to me it seems that they have much worse information than what is really the case. The remedy for this, my lord, you have talked about many times, and you know it much better than I could always write it here. It seems to me, Sir, that it would be God's service and yours to order it without delay. . . .

Sir, in many of these things I believe that I have been so far of help to you, and I wish to God that all would have the same willingness to see things reformed as I do, for with His help I think it would be done with little delay. And if I left the land, one of the reasons why I did was so that I could no longer be held responsible, even if I know that because of my departure the lord our king and you have now even more charges than before. If God will provide me with a good path, and my life here or there will return to its quiet state, I hope in Him that you will be relieved of any such charge which you at present have on account of me, and I [hope] to be of help in all the things that are in your service for the correction of these impediments.

If these things that I wrote here are not good nor well argued, I beg for your mercy and ask not to be held guilty of error, for I could not reason better, and if I did this it was more to obey your orders than because at present I was willing to talk of such things with you.

Your brother and servant,
Infante Dom Pedro

6. The Moroccan city of Ceuta (Ar. Sebta) was conquered by the Portuguese king João I in 1415, and it would remain in Portuguese hands until 1640.

78. MARRIAGE AND DIVORCE IN
MUSLIM GRANADA

The following two Arabic documents, a marriage contract (1438) and a divorce contract (1474), were drawn up for ordinary people in Granada. In contrast to the wealth of Christian documents surviving from the medieval period, relatively few everyday documents from Muslim Spain survive. Most of the Arabic documents that we do have come from the Naṣrid kingdom of Granada; these date from the fourteenth and fifteenth centuries. There are two primary reasons for this dearth of Arabic documentary material. First, medieval Muslim society did not place the same importance on the preservation of written records as was common in Christian regions. Although certain documents were preserved over time, there was never a Muslim archival tradition parallel to the highly organized Christian system. We know that written documents played an important role in Andalusi society, where they were employed to confirm all kinds of contracts, but these were rarely kept after the completion of the act or death of the participants. Second, even when documents had been carefully preserved, they were often lost or destroyed later as Muslims left the peninsula or converted to Christianity. (ORC)

A. Marriage Contract (1438)
Translated from Arabic by Olivia Remie Constable

This marriage contract records the legal bond represented in a marriage and gives particular attention to the transfer of property between the two parties. Because it is merely a legal document, it gives no hint of the ceremonies and festivities that would have surrounded the wedding. (ORC)

In the Name of God the Merciful and the Compassionate.

Blessings be upon our lord and protector Muḥammad and upon his family.

Praise be to God who created mankind from clay, made people from lowly water, and instituted marriage, inviting [people] to it and letting its excellence be known. God Most High has said "Marry as you wish either one, two, three, or four women." Blessings and peace upon Muḥammad his prophet, and upon his family and property, and upon his companions among the *muhājarūn*[1] and upon the *anṣār*,[2] his beloved friends and benefactors.

Translated from *Documentos arabigo-granadinos*, edited by Luis Seco de Lucena (Madrid: Imprenta del Instituto de Estudios Islámicos, 1961), pp. 8–9.

1. Those early believers who went with Muḥammad on his flight from Mecca to Medina in 622.

2. Supporters of Muḥammad who received him in Medina after his flight from Mecca.

'Alī ibn Mūsā ibn Ibrahīm ibn 'Ubaid Allah al-Lakhmī gives his daughter Fāṭima in marriage to Abū Ishāq Ibrahīm ibn Ahmad, known as al-Ḥakīm. She is a virgin, who has been under [her father's] care until he decided her marriage, and there are no impediments to be found [to the marriage]. The father of the bride, 'Alī, has received 375 dinars out of the total bride price of 610 dinars, and has acknowledged receipt of this from the groom, Ibn Ibrahīm [sic]. The remaining balance of 225 dinars is to be paid two years from the date of this document.[3]

'Ā'isha bint Abū 'Abd Allah ibn Mufaḍḍal, the mother of the groom and his guardian, gives her consent to this contract of marriage, and she wishes [for the couple] all the virtues and promised rewards [of marriage], with all its benefits of constancy and probity.

The bride receives as a gift [from the groom] a garden in the district of Almunia which is bordered on the south by property belonging to his sister, on the north by that of Abū al-Ḥasan, on the east by that of the heirs of Abū al-Ḥasan al-Murīd, and on the west by that of Abū 'Abd Allah ibn Musharrif and his daughter. This gift is required by the marriage contract.

It is witnessed that 'Alī, guardian and father of the bride, is of sound mind and has the legal right to give [his daughter in marriage]. Also, that the groom, Ibrahīm, and his mother, who is acting as his guardian in this matter, are both of sound mind and of legal capacity as regards this marriage contract. The groom, the contract itself, and the guardians that consent to it [are all sound].

Dated Saturday, 18 Jumāda al-Akhra, 842 [11 November 1438]

Signatures of witnesses

B. Divorce Contract (1474)

Translated from Arabic by Christopher S. Taylor

Muslim and Christian views of divorce were strikingly different. Divorce was strictly forbidden by Christian law but was permitted in both Muslim and Jewish law, though in each case it was almost exclusively a prerogative initiated by the husband. The document here is unusual in that it records a type of Islamic divorce agreement known as khul', *in which the woman secured a divorce from her husband, either by paying him a specified sum of money or by renouncing all or part of her dowry and*

---

3. Ten dinars have somehow been lost in this calculation.

Translated from *Documentos arábigo-granadinos,* edited by Luis Seco de Lucena (Madrid: Imprenta del Instituto de Estudios Islámicos, 1961), pp. 59–60. The translator acknowledges the kind assistance of Magda Ghaly and Hanna' Fahmy.

sometimes by forgoing other rights. Often the terms of a khulʿ *divorce were agreed on before the consummation of a marriage and incorporated into the original marriage contract. (CST)*

In the Name of God, the Merciful, the Compassionate.

May God bless and grant salvation to our master Muḥammad and to his family.

This is a copy of the divorce document drafted from the text of the marriage contract of Muḥammad ibn Aḥmad al-Ashkar, and ʿĀʾisha bint [the daughter of] Abū ʿUthmān Saʿad ibn Aḥmad al-Muʾadhin. The Text: Praise to God! The above-mentioned wife is divorced from her above-mentioned husband in this marriage, by completing her prescribed waiting period,[1] even if it should be prolonged; and by relinquishing all of her rights from him in this marriage contract, and otherwise, in terms of sustenance and the like. And if she is pregnant with his child she is released with the child from him on the same terms, prior to the child's birth and after the birth until either a male child reaches puberty or a female consummates marriage.[2] Moreover, their daughter Fāṭima is placed in the care and custody of her mother, who shall provide for and maintain her in every instance, including marrying her off and in anything else. No liability whatsoever will fall to her father until his maintenance obligation legally lapses. This in the presence of the wife's father and mother, Fāṭima bint Aḥmad al-Sharqī, and with their agreement on what is stated herein. Furthermore, the two of them undertake complete surety for all her liabilities whenever and whatever befalls her, including enfeeblement and destitution. If ever they should bring suit against the husband, they shall forsake all praise and censure will accrue to [the wife's] father. And in these two situations [enfeeblement or destitution], the parents will terminate her custody. [The wife] undertakes all of this willingly and voluntarily, without compulsion or any associated detriment. Her father completely forgoes whatever was incumbent on the husband owing to the period of his residence with her in the father's house in Bāb al-Bunūd within Granada. In view of all of this and because of it, the husband pronounces her divorced.[3] From

---

1. Islamic law provides for a mandated waiting period, known in Arabic as the *ʿidda*, during which a newly divorced or widowed woman may not contract a new marriage. The function of the *ʿidda* is to prevent questions over legal paternity. The waiting period for a widow is established in the Qurʾān (2:234) as lasting four months and ten days. For divorced premenopausal women the *ʿidda* extends through three menstrual cycles following the divorce. For postmenopausal women the waiting period is three months.

2. At which time the father's legal obligation to maintain the children of his divorced wife would lapse under the Mālikī rite of Islamic law.

3. The first, and a single, pronouncement of divorce is specified in the document. Islamic law permits men to unilaterally repudiate their wives and then subsequently revoke that

his possession he makes her the possessor of herself. They acknowledged his honorableness and made those who knew both of them, and who were sound and [legally] admissible, witness him [in this] on the eighth of Rabī' al-awwal of the year 879 [17 July 1474].

[The signatures are illegible.]

---

repudiation anytime prior to expiration of the mandated waiting period, 'idda, up to two times. Following a third pronouncement of divorce a husband may not lawfully take back his wife in marriage until she has first consummated marriage and been legally divorced from another man. In the case of a khul' divorce, such as in this text, the husband cannot revoke the divorce unilaterally during the 'idda having made the offer of khul' divorce and having accepted the terms of the divorce agreement under oath.

79. THREE LEGACIES FROM MUSLIM GRANADA
(1438)

Bequests of ʿĀ'isha bint Abū ʿAbd Allāh Muḥammad al-Jinjālī
Translated from Arabic by Amalia Zomeño

In February 1438, a dying woman in Granada called for a notary and dictated these three bequests from her property. Islamic law gives women control over their own property, but inheritance law dictates the rights of heirs and usually allows no more than one third of personal property to be given away at will. Notably, ʿĀ'isha chose to benefit other women in all three of her bequests. The documents indicate that ʿĀ'isha was a widow, and that her father was also dead, and we know nothing about whether she had children or other living relatives as heirs. These three texts are among a relatively large number of personal legal documents that survive from fifteenth-century Granada, and a very high percentage of these documents relate to women transacting business or exercising their property rights.[1] (ORC)

In the name of God, the Merciful, the Compassionate.

May God bless and grant salvation to our lord Muḥammad, his family and his companions.

ʿĀ'isha, the daughter of the late proud master Abū ʿAbd Allāh Muḥammad al-Jinjālī, makes a testament and expresses her will that when death will come on her, against which there is no remedy nor any secure refuge for any living creature, that there should be extracted from the third of her estate, whether real estate properties or other kind and in addition to what she already assigned in another document with the same date, five gold dinars at the common rate to be paid to Umm al-Fatḥ, the daughter of Muḥammad Faraj, so she will enjoy them in full domain. This legacy was written down in accordance with the legal principles that regulate the legacies and it was done with the intention to please God. This is a valid testament and she (the testator) knows its legal implications. She also called witnesses to testify that they know her and that, while she is sick and prostrated in her bed, she is sane and stable in her intellect and discernment. The document is legally valid.

The 29th of the venerable month of Shaʿbān of the year 841 [25 February 1438].

God knows the authenticity of this document.

English translation from Amalia Zomeño, "Notaries and Their Formulas: The Legacies from the University Library of Granada," in *From Al-Andalus to Khurasan: Documents from the Medieval Muslim World*, ed. Petra M. Sijpesteijn et al. (Leiden: Brill, 2007), pp. 62–65. Reprinted with permission of the publishers.
1. See Maya Shatzmiller, *Her Day in Court: Women's Property Rights in Fifteenth-Century Granada* (Cambridge, Mass.: Harvard University Press, 2007).

* * *

In the name of God, the Merciful, the Compassionate.

May God bless and grant salvation to our lord Muḥammad, his family and his companions.

The blessed ʿĀʾisha, the daughter of the venerable and proud master Abū ʿAbd Allāh Muḥammad al-Jinjālī, she is the one who was the wife of the knight Ibrāhīm al-Thānī, makes a testament and expresses her will that when she dies, there should be extracted from the third of her estate, whether real estate properties or other kind and in addition to what she already bequeathed in the same day in another document, twenty gold dinars of the common rate to be distributed for the trousseau of four virgin daughters of the orphans among the poor Muslims and giving to each of them an equal amount. This legacy was written down in accordance with the legal principles that regulate the legacies and it was done with the intention to please God, exalted, who is generous in his rewards. She assigned the supervision for the execution of this legacy and the distribution of what she specified for each of the girls, to the legal scholar and preacher of the Akhshārish [a suburb of Granada], whoever may be fulfilling this job (at the moment of her death). This is a valid testament and she knows its legal implications. She called witnesses to testify that they know her and that while she is sick and prostrated in her bed, she is sane and stable in her intellect and discernment, and therefore the document is legally valid.

The 29th of the venerable month of Shaʿbān of the year 841 [February 25, 1438].

God knows the authenticity of this document.

* * *

In the name of God, the Merciful, the Compassionate.

May God bless and grant salvation to our lord Muḥammad, his family and his companions.

The blessed ʿĀʾisha, the daughter of the proud and venerable master Abū ʿAbd Allāh Muḥammad al-Jinjālī, makes a testament and expresses her will that when God has decided on her death, that there should be extracted from the third of her estate, whether real estate properties or other kind, and in addition to what she already assigned the day of this document, but in another one, five gold dinars at the common rate to be paid to ʿĀʾisha, the daughter of ʿAbd Allāh ibn Zayd, so she will enjoy them in full domain. This legacy was written down in accordance with the legal principles that regulate the legacies and it was done with the intention to please God, exalted. This is a valid testament and she knows its legal implications. She has called witnesses to testify that they know her and that while she is sick and prostrated in her bed, she is sane, and stable in her mind and discernment. The document is legally valid.

The 29th of the venerable month of Sha'bān of the year 841 [25 February 1438]. God knows the authenticity of this document.

80. A MUDEJAR SUMMARY OF ISLAMIC LAW

Yça Gidelli, *Breviario sunni* (1462)
Translated from Aljamiado by L. P. Harvey

Yça Gidelli (also known as Ice or Iça de Gebir) was a Muslim judge in Segovia in the middle of the fifteenth century. His Breviario sunni *is a collection of maxims on Islamic law compiled for the use of Muslims in Castile because, according to the preface, they "have declined in their wealth and have lost their schools of Arabic, [and] in order to put right all these things which are wrong, many of my friends ... have pressed me hard, and have asked me to draw up and to copy out in Romance such an outstanding written work concerning our law and our* sunna: *what every good Muslim should know and have as his normal practice." Yça Gidelli wrote the book in* aljamiado, *an Arabized version of Spanish usually written in the Arabic alphabet that became an important tool for the transmission and preservation of Islamic culture in the Mudejar community. The* Breviario sunni *consists of thirteen chapters; the text translated here is the first. The book is a remarkable compilation of teachings that combines orthodox Islamic precepts with (often contradictory) ideas from Christian writings. As put by Harvey, "the contradictions of Ice's commandments and prohibitions are the product of the stresses of the Mudejar situation. What does shine through in this chapter is the determination of the Muslims of Christian Spain to continue to live in their religion" (pp. 90–91). (ORC)*

Principal Commandments and Prohibitions

Worship the Creator alone, attributing to him neither image nor likeness, and honoring his chosen and blessed Muḥammad.

Desire for your neighbor [*proximo*] that good which you desire for yourself.

Keep constantly pure by means of the minor and major ritual ablutions, and the five prayers.

Be obedient to your father and your mother, even though they be unbelievers.

Do not swear in the name of the Creator in vain.

Do not kill, do not steal, do not commit fornication with any creature.

Pay the canonical alms [*azaque*, i.e., *zakāt*].

Fast during the month of Ramadan.

Make the Pilgrimage [*ḥajj*].

Do not sleep with your wife unless both you and she are in a state of ritual purity.

Introductory information derived from L. P. Harvey, *Islamic Spain, 1250–1500* (Chicago: University of Chicago Press, 1990), pp. 78–97. English text reprinted from the same volume, pp. 88–90, with permission of the publisher.

Honor the day of Assembly [i.e., Friday], above all during the holy times, with all purity and with devout prayers, and with visits to the holy men of the law and to the poor.

Honor the scholars [of the law].

Serve in defense of the law both with your goods and with your person.

Honor your neighbor [vecino], whether he be a stranger or a relative or an unbeliever.

Give lodging willingly to the wayfarer and to the poor man.

Do not break your word, your oath, your bond, or your guarantee, unless it be something which be contrary to the law, when you must make an act of expiation.

Be faithful, do not trade in goods which you know to be stolen.

Do not cause sin or consent to sin, for if you do you participate in it.

Do not falsify weights and measures, nor be guilty of deceit or treachery, do not engage in usury.

Do not drink wine or any other intoxicating thing.

Do not eat pork, nor any carrion flesh, nor blood, nor any suspect thing, nor anything which has not been properly slaughtered, nor anything offered on an altar or to a creature [i.e., any sacrifice to a divinity other than God].

When you meet a Muslim, greet him with your *salāms,* and assist him in whatever is to God's service, and visit him when he is sick, and carry out his interment should he die.

Oppose any Muslim who transgresses the law or the *sunna* in any way.

Let anyone who speaks, speak well or keep silent, and let him not speak evil, even if it be the truth.

When you sit in judgment, be a faithful judge; do not take usury; abstain from covetousness; be faithful to your lord, even though he is not a Muslim, because he will become your heir should you have nobody else to inherit from you; pay him his due; honor the rich and do not despise the poor; beware of envy and wrath; be patient; do not follow enchanters nor fortune tellers, nor those who interpret omens, nor astrologers, nor those who cast lots, but your Lord alone.

Do not live in the land of the unbelievers, nor in any land without justice, nor among evil neighbors, nor should you keep company with bad Muslims.

Live among good men, and spend up to a third of your wealth, and more if you can do so without harm, and so long as you have no cause to regret it.

Do not play at draughts [checkers] or any other idle pastime.

Do not take pleasure in what is forbidden, and do not hanker in your heart
    after that which is not yours.

Beware of the Enemy: forgive him who leads you astray, and ask forgiveness
    of him whom you lead astray, and avoid overweening pride. Obey
    those who are older than you, be merciful on those who are younger,
    and be the brother of those who are the same age as yourself.

Do not be two-faced; be a peace-maker between people; put those who
    have gone astray back on the right path; calm down those who are
    angry, and please Allah.

Set the captive free with your wealth; bring aid to the orphan and to the
    widow, and you will be a neighbor to your Lord.

Learn the law, and teach it to everyone, for on Judgment Day you will be
    called to account for it, and sent to heaven or the flames of hell.

Stand in the way of those who are disobeying the law or *sunna*, because
    those who commit the sin and those who stand by and do nothing are
    equal in sin; strive in this respect, and you will please Allah.

If you are truly repentant, you will deserve everlasting praise.

Hold this world in contempt, and have worthy hope for the future, and you
    will receive everlasting life and blessings.

Do not employ the practices,[1] uses, or customs of the Christians, nor dress
    like them, nor should you have their images, nor those of the sinners,
    and you will be free from infernal sins.

You are to carry out and to preserve the sayings, teachings, uses, customs,
    habits, and way of dress of that excellent and blessed one, Muḥammad,
    on whom be benediction and peace, and those of his Companions, on
    whom Providence bestowed such grace, and on Judgment Day you will
    be one of those who enter paradise without being subjected to the test.

---

1. Here the word translated "practices" could possibly mean "conversations," but in the
context "practices" is the more likely interpretation.

81. TRANSLATING THE QUR'ĀN

A. Juan de Segovia Describes the Project
Translated from Latin by Anne Marie Wolf

*In his early adulthood, Juan Alfonso de Segovia (d. 1458), more commonly known
simply as Juan de Segovia, was a professor of theology at the University of Salamanca, although he would spend most of his adult years away from Spain. While
still in his native land he became curious about Islam and sought out well-informed
Muslims with whom he could discuss religious beliefs. Although he was interested,
ultimately, in converting Muslims, these discussions that he initiated with them
nonetheless seem to have been characterized by genuine interest and curiosity on his
part. In 1431 he left Salamanca on an errand to Rome. From there he went directly
to Basel and never returned to Spain. He was energetically involved in the Council
of Basel from 1433 until that body dissolved itself in 1449. During the council, he tried
to secure reliable translations of the Qur'ān and once borrowed a copy loaned to him
by Nicholas of Cusa. Although church reform controversies had dominated much of
his time for two decades, when the Ottoman Turks captured Constantinople in 1453
he abandoned other projects and dedicated his remaining years to convincing Christian leaders that renewed calls for crusade were not the answer to this threat, that
they should instead strive to convert Muslims to Christianity, and they should do this
through peaceful means.*

*Juan was convinced that Christian Europe was desperately in need of a new
and improved translation of the Qur'ān in order to pursue the goal of peaceful conversion. From his retirement in Aiton, in the French Alps in the Duchy of Savoy, he
wrote letters of inquiry, trying to find someone whose Arabic was strong enough to
produce one. These inquiries eventually achieved their goal when he arranged for
Yça Gidelli (also known as Iça de Gebir), a prominent teacher and scholar (faqīh),
to travel from Castile to Aiton to work on this project. We do not know precisely
how he pursued this goal, or which strings he pulled in Spain, but it appears that
he benefited from some intervention from the king. Yça Gidelli arrived at Juan de
Segovia's monastery in Aiton in December of 1455 and spent about four months as his
guest, as the texts below describe. The product of their collaboration was a trilingual
edition of the Qur'ān, containing the Arabic along with translations into Latin and
Spanish. Unfortunately, that work no longer exists, although the Preface that Juan
de Segovia wrote for it does. The three selections below document Juan de Segovia's
thoughts on the project. (AMW)*

Translated from Vatican City, Biblioteca Apostolica Vaticana (BAV), MS lat. 2923, fols.
190–191v. The translator is grateful to Damon Smith for his patient and capable assistance with
the Latin in several of these passages.

Selections from Juan de Segovia's Preface to a Trilingual Qur'ān

Therefore there was a need for additional work [toward a better translation of the Qur'ān], and then when a royal order had been issued to one of the senior *fuqahā*'[1] in the Kingdom of Castile, he responded that he could not do the translation because he lacked the knowledge needed and because the thing was not possible anyway. Then it pleased God that my wish, which was directed toward the glory of his name, be granted; and after my family and friends had offered security for [the man's] personal safety and for the salary he desired in exchange for his labors, on the fifth day of December, in the year 1455, he arrived at this place where I reside, the priory of Aiton, in the diocese of St. Jean de Maurienne, a man quite renowned among the Saracens of Castile, Yça Gidelli, the *faqīh* of Segovia, along with a companion belonging to his sect.

So it was fitting to attend to that one task, postponing everything else, that this master might complete the work for which he had come, having been called: to produce a translation of the book of the Qur'ān which conformed to the Arabic language and the text, without glosses, limitations, expositions, or insertions into the text, except for some very brief and rare [notes] in the margins to explain certain words.

Moreover, while he was here in this place for four months, he translated the Qur'ān for three of them, and in the fourth, we both read together, with me reviewing the Spanish and him the Arabic, which he himself had written. To be sure, he wrote quickly, both in Arabic and in Spanish. And the Arabic alphabet, not including *s* and *p*, which they lack entirely, contains twenty-nine letters, none of them vowels.[2] They indicate their *a*, *i*, and *u* by means of certain markings above or below their consonants, the *o*, moreover, signifying the *u* when the markings are doubled. The simple *o* is never pronounced in the Arabic language, but is rather *on*. And they indicate the *e*, the second vowel, by other markings that are either black or red. In designating these vowels, therefore, along with other markings, similar to accents and applied with different colors, [they introduce] variation in meaning. This work, which they call *axuclare*[3] and which only their masters do—and for a high salary—requires as much labor as the writing of the letters of their language. And they do not do both at the same time; indeed they cannot, since these markings, signs, and characters that are painted in above or below or on the

---

1. Islamic scholars.
2. This is a curious statement. Arabic does indeed lack a letter for *p*, but there are two different Arabic letters for *s*.
3. *Axuclare* is a Latinization of the Arabic verb *shakala*, one meaning of which is "to provide vowel marks." Thanks are due to Thomas Burman for this information.

side are not placed there in black, but rather in blue, red, green, or even a golden yellow.

Over the allotted space of three months, then, he wrote out the Qur'ān in the first, added vowels the next, and in the next he translated it into Spanish, writing out even the translation itself in his own hand, and very laboriously, as he demonstrated. For he sat in the chair every single day for at least twelve hours, except for the Saracen festival day on which the birth of their Prophet is celebrated. He would also get up often, interrupting his sleep, and write, lest he forget what had come to him. And in order that he could do the translation, he brought with him the books of his people's scholars explaining the Qur'ān.

*   *   *

But the master, having left behind a wife he had but recently married, was eager to leave here and return home, and intended to take with him the translation he had made. Writing the Spanish translation in a column beside the Arabic in a large and careful script, he was not able to finish the work quickly enough, so it was necessary, in order that a copy be left, to engage another copyist.

*   *   *

Once the translation was completed, as I have already mentioned, I urged strongly that the master remain with me for two more months so that I could make progress in learning Arabic, which I was beginning to read by sounding out the syllables, having learned to recognize the letters, but not all the signs and characters which either represent merely the accent or change the meaning of words. I also hoped that we might discuss matters of law together.

*   *   *

But he left, having received the packed and shaken down measure [Luke 6:38] of his pay, and he promised to try to persuade his unmarried brother, who was also a *faqīh*, to come to me so that he could finish teaching me Arabic. However, when the contractor [Gidelli himself] from Spain returned, even if he had promised to do it, [the brother] did not come, his spirit failing him, overwhelmed with fear where there was no cause for fear [Ps. 53:5], since indeed his Magnificence the duke had granted safe conduct, placing under his protection any from the sect of the Saracens who were coming to see me, staying, and returning.

In the Preface, Segovia described his struggles after Gidelli's departure. According to this account, he made two attempts to find another collaborator with the necessary facility in Arabic to help him complete the project. He wrote to leaders of the Franciscans, hoping that someone in that order who had lived in Muslim lands might be able to assist. He sent one man a test to see how well he could translate from the Arabic, and he was unimpressed with the results. Next he learned of a man who was a royal secretary in Cyprus for fifteen years and who had been an ambassador to the Muslims. This man told him that he would not be able to help because, just as among Christians there was a common language and also Latin, among the Muslims there was a common Arabic and also a more formal Arabic, which few even among them could understand. So Segovia was left to do the translation from Spanish to Latin alone and without a way to refer to the Arabic.[4]

Juan de Segovia's Letter About Yça Gidelli

The following is from a letter Juan de Segovia wrote about two years after Gidelli had left Aiton to a friend not named in the letter, although the recipient was probably Guillaume d'Orlyé, a hermit from one of Savoy's noble families who was affiliated with the Dominican house at Annecy. The letter bears the date 18 April, but gives no year. Internal evidence suggests that the year was 1458, making this letter one of the last things written by Juan de Segovia. He died about a month after writing this.

I am sending this work of introduction to you, my dear friend, having never sent it to the bishop[5] because it was just about then that the master *faqīh*, having come to me from Spain, began to translate, anxious with no small fear since he was in a foreign land. Because of this, from the outset he wished to be kept out of sight, but since no Saracen teacher of others, as he was, had ever been seen in Savoy (or at least not for a very long time), many came to visit the house in order to see him. And he, in accordance with his upbringing, as I was told, exercised all moderation both during the whole of Lent and on the days of fasting, when the house was fed on meager rations, never drinking wine, as had been his practice throughout his life. Indeed, when one day he had been served some pea soup, prepared as usual with a little wine,

---

4. His account of all these efforts is found in the Preface to the Qur'ān, which has been published in Darío Cabanelas Rodríguez, *Juan de Segovia y el problema islámico* (Madrid: Universidad de Madrid, 1952), pp. 292–93. This work was reprinted, with the same title and pagination, by the University of Granada in 2007.

    Translation from BAV, MS lat. 2923, fols. 197v–198.

5. The manuscript here reads "episcopo N." In his *Juan de Segovia y el problema islámico*, Darío Cabanelas Rodríguez identified this bishop as Jean Germain. Both Nicholas of Cusa and Jean Germain were bishops at the time, and Segovia had written to both regarding his thoughts on the proper strategy to employ with the Muslims. It is possible that the bishop Segovia was referring to here was Nicholas of Cusa, but it is more likely that it was Jean Germain, as Cabanelas thought, since Segovia's long letter to Germain was finished on 18 December 1455, not quite two weeks after Gidelli arrived in Aiton.

having learned this the next day, he ate just bread in the evening, as if doing penance. Truly their law—which does not make use of the sacraments because they are not able to allow any, nor anything like them—has this defect: the arbitrary permission that they may repent of things committed against God and neighbor which is laid down frequently in the book of the Qur'ān in that affirmation, "God turns toward them in mercy."[6]

Desiring to learn the secrets of their law, I could not hold back the hand . . . since I could not keep him here, with the purpose of discussing the contents of the law. At my fervent request, when he returned to Spain, he expounded on and sent to me twelve "doubts," matters which, he said, keep all Saracens back from the confession of the Catholic faith, and he demanded from me a satisfactory reply to them. So, attending to the Gospel teaching that the believer must give to all who ask [Luke 6:30], interrupting other work I had begun, as I wished now to send [a response] to Spain, I set my hand to the plow. But many things intervened, especially the illness which began in my shins nineteen months ago, but for the past half year has been in my liver, and day by day weakens the whole body along with the powers of the soul; I am unable to work as I wish, since my hands are weak. But I began, thinking that I would finish in two or three cisterns in Spanish, and now that the water I have collected is filling and overflowing the edges of the channel with its flood,[7] I would that God may be prevailed upon to give me life, that I might finish.

From Juan de Segovia's *Donatio*

This passage is from an inventory of the volumes in Juan de Segovia's library, including a description of the trilingual Qur'ān and instructions about where these volumes were to be sent upon his death. This document was dated 9 October 1457.

And because, in this way, it is important and indeed necessary for the suppression [of Islam] to accurately understand what the sect itself holds, the book of the Qur'ān, honored by the Saracens as if it were divine law, lest anything from it might be able to be concealed, having been newly translated by this Juan himself, at great labor and expense. This same Qur'ān has been written in three languages, namely Arabic, Spanish, and Latin, in a large volume of

---

6. This verse, or some version thereof, appears in several places in the Qur'ān (5:71, 9:117, 118). My thanks to Thomas Burman, who identified the passage and assisted in its translation.

7. This rather curious turn of phrase may reflect a metaphor that was common at the time.

Translated from Benigno Hernández Montes, *Biblioteca de Juan de Segovia: Edición y comentario de su escritura de donación* (Madrid: Consejo Superior de Investigaciones Científicas, Instituto "Francisco Suárez," 1984), pp. 107–8 n. 97.

considerable weight. And in the beginning of it is the Preface done by Juan concerning this same translation, and at the end a summary of all of the psalms[8] in Spanish, done by a master translator [of the Qur'ān], whose goal, as should be clear to the attentive [reader], was to praise his law beyond all measure.

B. Yça Gidelli, Letter to Juan de Segovia
Translated from Latin by Gerard Wiegers

This passage tells the story from the point of view of Yça Gidelli, written in a letter to Juan de Segovia dated 24 April 1454, over a year before Gidelli arrived in Aiton. In the letter, he discusses the feasibility of the proposed translation project. This letter is preserved in the Vatican library, as part of the same manuscript (MS lat. 2923) that also contains Juan de Segovia's work. The letter survives in a Latin translation, but it appears that it was originally written in Castilian, as indicated by the gloss on the Romance phrase de pe a pa. *(ORC)*

To the very reverend guide in perfection, John of Segovia, archbishop of Caesarea.

Most beloved and excellent occupant of the bishop's throne, seeker of the true perfection of the eternal kingdom. In the name of Him, in whom everything finds repose and completion.

From him who, with great desire, wishes to assist you in a decisive, angelic cause, to meet your honor and to open to you his hidden inner self, the *faqīh* Yça Gidelli, interpreter and teacher of the art of recitation of the Holy Qur'ān in the city of Segovia, who commends himself to your favor, hoping to accomplish your wish in a piece of work and in everything that leads to your honored perfection, etc.

You must know that your pupil conveyed to me your pious wish to know and found everything on a solid basis, and one thing above all, namely the Qur'ān interpreted in Romance *de pe a pa* (which in the Spanish vernacular amounts to saying "word for word") without any addition whatsoever, and, if possible, after the translation into Romance, to have the benefit of learning from the translator into Romance the meanings and explanations of its texts, etc.

---

8. The chapters of the Qur'ān.

English translation from Gerard Wiegers, *Islamic Literature in Spanish and Aljamiado: Yça of Segovia (fl. 1450), His Antecedents and Successors* (Leiden: Brill, 1994), pp. 232–35. For more discussion of the text, see Wiegers, pp. 100–107. Reprinted with permission of the publisher.

To these propositions [in general], and to each of them in particular I have answered as somebody who wishes to oblige your noble person, since the task is one of the seven called angelic. And although I have eventually sought as my lowest price 20 *doblas* exclusively for my work, my capability of translating and my attendance, without the necessary expenses and without the remuneration of the copyist, how then could it be, my lord, that, after this task is being completed truly and faithfully as the words demand, after calculating the length of time to do this, it should not work out to be more than it would cost to engage a gravedigger? Considering, however, the nature of the request, namely both by whom it was made, and also that it came from Him for whom my heart is open and before whom it is equally ready and although His administration was so outstanding in the past, since the entire reality of the things that had been and have to be until the end and the last extreme was perfect, I therefore. . . . It is so infinite, that I do not doubt that it is a miracle, and that from it the final complete perfection came about, not by necessity, but by a living policy: A Remover of uncertainties, with the true absolute perfection which shows one eternal Operator with might and wisdom, without change, may have been placed in the world, for the benefit of mankind on behalf of the necessary and the inevitable. Not that there is one without the other, nor that He has begun one thing without the other, or completed [it], as the one true goal is one whole, over which my heart and that of those who have some discretion must shed tears of blood. Confusion makes our judgments so poor, since the nature of our understanding changes through having one case of a temporary affair at hand. I tell you my desire in the awareness of my own fallibility, because my important function does not allow this poor judgment of mine to remain without effect, untested and isolated. I want this in order to serve [God's] administration and the enlightenment of my soul to be attained by study and [of the soul] of those for whom I have a responsibility. Because of what I am, I have changed my opinion. And you should emend the new [elements] in my explanations, for the true good is one highest good in which the good and the highest are one. Therefore the highest good is not in the bad . . . so that the good and the highest are one and the same thing. For this reason we are obliged to work and be grateful with nothing but the tenacity to do and to act in such a way as you also know, in that peace and quiet which is the true quiet of Him in whom all things rest: the final affair, the highest good, [supported by] the true knowledge of the composition of the world, namely that it is controlled by two poles of four . . . dispositions, which have been shown to us and which bring about the accidental things. They show that governments would be imperfect, etc.

With respect to your second petition, two things are required: in the first

place the change of residence with the consequence that I will come to stay
[with you]. This is not a drawback because it occurs in my great need, but
because there is nobody here to replace me, for I have an office. And your
love for your virtuous reputation is such a great good [that] I am afraid that
your delicate files and good work will sever all their ties and iron shackles.
Moreover, I feel obliged towards your pupil as well, in order to serve and
please you better.

The second thing would be to extend perfection to the infinite Scripture and its perfection of the Qur'ān. I believe that it is possible to make a
book containing glosses belonging to the subject matter, yet it would not be
possible to interpret it—and no one would permit that either—save in accordance with its eternal and constant meaning, with respect to which kings
jointly laid the foundation, together with high and important teachers, for
the sake of understanding the grammar of the Arabic language and the reasons for which its verses received their origin, [and] why it [the Qur'ān] was
sent [down]. And if I had true peace, then I would tell you as frankly as I
can about all these things, with the true love I have conceived for you in
accordance with the noble and outstanding virtues of a generous lord. And
that this is so appears from your request [for a translation of the Qur'ān],
although it is true, lord, that He put the Scripture in a perfect way in the
mouth of that great, deeply pious prophet Muḥammad at the time when the
heretics had the Sacred House full of idols, whilst He sent him [Muḥammad]
to warn them in a mysterious manner. He was thus enabled by God to provide the idolaters with knowledge of God and with the good of the prophet
Muḥammad He implemented that true guidance. Never will [the Muslims]
abandon the one good truth with the other true good, which is eternal:
one truth and one good. And the good and the truth had to be one single
thing: the sole, unique, perfect and necessary good, which serves mankind.
He [Muḥammad] never withdrew from keeping people off those who, as
your highness knows best, seduce us in a way hostile to the aforesaid two
things, to envy, desire, voracity, luxury, and malice, which were hostile to
him. And neither God nor the human will is able to protect someone against
this evil, and I have to confess that it [the human will] kept me chained and
captured in former times, but when it pleased God to enlighten me so that I
would understand His Sacred Scripture I found in it the secrets which exist
in many places owing to our deficiency but remain covered up. From that I
have learned that every sensible human being ought to have little confidence
in earthly goods, since he sees how quickly they decay and do not provide the
perfect good. And for that reason, and also, as I have said before, because of
your noble virtues which I have heard of, I am obliged to do everything you

have ordered me. And therefore, since I am, as it were, determined in this matter, I am sending you this letter, corroborated by my name, in the faith and the hope of your swift answer, if that be possible, so that I do not need to torment my soul with that wish.

Written at night, by candlelight, enlightened, as it were, by God. From Segovia, 24 April 1454. Very much willing to serve your honor.

82. HERESY AND INQUISITION

A. Descriptions of Two *Autos de Fe* (1486)
Translated from Castilian by Ronald Surtz

The auto de fe, *literally an "act of faith," was intended to be an edifying public spectacle that expressed hatred of heresy and faith in the mercy of the church. Penitents were marched through the streets to a scaffold from which their sentences were read and they publicly abjured their errors. By means of this ceremony, also known as reconciliation, repentant heretics were received back into the bosom of the church.*

Unrepentant heretics were executed. Burning at the stake was not normally a component of an auto de fe; *the emphasis was on reconciliation. Instead, executions took place during a subsidiary ceremony, usually held outside the city. As in the case of the medieval Inquisition, the church was forbidden to carry out the sentence of blood. Therefore, the guilty were turned over to the secular authorities for execution. (RS)*

Toledo, 12 February 1486

On Sunday, 12 February 1486, all the "reconciled" who lived in these seven parishes—Saint Vincent, Saint Nicholas, Saint John of the Milk, Saint Justa, Saint Michael, Saint Justus, [and] Saint Lawrence—marched in a procession; there were as many as 750 people [including] both men and women. And they marched in procession from [the monastery of] Saint Peter the Martyr in this fashion. The men were without cloaks, bareheaded, barefoot, and without hose. And because the weather was so cold they were ordered to wear linen soles under their otherwise bare feet, with unlit candles in their hands. And the women were without cloaks or any outer garment whatsoever, their faces uncovered,[1] barefoot like the men, and holding their candles. Many important and respected personages were among such people, and with the extremely cold temperature and the dishonor and disgrace they suffered on account of the great crowd that was watching them—because many people had come from the surrounding areas to see them—they went along shrieking with pain and weeping, and some tore out their hair (it is believed more because of the disgrace they were suffering than because of the offenses they had committed against God).

And thus they marched in great anguish through the entire city, following the same path as the Corpus Christi procession, until they arrived at the cathedral. At the door of the cathedral were two priests who made the sign of

Translated from Fidel Fita, "La inquisición toledana: Relación contemporánea de los autos y autillos que celebró desde el año 1485 hasta el de 1501," *Boletín de la Real Academia de la Historia* 2 (1887): 294–96, 299–300. In cases of doubt, the translator checked Fita's transcriptions against a microfilm of MS 9175, Biblioteca Nacional (Madrid).

1. Well-born Spanish women did not normally appear in public with their faces uncovered.

Figure 21. Pedro Berruguete (ca. 1450–1504), *Saint Dominic Presiding over an Auto de Fe*. Museo del Prado, Madrid. Photo credit: Erich Lessing/Art Resource, NY.

the cross on the forehead of each one of them, saying these words: "Receive the sign of the cross that you denied and lost through being grievously deceived." And they went into the cathedral up to a platform that was erected near the new gate. The father inquisitors were seated on the platform, and on another nearby platform was an altar where mass was said for them and a sermon was preached to them. And afterward a notary public arose and began to call each one by name, speaking in this way: "Is so-and-so there?" And the reconciled raised his candle and said: "Yes." And there in public he [the notary] read off all the things in which he [the reconciled] had Judaized, and likewise was done with the women.

And when this was done, there in public they were given their penance which was to march in a procession on six [consecutive] Fridays, whipping their backs with ropes of knotted hemp and without hose or hats, and [also] that they fast on those six Fridays. And it was ordered that as long as they should live they could hold no public office such as mayor or constable or alderman or magistrate or notary public or gatekeeper, and that those who held such offices should lose them, and that they could not be money changers or apothecaries or spice merchants, nor could they hold any suspicious post whatsoever, nor could they wear silk or fine scarlet wool or colored clothing or gold or silver or pearls or mother-of-pearl or coral or any jewel, nor could they act as witnesses, nor could they rent such things. They were ordered on penalty of being considered backsliders, that is, those who fall again into the same error as before, that if they used any one of the above-mentioned [forbidden] articles, they would be condemned to be burned at the stake. And when all these ceremonies were over, they left the cathedral at two in the afternoon.

Toledo, 16 August 1486

On Wednesday, 16 August of said year of 1486, twenty-five people were burned at the stake: twenty men and five women. Among those burned were Dr. Alonso Cota (a resident of Toledo), an alderman, a public prosecutor, a commander of the Order of Santiago, and other persons of high social standing. And they brought them out in this way: on foot and with conical miters on their heads, dressed in *sanbenitos* of yellow linen with the name of each one written on the *sanbenito*.[2] They read thus: "So and so, condemned

---

2. The *sanbenito* was a defamatory penitential garment that clearly indicated that its wearer had been convicted of heresy. Wearing the *sanbenito* for a certain period whenever the penitent went out in public was one of the punishments meted out to those reconciled. After the garment had been worn for the period specified by the Inquisition or after the execution of the condemned, the *sanbenito* was hung in the parish church with the heretic's name inscribed on it, so that everyone could see it. In this way the infamy of one generation was passed on to future generations.

heretic." Their hands were tied to the backs of their necks with pieces of rope. And they were brought to the square, where there was a tiered platform, upon which they were seated in order. And facing it was another platform where the inquisitors, notaries, and other people were [seated]. And there in public the dossier and the Judaizing acts of each one were read in a loud voice. And at the end of each dossier they proclaimed and condemned each one as a heretic and turned him over to the forces of justice and secular powers. And they spent from six in the morning until noon reading the dossiers. And when they had finished reading the dossiers, they turned them [the heretics] over to the secular authorities. And from there they were brought to the plain [outside the city], where they were burned, for not even a single bone remained that had not been burned to ashes.

Clergy can't spill blood — give to secular authority

B. Inquisitorial Trials of Inés López (1495–1496, 1511–1512)
Translated from Castilian by Ronald Surtz

Inés López was born in 1464 or 1466 to the shoemaker Diego López de Almodóvar and his wife Elvira González. She was tried twice by the Inquisition, once in 1495–1496 and again in 1511–1512. In 1494, when Inés was about twenty-nine, she married Alonso de Aguilera, but she was already a widow by the time her first trial began a year later. The couple had no children and Inés never remarried. There was no particular social or legal reason to prevent her from taking a second husband because Spanish law permitted remarriage after a year of mourning. Perhaps Inés preferred the relative freedom she could enjoy as a widow. Spanish law allowed widows to keep their own property and the dowry they brought to marriage.[1] Inés could thus live financially independent and subject to the will of no man.

Inés was about thirty years old at the time of her arrest. She was not the only member of her family to have dealings with the Inquisition. Her father, who died in 1481 when Inés was in her teens, was tried posthumously in 1484–1485. He was absolved, thanks to the efforts of his daughters, his son-in-law, and a good lawyer.[2] Inés's mother was also brought before the Inquisition and made to abjure her crimes of heresy. Inés's sister Leonor was tried in 1495–1496 and found guilty of Judaizing. She was condemned to life imprisonment and to public abjuration of her Jewish prac-

Translated from *Records of the Trials of the Spanish Inquisition in Ciudad Real*, edited by Haim Beinart, 4 vols. (Jerusalem: Israel Academy of Sciences and Humanities, 1974–1985), 2:59–125.

1. María Isabel Pérez de Tudela y Velasco, "La condición de la viuda en el medievo castellano-leonés," in *Las mujeres en las ciudades medievales*, edited by Cristina Segura Graiño (Madrid: Universidad Autónoma, 1984), pp. 87–101.
2. This was more than an instance of filial piety, for had the father been found guilty, his property—his children's inheritance—would have been confiscated and the whole family shamed.

tices. Inés's sisters Mayor and Violante were also tried by the Inquisition. Violante was burned at the stake in 1494, the year before Inés's own trial.

More than a formal trial in the modern sense, an Inquisitorial trial was a series of audiences. The accused was never told the reasons for his or her imprisonment. Instead, he or she was given three warnings, over a period of weeks, to confess. This was a strategy the Inquisition used to elicit spontaneous confessions of unreported instances of heresy. In her three confessions, Inés López admitted to observing some Jewish precepts, many of which had less to do with beliefs than with social and culinary customs. (RS)

[handwritten margin, left vertical:] Men had to be much more public practicing Judaism → easier for women + more common

[handwritten margin, left vertical:] Probably imprisoned (house arrest) October - January

[handwritten note next to (RS):] inquisitorial scribe

Confession of 22 October 1495

Most reverend Lords:

I, Inés López, a resident of Ciudad Real, wife of the late Alonso de Aguilera, appear before Your Reverences with the greatest contrition and repentance for my sins of which I am capable, and I beg Our Lord Jesus Christ for His pardon and mercy, and I beg of Your Reverences a saving penance for my soul, and for those [sins] that I have committed by which I have offended My Lord Jesus Christ and His Holy Catholic Faith, which are the following in this manner:

I declare, My Lords, that I did not do servile work on some Saturdays, and on Saturdays I put on clean clothes. And sometimes I ate food that was prepared on Friday for Saturday, and I lit candles on Friday evening in accordance with Jewish ritual.

Likewise, I observed some of the Jewish fasts, [fasting] until nightfall. Moreover, I sometimes observed Jewish holidays, when I found out about them from a cousin of mine named Isabel de Lobón, when I was [staying] with her, for she was a widow. And she told me to do so for the benefit of my soul, especially [to observe] Passover, for the aforementioned Isabel de Lobón every so often gave me [unleavened bread], warning me not to tell anyone. The aforementioned Isabel de Lobón has left Villarreal [Ciudad Real]; for where, no one knows.[3]

Likewise, I removed the fat from meat whenever I could.

Likewise, My Lords, I declare that I ate on low tables at funeral banquets. . . .

Additional Confession of 14 January 1496

My most reverend Lords:

I, Inés López, daughter of Diego López, a resident of Ciudad Real,

---

3. By accusing her cousin Isabel, Inés was able to satisfy the tribunal's demand that she report instances of heresy. However, Inés was able to do so without actually incriminating anyone, for Isabel had already fled from Spain and was safely ensconced in Constantinople.

appear before Your Reverences to say that, because I had made a confession of the sins I had committed against Our Lord in which I said that if any further sin came to mind I would declare and reveal it, I now declare, My Lords, that what I further remember is the following:

I declare and confess to Your Reverences that on some Friday nights my sister [Violante], the [wife] of [Pedro de] San Román, and I tidied up the house and cooked Saturday's food on those nights. We did this sometimes, and other times we didn't, so that we wouldn't be found out, etc.

Moreover, My Lords, I had little desire to eat pork, and when I could, I didn't eat it, and neither did my aforementioned sister, who told me that I shouldn't eat [it] nor anything cooked with it because I was younger than she.

Moreover, My Lords, sometimes when I went to Mass it was my custom and habit to chatter and not to pray. . . .

Moreover, My Lords, on Sundays and holidays I sometimes sewed things I needed and also performed other tasks. . . .

Moreover, My Lords, on days of abstinence in Lent and the vigils of other holidays and on ember days, I often prepared and ate food, and I saw that my aforementioned sisters ate meat and other [forbidden] delicacies.

Moreover, My Lords, I declare that when my father died, I saw Diego Díez's wife and Sezilla, the wife of Martín González, put a pot of water in the parlor where [his body] was. I don't know why, except that I heard it said that it was to bathe my aforementioned father, who was dirty. And I placed a basin of water and a cloth in said parlor—I don't remember who told me to do so, except that I believe that it was Mayor Álvarez, my sister, who was there.[4]

Moreover, I often lit candles on Friday nights in San Román's house, because I usually lived with San Román and his wife, my sister, for I was twelve or fifteen years old.

Moreover, my Lords, I saw that my mother did not spin on Saturdays, and I saw this during the whole time that I lived [with her]. . . .

Addition of 19 January 1496

My most reverend Lords:

I, Inés López, a resident of Ciudad Real, appear before Your Reverences and declare that, in addition to what I have declared and confessed to you, I often porged meat[5] and removed the tendons from legs of lamb.

---

4. According to Jewish custom, the bodies of the deceased were washed before burial.
5. That is, she removed the forbidden fat, veins, and sinews according to Jewish ritual.

On 17 September 1496 Inés was sentenced to be reconciled in an auto de fe. *As part of her sentence, Inés was required to wear a* sanbenito *whenever she went out in public. She was also sentenced to life imprisonment. This punishment actually meant a sort of house arrest, and even that was seldom enforced.*[6] *Also, such sentences were often commuted on payment of a fine. In any case, after her reconciliation and despite her sentence of life imprisonment, Inés seems to have enjoyed relative freedom of movement. Nonetheless, she continued to engage in Jewish religious practices and made some imprudent statements, which, in time, were duly noted and reported to the Inquisition by her friends and neighbors. Fifteen years after her first trial, Inés's imprudence caught up with her. On 4 June 1511, the Inquisitorial Court met in Toledo and, deeming the evidence sufficient for a trial, ordered the arrest of Inés López. She was imprisoned, and her property was confiscated.*

Arraignment: 16 September 1511

I. First, that the aforementioned Inés López, after her aforementioned false reconciliation and abjuration, often and at many times and in many places disclaimed the confession that she had spontaneously made, declaring and affirming that she had never perpetrated or committed the crimes of heresy that she had confessed to and for which she was reconciled, and [declaring] that false witnesses had imputed [such crimes] to her and to others, and that she had never done or committed such things, saying: "See how my life hangs on the words of a drunken man or a drunken woman" and that the Lord should preserve her from false witnesses, always declaring and affirming that she had never done any of those things for which she had been reconciled, and that she had only been reconciled so that they wouldn't burn her at the stake. . . .

II. Moreover, that the aforementioned Inés López, after her reconciliation and abjuration, defended and continued to defend many condemned heretics, declaring and affirming that they had been unjustly condemned, that they were no heretics, except that they had been falsely accused and condemned without their deserving it; in particular, she said that her mother and her sisters, who had been condemned, had been unjustly condemned, for they were good Christians and had not committed any crime of heresy whatsoever that would justify their being burned at the stake. . . .

[III. *Inés is also accused of defending certain deceased "heretics" whose bodies were discovered to be shrouded in the Jewish manner and buried without any crosses.*]

IV. Moreover, that the aforementioned Inés López, often speaking after

6. Henry Kamen, *Inquisition and Society in Spain in the Sixteenth and Seventeenth Centuries* (Bloomington: Indiana University Press, 1985), pp. 186–87.

her reconciliation about the Inquisition and about heretics, said that everything had been fabricated by false witnesses and that the Inquisition had been set up for the sole purpose of extracting money and robbing them. . . .

V. Moreover, that the aforementioned Inés López did not know how to cross herself nor did she ever cross herself, until such time eight or ten months ago when they said that the Inquisition was coming to Ciudad Real. And afterward, if she ever did make the sign of the cross, it was not done as a Christian, crossing herself and saying "In the name of the Father and of the Son, etc." And if ever they got her to say "In the name of the Father," she was reluctant and even refused to say "and of the Son" or "of the Holy Spirit."[7]

VI. Moreover, that the aforementioned Inés López, an unbeliever and a mocker of our holy Catholic Christian faith and of the things of the Church and the Eucharist, sometimes when she returned from hearing mass, which she only attended in order to look good in the eyes of her neighbors, would make jokes, saying that she had come from such and such a church and that she had heard a smoked mass, which she said because they had used incense. . . .

Inés was never told the names of those who had testified against her. However, as was standard procedure, on 17 February 1512 the judges gave the defense fifteen days to produce a list of tachas, that is, enemies of Inés López whose testimony should be discounted as biased. This section of the trial offers a glimpse of everyday life in a medieval Spanish village with all its gossip and petty arguments.

Questionnaire for Tachas Witnesses

IV. Moreover, if they know, etc., that the aforementioned Catalina Alonso was and continues to be an enemy of the aforementioned Inés López and has hatred and enmity toward her, because a daughter of the aforementioned Catalina Alonso was living with the aforementioned Inés López and the aforementioned Catalina Alonso removed her from the house, which caused them to quarrel, and the aforementioned Catalina Alonso went around saying that Inés López should be burned at the stake. And they also quarreled because the aforementioned Catalina Alonso stole a kneading trough from the aforementioned Inés López. . . .

VI. Moreover, if they know, etc., that Teresa Muñoz and the sacristan of Santa María and Catalina García, a companion of the aforementioned Teresa Muñoz, were and continue to be enemies of the aforementioned Inés López, because the aforementioned Teresa Muñoz stole two pieces of ribbon from

---

7. This practice was common among Judaizing *conversos* because they abhorred the notion of three divinities embodied in the Christian Trinity and preferred to pray to one God only, in this case the Father.

the aforementioned Inés López, who quarreled with her and called her a whore and a procuress and a sorceress, as she is, for she [Teresa] procured a daughter of Pedro Amarillo for the aforementioned sacristan, and likewise she [Inés] quarreled with the aforementioned Catalina García because she [Catalina] had the aforementioned Teresa Muñoz [living] in her house, which is why all three had it in for her [Inés].

VII. Also, if they know, etc., that the aforementioned Juana de Torres, a holy woman, was and continues to be an enemy of the aforementioned Inés López because she [Juana] stole a lace-trimmed piece of cloth from her, and she fell out [with her] over that, and [also] because the aforementioned Inés López discovered and disclosed that the aforementioned Juana de Torres had given birth [out of wedlock] to a son and a daughter, and out of enmity she [Inés] made the whole matter public, and from that moment on they [Juana and her children] had great enmity toward her. . . .

IX. Also, if they know that the aforementioned Alonso de Carmona [Camargo] was and continues to be an enemy of the aforementioned Inés López and holds hatred and enmity toward her, because while the aforementioned Camargo was away traveling, the aforementioned Inés López lived in Camargo's house, and as soon as she took possession of it, she made off with a wardrobe she was renting from him, concerning which the aforementioned Alonso de Camargo summoned the aforementioned Inés López to appear in court, and also concerning a certain pile of manure that she left in the house, about which they fell out and ended up enemies. . . .

XVI. Also, Catalina de Salzedo is her enemy, because she adopted the honorific title "Doña" and the aforementioned Inés López said: "Confound it!" for since she [Catalina] was the daughter of a purse-maker, she had no right to call herself "Doña." And the aforementioned Catalina de Salzedo found out about it and showed and continued to show enmity toward her. . . .

XXII. Also, Marina, the wife of Monteagudo is her enemy, because when she was Monteagudo's mistress, the two of them quarreled and the aforementioned Inés López called the aforementioned Marina a whore. . . .

XXVIII. Also, if they know that Elvira González, mother of the aforementioned Inés López, was and continues to be her enemy, for she would say publicly that the aforementioned Inés López was no daughter of hers, and she [Elvira] is a woman who often has bouts of delirium.

In Toledo on 1 and 2 March 1512, witnesses testified that to the best of their knowledge the persons Inés claimed were hostile to her were not, in fact, her enemies. On 3 and 5 July the Inquisitors met and voted that Inés's property be confiscated and that she be turned over to the secular authorities to be burned at the stake.

83. MUSLIMS AND CHRISTIANS IN VALENCIA

A. Socializing and Violence on Corpus Christi Day (1491)
Translated from Catalan by Mark Meyerson

Many historians would maintain that by the later fifteenth century Christian-Muslim coexistence in the Spanish Christian kingdoms was practically impossible for a number of reasons: Christians despised Muslims as infidels; Christians feared the Muslims in their midst as a fifth column who would aid the Christian kingdoms' Muslim enemies when the opportunity presented itself; Muslims in regions like the kingdom of Valencia could speak only Arabic and therefore could not socialize with Christians; and Christians had grown more intolerant of non-Christians in general. The following excerpts suggest that this viewpoint is debatable and that the state of Muslim-Christian relations was more complex. These excerpts are from the trial of Açen Muça, a Muslim accused of murdering another Muslim, Abdalla Centido, who had killed his half brother. The murder took place as Christians and Muslims were watching the Corpus Christi procession together. The attendance of members of both faiths at an important Christian religious festival indicates the breaching of religious and social barriers. However, the readiness of Christians to take up arms against the Muslims after the murder had been committed points to the fragility of the modus vivendi between Muslims and Christians. (MM)

On 3 June 1491, before the court of the bailiff general of the kingdom of Valencia, Mariem, widow of the murdered Abdalla Centido, and Abdalla's two sisters, Axa and Nuça, all Muslims of the village of Alacuas, with the assistance of the royal prosecutors, make the following accusations against the defendant Açen Muça, Muslim of the village of Serra.

Some time ago the defendant had conceived, for no reason, great hatred, rancor, and ill will against the said Abdalla Centido, thinking about how he might kill him or gravely wound him. And this is true and public knowledge. . . . On the day of Corpus Christi—on which day is made a great celebration and ceremony of the precious body of our [the scribe's] Lord God Jesus Christ [and] on which day many Muslims and Christians from diverse parts of the kingdom come to see the great celebration—the said Abdalla Centido, along with his wife and others from the village of Alacuas, came to the present city [of Valencia] to see the said celebration simply and without any fear of the said defendant. And this is true and public knowledge. . . . The said defendant, knowing that the said Abdalla Centido was in the present city to

Translated from Archive of the Kingdom of Valencia, Bailiff General, Reg. 1431, fols. 64v–99r (3–28 June 1491).

see the celebration without fear of him and therefore without carrying arms, seized a large dagger and went searching for the said victim [Abdalla] in the *boçeria* [pursemaking center] and other places where the Corpus Christi procession passed in order to kill him. And this is true and public knowledge. . . . The defendant, seeing the said Abdalla Centido standing near the butcher shop of the *morería* [Muslim quarter] and watching the said procession, drew his dagger from under his cape and approached Abdalla Centido. . . . And so the said defendant . . . stabbed Abdalla Centido in the chest . . . from which the said Abdalla Centido quickly died and passed from the present life into the next. And this is true and public knowledge. . . .

Because of the very foul deed committed by the said defendant on the person of the said Abdalla Centido, a great disturbance was caused in the present city, especially in the *boçeria*, *morería*, and other places near where the said foul deed was done, inasmuch as all the [Christian] people moved to take arms against the Muslims. Were it not for the assistance of the officials of the present city, a very great inconvenience would have occurred in the present city. And this is true and public knowledge.

On 7 June 1491, witnesses for the prosecution testify. The following is the testimony of Miquel de la Serra, a Christian tailor of Valencia.

And he said that it is true that on the day that the said Centido, Muslim, arrived in the present city of Valencia it was the day of Corpus Christi. In the morning he [Abdalla Centido] came with other Muslim lads to eat in the home of the witness . . . and while they ate the said [Muslim] lads said they were from Chiva [Alacuas; the witness was incorrect], and they asked the said witness and others to accompany them to the celebration. . . . And so the said witness and the others went with them. And while they were watching a certain wagon or float [on which biblical stories were enacted for the edification of the crowd] they heard a commotion; and then the said witness went toward the commotion and discovered how the said Centido had been stabbed.

On 9 June 1491, another witness for the prosecution, Joan de Bolea, a Christian weaver of Valencia, made the following testimony.

The said witness along with a neighbor named Bernat Canon [another Christian weaver] came [to watch the Corpus Christi procession] in the company of certain Muslims from Alacuas and of the deceased Muslim [Abdalla Centido], who said they had come to see the celebration. When they were near the butcher shop of the *morería*, the said deceased Muslim said that the sun was in his face and that they should move to the shade. And so the said witness and the said Bernat Canon and the said deceased Muslim moved to the wall of the house of the apothecary Monsoriu, and the three of them leaned there and spoke among themselves. . . . And so the said witness, while he was there with him [Abdalla Centido], saw coming behind him a Muslim dressed in a cape [Açen Muça]; the Muslim came on furiously . . . and with great violence stabbed the said deceased Muslim in the chest. And the said witness stood there shocked, and then turned toward the victim and saw a great amount of blood gushing from his chest. And then the witness ran after the said Muslim [Açen Muça] to apprehend him.

On 28 June 1491, the bailiff general finds Açen Muça guilty of the murder of Abdalla Centido and sentences him to have his right hand amputated in the place where he committed the murder, to pay a fine of 200 morabatins—100 to the royal authorities and 100 to the heirs of Abdalla Centido—and to banishment from the kingdom of Valencia. Among the factors considered by the bailiff was the fact that the murder had been committed by "an infidel on a day so solemn and of such great celebration, in honor and reverence of the holy body of our Lord Redeemer Jesus Christ, and in the place of the procession and celebration and in such great disregard of the said holiday and with commotion, disturbance, and danger of scandal in the present city."   Harsher punishment due to Muslim + Christian holy day

(Muslim kills Muslim, Christians say "let's kill Muslim.")

B. Confessions of a Muslim Prostitute (1491)
Translated from Catalan by Mark Meyerson

The religious and social order of the Spanish Christian kingdoms left Muslim women particularly vulnerable to exploitation by Christian men. According to the laws of the kingdom of Valencia (the Furs), if a Muslim man slept with a Christian woman, both parties were to be burned alive; however, if a Christian man slept with a Muslim woman, the Christian man received no punishment at all, while the woman was punished according to Islamic law for fornication or adultery—that is, by flogging or death by stoning. The royal authorities usually commuted these Islamic penalties to enslavement to the crown. Muslim women thus enslaved were then sold and frequently forced into prostitution by their Christian masters. The royal policy regarding prostitution—Muslim or Christian—was to license it, regulate it, and tax it. By the fifteenth century, the royal authorities seem to have become avid to acquire Muslim prostitutes in particular to staff royal brothels. However, they went beyond apprehending the few Muslim women who had slept with Christian men. Realizing

Translated from Archive of the Kingdom of Valencia, Bailiff General, Reg. 1431, fols. 57r–61v (23 June 1491).

that in Muslim society the honor of the family was to a significant degree dependent on the sexual purity of its womenfolk and that Muslim women who had been involved in premarital or adulterous liaisons with Muslim men were spurned by their own families and communities and then condemned by Islamic courts, the royal authorities focused their attention on these marginalized Muslim women and again intervened to commute the Islamic penalties to enslavement to the crown. Royal mercy often meant a life of prostitution for these women. (MM)

[23 June 1491] Confessions exacted from the prostitute Mariem, Muslim woman [*mora*] of Alasquer [in the kingdom of Valencia].

First she was asked her name. She answered that it is Mariem.

She was asked whose daughter she is. She answered that she is the daughter of Yuseff Algumeli,[1] Muslim of the village of Alasquer.

She was asked how she came here [that is, to the city of Valencia]. She answered that it was because of her mother, for her mother had forced her to return to her husband.

She was asked with whom did she come [to Valencia]. She answered that [she came] with a procurer by the name of Cutaydal [a Muslim], whose place of origin, she said, is unknown to her.

She was asked if she is with that one [Cutaydal] freely or by compulsion. She answered that presently she is no longer with him, since he mistreated her; however, previously she was and came with him out of her own free will, for he had promised to make her his wife.

She was asked if he [Cutaydal] put her to work [as a prostitute] with her free consent or by compulsion. She answered that in the beginning she, the said defendant, traveled with the said Cutaydal voluntarily, for he had promised to make her his wife.

She was asked if she, the said defendant, is in the brothel voluntarily or if the said Cutaydal was forcing her to be there. And she answered that before she, the said defendant, became a prostitute, the said Cutaydal threatened her, telling her that the agents of the lord cardinal [of Valencia; a major landholder in the kingdom with a reputation for mistreating Muslims] would enslave her. And therefore it was decided [by Mariem and Cutaydal] that she should be sold to the noble Don Altobello [de Centelles] and that thus she would be secure [that is, safe from the cardinal's men as Don Altobello's slave, a more benign master]. And so she was led to believe that she had been sold to Don Altobello, and thus they have put her in the brothel. And thus she has had to endure being there and is there voluntarily.

She was asked if she would like to return to the custody of her husband

---

1. The spelling of names in this translation follows the spelling in the original document.

or of her mother and return to freedom, instead of being where she is. She answered that she does not wish to return to her husband, but that she desires to return to her mother rather than being where she is.

She was asked for what quantity [of money] she was sold to the said Don Altobello. She answered that the said Cutaydal led her to believe that he had sold her for twenty pounds, but that the said Don Altobello has told her that it was for thirty pounds.

She was asked what she does with her earnings [from prostitution]. She answered that she has worked for two days, and that everything she earns she gives to Don Altobello. And that he [Don Altobello] has told her that he will take her earnings into account toward her ransom.

She was asked if she has taken any clothing or jewelry from the said village of Alasquer. She answered that she has not taken anything other than the clothes she is wearing.

Mariem is released into the custody of Cahat Bellvis and Yuçeff Maymo, councillors of the Muslim community of Valencia, and of the representative of Don Rodrigo de Mendoza, the lord of Alasquer. The questioning of Mariem resumes on 4 July 1491.

She was asked if she is married and has a husband. She answered yes, she was married with a letter of *ṣadāq* [Arabic, dower], according to the custom of the Muslims. Her husband is named Mahomat Jahupi.

She was asked if she has worked [as a prostitute] and has committed adultery with any Muslim in the present city of Valencia. She answered that she has been a prostitute and has worked in the brothel of the *morería* [Muslim quarter] of Valencia.

She was asked if she had committed adultery before she was put in the brothel of the *morería* of Valencia. She answered yes, that is, that she slept with the said Cutaydal in the city of Valencia.

She was asked if she was adhering to the aforesaid confessions. She answered yes, that she will always adhere to them.

important family

Joan Sobrevero, the representative of Don Rodrigo de Mendoza, lord of Alasquer, appears before the bailiff general and argues that Mariem was unlawfully sold to Don Altobello de Centelles, since she was a free vassal of Don Rodrigo. Sobrevero also produces evidence that Mariem purchased a license to practice prostitution from the bailiff general, and maintains that therefore she cannot be penalized for unlicensed prostitution. The bailiff general concurs with Sobrevero's arguments and nullifies the sale of Mariem to Don Altobello. He frees Mariem to practice prostitution or to return to her parents or husband.

84. THE CHRISTIAN CONQUEST OF GRANADA
(1492)

A. Hernando del Pulgar (1436–1492), *Crónicas de los reyes de Castilla* (1492)

Translated from Castilian by Teofilo Ruiz

In the last days of 1491, with the city of Granada besieged by Christian armies, its ruler, Muḥammad XII (or Abū ʿAbd Allah, hence he was commonly called Boabdil by Christians), began to negotiate the surrender of his kingdom. Hernando del Pulgar's chronicle provides a brief but dramatic narrative of the Christians' victorious entry into the city and of the end of Muslim rule in the peninsula on 2 January 1492. His account captures the emotional character of the closing of the reconquista *and inscribes the chivalric culture of the age. (TR)*

In the month of December, not having enough provisions left, the citizens of Granada requested a parlay with the Christians. The negotiations [between the Muslims and the Christians] lasted thirty days and on 30 December [1491], the Moors surrendered the fortresses held by their king—the most important of which was the Alhambra—to the king Don Fernando and to the queen Doña Isabel. The terms of the treaty allowed the Moors to keep their religion and property, as well as other privileges. The Moors also gave concessions [to the Christians] and, to guarantee the surrender of the fortresses and of all their weapons, many of Granada's most important citizens were surrendered as hostages.

A mad Moor went around the streets of Granada, clamoring for the people of Granada to reject the treaty, and so many followed him that the Moorish king [Boabdil] did not dare to leave. Thus, on Saturday, the king of Granada gathered his counselors, as well as those in the city who were rioting. He spoke to them with such words as to pacify them, explaining that the time was already past for such actions, because they no longer had the supplies to withstand the Christian siege. Since they [the people of Granada] had no hope of help and had given hostages, resistance would bring harm rather than any remedy. Having said that, the Moorish king returned to the Alhambra, which he had agreed to surrender on the Day of the Epiphany [6 January 1492]. And [then] the Moorish king wrote to the [Christian] king to give

Translated from Hernando del Pulgar, "Crónica de los señores reyes católicos Don Fernando y Doña Isabel," in *Crónicas de los reyes de Castilla* III, Biblioteca de Autores Españoles 70 (Madrid: Atlas, 1953), pp. 510–11.

Figure 22. Pedro Marcuello, *Portrait of the Catholic Monarchs Fernando and Isabel with Their Daughter Juana*. From the *Devotional of Queen Juana la Loca*, MS 604, fol. 30v, Musée Condé, Chantilly. Photo credit: Réunion des Musées Nationaux/Art Resource, NY.

Figure 23. Departure of Boabdil from Granada. Carved wooden alterpiece from the Capilla Real, Granada. Photo credit: DeA Picture Library/Art Resource, NY.

assurance that he would comply with the terms of surrender and advising that it be carried out as soon as possible.

Reading this, on 2 January the king and queen led their army to Granada. The queen, the prince [the infante] heir to the throne, and the infanta Doña Juana remained on a hill overlooking Granada, while the king and his men rode to a place across the river Genil from the city. The Moorish king came out to surrender [to King Fernando] the keys of the city. While doing so, Boabdil tried to descend from his horse and kiss Don Fernando's hand, which the Christian king did not allow. Instead Boabdil kissed the king's arm and gave him the keys [to the city]. And Don Fernando gave them to the count of Tendilla, to whom he had given authority [*alcaydía*] over Granada and to Don Gutierre de Cardenas, *comendador* major of León. They [these two officials and their troops] entered the Alhambra; on top of the tower of Comares they raised the cross and the royal banners, and the heralds cried out: "Granada, Granada for the kings Don Fernando and Doña Isabel."

Once the queen saw the cross, her clergymen sang a *Te Deum laudamus*. And such was the happiness that they all began to cry. Later [that day] all the great lords, who were with the king, went to where the queen was and kissed her hand [in obeisance] as queen of Granada. And next to the royal banners also rose the banner of the Order of Santiago which had been brought to Granada by the Master of the Order.

Figure 24. Fernando and Isabel entering Granada. Carved wooden alterpiece from the Capilla Real, Granada. Permission and photograph credit: Cabildo de la Capilla Real, Granada.

[handwritten in left margin: Cultural separation of Muslims & Christians]

B. Capitulations of Granada (1491)
Translated from Castilian by L. P. Harvey

Versions of this text survive in both Arabic and Castilian, but the Castilian versions are by far the more complete and include official transcripts dating from 1492. The text records the terms for the surrender of Granada laid out in 1491 and arrangements for the subsequent treatment of its Muslim inhabitants. Because of the length of the text, some clauses have been translated in full (indicated by [F]) whereas others have been summarized (indicated by [S]). (ORC)

"*Firstly* that the Moorish king and his *alcaides* [*sic*] and lawyers, judges, *muftīs*, ministers, learned men, military leaders, good men, and all the common folk of the city of Granada and of its Albaicín and other suburbs will in love, peace, goodwill, and with all truthfulness in their dealings and their actions yield and surrender to their highnesses, or to a person by them appointed, within forty days from this date, the fortress of the Alhambra and the Alhizan with all towers, gates to the city and the Albaicín and to suburbs connecting directly with the open country, so that they may occupy them in their name with their own troops, at their own free will, on condition that orders be issued to the justices that they should not permit the Christians to climb onto the wall between the Alcazaba and the Albaicín from where the houses of the Moors may be seen; and if anybody should climb up there, he should be punished immediately and sternly." [F]

2. The second clause related to the arrangements for the actual surrender: it should be carried out within forty days "freely and spontaneously," and in order to ensure against trouble, one day before the actual handover, Aben Comixa [Yūsuf ibn Kumāsha] and fifty other hostages from important families should give themselves up (once the city, etc., was surrendered, they were to be released). [S]

3. Isabel, Fernando, and Prince Juan (their son) would after the surrender accept all Granadans, from King Abi Abdilehi [Abū 'Abd Allah; Muḥammad XII] own, "great and small, men and women," as their vassals and natural subjects. In return the monarchs guaranteed to let them remain in their "houses, estates and hereditaments now and for all time and for ever, nor would they allow any harm to be done to them without due legal process and without cause, nor would they have their estates and property nor any part thereof taken from them, rather would they be honored and respected by all their vassals." [S]

Introductory information derived from L. P. Harvey, *Islamic Spain, 1250–1500* (Chicago: University of Chicago Press, 1990), pp. 314–15. English text reprinted from the same volume, pp. 315–21, with permission of the publisher.

4. To avoid creating an uproar *(escándalo)*, those who came to take over the Alhambra would enter by two named gates or from the side facing the country. [S]

5. The same day that Boabdil [Abū ʿAbd Allah] surrendered the fortresses, the king and queen would return to him his son and all the other hostages and their families, unless they had turned Christian. [S]

6. "Their highnesses and their successors will ever afterwards [*para siempre jamás*] allow King Abi Abdilehi and his *alcaides,* judges, *muftīs, alguaciles,* military leaders, and good men, and all the common people, great or small, to live in their own religion, and not permit that their mosques be taken from them, nor their minarets nor their muezzins, nor will they interfere with the pious foundations or endowments which they have for such purposes, nor will they disturb the uses and customs which they observe." [F]

7. "The Moors shall be judged in their laws and law suits according to the code of the *sharīʿa* which it is their custom to respect, under the jurisdiction of their judges and *qāḍīs.*" [F]

8. "Neither now nor at any future time will their arms or their horses be taken from them, with the exception of cannons, both large and small, which they will within a short space of time hand over to whomsoever their highnesses appoint for that purpose." [F]

9. "Those Moors, both great and small, men and women, whether from Granada or from the Alpujarra and all other places, who may wish to go to live in Barbary or to such other places as they see fit, may sell their property, whether it be real estate or goods and chattels, in any manner and to whomsoever they like, and their highnesses will at no time take them away, or take them from those who may have bought them." [S]

10. Those who wished to leave with their families and all their possessions of any kind whatsoever, except firearms, might do so. Those wishing to cross immediately might make use of the ten large ships provided for the purpose for the next seventy days from the port of their choice to "those ports of Barbary where Christian merchants normally trade." After this, and for three years, ships would be made available free at fifty days' notice. [S]

11. After the end of the three years, they should be free to go, but would have to pay one ducat a head and also the cost of the passage. [S]

12. If those going to Barbary were not able to sell their real estate in Granada (etc.) they could leave it in the hands of a trustee who would be entirely free to remit to Barbary any proceeds. [S]

13. "Neither their highnesses nor the Prince Juan their son nor those who may follow after them for all time will give instructions that those Moors

who are their vassals shall be obliged to wear distinctive marks like those worn by the Jews." [F]

14. Neither Boabdil nor any other Moor of Granada would have to pay taxes on their houses, etc., for three years, they would simply have to pay a tax of one-tenth in August and in autumn and one-tenth on cattle in their possession in April and May "as the Christians are accustomed to pay." [S]

15. All Christian captives were to be handed over at the moment of surrender, with no entitlement for ransom or compensation, although if the Granadan owner of the captive had taken him to North Africa and already sold him before the Capitulations came into force, he would not have to hand him back. [S]

16. Boabdil and his principal officers, etc., were exempt from having their transport animals requisitioned for any form of service (apart from work willingly undertaken for payment). [S]

17. No Christians might enter mosques where the Muslims perform their prayer without permission of the *alfaquíes*: anyone entering otherwise was to be punished. [S]

18. Their highnesses would not permit the Jews to have power or command over the Moors, or to be collectors of any tax. [S]

19. King Boabdil and all his dignitaries, and all the common people of Granada, etc., would be well treated by their highnesses and their ministers, "and that what they have to say will be listened to, and their customs and rites will be preserved, and all *alcaides* and *alfaquíes* will be allowed to collect their incomes and enjoy their preeminences and their liberties such as by custom they enjoy, and it is only right that they should continue to enjoy." [S]

20. "Their highnesses order that the Moors should not against their will have boarders forced upon them, nor have their linen, or their poultry or their animals or supplies of any sort taken from them." [F]

21. "Law suits which arise between Moors will be judged by their law *sharī'a*, which they call of the *sunna,* and by their *qāḍīs* and judges, as they customarily have, but if the suit should arise between a Christian and a Moor, then it will be judged by a Christian judge and a Moorish *qāḍī*, in order that neither side may have any grounds for complaint against the sentence." [F]

22. No Moor may be tried for another. [S]

23. A general pardon would be accorded to Moors found in the prison of Hamet Abi Ali "his vassal," and neither they nor the villages of Captil would be prosecuted for any Christians they had killed, nor would any harm be done to them, nor would they have to restore stolen goods. [S]

24. Any Moorish captives in Christian hands who succeeded in fleeing to Granada or other places included in these Capitulations would become free,

and their owners were barred from attempts to recover them making use of the law. Not included under this clause were Canary Islanders, and negroes from "the islands" (Cape Verde?). [S]

25. "That the Moors will not be obliged to give or pay more tribute to their highnesses than they used to give to the Moorish kings." [F]

26. Any Granadan Moors in North Africa could, if they wished, be included in the terms of the Capitulations; they had three years to return if they wished to do so. (If they had had Christian slaves and sold them, they would not be obliged to return them or the money so obtained.) [S]

27. If any Moor were to go to North Africa and then find he did not like the way of life, he could return and have all the benefits of the Capitulations, so long as he returned within three years. [S]

28. Any Moors accepting the Capitulations who wished to cross to North Africa for purposes of trade would be freely permitted to do so; also to any places in Castile or Andalusia, with no tolls to pay other than those commonly paid by Christians. [S]

29. Nobody would be permitted to abuse by word or by deed any Christian man or woman who before the date of the Capitulations had turned Moor, and if any Moor had taken a renegade for his wife, she would not be forced to become a Christian against her will, but might be questioned in the presence of Christians and Moors, and be allowed to follow her own will; the same was to be understood of children born of a Christian mother and a Moor. [S]

30. "No Moor will be forced to become Christian against his or her will, and if for reasons of love an unmarried girl or a married woman or a widow should wish to become Christian, she will not be received [into the church] until she has been questioned. And if she has taken away from her parents' house clothing or jewels, these will be restored to the rightful owner, and guilty persons will be dealt with by the law." [F]

31. Neither the King Abi Abdilehi nor any of the Muslims included in the Capitulations might be called to account for any cattle, property, etc., taken during the war, whether from Christians or from Muslims who were Mudejars or who were not Mudejars. If any persons recognized objects as theirs, they were not entitled to ask for them back and indeed could be punished if they did. [S]

32. If any Moor had wounded or insulted any Christian man or woman held in captivity, no legal proceedings could be instituted against him ever. [S]

33. After the initial three-year tax holiday the Muslims would not have heavier taxes imposed on them than was just, bearing in mind value and quality. [S]

34. "The judges, *alcaides,* and governors which their highnesses appoint in the city and region of Granada will be persons such as will honor the Moors and treat them kindly [*amorosamente*], and continue to respect these Capitulations. And if anyone should do anything which he ought not to do, their highnesses will have him moved from his post and punished." [F]

35. Neither Boabdil nor anybody else would be called to account for things done before the city surrendered. [S]

36. "No *alcaide,* squire, or servant of the king al-Zagal[1] may hold any office or command at any time over the Moors of Granada." [F]

37. As a favor to King Abi Abdilehi and the inhabitants both men and women of Granada, the Albaicín, and other suburbs [no mention of the Alpujarras here], they would give orders for the release of all Moorish prisoners, whether male or female, without any payment at all: those in Andalusia within five months, those in Castile, eight. Within two days of the handover by the Moors of any Christian captives in Granada, their highnesses would have two hundred Moorish men and women released. "And in addition we will place at liberty Aben Adrami, who is held by Gonzalo Hernández de Córdoba, and Hozmin ['Uthmān] who is held by the count of Tendilla, and Ben Reduan, held by the count of Cabra, and Aben Mueden and the *alfaquí* Hademi's son, all of them leading residents of Granada, also the five shield-bearers [*escuderos*] who were taken when Brahem Abencerrax [Ibrāhīm Ibn Sarrāj] was defeated, if their whereabouts can be discovered." [S]

38. The Moors of the Alpujarras who had accepted vassalage would surrender all their Christian captives within two weeks for no payment. [S]

39. "Their highnesses will order that the customs of the Moors relating to inheritances will be respected, and in such matters the judges will be their own *qāḍīs*." [F]

40. "All Moors other than those included in this agreement who desire to enter their highnesses' service within thirty days may do so and enjoy all the benefits of it, other than the three-year period of tax exemption." [F]

41. "The pious endowments [*habices*] and the emoluments of the mosques, and the alms and other things customarily given to colleges [*madrasas*] and schools where children are taught will be the responsibility of the *alfaquíes,* to distribute them as they see fit, and their highnesses and their ministers will not interfere in this nor any aspect of it, nor will they give orders with regard to their confiscation or sequestration at any time ever in the future." [F]

42. North African ships in Granadan ports would, so long as they carried

---

1. Muḥammad XIII, known as 'Abd Allah al-Zajal, was Boabdil's uncle.

no Christian captives, be free to leave, and while in port were free from vexation and requisition of property, but they must submit to inspection on departure. [S]

43. Muslims would not be conscripted for military service against their will, and if their highnesses wished to recruit cavalry [no mention of infantry] for service in Andalusia, they would be paid from the day they left home until the date of return. [S]

44. No changes would be made in regulations affecting water courses and irrigation channels, and anybody throwing any unclean thing in a channel would be prosecuted. [S]

45. If any Moorish captive had arranged for someone else to stand as proxy for him in captivity and had then absconded, neither of them would have to pay a ransom. [S]

46. Nobody as a result of the change of sovereignty would be allowed to escape from contractual debt obligations. [S]

47. Christian slaughterhouses would be separated from Muslim ones. [S]

48. "The Jews native to Granada, Albaicín, and other suburbs, and of the Alpujarras and all other places contained in these Capitulations, will benefit from them, on condition that those who do not become Christians cross to North Africa within three years counting from December 8 of this year." [F]

"And their highnesses will give orders for the totality of the contents of these Capitulations to be observed from the day when the fortresses of Granada are surrendered onwards. To which effect they have commanded that their royal charter and deed should be signed with their names and sealed with their seal and witnessed by Hernando de Zafra their secretary, and have so done, dated in the *vega* of Granada on this 28th day of the month of November of the year of our salvation 1491." [F]

C. *Nubdhat al-ʿaṣr*

Translated from Arabic by L. P. Harvey

There is much less information on the surrender of Granada from the Muslim point of view than that provided by Christian sources. However, the anonymous Arabic chronicle Nubdhat al-ʿaṣr describes the process of public debate that led to the decision to surrender the city to Fernando and Isabel. (ORC)

English text from L. P. Harvey, *Islamic Spain, 1250–1500* (Chicago: University of Chicago Press, 1990), pp. 310–11. Reprinted with permission of the publisher. For further discussion of this text, see the same volume, pp. 307–14.

When the month of Safar of the year in question [897 = 1491] came, the situation of the people became very much worse because of starvation and lack of food supplies, even many rich people being affected by hunger.

So there came together the leading men, nobles [*khāṣṣa*] and common folk alike, with the Islamic lawyers [*fuqahāʾ*], the guild wardens, the elders, learned men, such courageous knights [*anjād al-fursān*] as were still alive, and anybody in Granada with some insight into affairs. They all went to see their amīr Muḥammad ibn ʿAlī [Boabdil], and informed him of the condition of the people, how weak they were, and how afflicted by hunger, how little food there was. Their city was a great one, for which normal food imports were hardly sufficient, so how could it manage when nothing was being brought in at all? The route used to bring in food and fruit supplies from the Alpujarras had been cut. The best of the knights were all dead and passed away, and those that remained were weakened by wounds. The people were prevented from going out to seek food, or to cultivate the land, or to plough. Their heroes had been killed in the battles.

They then went on to say to him: "Our brethren the Muslims who live across the sea in the Magrib have already been approached, and none of them have come to help or risen to our assistance. Our enemy has already constructed siege works and is getting ever stronger, whereas we are getting weaker. They receive supplies from their own country, we receive nothing. The winter season has already begun, and the enemy's army has dispersed and is thus not at full strength, and military operations against us have been suspended. If we were to open talks with them now, our approach would be well received, and they would agree to what we ask. If we wait till spring has come, his armies will assemble to attack us, and we will be weaker still, and the famine even worse. He will not again be prepared to agree to the terms we are seeking, and we and our city may not be saved from military conquest. What is more, many of our folk have fled to his camp, and they will act as guides to point out to him our vulnerable spots, and he will make use of them against us."

The amīr Muḥammad ibn ʿAlī [Boabdil] said to them, "Give consideration to what seems best to you, and reach a unanimous agreement on what will be to your good."

It was agreed by nobles and commoners alike that they should send an emissary to have talks with the Christian king about their concerns, and those of the city.

Many people alleged that the amīr of Granada and his ministers and military chiefs had already made an agreement to hand over the city to the Christian king who was invading them, but they feared the common people, and so kept them duped, and simply told them what they wanted to hear. This was why, when they [the people] came saying what the king and his ministers had been keeping secret from them, they pardoned them on the spot. This was why military operations had been suspended at that time, to give scope for them to find a way of introducing the idea to the common people. So when they sent to the king of the Christians, they found he readily agreed, and was happy to grant all their requests and all their stipulations.

85. THE EXPULSION OF THE JEWS

After the surrender of Granada in January 1492, Fernando and Isabel decided to expel the Jews from their joint kingdoms of Castile and Aragón. The three texts below document this event, first in the charter issued by the Catholic Monarchs in March 1492, second in an anonymous account from Italy (where many of the exiled Iberian Jews found refuge) written in 1495, and third in a poem by Judah Abravanel from 1503. (ORC)

A. Charter of Expulsion (1492)
Translated from Castilian by Edward Peters

This charter is noteworthy in numerous respects. First, it is as broadly addressed as any document that Fernando and Isabel ever issued. Its prologue, or arenga *(the first part of a charter in which the general reasons for its issuance are given) states that Christians (i.e.,* conversos, *although they are not categorized as such) have apostatized because Jews have attempted successfully to (re)convert them to Judaism. The kings note that they have been concerned with this problem since as early as 1480; in the cortes of Toledo that year they had given instructions that Jews were to be separated from Christians and settled in* aljamas, *Jewish quarters of residence. The Spanish Inquisition was established precisely because of the problem of relations between* conversos *and Jews, and one of its results was the list of criminal acts allegedly committed by Jews against Christians. Even the expulsion of the Jews from Andalusia had proved insufficient to stop Christian apostatizing; nothing had changed between 1480 and 1492. Just as every organization whose members committed criminal acts was dissolved or expelled from the kingdom, regardless of the innocence of some of its members, so the Jews were expelled from the realms of Fernando and Isabel.*

The last part of the arenga, *immediately preceding the dispository clauses—the bulk of any charter containing its actual terms or commands—is an important indication of the rulers' use of contemporary criminal legal theory concerning punitive exile and the expulsion of criminals in general, as well as the problem of the legal disposition of criminal groups or corporations. The charges against Jews made as a result of the activities of the Inquisition laid the groundwork for the application to Jews of other criminal legal doctrine, since the offenses with which Jews were charged were precisely those that brought Jews under the jurisdiction of the Inquisition. This*

Translation based on the fullest version of the text, *Documentos acerca de la expulsion de los judios,* edited by Luis Suárez-Fernández (Valladolid: C.S.I.C., 1964), no. 177, pp. 391–95. One necessary emendation has been made based on Fidel Fita, "Edicto de los Reyes Católicos (31 marzo 1492) desterrando de sus estados a todos los judios," *Boletín de la Real Academia de la Historia* 11 (1887): 512–28. English text from Edward Peters, "Jewish History and Gentile Memory: The Expulsion of 1492," *Jewish History* 9 (1995): 9–34, at 23–28. Reprinted with permission of the publisher.

religious argument, bolstered by the terminology of contemporary criminal legal theory and practice, constitutes the rulers' justification for the expulsion. The boiler-plate character of much of the charter's language indicates a remarkable degree of inclusiveness and thoroughness in imposing sanctions.

Although the charter is dated 31 March 1492, it was not actually issued until a month later, thereby giving Spanish Jews only three months, instead of the original four, in which to prepare for the expulsion. The delay may have been caused by attempts to persuade the monarchs to rescind the order, for which there is substantial contemporary evidence. In the end, these attempts failed. (EP)

31 March 1492. Granada

[1] Lord Fernando and Lady Isabel, by the grace of God king and queen of Castile, León, Aragón, Sicily, Granada, Toledo, Valencia, Galicia, the Balearic Islands, Seville, Sardinia, Córdoba, Corsica, Murcia, Jaén, of the Algarve, Algeciras, Gibraltar, and of the Canary Islands, count and countess of Barcelona and lords of Biscay and Molina, dukes of Athens and Neopatria, counts of Rousillon and Cerdaña, marquises of Oristan and of Gociano, to the prince Lord Juan, our very dear and much loved son, and to the [other] royal children, prelates, dukes, marquises, counts, masters of [military] orders, priors, grandees, knight commanders, governors of castles and fortified places of our kingdoms and lordships, and to councils, magistrates, mayors, constables, district judges, knights, official squires, and all good men of the noble and loyal city of Burgos and other cities, towns, and villages of its bishopric and of other archbishoprics, bishoprics, dioceses of our kingdoms and lordships, and to the residential quarters of the Jews of the said city of Burgos and of all the aforesaid cities, towns, and villages of its bishopric and of the other cities, towns, and villages of our aforementioned kingdoms and lordships, and to all Jews and to all individual Jews of those places, and to barons and women of whatever age they may be, and to all other persons of whatever law, estate, dignity, preeminence, and condition they may be, and to all to whom the matter contained in this charter pertains or may pertain. Salutations and grace.

[2] You know well, or ought to know, that whereas we have been informed that in these our kingdoms there were some wicked Christians who Judaized and apostatized from our holy Catholic faith, the great cause of which was interaction between the Jews and these Christians, in the cortes which we held in the city of Toledo in the past year of one thousand, four hundred and eighty, we ordered the separation of the said Jews in all the cities, towns, and villages of our kingdoms and lordships and [commanded] that they be given Jewish quarters and separated places where they should live, hoping that by their separation the situation would remedy itself. Furthermore, we procured

and gave orders that inquisition should be made in our aforementioned kingdoms and lordships, which as you know has for twelve years been made and
is being made, and by it many guilty persons have been discovered, as is very
well known, and accordingly we are informed by the inquisitors and by other
devout persons, ecclesiastical and secular, that great injury has resulted and
still results, since the Christians have engaged in and continue to engage in
social interaction and communication they have had and continue to have
with Jews, who, it seems, seek always and by whatever means and ways they
can to subvert and to steal faithful Christians from our holy Catholic faith and
to separate them from it, and to draw them to themselves and subvert them
to their own wicked belief and conviction, instructing them in the ceremonies
and observances of their law, holding meetings at which they read and teach
that which people must hold and believe according to their law, achieving that
the Christians and their children be circumcised, and giving them books from
which they may read their prayers and declaring to them the fasts that they
must keep, and joining with them to read and teach them the history of their
law, indicating to them the festivals before they occur, advising them of what
in them they are to hold and observe, carrying to them and giving to them
from their houses unleavened bread and meats ritually slaughtered, instructing them about the things from which they must refrain, as much in eating as
in other things in order to observe their law, and persuading them as much as
they can to hold and observe the law of Moses, convincing them that there
is no other law or truth except for that one. This proved by many statements
and confessions, both from these same Jews and from those who have been
perverted and enticed by them, which has redounded to the great injury, detriment, and opprobrium of our holy Catholic faith.

[3] Notwithstanding that we were informed of the great part of this before now and we knew that the true remedy for all these injuries and inconveniences was to prohibit all interaction between the said Jews and Christians
and banish them [the Jews] from all our kingdoms, we desired to content
ourselves by commanding them to leave all cities, towns, and villages of Andalusia where it appears that they have done the greatest injury, believing that
that would be sufficient so that those of other cities, towns, and villages of
our kingdoms and lordships would cease to do and commit the aforesaid acts.
And since we are informed that neither that step nor the passing of sentence
[of condemnation] against the said Jews who have been most guilty of the
said crimes and delicts against our holy Catholic faith have been sufficient
as a complete remedy to obviate and correct so great an opprobrium and
offense to the faith and the Christian religion, because every day it is found
and appears that the said Jews increase in continuing their evil and wicked

purpose wherever they live and congregate, and so that there will not be any place where they further offend our holy faith, and corrupt those whom God has until now most desired to preserve, as well as those who had fallen but amended and returned to Holy Mother Church, the which according to the weakness of our humanity and by diabolical astuteness and suggestion that continually wages war against us may easily occur unless the principal cause of it be removed, which is to banish the said Jews from our kingdoms. Because whenever any grave and detestable crime is committed by members of any organization or corporation, it is reasonable that such an organization or corporation should be dissolved and annihilated and that the lesser members as well as the greater and everyone for the others be punished, and that those who perturb the good and honest life of cities and towns and by contagion can injure others should be expelled from those places and even if for lighter causes that may be injurious to the Republic, how much more for those greater and most dangerous and most contagious crimes such as this.

[4] Therefore, we, with the counsel and advice of prelates, great noblemen of our kingdoms, and other persons of learning and wisdom of our council, having taken deliberation about this matter, resolve to order the said Jews and Jewesses of our kingdoms to depart and never to return or come back to them or to any of them. And concerning this we command this our charter to be given, by which we order all Jews and Jewesses of whatever age they may be, who live, reside, and exist in our said kingdoms and lordships, as much those who are natives as those who are not, who by whatever manner or whatever cause have come to live and reside therein, that by the end of the month of July next of the present year, they depart from all of these our said realms and lordships, along with their sons and daughters, manservants and maidservants, Jewish familiars, those who are great as well as the lesser folk, of whatever age they may be, and they shall not dare to return to those places, nor to reside in them, nor to live in any part of them, neither temporarily on the way to somewhere else nor in any other manner, under pain that if they do not perform and comply with this command and should be found in our said kingdom and lordships and should in any manner live in them, they incur the penalty of death and the confiscation of all their possessions by our Chamber of Finance, incurring these penalties by the act itself, without further trial, sentence, or declaration. And we command and forbid that any person or persons of the said kingdoms, of whatever estate, condition, or dignity that they may be, shall dare to receive, protect, defend, nor hold publicly or secretly any Jew or Jewess beyond the date of the end of July and from henceforth forever, in their lands, houses, or in other parts of any of our said kingdoms and lordships, under pain of losing all their possessions, vassals,

fortified places, and other inheritances, and beyond this of losing whatever financial grants they hold from us by our Chamber of Finance.

[5] And so that the said Jews and Jewesses during the stated period of time until the end of the said month of July may be better able to dispose of themselves, and their possessions, and their estates, for the present we take and receive them under our security, protection, and royal safeguard, and we secure to them and to their possessions that for the duration of the said time until the said last day of the said month of July they may travel and be safe, they may enter, sell, trade, and alienate all their movable and rooted possessions and dispose of them freely and at their will, and that during the said time, no one shall harm them, nor injure them, no wrong shall be done to them against justice, in their persons or in their possessions, under the penalty which falls on and is incurred by those who violate the royal safeguard. And we likewise give license and faculty to those said Jews and Jewesses that they be able to export their goods and estates out of these our said kingdoms and lordships by sea or land as long as they do not export gold or silver or coined money or other things prohibited by the laws of our kingdoms, excepting merchandise and things that are not prohibited.

[6] And we command all councils, justices, magistrates, knights, squires, officials, and all good men of the said city of Burgos and of the other cities, towns, and villages of our said kingdoms and lordships and all our new vassals, subjects, and natives that they preserve and comply with and cause to be preserved and complied with this our charter and all that is contained in it, and to give and to cause to be given all assistance and favor in its application under penalty of [being at] our mercy and the confiscation of all their possessions and offices by our Chamber of Finance. And because this must be brought to the notice of all, so that no one may pretend ignorance, we command that this our charter be posted in the customary plazas and places of the said city and of the principal cities, towns, and villages of its bishopric as an announcement and as a public document. And no one shall do any damage to it in any manner under penalty of being at our mercy and the deprivation of their offices and the confiscation of their possessions, which will happen to each one who might do this. Moreover, we command the [man] who shows them this our charter that he summon [those who act against the charter] to appear before us at our court wherever we may be, on the day that they are summoned during the fifteen days following the crime under the said penalty, under which we command whichever public scribe who would be called for the purpose of reading this our charter that the signed charter with its seal should be shown to you all so that we may know that our command is carried out.

[7] Given in our city of Granada, the XXXI day of the month of March,

the year of the birth of our lord Jesus Christ one thousand four hundred and ninety-two years. I, the king, I, the queen, I, Juan de Coloma, secretary of the king and queen our lords, have caused this to be written at their command. Registered by Cabrera, Almacan chancellor.

B. Jewish Account of the Expulsion (1495)
Translated from Hebrew by Jacob R. Marcus

This anonymous account of the expulsion was written in Italy in the spring of 1495.

And in the year 5252 [1492], in the days of King Fernando, the Lord visited the remnant of his people a second time and exiled them.[1] After the King had captured the city of Granada from the Moors, and it had surrendered to him on the 7th of January[2] of the year just mentioned, he ordered the expulsion of all the Jews in all parts of his kingdom—in the kingdoms of Castile, Catalonia, Aragón, Galicia, Mallorca, Minorca, the Basque provinces, the islands of Sardinia and Sicily, and the kingdom of Valencia. Even before that the Queen had expelled them from the kingdom of Andalusia [1483].

The King gave them three months' time in which to leave. It was announced in public in every city on the first of May, which happened to be the 19th day of the *Omer*, and the term ended on the day before the 9th of Ab.[3]

About their number there is no agreement, but, after many inquiries, I found that the most generally accepted estimate is 50,000 families, or, as others say, 53,000. They had houses, fields, vineyards, and cattle, and most of them were artisans. At that time there existed many [Talmudic] academies in Spain, and at the head of the greatest of them were Rabbi Isaac Aboab in Guadalajara, Rabbi Isaac Veçudo in León, and Rabbi Jacob Habib in Salamanca. In the last named city there was a great expert in mathematics, and whenever there was any doubt on mathematical questions in the Christian academy of that city they referred them to him. His name was Abraham Zacuto. . . .[4]

In the course of the three months' respite granted them they endeavored to effect an arrangement permitting them to stay on in the country,

Translation from Jacob R. Marcus, *The Jew in the Medieval World: A Source Book, 315–1791* (New York: Atheneum, 1979), pp. 51–55. Reprinted with permission of the copyright holder.
    1. For the first visitation, the author probably refers to the pogroms of 1391.
    2. Actually, the second of January.
    3. The forty-nine days between the second of Passover and Shabuot are called Omer days. The actual decree of expulsion was signed on 31 March and announced on 1 May, 19th day of the Omer. The Jews were to leave during May, June, and July and be out of the country by 1 August, 8th of Ab.
    4. This famous astronomer encouraged the expedition of Vasco da Gama.

and they felt confident of success. Their representatives were the rabbi, Don Abraham Seneor, the leader of the Spanish congregations, who was attended by a retinue on thirty mules, and Rabbi Meïr Melamed, who was secretary to the King, and Don Isaac Abravanel, who had fled to Castile from the King of Portugal, and then occupied an equally prominent position at the Spanish royal court.[5] He, too, was later expelled, went to Naples, and was highly esteemed by the King of Naples. The aforementioned great rabbi, Rabbi Isaac of León, used to call this Don Abraham Seneor: "Soné Or"[6] because he was a heretic, and the end proved that he was right, as he was converted to Christianity at the age of eighty, he and all his family, and Rabbi Meïr Melamed with him.[7] Don Abraham had arranged the nuptials between the King and the Queen. The Queen was the heiress to the throne, and the King one of the Spanish nobility. On account of this, Don Abraham was appointed leader of the Jews, but not with their consent.

The agreement permitting them to remain in the country on the payment of a large sum of money was almost completed when it was frustrated by the interference of a prior who was called the Prior of Santa Cruz.[8] Then the Queen gave an answer to the representatives of the Jews, similar to the saying of King Solomon: "The king's heart is in the hand of the Lord, as the rivers of water. God turneth it withersoever He will" [Prov. 21:1]. She said furthermore: "Do you believe that this comes upon you from us? The Lord hath put this thing into the heart of the king."

Then they saw that there was evil determined against them by the King, and they gave up the hope of remaining. But the time had become short, and they had to hasten their exodus from Spain. They sold their houses, their landed estates, and their cattle for very small prices, to save themselves. The King did not allow them to carry silver and gold out of his country, so that they were compelled to exchange their silver and gold for merchandise of cloths and skins and other things.

One hundred and twenty thousand of them went to Portugal, according to a compact which a prominent man, Don Vidal bar Benveniste del Cavalleria, had made with the King of Portugal, and they paid one ducat for every soul, and the fourth part of all the merchandise they had carried thither; and he allowed them to stay in his country six months. This King acted much worse toward them than the King of Spain, and after the six months had

---

5. Isaac Abravanel (1437–1508) was the father of Judah Abravenel, author of the poem.
6. "Hater of Light," a Hebrew pun on Seneor.
7. Seneor and his son-in-law Meïr were converted 15 June 1492; Fernando and Isabel were among the sponsors.
8. Tomás de Torquemada was prior of the convent of Santa Cruz.

[handwritten margin note: anti-refugee laws not from marriage]

elapsed he made slaves of all those that remained in his country, and banished seven hundred children to a remote island to settle it, and all of them died. Some say that there were double as many. Upon them the Scriptural word was fulfilled: "Thy sons and thy daughters shall be given unto another people, etc."[9] He also ordered the congregation of Lisbon, his capital, not to raise their voice in their prayers, that the Lord might not hear their complaining about the violence that was done unto them.

Many of the exiled Spaniards went to Mohammedan countries, to Fez, Tlemçen, and the Berber provinces, under the king of Tunis. On account of their large numbers the Moors did not allow them into their cities, and many of them died in the fields from hunger, thirst, and lack of everything. The lions and bears, which are numerous in this country, killed some of them while they lay starving outside of the cities. A Jew in the kingdom of Tlemçen, named Abraham, the viceroy who ruled the kingdom, made part of them come to this kingdom, and he spent a large amount of money to help them. The Jews of Northern Africa were very charitable toward them. A part of those who went to Northern Africa, as they found no rest and no place that would receive them, returned to Spain, and became converts, and through them the prophecy of Jeremiah was fulfilled: "He hath spread a net for my feet, he hath turned me back" [Lam. 1:13]. For, originally, they had all fled for the sake of the unity of God; only a very few had become converts throughout all the boundaries of Spain; they did not spare their fortunes; yea, parents escaped without having regard to their children.

When the edict of expulsion became known in the other countries, vessels came from Genoa to the Spanish harbors to carry away the Jews. The crews of these vessels, too, acted maliciously and meanly toward the Jews, robbed them, and delivered some of them to the famous pirate of that time who was called the Corsair of Genoa. To those who escaped and arrived at Genoa the people of the city showed themselves merciless, and oppressed and robbed them, and the cruelty of their wicked hearts went so far that they took the infants from the mothers' breasts.

Many ships with Jews, especially from Sicily, went to the city of Naples on the coast. The King of this country was friendly to the Jews, received them all, and was merciful towards them, and he helped them with money. The Jews that were at Naples supplied them with food as much as they could, and sent around to the other parts of Italy to collect money to sustain them. The

9. Deuteronomy 28:32. All Spanish Jews who were still in Portugal in 1493 were enslaved by King João (1481–1495). The children were sent to the isle of St. Thomas, off the coast of Africa.

marranos in this city lent them money on pledges without interest; even the Dominican Brotherhood acted mercifully toward them. On account of their very large number, all this was not enough. Some of them died by famine, others sold their children to Christians to sustain their life. Finally, a plague broke out among them, spread to Naples, and very many of them died, so that the living wearied of burying the dead.

Part of the exiled Spaniards went over sea to Turkey. Some of them were thrown into the sea and drowned, but those who arrived there the King of Turkey received kindly, as they were artisans. He lent them money and settled many of them on an island, and gave them fields and estates.

A few of the exiles were dispersed in the countries of Italy, in the city of Ferrara, in the [papal] countries of Romagna, the March, and Patrimonium, and in Rome. . . .

He who said unto His world, Enough, may He also say Enough unto our sufferings, and may He look down upon our impotence. May He turn again, and have compassion upon us, and hasten our salvation. Thus may it be Thy will.

C. Judah Abravanel, Poem to His Son (1503)
Translated from Hebrew by Raymond P. Scheindlin

This Hebrew poem by Judah Leon Abravanel (ca. 1460 –ca. 1535; also known as Leone Ebreo) is an anguished expression of the dislocation experienced by a prominent Jewish aristocrat caught up in the expulsion of the Jews from Spain. It was written in Italy in 1503 and addressed to the poet's twelve-year-old son Isaac, then living in Portugal. The family had originally lived in Portugal, then moved to Castile in 1483 when Judah's father, Isaac, fell from grace at the Portuguese court. After the 1492 Edict of Expulsion in Castile, however, the infant Isaac was sent to live with relatives in Portugal for safety, while his father and grandfather later fled to Italy. Unfortunately, Manuel I of Portugal ordered the forced baptism of Jewish refugee children in 1497, an edict that applied to young Isaac. This letter was written to Isaac while Judah was serving as a doctor to the Spanish viceroy in Naples, and it may have been prompted by the expectation of bringing Isaac to Italy. In the poem, Judah not only rails against fate, but admonishes his son to live up to family traditions. Clearly, as with many marranos *[Jews who had converted to Christianity under pressure but still considered themselves Jewish], Isaac had access to some Jewish education despite his conversion. We do not know what happened next, or whether father and son were ever reunited. Isaac may have left Portugal in 1507, when* marranos *were given permission to leave the country, and a Jew bearing his name turned up in Salonica in 1558. (ORC & RPS)*

Hebrew text published by Hayim Schirmann, *Mivhar hashira ha'ivrit beitalya* (Berlin: Schocken, 1934), pp. 217–22. English text from "Judah Abravanel to His Sons," *Judaism* 41 (Spring 1992). Reprinted with permission of the American Jewish Congress.

Time with his pointed shafts has hit my heart
and split my gut, laid open my entrails,
landed me a blow that will not heal,
knocked me down, left me in lasting pain.
Time wounded me, wasted away my flesh,
used up my blood and fat in suffering,
ground my bones to meal, and rampaged, leapt,
attacked me like a lion in his rage.

*   *   *

He did not stop at whirling me around,
exiling me while yet my days were green,
sending me stumbling, drunk, to roam the world,
spinning me dizzy round about its edge -
so that I've spent two decades on the move
without my horses ever catching breath—
so that my palms have measured oceans, weighed
the dust of continents—so that my spring
is spent—
        no, that was not enough:
He chased my friends from me, exiled
my age-mates, sent my family far
so that I never see a face I know—
father, mother, brothers, or a friend.
He scattered everyone I care for northward,
eastward, or to the west, so that
I have no rest from constant thinking, planning—
and never a moment's peace, for all my plans.
Now that I see my future in the East,
their separation clutches at my heels.
My foot is turned to go, but my heart's at sea;
I can't tell forward from behind.
                Yes, Time—
my bear, my wolf!—ate up my heart, cleft
it in two and cut it into bits, so that it aches with groaning, panic, plunder,
confiscation, loss, captivity.
But even this was not enough for him; he also seeks
to snuff my spark, exterminate my line.

Two sons were born to me, two splendid sons,
two precious, noble, handsome boys.
The younger I named Samuel. Time,
my watchful overseer, confiscated him,
struck him down, just five years old,
and all that grew from him was misery.
The elder I called Isaac Abravanel,
after the quarry where I myself was hewn,
after one of Israel's greats, his grandfather,
a man a match for David, Lamp unto the West.
At birth I saw that he was good,
his heart a fitting site for wisdom, apt
repository for the goods
his forebears handed down through me.
He was just one year old—alas!—when Time,
the enemy ever at my heels, took him away.
The day the King of Spain expelled the Jews
he ordered that a watch be set for me
so that I not slip away through mountain passes,
and that my child, still nursing, should be seized
and brought into his faith on his behalf.
A good man got word to me in time, a friend;
I sent him with his wet-nurse in the dark
of midnight—just like smuggled goods!—
to Portugal, then ruled by a wicked king
who earlier had nearly ruined me.
For in his father's time—a worthy king!—
my father had achieved success and wealth.
Then this one followed him, a grasping thing,
a man but with the cravings of a dog.
His courtiers and his brother schemed revolt.
He thwarted them and killed his brother; then,
alleging that my father was with them,
he tried to kill him too![1] But God,
the Rider of the clouds, preserved his life.
My father fled to Castile, home of my ancestors,

---

1. Judah Abravanel's father was Don Isaac Abravanel, a courtier and financier of Fernando and Isabel and a rabbi of great renown. His commentaries on the Bible are classic works of Jewish religious scholarship.

my family's source. But as for me,
the King seized all my gold and silver,
took as forfeit everything I owned.

*   *   *

Now, seeing that my child was in his land,
and learning that I planned
to join my father's house in Italy,
the King detained my child and gave command
that none should send my stray lamb back to me.
After he died a foolish king arose,
fanatical and hollow in the head,
who violated all the House of Jacob,
turned my noble people to his faith.
Many killed themselves, rather than
transgress the Law of God, our help in need.
My darling boy was taken, and his good name,
the name of the rock from which I was hewn changed!
He's twelve years old; I haven't seen him since—
so are my sins repaid!
I rage, but only at myself;
There's no one else but me to bear the blame.
I chased him from mere troubles to a trap,
I drove him from mere sparks into a flame.
I hope to see him, heartsick with my endless hope.

*   *   *

O dear gazelle! What makes you tarry so?
Why do you thus crush a father's heart?
Why do you aim your arrows at my inmost parts?
Why do you dim the light by sending clouds
and make the shining seem like night to me?
The moon is always darkened in my sight,
my star is blotted out by clouds;
no sun's ray ever penetrates my home,
or crosses my doorsill to reach my beams.
My roses never bloom on Sharon's plain,
my grasses never feel the driving rain.

You steal my very sleep with the thought of you—
am I sleeping or awake? I cannot tell.
I cannot touch my food, for even honey
stings, and sweets taste venomous to me.
Miserably I nibble coal-burnt crusts,
moistening with tears my dried-out bread.
My only drink is water mixed with tears;
the blood of grapes does not come near my mouth.
I'm drunk with nothing more than water,
like a Nazirite or one of Rechab's sons.

*   *   *

But when I dream of your return, and when
I picture in my mind's eye how you look,
how good my fortune seems! The rose returns
to dress my cheek in sanguine once again.
I sleep and find sleep sweet; I wake
refreshed, delighting in your lingering image.
The water that I drink is sweet, and even earth
tastes sweet when I imagine you are here.
But when I think about our separation,
heat blasts my heart, a desert wind within.
I seem like one dismayed or in a faint,
diminished somehow and reduced in size.
The thought of you is joy to me and pain,
tonic and torment are from you, balm and bane.
I have your image graven on my heart,
but also our separation in my core,
and any joy your image brings to me
cannot outweigh the reproach your absence speaks.
Your absence frustrates all my plans,
your exile blocks, diverts my roads.

*   *   *

Let me go back to speaking to my boy,
for that will make him leave off hurting me.
Now pay attention, son: Know that you
descend from scholars, men with minds

developed to the point of prophecy.
Wisdom is your heritage, so do not waste
your boyhood, precious boy.
Think of your studies as pleasure: learning Scripture,
conning the commentators, memorizing
Mishna, reasoning out the Talmud
with the Thirteen Principles, guided by
the glosses of the ancient Schools . . .[2]
—But how can I control myself when *he* is lost?
That is the thought that sickens, strangles, slashes me;
that is the razor, sharper than any barber's blade,
that rips the membrane of my aching heart,
that brings into my miserable heart
into my very gut the naming sword:
To whom will I hand on my scholarship?
To whom can I pour the nectar from my vines?
Who will taste and eat the fruit of all
my learning, of my books, when I am gone?
Who will penetrate the mysteries
my father put into his sacred books?
Who will slake his thirst at my father's well?
Who will drink at all in this time of drought?
Who will pluck the blooms of my own garden,
hew and harvest my own wisdom's tree?
Who will take my undone works in hand?
Who will weave my writings' woof and warp?
Who will wear the emblem of my faith
when once I die?
Who will mount my mule or ride my coach?—
Only you, my soul's delight, my heir,

---

2. The curriculum Judah is recommending to young Isaac was the standard curriculum of rabbinic education, indeed, of Jewish religious education in general, from the Middle Ages until recent times.

Mishna is the fundamental text of rabbinic law, the basis of all later legal compilations and codes. It was composed in the last part of the second century by Rabbi Juday the Prince.

The Talmud is the great compendium of rabbinic lore, organized as a commentary on the Mishna, but actually constituting an independent work of considerable complexity. Its study is the main subject of advanced religious training in Judaism. There are in fact two different works called the Talmud, one compiled in Palestine around A.D. 400 and the other in Iraq around A.D. 500. The latter is the one usually meant.

The Thirteen Principles are the hermeneutical techniques used by the early rabbis in deriving legal rulings from the laws of the Torah. Their formulation is attributed to Rabbi Ismael ibn Elisha (early second century A.D.).

the pledge for everything I owe to God.
   For you, my son, my heart is thirsting, burning;
in you I quell my hunger and my thirst.
My splendid skills are yours by right, my knowledge,
and the science that has gotten fame for me.
Some of it my mentor, my own father
bequeathed to me—a scholar's scholar he;
the rest I gained by struggling on my own,
subduing wisdom with my bow and sword,
plumbing it with my mind. Christian scholars
are grasshoppers next to me. I've seen their colleges—
they've no one who can best me in the duel of words.
I beat down any man who stands against me,
crush and hush my opponent, prove him wrong.
Who but me would dare to tell the mysteries
of the Creation, of the Chariot, of its Rider?
My soul excels, surpasses all the souls
of my contemporaries in this wretched age.
My Form is fortified by God, my Rock,
locked, imprisoned in my body's cage.
It yearns for you to surpass my degree;
I always hoped that you would outdo me.

*   *   *

Dear one, what keeps you with an unclean folk,
an apple tree alone amid the carobs,
a pure soul lost among the nations,
a rose among the desert thorns and weeds?
Set out upon the road to me, my dear.
Fly, bound like a fawn or a gazelle,
and make your way to your father's house, who sired you
(may God protect you, Who protected me!).
May the Lord give you smooth roads to travel,
lift you out of straits to my ample court,
heap upon your head my forefathers' bounty,
besides my father's and my grandfather's wealth.
Then He will light my spirit in its darkness,
and redirect my footsteps to the plain.
I now commend my son to God, my shepherd,

and cast my burden on my Highest Father.
He will bring my dear son to my presence:
When I call my darling boy will hear.
Then I will sing a love-song to my Maker,
hymning my passion to Him while I live,
bringing my offering, setting my gift before Him.
My song it is that binds me to my Holy One.
The best of me is in it: my heart and eyes.
O may it please Him like the Temple rams;
my hymn, my words, like bulls upon His altar.
And may He show me Zion in her splendor,
the royal city of my anointed king,
and over it, two luminaries, equals:
Messiah, son of David and Elijah.
May never enemy again divide her,
or nomad pitch his tent in her again.

86. THE CASTILIAN NEW WORLD

Letter from Christopher Columbus to the Catholic Monarchs (1493)

Translated from Castilian by William Phillips

Few of the autograph writings of Christopher Columbus remain today; scholars must rely on copies or summaries made by others. This is true of one of his most famous letters, that announcing the momentous results of his first transatlantic voyage. Since 1493, the most familiar version was the letter to Luis de Santángel, royal councillor. Printed many times, it contained alterations and inconsistencies, probably introduced by officials of Fernando and Isabel to disguise the true location of the islands Columbus found. In 1986, a purported sixteenth-century copy of Columbus's first letter directly to the Spanish monarchs appeared in a bookstore in Tarragona. The Spanish government purchased it and it has been transcribed and printed in at least two editions. Scholars are not unanimously convinced of its authenticity, but its contents appear consistent with its having been written by Columbus.

In the letter, we get a first glimpse of the Americas and the Americans, previously unknown to Europeans. Columbus reported on the islands he found, praising their beauty and exaggerating their size while extolling their potential for lucrative trade. His view of the people he dubbed Indians is varied and ambivalent. He believed that most were docile and peaceful, but they were threatened by others, the warlike and cannibalistic men of "Caribo." Medieval tales of monstrous races made up part of the speculative geography Columbus shared with his contemporaries, and he reported Amazons, people born with tails, and hairless Jamaicans, without having seen them.

He was not reluctant to express his personal concerns, a mixture of spiritualism and ambition for wealth and position. The letter contains his proposal to raise an army for the Christian reconquest of Jerusalem and his request to have his young son made a cardinal.

In this short letter, the complexity of Columbus is readily apparent. Equally, the seeds of the multifacted and ambivalent relations between Europeans and Americans can be discerned within it. (WP)

Sea of Spain, 4 March 1493

Most Christian and exalted and powerful princes:

That eternal God who has given so many victories to Your Highnesses, now gave you the highest that he has given to princes up to now. With the armada that Your Highnesses gave me, I come from the Indies, where I went in thirty-three days after I left your kingdoms; and fourteen of these

Translated from Cristóbal Colón, *Textos y documentos completos,* edited by Consuelo Varela, *Nuevas cartas,* edited by Juan Gil (Madrid: Alianza Editoriál, 1992), 227–35.

thirty-three were calm in which I made little headway. I found people with-
out number and very many islands, of which I took possession in the name of
Your Highnesses, with a proclamation and with your royal banner extended;
and I was not contradicted. To the first I gave the name of the island of San
Salvador [Holy Savior] in memory of his high majesty; to the second that of
Santa María de la Concepción [Saint Mary of the Conception]; to the third,
Fernandina; to the fourth, Isabel; to the fifth, Juana; and thus to the others
new names. After I arrived at Juana [Cuba], I followed its coast to the west
and found it so large that I thought that it might not be an island but the
mainland and that it would be the province of Cathay, but I could obtain no
news of it, because at each promontory that I reached the people fled and I
could not have conversation. And because I could not find a notable population, I believed that, going along the coast, I could not fail to find some town
or large city, as those who have been in that province by land have recounted.
After I had coasted this land a long time, I found [that because of the shape
of the coastline] I was being forced off my westerly course and carried to the
north, and I found the wind that came from there, . . . [and] I did not wish
to delay until another came, for it was already winter incarnate, and I had no
alternative but to flee from it to the south. Thus I made the return in this
way. Already I understood something of the words and signs of some Indians
I had taken on the island of San Salvador, and I understood that it was still
this island. And thus I came upon a very good port, from which I sent two
men inland for three days, with one of the Indians I had with me, who had
taken amnesty with me, in order that they could see and find out if there
were cities or large populations, and what land it was and what there was in
it. They found many settlements and people without number, but nothing
of a large government, and thus they returned. I left and took, in the said
port, certain Indians, because therefore I could through them understand or
comprehend about the said lands. And thus I followed the sea coast of this
island to the east for one hundred seven leagues, until its end. And before
I departed from it, I saw another island to the east, eighteen leagues away,
which I later named Española [Hispaniola]. And I later went to it and followed the northern part of its coast, like that of Juana, always straight to the
east one hundred eighty-eight large leagues. And I anchored in many ports,
in which and in all the others of the other islands I put a great cross in the
most appropriate place, and in many places I took translators. After I had
traveled in this way until the sixteenth of January, I determined to return to
Your Highnesses, because of having found most of what I had wished for,
and because then I had only one caravel [small merchant vessel], for the ship
[a *nao*, a large merchant vessel] that I had brought I left with the people

in the town of La Navidad of Your Highnesses, fortifying themselves in it, as I will later tell; and the other caravel, a person of Palos [Martín Alonso Pinzón], to whom I had given charge of it expecting good service, had taken it and left me, with thought of taking much gold from an island of which an Indian had given him news. . . .

The sea is the most sweet for sailing that there is in the world and with less danger for ships of all sorts, but for discovery the caravels are the best, because traveling along the coast and up rivers by necessity, to discover a great deal, they need little depth and can be aided by oars. Nor is there ever a storm, for in every cape where I have been I saw that the grass and the trees reached into the water.

Beyond the above-mentioned islands I have found many others in the Indies, of which I do not care to say in the present letter. Those with these others are of such fertility that, although I know to say it, it would not be a marvel to place doubt in the belief. The most temperate airs, the trees and fruits and grasses are beautiful in the extreme and very different from ours. The rivers and ports are so numerous and so much better than those in Christendom that it is a marvel. All these islands are heavily populated by the best sinless and guileless people there are under heaven. All, men and women alike, go around as naked as their mothers bore them, although some women wear some little thing of cotton or a girdle of grass with which they cover themselves. They have no iron nor weapons, except some cane tops at the end of which they put a thin, sharp stick; all that they make is with stones. And I could not find out if anyone has private property, because some days that I spent with a king in the town of La Navidad, I saw that all the town, and especially the women, brought him "agis," which is a food they eat, and he ordered them to be distributed, very singular sustenance.

In no part of these islands do the people know any sect or idolatry nor does the language differ from one to the others, since all understand each other. I know that they are aware that in heaven are all the forces, and generally, in whatever lands I traveled, they believed and still believe that I had come from heaven with these people and ships, and with this view they received me. And still today they hold the same belief, nor have they abandoned it, despite repeated conversations; and later arriving at whatever settlement, the men and women and children went shouting among the houses, "Come, come to see the people from heaven." Whatever they have they give for whatever is shown them, so far as to take a piece of glass or a broken bowl or something similar for either gold or something else of value. In exchange for the metal ends of shoelaces a sailor got more than two and a half *castellanos* [small Castilian coins]. And of these things there are ten thousand to tell.

These islands are all very flat and the land is very low-lying, except for Juana and Española: these two have highlands, and in them are sierras and very high mountains, beyond comparison with those of the island of Tenerife. The mountains are all of a thousand shapes and all most beautiful and most fertile and walkable and full of trees; it seems they reach to heaven. The one and the other of these islands are very large that, as I have said, I traveled straight for one hundred seven leagues along Juana, and two provinces still remained for me to travel to the northwest point, in which, according to what I could understand from these Indians, that its length could have no less than fifty to sixty leagues, thus arguably it is much larger than England and Scotland together. This other Española is larger in circumference than all Spain, which, as I said above, traveling in a straight line from west to east one hundred eighty-eight great leagues are in that quarter. Juana has many rivers, and in it are great mountains and most grand valleys and plains and fields, and all full of trees and very large palms and marvelous in a thousand ways. Española has an advantage in everything: the trees are not as tall nor of the same quality, but very fruitful and ample; and delectable lands for all things and for seeding and planting and raising livestock, of which in no island have I seen any species. The island has airs that are marvelously moderate, and plains and fields to be marveled at and without comparison with those of Castile, and the rivers are the same: large and good waters, and most are gold-bearing. The seaports are so many and so good that you would not believe it without seeing it. In these and the other islands I did not detain myself for many reasons, as I said above, especially because it happened to be winter when I went along these coasts, which did not allow me to go to the south, for I was in the northern part of them and the winds were almost always from the east, which were contrary to the pursuit of my navigation; afterwards I did not understand these people or they me, save as much as free-will taught, since they took pains and I much more because I wanted to have good information about everything. And the assistance that I had for it was the Indians that I had, for they learned our language and we theirs, and later, so that the other voyage should be known, I had no reason to detain myself in any port because of how much I had to navigate. And also, as I have said, the vessels I had were very large and heavy for their type, and especially the *nao* I had, about which I was quite skeptical before I left Castile. I would prefer to take small caravels, but because this was the first voyage and the crew were fearful of finding heavy seas and dubious about the voyage, and I had already had so many contrarieties and whoever dared to contradict this path and put in it a thousand dangers, without any reason they could give for it, made me deny my will and do everything to make those I had with me want to go, in order to finally make the voyage and find land. But Our Lord, who is the light and force of all who strive for a good goal and who gives them victory in things that seem impossible, wished to order that I would find and have found gold and mines of it and spices and people without number, some disposed to become Christians and others for the Christians [illegible word] to them, and with a visible miracle he gave me a place where I made the fortress, which now is or should be finished, and I ordered that the people whom I had in the *nao* and some from the caravels should go into it, in possession of the town of La Navidad, supplied with provisions for more than a year and a good amount of artillery and quite without danger from anyone, because of the great friendship of the local king, he who bragged of calling me and considering me a brother; he who always demonstrated having the best happiness in the world, as I said, and the others are like the king, such that the people I left there are sufficient for subjugating the entire island without danger. This island is in a place, as I have said, indicated by the hands of Our Lord; from where I hope that His Majesty will give Your Highnesses as much gold as you need; spicery, from pepper, as many cargoes as Your Highnesses order loaded, and mastic as much as you wish to load, which has not been found until now except on the island of Chios in Greece and they sell as much of it as they wish in the lordship [of Genoa], and I believe that they make more than forty-five thousand ducats from it each year; and aloe as much as you order to be loaded, and cotton as much as you order to be loaded, and so many slaves that they are numberless, and they will be from the idolaters; and I believe I have found rhubarb and cinnamon. All this now I found while traveling hurriedly, but I hope in God that on the return the people I left there will have found another thousand things of substance, for I charged them to do so, and I left them a boat [*barca*] and the rigging for it and for making other boats and masters of all the arts of the sea. And above all, I hold for Your Highnesses all the above-mentioned islands, and they may be made use of . . . more completely than the kingdoms of Castile, and especially this Española.

I conclude here that, through the divine grace of He who is the beginning of all things virtuous and good and who gives favor and victory to all those who walk in his footsteps, that in seven years from today I can provide Your Highnesses with five thousand mounted troops and fifty thousand foot soldiers for the war and conquest of Jerusalem, upon which proposition this enterprise was undertaken; and after five more years another five thousand cavalry and fifty thousand foot, and this with the very little cost that now you have expended in this beginning, because all the Indies are held and that which is in them is in the hand, which I will later personally tell Your

Highnesses. And for this I am right and do not speak uncertainly, and it is not necessary to sleep on it, as was done in the establishment of this enterprise, for which may God forgive the one who was the cause of it.

Most powerful princes, all Christians should make very great celebrations and especially the church of God for having found such a multitude of peoples so approachable, so that for little work they would turn themselves to our holy faith, and so many lands full of so many goods very necessary to us, in which all Christians will have refuge and gain, where all was unknown nor was anything told about it except in the manner of fables. Your Highnesses should order great celebrations and festivals in the churches and great thanks to the Holy Trinity to be held in all of your kingdoms and lordships for the great love that has been shown you, more than to any other prince.

Now, most serene princes, remember, Your Highnesses, that I left wife and children and came from my land to serve you, where I spent what I had and expended seven years of time and received a thousand rebuffs with defamation and I suffered great deprivations, and I did not wish to reach agreements with other princes who implored me, inasmuch as Your Highnesses have financed this voyage, which has been more from my importunity than for any other thing, and because I have only been given support, but what I had been promised is still not completed. I do not request a grant to enrich me, because I have no other condition but to serve God and Your Highnesses and to carry this business of the Indies to completion, as time will tell; and thus I pray that the honor be given me according to the service.

Also the church of God must be involved in this: to provide prelates and clerics and religious experts: and because the thing is so large and of such quality that it is right that the Holy Father provide prelates who are completely above greed for worldly goods, and very proper to the service of God and Your Highnesses, and therefore I pray that, in the letter you write of this victory, that you demand of him a cardinalate for my son and that, because he is not yet of a suitable age, that he be given it, since there is little difference in age between him and the son of the head of the Medicis of Florence, to whom a hat was given without his serving or being appropriate for such a Christian honor; and that I be given the grant of the letter about this, because I should send to procure it. . . .

Therefore it is proper for Your Highnesses to know that the first island of the Indies reached from Spain is totally populated by women without a single man, and their manner is not feminine, but to use arms and other manly exercises. They carry bows and arrows and adorn themselves with sheets of copper, a metal they have in abundance. They call this island Mateninó. The second they call Caribo, [illegible] leagues distant from the other. Here are those peoples, who are feared by all the other islands of India. They eat human flesh. They are great archers. They have many canoes, almost as large as oared lighters, with which they travel all the islands of India, and they are so feared that to one a hundred are not equal. They go about as naked as the others, except that they wear their hair very long, like women. I believe that the enormous cowardice of the peoples of the other islands, which is without remedy, make them say the people of Caribo are daring, but I hold them in the same estimation as the others; and when Your Highnesses order that I send you slaves, I hope to bring or send the major part from these. These are those who treat with the women of Mateninó; they, if they give birth to a girl, keep her with them and, if a boy, care for him until he can eat for himself and then send him to Caribo. Between these islands of Caribo and Española is another island that they call Boriquén, and all is little distance from the other part of the island of Juana, which they call Cuba. In the most western part, in one of the two provinces I failed to visit, which is called Faba, everyone is born with a tail. Behind this island of Juana, within sight, there is another, which these Indians assure me is larger, that they call Jamaica, where all the people lack hair; on it there is gold beyond measure. And now I bring Indians with me who have been on the ones and the others [of the islands] and know the language and the customs. Nothing more, except that may the Most Holy Trinity keep and increase the royal estate of Your Highnesses in His holy service. Dated in the sea of Spain on the fourth day of March of fourteen ninety-three, at sea.

87. THE PORTUGUESE NEW WORLD AND INDIA

Letter Describing a Voyage to Brazil and India (1505)
Translated from Italian by Sergio J. Pacifici

When the Portuguese explorer Vasco da Gama returned to Lisbon from India in the summer of 1499, he proved at long last that the spices of India could be brought to Europe by a sea route around the Cape of Good Hope. The Portuguese king, Manuel I (r. 1495–1521), lost no time attempting to exploit this new route and sent a fleet of thirteen ships to India in 1500 under the command of Pedro Álvares Cabral, a member of one of Portugal's noble families. This voyage was not only the first successful Portuguese commercial expedition to reach India around the Cape of Good Hope; Cabral's route also touched the coast of Brazil on his outward journey, thereby establishing Portuguese interests in the New World. After Cabral's first voyage in 1500, three more Portuguese expeditions set forth to India in the next four years.

In 1505, the text of this "letter" appeared in Rome, under the title "Copy of a Letter of the King of Portugal Sent to the King of Castile Concerning the Voyage and Success of India." Although the spectacular title may not be accurate, this report provides a contemporary account of the first Portuguese voyages to India and contains the first printed reference to the discovery of Brazil. The excerpt included here describes the first part of the voyage. (ORC)

Although, my Catholic King and Lord, I have advised more than once Your Most Serene Majesty of our success in other letters of mine, after we had already begun our traffic and trade in the lands of India in our name, yet, at the present time, because of the arrival of some of our ships, it has seemed opportune to me to make a report of their news. And repeating whatever we have written in our previous letters, in order that you might be excellently informed of everything, it has seemed opportune to me to recall all the information from the time of our first armada right up to the present armada. The first ships we sent to those lands were twelve in number, plus a caravel full of provisions. These ships left our port of Lisbon in the year 1500, on the 8th day of March, to go and trade in spices and drugs in the lands of India, beyond the Red and the Persian Seas, to a city called Calicut. Of the King, site, customs, and manners of these lands we shall speak later on. Pedro Álvares Cabral was the Captain General of the afore-mentioned armada. Sailing past Cape Verde, they sighted a land which had recently come to be known in our Europe, to which they gave the name of Santa Cruz, and this because they

English text from *Copy of a Letter of the King of Portugal Sent to the King of Castile Concerning the Voyage and Success of India*, translated by Sergio J. Pacifici (Minneapolis: University of Minnesota Press, 1955), pp. 3–7. Reprinted with permission of the publisher.

had a very high cross erected on its shore. Others call it New Land, that is, New World. This land, where they came ashore, is situated on the 14th meridian beyond the Tropic of Cancer, as the sailors found its position by means of their quadrants and astrolabes, since they sail in those parts with astrological instruments. This land is situated 400 leagues west-southwest of the afore-mentioned Cape Verde. We have previously advised Your Lordship of its inhabitants, fertility, size, and condition and whether it is an island or a continent. The armada, upon its departure, left two Christians to chance. It was carrying 20 convicts, previously condemned to death, to be left wherever the Captain might deem fitting. Later on, one of these two Christians came back with another armada we had sent directly to that land. This man knew their language and gave information about everything. From there the Captain sent back the caravel carrying the provisions. On the 2nd of May they sailed toward the Cape of Good Hope and on the 12th they sighted that Cape, situated 1200 miles away. This Cape of Good Hope is situated on the 31st meridian beyond the Equinox, and Ptolemy in his outline of Africa leaves it as unexplored land. The coast is inhabited by people not too black, and is fertile and abundant with every fruit and water. From the observations made by the sailors, its people have journeyed to the Antarctic Pole, and know Aquarius and most other constellations, of which they have the descriptions. While sailing toward Africa, for ten consecutive nights the sailors saw a very large comet. Also they saw the celestial arc right in the middle of the night—something unheard of amongst our people. On the 24th day of the same month, the weather being good, as they were sailing round the mentioned Cape Verde, they suddenly met with a very strong wind which sank right there four of the ships together with all their crews. Two more got lost; the rest, carried off by a following wind, with sails, rigging, rods, and masts torn, were left to chance for five days. Finally, once the sea had calmed down, the ships, which were six in number, came together. Sailing by the coast they passed Sofala. This is an island at the mouth of a river, and is inhabited by many merchants. There gold is abundant and is brought to them from the interior of Africa by men small in body, strong, and very ugly, and with small voices, who eat human flesh, mainly that of their enemies. This is the same manner in which gold is brought to our mine in Guinea. This island, too, belongs to the King of Quiloa. Past this island, they found two big ships coming from Sofala and going to the King. These two ships were held by our Captain, but once he understood that they belonged to the aforesaid King he let them go free, taking from them only a pilot to guide them to Quiloa. Arriving in Quiloa, principal city of this great and well-populated kingdom, with a safe-conduct, the Captain was much honored by that King because he was carrying our letters written in Arabic, and our directives to the King to grant him the traffic and trade of this island. And this was granted to him. But since two ships which were to remain there were being held, he did not demand any ransom. Quiloa is a city in Arabia, situated on a small island connected with the Continent, well populated by Negro merchants, and built in our ways. Here there is an abundance of gold, silver, amber, musk, and pearls, and the people wear silk and fine cotton clothes without excess. Leaving from there, they sailed towards the kingdom of Malindi, to the King of which they were similarly bringing my letters and message since he had graciously received don Vasco [da Gama], who was the first to discover this coast. There, in the harbor of Malindi, they found three ships of Cambay of 200 barrels each. They are ships built with canes above and wood shiplaps tied with ropes and pitch at the bottom, since they do not have nails. All the ships in those lands are of this kind. They always sail with wind astern because they cannot go into the wind; they have a quarter-deck. The King talked with our Captain through interpreters, and signed a pact of good friendship between us, giving the Captain a pilot to lead him to Calicut. There two other convicts remained, one of whom was to remain in Malindi, the other to seek refuge elsewhere on the land. These two kingdoms, Quiloa and Malindi, are on the west side of the Red Sea, adjacent to the territories of the Gentiles and Prester John, whom they call *Abechi* in their language—which means iron-branded, because in this fashion in fact they brand themselves with hot steel and thus they are baptized without water. The 7th day of August they left for Calicut and passed a gulf 700 leagues wide. They sighted Calicut the 12th of September, six months after their departure from Lisbon. One league from the harbor of Calicut, the citizens and gentlemen of the King came to greet them with great festivities. They docked before the city and fired the artillery, which caused great admiration among the inhabitants. Calicut is in India, and to it are brought spices and drugs; it is densely populated with Gentiles. For this reason, there are merchants of these goods from many lands and trades, like Bruges in Flanders or Venice in Italy. The following day the Captain sent to land four Indians whom he had brought from Lisbon, and who spoke Portuguese fluently. They received a safe-conduct from the King in order that our people might be allowed to land as the Captain had ordered. So Alfonso Furtado came ashore and he agreed with the King that five gentlemen should be sent to the ships as hostages, in order that the Captain might land safely and parley with him. The Captain landed, leaving in his place Sancho de Tovar in charge of the ships. The King, carried on a litter, came to the shores to receive the Captain, who was carried in the arms of the King's gentlemen right up to the King's presence. The King was lying down in a litter covered by a purple silk cloth. From his waist up he was naked, from the waist down he was clothed with a cloth of cotton, worked with gold and silver. He had on his head a cap of brocade made like an antique helmet. From his ears there hung two pearls, as big as hazelnuts, one round and the other pear-shaped. He wore two gold bracelets with many jewels and pearls and an infinite number of rings on his hands. All those gems were very precious and of great price. There was also a large chair made completely of silver. Its armrests and the back were of gold with many precious stones. There were 20 trumpets of silver and three of gold, a third longer than ours and quite loud. In the room there were six Moorish lamps of silver, which burned day and night. No one of the bystanders can approach the King nearer than six paces, out of reverence, but the Captain came closer than the others and, sitting down, relayed his message and gave the King our letters written both in Arabic and in our tongue. And at once the Captain sent for our presents, which were as follows: first, a basin and a large gilded silver jug, worked with many figures in relief; a large covered bowl and a large gold cup worked with figures; two silver maces with their own chains; four cushions, two of brocade and two of crimson velvet; a baldachin of brocade with gold and crimson fringes; a large carpet; two cloths of fine satin, one with foliage, the other with figures. The King graciously received these gifts because these things are unusual in those lands, and concluded a pact of peace and friendship.

88. THE EXPULSION OF MUSLIMS FROM CASTILE AND LEÓN

Royal Edict of Expulsion (1502)

Translated from Castilian by Dayle Seidenspinner-Nuñez

In spite of the terms laid out in the Capitulations of Granada (Chapter 84B), which allowed the Muslims of Granada to practice their customs and religion freely under Christian rule, or to emigrate abroad if they wished, tensions escalated in newly Christian Granada. Critical of the tolerant implementation of the Capitulations by the archbishop of Granada, Francisco Jiménez de Cisneros's harassing of the elches (Christian converts to Islam), attempts to terrorize the Islamic elite into conversion, and burning of Arabic books led to Muslim uprisings in 1499–1501. These revolts provided an opportunity for Christian authorities to rid themselves of the Capitulations and to modify or rescind the Mudejar status of other Muslims elsewhere. The Charter of Expulsion of Muslims from the kingdoms of Castile and León was promulgated in Granada on 20 July 1501 and in Seville on 12 February 1502; forced conversions were subsequently implemented in Aragónand Valencia in the 1520s. (DSN)

Considering the great scandal (spiritual danger)[1] that the presence of Muslims in our realms and domains holds for the newly converted as well as for all our natural subjects and how such scandal could endanger their public well being and seeing that we have worked so hard in the kingdom of Granada, where once everyone was an infidel, to ensure that none remain, and that with the help of our Lord we have removed from there the head of opprobrium of our faith, which this sect represents throughout Spain, it is an obstacle to our efforts to permit members of this sect to inhabit our realms. And since it pleased our Lord in our time to overthrow our ancient enemies from said kingdom, who for so many years battled against our faith and against our kings who preceded us and against our realms, it is right that we, showing our gratitude for our victory and for all the other blessings that we have received from our Lord, expel from our realms (of Castile and León) the enemies of his holy name and that we no longer permit people who follow reprobate laws to reside in our realms.

Considering also how we have seen in our realms that the greatest cause of subversion of many Christians was their interaction and communication

Reconquista

Translated from F. Fernández y González, *Estado social y político de los mudéjares de Castilla* (Madrid: Impr. J. Muñoz, 1866) 432–34.

1. *Escandalo* (from Latin *scandalum*) is a religious term to denote damage and spiritual ruin inflicted on another.

Figure 25. Baptizing Muslim women after the fall of Granada. Carved wooden alterpiece from the Capilla Real, Granada. Permission and photograph credit: Cabildo de la Capilla Real, Granada.

Figure 26. A Morisca girl and a woman in Granada (early sixteenth century). Christophe Weiditz, *Authentic Everyday Dress in the Renaissance: All 154 Plates from the "Trachtenbuch"* (New York: Dover, 1994), plates 83, 84. Reproduced with the permission of Dover Books. Photo credit: University of Notre Dame, Rare Books Department.

with the Jews, there is similarly much danger in the interaction of said Muslims in our realms with the newly converted, which can cause the newly converted to be tempted or induced to leave our faith and return to their original errors. This (relapse), given the weakness of our humanity and the diabolic temptation which continuously assails us, may easily happen, as we already have seen by experience in our kingdom and beyond, if the principal cause is not removed, which is to expel said Muslims from our realms and domains.[2] And since it is better to prevent with a remedy than to wait to punish errors once crimes are done and committed, given the scandal and danger of

2. Much of the rationale and phrasing of the Charter of Expulsion of the Muslims from Castile and León is modeled on the 1492 charter expelling the Jews (Chapter 85A), where *converso* corruption, "according to the weakness of our humanity and by diabolical astuteness and suggestion that continually wages war against us may easily occur unless the principal cause of it be removed, which is to banish the said Jews from our kingdoms." Many of the subsequent paragraphs may also be fruitfully compared, in terms of language, process, and intention, with the 1492 charter.

Muslim residence and the need for their departure or expulsion, even if they are peaceful and live quietly, it is right that the lesser as well as the greater be expelled from our lands and that everyone on account of some in this be punished and chastised.

Therefore we, with the counsel and advice of prelates and grandees of our realms, knights and other people of learning and conscience of our council, having had much deliberation on this issue, resolve to order that all said Muslim men and women depart from our realms of Castile and León and that they never come back or return to them. And concerning this we command that this our charter be given, by which we command that all Muslim men of fourteen years of age and above and all Muslim women of twelve years of age and above, who live and reside in our said realms of Castile and León, both natural-born residents and otherwise, who by whatever manner and for whatever reason have arrived and live on our lands, with the exception of captive Muslims who will wear chains so they are recognized, by the end of the month of April of this current year of 1502, abandon all our said realms and domains and depart from them with the possessions that they wish to take as long as neither they, nor others on their behalf, carry away or take outside our realms gold or silver or any other goods forbidden or prohibited by us. And they must depart, and leave and take away their possessions only through the ports of our county of Viscaya, and not through any other ports or places; accordingly we order that persons charged with overseeing what is being taken away be stationed in said ports with the penalty that, if they leave through another port or take away gold or silver or any other forbidden item through the Viscayan ports, by this deed they fall under and incur the penalty of death and forfeiture of all their goods for our Chamber of Finance.

And we order that said Muslims cannot travel by sea or by land to our realms of Aragón or Valencia, the principality of Catalonia, or the kingdom of Navarre and that no one dare convey them to these lands. And because we are engaged in war with the Muslims of Africa and with the Turks, they cannot go to these parts of Africa or Turkish territory, under said penalty of death and confiscation of goods. However, we do permit them to go, if they wish, to the lands of the Sultan and to whatever other lands they wish that are not prohibited by us above.

And we order that said Muslims or Muslims by birth or otherwise of these our realms, not being captives, not dare to arrive or return or be in these our realms or in any part of them, by residence or passing through or any other manner, forever and ever, with the penalty that, if they were to do so and were found to be in our realms and domains or to enter them in any manner, they will incur by this deed, with no other legal trial or sentence or declaration, said penalty of death and confiscation of all their goods for our Chamber of Finance.

And we command and prohibit that any persons of our said realms, of whatever estate, preeminence or dignity, dare to welcome, receive, or harbor or publicly or secretly defend the above mentioned Muslim men or women, after the deadline of the end of the month of April nor thereafter forever and ever, on their lands or in their homes or in any other part of our said realms and domains, under penalty of forfeiture of all their goods, vassals, and fortresses and other inheritances; and also loss of any subsidy they may have from us, and that all these goods be applied to our Chamber of Finance.

And we order that none of the captive Muslims or Muslim women or any other person dare to say anything or speak to the new converts to our holy Catholic faith that may attract them to leave our faith, under penalty of death.

89. MORISCO APPEAL TO THE OTTOMAN SULTAN

Verses to Bayazid II (ca. 1502)

Translated from Arabic by James T. Monroe

In spite of the terms laid out in the Capitulations of Granada (Chapter 84B), which allowed the Muslims of Granada to practice their customs and religion freely under Christian rule, or to emigrate abroad if they wished, tensions escalated in newly Christian Granada. A Muslim uprising in 1499, and the crushing of this revolt in 1501, led to an edict that Muslims had to convert to Christianity or leave the peninsula. Shortly afterward, an anonymous Granadan Muslim composed this verse appeal to the Ottoman sultan Bayazid II (r. 1481–1512), then the most powerful ruler in the Islamic world. The writer described the intolerable situation in Granada, where mosques were being converted to churches and priests were teaching Christianity to Muslim children. At the same time, lest other Muslims suspect them of apostasy, he stressed that Andalusi Muslims had been converted entirely against their will. He also pointed out that the Mozarabs had never been similarly oppressed under Muslim rule. The poet repeatedly appealed to Bayazid to intercede with Christian authorities on behalf of Granadan Muslims, asking that they be allowed either to practice Islam or to leave Spain with all their possessions. (ORC)

A noble, enduring, ever-renewed peace do I attribute exclusively to his
    highness, the best of Caliphs.
Peace be upon his highness, the possessor of glory and lofty stature, who
    has clothed the infidel in a robe of humility;
Peace be upon him whose kingship God has expanded, supporting him with
    victory in every region;
Peace be upon his majesty, the capital of whose realm is Constantinople.
    What a noble city it is!
Peace be upon him whose kingdom God adorned with armies and subject
    populations of Turks;
Peace be upon you. May God exalt your rank and may He also make you a
    king over every nation.
Peace be upon the judge and upon whomsoever of the noble, exalted men
    of learning resemble him;
Peace be upon the men of religion and piety and upon whomsoever among
    the counselors is gifted with sound judgment.
Peace be upon you on behalf of some slaves who have remained in a land of
    exile, in Andalus in the west,

English text from *Hispano-Arabic Poetry*, translated by James T. Monroe (Berkeley: University of California Press, 1974), pp. 376–88. Reprinted with permission of the publisher.

Whom the swelling sea of Rūm as well as a deep, gloomy, and fathomless
    ocean encompasses.

Peace be upon you on behalf of some slaves smitten by a dire misfortune.
    What a misfortune it was!

Peace be upon you on behalf of some old men whose white hair has come
    to be torn from [much] plucking, after [they have enjoyed a life of]
    glory;

Peace be upon you on behalf of some faces that have been bared to the
    company of non-Arabs after having been veiled;

Peace be upon you on behalf of some young girls whom the priest drives by
    force to a bed of shame;

Peace be upon you on behalf of some old women who have been compelled
    to eat pork and flesh not killed according to ritual prescriptions.

We all kiss the ground of your royal court and we call down blessings upon
    you at all moments.

May the Lord cause your royal power and life to endure, and may He
    preserve you from every trial and misfortune;

May He strengthen you with support and victory over the enemy, and
    lodge you in the abode of [His] pleasure and regard [for you].

We have complained to you, your majesty, of the harm, the misfortune and
    the enormous calamity that has afflicted us.

We have been betrayed and converted to Christianity; our religion has been
    exchanged for another; we have been oppressed and treated in every
    shameful way.

Yet under the Prophet Muḥammad's religion we used to oppose the agents
    of the Cross with our inner intentions,

Facing grave dangers in Holy War because of killing and capturing, hunger
    and dearth.

But the Christians attacked us from all sides in a vast torrent, company after
    company

Smiting us with zeal and resolution like locusts in the multitude of their
    cavalry and weapons.

Nevertheless, for a long time we withstood their armies and killed group
    after group of them,

Although their horsemen increased every moment, whereas ours were in a
    state of diminution and scarcity,

Hence, when we became weak, they camped in our territory and smote us,
    town after town,

Bringing many large cannons that demolished the impregnable walls of the
    towns,

Attacking them energetically during the siege for many months and days;
    with zeal and determination.

So when our cavalry and foot soldiers had perished and we observed that no
    rescue was forthcoming from our brethren,

And when our victuals had diminished and our lot had become hard indeed,
    we complied, against our will, with their demands, out of fear of disgrace,

And fearing for our sons and daughters, lest they be taken captive or cruelly
    slaughtered,

On the condition that we were to remain like the Mudejars before us,
    namely the inhabitants of the old territory,

And that we were to be allowed to remain in enjoyment [of the right] to
    call to prayer and [to celebrate] our ritual oration, while we were not
    [to be required] to abandon any of the prescriptions of the Religious
    Law;

And that whosoever among us desired [to cross] the sea was to [be allowed
    to] do so in safety, to the land on the [African] coast with all the
    property he wished [to take],

As well as many other stipulations, surpassing fifty by the number of five.

Then their Sultan[1] and grandee said to us: "What you have stipulated is
    granted to you in more than its entirety,"

Showing us documents containing a pact and a treaty, saying to us: "This is
    my amnesty and my protection [over you],

So remain in enjoyment of your possessions and homes as you were before,
    unharmed."

Yet when we came under their treaty of protection, their treachery toward
    us became apparent for [he] broke the agreement.

He broke the compacts he had deceived us with and converted us to
    Christianity by force, with harshness and severity,

Burning the books we had and mixing them with dung or with filth,

Though each book was on the subject of our religion. Yet they were cast
    into the fire with scorn and derision,

Nor did they spare a single volume belonging to any Muslim, or any tome
    which one could read in solitude.

Whosoever fasted or prayed and his state came to be known, was in every
    instance cast into the fire,

And whosoever of us failed to go to their place of unbelief, him did the
    priest severely punish,

Slapping him on both cheeks, confiscating his property, and imprisoning
    him in a wretched state.

1. Fernando of Aragón.

during baptism.

Moreover, during Ramadan, they spoiled our fast time after time with food
and drink,
And they ordered us to curse our Prophet and to refrain from invoking him
in times of ease or hardship.
They even overheard a group chanting his name, and the latter suffered a
grievous injury at their hands,
For their judges and governors punished them with beatings, fines,
imprisonment, and humiliation.
Whosoever lay dying, and did not have in attendance one who could preach
[their religion to him], in their deceit, they would refuse to bury him,
Instead, he was left lying prostrate on a dung heap like a dead donkey or
[some other] animal.
[They committed] many other similar, shameful deeds, as well as numerous
wicked acts.
Our names were changed and given a new form with neither our consent
nor our desire.
Therefore, alas for the exchanging of Muḥammad's religion for that of the
Christian dogs, the worst of creatures!
Alas for our names when they were exchanged for those of ignorant
non-Arabs!
Alas for our sons and daughters who go off every morning to a priest   *Christianizing next gen*
Who teaches them unbelief, idolatry, and falsehood while they are entirely
unable to circumvent [the Christians] by any trick!
Alas for those mosques that have been walled up to become dung heaps for
the infidel after having enjoyed ritual purity![2]
Alas for those minarets in which the bells [of the Christians] have been
hung in place of the Muslim declaration of faith [being announced
from them]!
Alas for those towns and their beauty! Through unbelief they have grown
very dark!
They have become strongholds for the worshipers of the Cross, and in them
the latter are safe against the occurring of raids.
We have become slaves; not captives who may be ransomed, nor even
Muslims who pronounce their declaration of faith!
Hence, were your eyes to see what has become of our lot, they would
overflow with abundant tears.
So alas! Alas for us! Alas for the misfortune that struck us, namely harm,
sorrow, and the robe of oppression!

---

2. Between 1492 and 1499 Archbishop Talavera turned the main mosque of Granada
into the Sagrario, that of Albaicín into the church of El Salvador.

We besought you, your majesty, by the Lord our God, and by the chosen,
the elect, the best of creatures,
And by those goodly lords, the family of Muḥammad and his companions—
what noble companions are they!—
And by the lord al-'Abbās, our Prophet's paternal uncle, by his white hair,
the most excellent white hair,
By those upright ones who grant recognition to their Lord, and by every
excellent saint endowed with nobility.
Perchance you will look upon us and what has smitten us; perhaps the God
of the Throne will bring mercy,
For your speech is hearkened to and your order is effective, while everything
you command is swiftly executed.
As for the Christian faith, its [place of] origin is ruled by your authority, and
it was from there that it spread to them in every region.
So, by God, your highness, be pleased to favor us with some advice or some
words of protest,
For you possess excellence, glory, rank, and [the power] to rescue God's
worshipers from all evil.
Therefore ask their Pope, that is to say, the ruler of Rome, why they
permitted treason after having [granted] amnesty,
And why they harmed us with their betrayal with no wrong or crime on our
part?
When their people who had been conquered [by us] were under the
safeguard of our religion and the protection of [our] glorious kings
who fulfilled their promises,
Neither were they converted from their faith, nor expelled from their
homes, nor did they suffer betrayal or dishonor.
As for him who grants a treaty and then betrays it, that is a deed forbidden
by every faith,
Especially on the part of kings, for it is a disgraceful, infamous deed;
unlawful everywhere.
Your letter to them arrived, yet they did not heed one single word of it all;
It only increased their enmity and boldness against us as well as their
perseverance in all kinds of wicked deeds.
The envoys of Egypt reached them and they were not treated with
treachery or dishonor,[3]

3. Some emissaries from Mamluk Egypt were sent to Spain in 1500 after the Egyptian
sultan had been urged to interfere on behalf of the Moriscos. They informed the Spanish monarchs that if the Moriscos were forced to convert to Christianity, the Mamluk sultan would
retaliate by persecuting the Christian populations of his realm.

Yet [the Christians] informed those envoys on our behalf, that we had
    voluntarily accepted the religion of unbelief,
And they brought out some [token] conversions to idolatry, of those
    who had submitted to them; yet, by God, we will never accept that
    declaration of faith!
They have lied about us with the greatest of falsehood in their words and
    arguments in saying that.
Rather, it was the fear of death and of burning that caused us to convert. We
    speak just as they spoke [to us]. It happened contrary to our intention,
While the faith of God's Prophet has not been extinguished among us, since
    in every glance our recognition of God's monotheism can be observed.
Moreover, by God, we accept neither our change of religion nor what they
    say on the subject of the Trinity,
And if they claim that we have accepted their religion unharmed by them,
Then ask Huéjar[4] about its inhabitants: how they became captives and
    slaughterlings under [the burden] of humiliation and misfortune,
And ask Belefique[5] what was the outcome of their affair: they were cut to
    pieces by the sword after undergoing anxiety.
As for Munyāfa,[6] its inhabitants were sundered by the sword. The same was
    done to the people of Alpujarra.
As for Andarax,[7] its people were consumed by fire. It was in their mosque
    that they all became like charcoal.
Lo, your majesty, we complain to you, what we have encountered is the
    worst form of estrangement.
Could our religion not be left to us as well as our ritual prayer, as they
    swore to do before the agreement was broken?
If not let them allow us to emigrate from their land to North Africa, the
    homeland of our dear ones, with our belongings.
For expulsion is better for us than remaining in unbelief, enjoying power
    but having no religion.
This is what we hope for from the glory of your rank. May every need of
    ours be satisfied by you!
From you do we hope for an end to our anxieties and to the evil lot and
    humiliation that have overcome us,

---

4. Huéjar was a town where rebellion was suppressed by the Christians in 1501. Its inhabitants were all massacred.
    5. Belefique was another center of insurrection in Las Alpujarras. The count of Cifuentes had its men massacred and its women sold as slaves.
    6. Munyāfa is an unidentified site.
    7. In 1500 the count of Lerin laid siege to the fortress of Laujar in Andarax. He used gunpowder to blow up a mosque where the Muslim women and children had sought refuge.

For you, praise be to God, are the best of our kings while your glory rises
   above all other glories.

Therefore we ask our Lord to prolong your life in kingship and glory, in joy
   and prosperity;

And [to grant you] peace in your realms, victory over your enemies,
   abundant troops, wealth, and magnificence,

Finally, may God's peace, followed by His mercy, be ever upon you for the
   duration of Time!

Chronology

410	Visigoths attack Rome.
456	Visigoths defeat the Suevi in the Iberian Peninsula and lay the foundations for their control of the region. Visigothic rule becomes well established in the Iberian Peninsula by 476.
ca. 575	Toledo becomes the Visigothic capital during the reign of Leovigild, the last Arian ruler (569–586).
589	Visigothic conversion from Arianism to Catholicism at the Third Council of Toledo (Chapter 3).
622	Foundation of Islam with the flight of the prophet Muḥammad and his followers from Mecca to Medina.
711	Muslim armies arrive in the Iberian Peninsula (Chapter 6).
722	Pelayo resists Muslim forces at Covadonga (Chapter 9).
732	Charles Martel defeats Muslim forces from al-Andalus at the Battle of Poitiers.
ca. 750	Kingdom of Asturias established under Alfonso I (739–757).
756	'Abd al-Raḥmān I establishes a new branch of the Umayyad dynasty in al-Andalus.
781	Charlemagne establishes Spanish March in Catalonia.
801	Charlemagne takes Barcelona.
850–859	Christian martyr movement in Córdoba (Chapter 12).
880	Start of rebellion of 'Umar ibn Ḥafṣūn against Umayyad rule. This revolt continues until 928 (Chapters 14 and 15).
929	'Abd al-Raḥmān III establishes Umayyad caliphate in al-Andalus (Chapter 15).
976	Al-Manṣūr takes over effective rule in al-Andalus during the minority of the caliph Hishām, until his death in 1002 (Chapter 16).
997	Al-Manṣūr leads a raid on Santiago de Compostela (Chapter 17).
1009–1031	Civil war in al-Andalus ends the period of Umayyad rule and opens the Taifa period (Chapter 18).
1035	Beginning of the Almoravid movement in North Africa. The Almoravids establish their first capital at Sijilmasa in 1055, then found a new capital at Marrakesh in 1062.

1039	Fernando I (1035-1065) unites Castile and León, then partitions his kingdom at his death among his three sons.
1066	Massacre of Jews in Granada (Chapter 21).
1080	Council of Burgos establishes the Roman Rite in the Iberian Peninsula.
1085	Alfonso VI of León-Castile captures Toledo. In response, Taifa rulers seek military assistance from the Almoravids (Chapters 22 and 24).
1086	Almoravid forces arrive in Spain and win a victory over Alfonso VI at the battle of Zallāqa (Chapter 23). The Almoravids establish their rule in al-Andalus shortly thereafter.
1094	The Cid captures Valencia and holds it until his death in 1099 (Chapter 25).
1095	Pope Urban II launches the First Crusade to the Holy Land.
1108	Almoravid victory in the battle of Uclés.
1110	Almoravids take control of the Taifa of Zaragoza.
1118	Alfonso I of Aragón captures Zaragoza.
1121	Ibn Tumart begins to preach the Almohad doctrine in the Maghrib (Chapters 42 and 43).
1128	Afonso Henriques establishes his rule in Portugal (Chapter 30).
1135	Alfonso VII declares himself emperor in León (Chapter 30).
1137	Union of Aragón and Catalonia with the marriage of Petronila and Count Ramon Berenguer IV. The latter commissions the compilation of the *Usatges of Barcelona* during his reign (Chapter 28).
1144	Demise of Almoravid power in al-Andalus.
1147	Christian capture of Lisbon (Chapter 31).
1147	The Almohads arrive in al-Andalus from North Africa. Strict Almohad policies lead to an exodus of Jews from al-Andalus, and many seek refuge in the Christian North (Chapter 46).
1170	Foundation of the Order of Santiago (Chapter 35).
1178	Treaty of Cazola partitions Muslim territories to be conquered in the future by Castile and Aragón (Chapter 36).
1195	Almohad victory over Castile at the Battle of Alarcos.
1212	Combined forces of Castile, Aragón, and Navarre defeat the Almohads at the Battle of Las Navas de Tolosa.
1228	The Almohads depart from al-Andalus.
1229	Jaume I of Aragón captures Mallorca (Figure 10).
1230	Permanent union of Castile and León under Fernando III.

ca. 1235	Naṣrid dynasty established in Granada.
1236	Fernando III of Castile-León captures Córdoba.
1238	Jaume I of Aragón captures Valencia, but solidification of his rule over the Valencian region takes several more decades (Chapters 48, 49, and 50).
1248	Fernando III of Castile-León captures Seville (Chapter 51).
1252	Alfonso X of Castile-León takes the throne after the death of his father, Fernando III. Known as "el Sabio" (the Wise), Alfonso becomes famous as a patron of learning and commissioner of texts, including the *Cantigas de Santa María* (Chapter 60; Figures 14–18) and the *Siete Partidas* (Chapters 62, 65, and 66).
1258	Treaty of Corbeil assigns Provence to France and gives the Spanish March to the Crown of Aragón.
1263	Disputation staged in Barcelona between Moses Nahmanides and Paul Christiani (Chapter 57).
1266	Alfonso X of Castile-León captures Murcia.
1282	War of the Sicilian Vespers begins Aragonese rule in Sicily.
1295	Treaty of Anagni compels Jaume II of Aragón to obey papal wishes and abandon his claims in Sicily. His brother, however, refuses to comply with the treaty and rules the island as Federico III (1295-1337).
1309	Ineffectual alliance between the Crowns of Castile and Aragón against Granada. Castile briefly holds Gibraltar (Chapter 54).
1348	The Black Death arrives in the Mediterranean world and Europe.
1369	Enrique II de Trastámara takes over the throne of the Crown of Castile from his half-brother, Pedro the Cruel (Chapter 73).
1385	Battle of Aljubarrota solidifies the Portuguese independence from Castile (Chapter 75).
1391	Jewish pogroms throughout the Christian peninsula.
1412	Castilian prince Fernando de Antequera is elected ruler of Aragón at the Compromise of Caspe. After this, both Castile and Aragón are ruled by members of the Trastámara dynasty.
1469	Wedding of Isabel of Castile and Fernando of Aragón (later known as "the Catholic Monarchs").
1478	Establishment of the Inquisition in Spain (Chapter 82).
1479	Official union between Castile and Aragón under Fernando and Isabel.
1491	Fernando and Isabel capture Granada in late December. The

	city officially surrenders to the Catholic Monarchs in January 1492 (Chapter 84; Figures 23 and 24).
1492	Jews expelled from Castile and Aragón (Chapter 85).
1492	Christopher Columbus reaches the Americas (Chapter 86).
1496	Jews expelled from Portugal.
1498	Jews expelled from Navarre.
1498	Vasco da Gama reaches India by sea from Portugal (Chapter 87).
1502	After a period of rebellions, the Muslims of Castile and León are forced to choose between exile or conversion to Christianity (Chapters 88 and 89).
1525	Muslims in the Crown of Aragón are likewise forced to choose between exile and conversion.
1609–1614	Moriscos expelled from the Iberian Peninsula.

Genealogical Tables

TABLE I   UMAYYAD AMĪRS AND CALIPHS IN CÓRDOBA (756–1031)

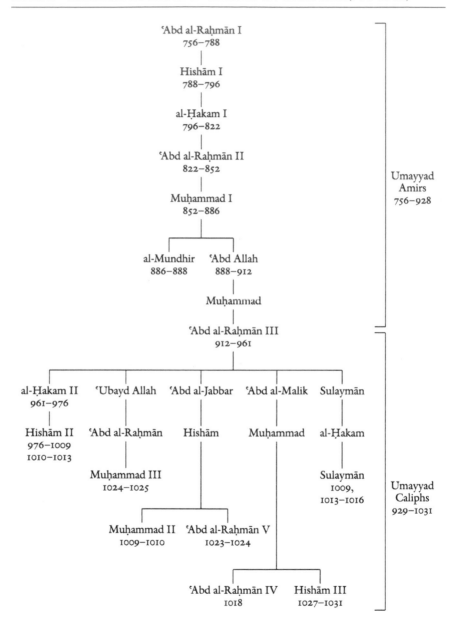

TABLE 2. ZIRID RULERS OF TAIFA GRANADA (CA. 1026–1090)

Ḥabbūs b. Māksan
(ca. 1026–1038)

Buluggīn

Bādīs b. Ḥabbūs
(1038–1073)

Buluggīn b. Bādīs
(called Sayf al-Dawla)
(died 1064)

ʿAbd Allah b. Buluggīn
(1073–1090)

TABLE 3 ALMORÁVID RULERS IN AL-ANDÁLUS (CA. 1086–1145)

Yūsuf b. Tāshufīn, (ca.1086–1106)

ʿAlī b. Yūsuf (1106–1143)

Tāshufīn b. ʿAlī (1143–1145)

TABLE 4 ALMOHAD RULERS IN AL-ANDALUS (1121–1223)

(Ibn Tumart)

ʿAbd al-Muʾmin (1130–1163)

Abū Yaʿqūb Yūsuf I (1163–1184)

Abū Yūsuf Yaʿqūb al-Manṣūr (1184–1199)

Muḥammad al-Nāṣir (1199–1213)

Abū Yaʿqūb Yūsuf II (1213–1223)

For a complete list of Taifa kingdoms and their rulers, see David Wasserstein, *The Rise and Fall of the Party Kings* (Princeton, N.J.: Princeton University Press, 1985), pp. 82–98. The Zirid genealogy is provided because the family is relevant to several texts in this collection.

Table 5 RULERS OF NAṢRID GRANADA (1232–1492)

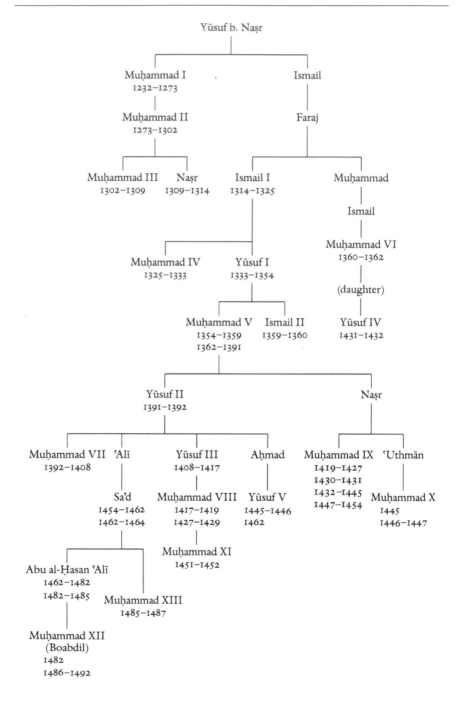

Yūsuf b. Naṣr

Muḥammad I
1232–1273

Ismail

Muḥammad II
1273–1302

Faraj

Muḥammad III
1302–1309

Naṣr
1309–1314

Ismail I
1314–1325

Muḥammad

Ismail

Muḥammad VI
1360–1362

Muḥammad IV
1325–1333

Yūsuf I
1333–1354

(daughter)

Muḥammad V
1354–1359
1362–1391

Ismail II
1359–1360

Yūsuf IV
1431–1432

Yūsuf II
1391–1392

Naṣr

Muḥammad VII
1392–1408

'Alī

Yūsuf III
1408–1417

Aḥmad

Muḥammad IX
1419–1427
1430–1431
1432–1445
1447–1454

'Uthmān

Saʿd
1454–1462
1462–1464

Muḥammad VIII
1417–1419
1427–1429

Yūsuf V
1445–1446
1462

Muḥammad X
1445
1446–1447

Muḥammad XI
1451–1452

Abu al-Ḥasan ʿAlī
1462–1482
1482–1485

Muḥammad XIII
1485–1487

Muḥammad XII
(Boabdil)
1482
1486–1492

TABLE 6   RULERS OF ASTURIAS-LEÓN, THEN PORTUGAL, LEÓN, AND
CASTILE (EIGHTH–THIRTEENTH CENTURIES)

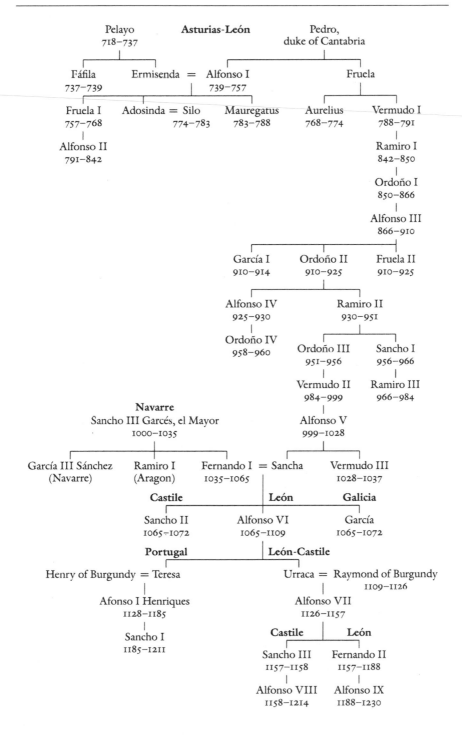

Asturias-León

Pelayo
718–737

Pedro,
duke of Cantabria

Fáfila
737–739

Ermisenda = Alfonso I
739–757

Fruela

Fruela I
757–768

Adosinda = Silo
774–783

Mauregatus
783–788

Aurelius
768–774

Vermudo I
788–791

Alfonso II
791–842

Ramiro I
842–850

Ordoño I
850–866

Alfonso III
866–910

García I
910–914

Ordoño II
910–925

Fruela II
910–925

Alfonso IV
925–930

Ramiro II
930–951

Ordoño IV
958–960

Ordoño III
951–956

Sancho I
956–966

Vermudo II
984–999

Ramiro III
966–984

Navarre

Sancho III Garcés, el Mayor
1000–1035

Alfonso V
999–1028

García III Sánchez
(Navarre)

Ramiro I
(Aragon)

Fernando I = Sancha
1035–1065

Vermudo III
1028–1037

Castile   **León**   **Galicia**

Sancho II
1065–1072

Alfonso VI
1065–1109

García
1065–1072

Portugal   **León-Castile**

Henry of Burgundy = Teresa

Urraca = Raymond of Burgundy
1109–1126

Afonso I Henriques
1128–1185

Alfonso VII
1126–1157

Sancho I
1185–1211

Castile   **León**

Sancho III
1157–1158

Fernando II
1157–1188

Alfonso VIII
1158–1214

Alfonso IX
1188–1230

TABLE 7   RULERS OF NAVARRE, ARAGÓN, AND CATALONIA (NINTH-THIRTEENTH CENTURIES)

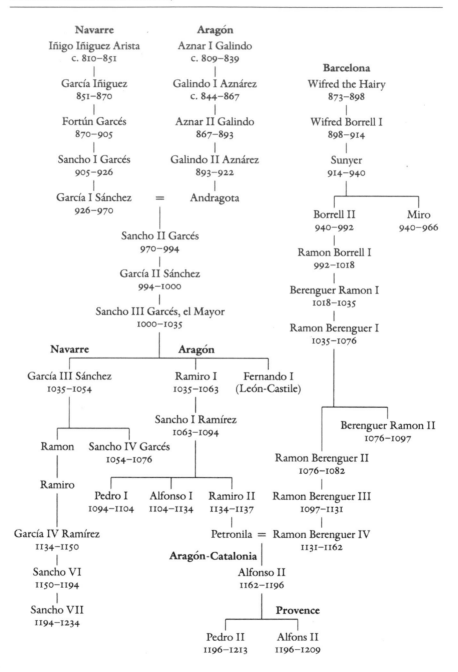

TABLE 8   RULERS OF PORTUGAL (1185–1521)

Sancho I
1185–1211

Afonso II
1211–1223

Sancho II   Afonso III
1223–1248   1248–1279

Dinis
1279–1325

Afonso IV
1325–1357

Pedro
1357–1367

                              John of Gaunt

Fernando   João I of Avis = Philippa
1367–1383   1385–1433

Juan I of = Beatriz
Castile

              Duarte   Henry the   Pedro of
              1433–1438   Navigator   Coimbra

                                                Pedro the
                                                Constable

Afonso V   Fernando
1438–1481

João II   Manuel I
1481–1495   1495–1521

TABLE 9   RULERS OF THE CROWN OF ARAGÓN (1196–1516)

RULERS OF THE CROWN OF ARAGÓN (1196–1516)

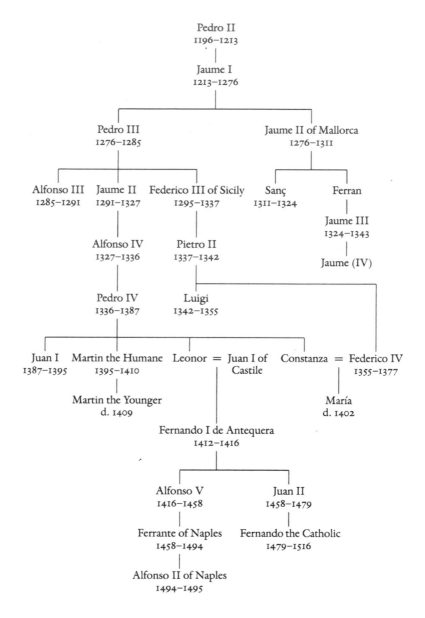

TABLE 10   RULERS OF LEÓN-CASTILE (1157–1504)

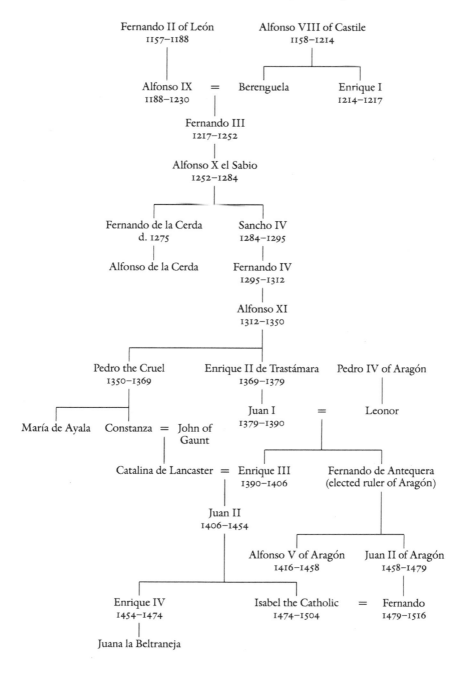

RULERS OF LEÓN-CASTILE (1157–1504)

Fernando II of León
1157–1188

Alfonso VIII of Castile
1158–1214

Alfonso IX   =   Berenguela   Enrique I
1188–1230   1214–1217

Fernando III
1217–1252

Alfonso X el Sabio
1252–1284

Fernando de la Cerda   Sancho IV
d. 1275   1284–1295

Alfonso de la Cerda   Fernando IV
1295–1312

Alfonso XI
1312–1350

Pedro the Cruel   Enrique II de Trastámara   Pedro IV of Aragón
1350–1369   1369–1379

Juan I   =   Leonor
1379–1390

María de Ayala   Constanza = John of
Gaunt

Catalina de Lancaster = Enrique III   Fernando de Antequera
1390–1406   (elected ruler of Aragón)

Juan II
1406–1454

Alfonso V of Aragón   Juan II of Aragón
1416–1458   1458–1479

Enrique IV   Isabel the Catholic   =   Fernando
1454–1474   1474–1504   1479–1516

Juana la Beltraneja

Glossary

A = Arabic
L = Latin
H = Hebrew
V = Vernacular (usually Castilian)

acequiero—(V) Irrigation officer.
adalid—(V) Scout (from Arabic *dalīl*).
al-Andalus—(A) Iberian territory under Muslim rule.
al-Murābiṭ—See Almoravid.
al-Muwahhid—See Almohad.
alcalde—(V) Municipal official who filled a number of different roles
     according to place and period. The *alcalde* could dispense justice, act
     as parish representative, lead the urban militia, collect royal taxes, and
     more.
alcaría—(V) Also spelled *alquería* (from Arabic *al-qarya*), this was a rural
     settlement or hamlet inhabited by several families, generally a tribal
     clan. It was held under a lord or by collective ownership.
aldea—(V) Village.
alfaba—(V) Unit of valuation of land (from Arabic *al-ḥabba*).
alfaquíes—(V) Castilian version of *faqīh*, a Muslim judge.
alférez—(V) Royal standard-bearer.
Alhambra—Palace complex and fortress of the Naṣrid rulers in Granada.
aljama—(V) Community or neighborhood (from Arabic *al-jamaʿ*). Usually
     a community of Jews or Muslims living under Christian rule.
Aljamiado—Version of Castilian used by the Mudejar population and
     written in Arabic characters.
Almohad—From the Arabic name al-Muwahhid (meaning "those who
     affirm the unity of God"), this Berber movement was established under
     the reforming leader Ibn Tumart in the early twelfth century. The
     Almohad dynasty came to control much of western North Africa and
     al-Andalus. They withdrew from the Iberian Peninsula in 1223.
Almoravid—North African Muslim Berber dynasty ruling in al-Andalus
     from 1086 until 1147. The English name comes from the Arabic

al-Murābiṭ, a word linked to the institution of the *ribaṭ*, a Muslim house of religious retreat.

alod—Freely held parcel of land.

alquería—(V) See *alcaria*.

amīr—(A) Muslim ruler or noble.

aranzada—(V) Unit of land measurement equal to about an acre, or five hectares.

Arianism—Christian heresy that questioned the full divinity of Christ and held him to be neither coequal nor coeternal with the Father. Although Arian views were declared heretical at the Council of Nicaea in 325, they persisted in Gothic Europe until the sixth century. Arianism was espoused by the Visigoths until their conversion to Catholicism under King Reccared in 589.

Averroes—Latin name of the Muslim philosopher Ibn Rushd, who worked at the Almohad court. He was particularly known for his commentaries on the work of Aristotle.

boni homines—(L) Citizens, literally "good men," this was a common designation for men deemed appropriate to serve in urban government or other public functions.

caballero—(V) Knight.

caliph—Title of the supreme ruler of the Muslim community in both religious and secular affairs (from Arabic *khalīfa*, the "successor" to Muḥammad). Traditionally, there was only one caliph at a time in the Muslim world, but this tradition was broken by the declaration of a Fatimid caliphate in North Africa and an Umayyad caliphate in al-Andalus (under ʿAbd al-Raḥmān III) in the early tenth century.

cavalleria—(V) Unit of land measurement equal to about ninety-five acres.

Chaldean—Medieval Latin term for Muslim.

conversos—(V) Jews converted to Christianity.

convivencia—Meaning "living together" in modern Castilian, this term has been used by historians to describe the harmonious coexistence of Muslims, Christians, and Jews in the medieval Iberian Peninsula.

cortes—(V) (Catalan *corts*) Parliamentary assembly of representatives from the nobility, clergy, and towns. The cortes was supposed to be called by the ruler at regular intervals in order to decide matters of legislation, taxation, and other issues.

dār al-Islām—(A) Islamic world.

dhimma—(A) An agreement according protection to Christians and Jews (*dhimmīs*) living under Islamic rule.

dhimmī—(A) A Christian or Jew living under Islamic rule. *Dhimmīs* were

also called "people of the book" (*ahl al-kitāb*) because followed a
written religious text. Although subject to special restrictions and taxes,
dhimmīs could not be forcibly converted to Islam.

dinar—(A) Muslim gold coin.

dirham—(A) Muslim silver coin.

dobla—(V) Christian heavy gold coin modeled on Almohad "double
dinars."

elches—(V) Derogatory term for Christian converts to Islam.

emir—(A) see amīr

fanecate—(V) Unit of land measurement (from Arabic).

faqīh—(A) Muslim religious scholar and judge.

fils—(A) Small coin, usually made of copper.

fuero—(V) (Catalan *furs*) Charter of urban laws and freedoms granted to a
town by the ruler.

ḥadīth—(A) Traditions relating to the Prophet Muḥammad.

ḥājib—(A) Muslim palace official, generally translated as chamberlain,
regent, or vizier. Under the last Umayyad ruler, real power in the realm
was held by the *ḥājib* al-Manṣūr.

ḥajj—(A) Muslim pilgrimage to Mecca.

hidalgo—(V) Member of the lower nobility.

Hijra—(A) Muḥammad's flight from Mecca to Medina in 622, the starting
date for the Muslim calendar.

ḥisba—(A) See *muḥtasib*.

Hispano-Romans—Latin-speaking Catholics living in the Iberian Peninsula
at the time of the Visigoths' arrival and continuing to live there under
Visigothic rule.

huerta—(V) Garden or area of irrigated agricultural land.

imām—(A) Muslim religious leader or preacher.

infante/infanta—(V) Prince/princess.

iurates/jurates—(L) Sworn witnesses.

jizya—(A) Tax paid by People of the Book (*dhimmī*) living under Muslim
rule.

Judeo-Arabic—Arabic written in Hebrew characters.

judería—(V) Jewish quarter in a Christian town.

kātib—(A) Muslim scribe or administrator.

mahdi—(A) Literally "the rightly guided one," this term designated a
Muslim apocalyptic leader.

Mālikī—(A) One of the four primary schools of Islamic law, the Mālikī
school was dominant in al-Andalus and North Africa for most of the
medieval period.

maravedi—(V) Castilian gold coin, or more usually, money of account (related to morabetin).

Marranos—Jewish converts to Christianity.

mithqāl—(A) Term referring to a gold coin (*dinar*), or to a unit of monetary weight.

morabatin (or morabetin)—(V) Christian gold coin modeled on Almoravid dinars.

morería—(V) Muslim quarter in a Christian town.

Moriscos—Muslims converted to Christianity and living in Christian Spain in later Middle Ages.

mosque—Building for Muslim worship.

Mozarabs—Term usually applied to Arabized Christians living in al-Andalus or in the northern Christian kingdoms.

Mudejars—Muslims living under Christian rule. The term "mudejar" is also applied to an architectural style associated with mudejar builders.

muezzin—(A) Person giving the call to Muslim prayers.

muftī—(A) Muslim scholar and judge.

muḥtasib—(A) Muslim market inspector. The *muḥtasib* was responsible for the economic and moral probity of the marketplace and other urban areas, and for overseeing the *ḥisba* (the promotion of good and prevention of evil) from which the office takes its name.

muwallad—(A) Sometimes called "neo-Muslims," these were Iberian Christians converted to Islam after the Muslim conquest in 711.

nagid—(H) Revered leader, or "prince," of the Jewish community.

nasi—(H) Traditionally meaning "patriarch," this term was used as a title of high honor in the Iberian Jewish community.

Naṣrid—Muslim dynasty ruling in Granada from 1232 until 1492.

probi homines—(L) Citizens (see *boni homines*).

qāḍī—(A) Muslim judge.

qāʾid—(A) Muslim military leader or governor.

Qurʾān—(A) The Muslim holy book revealed to the Prophet Muḥammad in the early seventh century.

rahal—(V) Private estate (from Arabic).

raʾīs—(A) Muslim commander, admiral, or person in authority.

raṭl—(A) A measure of weight.

reconquista—(V) Iberian Christian military effort to retake territory from the Muslims.

repartimiento—(V) (Catalan *repartiment*) Division of conquered Muslim land and houses among Christian conquerors and new settlers. This division is recorded in extensive registers (*Libros de repartimiento* in Castilian, or *Llibres del repartiment* in Catalan).

Sefarad—Hebrew name for Spain; hence "Sefardic" is used for Iberian Jews or Jews who trace their heritage to the Iberian Peninsula.

Shāfiʿī—One of the four primary schools of Islamic law.

sharīʿa—(A) Muslim law.

Shiʿī—(A) A branch of Islam whose believers support the claims of ʿAlī, Muḥammad's cousin and son-in-law, and ʿAlī's descendants, to the Muslim caliphate. Although Shiʿism was very influential elsewhere in the medieval Islamic world, it never gained much of a foothold in al-Andalus.

solidus— (L) Christian gold coin (or unit of account).

Sunnī—(A) The word comes from the *sunna* (literally "tradition" or "habit") of Muḥammad and applies to the followers of mainstream Muslim belief. Almost all Muslims in al-Andalus were Sunnī.

tahulla—(V) Unit of land measurement (from Arabic *tahwīla*).

Taifa kingdoms—Small kingdoms that formed in al-Andalus following the breakup of centralized Umayyad rule in 1031. The Taifa period lasted until the arrival of the Almoravids in the Iberian Peninsula in 1086.

Trastámara—Castilian dynasty established by Enrique II, who seized the throne from his half brother, Pedro I, in 1369. Following the election of Fernando de Antequera to the throne of Aragón in 1412, the Crowns of Castile and Aragón were both ruled by members of the Trastámara dynasty.

Umayyad—Muslim dynasty ruling in al-Andalus from 756 until 1031. Their rule was established when ʿAbd al-Raḥmān I arrived from Syria.

vega—(V) Cultivated land outside the walls of a town.

Visigoths—A Germanic people who ruled the Iberian Peninsula from the middle of the fifth century until the arrival of the Muslims in 711.

vizir (or vizier)—(A) Councillor or high administrator in a Muslim court.

wazīr—(A) See *vizir*.

Ẓāhirī—(A) School of Islamic law emphasizing the literal interpretation of the Qurʾān and *hadīth*.

zakāt—(A) Alms tax paid by Muslims in an Islamic state.

zalmedina—(V) Aragonese urban official or magistrate (from Arabic).

Bibliography

The bibliography provides a selection of books in English on medieval Iberian history. Most are modern monographs, although a few classics and collected volumes have also been included. Entries are divided roughly according to the general topic or period they cover. There are, of course, many excellent works in other languages, as well as older studies in the field. Interested readers will find references to these in the notes and bibliographies of the books listed below. Readers looking for primary texts and translations will find these in the same places, as well as in the sources cited for many of the translations in this collection. Readers may also want to consult the Library of Iberian Resources Online (LIBRO) at http://libro.uca.edu.

GENERAL HISTORY AND HISTORIOGRAPHY

Bisson, Thomas N. *The Medieval Crown of Aragon: A Short History*. Oxford: Clarendon Press, 1986.

Castro, Américo. *The Spaniards: An Introduction to Their History*. Trans. Willard F. King and Selma Margaretten. Berkeley: University of California Press, 1971.

———. *The Structure of Spanish History*. Trans. Edmund L. King. Princeton, N.J.: Princeton University Press, 1954.

Collins, Roger. *Spain: An Oxford Archaeological Guide*. New York: Oxford University Press, 1998.

Corfis, Ivy A., and Ray Harris-Northall, eds. *Medieval Iberia: Changing Societies and Cultures in Contact and Transition*. Woodbridge: Tamesis, 2007.

Dodds, Jerrilynn, María Rosa Menocal, and Abigail Krasner Balbale, eds. *The Arts of Intimacy: Christians, Jews, and Muslims in the Making of Castilian Culture*. New Haven, Conn.: Yale University Press, 2008.

Doubleday, Simon, and David Coleman, eds. *In the Light of Medieval Spain: Islam, the West, and the Relevance of the Past*. New York: Palgrave Macmillan, 2008.

Ecker, Heather. *Caliphs and Kings: The Art and Influence of Medieval Spain*. Washington, D.C.: Smithsonian Institution Press, 2004.

Gerli, Michael, ed. *Medieval Iberia: An Encyclopedia*. New York: Routledge, 2003.

Glick, Thomas F. *From Muslim Fortress to Christian Castle: Social and Cultural Change in Medieval Spain*. Manchester: Manchester University Press, 1995.

———. *Islamic and Christian Spain in the Early Middle Ages*. Princeton, N.J.: Princeton University Press, 1979. 2nd ed. Leiden: Brill, 2005.

Grieve, Patricia E. *The Eve of Spain: Myths of Origins in the History of Christian, Muslim, and Jewish Conflict*. Baltimore: Johns Hopkins University Press, 2009.

Hillgarth, J. N. *The Mirror of Spain, 1500–1700: The Formation of a Myth.* Ann Arbor: University of Michigan Press, 2000.

Jackson, Gabriel. *The Making of Medieval Spain.* New York: Harcourt Brace Jovanovich, 1972.

Kamen, Henry. *Imagining Spain: Historical Myth and National Identity.* New Haven, Conn.: Yale University Press, 2008.

Linehan, Peter. *History and the Historians of Medieval Spain.* Oxford: Clarendon Press, 1993.

Mann, Vivian B., Thomas F. Glick, and Jerrilynn D. Dodds, eds. *Convivencia: Jews, Muslims, and Christians in Medieval Spain.* New York: Braziller, 1992.

Menéndez Pidal, Ramón. *The Spaniards in Their History.* Trans. Walter Starkie. New York: Norton, 1950.

Menocal, María Rosa. *The Arabic Role in Medieval Literary History: A Forgotten Heritage.* Philadelphia: University of Pennsylvania Press, 2004.

———. *The Ornament of the World. How Muslims, Jews, and Christians Created a Culture of Tolerance in Medieval Spain.* Boston: Little, Brown, 2002.

Monroe, James T. *Islam and the Arabs in Spanish Scholarship.* Leiden: Brill, 1970.

Nepaulsingh, Colbert. *Towards a History of Literary Composition in Medieval Spain.* Toronto: University of Toronto Press, 1986.

O'Callaghan, Joseph F. *A History of Medieval Spain.* Ithaca, N.Y.: Cornell University Press, 1975.

Reilly, Bernard F. *The Medieval Spains.* Cambridge: Cambridge University Press, 1993.

Vicens Vives, Jaime. *Approaches to the History of Spain.* Trans. Joan C. Ullman, 2nd ed. Berkeley: University of California Press, 1970.

———. *An Economic History of Spain.* Trans. F. M. López Morillas. Princeton, N.J.: Princeton University Press, 1969.

VISIGOTHS AND THE EARLY MEDIEVAL PERIOD

Bowes, Kimberley D., and Michael Kulikowski, eds. *Hispania in Late Antiquity: Current Perspectives.* Leiden: Brill, 2005.

Carr, Karen Eva. *Vandals to Visigoths: Rural Settlement Patterns in Early Medieval Spain.* Ann Arbor: University of Michigan Press, 2002.

Collins, Roger. *The Arab Conquest of Spain, 710–797.* Oxford: Blackwell, 1989.

———. *Early Medieval Spain: Unity in Diversity, 400–1000.* London: Macmillan, 1983.

———. *Law, Culture, and Regionalism in Early Medieval Spain.* Aldershot: Variorum, 1992.

———. *Visigothic Spain, 409–711.* Malden, Mass.: Blackwell, 2004.

Ferreiro, Alberto. *The Visigoths: Studies in Culture and Society.* Leiden: Brill, 1999.

———. *The Visigoths in Gaul and Iberia: A Supplemental Bibliography 1984–2003.* Leiden: Brill, 2006.

———. *The Visigoths in Gaul and Iberia: A Supplemental Bibliography 2004–2006.* Leiden: Brill, 2008.

Heather, Peter J., ed. *The Visigoths from the Migration Period to the Seventh Century: An Ethnographic Perspective.* Woodbridge: Boydell, 1999.

James, Edward, ed. *Visigothic Spain: New Approaches*. New York: Oxford University Press, 1980.

Katz, Solomon. *The Jews in the Visigothic Kingdoms of Gaul and Spain*. Cambridge, Mass.: Medieval Academy of America, 1937.

King, P. D. *Law and Society in the Visigothic Kingdom*. Cambridge: Cambridge University Press, 1972.

Kulikowski, Michael. *Late Roman Spain and Its Cities*. Baltimore: Johns Hopkins University Press, 2004.

Lewis, Archibald. *The Development of Southern French and Catalan Society, 718–1050*. Austin: University of Texas Press, 1965.

Livermore, Harold V. *The Origins of Spain and Portugal*. London: Allen and Unwin, 1971.

Martyn, John R. C. *King Sisebut and the Culture of Visigothic Spain*. Lewiston, N.Y.: Edward Mellon, 2008.

Roth, Norman. *Jews, Visigoths, and Muslims in Medieval Spain: Cooperation and Conflict*. Leiden: Brill, 1994.

Stocking, Rachel. *Bishops, Councils, and Consensus in the Visigothic Kingdom, 589–633*. Ann Arbor: University of Michigan Press, 2000.

Thompson, E. A. *The Goths in Spain*. Oxford: Clarendon Press, 1969.

Ziegler, Aloysius K. *Church and State in Visigothic Spain*. Washington, D.C.: Catholic University of America Press, 1930.

AL-ANDALUS FROM THE NINTH TO THE THIRTEENTH CENTURY

Anderson, Glaire D., and Mariam Rosser-Owen, eds. *Revisiting al-Andalus: Perspectives on the Material Culture of Iberia and Beyond*. Leiden: Brill, 2007.

Ashtor, Eliyahu. *The Jews of Moslem Spain*. 3 vols. Philadelphia: Jewish Publication Society of America, 1973–1984.

Brann, Ross. *Power in the Portrayal: Representations of Jews and Muslims in Eleventh and Twelfth-Century Islamic Spain*. Princeton, N.J.: Princeton University Press, 2002.

Chejne, Anwar G. *Muslim Spain: Its History and Culture*. Minneapolis: University of Minnesota Press, 1974.

Christys, Ann. *Christians in al-Andalus, 711–1000*. Richmond, Surrey: Curzon, 2002.

Colbert, Edward P. *The Martyrs of Córdoba: A Study of the Sources*. Washington, D.C.: Catholic University of America Press, 1962.

Constable, Olivia R. *Trade and Traders in Muslim Spain: The Commercial Realignment of the Iberian Peninsula, 900–1500*. Cambridge: Cambridge University Press, 1994.

Coope, Jessica A. *The Martyrs of Córdoba: Community and Family Conflict in an Age of Mass Conversion*. Lincoln: University of Nebraska Press, 1995.

Dodds, Jerrilynn D. *Architecture and Ideology in Early Medieval Spain*. University Park: Pennsylvania State University Press, 1990.

———, ed. *Al-Andalus: The Art of Islamic Spain*. New York: Metropolitan Museum of Art, 1992.

Fierro, Maribel. *'Abd al-Rahman III: The First Cordoban Caliph*. Oxford: Oneworld, 2005.

Fletcher, Richard. *Moorish Spain*. New York: Holt, 1992.

Handler, Andrew. *The Zirids of Granada*. Coral Gables, Fla.: University of Miami Press, 1974.

Hitchcock, Richard. *Mozarabs in Medieval and Early Modern Spain*. Aldershot: Ashgate, 2008.

Imamuddin, S.M. *Muslim Spain, 711–1492 A.D.: A Sociological* Study. Leiden: Brill, 1981.

———. *Some Aspects of the Socio-Economic and Cultural History of Muslim Spain, 711–1492 A.D.* Leiden: Brill, 1965.

Jayyusi, Salma K., ed. *The Legacy of Muslim Spain*. Leiden: Brill, 1992.

Kennedy, Hugh. *Muslim Spain and Portugal: A Political History of al-Andalus*. Harlow: Longman, 1996.

Le Tourneau, Roger. *The Almohad Movement in North Africa in the Twelfth and Thirteenth Centuries*. Princeton, N.J.: Princeton University Press, 1969.

Marín, Manuela, ed. *The Formation of al-Andalus*. 2 vols. Aldershot: Ashgate, 1998.

O'Connor, Isabel A. *A Forgotten Community: The Mudejar Aljama of Xàtiva, 1240–1327*. Leiden: Brill, 2003.

Robinson, Cynthia. *In Praise of Song: The Making of Courtly Culture in al-Andalus and Provence, 1005–1134 AD*. Leiden: Brill, 2002.

———. *Medieval Andalusian Courtly Culture in the Mediterranean*. New York: Routledge, 2007.

Ruggles, D. Fairchild. *Gardens, Landscape, and Vision in the Palaces of Islamic Spain*. University Park: Pennsylvania State University Press, 2000.

Safran, Janina M. *The Second Umayyad Caliphate: The Articulation of Caliphal Legitimacy in al-Andalus*. Cambridge, Mass.: Harvard University Press, 2000.

Scales, Peter. *The Fall of the Caliphate of Córdoba: Berbers and Andalusis in Conflict*. Leiden: Brill, 1994.

Wasserstein, David J. *The Caliphate in the West: An Islamic Political Institution in the Iberian Peninsula*. Oxford: Clarendon Press, 1993.

———. *The Rise and Fall of the Party Kings: Politics and Society in Islamic Spain, 1002–1086*. Princeton, N.J.: Princeton University Press, 1985.

Watt, W. Montgomery, and Pierre Cachia. *A History of Islamic Spain*. Edinburgh: Edinburgh University Press, 1965.

Wolf, Kenneth B. *Christian Martyrs in Muslim Spain*. Cambridge: Cambridge University Press, 1988.

CHRISTIAN IBERIA FROM THE NINTH TO THE THIRTEENTH CENTURY

Baer, Yitzhak. *A History of the Jews in Christian Spain*. Trans. Louis Schiffman. 2 vols. Philadelphia: Jewish Publication Society of America, 1961–1966.

Barton, Simon. *The Aristocracy in Twelfth-Century León and Castile*. Cambridge: Cambridge University Press, 1997.

Bensch, Stephen P. *Barcelona and Its Rulers, 1096–1291*. Cambridge: Cambridge University Press, 1994.

Bishko, Charles Julian. *Spanish and Portuguese Monastic History, 600–1300*. London: Variorum, 1984.

———. *Studies in Medieval Spanish Frontier History*. London: Variorum, 1980.

Bisson, Thomas N. *Tormented Voices: Power, Crisis, and Humanity in Rural Catalonia, 1140–1200*. Cambridge, Mass.: Harvard University Press, 1998.

Bowman, Jeffrey A. *Shifting Landmarks: Property, Proof, and Dispute in Catalonia Around the Year 1000*. Ithaca, N.Y.: Cornell University Press, 2004.

Brodman, James W. *Charity and Welfare: Hospitals and the Poor in Medieval Catalonia*. Philadelphia: University of Pennsylvania Press, 1998.

———. *Ransoming Captives in Crusader Spain: The Order of Merced on the Christian-Islamic Frontier*. Philadelphia: University of Pennsylvania Press, 1986.

Burman, Thomas E. *Reading the Quran in Latin Christendom, 1140–1560*. Philadelphia: University of Pennsylvania Press, 2007.

———. *Religious Polemic and the Intellectual History of the Mozarabs, c. 1050–1200*. Leiden: Brill, 1994.

Burns, Robert I. *The Crusader Kingdom of Valencia: Reconstruction on a Thirteenth-Century Frontier*. 2 vols. Cambridge, Mass.: Harvard University Press, 1967.

———. *Foundations of Crusader Valencia: Revolt and Recovery, 1257–1263*. Princeton, N.J.: Princeton University Press, 1991.

———. *Islam Under the Crusaders: Colonial Survival in the Thirteenth-Century Kingdom of Valencia*. Princeton. N.J.: Princeton University Press, 1991.

———. *Jews in the Notarial Culture: Latinate Wills in Mediterranean Spain, 1250–1350*. Berkeley: University of California Press, 1996.

———. *Medieval Colonialism: Postcrusade Exploitation of Islamic Valencia*. Princeton, N.J.: Princeton University Press, 1975.

———. *Moors and Crusaders in Mediterranean Spain*. London: Variorum, 1978.

———. *Muslims, Christians, and Jews in the Crusader Kingdom of Valencia*. Cambridge: Cambridge University Press, 1984.

———, ed. *Emperor of Culture: Alfonso X the Learned of Castile and His Thirteenth-Century Renaissance*. Philadelphia: University of Pennsylvania Press, 1990.

———. *The Worlds of Alfonso the Learned and James the Conqueror*. Princeton, N.J.: Princeton University Press, 1985.

Burns, Robert I., and Paul E. Chevedden. *Negotiating Cultures: Bilingual Surrender Treaties in Muslim-Crusader Spain*. Leiden: Brill, 1999.

Caputo, Nina. *Nahmanides in Medieval Catalonia: History, Community, and Messianism*. Notre Dame, Ind.: Notre Dame University Press, 2007.

Catlos, Brian A. *The Victors and the Vanquished: Christians and Muslims of Catalonia and Aragon, 1050–1300*. Cambridge: Cambridge University Press, 2004.

Chazan, Robert. *Barcelona and Beyond: The Disputation of 1263 and Its Aftermath*. Berkeley: University of California Press, 1992.

Chevedden, Paul, Donald Kagay, and P. Padilla, eds. *Iberia and the Mediterranean World of the Middle Ages: Studies in Honor of Robert I. Burns*. Vol. 2. Leiden: Brill, 1996.

Dillard, Heath. *Daughters of the Reconquest: Women in Castilian Town Society, 1100–1300*. Cambridge: Cambridge University Press, 1984.

Fletcher, Richard. *The Episcopate in the Kingdom of León in the Twelfth Century*. Oxford: Oxford University Press, 1978.

———. *The Quest for El Cid*. New York: Knopf, 1990.

Freedman, Paul H. *Church, Law, and Society in Catalonia, 900–1500*. Aldershot: Variorum, 1994.

————. *The Diocese of Vic: Tradition and Regeneration in Medieval Catalonia*. New Brunswick, N.J.: Rutgers University Press, 1983.

————. *The Origins of Peasant Servitude in Medieval Catalonia*. Cambridge: Cambridge University Press, 1991.

Keller, John E., and Annette G. Cash. *Daily Life Depicted in the Cantigas de Santa Maria*. Lexington: University Press of Kentucky, 1998.

Klein, Elka. *Jews, Christian Society and Royal Power in Medieval Barcelona*. Ann Arbor: University of Michigan Press, 2006.

Kosto, Adam. *Making Agreements in Medieval Catalonia*. Cambridge: Cambridge University Press, 2001.

Lay, Stephen. *The Reconquest Kings of Portugal: Political and Cultural Reorientation on the Medieval Frontier*. New York: Palgrave Macmillan, 2009.

Linehan, Peter. *The Ladies of Zamora*. University Park: Pennsylvania State University Press, 1997.

————. *Past and Present in Medieval Spain*. Aldershot: Variorum, 1992.

————. *The Processes of Politics and the Rule of Law: Studies on the Iberian Kingdoms and Papal Rome in the Middle Ages*. Aldershot: Ashgate, 2002.

————. *Spain, 1157–1300. A Partible Inheritance*. Oxford: Blackwell, 2008.

————. *The Spanish Church and the Papacy in the Thirteenth Century*. Cambridge: Cambridge University Press, 1971.

————. *Spanish Church and Society, 1150–1300*. London: Variorum, 1983.

Lomax, D. W. *The Reconquest of Spain*. New York: Longman, 1978.

Lomax, D. W., and D. Mackenzie, eds. *God and Man in Medieval Spain*. Warminster: Aris and Phillips, 1989.

Menéndez Pidal, Ramón. *The Cid and His Spain*. Trans. Harold Sunderland. London: John Murray, 1934.

Mirrer, Louise. *Women, Jews, and Muslims in the Texts of Reconquest Castile*. Ann Arbor: University of Michigan Press, 1996.

Neuman, Abraham A. *The Jews in Spain: Their Social, Political, and Cultural Life During the Middle Ages*. 2 vols. Philadelphia: Jewish Publication Society of America, 1942–1944.

O'Callaghan, Joseph F. *Alfonso X and the Cantigas de Santa Maria: A Poetic Biography*. Leiden: Brill, 1998.

————. *The Cortes of Castile-León, 1188–1350*. Philadelphia: University of Pennsylvania Press, 1989.

————. *The Learned King: The Reign of Alfonso X of Castile*. Philadelphia: University of Pennsylvania Press, 1993.

————. *Reconquest and Crusade in Medieval Spain*. Philadelphia: University of Pennsylvania Press, 2003.

Pick, Lucy K. *Conflict and Coexistence: Archbishop Rodrigo and the Muslims and Jews in Medieval Spain*. Ann Arbor: University of Michigan Press, 2004.

Powers, James F. *A Society Organized for War: The Iberian Municipal Militias in the Central Middle Ages, 1000–1284*. Berkeley: University of California Press, 1988.

Procter, Evelyn S. *Alfonso X of Castile: Patron of Literature and Learning*. Oxford: Clarendon Press, 1961.

————. *Curia and Cortes in León and Castile, 1072–1295*. Cambridge: Cambridge University Press, 1980.

————. *The Judicial Use of the "Pesquisa" (Inquisition) in León and Castilla, 1157–1369.* London: Longman, 1966.

Ray, Jonathan. *The Sephardic Frontier: The Reconquista and the Jewish Community in Medieval Iberia.* Ithaca, N.Y.: Cornell University Press, 2006.

Reilly, Bernard F. *The Contest of Christian and Muslim Spain, 1031–1157.* Oxford: Blackwell, 1992.

————. *The Kingdom of León-Castilla Under King Alfonso VI, 1065–1109.* Princeton, N.J.: Princeton University Press, 1988.

————. *The Kingdom of León-Castilla Under King Alfonso VII, 1126–1157.* Philadelphia: University of Pennsylvania Press, 1998.

————. *The Kingdom of León-Castilla Under Queen Urraca, 1109–1126.* Princeton, N.J.: Princeton University Press, 1982.

Robinson, Cynthia, and Leyla Rouhi, eds. *Under the Influence: Questioning the Comparative in Medieval Castile.* Leiden: Brill, 2005.

Ruiz, Teofilo F. *From Heaven to Earth: The Reordering of Castilian Society, 1150–1350.* Princeton, N.J.: Princeton University Press, 2004.

Shideler, John. *A Medieval Catalan Noble Family: The Moncadas, 1000–1250.* Berkeley: University of California Press, 1983.

Simon, Larry J., ed. *Iberia and the Mediterranean World of the Middle Ages: Studies in Honor of Robert I. Burns.* Vol. 1. Leiden: Brill, 1995.

Smith, Colin. *The Making of the "Poema de mío Cid."* Cambridge: Cambridge University Press, 1983.

Stalls, Clay. *Possessing the Land: Aragon's Expansion in Islam's Ebro Frontier Under Alfonso the Battler, 1104–1134.* Leiden: Brill, 1995.

Vann, Theresa, ed. *Queens, Regents and Potentates.* Dallas: Academia, 1993.

Vose, Robin. *Dominicans, Muslims and Jews in the Medieval Crown of Aragon.* Cambridge: Cambridge University Press, 2009.

THE IBERIAN PENINSULA IN THE LATER MIDDLE AGES

Abulafia, David. *A Mediterranean Emporium: The Catalan Kingdom of Majorca.* Cambridge: Cambridge University Press, 1994.

————. *The Western Mediterranean Kingdoms, 1200–1500.* London: Longman, 1997.

Alcalá, Angel, ed. *The Spanish Inquisition and the Inquisitorial Mind.* New York: Columbia University Press, 1987.

Beinart, H. *Conversos on Trial: The Inquisition in Ciudad Real.* Jerusalem: Magnes Press, 1981.

Blumenthal, Debra. *Enemies and Familiars: Slavery and Mastery in Fifteenth-Century Valencia.* Ithaca, N.Y.: Cornell University Press, 2009.

Boswell, John. *The Royal Treasure: Muslim Communities Under the Crown of Aragon in the Fourteenth Century.* New Haven, Conn.: Yale University Press, 1977.

Boxer, C. R. *The Portuguese Seaborne Empire, 1415–1825.* London: Hutchinson, 1969.

Catz, Rebecca. *Christopher Columbus and the Portuguese, 1476–1498.* Westport, Conn.: Greenwood Press, 1993.

Chejne, Anwar. *Islam and the West: The Moriscos, a Cultural and Social History.* Albany: State University of New York Press, 1983.

Doñate Sebastiá, José María. *Three Jewish Communities in Medieval Valencia.* Jerusalem: Magnes Press, 1990.

Doubleday, Simon. *The Lara Family: Crown and Nobility in Medieval Spain.* Cambridge, Mass.: Harvard University Press, 2001.

Earenfight, Theresa. *The King's Other Body: Maria of Castile and the Crown of Aragon.* Philadelphia: University of Pennsylvania Press, 2009.

———, ed. *Queenship and Political Power in Medieval and Early Modern Spain.* Aldershot: Ashgate, 2005.

Echevarría, Ana. *The Fortress of Faith: The Attitude Towards Muslims in Fifteenth Century Spain.* Leiden: Brill, 1999.

———. *Knights on the Frontier: The Moorish Guard of the Kings of Castile (1410–1467).* Leiden: Brill, 2009.

Edwards, John. *Christian Córdoba: The City and Its Regions in the Late Middle Ages.* Cambridge: Cambridge University Press, 1982.

———. *The Spain of the Catholic Monarchs, 1474–1520.* Malden, Mass.: Blackwell, 2000.

Ehlers, Benjamin. *Between Christians and Moriscos: Juan de Ribera and Religious Reform in Valencia, 1568–1614.* Baltimore: Johns Hopkins University Press, 2006.

Estow, Clara. *Pedro the Cruel of Castile, 1350–1369.* Leiden: Brill, 1995.

Fernández-Armesto, Felipe. *Columbus.* Oxford: Oxford University Press, 1991.

Gampel, Benjamin R. *Crisis and Creativity in the Sephardic World, 1391–1648.* New York: Columbia University Press, 1997.

———. *The Last Jews on Iberian Soil: Navarrese Jewry, 1479–1498.* Berkeley: University of California Press, 1989.

Gomes, Rita Costa. *The Making of a Court Society: Kings and Nobles in Late Medieval Portugal.* Cambridge: Cambridge University Press, 2003.

Grabar, Oleg. *The Alhambra.* Cambridge, Mass.: Harvard University Press, 1978.

Hames, Harvey J., ed. *Jews, Muslims, and Christians in and around the Crown of Aragon. Studies in Honor of Elena Lourie.* Leiden: Brill, 2004.

Hamilton, Earl. *Money, Prices, and Wages in Valencia, Aragon, and Navarre, 1351–1500.* Cambridge, Mass.: Harvard University Press, 1936.

Harvey, L. P. *Islamic Spain, 1250–1500.* Chicago: University of Chicago Press, 1990.

———. *Muslims in Spain, 1500–1614.* Chicago: University of Chicago Press, 2005.

Hillgarth, J. N. *The Spanish Kingdoms, 1250–1516.* 2 vols. Oxford: Clarendon Press, 1976–1978.

Hinojosa Montalvo, José. *The Jews of the Kingdom of Valencia, from Persecution to Expulsion, 1391–1492.* Jerusalem: Magnes Press, 1993.

Kamen, Henry. *The Spanish Inquisition: An Historical Revision.* London: Weidenfeld and Nicolson, 1997.

Kedourie, Elie, ed. *Spain and the Jews: The Sephardi Experience, 1492 and After.* New York: Thames and Hudson, 1992.

Klein, Julius. *The Mesta: A Study in Spanish Economic History, 1273-1836.* Cambridge, Mass.: Harvard University Press, 1920.

Lea, Henry Charles. *A History of the Inquisition of Spain.* 4 vols. New York: Macmillan, 1906–1907.

Leroy, Beatrice. *The Jews of Navarre in the Late Middle Ages.* Jerusalem: Magnes Press, 1985.

Lourie, Elena. *Crusade and Colonization: Muslims, Christians, and Jews in Medieval Aragon.* Aldershot: Variorum, 1990.

MacKay, Angus. *Money, Prices, and Politics in Fifteenth-Century Castile*. London: Royal Historical Society, 1981.

———. *Society, Economy, and Religion in Late Medieval Castile*. London: Variorum, 1987.

———. *Spain in the Middle Ages: From Frontier to Empire, 1000–1500*. London: Macmillan, 1977.

Meyerson, Mark D. *A Jewish Renaissance in Fifteenth-Century Spain*. Princeton, N.J.: Princeton University Press, 2004.

———. *Jews in an Iberian Frontier Kingdom: Society, Economy, and Politics in Morvedre, 1248–1391*. Leiden: Brill, 2004.

———. *The Muslims of Valencia in the Age of Fernando and Isabel: Between Coexistence and Crusade*. Berkeley: University of California Press, 1991.

Miller, Kathryn A. *Guardians of Islam: Religious Authority and Muslim Communities in Late Medieval Spain*. New York: Columbia University Press, 2008.

Netanyahu, Benzion. *The Origins of the Inquisition in Fifteenth-Century Spain*. New York: Random House, 1995.

Nirenberg, David. *Communities of Violence: Persecution of Minorities in the Middle Ages*. Princeton, N.J.: Princeton University Press, 1996.

Oliveira Marques, A. H. de. *Daily Life in Portugal in the Late Middle Ages*. Trans. S. S. Wyatt. Madison: University of Wisconsin Press, 1971.

Perry, Mary Elizabeth. *The Handless Maiden: Moriscos and the Politics of Religion in Early Modern Spain*. Princeton, N.J.: Princeton University Press, 2005.

Phillips, Carla Rahn, and William D. Phillips. *The Worlds of Christopher Columbus*. Cambridge: Cambridge University Press, 1992.

Powell, James M., ed. *Muslims Under Latin Rule*. Princeton, N.J.: Princeton University Press, 1990.

Rodriguez, Jarbel. *Captives and Their Saviors in the Medieval Crown of Aragon*. Washington, D.C.: Catholic University of America Press, 2007.

Roth, Norman. *Conversos, Inquisition, and Expulsion of the Jews from Spain*. Madison: University of Wisconsin Press, 1995.

Ruiz, Teofilo F. *Crisis and Continuity: Land and Town in Late Medieval Castile*. Philadelphia: University of Pennsylvania Press, 1994.

———. *Spain's Centuries of Crisis: 1300–1474*. Oxford: Blackwell, 2007.

———. *Spanish Society, 1400–1600*. Harlow: Longman, 2001.

Russell, P. E. *The English Intervention in Spain and Portugal at the Time of Edward III and Richard II*. Oxford: Clarendon Press, 1995.

Shatzmiller, Maya. *Her Day in Court: Women's Property Rights in Fifteenth-Century Granada*. Cambridge, Mass.: Harvard University Press, 2007.

Soyer, François. *The Persecution of the Jews and Muslims of Portugal: King Manuel I and the End of Religious Tolerance (1496–97)*. Leiden: Brill, 2007.

Surtz, Ronald E. *Writing Women in Late Medieval and Early Modern Spain: The Mothers of Saint Teresa of Avila*. Philadelphia: University of Pennsylvania Press, 1995.

Trautner-Kromann, Hanne. *Shield and Sword: Jewish Polemics Against Christianity and Christians in France and Spain from 1100–1500*. Tübingen: Mohr, 1993.

Tueller, James B. *Good and Faithful Christians: Moriscos and Catholicism in Early Modern Spain*. New Orleans: University Press of the South, 2002.

VanLandingham, Marta. *Transforming the State: King, Court, and Political Culture in the Realms of Aragon (1213–1387)*. Leiden: Brill, 2002.

Webster, Jill. *Els menorets: The Franciscans in the Realms of Aragon from St. Francis to the Black Death.* Toronto: Pontifical Institute of Medieval Studies, 1993.

Weissberger, Barbara F. *Queen Isabel I of Castile: Power, Patronage, Persona.* Woodbridge: Tamesis, 2008.

Wiegers, Gerard. *Islamic Literature in Spanish and Aljamiado: Yça of Segovia (fl. 1450), His Antecedents and Successors.* Leiden: Brill, 1994.

Index of Texts According to Genre

Chapters listed below contain one or more texts in a given genre. In several cases, chapters and texts are listed under more than one genre.

Index

Personal and place-names are generally given in their modern Castilian versions, except in the case of some regional or medieval spellings. Personal names are alphabetized by first name. Page numbers in bold refer to original texts. Page numbers in italics refer to illustrations. An additional listing of subjects is included in the Table of Contents According to Subject.

Acknowledgments

In creating this second edition, special thanks are due to my research assistant, Damian Zurro, whose help has been invaluable in collecting, scanning, proofreading, and organizing the many new texts. I owe deep gratitude, likewise, to those colleagues who have generously contributed new translations to the second edition (as well as ongoing thanks to those who originally provided texts for the first edition). Thanks are also due to my many students, both undergraduates and graduate students, who have used and commented on the first edition since its appearance over a decade ago. Finally, my thanks to Jerry Singerman and the University of Pennsylvania Press for ongoing enthusiasm and support of this project, and to the Institute for Scholarship in the Liberal Arts, at the University of Notre Dame, for providing necessary funding.